OPTICS

OPTICS

Principles and Applications

by

K. K. Sharma

ACADEMIC PRESS
An Imprint of Elsevier

Optics: Principles and Applications
Sharma

ACADEMIC PRESS
An Imprint of Elsevier
30 Corporate Drive, Suite 400, Burlington, MA 01803, USA
525 B Street, Suite 1900, San Diego, California 92101-4495, USA
84 Theobald's Road, London WC1X 8RR, UK

Original ISBN: 978-0-12-370611-9

First Printed in India 2006
Reprinted 2010

Indian Reprint ISBN: 978-81-312-0651-5

Published by Elsevier, a division of Reed Elsevier India Private Limited.

Registered Office: Gate No. 3, Building No. A-1, 2 Industrial Area, Kalkaji, New Delhi 110 019
Corporate Office: 14th floor, Building No. 10B, DLF Cyber City Phase - II, Gurgaon, Haryana, India - 122002.

Printed and bound in India by Sanat Printers, Kundli - 131 028

Dedicated to the memory of my parents

Bliss is the inseparable
companion of knowledge
-Upanishads

CONTENTS

PREFACE

The driving force to write a book is the urge in author's mind to present his/her way of treating the subject matter. In the process, the book may succeed in emphasizing aspects which may or may not have received due attention. Excellent books on optics exist. For example, *Principles of Optics* by Max Born and Emil Wolf contains practically everything that a book on classical optics should have. Today, optics may be as relevant to engineering students as to students of physics. This textbook, an outcome of my experience of teaching optics courses at Indian Institute of Technology Kanpur, strives to meet the needs of both streams of students. Not that other authors have not paid sufficient attention to this aspect, the emphasis and visibility of topics may, however, differ from book to book. Admittedly, a textbook on optics cannot over-emphasize topics of engineering interest without compromising on basics of optics. Pedagogy is the other thought process that has guided the preparation of the manuscript. The collection and sequencing of the material have been done to ensure continuity in the learning process. By and large, all selected topics have been treated rigorously, in depth, and as far as possible completely. Motivated students should benefit through self-study, but teacher's exposition is perhaps essential. The book is primarily aimed for senior undergraduate and beginning postgraduate students. Students at that level with sufficiently advanced skills may not need solved examples and illustrations. However, first few problems of most chapters are relatively easy and should essentially serve that purpose.

Consulting different books is an enriching experience for students and teachers alike, but availability of a textbook which can delineate broad outlines of a course or courses may be desirable. Leaving a few topics and emphasizing some others should provide the necessary flexibility to adopt this textbook for different courses on optics, applied optics, and photonics. The reader may find sequencing of some topics a bit unusual. Coherence of light, for example, is taken up much before diffraction. This is to make students realize that real light is polychromatic and only partially coherent. Treating light through plane waves throughout the book and bringing in polychromaticity and partial coherence towards the end defeats this purpose. Introducing coherence early on puts students in an advantageous position to deal with real light in basic optics, as for example in interference studies.

As in other fields, consistency and uniqueness of notations do not exist in optics. My choice of notations may reflect personal bias and quite possibly may not be the choice of the majority in the field. I have, however, tried to use simple and consistent notations, but at times deliberate departures could not be avoided. With very few exceptions, function variations shown in the book are actual plots drawn on MATLAB. The figures are drawn using Xfig software. The book contains eight original photographs besides three photographs (Figs. 11.10, 13.22, and 13.24) borrowed from literature, for which I am indebted to the original authors and publishers. Wherever I leaned substantially on a certain approach, original authors are acknowledged. I apologize for inadvertent omissions. Most derivations in the book are sufficiently detailed. Utmost care was exercised to eliminate errors, but this cannot be guaranteed. Hopefully, serious mistakes should not be too many. Effort has been made, as far as possible, to make each chapter self contained.

Chapter 1 deals with light propagation in isotropic and anisotropic media. This is a bit of a departure from tradition. Usually, light propagation in anisotropic media is considered much later. Anisotropic media, however, provide a more general (and beautiful) example of light propagation and their discussion at this stage seems quite appropriate. Likewise, coherence of light waves is introduced in Chapter 2 to help develop a realistic appreciation of real light at an early stage. Elementary knowledge of Fourier transforms and Fraunhofer diffraction should suffice to follow the contents of this chapter. Chapters 3–8 cover bulk of standard linear optics except Fraunhofer diffraction which is taken up in Chapter 10. The Jones vectors, Stokes parameters, matrix techniques for the description of optical instruments and laser resonators, lens aberrations, two- and multi-wave interference, thin optical coatings, diffraction theories, and Fresnel diffraction are among the topics discussed in these chapters. Chapters 10–13 on Fraunhofer diffraction, image formation and processing, transfer functions, and holography may constitute the section on Fourier optics. Fourier transforms, convolution and correlation operations, needed for the discussions in these chapters are reviewed in Chapter 9. Nonlinear optics is introduced in the last chapter (Chapter 14) of the book. First twenty five pages of this chapter develop fairly rigorously the theoretical framework, followed by a discussion on some of the commonly observed nonlinear effects such as the sum-frequency generation, upconversion, second-harmonic generation, parametric amplification and optical phase conjugation. The chapter ends with a discussion on optical Kerr and electrooptic effects. Each chapter has a set of problems which should help students extend their working knowledge of optics. Major omissions of the book include fiber optics, lasers, and quantum optics. Full justification to these topics without substantially increasing the size of the book is not possible, hence their exclusion.

K K Sharma
Panchkula, India
2006
(Formerly at Indian Institute of Technology Kanpur)

ACKNOWLEDGEMENTS

First of all, I wish to acknowledge students of my optics courses over the years because the inspiration to write the book came from my interaction with them. My many colleagues at Indian Institute of Technology Kanpur must be thanked for their encouragement. David Joseph deserves special thanks for help at different stages of manuscript preparation. Sandhya Agnihotri showed exceptional patience in typing and re-typing (in LaTeX) many revisions of the manuscript. I express my gratitude to her. Thanks are also due to Shikha, Seema, and Atul for typing the difficult chapter on nonlinear optics. I am grateful to Vivek Mishra and Sachin Ganu for MATLAB work, to Harjeet and Ruchika for Xfig drawings, to David Joseph for setting diffraction experiments, to Om Prakash for workshop assistance, and to the staff of the TV Centre of the Institute for photography. I am indebted to Greg Gbur for a careful reading of the manuscript and for his suggestions. I acknowledge my gratitude to Indian Institute of Technology Kanpur for providing facilities and congenial environment. I am thankful to the Department of Science and Technology, New Delhi for financial support during the latter phase of book-writing. Most of all, I thank my wife Tripta not only for her immense patience and forbearance, but also for keeping me free from family tasks so that I could remain focused on this endeavor. I cherish the moral support I have recieved from my extended family, our children Shikha, Seema, Atul, and Anjali, and also from Amit and Sachin. The smiles from Neha and Arushi helped to cheer me up when there were reasons to feel otherwise. I put on record the pleasure of interacting with Tim Pitts, Rachel Roumeliotis, Brandy Lilly and Priyaa H Menon of the editorial staff of Elsevier. There is a long list of individuals who have helped me in many ways, I thank them collectively.

CHAPTER 1

Light Waves

1.1 INTRODUCTION

Visible light constitutes a small, albeit an important, segment of the broad spectrum of electromagnetic waves encompassing γ-rays on one extreme and radio waves on the other. Between these two extremes, lie X-rays, ultraviolet radiation, visible light, infrared radiation and microwaves in decreasing order of frequency (Table 1.1). At the present stage of development of the field of optics, it is really not necessary to justify the wave nature of light. Having said that, it must also be mentioned that the original controversy between the two protagonists (Sir Issac Newton and Christian Huygens) representing two schools of thought – light being corpuscular and light having wave nature – took a new twist with the development of quantum mechanics. Light, like matter, is now understood to have a dual character – the wave-like behavior as well as the particle-like (photon) behavior. Both attributes may not be revealed in a single measurement. Broadly speaking, light propagation in free space and in other media can be described in classical terms whereas light–matter interaction (absorption and emission of light) can be understood only in the quantum mechanical description. In this book, we are primarily concerned with light propagation and hence the classical description in terms of Maxwell's equations is quite adequate. Maxwell's equations predict the velocity of propagation of electromagnetic waves in vacuum which is in close agreement with the measured velocity of light. This observation firmly establishes light in the realm of the electromagnetic waves.

1.2 MAXWELL'S EQUATIONS

All electromagnetic phenomena, including light propagation, can be fully described in terms of Maxwell's equations (written here, in the SI units):

$$\nabla \cdot \vec{E} = \rho/\epsilon_0,$$

$$\nabla \cdot \vec{B} = 0,$$

Table 1.1. The electromagnetic spectrum.

Spectral Region	Approximate Frequency Range
Gamma rays	$>10^{20}$ Hz
X-rays	$10^{17}-10^{20}$ Hz
Ultraviolet	$10^{15}-10^{17}$ Hz
Visible	$(3.5-7.5)\times 10^{14}$ Hz
Infrared	$10^{12}-10^{14}$ Hz
Microwaves	$10^{9}-10^{12}$ Hz
Radiofrequency	$<10^{9}$ Hz

$$\nabla\times\vec{E}=-\frac{\partial\vec{B}}{\partial t},$$

$$\nabla\times\vec{B}=\mu_0\left(\vec{J}+\epsilon_0\frac{\partial\vec{E}}{\partial t}\right), \tag{1.1}$$

where μ_0 and ϵ_0 are, respectively, the permeability and permittivity of vacuum; ρ and $\vec{J}$ are the charge and current densities, respectively.

There is a need to distinguish between the microscopic and macroscopic forms of Maxwell's equations. The charge and current densities in the microscopic form of Maxwell's equations are those which exist at the atomic level. Consequently, the electric field $\vec{E}$ and magnetic field $\vec{B}$ are expected to show rapid variations over atomic and subatomic distances. Visible light with wavelength range between 400 and 800 nm cannot probe the charge and current distributions at the atomic level. X-rays and γ-rays with much shorter wavelengths are better suited to probe atomic distributions. Light waves can provide information on charge and current distributions in matter averaged over distances of the order of the wavelength of light. In that sense, light is a rather crude probe to interrogate matter at the atomic level. Light waves perceive a medium more like a continuum, and not a medium packed with discrete particles. The macroscopic form of Maxwell's equations uses the charge and current densities which are averaged over microscopically large, but macroscopically small volumes. Macroscopically averaged fields vary smoothly in space and are mathematically well behaved. The Gauss and Stokes vector theorems can be applied to these fields. In this book, we shall deal with the macroscopic form of Maxwell's equations. Maxwell's equations in the differential form (Eq. 1.1) can be derived from the empirical integral formulation of the laws of electromagnetism developed over centuries by Gauss, Ampère, Faraday and others. Maxwell brought symmetry to these equations by introducing the displacement current density $\epsilon_0\partial\vec{E}/\partial t$. No wonder, these equations are known as Maxwell's equations. In the context of the macroscopic form of Maxwell's equations, it is necessary to distinguish between the free and bound charge and current densities. The free electrons in conductors generate the free charge density (ρ_f). In addition, it may also happen that the centers of the positive and negative charges in a small macroscopic volume may not coincide. If this happens, an electric dipole moment can be associated with this volume and the medium is said to be polarized. The electric polarization $\vec{P}$ is defined as

$$\vec{P} = \frac{\text{net electric dipole moment in a macroscopically small volume } V}{\text{volume } V}. \tag{1.2}$$

The bound charge density in a polarized medium is given by

$$\rho_\mathrm{b} = -\nabla \cdot \vec{P}. \tag{1.3}$$

The bound charge density ρ_b is non-zero only if polarization $\vec{P}$ is spatially changing. Electric polarization can be created in a medium either by aligning its polar molecules or by displacing its negative charge with respect to the positive charge by the application of an external electric field. The movement of the free charges in a conductor gives rise to the free current density ($\vec{J}_\mathrm{f}$), and the changing displacements of the bound charges from their equilibrium positions give rise to the bound current density

$$\vec{J}_\mathrm{b} = \frac{\mathrm{d}\vec{P}}{\mathrm{d}t}.$$

We should also recognize the existence of the magnetic dipole moments in magnetic materials. The bound current density can be generalized to include these contributions as well;

$$\vec{J}_\mathrm{b} = \frac{\mathrm{d}\vec{P}}{\mathrm{d}t} + \nabla \times \vec{M}, \tag{1.4}$$

where magnetization $\vec{M}$ is the magnetic moment per unit volume defined in the manner of Eq. (1.2). We now write Maxwell's equations indicating these contributions explicitly:

$$\nabla \cdot \vec{E} = (\rho_\mathrm{f} + \rho_\mathrm{b})/\epsilon_0, \tag{1.5a}$$

$$\nabla \cdot \vec{B} = 0, \tag{1.5b}$$

$$\nabla\times\vec{E}=-\frac{\partial\vec{B}}{\partial t},\tag{1.5c}$$

$$\nabla\times\vec{B}=\mu_0\left(\vec{J}_{\mathrm{f}}+\vec{J}_{\mathrm{b}}+\epsilon_0\frac{\partial\vec{E}}{\partial t}\right).\tag{1.5d}$$

These equations along with the defining equations for the bound charge and bound current densities constitute a formidable set of equations to deal with. They can be made more compact by introducing two additional fields,

$$\vec{D}=\epsilon_0\vec{E}+\vec{P},\tag{1.6a}$$

$$\vec{H}=\frac{\vec{B}}{\mu_0}-\vec{M},\tag{1.6b}$$

where $\vec{D}$ is the electric displacement field and $\vec{H}$ is the magnetic field. The field $\vec{B}$ is usually called the magnetic induction or the magnetic flux density. The term magnetic field is often used to refer either of the $\vec{B}$ or $\vec{H}$ field. Maxwell's equations (Eqs 1.5) can now be put in the form:

$$\nabla\cdot\vec{D}=\rho_{\mathrm{f}},\tag{1.7a}$$

$$\nabla\cdot\vec{B}=0,\tag{1.7b}$$

$$\nabla\times\vec{E}=-\frac{\partial\vec{B}}{\partial t},\tag{1.7c}$$

$$\nabla\times\vec{H}=\vec{J}_{\mathrm{f}}+\frac{\partial\vec{D}}{\partial t}.\tag{1.7d}$$

Despite the presence of the source terms, Maxwell's equations should not be conceptualized in terms of the cause and effect, where the fields are determined by the sources of the charge and current present in the medium. The sources and fields are, in fact, inter-dependent – each affecting the other. True, the free charges do not depend on the fields, but the bound charges and currents are field dependent. The bound charges and currents change the fields and are in turn modified by the changing fields.

Equations (1.7) appear deceptively simple but are actually unmanageable primarily because, notwithstanding Eqs (1.6), no simple relationships exist between the electric fields $\vec{E}$ and $\vec{D}$ and between the magnetic fields $\vec{B}$ and $\vec{H}$. Fortunately, the elementary magnetic moments are not of much concern at the optical frequencies. Consequently, the magnetization $\vec{M}$ can be ignored and the relationship between the $\vec{B}$ and $\vec{H}$ fields for materials of optical interest is rather simple:

$$\vec{B} = \mu \vec{H}.$$

The permeability μ of optical materials is essentially field independent and differs only slightly from vacuum permeability μ_0. However, the electric polarization $\vec{P}$ must be reckoned with and cannot be ignored. In the absence of a detailed understanding in classical terms, the electric polarization $\vec{P}$ is usually expanded as a power series in the electric field:

$$P_i = \epsilon_0 \left[\chi_{ij}^{(1)} E_j + \chi_{ijk}^{(2)} E_j E_k + \chi_{ijkl}^{(3)} E_j E_k E_l + \cdots \right], \tag{1.8}$$

where E_i, E_j, E_k are the components of the electric field contributing to the ith component of the polarization $\vec{P}$. The coefficients $\chi^{(n)}$ with $n = 1, 2, 3, \ldots$ are the electric susceptibility tensors describing intrinsic material properties and are best understood in quantum mechanical terms. Alternatively, they may be treated as parameters to be determined empirically. Equation (1.8) is actually more complicated than it appears because the polarization $\vec{P}$ at a certain space-time point $(\vec{r}, t)$ may depend, in addition to field $\vec{E}$ at point $\vec{r}$ and time t, on fields in the spatial neighborhood of this point and may also depend on fields at times prior to the chosen time t. We shall ignore such complications. Here, we assume polarization $\vec{P}(\vec{r}, t)$ to depend linearly on the local and instantaneous field only. Hence, we can write

$$\vec{P}(\vec{r}, t) = \epsilon_0 \chi^{(1)} \vec{E}(\vec{r}, t). \tag{1.9a}$$

This is the regime of linear optics to which most of this book is devoted. The remaining terms in Eq. (1.8) form the basis of the exciting field of nonlinear optics (Chapter 14). Equation (1.9a) is equivalent to

$$\vec{D}(\vec{r}, t) = \epsilon \vec{E}(\vec{r}, t), \tag{1.9b}$$

where

$$\epsilon = \epsilon_0 (1 + \chi^{(1)}) \tag{1.9c}$$

is the medium permittivity. Except for vacuum ($\chi^{(1)} = 0$), the linear susceptibility $\chi^{(1)}$ and permittivity ϵ are in general complex suggesting the polarization $\vec{P}$ and displacement field $\vec{D}$ do not always remain in phase with the electric field $\vec{E}$. For conducting media, the so-called constitutive relations (Eqs 1.6) need to be supplemented by

$$\vec{J} = \sigma \vec{E}, \tag{1.6c}$$

where σ is the electrical conductivity of the medium. A homogeneous medium is characterized by constant values of ϵ, μ and σ, and an inhomogeneous medium admits changes in these quantities from point to point in a smooth manner. For linear optical materials ($\rho_f = 0$, $\vec{J}_f = 0$, $\sigma = 0$), Eqs (1.7) can be re-cast into the form:

$$\nabla \cdot \epsilon \vec{E} = 0, \tag{1.10a}$$

$$\nabla \cdot \vec{B} = 0, \tag{1.10b}$$

$$\nabla \times \vec{E} = -\frac{\partial \vec{B}}{\partial t}, \tag{1.10c}$$

$$\nabla \times \vec{B} = \mu\epsilon \frac{\partial \vec{E}}{\partial t}. \tag{1.10d}$$

We note that for linear optical materials, only two fields $\vec{E}$ and $\vec{B}$ need to be dealt with, but the permittivity ϵ and to some extent the permeability μ are unknown quantities to be determined with reference to experimental observations. It must be appreciated that the averaging process has transferred the information on the electromagnetic behavior of the medium at the atomic level to the macroscopic or bulk properties of the medium – the permittivity ϵ and permeability μ in the context of optical materials.

All electromagnetic fields including the light fields must be consistent with Maxwell's equations, but on their own these equations do not suggest the existence of fields of any particular kind. One needs to postulate specific forms of the fields and then obtain conditions for their existence. Another point to be noted is that these equations describe relationships for the spatial and temporal variations of the fields, but do not provide any clue as to how these fields are generated in the first place.

1.3 THE WAVE EQUATION

The electric and magnetic fields appear coupled in Maxwell's equations. It is possible to de-couple them. The decoupling process brings out some of the most exciting aspects of electromagnetism. For a homogeneous medium, except at its boundaries, Eq. (1.10a) reduces to

$$\nabla \cdot \vec{E} = 0. \tag{1.10e}$$

This result in conjunction with Eq. (1.5a) suggests that a linear homogeneous medium, with no free charge inside, cannot sustain any bound charge except (may be) at its boundaries. We shall have to fall back to Eq. (1.10a) when the boundaries of a homogeneous medium are approached. With Eq. (1.10e), the $\nabla \times \nabla \times \vec{E}$ simplifies to

$$\nabla \times \nabla \times \vec{E} = \nabla(\nabla \cdot \vec{E}) - \nabla^2 \vec{E} = -\nabla^2 \vec{E}.$$

Taking curl of Eq. (1.10c), interchanging ∇ and $\partial/\partial t$ operations on the right-hand side and combining it with Eq. (1.10d) leads to the well-known wave equation

$$\nabla^2 \vec{E} - \mu\epsilon \frac{\partial^2 \vec{E}}{\partial t^2} = 0. \tag{1.11a}$$

In a similar manner, we can obtain

$$\nabla^2 \vec{B} - \mu\epsilon \frac{\partial^2 \vec{B}}{\partial t^2} = 0. \tag{1.11b}$$

Notwithstanding this apparent separation, the electric field $\vec{E}$ and magnetic field $\vec{B}$ of an electromagnetic wave remain dependent on each other through Maxwell's equations.

The wave equations (1.11) describe wave motion in a variety of situations, as for example the waves in an elastic medium. We can interpret Eqs (1.11) to describe the propagation of the electric and magnetic fields or more appropriately, the propagation of the electromagnetic waves. Extending the similarity with the elastic waves a bit further, one may postulate the existence of some kind of an elastic medium pervading all space which makes it possible for the electromagnetic waves to propagate. Aether was thought to be such a medium. It must necessarily be a thin medium since electromagnetic waves do propagate in essentially free space. At the same time, aether must be sufficiently elastic for wave propagation to take place. These are some of the internal inconsistencies of the aether postulate. The results of an ingenious experiment performed by Michelson and Morley were not consistent with the aether postulate. Aether has no place in the special theory of relativity developed by Albert Einstein.

Electromagnetic waves including the light waves can propagate in absolutely empty space. They do not require matter to facilitate propagation. The changing electric and magnetic fields associated with an electromagnetic wave are capable of sustaining each other. A comparison of the wave equation with its counterpart for mechanical waves suggests that the product $\mu\epsilon$ must represent the inverse of the square of the speed of propagation of electromagnetic waves. A medium is not necessary for the propagation of electromagnetic waves. However, the velocity of propagation of electromagnetic waves in a given medium is determined by its permeability and permittivity. The vacuum with permeability $\mu_0 = 4\pi \times 10^{-7}\,\mathrm{N\,s^2\,C^{-2}}$ and permittivity $\epsilon_0 = 8.85 \times 10^{-12}\,\mathrm{C^2\,N^{-1}\,m^{-2}}$ has velocity $c = 2.99 \times 10^8\,\mathrm{m\,s^{-1}}$ for the propagation of electromagnetic waves. This value agrees very closely with the velocity of light measured in the laboratory. This brings light within the domain of applicability of Maxwell's equations.

The wave equation (1.11) is a linear, homogeneous, second-order differential equation. The linearity of the wave equation leads to the superposition principle which states that if $\vec{E}_j$ $(j = 1, 2, 3, \ldots, n)$ are solutions of the wave equation, then $\sum_j a_j \vec{E}_j$ is also a solution of the wave equation, where a_j are arbitrary constants (real or complex). The wave equation admits a variety of solutions – some extremely simple in form, others sufficiently intricate. The implication of this statement needs to be appreciated. All light fields in a homogeneous medium must be solutions of the wave equation. However, external conditions must be accurately controlled to generate light fields to correspond to a particular solution of the wave equation. Some solutions may be mathematically easy to handle, but difficult to realize in practice. Fortunately, external conditions can often be manipulated to favor a particular kind of solution – generation of coherent light in a laser is an important step in this direction. The plane wave solution

$$\vec{E}(\vec{r}, t) = \vec{E}_0\, \mathrm{e}^{\mathrm{i}(\vec{k}.\vec{r} - \omega t)}$$

is perhaps the simplest solution and the lowest order Bessel wave solution [1.2]

$$E(\vec{r}, t) = E_0 J_0(\alpha\rho)\mathrm{e}^{\mathrm{i}(\beta z - \omega t)},$$

representing a nonspreading beam with $\alpha^2 + \beta^2 = (\omega/c)^2$, is one of the non-trivial solutions of the wave equation.

A plane wave is actually unphysical in the sense that no experimental effort can succeed to generate a plane wave. Notwithstanding this 'awkwardness', the plane wave solution of the wave equation is an extremely useful solution. In the backdrop of these remarks, we now discuss some monochromatic (single frequency) solutions of the wave equation in a homogeneous medium. The quasi-monochromatic and polychromatic wave solutions can be constructed in terms of the monochromatic wave solutions. This will be the subject matter of the next chapter.

1.3.1 Plane Wave Solution

The general solution of the wave equation (1.11) can be written in the form

$$\vec{E}(\vec{r}, t) = \vec{E}_0(\vec{r}, t)e^{i\phi(\vec{r}, t)}, \tag{1.12}$$

where $\vec{E}_0(\vec{r}, t)$ and $\phi(\vec{r}, t)$ are the amplitude and phase of the wave, respectively. A plane wave is characterized by phase $\phi(\vec{r}, t)$ which, at any given time, remains constant in a plane perpendicular to the direction of propagation of the wave. The phase

$$\phi(\vec{r}, t) = \vec{k} \cdot \vec{r} - \omega t$$

satisfies this condition since the dot product $\vec{k} \cdot \vec{r}$ remains constant $(= kr_0)$ as the tip of the position vector $\vec{r}$ moves over a given plane perpendicular to the direction of propagation $\vec{k}$; r_0 is the component of $\vec{r}$ in the direction of $\vec{k}$ (Fig. 1.1). The amplitude $\vec{E}_0$ of a plane wave does not depend on position vector $\vec{r}$ and time t.

A surface (in this case a plane) of constant phase is called a wavefront or an equiphase surface. Let plane I in Fig. 1.1 represent the wavefront at the space-time point (r_0, t_0) with phase

$$\phi_0 = \vec{k} \cdot \vec{r} - \omega t = kr_0 - \omega t_0.$$

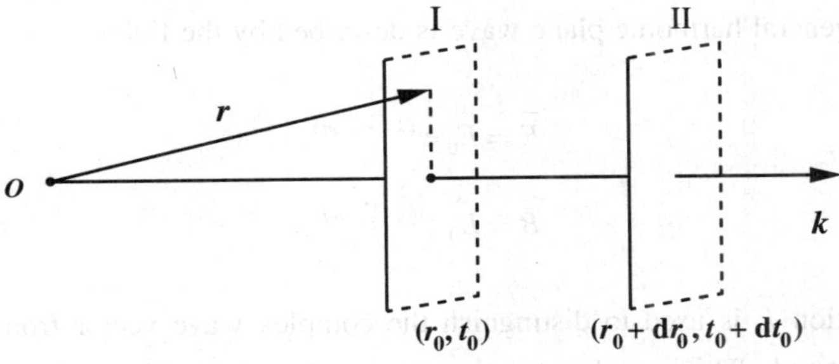

Fig. 1.1: Moving wavefront of a plane wave.

This wavefront moves along with the wave and plane II is its subsequent position at the neighboring space-time point $(r_0 + \mathrm{d}r_0, t_0 + \mathrm{d}t_0)$. Therefore,

$$\phi_0 = kr_0 - \omega t_0 = k(r_0 + \mathrm{d}r_0) - \omega(t_0 + \mathrm{d}t_0).$$

The velocity of propagation of the wavefront is given by

$$v_\mathrm{p} = \frac{\mathrm{d}r_0}{\mathrm{d}t_0} = \frac{\omega}{k}.$$

This is the phase velocity or the wave velocity. We could have defined the phase of a plane wave with a negative sign before $\vec{k} \cdot \vec{r}$. That choice represents another plane wave propagating in just the opposite direction. In fact, any well-behaved mathematical function of $(\pm k \cdot r - \omega t)$ can represent a plane wave. A particularly useful form of the plane wave is the harmonic plane wave

$$\vec{E}_\mathrm{r} = \vec{E}_{0\mathrm{r}} \cos(\vec{k} \cdot \vec{r} - \omega t + \phi_0) \tag{1.13a}$$

in the real field notation or

$$\vec{E} = \vec{E}_{0\mathrm{r}}\, \mathrm{e}^{\mathrm{i}(\vec{k} \cdot \vec{r} - \omega t + \phi_0)} \tag{1.13b}$$

in the complex field notation, where ϕ_0 is a constant called the phase constant. To avoid trigonometric complications, we prefer to employ the complex field notation. The real field can always be recovered from the complex field and its complex conjugate:

$$\vec{E}_\mathrm{r} = \frac{1}{2}\, \vec{E}_{0\mathrm{r}}\, \mathrm{e}^{\mathrm{i}(k \cdot r - \omega t + \phi_0)} + \frac{1}{2}\, \vec{E}_{0\mathrm{r}}\, \mathrm{e}^{-\mathrm{i}(\vec{k} \cdot \vec{r} - \omega t + \phi_0)}. \tag{1.14}$$

A more general harmonic plane wave is described by the fields

$$\vec{E} = \vec{E}_0\, \mathrm{e}^{\mathrm{i}(\vec{\tilde{k}} \cdot \vec{r} - \omega t)}, \tag{1.15a}$$

$$\vec{B} = \vec{B}_0\, \mathrm{e}^{\mathrm{i}(\vec{\tilde{k}} \cdot \vec{r} - \omega t)}. \tag{1.15b}$$

The notation $\vec{\tilde{k}}$ is used to distinguish the complex wave vector from the real wave vector $\vec{k}$. The complex wave vector or the propagation vector $\vec{\tilde{k}}$ allows for the attenuation (or the gain) of the amplitude of a wave as it propagates in the medium. For complex $\vec{E}_0$ and $\vec{B}_0$, the electric and magnetic fields may not always remain in phase. The complex propagation vector may be expressed as

$$\vec{\tilde{k}} = \vec{k} + \mathrm{i}\,\vec{a}, \tag{1.16}$$

where $\vec{k}$ is the real part of the propagation vector and $\vec{a}$ is a real vector called the attenuation vector. For the harmonic plane wave solution to be consistent with Maxwell's equations in a homogeneous medium, following conditions must be satisfied:

$$\vec{\tilde{k}} \cdot \vec{E}_0 = 0, \tag{1.17a}$$

$$\vec{\tilde{k}} \cdot \vec{B}_0 = 0, \tag{1.17b}$$

$$\vec{B}_0 = \frac{\vec{\tilde{k}} \times \vec{E}_0}{\omega}, \tag{1.17c}$$

$$\vec{E}_0 = -\frac{\vec{\tilde{k}} \times \vec{B}_0}{\mu\epsilon\omega}. \tag{1.17d}$$

Equations (1.17a) and (1.17b) specify the transversality condition of the complex field amplitudes $\vec{E}_0$ and $\vec{B}_0$. However, it must be understood that the electric and magnetic fields are transverse to the real wave vector k only when the medium is non-absorbing ($\vec{a} = 0$). Combining Eqs (1.17c) and (1.17d) and making use of the vector triple product, we get

$$\tilde{k}^2 = \vec{\tilde{k}} \cdot \vec{\tilde{k}} = \mu\epsilon\omega^2 = \tilde{n}^2 \frac{\omega^2}{c^2}, \tag{1.18a}$$

where

$$\tilde{n}^2 = \mu\epsilon c^2. \tag{1.18b}$$

The real and imaginary parts of the complex refractive index

$$\tilde{n} = n + \mathrm{i}\kappa \tag{1.19}$$

are known as the refractive and extinction indices of the medium, respectively. The real and imaginary parts of the complex wave vector $\tilde{k}$ and complex refractive index $\tilde{n}$ satisfy the following relations:

$$k^2 - a^2 = (n^2 - \kappa^2)\frac{\omega^2}{c^2}, \tag{1.20a}$$

$$\vec{k} \cdot \vec{a} = n\kappa\frac{\omega^2}{c^2}. \tag{1.20b}$$

It should be noted that in place of permittivity and permeability, the complex refractive index now describes the bulk properties of an optical material.

1.3.2 Spherical and Cylindrical Wave Solutions

A point source embedded in an isotropic medium generates a spherical wave which propagates radially outward. The surfaces of constant phases for a spherical wave are spherical, centered at the source point. The scalar electric field of a harmonic spherical wave in the complex notation has the form

$$E(r) = \frac{A}{r}\mathrm{e}^{\mathrm{i}(kr-\omega t)}, \tag{1.21a}$$

where A is the amplitude of the spherical wave at unit distance from the point source. The $1/r$ dependence of the field can be easily derived by integrating the wave equation after expressing it in spherical polar coordinates. However, this dependence follows from consideration of energy conservation. Equation (1.21a) represents a diverging or an expanding spherical wave diverging from point $r = 0$, and the spherical wave converging to point $r = 0$ is

$$E(r) = \frac{A}{r}\mathrm{e}^{\mathrm{i}(-kr-\omega t)}. \tag{1.21b}$$

The harmonic cylindrical wave solutions of the wave equation have the form

$$E(r) = \frac{A}{\sqrt{r}}\mathrm{e}^{\mathrm{i}(\pm kr-\omega t)}, \tag{1.21c}$$

where the wavefronts are in the form of coaxial cylindrical surfaces travelling outward from an infinite line source at $r = 0$ or travelling inward to converge on a line at $r = 0$.

1.3.3 Beam-Like Solutions

Laser light possesses a high degree of directionality resembling closely the directionality of a plane wave. But unlike for a plane wave, the field amplitude of laser light decreases rapidly in the transverse plane. Laser light diverges as it propagates, but for short distances the divergence of laser light is much smaller than the divergence of a spherical wave. Of course, laser light is not monochromatic but it is the closest approximation we have for monochromatic light. We now seek a monochromatic solution of the wave equation which is highly directional and possesses a low degree of divergence. It is hoped that such a solution may provide at least an approximate description of laser light. Here, we disregard the fact that the wave equation (1.11) is a vector equation. Instead, we treat the electric and magnetic fields as scalar fields. By doing so, we lose all information about the state of polarization of light to which this solution may correspond. The solution may still be useful to describe interference and diffraction phenomena. We begin by requiring that the beam-like solution be monochromatic, so that

$$E(\vec{r}, t) = E(\vec{r})\mathrm{e}^{-\mathrm{i}\omega t}.$$

On substituting this solution, the wave equation (1.11a) reduces to Helmholtz equation

$$(\nabla^2 + k^2)E(\vec{r}) = 0, \tag{1.22}$$

where

$$k^2 = \mu\epsilon\omega^2 = \omega^2/v^2 = n^2\frac{\omega^2}{c^2}.$$

The propagation vector and index of refraction are assumed real in the present context. To retain the beam-like character of the solution, we write

$$E(\vec{r}) = \varepsilon(\vec{r})\mathrm{e}^{ikz}. \tag{1.23}$$

The wave propagates in the z-direction with wave number $k = n(\omega/c)$. Noting that

$$\frac{\partial^2}{\partial z^2}\left(\varepsilon(\vec{r})\mathrm{e}^{ikz}\right) = \left[\frac{\partial^2}{\partial z^2} + 2\mathrm{i}k\frac{\partial}{\partial z} - k^2\right]\varepsilon(\vec{r})\mathrm{e}^{ikz},$$

Eq. (1.22) can be recast into the form

$$\nabla_t^2\varepsilon(\vec{r}) + \frac{\partial^2\varepsilon(\vec{r})}{\partial z^2} + 2\mathrm{i}k\frac{\partial\varepsilon(\vec{r})}{\partial z} = 0, \tag{1.24}$$

where

$$\nabla_t^2 = \frac{\partial^2}{\partial x^2} + \frac{\partial^2}{\partial y^2}.$$

Making use of the slowly varying envelope approximation (SVEA)

$$\frac{\partial^2 \varepsilon(\vec{r})}{\partial z^2} \ll k \frac{\partial \varepsilon(\vec{r})}{\partial z},$$

Eq. (1.24) can be approximated to

$$\nabla_t^2 \varepsilon(\vec{r}) + 2\mathrm{i}k \frac{\partial \varepsilon(\vec{r})}{\partial z} = 0. \tag{1.25}$$

The SVEA ensures slow variation (on the wavelength scale) of the field amplitude $\varepsilon(r)$ and its derivatives in the direction of propagation. However, appreciable changes in the amplitude over long distances are still permitted. Equation (1.25) admits many beam-like solutions. We look for the one which manifests cylindrical symmetry about the direction of propagation. This may be the simplest, but not the only interesting beam-like solution the wave equation possesses. For the present, it suffices to solve the equation

$$\frac{1}{\rho}\frac{\partial}{\partial \rho}\left(\rho \frac{\partial \varepsilon(\vec{r})}{\partial \rho}\right) + 2\mathrm{i}k \frac{\partial \varepsilon(\vec{r})}{\partial z} = 0, \tag{1.26}$$

where $\rho = (x^2 + y^2)^{1/2}$. A possible solution to this equation may have the form

$$\varepsilon(\rho, z) = A\,\mathrm{e}^{\mathrm{i}[p(z) + \frac{1}{2}(k\rho^2)/(q(z))]}, \tag{1.27}$$

where A is a constant. For real $p(z)$ and $q(z)$, the beam intensity is independent of ρ and z. This is not the kind of solution we are seeking. Hence, we expect either one or both of these functions to be complex. Substituting Eq. (1.27) into Eq. (1.26) gives

$$2k\left(\frac{\mathrm{i}}{q(z)} - \frac{\mathrm{d}p(z)}{\mathrm{d}z}\right) + \frac{k^2\rho^2}{q^2(z)}\left(\frac{\mathrm{d}q(z)}{\mathrm{d}z} - 1\right) = 0. \tag{1.28}$$

This equation is satisfied if

$$\frac{\mathrm{d}q(z)}{\mathrm{d}z} = 1, \tag{1.29a}$$

$$\frac{\mathrm{d}p(z)}{\mathrm{d}z} = \frac{\mathrm{i}}{q(z)}. \tag{1.29b}$$

The solution of Eq. (1.29a) is

$$q(z) = z - \mathrm{i}z_0. \tag{1.30}$$

For convenience, the constant of integration has been taken as $-\mathrm{i}z_0$. Integration of Eq. (1.29b) yields

$$p(z) = \mathrm{i}\,\ln(1 + \mathrm{i}z/z_0), \tag{1.31}$$

where the constant of integration has been chosen to make $p(0) = 0$. With this choice, this beam-like solution has exactly the phase (but not the amplitude) of the plane wave at $z = 0$. In other words, the wavefront at $z = 0$ is planar. Equation (1.31) can be expressed as

$$\begin{aligned} \mathrm{e}^{\mathrm{i}pz} &= \left(1 + \mathrm{i}\frac{z}{z_0}\right)^{-1} \\ &= \frac{1}{\sqrt{1 + \frac{z^2}{z_0^2}}}\,\mathrm{e}^{-\mathrm{i}\phi(z)}, \end{aligned} \tag{1.32}$$

where $\phi(z) = \tan^{-1} z/z_0$. Equation (1.30) can be written in an equivalent form

$$\begin{aligned} \frac{1}{q(z)} &= \frac{z}{z^2 + z_0^2} + \mathrm{i}\frac{z_0}{z^2 + z_0^2} \\ &= \frac{1}{R(z)} + \frac{2\mathrm{i}}{k}\frac{1}{w^2(z)}, \end{aligned} \tag{1.33}$$

where

$$R(z) = z + \frac{z_0^2}{z}, \tag{1.34a}$$

$$w^2(z) = w_0^2\left(1 + z^2/z_0^2\right), \tag{1.34b}$$

$$w_0^2 = \frac{2z_0}{k}. \tag{1.34c}$$

Combining these results, the beam-like solution of the wave equation possessing cylindrical symmetry about the direction of propagation can be written as

$$E(\vec{r}, t) = A\frac{w_0}{w(z)}\,\mathrm{e}^{-\rho^2/w^2(z)}\,\mathrm{e}^{\mathrm{i}k\rho^2/2R(z)}\,\mathrm{e}^{\mathrm{i}(kz - \phi(z) - \omega t)}, \tag{1.35a}$$

$$= A\frac{w_0}{w(z)}\,\mathrm{e}^{-\rho^2/w^2(z)}\,\mathrm{e}^{\mathrm{i}k(z + (\rho^2/2R(z)))}\,\mathrm{e}^{-\mathrm{i}\phi(z)}\mathrm{e}^{-\mathrm{i}\omega t}. \tag{1.35b}$$

The two equivalent expressions (1.35a) and (1.35b) have been written to bring out two complementary features of the beam-like solution. The phase factor $(kz - \phi(z) - \omega t)$ in Eq. (1.35a) reminds us of the plane wave solution since $\phi(z)$ is a slowly varying function of z, changing from zero to $\pi/4$ as z goes from zero to z_0. On the other hand, for visible light, kz varies by nearly 10^5 radians over a distance of 1 cm. However, the solution differs from a plane wave because the amplitude of the wave does not remain constant. The expression (1.35b), on the other hand, possesses some implicit resemblance to a spherical wave. The phase factor $k(z+\rho^2/2R(z))$ will be shown to approximate the phase factor kr of a spherical wave in the limit of large r. Furthermore, $w(z)$ varies linearly with z for large z suggesting an inverse dependence of the amplitude on distance as for a spherical wave. But for z, not too large, this solution has much lower divergence as compared to the divergence of a spherical wave. The amplitude

$$E_0(\vec{r}) = A\frac{w_0}{w(z)}\,\mathrm{e}^{-(x^2+y^2)/w^2(z)}$$

of the beam-like solution varies with x, y, z. For a fixed value of z, it has a Gaussian profile in the transverse plane. The amplitude falls to $1/e$ of its maximum value at a distance $\rho = (x^2+y^2)^{1/2} = w(z)$ from the axis of symmetry (Fig. 1.2).

The transverse profile of the beam-like solution changes as the wave propagates. It has minimum spread at $z = 0$. The width of the transverse profile of the beam increases non-linearly with z on either side of the point $z = 0$. However,

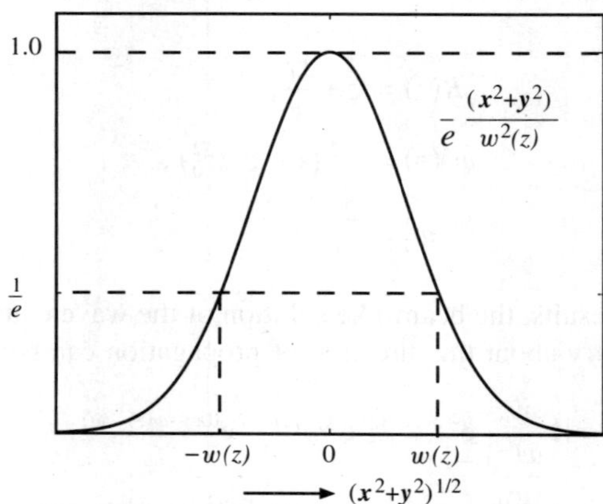

Fig. 1.2: Gaussian profile of the amplitude of the beam-like solution.

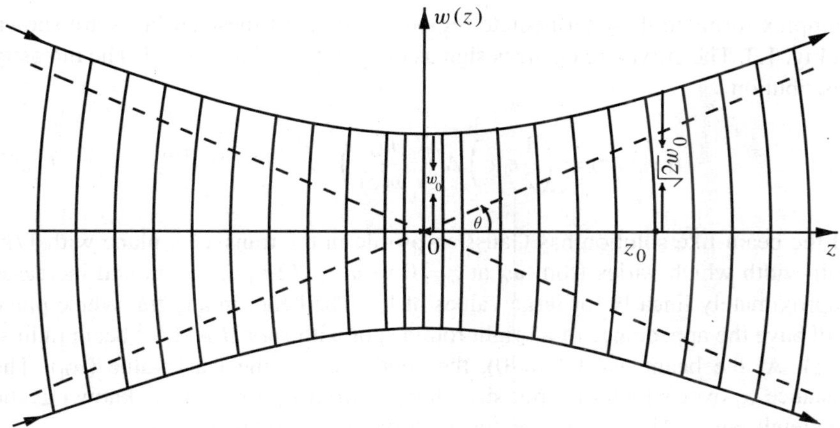

Fig. 1.3: Variation of the transverse profile of the beam-like solution; w_0 is beam waist and z_0 is Rayleigh range.

for $|z| \gg z_0$, the transverse profile shows a linear dependence on z. This behavior of the solution is shown in Fig. 1.3.

We next consider the spatial phase of the wave,

$$\Phi(x, y, z) = k\left(z + \frac{x^2 + y^2}{2R(z)}\right). \tag{1.36a}$$

This phase is obviously not constant for a given value of z. The equiphase surfaces are curved, but not necessarily spherical (Fig. 1.3). For comparison, we write the spatial phase of a spherical wave in the limit $x, y \ll z$:

$$\begin{aligned}\Phi_{\text{sph}}(x, y, z) &= kr \\ &= k[x^2 + y^2 + z^2]^{1/2} \\ &\approx k[z + \frac{x^2 + y^2}{2z}].\end{aligned} \tag{1.36b}$$

Only the first term in the binomial expansion has been retained. The expressions (1.36a) and (1.36b) are similar since $R(z) \sim z$ for large z. One may therefore conclude that for points in the transverse plane, not too far from the axis of symmetry, the curvature of the equiphase surface of the beam-like solution approaches sphericity for large values of z. It is tempting to identify the factor $1/R(z)$ with the curvature of the equiphase surface. The curvature changes continuously from planar at $z = 0$ to near-spherical for large z, taking more complex forms in the intermediate region. Sections of these surfaces are shown in Fig. 1.3. The curvature changes sign as the point $z = 0$ is crossed. The intensity distribution

$$I(x, y, z) = \left(\frac{1}{2}\epsilon_0 c\right) A^2 \left(\frac{w_0}{w(z)}\right)^2 \mathrm{e}^{-2(x^2+y^2)/(w^2(z))} \tag{1.37}$$

of the beam-like solution has Gaussian profile in the transverse plane with $1/e^2$ half-width which varies from w_0 at $z = 0$ to $w = \sqrt{2}w_0$ at $z = z_0$ and increases approximately linearly for large values of $|z|$. The beam in any transverse plane will have the appearance of a bright round spot with *spot size* ($1/e^2$ beam radius) $w(z)$. At the beam waist ($z = 0$), the spot size has the least value (w_0). The distance z_0 over which the spot size changes from w_0 to $\sqrt{2}w_0$ is known as the Rayleigh range. The beam divergence, defined asymptotically, is

$$\theta(\text{divergence}) = \lim_{z\to\infty} \frac{\mathrm{d}w(z)}{\mathrm{d}z} = \frac{w_0}{z_0} = \frac{\lambda_v}{\pi n w_0},$$

where λ_v is wavelength of light in a vacuum and n is refractive index of the medium. Typical divergence angle of the beam of a commercial laser is in milliradians.

As mentioned earlier, we have considered only the lowest order beam-like solution (TEM_{00}mode) of the wave equation which has been found to resemble in some way a plane wave for $z \to 0$ and a spherical wave for $z \to \pm\infty$. Higher order solutions of the wave equation with beam-like character also exist. They are described in terms of the Hermite polynomials [1.1, 1.2].

1.4 HOMOGENEOUS AND INHOMOGENEOUS WAVES

A vacuum is a perfectly transparent medium for the entire range of the electromagnetic spectrum. Other media may approach complete transparency over limited spectral bandwidths. Perfect transparency exists in an optical medium when the index of refraction is purely real ($\kappa = 0$). This need not necessarily imply a purely real propagation vector (a non-absorbing medium). For perfect transparency, Eq. (1.20b) requires

$$\vec{k} \cdot \vec{a} = 0. \tag{1.38}$$

This condition can be met in two ways. The attenuation vector may be a null vector ($\vec{a} = 0$), in which case, the plane wave solution takes the form

$$\begin{aligned}\vec{E} &= \vec{E}_0\ \mathrm{e}^{\mathrm{i}(\vec{k}\cdot\vec{r}-\omega t)},\\ \vec{B} &= \vec{B}_0\ \mathrm{e}^{\mathrm{i}(\vec{k}\cdot\vec{r}-\omega t)},\end{aligned} \tag{1.39}$$

where $\vec{k}$ is now a real vector of magnitude

$$k = n\frac{\omega}{c}. \tag{1.40}$$

These fields represent a homogeneous plane wave with coincident surfaces of constant amplitude ($\vec{E}_0 =$ constant, $\vec{B}_0 =$ constant) and constant phase ($\vec{k}\cdot\vec{r} =$ constant). These surfaces are planes perpendicular to the real wave vector $\vec{k}$. Equations (1.39) represent a wave with unchanging amplitude propagating with speed

$$v = \frac{\omega}{k} = \frac{c}{n}. \tag{1.41}$$

In this case, Eqs. (1.17) have clear physical interpretation. The real and imaginary parts of the $\vec{E}$ and $\vec{B}$ fields are transverse to the direction of propagation. It should be understood that we have used the complex notation for the fields only for the sake of convenience. The physical electric and magnetic fields being real are not only transverse to the direction of propagation, but are also transverse to each other in the present case. Such a wave is called a TEM wave, where TEM stands for transverse electric and magnetic fields (Fig. 1.4). The electric and magnetic fields remain in phase and their amplitudes are related by

$$B_0 = \frac{n}{c}E_0. \tag{1.42}$$

For a perfectly transparent medium ($\kappa = 0$), the condition (1.38) can also be met for a non-zero value of the attenuation vector $\vec{a}$ provided the real and imaginary parts of the complex wave vector $\vec{\tilde{k}}$ are orthogonal to each other. In this case, the plane wave solution takes the form

$$\vec{E}(\vec{r}, t) = \vec{E}_0\ \mathrm{e}^{-\vec{a}\cdot\vec{r}}\ \mathrm{e}^{\mathrm{i}(\vec{k}\cdot\vec{r}-\omega t)}. \tag{1.43}$$

The wave now propagates in the direction of $\vec{k}$ with somewhat diminished velocity as compared to the velocity of the homogeneous wave ($\vec{a} = 0$). The surfaces of constant phase and constant amplitude are no longer coincident. The surfaces

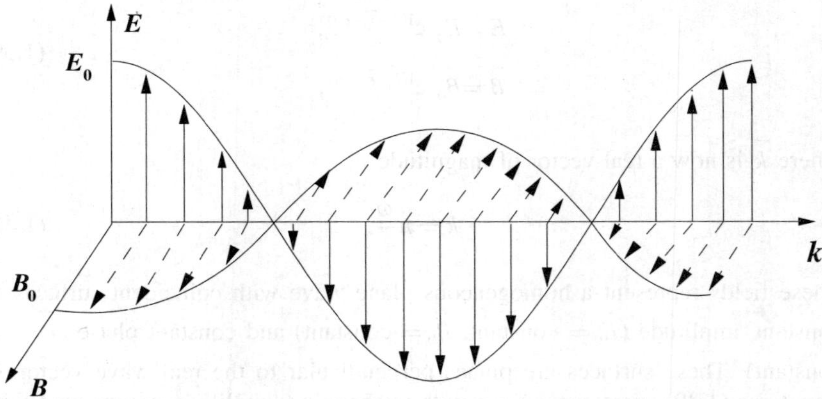

Fig. 1.4: A homogeneous harmonic plane wave; electric and magnetic fields are transverse to the direction of propagation and also to each other.

of constant phase remain perpendicular to the direction of propagation $\vec{k}$, but the surfaces of constant amplitude ($\vec{E}_0\ e^{-\vec{a}\cdot\vec{r}}$ = constant) are now planes perpendicular to the direction of the attenuation vector $\vec{a}$ since $\vec{a} \cdot \vec{r}$ remains constant in a plane normal to $\vec{a}$. The amplitude of the wave decreases in the direction of $\vec{a}$. This is the inhomogeneous wave. Figure 1.5 compares a homogeneous wave with an inhomogeneous wave of this kind. A wave is inhomogeneous if the surfaces of constant amplitude and constant phase are not coincident. The field configurations are not easy to visualize for the inhomogeneous waves. For the TE mode, the real and imaginary parts of the electric field $\vec{E}$ are perpendicular to the plane containing the propagation vector $\vec{k}$ and attenuation vector $\vec{a}$. It can be shown (see Problem 1.4) that the magnetic field for the TE mode is elliptically polarized. For the TM mode, the real and imaginary parts of the magnetic field $\vec{B}$ are perpendicular to the plane of $\vec{k}$ and $\vec{a}$. Any field configuration can be expressed as a superposition of TE and TM modes. An example of an inhomogeneous wave is the evanescent wave to be considered later in this chapter.

For the more general case of non-zero extinction index κ, the attenuation vector $\vec{a}$ is not normal to the propagation vector $\vec{k}$ and the amplitude of the inhomogeneous wave decreases in the direction of propagation as well. The surfaces of constant phase and constant amplitude are neither coincident nor orthogonal. Electromagnetic waves in metals behave in this manner.

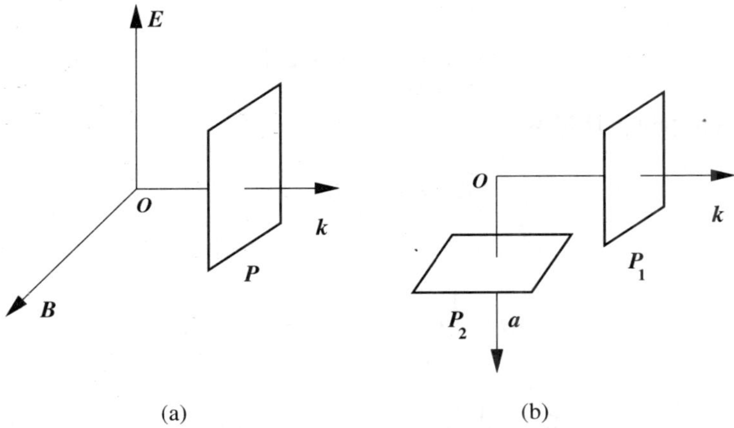

Fig. 1.5: (a) A homogeneous plane wave; planes of constant phase and planes of constant amplitude are coincident (P). (b) An inhomogeneous plane wave; planes of constant phase (P_1) are perpendicular to propagation vector $\vec{k}$ and planes of constant amplitude (P_2) are perpendicular to attenuation vector $\vec{a}$.

1.5 ENERGY DENSITY AND POYNTING VECTOR

A wave carries energy as it propagates in a medium. The instantaneous energy density stored in the medium due to the presence of the wave is given by[1]

$$u = \frac{1}{2}\epsilon(E^{(\mathrm{r})})^2 + \frac{1}{2\mu}(B^{(\mathrm{r})})^2 \tag{1.44a}$$

and the instantaneous energy crossing per unit area per unit time is given by the Poynting vector

$$\vec{S} = \frac{\vec{E}^{(\mathrm{r})} \times \vec{B}^{(\mathrm{r})}}{\mu}, \tag{1.44b}$$

where $\vec{E}^{(\mathrm{r})}$ and $\vec{B}^{(\mathrm{r})}$ are real time-dependent fields. The more relevant quantities for light fields are their time averaged values. In the complex notation,

$$\langle u \rangle = \frac{1}{4} Re\left[\epsilon \vec{E} \cdot \vec{E}^{*} + \frac{1}{\mu} \vec{B} \cdot \vec{B}^{*}\right]$$

[1] Introduction to Electrodynamics by David J. Griffiths.

and

$$\langle \vec{S} \rangle = \frac{1}{2\mu} Re[\vec{E} \times \vec{B}^*].$$

For a propagating TEM wave,

$$\epsilon \vec{E} \cdot \vec{E}^* = \frac{1}{\mu} \vec{B} \cdot \vec{B}^*,$$

so that

$$\langle u \rangle = \frac{1}{2} \epsilon \vec{E} \cdot \vec{E}^* = \epsilon \langle (E^{(\mathrm{r})})^2 \rangle$$

and

$$\langle \vec{S} \rangle = \frac{1}{2\mu} Re \langle \vec{E} \times \vec{B}^* \rangle = \frac{1}{2\mu v} EE^* \hat{s},$$

where the symbol $\langle\,\rangle$ represents the average over a time needed to make a measurement which is much longer than the period of a light wave and $\hat{s}$ is a unit vector in the direction of $\vec{S}$. The intensity of a wave, defined as the magnitude of the time averaged Poynting vector, is given by

$$I = \langle S \rangle = \frac{1}{2\mu v} EE^* = \frac{1}{2} \epsilon v E E^*, \tag{1.45}$$

where v is the velocity of the wave in the medium. The expression

$$I = \frac{1}{2} n \epsilon_0 c |E|^2, \tag{1.46}$$

commonly used in literature makes the reasonable assumption of $\mu \approx \mu_0$ for an optically transparent medium of refractive index n. A useful relation between the energy density and intensity of a plane wave is

$$I = v \langle u \rangle. \tag{1.47}$$

1.6 BOUNDARY CONDITIONS

We have so far been considering wave propagation in a source-free infinite homogeneous medium. In practice, one encounters wave propagation in a medium of finite extent. We need to address ourselves to the question of matching the solutions of the wave equation at the interface between two media. It is convenient to assume a plane boundary separating the two media. This assumption may actually be not as restrictive as it appears at first sight. As mentioned earlier, the macroscopically averaged electric and magnetic fields satisfy Gauss and Stokes theorems everywhere in the two media including the region surrounding the boundary between them. The restrictions imposed by these theorems on the fields on the two sides of the interface are called the boundary conditions.

1.6.1 Continuity of the Normal Components

Consider a small pillbox around the interface between two media of permittivities ϵ_1 and ϵ_2 (Fig. 1.6a). The height h of the pillbox is infinitesimally small bringing the flat surfaces of the pillbox very close, but on the opposite sides of the boundary. We apply Gauss' theorem

$$\oint\!\!\oint_S \vec{D} \cdot \mathrm{d}\vec{A} = \iiint_V \nabla \cdot \vec{D}\, \mathrm{d}V$$

to the displacement field $\vec{D}$ over this pillbox. The integral on the left-hand side is over the closed surface S bounding the volume V. The volume integral on the right-hand side vanishes when the volume of the pillbox approaches zero as $h \to 0$. In the same limit, the contribution to the surface integral from the curved surface of the pillbox is vanishingly small. The flat surfaces of the pillbox are taken sufficiently small so that the normal component of the displacement field contributing to the surface integral in each medium remains constant. Therefore,

$$\epsilon_1 \vec{E}_1 \cdot \hat{n}' + \epsilon_2 \vec{E}_2 \cdot \hat{n} = 0,$$

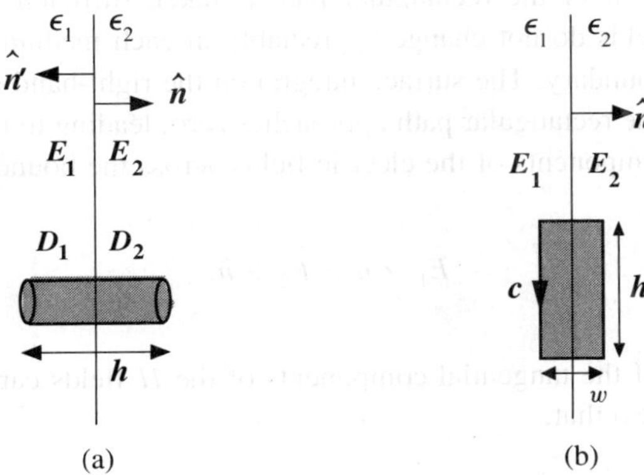

Fig. 1.6: Plane boundary between two homogeneous media.

where the unit vectors $\hat{n}'$ and $\hat{n}$ are normal to the boundary as shown in the figure. With $\hat{n}' = -\hat{n}$, the above condition, expressed as

$$\epsilon_1 \vec{E}_1 \cdot \hat{n} = \epsilon_2 \vec{E}_2 \cdot \hat{n}, \tag{1.48a}$$

is a statement of the continuity of the normal components of the displacement fields across the boundary between two homogeneous media. A similar condition holds for the normal components of the $\vec{B}$ fields, i.e.,

$$\vec{B}_1 \cdot \hat{n} = \vec{B}_2 \cdot \hat{n}. \tag{1.48b}$$

1.6.2 Continuity of the Tangential Components

Next, we apply Stokes' theorem

$$\oint_c \vec{E} \cdot \mathrm{d}\,\vec{l} = \int\int_{\Sigma} \nabla \times \vec{E} \cdot \mathrm{d}\,\vec{A}$$
$$= -\frac{\partial}{\partial t} \int\int_{\Sigma} \vec{B} \cdot \mathrm{d}\,\vec{A}$$

to the electric field, where the closed path c encloses the boundary between the two media as shown in Fig. 1.6b. Here, $\sum$ is a surface bounded by the closed path c. The side h of the rectangular path is taken sufficiently small so that the tangential fields do not change appreciably in each medium over the paths parallel to the boundary. The surface integral on the right-hand side vanishes as the width w of the rectangular path approaches zero, leading to the continuity of the tangential components of the electric fields across the boundary, i.e.,

$$\vec{E}_1 \times \hat{n} = \vec{E}_2 \times \hat{n}. \tag{1.48c}$$

The continuity of the tangential components of the $\vec{H}$ fields can be shown in a similar manner. So that,

$$\vec{H}_1 \times \hat{n} = \vec{H}_2 \times \hat{n}$$

or equivalently

$$\frac{\vec{B}_1}{\mu_1} \times \hat{n} = \frac{\vec{B}_2}{\mu_2} \times \hat{n}, \tag{1.48d}$$

where μ_1 and μ_2 are the permeabilities of the two media. We may make the reasonable assumption that for the optically transparent media $\mu_1 \approx \mu_2 = \mu_0$. These four relations (Eqs 1.48) constitute the boundary conditions which must be satisfied across an interface between two homogeneous media.

1.7 REFLECTION AND TRANSMISSION AT A BOUNDARY

The boundary conditions obtained in Section 1.6 can be used to obtain relationships among the amplitudes of the reflected, transmitted and incident waves at the boundary between two homogeneous media (Fig. 1.7). This exercise can be quite tedious. Our approach here is to avoid mathematical complications as far as possible, but at the same time not to miss the essential features of what goes on at the interface. Following Stone [1.3], we consider light incidence from a perfectly transparent ($\kappa_1 = 0$) and non-absorbing ($\vec{a}_1 = 0$) medium of refractive index n_1 to a medium for which the refractive index $\tilde{n}$ and wave vector $\vec{\tilde{k}}$ may be complex.

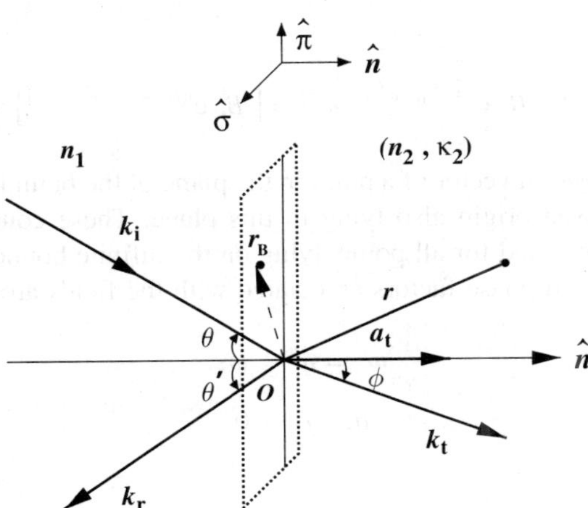

Fig. 1.7: Reflection and transmission of a wave at a plane boundary.

The incident wave is therefore homogeneous. We can anticipate the reflected wave to be homogeneous as well, but the transmitted wave in general will be inhomogeneous. Accordingly, the fields in the two media can be expressed as Incident wave:

$$\vec{E}_{\text{in}} = \vec{E}_{\text{i}}\ \mathrm{e}^{\mathrm{i}(\vec{k}_{\text{i}}\cdot\vec{r}-\omega t)}, \qquad \vec{B}_{\text{in}} = \vec{B}_{\text{i}}\ \mathrm{e}^{\mathrm{i}(\vec{k}_{\text{i}}\cdot\vec{r}-\omega t)}, \tag{1.49a}$$

Reflected wave:

$$\vec{E}_{\text{re}} = \vec{E}_{\text{r}}\ \mathrm{e}^{\mathrm{i}(\vec{k}_{\text{r}}\cdot\vec{r}-\omega' t)}, \qquad \vec{B}_{\text{re}} = \vec{B}_{\text{r}}\ \mathrm{e}^{\mathrm{i}(\vec{k}_{\text{r}}\cdot\vec{r}-\omega' t)}, \tag{1.49b}$$

Transmitted wave:

$$\vec{E}_{\text{tr}} = \vec{E}_{\text{t}}\ \mathrm{e}^{\mathrm{i}[(\vec{k}_{\text{t}}+\mathrm{i}\vec{a}_{\text{t}})\cdot\vec{r}-\omega'' t]}, \qquad \vec{B}_{\text{tr}} = \vec{B}_{\text{t}}\ \mathrm{e}^{\mathrm{i}[(\vec{k}_{\text{t}}+\mathrm{i}\vec{a}_{\text{t}})\cdot\vec{r}-\omega'' t)]}, \tag{1.49c}$$

where the amplitude vectors $\vec{E}_{\text{i}}$, $\vec{B}_{\text{i}}$, $\vec{E}_{\text{r}}$, $\vec{B}_{\text{r}}$, $\vec{E}_{\text{t}}$, and $\vec{B}_{\text{t}}$ are in general complex. The boundary conditions (1.48c) and (1.48d) require

$$\left[\vec{E}_{\text{i}}\ \mathrm{e}^{\mathrm{i}(\vec{k}_{\text{i}}\cdot\vec{r}_{\text{B}}-\omega t)} + \vec{E}_{\text{r}}\ \mathrm{e}^{\mathrm{i}(\vec{k}_{\text{r}}\cdot\vec{r}_{\text{B}}-\omega' t)}\right]\times\hat{n} = \left[\vec{E}_{\text{t}}\ \mathrm{e}^{\mathrm{i}[(\vec{k}_{\text{t}}+\mathrm{i}\vec{a}_{\text{t}})\cdot\vec{r}_{\text{B}}-\omega'' t]}\right]\times\hat{n} \tag{1.50a}$$

and

$$\left[\vec{B}_{\text{i}}\ \mathrm{e}^{\mathrm{i}(\vec{k}_{\text{i}}\cdot\vec{r}_{\text{B}}-\omega t)} + \vec{B}_{\text{r}}\ \mathrm{e}^{\mathrm{i}(\vec{k}_{\text{r}}\cdot\vec{r}_{\text{B}}-\omega' t)}\right]\times\hat{n} = \left[\vec{B}_{\text{t}}\ \mathrm{e}^{\mathrm{i}[(\vec{k}_{\text{t}}+\mathrm{i}\vec{a}_{\text{t}})\cdot\vec{r}_{\text{B}}-\omega'' t]}\right]\times\hat{n}. \tag{1.50b}$$

Here, $\vec{r}_{\text{B}}$ is the position vector of a point in the plane of the boundary with respect to a suitably chosen origin also lying in this plane. These conditions must be satisfied at all times and for all points lying on the infinite boundary plane. This can be ensured if all phase factors associated with the fields are equal. Hence

$$\omega'' = \omega' = \omega, \tag{1.51a}$$

$$\vec{a}_{\text{t}}\cdot\vec{r}_{\text{B}} = 0 \tag{1.51b}$$

and

$$\vec{k}_{\text{i}}\cdot\vec{r}_{\text{B}} = \vec{k}_{\text{r}}\cdot\vec{r}_{\text{B}} = \vec{k}_{\text{t}}\cdot\vec{r}_{\text{B}}\,. \tag{1.51c}$$

The boundary conditions therefore require the incident, reflected, and transmitted waves to have the same frequency. The magnitudes of the wave vectors of the incident and reflected waves, being in the same medium, are equal, i.e.,

$$|\vec{k}_{\rm i}| = |\vec{k}_{\rm r}| = k = n_1 \frac{\omega}{c}. \tag{1.51d}$$

Equation (1.51b) requires the attenuation vector in the second medium to be directed along the normal to the plane of the boundary, i.e.,

$$\vec{a}_{\rm t} = a_{\rm t}\hat{n}. \tag{1.51e}$$

The condition (1.51c) can be re-expressed as,

$$\vec{k}_{\rm i} \cdot \hat{n} \times \vec{r} = \vec{k}_{\rm r} \cdot \hat{n} \times \vec{r} = \vec{k}_{\rm t} \cdot \hat{n} \times \vec{r}, \tag{1.51f}$$

where $\hat{n}\times \vec{r}$ is a convenient representation for vector $\vec{r}_{\rm B}$ lying in the plane of the boundary in terms of an arbitrary position vector $\vec{r}$ (see Fig. 1.7). Manipulation of the scalar triple product leads to the important result:

$$\vec{k}_{\rm i} \times \hat{n} = \vec{k}_{\rm r} \times \hat{n} = \vec{k}_{\rm t} \times \hat{n}. \tag{1.52}$$

This is the statement of the coplanarity of the wave vectors $\vec{k}_{\rm i}$, $\vec{k}_{\rm r}$, $\vec{k}_{\rm t}$, and the normal $\hat{n}$ to the plane of the interface. In addition, Eq. (1.52) requires

$$\theta' = \theta \tag{1.53a}$$

and

$$k_{\rm t} \sin\phi = k \sin\theta, \tag{1.53b}$$

where θ, θ', and ϕ are the angles of incidence, reflection, and refraction, respectively. These equations ensure the equality of the angles of incidence and reflection, but leave the angle of refraction ϕ and magnitude $k_{\rm t}$ of the real part of the propagation vector in the second medium undetermined – only the product $k_{\rm t} \sin\phi$ is determined. Equations (1.52) and (1.53b) describe the laws of reflection and refraction of light across an interface. Combining Eqs (1.16), (1.18), and (1.19), we get

$$(k_{\rm t} \cos\phi + {\rm i}a_{\rm t})^2 + (k_{\rm t} \sin\phi)^2 = \frac{\omega^2}{c^2}(n_2 + {\rm i}\kappa_2)^2. \tag{1.54}$$

Knowing n_1, n_2, and κ_2, Eqs (1.53b) and (1.54) suffice to determine ϕ, k_t, and a_t. With the equality of the phase factors guaranteed by Eqs (1.51), the restrictions (Eqs 1.50a and 1.50b) on the fields go over to the restrictions on the corresponding field amplitudes. Therefore,

$$(\vec{E}_i + \vec{E}_r)_{\text{boundary}} \times \hat{n} = (\vec{E}_t)_{\text{boundary}} \times \hat{n}, \tag{1.55a}$$

$$(\vec{B}_i + \vec{B}_r)_{\text{boundary}} \times \hat{n} = (\vec{B}_t)_{\text{boundary}} \times \hat{n}. \tag{1.55b}$$

Expressing the electric fields in terms of the Cartesian components, we have

$$\vec{E}_i = E_{in}\hat{n} + E_{i\pi}\hat{\pi} + E_{i\sigma}\hat{\sigma}, \tag{1.56a}$$

$$\vec{E}_r = E_{rn}\hat{n} + E_{r\pi}\hat{\pi} + E_{r\sigma}\hat{\sigma}, \tag{1.56b}$$

$$E_t = E_{tn}\hat{n} + E_{t\pi}\hat{\pi} + E_{t\sigma}\hat{\sigma}, \tag{1.56c}$$

where the unit vectors $\hat{\pi}$, $\hat{\sigma}$, $\hat{n}$ constitute a right-handed Cartesian coordinate system with the unit vectors $\hat{\pi}$ and $\hat{\sigma}$ lying in the plane of the boundary and unit vector $\hat{n}$ pointing normal to it (Fig. 1.7). We can choose the unit vector $\hat{\pi}$ to lie in the plane of incidence (plane containing $\vec{k}_i$, $\vec{k}_r$, $\vec{k}_t$, $\hat{n}$). Similarly, decomposing the propagation vectors of the three waves in the chosen system of coordinates, we have

$$\vec{k}_i = (k\cos\theta)\hat{n} - (k\sin\theta)\hat{\pi}, \tag{1.57a}$$

$$\vec{k}_r = -(k\cos\theta)\hat{n} - (k\sin\theta)\hat{\pi}, \tag{1.57b}$$

$$\vec{k}_t = (k_t\cos\phi)\hat{n} - (k_t\sin\phi)\hat{\pi}. \tag{1.57c}$$

The transversality conditions (1.17a,b) require

$$E_{in} = E_{i\pi}\tan\theta, \tag{1.58a}$$

$$E_{rn} = -E_{r\pi}\tan\theta, \tag{1.58b}$$

$$E_{tn} = \frac{k_t\sin\phi}{k_t\cos\phi + ia_t}E_{t\pi}. \tag{1.58c}$$

Using Eqs (1.17), (1.56), and (1.57), the magnetic field vectors associated with the incident, reflected, and transmitted waves can be expressed in terms of the components of the corresponding electric field vectors. So that,

$$\vec{B}_{\mathrm{i}} = \frac{k}{\omega}[-(E_{\mathrm{i}\sigma}\sin\theta)\hat{n} - (E_{\mathrm{i}\sigma}\cos\theta)\hat{\pi} + (E_{\mathrm{i}n}\sin\theta + E_{\mathrm{i}\pi}\cos\theta)\hat{\sigma}], \tag{1.59a}$$

$$\vec{B}_{\mathrm{r}} = \frac{k}{\omega}[-(E_{\mathrm{r}\sigma}\sin\theta)\hat{n} + (E_{\mathrm{r}\sigma}\cos\theta)\hat{\pi} + (E_{\mathrm{r}n}\sin\theta - E_{\mathrm{r}\pi}\cos\theta)\hat{\sigma}], \tag{1.59b}$$

$$\vec{B}_{\mathrm{t}} = \frac{1}{\omega}[-(E_{\mathrm{t}\sigma}k_{\mathrm{t}}\sin\phi)\hat{n} - (E_{\mathrm{t}\sigma}k_{\mathrm{t}}\cos\phi + \mathrm{i}E_{\mathrm{t}\sigma}a_{\mathrm{t}})\hat{\pi} + (E_{\mathrm{t}\pi}k_{\mathrm{t}}\cos\phi + E_{\mathrm{t}n}k_{\mathrm{t}}\sin\phi + \mathrm{i}E_{\mathrm{t}\pi}a_{\mathrm{t}})\hat{\sigma}]. \tag{1.59c}$$

The field components of the incident wave are determined by its state of polarization and are therefore known. The boundary conditions (1.55a,b) impose the following restrictions on the components of the reflected and transmitted fields:

$$(E_{\mathrm{i}\pi} + E_{\mathrm{r}\pi})_{\mathrm{boundary}} = (E_{\mathrm{t}\pi})_{\mathrm{boundary}}, \tag{1.60a}$$

$$(E_{\mathrm{i}\sigma} + E_{\mathrm{r}\sigma})_{\mathrm{boundary}} = (E_{\mathrm{t}\sigma})_{\mathrm{boundary}}, \tag{1.60b}$$

$$(B_{\mathrm{i}\pi} + B_{\mathrm{r}\pi})_{\mathrm{boundary}} = (B_{\mathrm{t}\pi})_{\mathrm{boundary}}, \tag{1.60c}$$

$$(B_{\mathrm{i}\sigma} + B_{\mathrm{r}\sigma})_{\mathrm{boundary}} = (B_{\mathrm{t}\sigma})_{\mathrm{boundary}}. \tag{1.60d}$$

Equations (1.60c,d) involving the tangential components of the magnetic fields can be expressed in terms of the tangential components of the electric fields:

$$k(E_{\mathrm{i}\sigma} - E_{\mathrm{r}\sigma})\cos\theta = (k_{\mathrm{t}}\cos\phi + \mathrm{i}a_{\mathrm{t}})E_{\mathrm{t}\sigma}, \tag{1.61a}$$

$$\frac{k}{\cos\theta}(E_{\mathrm{i}\pi} - E_{\mathrm{r}\pi}) = \frac{(\vec{k}_{\mathrm{t}} + \mathrm{i}\,\vec{a}_{\mathrm{t}})^2}{k_{\mathrm{t}}\cos\phi + \mathrm{i}a_{\mathrm{t}}}E_{\mathrm{t}\pi}. \tag{1.61b}$$

Equations (1.58), (1.60a,b), and (1.61) can now be solved to obtain the amplitude reflection and transmission coefficients:

$$r_{\sigma} = \left(\frac{E_{\mathrm{r}\sigma}}{E_{\mathrm{i}\sigma}}\right)_{\mathrm{boundary}} = \frac{k\cos\theta - k_{\mathrm{t}}\cos\phi - \mathrm{i}a_{\mathrm{t}}}{k\cos\theta + k_{\mathrm{t}}\cos\phi + \mathrm{i}a_{\mathrm{t}}}, \tag{1.62a}$$

$$r_{\pi} = \left(\frac{E_{\mathrm{r}\pi}}{E_{\mathrm{i}\pi}}\right)_{\mathrm{boundary}} = \frac{n_1^2(k_{\mathrm{t}}\cos\phi + \mathrm{i}a_{\mathrm{t}}) - (n_2 + \mathrm{i}\kappa_2)^2 k\cos\theta}{n_1^2(k_{\mathrm{t}}\cos\phi + \mathrm{i}a_{\mathrm{t}}) + (n_2 + \mathrm{i}\kappa_2)^2 k\cos\theta}, \tag{1.62b}$$

$$r_{n} = \left(\frac{E_{\mathrm{r}n}}{E_{\mathrm{i}n}}\right)_{\mathrm{boundary}} = -r_{\pi}, \tag{1.62c}$$

$$t_\sigma = \left(\frac{E_{t\sigma}}{E_{i\sigma}}\right)_{\text{boundary}} = \frac{2k\cos\theta}{k\cos\theta + k_t\cos\phi + ia_t}, \tag{1.62d}$$

$$t_\pi = \left(\frac{E_{t\pi}}{E_{i\pi}}\right)_{\text{boundary}} = \frac{2n_1^2(k_t\cos\phi + ia_t)}{n_1^2(k_t\cos\phi + ia_t) + (n_2 + i\kappa_2)^2 k\cos\theta}, \tag{1.62e}$$

$$t_n = \left(\frac{E_{tn}}{E_{in}}\right)_{\text{boundary}} = \frac{k\cos\theta}{k_t\cos\phi + ia_t} t_\pi. \tag{1.62f}$$

We note that the reflection and transmission coefficients are complex, implying that the reflected and transmitted fields are in general not in phase with the incident field. Some care needs to be exercised to distinguish between the $\hat{n}$- and $\hat{\pi}$-polarizations – both lying in the plane of incidence. Their reflection coefficients have equal magnitudes but are 180° out of phase at all angles of incidence whereas the transmission coefficients for these polarizations differ in phase as well as in magnitude at all angles of incidence.

In the present example, the reflection and transmission coefficients were obtained from the continuity of the tangential components of the fields (Eqs 1.48c,d) at the interface and some intuition concerning the incident and reflected fields in the first medium. In other situations, it may be necessary to use the continuity of the normal components (Eqs 1.48a,b) also.

1.7.1 External Reflections

We first consider the case when light crosses an interface from an optically rare medium to an optically dense medium ($n_1 < n_2$). Reflections under these conditions are known as external reflections. If the second medium is also perfectly transparent ($\kappa_2 = 0$), then Eq. (1.54) when combined with Eq. (1.53b) gives

$$k_t\cos\phi + ia_t = \frac{\omega}{c}(n_2^2 - n_1^2\sin^2\theta)^{1/2}. \tag{1.63}$$

For $n_2 > n_1$, the right-hand side of Eq. (1.63) remains real for all angles of incidence. Therefore, the attenuation vector must vanish, i.e.,

$$a_t = 0$$

and

$$k_t\cos\phi = \frac{\omega}{c}(n_2^2 - n_1^2\sin^2\theta)^{1/2}.$$

In this case the transmitted wave in the second medium is also homogeneous with

$$k_t = n_2\frac{\omega}{c}, \tag{1.64a}$$

and Eq. (1.53b) takes the more familiar form

$$n_2 \sin\phi = n_1 \sin\theta. \tag{1.64b}$$

This is the well-known Snell's law which holds at the interface between two perfectly transparent media under conditions of external reflections ($n_2 > n_1$). It is not obvious at this stage whether Snell's law in its present form will hold when light is incident from an optically more dense medium to an optically less dense medium. Equations (1.53b) and (1.54) may be taken together to represent the more general form of Snell's law. For external reflections, Eqs (1.62) simplify to

$$r_\sigma = \frac{n_1\cos\theta - n_2\cos\phi}{n_1\cos\theta + n_2\cos\phi}, \tag{1.65a}$$

$$r_\pi = \frac{n_1\cos\phi - n_2\cos\theta}{n_1\cos\phi + n_2\cos\theta}, \tag{1.65b}$$

$$r_n = -r_\pi, \tag{1.65c}$$

$$t_\sigma = \frac{2n_1\cos\theta}{n_1\cos\theta + n_2\cos\phi}, \tag{1.65d}$$

$$t_\pi = \frac{2n_1\cos\phi}{n_1\cos\phi + n_2\cos\theta}, \tag{1.65e}$$

$$t_n = \frac{n_1\cos\theta}{n_2\cos\phi} t_\pi. \tag{1.65f}$$

Equations (1.65) constitute the Fresnel relations. They are applicable when light enters from a perfectly transparent medium of smaller index of refraction into another perfectly transparent medium of higher index of refraction. Some of these relations may differ from the standard form of Fresnel relations given in many texts. We shall return to these differences shortly.

It will be shown in Section 6.5.1 that if the direction of incidence is reversed, i.e., if light enters the medium of index of refraction n_1 from medium of index of refraction n_2, then the new reflection coefficients r'_σ, r'_π and the new transmission coefficients t'_σ, t'_π satisfy the following relationships:

$$r'_\sigma = -r_\sigma, \tag{1.65g}$$

$$r'_\pi = -r_\pi, \tag{1.65h}$$

$$t_\sigma t'_\sigma = 1 - r_\sigma^2, \tag{1.65i}$$

$$t_\pi t'_\pi = 1 - r_\pi^2. \tag{1.65j}$$

1.7.1.1 Brewster Angle

Fresnel relations reveal an interesting consequence of the boundary conditions. The reflection coefficient for σ-polarized light does not become zero for any angle of incidence, but the reflection coefficients for π- and n-polarizations vanish for angle of incidence θ_B, satisfying the condition

$$n_1 \cos\phi = n_2 \cos\theta_B. \tag{1.66a}$$

This result when combined with Snell's law gives

$$\phi = \frac{\pi}{2} - \theta_B. \tag{1.66b}$$

Accordingly, the reflection coefficient of light polarized in the plane of incidence becomes zero when the angle between the directions of propagation of the reflected and transmitted light waves becomes 90°. The angle of incidence θ_B satisfying this condition is known as Brewster angle. The π- and n-polarized waves at this angle of incidence do not undergo any reflection and are therefore fully transmitted. The σ-polarized light, on the other hand, is partially transmitted and partially reflected at all angles of incidence including the Brewster angle. Equations (1.66) give for the Brewster angle, the condition

$$\tan\theta_B = \frac{n_2}{n_1}. \tag{1.67}$$

If unpolarized light is incident at this angle, the reflected light appears in pure σ-polarization. However, for $n_2/n_1 = 1.5$, as for the air–glass interface, $\theta_B = 56.3°$, and only 15% of the incident energy appears in the reflected light. Notwithstanding this rather low polarizing efficiency, the Brewster angle is also known as the polarizing angle. Lasers make a very effective use of incidence at Brewster angle for controlling the state of polarization of laser light. This is shown in Fig. 1.8. Glass or quartz windows are fused to the plasma tube of a laser at both ends at the Brewster angle. At each of the four interfaces, σ-polarized

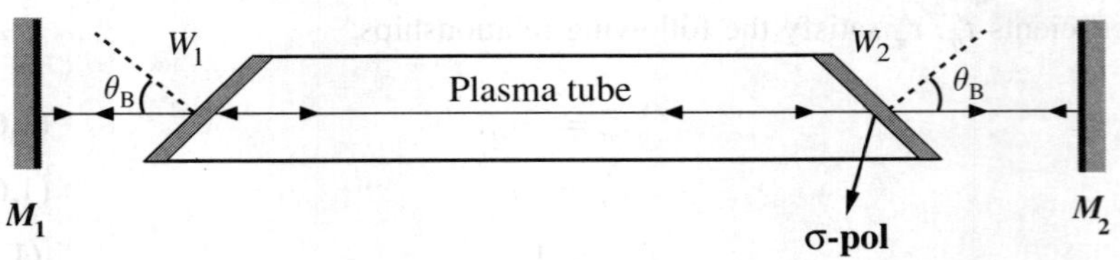

Fig. 1.8: Brewster windows (W_1, W_2) of the plasma tube of a laser.

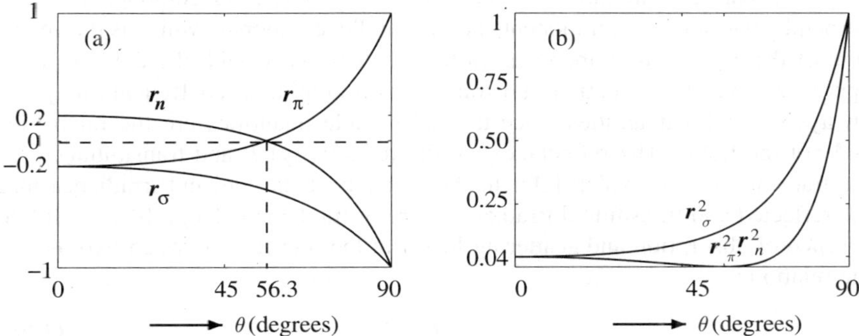

Fig. 1.9: Variations of reflection coefficients (a) and their squares (b) with angle of incidence for external reflections ($n_2/n_1 = 1.5$).

light suffers substantial (15% for glass windows) reflection losses whereas light polarized in the plane of incidence is transmitted without any reflection loss. The laser cavity (mirrors M_1, M_2 and the active medium filling the plasma tube) is unable to sustain oscillations for the σ-polarized light in the presence of these losses. Consequently, light coming out of a laser with Brewster windows is polarized in the plane of incidence. The σ-polarized light with electric field perpendicular to the plane of incidence is eliminated in the process.

Variations of the reflection coefficients and their squares with the angle of incidence are shown in Fig. 1.9 for the three states of polarization. The reflection coefficient is rather small at normal incidence (0.2 for $n_2/n_1 = 1.5$), but approaches unit value at grazing incidence ($\theta \longrightarrow 90°$). The three polarization states behave differently. The σ-polarized light suffers 180° phase change on reflection at all angles of incidence. The π-polarized light, however, undergoes phase reversal only up to the Brewster angle, and no phase change for incidence beyond this angle. The n-polarized light has the behavior just opposite to that of the π-polarized light (Fig. 1.9a).

The reflection coefficients and their squares vanish at the Brewster angle for π- and n-polarizations. The reflected light is richer in σ polarization, except for incidence at normal and grazing angles.

1.7.2 Reflectance and Transmittance

It was mentioned that the Fresnel relations in their present form (Eqs 1.62) may differ somewhat from Fresnel relations given elsewhere. The difference lies in the fact that we have decomposed the field vectors into three components along the $\hat{\pi}$-, $\hat{\sigma}$-, and $\hat{n}$-directions. In most texts, the in-plane ($\hat{\pi}$- and $\hat{n}$-) components are not separated. Instead, one deals with only two field components – the perpendicular or the σ-component and the parallel component which is the vector sum of the π- and n-components. In this context, we would like the readers to appreciate that the reflection and transmission amplitude coefficients may not always be useful quantities since the measurable quantities are the intensities and not the fields. The reflectance (or the reflectivity) R and transmittance (or the transmitivity) T, which refer to the division of the incident irradiance into the reflected and transmitted irradiances, are of fundamental significance. In the absence of absorption and scattering losses at the interface between two media, the relation

$$R + T = 1 \tag{1.68}$$

must hold for reasons of energy conservation. The incident, reflected and transmitted energies crossing per unit time per unit area of the interface are

$$\begin{aligned} I_{\text{in}} &= \vec{S}_{\text{i}} \;.\hat{n} = S_{\text{i}} \cos\theta, \\ I_{\text{re}} &= \vec{S}_{\text{r}} \;.\hat{n} = S_{\text{r}} \cos\theta, \\ I_{\text{tr}} &= \vec{S}_{\text{t}} \;.\hat{n} = S_{\text{t}} \cos\phi, \end{aligned}$$

respectively. So that

$$R = \frac{I_{\text{re}}}{I_{\text{in}}} = \frac{S_{\text{r}} \cos\theta}{S_{\text{i}} \cos\theta} = \left(\frac{E_{\text{r}}}{E_{\text{i}}}\right)^2 = r^2, \tag{1.69a}$$

$$T = \frac{I_{\text{tr}}}{I_{\text{in}}} = \frac{S_{\text{t}} \cos\phi}{S_{\text{i}} \cos\theta} = \frac{n_2 \cos\phi}{n_1 \cos\theta}\left(\frac{E_{\text{t}}}{E_{\text{i}}}\right)^2 = \frac{n_2 \cos\phi}{n_1 \cos\theta} t^2, \tag{1.69b}$$

where S_{i}, S_{r}, and S_{t} are the magnitudes of the incident, reflected and transmitted Poynting vectors at the interface, respectively. For perpendicular (σ-) polarization,

$$R_\sigma = r_\sigma^2 = \left(\frac{n_1 \cos\theta - n_2 \cos\phi}{n_1 \cos\theta + n_2 \cos\phi}\right)^2, \tag{1.70a}$$

$$T_\sigma = \frac{n_2 \cos\phi}{n_1 \cos\theta} t_\sigma^2 = \frac{n_2 \cos\phi}{n_1 \cos\theta}\left(\frac{2n_1 \cos\theta}{n_1 \cos\theta + n_2 \cos\phi}\right)^2. \tag{1.70b}$$

It can be seen that the condition

$$R_\sigma + T_\sigma = 1$$

holds. For the in-plane or the so-called parallel polarization, we need to combine the n- and π-components since they do not represent independent waves. Therefore,

$$\begin{aligned} R_{\mathrm{p}} &= r^2(\text{parallel polarization}) \\ &= \frac{E_{\mathrm{r}n}^2 + E_{\mathrm{r}\pi}^2}{E_{\mathrm{i}n}^2 + E_{\mathrm{i}\pi}^2} \\ &= \frac{r_n^2 E_{\mathrm{i}n}^2 + r_\pi^2 E_{\mathrm{i}\pi}^2}{E_{\mathrm{i}n}^2 + E_{\mathrm{i}\pi}^2} \\ &= \left(\frac{n_1\cos\phi - n_2\cos\theta}{n_1\cos\phi + n_2\cos\theta}\right)^2 \end{aligned} \tag{1.71a}$$

and

$$\begin{aligned} T_{\mathrm{p}} &= \frac{n_2}{n_1}\left(\frac{E_{\mathrm{t}n}^2 + E_{\mathrm{t}\pi}^2}{E_{\mathrm{i}n}^2 + E_{\mathrm{i}\pi}^2}\right)\left(\frac{\cos\phi}{\cos\theta}\right) \\ &= \frac{4n_1 n_2\cos\phi\cos\theta}{(n_1\cos\phi + n_2\cos\theta)^2}. \end{aligned} \tag{1.71b}$$

Once again, it can be seen that $R_{\mathrm{p}} + T_{\mathrm{p}} = 1$. Figure 1.10 shows the variations in the reflectance and transmittance with the angle of incidence for external reflections ($n_2/n_1 = 1.5$).

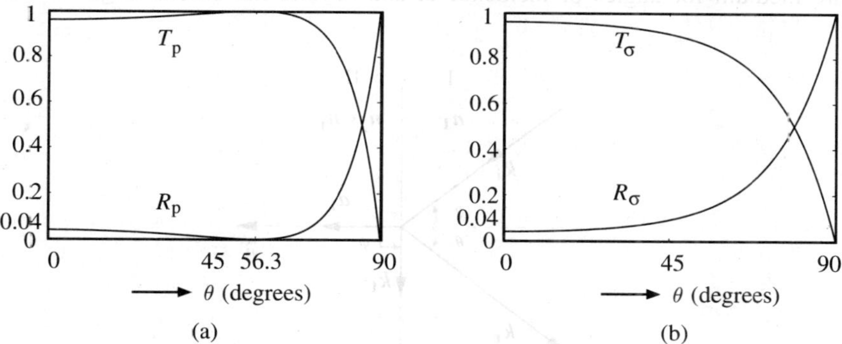

Fig. 1.10: Reflectance and transmittance changes with angle of incidence for external reflections ($n_2/n_1 = 1.5$); (a) parallel or in-plane polarization, (b) perpendicular polarization.

1.7.3 Internal Reflections

When the refractive index n_2 of the second medium is lower than the refractive index n_1 of the first medium, the right-hand side of Eq. (1.63) cannot remain real for all angles of incidence. Beyond a certain angle of incidence, called the critical angle θ_c defined by

$$n_2 = n_1 \sin\theta_c, \tag{1.72}$$

the right-hand side becomes purely imaginary. For incident angles smaller than the critical angle, the attenuation vector $\vec{a}_t$ vanishes as the right-hand side is real, and the transmitted wave in the second medium is homogeneous with the magnitude of the wave vector $k_t = n_2\omega/c$, just as for the external reflections. Except for the fact that the angle of refraction exceeds the angle of incidence, there is no qualitative difference in external and internal reflections as long as the angle of incidence remains smaller than the critical angle. In fact, the π- and n-polarizations go through zero reflectivity at the corresponding Brewster angle in this case as well. Brewster angle is always smaller than the critical angle (for $n_1/n_2 = 1.5$, $\theta_B = 33.7°$ and $\theta_c = 41.8°$). However, the situation changes non-trivially as the critical angle is approached. At the critical angle, the right-hand side of Eq. (1.63) vanishes, forcing $k_t \cos\phi$ and a_t to take zero values. This happens when the angle of refraction ϕ becomes 90° and wave propagation in the second medium takes place along the interface only (Fig. 1.11). Equations (1.65) give reflection coefficient of unit magnitude at this angle of incidence, irrespective of the state of polarization. Light is therefore totally reflected back into the first medium; hence the use of the term total internal reflection to describe wave propagation from an optically dense to an optically rare medium for angles of incidence at and beyond the critical angle. It may

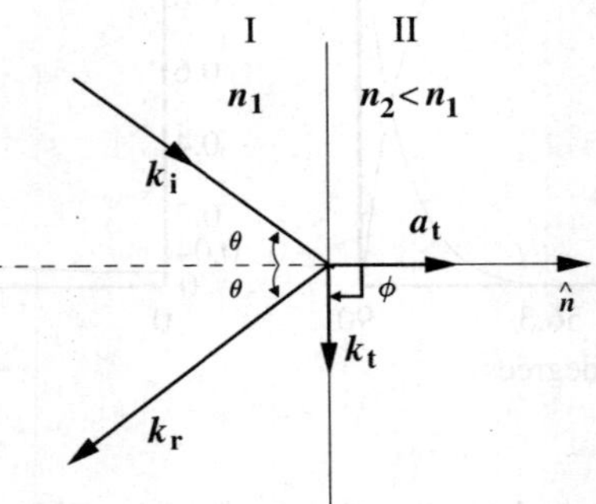

Fig. 1.11: Geometry for internal reflections. Wave in second medium is inhomogeneous for angles of incidence exceeding the critical angle.

appear confusing that the wave is totally reflected back into the first medium despite wave propagation taking place along the interface ($\phi = 90°$). We shall return to this point shortly. The wave propagating along the interface is called the evanescent (tending to vanish) wave.

As the angle of incidence exceeds the critical angle, the right-hand side of Eq. (1.63) becomes purely imaginary and the transmitted wave continues to propagate along the interface with propagation vector $\vec{k}_t$ of magnitude (Eq. 1.53b)

$$k_t = n_1 \frac{\omega}{c} \sin\theta, \tag{1.73}$$

but now with an attenuation vector $\vec{a}_t$ of magnitude

$$a_t = \frac{\omega}{c}(n_1^2 \sin^2\theta - n_2^2)^{1/2} \tag{1.74}$$

directed normal (Eq. 1.51e) to the plane of the boundary (Fig. 1.11). Equation (1.49c) for the transmitted wave now takes the form

$$\vec{E}_{tr} = \vec{E}_t \, e^{i[(\vec{k}_t + i\vec{a}_t).\vec{r} - \omega t]}. \tag{1.75}$$

Substituting k_t and a_t from Eqs (1.73) and (1.74) gives

$$\vec{E}_{tr} = \vec{E}_t \, e^{-\frac{\omega}{c}(n_1^2 \sin^2\theta - n_2^2)^{1/2} z} \, e^{i(\frac{n_1\omega}{c} x \sin\theta - \omega t)}. \tag{1.76}$$

The transmitted wave (evanescent wave) propagates in the x direction. The amplitude of the wave in the second medium decreases exponentially with z, falling to $1/e$ of its value at the interface at a distance

$$\delta = \frac{1}{a_t} = \frac{\lambda_v}{2\pi(n_1^2 \sin^2\theta - n_2^2)^{1/2}} \tag{1.77}$$

away from the interface. The beam attenuation increases with increasing angle of incidence beyond the critical angle. For the glass–air interface, $\delta = 2.3 \times 10^{-5}$ cm for $\theta = 45°$ and $\lambda_v = 500$ nm. The penetration depth δ in the second medium is only a fraction of the wavelength of light. The surfaces of constant phase (normal to $\vec{k}_t$) are normal to the plane of the interface and the surfaces of constant amplitude (normal to $\vec{a}_t$) are parallel to the plane of the interface.The evanescent wave in the second medium is therefore an inhomogeneous wave with the phase velocity ($\omega/k_t = c/(n_1 \sin\theta)$) exceeding the velocity of light (c/n_1) in the medium. Total internal reflection makes it possible for light to propagate in optical fibers and optical wave guides.

The reflection and transmission coefficients for internal reflections for $\theta < \theta_c$ are still given by Eqs (1.65), just as for the external reflections. But now n_2 being smaller than n_1, the signs of the reflection coefficients are opposite to those for the external reflections. For $\theta > \theta_c$, Eqs (1.62) give the following expressions for the reflection coefficients:

$$r_\sigma = \frac{n_1 \cos\theta - \mathrm{i}(n_1^2 \sin^2\theta - n_2^2)^{1/2}}{n_1 \cos\theta + \mathrm{i}(n_1^2 \sin^2\theta - n_2^2)^{1/2}} = \mathrm{e}^{-\mathrm{i}2\phi_0}, \tag{1.78a}$$

$$r_\pi = \frac{-n_2^2 \cos\theta + \mathrm{i}n_1(n_1^2 \sin^2\theta - n_2^2)^{1/2}}{n_2^2 \cos\theta + \mathrm{i}n_1(n_1^2 \sin^2\theta - n_2^2)^{1/2}} = \mathrm{e}^{-\mathrm{i}(2\psi_0+\pi)}, \tag{1.78b}$$

where

$$\tan\phi_0 = \frac{(n_1^2 \sin^2\theta - n_2^2)^{1/2}}{n_1 \cos\theta}, \tag{1.79a}$$

$$\tan\psi_0 = \left(\frac{n_1}{n_2}\right)^2 \frac{(n_1^2 \sin^2\theta - n_2^2)^{1/2}}{n_1 \cos\theta}. \tag{1.79b}$$

The reflection coefficients are now complex with unit magnitude for any state of polarization for all angles exceeding the critical angle. The reflection is therefore total. For internal reflections, the variations of the reflection coefficients and reflectances with the angle of incidence are shown in Fig. 1.12. The phase changes for the reflected fields are different for the π- and σ-polarizations. Accordingly, linearly polarized light, polarized along directions other than $\hat{\pi}$- and $\hat{\sigma}$-directions, becomes elliptically polarized after an internal reflection. The phase for σ-polarization changes from $2\phi_0 = 0$ at $\theta = \theta_c$ to $2\phi_0 = \pi$ at $\theta = 90°$. The π-polarization, on the other hand, undergoes a 180° phase change (change

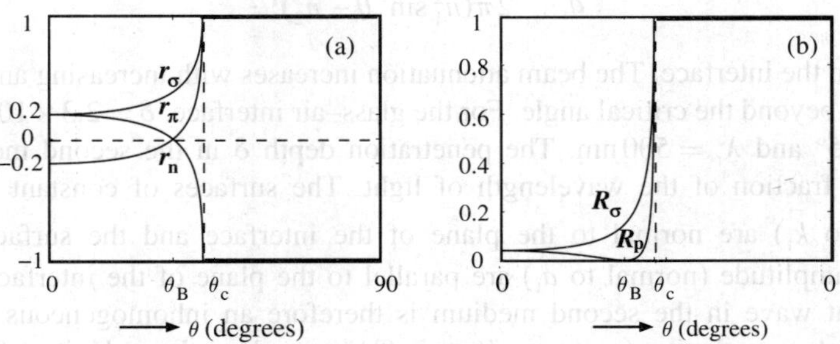

Fig. 1.12: Variation of reflection coefficients (a) and reflectances (b) with angle of incidence for internal reflection ($n_1/n_2 = 1.5$); $\theta_B = 33.7°$, $\theta_c = 41.8°$.

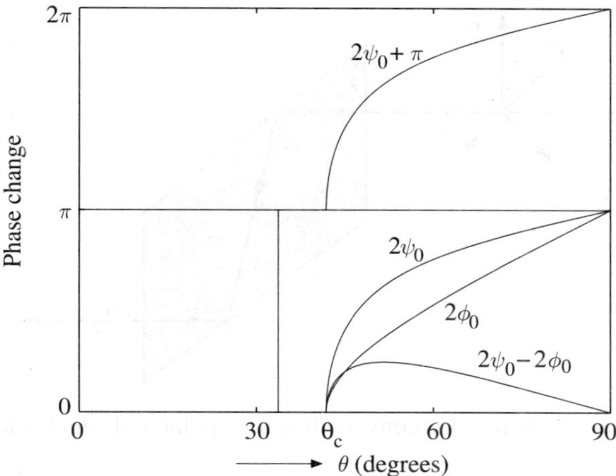

Fig. 1.13: Phase changes during internal reflections with angle of incidence ($n_1/n_2 = 1.5$); ψ_0 is for π-polarization and ϕ_0 is for σ-polarization.

of sign) at the Brewster angle. Additional phase changes take place beyond the critical angle. The net phase of π-polarized wave varies from $2\psi_0 + \pi = \pi$ at $\theta = \theta_c$ to $2\psi_0 + \pi = 2\pi$ at $\theta = 90°$. These phase changes are shown in Fig. 1.13. The same figure also shows the variations of $2\psi_0$ and $2\psi_0 - 2\phi_0$.

The phase difference $2(\psi_0 - \phi_0)$ between π- and σ-polarizations can be obtained from

$$\tan(\psi_0 - \phi_0) = \frac{\cos\theta}{\sin^2\theta}\left(\sin^2\theta - \frac{n_2^2}{n_1^2}\right)^{1/2}. \tag{1.80}$$

For $n_1/n_2 = 1.5$, the maximum value of $(2\psi_0 - 2\phi_0)$ of 45.2° occurs at $\theta = 54°$.

1.7.3.1 Fresnel Rhomb

This device, first conceived by Fresnel, is used to change the state of polarization of light from linear to circular by introducing a phase difference of 90° between the π- and σ-polarized light waves through two successive internal reflections in a rhomb, cut with an apex angle which allows 45° phase change in each internal reflection (Fig. 1.14). The incident beam, linearly polarized at 45° with the face edge, enters the rhomb normally. The beam suffers two internal reflections inside the rhomb and leaves through the opposite face of the rhomb normally, but now circularly polarized. Unlike a quarter-wave plate

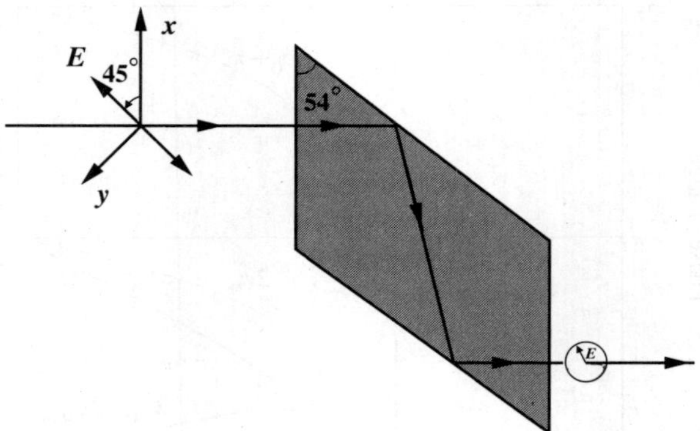

Fig. 1.14: Fresnel rhomb to convert linearly polarized light into circularly polarized light.

(see Section 3.3.2), Fresnel rhomb is much less sensitive to changes in the wavelength of light.

1.7.4 Frustrated Total Internal Reflection

We have seen that despite the existence of the evanescent wave along the interface, light is fully reflected back into the first medium. Consequently, no energy can flow into the second medium. This, as a matter of fact, is a correct statement and can be proved by showing that the time averaged value of the z-component of the Poynting vector in the semi-infinite second medium is actually zero. This, however, does not fully clarify the situation. There is a need to further explore what actually happens in the neighborhood of the interface. It has already been mentioned that light does penetrate into the second medium, but the depth of penetration is rather small. This can be verified. Consider a thin slab of lower refractive index n_2 sandwiched between thicker slabs of a medium of higher refractive index n_1 as shown in Fig. 1.15.

Let the thickness d of the sandwiched slab be comparable to the penetration depth of the wave. For incidence at the first interface at an angle greater than the critical angle, the transmitted wave can be detected beyond the second interface. The amplitude of the transmitted wave depends on the actual thickness of the sandwiched slab; thinner the sandwiched slab, larger the amplitude of the transmitted wave. However, to avoid multiple reflections in the sandwiched medium, its thickness should be somewhat larger than the penetration depth δ. It is therefore clear that notwithstanding what has been said earlier, light is partially transmitted in an internal reflection. However, if the thickness of the sandwiched slab is made sufficiently large, the transmitted wave after travelling

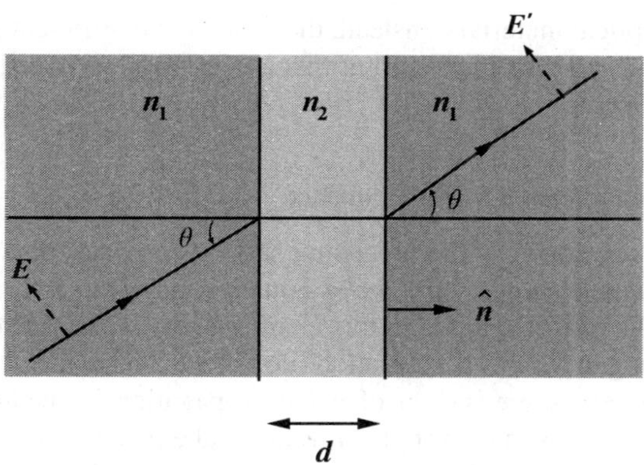

Fig. 1.15: Geometry to frustrate total internal reflection ($n_2 < n_1$).

a short distance in this medium apparently bends and re-enters the first medium, somewhat shifted from the position of entry into the second medium (Goos-Hanchan shift [1.4]). Thus, no net energy flows into the second medium making internal reflection total, indeed. But the time averaged component of the Poynting vector along the interface is non-zero (the evanescent wave). It is possible to frustrate the total internal reflection (make it less than total) by reducing the thickness of the middle slab. Arrangements of the type shown in Fig. 1.15 can control the amount of energy being coupled from one medium to the other. For σ-polarized light of amplitude E_σ entering the first interface, amplitude of the wave leaving the second interface (see Eq. 1.65i), is

$$\begin{aligned} E'_\sigma &= t_\sigma t'_\sigma \, \mathrm{e}^{-d/\delta} E_\sigma \\ &= (1 - r_\sigma^2)\, \mathrm{e}^{-d/\delta} E_\sigma \\ &= (1 - \mathrm{e}^{-\mathrm{i}4\phi_0})\, \mathrm{e}^{-d/\delta} E_\sigma, \end{aligned}$$

where ϕ_0 is as defined in Eq. (1.78a), δ the penetration depth (Eq. 1.77) and d the thickness of the sandwiched slab. It must be mentioned that bringing in the second interface as in Fig. 1.15 changes the original problem altogether. The boundary conditions at the first interface get modified due to the presence of the second interface.

We end this discussion by recalling that the external and internal reflections have been investigated here under the assumption of perfect transparency of the media on the two sides of the interface. Real optical materials are not perfectly transparent. For sufficiently high transparency ($\kappa \to 0$), the results obtained in this chapter may be used as such or with slight modification. For example, complete absence of π-polarized light on reflection at Brewster angle may not happen in real optical materials. Instead, the reflection coefficient for π-polarized light goes through a sharp minimum at this angle. Similar modifications may be expected elsewhere.

1.7.5 Reflection from a Metallic Surface

The formalism developed in the preceding sections can describe reflection from a metallic surface. However, the wave equation applicable to metals is quite different from the one developed in this chapter because the free charge and free currents appearing in Maxwell's equations do not vanish for metals. Nevertheless, it is possible to gain some insight of wave propagation in metals from Fresnel relations if allowance is made for absorption to take place in the second medium [1.5, 1.6]. Metals are generally opaque to visible light unless thin metallic films no more than a few nanometers (10^{-7} cm) in thickness are employed. Special care needs to be exercised for the preparation of thin metallic films if they are to faithfully represent the behavior of bulk metals. Thin metallic films are partially transparent in some regions of the visible spectrum. For example, gold and copper with yellow luster are somewhat transparent to blue-green light if used in the form of thin films. Table 1.2 gives real and imaginary parts of the index of refraction of some metals in the visible region.

For good conductors, the imaginary part of the refractive index is much larger than the real part, and an approximate expression

$$\sin\phi = \frac{\sin\theta}{\kappa} \tag{1.81}$$

holds for the angle of refraction ϕ, where θ is the angle of incidence. For incidence at 60°, the angle of refraction for aluminum is merely 7°. Thus for good conductors, the transmitted wave propagates essentially along the normal to the plane of the interface. The propagation vector $\vec{k}_t$ and attenuation vector $\vec{a}_t$ are nearly coincident. Therefore, the wave in a good conductor is very nearly

Table 1.2. Complex refractive index $\tilde{n} = n + i\kappa$ of some metals.

Metal	λ (nm)	n	κ
Al	650	1.30	7.11
Pd	550	1.8	4.0
Cu	548	0.76	2.46
Ag	584	0.055	3.32
Na	546	0.05	2.20
Au	546	0.4	2.3

a homogeneous wave, despite severe attenuation. This is in contrast to the evanescent wave discussed earlier.

Reflection at the boundary between an optically transparent medium and a metal can be described by Fresnel relations provided the real index of refraction n_2 of the second medium is replaced by the complex refractive index $\tilde{n}_2 = n_2 + i\kappa_2$ and the angle of refraction ϕ is allowed to become complex (see [1.5]). Defining

$$\tilde{n}_2 \cos\phi = u + iv \tag{1.82}$$

and using $\tilde{n}_2 \sin\phi = n_1 \sin\theta$, the reflection coefficient for σ-polarized light takes the form

$$r_\sigma = \frac{n_1 \cos\theta - u - iv}{n_1 \cos\theta + u + iv}, \tag{1.83}$$

where

$$u^2 - v^2 = n_2^2 - \kappa_2^2 - n_1^2 \sin^2\theta, \tag{1.84}$$
$$uv = n_2 \kappa_2.$$

The reflection coefficient for π-polarization can be expressed as

$$\begin{aligned} r_\mathrm{p} &= \frac{n_1 \cos\phi - \tilde{n}_2 \cos\theta}{n_1 \cos\phi + \tilde{n}_2 \cos\theta} \\ &= \frac{n_1 \tilde{n}_2 \cos\phi - \tilde{n}_2^2 \cos\theta}{n_1 \tilde{n}_2 \cos\phi + \tilde{n}_2^2 \cos\theta} \\ &= \frac{n_1(u + iv) - (n_2 + i\kappa_2)^2 \cos\theta}{n_1(u + iv) + (n_2 + i\kappa_2)^2 \cos\theta}. \end{aligned} \tag{1.85}$$

The magnitude and phase of the reflection coefficient of a metal as a function of the angle of incidence can be obtained from Eqs (1.83) and (1.85). The phase changes for $\hat{\pi}$- and $\hat{\sigma}$-polarizations are in general different. Therefore, on reflection from a metal, light linearly polarized in an arbitrary direction becomes elliptically polarized.

The reflectance of a metal for normal incidence is

$$\begin{aligned} R\,(\text{Metal}) = |r^2| &= \left| \frac{n_1 - (n_2 + i\kappa_2)}{n_1 + (n_2 + i\kappa_2)} \right|^2 \\ &= \frac{(n_1 - n_2)^2 + \kappa_2^2}{(n_1 + n_2)^2 + \kappa_2^2}. \end{aligned} \tag{1.86}$$

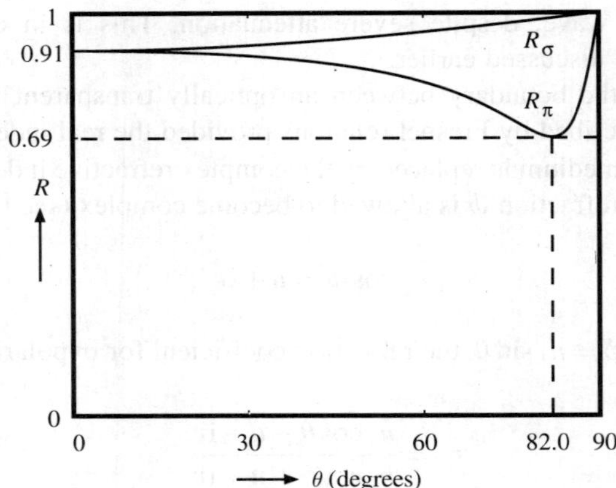

Fig. 1.16: Changes in the reflectance of aluminum with angle of incidence.

For normal incidence, the reflectance at the air–aluminum interface is 0.91. Figure 1.16 shows the variation of reflectance of aluminum as a function of the angle of incidence. As expected, the reflectance is generally high and not very sensitive to the angle of incidence. The counterpart of Brewster angle, called the principal angle of incidence, is marked by a broad dip in the reflectivity of π-polarized light. At this angle of incidence, the phase difference between $\hat{\pi}$- and $\hat{\sigma}$-polarizations is nearly 90°.

1.8 PASSAGE OF LIGHT THROUGH A PRISM

A beam of monochromatic light is laterally shifted in passing through a transparent block with parallel faces, but emerges undeviated from its original direction

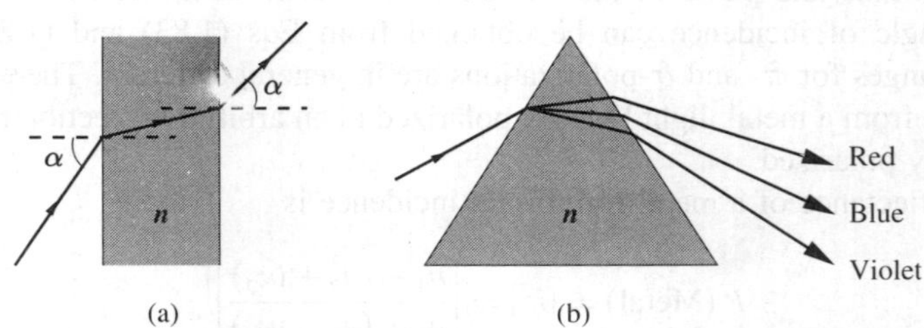

Fig. 1.17: Passage (a) of monochromatic light through a transparent block and (b) of white light through a prism.

of propagation (Fig. 1.17a). Similarly, a parallel beam of white light which has wavelength spread from about 400 to 800 nm continues to move undeviated after passing through such a slab. A prism, on the other hand, bends different wavelengths of white light through different angles (Fig. 1.17b). Separation of white light into its spectral components is called dispersion. Figure 1.17b is a case of normal dispersion which results from a slight decrease in the index of refraction of optically transparent media with increasing wavelength. Violet light is deviated most and red light undergoes least deviation. Other colors occupy positions in between in the sequence VIBGYOR[2]. The Cauchy dispersion formula

$$n(\lambda) = A + \frac{B}{\lambda^2} + \frac{C}{\lambda^4} + \cdots \tag{1.87}$$

describes the dependence of the index of refraction of such media on wavelength, where A, B, C are constants to be determined empirically for a given material. Normal dispersion (negative $\mathrm{d}n/\mathrm{d}\lambda$) occurs at wavelengths not too close to an atomic transition. In the close neighborhood of an atomic transition, $\mathrm{d}n/\mathrm{d}\lambda$ may become positive and dispersion in this region is called anomalous dispersion, although there is nothing anomalous about it except that it is accompanied by substantial absorption whereas much less absorption takes place in the spectral range of normal dispersion (see Fig. 1.21). A lens also disperses white light. Whereas the dispersion produced by a prism (in a prism spectrometer) and by a grating (in a grating spectrometer) is useful in determining the spectral (wavelength) composition of incident light, the dispersion in the image formed by a lens is undesirable, and is therefore called the chromatic aberration of the lens. As an application of light propagation through a prism, we show how the index of refraction of the material of the prism can be determined quite accurately from the deviation the prism produces in the path of a ray (Fig. 1.18).

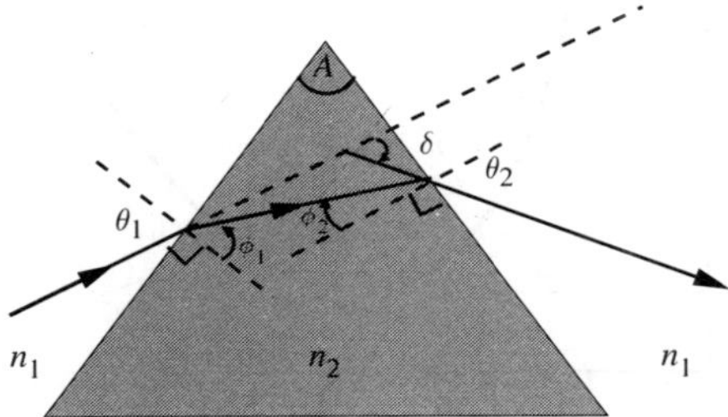

Fig. 1.18: Deviation of a monochromatic wave in passing through a prism.

[2] VIBGYOR stands for violet, indigo, blue, green, yellow, orange and red colours.

The deviation of a ray passing through a prism is given by

$$\delta = \theta_1 + \theta_2 - \phi_1 - \phi_2, \tag{1.88}$$

where θ_1 and θ_2 are the angles of incidence and emergence, respectively, ϕ_1 the angle of refraction at the first interface, and ϕ_2 the angle of incidence at the second interface. We note that

$$\phi_1 + \phi_2 + \pi - A = \pi$$

or

$$\phi_1 + \phi_2 = A, \tag{1.89}$$

where A is the angle of the prism. Accordingly,

$$\begin{aligned}\delta &= \theta_1 + \theta_2 - A \\ &= \theta_1 + \sin^{-1}\left[\frac{n_2}{n_1}\sin\left\{A - \sin^{-1}\left(\frac{n_1}{n_2}\sin\theta_1\right)\right\}\right] - A,\end{aligned} \tag{1.90}$$

where n_2 is the index of refraction of the material of the prism and n_1 is the index of refraction of the medium on the two sides of the prism. The dependence of the angle of deviation on the angle of incidence for $n_1 = 1.0$, $n_2 = 1.5$, and $A = 60°$ is shown in Fig. 1.19.

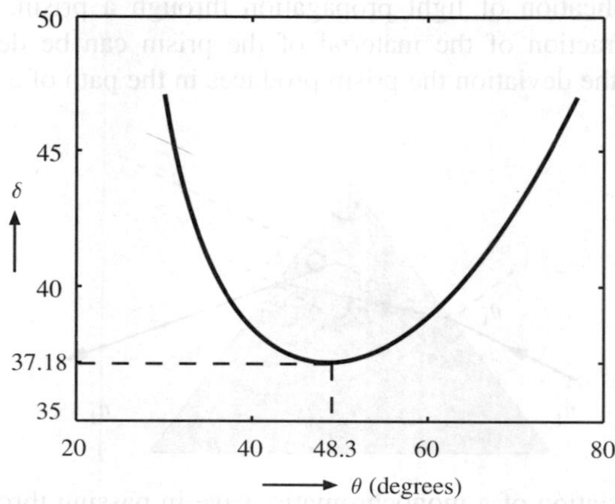

Fig. 1.19: Dependence of angle of deviation (δ) on angle of incidence for a prism with $n_2 = 1.5$, $A = 60°$.

The deviation in the direction of a ray goes through a minimum value ($\delta_{\min}$) as the angle of incidence is increased. At minimum deviation,

$$\frac{d(\delta)}{d\theta_1} = 1 + \frac{d\theta_2}{d\theta_1} = 0. \tag{1.91}$$

Applying Snell's law at the entrance and emergence of the ray, we have

$$n_1 \cos\theta_1 \, d\theta_1 = n_2 \cos\phi_1 \, d\phi_1,$$
$$n_1 \cos\theta_2 \, d\theta_2 = n_2 \cos\phi_2 \, d\phi_2.$$

So that

$$\begin{aligned}\frac{d\theta_1}{d\theta_2} &= \frac{\cos\phi_1}{\cos\phi_2}\frac{\cos\theta_2}{\cos\theta_1}\frac{d\phi_1}{d\phi_2} \\ &= -\frac{\cos\phi_1 \cos\theta_2}{\cos\phi_2 \cos\theta_1}.\end{aligned} \tag{1.92}$$

Therefore, the condition for minimum deviation is

$$\frac{\cos\theta_2}{\cos\theta_1} = \frac{\cos\phi_2}{\cos\phi_1}, \tag{1.93}$$

requiring $\theta_1 = \theta_2 = \theta$, and $\phi_1 = \phi_2 = \phi$. These conclusions follow if Snell's law is applied after expressing Eq. (1.92) in terms of the sines of the angles. Therefore,

$$\delta_{\min} = 2\theta - A$$

or

$$\theta = (\delta_{\min} + A)/2$$

and $\phi = A/2$. So that

$$\begin{aligned}\frac{n_2}{n_1} &= \frac{\sin\theta_1}{\sin\phi_1} \\ &= \frac{\sin\left(\frac{\delta_{\min}+A}{2}\right)}{\sin(A/2)}.\end{aligned} \tag{1.94}$$

The angle of minimum deviation and the angle of the prism can be measured quite accurately even with an undergraduate laboratory prism spectrometer, giving a precise estimate of the index of refraction of the material of the prism.

Prism combinations in the various forms are put to a variety of uses. The combination may consist of different prisms cemented together or it may be a single block representing several prisms juxtaposed. Combinations of oppositely oriented prisms of crown and flint glasses (Fig. 1.20a) can have non-zero deviation with no dispersion for two wavelengths (achromatic combination), or non-zero dispersion with minimal deviation (direct vision combination). The Pellin-Broca prism, commonly used in constant deviation spectrometers, consists of three right-angled prisms (30°–60°–90°, 45°–45°–90°, 30°–60°–90°) built into a single block (Fig. 1.20b). The wavelength for which light travels parallel to the bases of all three constituent prisms undergoes a deviation of 90°. Accordingly, the source of light and detector in a spectrometer using a Pellin-Broca prism can have fixed positions. Rotation of the prism brings different wavelengths in succession in line with the detector, thus providing dispersion at constant deviation for all wavelengths. The Porro, Dove and Amici prisms are variants of the right-angled prism for special applications.

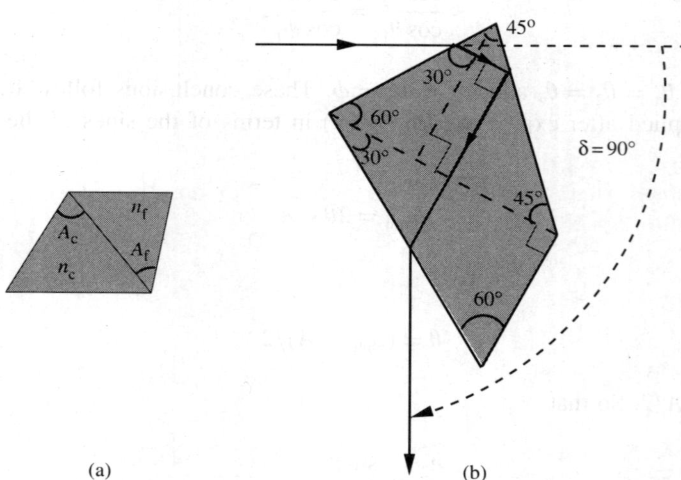

Fig. 1.20: (a) Crown glass prism of index of refraction n_c cemented to flint glass prism of index of refraction n_f, (b) Pellin-Broca constant deviation prism ($\delta = 90°$).

The minimum deviation of a small angle prism can be approximated to

$$\delta = \left(\frac{n_2}{n_1} - 1\right) A = (n-1)A. \tag{1.95}$$

The dispersive power of a prism is defined as the ratio of the angular separation of the F and C Fraunhofer lines and the deviation of the Fraunhofer D line[3], i.e.,

$$\text{Dispersive power} = \frac{1}{w} = \frac{\delta_F - \delta_C}{\delta_D} = \frac{n_F - n_C}{n_D - 1}, \tag{1.96}$$

where n_F, n_D, n_C are the indices of refraction of the prism material at wavelengths corresponding to the Fraunhofer lines F ($\lambda = 486.1\,\text{nm}$), D ($\lambda = 589.3\,\text{nm}$), and C ($\lambda = 656.3\,\text{nm}$), respectively. An achromatic combination (zero dispersion) of the crown and flint glass prisms (Fig. 1.20a) will have

$$\delta_F - \delta_C = 0, \tag{1.97}$$

where

$$\delta_F = (n_F^{\text{c}} - 1)A_{\text{c}} - (n_F^{\text{f}} - 1)A_{\text{f}},$$
$$\delta_C = (n_C^{\text{c}} - 1)A_{\text{c}} - (n_C^{\text{f}} - 1)A_{\text{f}}$$

are the deviations for the F and C lines, respectively, if

$$\frac{A_{\text{c}}}{A_{\text{f}}} = \frac{n_F^{\text{f}} - n_C^{\text{f}}}{n_F^{\text{c}} - n_C^{\text{c}}}, \tag{1.98}$$

where the small letters c and f refer to crown and flint glasses, respectively. The mean deviation of an achromatic combination is

$$\delta_D = (n_F^{\text{c}} - n_C^{\text{c}})(w_{\text{c}} - w_{\text{f}})A_{\text{c}}, \tag{1.99}$$

where w_{c} and w_{f} are the dispersive powers of the crown and flint glass prisms, respectively. Similarly for a direct vision prism combination, the mean deviation

$$\delta_D = \delta_D^{\text{c}} - \delta_D^{\text{f}} = 0 \tag{1.100}$$

[3] Fraunhofer lines are the dark lines appearing in the solar spectrum. They arise due to absorption of solar radiation by atomic species (Hydrogen atoms for the F and C lines and sodium atoms for the D line) present in sun's atmosphere.

if

$$\frac{A_c}{A_f} = \frac{n_D^f - 1}{n_D^c - 1}, \tag{1.101}$$

giving the angular separation between the F and C lines as

$$\delta_F - \delta_C = (n_D^c - 1)\left(\frac{1}{w_c} - \frac{1}{w_f}\right) A_c. \tag{1.102}$$

1.9 DISPERSION

We have seen in Section 1.8 how a prism separates different colors of white light. Dispersion (separation of colors or more appropriately, variation of the index of refraction with wavelength) and absorption of light are closely related. It was noted in the introduction that absorption of light cannot be understood in classical terms, where matter is described by its bulk properties such as the permittivity and permeability. We also gave an equivalent description in terms of the complex index of refraction of the medium which provided a phenomenological basis for absorption of light during propagation. Though not explicitly stated, one may not be wrong to conclude from our treatment so far that the permittivity and index of refraction of a medium do not change with the frequency of the light field. This, however, is not true, and it is the frequency dependence of the velocity ($v = c/n(\omega)$) of light in a medium which gives rise to the phenomenon of dispersion. Velocity of light in vacuum is independent of its frequency. A vacuum is therefore a non-dispersive medium. To explore the frequency dependence of the index of refraction of other media, we need to return to the atomistic nature of matter, where atoms and molecules are essentially dispersed in vacuum. An atom consists of a positively charged nucleus surrounded by a charged cloud of electrons. In the absence of external radiation, an atom has no dipole moment since the centers of positive and negative charges coincide. This equilibrium is disturbed by the external field and the atom acquires a dipole moment. The nucleus, being heavy, is sluggish to respond to the rapidly changing optical fields. Therefore, the dipole moment of an atom can be thought to arise from the displacement of the electron from its equilibrium position (Lorentz model). For the time being, only one electron per atom is assumed. This restriction will be eventually relaxed. Intra-atomic restoring forces make the electron undergo forced oscillations about its equilibrium position (at the frequency of the light field). Since absorption cannot be accounted in the classical description, we introduce a damping term to allow for energy dissipation in the medium and for the radiative loss. The induced atomic dipole moment generates a time varying polarization in the medium. A molecule, on the other hand, may or may not have a dipole moment in the absence of the external field. Molecular polarization is, however, more pronounced in the infrared region. Nevertheless, the ensuing discussion is applicable to molecules as well.

The motion of the oscillating electron, assuming only a linear restoring force, is described by the equation

$$\frac{d^2 \vec{r}}{dt^2} + \gamma \frac{d \vec{r}}{dt} + \omega_0^2 \vec{r} = \frac{q}{m} \vec{E}', \tag{1.103}$$

where ω_0 is the natural frequency of oscillation of the electron (charge q, mass m), γ the damping constant, and $\vec{E}'$ the net electric field or the local field acting on the electron. In a dilute gas,

$$\vec{E}' = \vec{E}$$

and in a dense medium (Lorentz's correction),

$$\vec{E}' = \vec{E} + \frac{\vec{P}}{3\epsilon_0}, \tag{1.104}$$

where $\vec{E}$ is the external field and $\vec{P}$ is the medium polarization. The derivation of Lorentz' correction can be found in texts on electromagnetism.[4] Assuming

$$\vec{E}' = \vec{E}_0' \, e^{-i\omega t},$$

$$\vec{r} = \vec{r}_0 \, e^{-i\omega t},$$

the amplitude of oscillation of the electron is found to be

$$r_0 = \frac{qE_0'/m}{\omega_0^2 - \omega^2 - i\gamma\omega}.$$

The induced atomic polarization is

$$P = Nqr_0 = \frac{(Nq^2/m)E_0'}{\omega_0^2 - \omega^2 - i\gamma\omega}, \tag{1.105}$$

---

[4] Classical electrodynamics by John David Jackson.

where N is the number of electrons per unit volume of the medium. Combining Eqs (1.9a,c), (1.18), (1.105), the complex index of refraction of the medium can be expressed as

$$\tilde{n}^2 = \frac{\epsilon}{\epsilon_0} = 1 + \chi^{(1)}$$

$$= 1 + \frac{(Nq^2/m\epsilon_0)}{\omega_0^2 - \omega^2 - \mathrm{i}\gamma\omega}. \tag{1.106}$$

In view of the fact that an atom may have several oscillating electrons, Eq. (1.106) may be modified as

$$\tilde{n}^2 = 1 + \frac{Nq^2}{m\epsilon_0} \sum_j \frac{f_j}{\omega_{0j}^2 - \omega^2 - \mathrm{i}\gamma\omega}, \tag{1.107}$$

where the oscillator strength f_j (<1), introduced for each oscillating electron, is related to the quantum mechanical transition probability. Equation (1.107) is called Sellemeier's equation.

1.9.1 Dispersion in Dilute Gases

For low-pressure gases, $\tilde{n} \approx 1$. Assuming only one electron per atom, Eq. (1.106) can be approximated (by retaining only the first term in the binomial expansion) to

$$\tilde{n} = 1 + \frac{(Nq^2/2m\epsilon_0)}{\omega_0^2 - \omega^2 - \mathrm{i}\gamma\omega} \tag{1.108a}$$

$$= 1 + \frac{1}{2}\frac{\omega_p^2}{\omega_0^2 - \omega^2 - \mathrm{i}\gamma\omega}, \tag{1.108b}$$

where the plasma frequency $\omega_\mathrm{p} = (Nq^2/m\epsilon_0)^{1/2}$. The real and imaginary parts of the complex index of refraction (Eq. 1.19) of a low-pressure gas are obtained as

$$n = 1 + \frac{1}{2}\frac{\omega_\mathrm{p}^2(\omega_0^2 - \omega^2)}{(\omega_0^2 - \omega^2)^2 + \gamma^2\omega^2}, \tag{1.109a}$$

$$\kappa = \frac{1}{2}\frac{\gamma\omega_\mathrm{p}^2\omega}{(\omega_0^2 - \omega^2)^2 + \gamma^2\omega^2}. \tag{1.109b}$$

Far below resonance ($\omega_0^2 - \omega^2 \gg \gamma\omega$), Eq. (1.109a) is reduced to

$$n = 1 + \frac{1}{2}\frac{\omega_p^2}{\omega_0^2 - \omega^2},$$

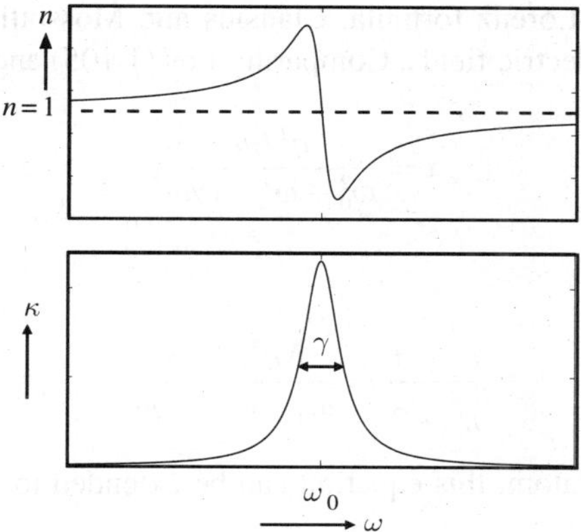

Fig. 1.21: Spectral behavior of the real and imaginary parts of the index of refraction of a dilute gas.

so that for a dilute gas below resonance ($\omega < \omega_0$), $n > 1$ and $\mathrm{d}n/\mathrm{d}\omega$ is positive. This is the spectral region of normal dispersion and low absorption. At resonance ($\omega = \omega_0$), $n = 1$ and absorption is at its maximum value. Above resonance ($\omega > \omega_0$), $n < 1$. For the spectral range $(\omega_0 - \frac{\gamma}{2}) < \omega < (\omega_0 + \frac{\gamma}{2})$, $\mathrm{d}n/\mathrm{d}\omega$ is negative. This is the region of anomalous dispersion and high absorption. Beyond $\omega = \omega_0 + \frac{\gamma}{2}$, $\mathrm{d}n/\mathrm{d}\omega$ is positive and dispersion is once again normal. These features are shown in Fig. 1.21.

1.9.2 Dispersion in Dense Media

For gases at high pressure, liquids and dielectrics, we must return to Eq. (1.06). Expressing polarization of the medium in terms of the mean polarizability α of its molecules,

$$P = N\alpha E_0' \tag{1.110}$$

and combining it with Eqs (1.9a) and (1.104), we obtain

$$\tilde{n}^2 = \frac{\epsilon}{\epsilon_0} = \frac{1 + 2N\alpha/3\epsilon_0}{1 - N\alpha/3\epsilon_0}, \tag{1.111}$$

giving the mean molecular polarizability as

$$\alpha = \frac{3\epsilon_0}{N}\frac{\tilde{n}^2 - 1}{\tilde{n}^2 + 2}. \tag{1.112}$$

This is the Lorentz–Lorenz formula. Clausius and Mossotti obtained the same result for the static electric fields. Comparing Eqs (1.105) and (1.110), we obtain

$$\alpha = \frac{q^2/m}{\omega_0^2 - \omega^2 - \mathrm{i}\gamma\omega}, \tag{1.113}$$

yielding

$$\frac{\tilde{n}^2 - 1}{\tilde{n}^2 + 2} = \frac{Nq^2/3\epsilon_0 m}{\omega_0^2 - \omega^2 - \mathrm{i}\gamma\omega}. \tag{1.114}$$

For a multi-electron atom, this equation can be extended to

$$\frac{\tilde{n}^2 - 1}{\tilde{n}^2 + 2} = \frac{Nq^2}{3\epsilon_0 m} \sum_j \frac{f_j}{\omega_{0j}^2 - \omega^2 - \mathrm{i}\gamma\omega}. \tag{1.115}$$

In conclusion, the index of refraction and hence the velocity of propagation of a wave in dilute as well as in dense media changes with the frequency of the light field.

Separation of the real and imaginary parts of the index of refraction for dense media is more involved and will not be attempted here. However, their spectral behavior (Fig. 1.22) is qualitatively similar to the one observed in dilute gases. Optically transparent materials have absorption bands (resonant frequencies ω_{0j}) in the ultraviolet. Therefore their index of refraction is less than 1 beyond the ultraviolet spectral region (see Table 1.1). As can be seen from Fig. 1.22, X-rays will undergo total external reflection (i.e. from air back to air) from optically transparent materials such as glasses.

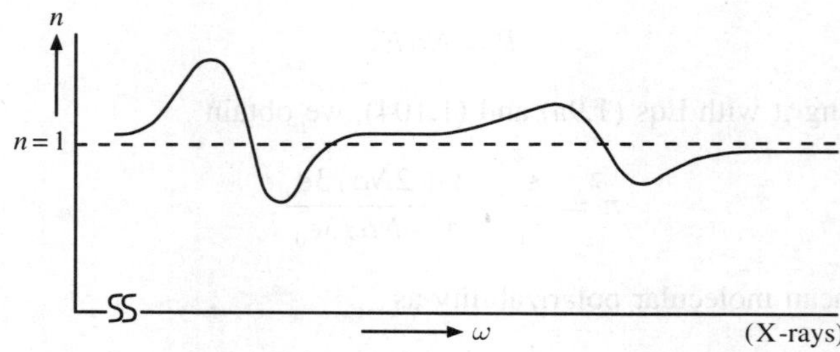

Fig. 1.22: Spectral behavior of the real part of the index of refraction of dense media; $n < 1$ in the X-ray region.

1.9.3 Group and Signal Velocities

Dispersion analysis has shown that the real part of the index of refraction of a medium can fall below 1 in certain spectral regions. Therefore the phase velocity (c/n) of a monochromatic wave can exceed velocity of light in vacuum in those spectral regions. This must be reconciled against the theory of relativity, according to which signals must propagate at velocities less than the velocity of light in vacuum. A monochromatic wave does not really exist and even if it exists, it cannot carry a signal and still remain monochromatic. Hence this question needs to be addressed in the context of propagating pulses and wave packets. The simplest wave packet is a superposition of two waves of equal amplitudes, but different frequencies:

$$\begin{aligned} E(z,t) &= E_0[\mathrm{e}^{\mathrm{i}(k_1 z-\omega_1 t)} + \mathrm{e}^{\mathrm{i}(k_2 z-\omega_2 t)}] \\ &= 2E_0 \cos\left(\frac{\Delta k}{2}z - \frac{\Delta\omega}{2}t\right)\mathrm{e}^{\mathrm{i}(\bar{k}z-\bar{\omega}t)}, \end{aligned} \tag{1.116}$$

where

$$k_1 = \bar{k} - \frac{\Delta k}{2}, \quad k_2 = \bar{k} + \frac{\Delta k}{2},$$
$$\omega_1 = \bar{\omega} - \frac{\Delta\omega}{2}, \quad \omega_2 = \bar{\omega} + \frac{\Delta\omega}{2},$$

and $\bar{\omega}$ and $\bar{k}$ are, respectively, the mean frequency and mean wave number of the wave packet. The phase velocity of this wave packet is $\bar{\omega}/\bar{k}$. We may define the group velocity of the wave packet as the velocity with which the modulation envelope (Fig. 1.23) of the wave packet moves, viz.,

$$v_{\mathrm{g}} = \frac{\Delta\omega}{\Delta k}.$$

In a non-dispersive medium, the velocity of a wave is independent of its frequency. Therefore,

$$v_{\mathrm{g}} = \frac{\Delta\omega}{\Delta k} = \frac{\omega_2-\omega_1}{k_2-k_1} = \frac{v(k_2-k_1)}{k_2-k_1} = v_{\mathrm{p}}.$$

Hence, there is no distinction between phase velocity and group velocity in a non-dispersive medium. Since all waves move with the same velocity in a non-dispersive medium, the constituent waves of the wave packet maintain their initial relative phases. The wave packet therefore propagates retaining its original profile. The situation is quite different in a dispersive medium where

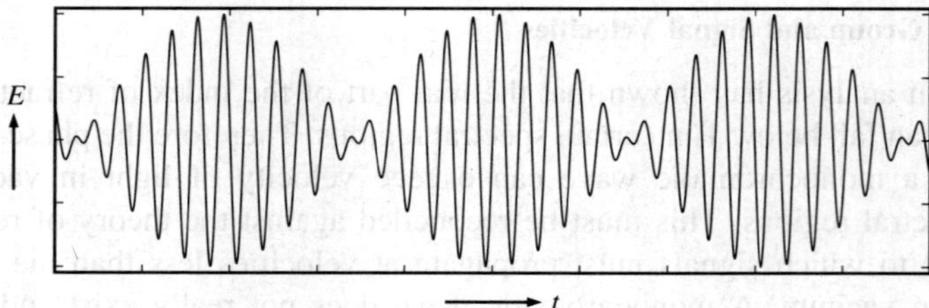

Fig. 1.23: Superposition of two waves ($\omega_2/\omega_1 = 1.1$) of equal amplitudes.

the constituent waves get out of phase with time due to their different velocities, resulting in a changing profile of the wave packet during propagation.

For a more general wave packet propagating in a dispersive medium, we can write

$$v_g = \frac{d\omega}{dk}, \tag{1.117a}$$

$$\omega(k) = kv(k), \tag{1.117b}$$

giving

$$\begin{aligned} v_g &= v + k\frac{dv}{dk} \\ &= \frac{c}{n} - \frac{kc}{n^2}\frac{dn}{dk} \\ &= \frac{c}{n} - \frac{\omega}{n}v_g\frac{dn}{d\omega}, \end{aligned}$$

so that

$$\begin{aligned} v_g &= \frac{c}{n + \omega\frac{dn}{d\omega}} \\ &= v_p\left(1 + \frac{\omega}{n}\frac{dn}{d\omega}\right)^{-1}. \end{aligned} \tag{1.118}$$

For normal dispersion with $n > 1$ and positive $dn/d\omega$, the phase velocity and the group velocity are both smaller than velocity of light in vacuum. The group velocity, which is the velocity of any point on the modulation envelope, equals the signal velocity in normal dispersion. During anomalous dispersion ($n < 1$ and negative $dn/d\omega$), the phase velocity as well as the group velocity exceeds velocity of light in vacuum. Group velocities greater than the velocity of light in

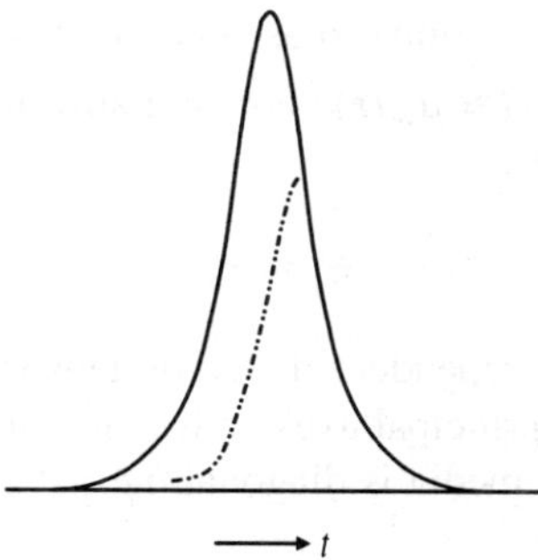

Fig. 1.24: Excessive absorption of the trailing edge of a light pulse during anomalous dispersion effectively pushes the peak forward.

vacuum have been measured for laser pulses propagating in dispersive media. In the spectral region of anomalous dispersion, absorption is very high. But since it takes some time for the absorption to set in, the trailing edge of the pulse is excessively absorbed, resulting in effective forward movement of the peak of the pulse (Fig. 1.24). The group velocity may therefore exceed velocity of light in vacuum. Group velocity under conditions of anomalous dispersion is not the signal velocity which is always less than c.

1.10 PROPAGATION OF LIGHT IN ANISOTROPIC MEDIA

The formulation of the previous sections is restricted to light propagation in linear and electrically and magnetically isotropic media, for which Eqs (1.9) ensure parallelism between the displacement and electric fields. In crystalline solids with direction-dependent inter-atomic forces, the displacement field may be proportional to the electric field, but not always parallel to it. For optically transparent anisotropic media, the permittivity ϵ in $\vec{D}= \epsilon \vec{E}$ (Eq. 1.9b) is not a scalar but more likely a tensor (called the permittivity or the dielectric tensor) of the second rank with nine components, i.e.,

$$\epsilon = \begin{pmatrix} \epsilon_{xx} & \epsilon_{xy} & \epsilon_{xz} \\ \epsilon_{yx} & \epsilon_{yy} & \epsilon_{yz} \\ \epsilon_{zx} & \epsilon_{zy} & \epsilon_{zz} \end{pmatrix}, \tag{1.119}$$

so that each component of the displacement field can be expressed as

$$D_i = \sum_j \epsilon_{ij} E_j, \tag{1.120}$$

where $(i, j) = x, y, z$. We continue to assume our anisotropic media to be magnetically isotropic ($\vec{B} = \mu \vec{H} \approx \mu_0 \vec{H}$). For non-absorbing anisotropic media, ϵ_{ij} are real and symmetric, i.e.,

$$\epsilon_{ij}^* = \epsilon_{ji},$$

reducing the number of independent dielectric tensor components to six. A set of x, y, z axes, called the principal axes, exists in which the dielectric tensor for non-absorbing anisotropic media is diagonal, i.e.,

$$\epsilon = \begin{pmatrix} \epsilon_x & 0 & 0 \\ 0 & \epsilon_y & 0 \\ 0 & 0 & \epsilon_z \end{pmatrix} \tag{1.121}$$

and Eq. (1.120) simplifies to

$$\begin{aligned} D_x &= \epsilon_x E_x, \\ D_y &= \epsilon_y E_y, \\ D_z &= \epsilon_z E_z. \end{aligned} \tag{1.122}$$

Despite this simplification, the displacement field in an anisotropic medium is not parallel to the electric field, unless the latter is along one of the principal axes of the dielectric tensor. The energy density in this coordinate system takes the form

$$u = \vec{D} \cdot \vec{E} = \frac{D_x^2}{\epsilon_x} + \frac{D_y^2}{\epsilon_y} + \frac{D_z^2}{\epsilon_z} \tag{1.123}$$

For the harmonic plane wave solution (Eq. 1.15) to be consistent with Maxwell's equations (1.7) in a source-free, non-absorbing anisotropic medium, we must have

$$\begin{aligned} \vec{k} \cdot \vec{D} &= 0, \\ \vec{k} \cdot \vec{B} &= 0, \\ \vec{B} &= \frac{\vec{k} \times \vec{E}}{\omega}, \\ \vec{D} &= -\vec{k} \times \vec{H}, \end{aligned} \tag{1.124}$$

where $\vec{k}$ is the real propagation vector. Note that Maxwell's equations do not constrain the electric field $\vec{E}$ to be perpendicular to the propagation vector in an anisotropic medium. Combining the last two results of Eq. (1.124) gives the relationship between the $\vec{E}$ and $\vec{D}$ fields:

$$\begin{aligned}\vec{D} &= \frac{k^2}{\mu_0\omega^2}\left[\vec{E} - \hat{k}(\hat{k}\cdot\vec{E})\right] \\ &= \epsilon_0 n^2\left[\vec{E} - \hat{k}(\hat{k}\cdot\vec{E})\right],\end{aligned} \tag{1.125}$$

where $\hat{k}$ is a unit vector in the direction of propagation and n is the corresponding index of refraction of the anisotropic medium at frequency ω. Similarly, the Poynting vector for an anisotropic medium can be expressed as

$$\begin{aligned}\vec{S} &= \frac{1}{\mu_0\omega}\vec{E}\times(\vec{k}\times\vec{E}) \\ &= \frac{k}{\mu_0\omega}E^2[\hat{k} - (\hat{E}\cdot\hat{k})\hat{E}],\end{aligned} \tag{1.126}$$

where $\hat{E}$ is a unit vector in the direction of $\vec{E}$. Since Eqs (1.124) do not require the electric field $\vec{E}$ to be perpendicular to the propagation vector $\vec{k}$, the Poynting vector is generally not collinear with the propagation vector in anisotropic media. This is one major difference of light propagation in isotropic and anisotropic media. The phase velocity, as defined earlier, is the velocity with which the wavefront of the wave advances, i.e.,

$$\vec{v}_\mathrm{p} = \frac{c}{n}\hat{k}. \tag{1.127a}$$

The Poynting vector, on the other hand, defines the direction of a ray along which energy propagates in a medium under conditions of normal dispersion. The phase velocity is the projection of the ray velocity in the direction of the wave normal. Therefore,

$$v_\mathrm{r} = \frac{v_\mathrm{p}}{\cos\alpha}, \tag{1.127b}$$

where α is the angle between the propagation vector $\vec{k}$ and Poynting vector $\vec{S}$. In isotropic media, there is no distinction between the ray and wave velocities ($\alpha = 0$). From the preceding discussion, it follows that the vectors $\vec{k}$, $\vec{D}$ and $\vec{B}$ are

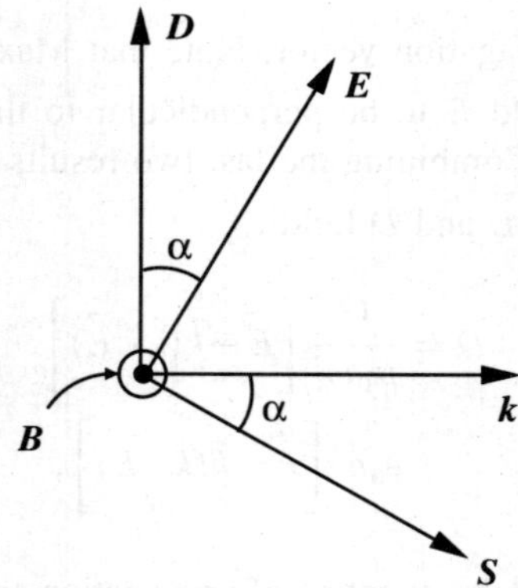

Fig. 1.25: Directions of $\vec{D}$, $\vec{E}$, $\vec{k}$, $\vec{S}$ and $\vec{B}$ vectors in an anisotropic medium.

mutually orthogonal and so are the vectors $\vec{S}$, $\vec{E}$ and $\vec{B}$. The vectors $\vec{D}$, $\vec{E}$, $\vec{k}$ and $\vec{S}$ are coplanar since they are all perpendicular to $\vec{B}$ (Fig. 1.25). The harmonic plane wave solutions of the wave equation in non-absorbing anisotropic media must meet these requirements, imposed by the Maxwell's equations.

1.10.1 Fresnel Equation

Combining Eqs (1.122) and (1.125), the components of the electric field along the principal axes of the dielectric tensor can be expressed as

$$E_j = \frac{n^2 \hat{k}_j (\hat{k} \cdot \vec{E})}{n^2 - \frac{\epsilon_j}{\epsilon_0}}, \tag{1.128}$$

where $j = x, y, z$ and $\hat{k}_j$ is the jth component of the unit vector $\hat{k}$. Multiplying both sides of this equation by $\hat{k}_j$ and summing over j gives the identity:

$$(\hat{k} \cdot \vec{E}) = \left[\frac{n^2 \hat{k}_x^2}{n^2 - \dfrac{\epsilon_x}{\epsilon_0}} + \frac{n^2 \hat{k}_y^2}{n^2 - \dfrac{\epsilon_y}{\epsilon_0}} + \frac{n^2 \hat{k}_z^2}{n^2 - \dfrac{\epsilon_z}{\epsilon_0}} \right] (\hat{k} \cdot \vec{E}).$$

For $\hat{k} \,.\, \vec{E} \neq 0$, we obtain the Fresnel equation

$$\frac{1}{n^2} = \frac{\hat{k}_x^2}{n^2 - \frac{\epsilon_x}{\epsilon_0}} + \frac{\hat{k}_y^2}{n^2 - \frac{\epsilon_y}{\epsilon_0}} + \frac{\hat{k}_z^2}{n^2 - \frac{\epsilon_z}{\epsilon_0}}. \tag{1.129a}$$

Multiplying Eq. (1.129a) by n^2 and replacing 1 on the left-hand side by $\hat{k}_x^2 + \hat{k}_y^2 + \hat{k}_z^2$, gives an equivalent form of the Fresnel equation:

$$\frac{\hat{k}_x^2}{v_\mathrm{p}^2 - v_x^2} + \frac{\hat{k}_y^2}{v_\mathrm{p}^2 - v_y^2} + \frac{\hat{k}_z^2}{v_\mathrm{p}^2 - v_z^2} = 0, \tag{1.129b}$$

where v_p is the phase velocity in the direction of the propagation vector $\hat{k}$, and

$$v_x = c\left(\frac{\epsilon_x}{\epsilon_0}\right)^{-1/2} = \frac{1}{\sqrt{\mu_0 \epsilon_x}}, \quad v_y = \frac{1}{\sqrt{\mu_0 \epsilon_y}}, \quad v_z = \frac{1}{\sqrt{\mu_0 \epsilon_z}}$$

are the phase velocities along the principal axes. Eq. (1.128), when expressed in terms of the phase velocities, takes the form

$$E_j = \frac{v_j^2}{v_j^2 - v_\mathrm{p}^2} \hat{k}_j (\hat{k} \,.\, \vec{E}), \tag{1.130}$$

where $j = x, y, z$. Fresnel equation (1.129a) is quadratic in n^2 (coefficient of n^6 is zero) and Eq. (1.129b) is quadratic in v_p^2, giving two values for the index of refraction (n_1, n_2) and hence two values for the phase velocity $(v_\mathrm{p}', v_\mathrm{p}'')$ for wave propagation in a given direction in an anisotropic medium. For each of the phase velocities, the ratios of the components of $\vec{E}$ (and hence of $\vec{D}$) along the principal axes, obtained from Eq. (1.130), are real and constant. Therefore, there are two linearly polarized waves (see Section 3.1.2) propagating in any direction in an anisotropic medium. These waves are orthogonally polarized $(\vec{D}_1 \cdot \vec{D}_2 = 0)$. To prove this statement, let us express

$$\vec{E} = \vec{E}_\parallel + \vec{E}_\perp,$$

where $\vec{E}_\parallel$ and $\vec{E}_\perp$ are, respectively, parallel and perpendicular to the direction of the propagation vector $\hat{k}$. Since the displacement field $\vec{D}$ is perpendicular to $\hat{k}$, Eq. (1.125) gives

$$D_1 = \epsilon_0 n_1^2 E_{1\perp}, \quad D_2 = \epsilon_0 n_2^2 E_{2\perp}. \tag{1.131}$$

Further since $\epsilon_{ij} = \epsilon_{ji}$,

$$\vec{E}_2 \cdot \vec{D}_1 = \sum_i E_{2i} D_{1i} = \sum_i \sum_j E_{2i} \epsilon_{ij} E_{1j}$$

$$= \sum_i \sum_j E_{1j} \epsilon_{ji} E_{2i} = \vec{E}_1 \cdot \vec{D}_2 . \tag{1.132}$$

Therefore

$$\epsilon_0 n_1^2 \vec{E}_2 \cdot \vec{E}_{1\perp} = \epsilon_0 n_2^2 \vec{E}_1 \cdot \vec{E}_{2\perp}$$

or

$$n_1^2 \vec{E}_{2\perp} \cdot \vec{E}_{1\perp} = n_2^2 \vec{E}_{1\perp} \cdot \vec{E}_{2\perp} .$$

For $n_1 \neq n_2$, $\vec{E}_{1\perp} \cdot \vec{E}_{2\perp} = 0$ and hence

$$\vec{D}_1 \cdot \vec{D}_2 = 0. \tag{1.133}$$

1.10.2 Geometrical Constructions

There are a number of geometrical constructions to illustrate the various aspects of wave propagation in an anisotropic medium. We consider two such constructions.

1.10.2.1 Index Ellipsoid

Equation (1.123) may be written in the form

$$\frac{D_x^2}{u\epsilon_x} + \frac{D_y^2}{u\epsilon_y} + \frac{D_z^2}{u\epsilon_z} = 1, \tag{1.134}$$

where D_x, D_y, D_z are the components of the displacement field along the principal axes of the dielectric tensor, u the energy density and ϵ_x, ϵ_y, ϵ_z are the principal dielectric constants. Equation (1.134) represents an ellipsoid in the space spanned by D_x, D_y, D_z (Fig. 1.26), whose semi-axes at a given frequency are proportional to the square roots of the principal dielectric constants or to the principal indices of refraction ($n_x^2 = \epsilon_x/\epsilon_0$, $n_y^2 = \epsilon_y/\epsilon_0$, $n_z^2 = \epsilon_z/\epsilon_0$). This ellipsoid is variously known as the ellipsoid of wave normals, optical indicatrix, etc. The semi-axes and orientation of the index ellipsoid change with the frequency of the wave since the principal dielectric constants are frequency dependent. The index ellipsoid is helpful in determining the phase velocities (or equivalently the indices of

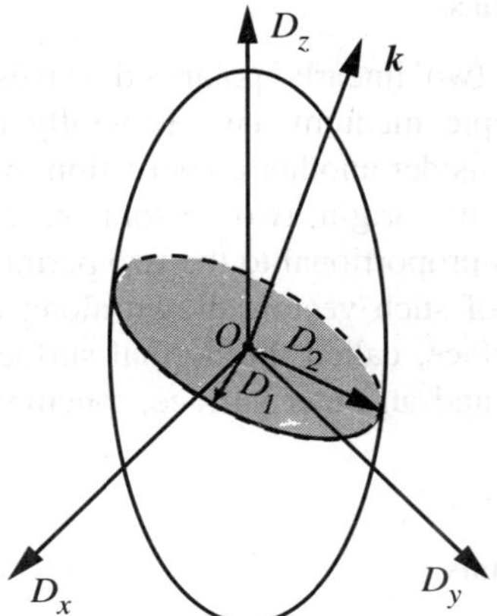

Fig. 1.26: Index ellipsoid; polarization directions of the waves propagating along $\vec{k}$ are along the semi-axes of the ellipse ($\vec{D}_1$ and $\vec{D}_2$).

refraction) and the permissible directions of polarizations (directions of $\vec{D}$) of waves propagating in anisotropic media. Figure 1.26 shows the propagation vector $\vec{k}$ drawn from the center O of the index ellipsoid. The intersection of the plane, passing through O and perpendicular to the direction of propagation, with the index ellipsoid is in general an ellipse. The displacement fields for the two waves propagating along $\vec{k}$ oscillate along the semi-axes of this ellipse. The semi-axes of the ellipse being perpendicular to each other, the two waves have orthogonal polarizations as required by Eq. (1.133). The phase velocities of the waves can be obtained from the lengths of the semi-axes of the ellipse.

There are at most two directions of propagation in a crystal, for which the intersecting ellipse degenerates into a circle. These are the directions of the optic axes in a crystal. The crystals belonging to the orthorhombic, monoclinic, and triclinic crystallographic systems have no two directions which are crystallographically equivalent. These are the biaxial crystals with two optic axes. The uniaxial crystals belong to the trigonal, tetragonal, and hexagonal systems and can have two or more crystallographically equivalent directions. There is only one optic axis for a uniaxial crystal. The phase velocities of the waves propagating along an optic axis are equal, and any two mutually orthogonal directions can be chosen to describe their polarization states. Cubic crystals have three mutually perpendicular directions which are crystallographically equivalent. They are optically isotropic since $\epsilon_x = \epsilon_y = \epsilon_z$.

1.10.2.2 Normal Surface

We have seen that the two linearly polarized waves travelling in any given direction in an anisotropic medium have generally unequal phase velocities. With this in mind, we consider another construction in which from a fixed point in the medium, taken as the origin, two vectors are drawn in each direction of propagation with lengths proportional to the two permissible phase velocities for that direction. The tips of such vectors drawn along all different directions of propagation lie on a surface, called the normal surface, which as we shall see breaks up into an inner and an outer surface, touching each other at points on the optic axes.

1.10.3 Uniaxial Crystals

The axis of symmetry of a uniaxial crystal is also its optic axis. Let the z-axis of the principal axis system coincide with the optic axis. The principal dielectric constants must display the symmetry of the crystal. Therefore, $\epsilon_x = \epsilon_y$ and $v_x = v_y$. Anticipating results, we define

$$v_x = v_y = v_\mathrm{o}, \quad v_z = v_\mathrm{e},$$

where the subscripts o and e refer to the ordinary and extraordinary waves, respectively. With this choice, Eq. (1.129b) takes the form

$$(v_\mathrm{p}^2 - v_\mathrm{o}^2)[(v_\mathrm{p}^2 - v_\mathrm{e}^2)(\hat{k}_x^2 + \hat{k}_y^2) + (v_\mathrm{p}^2 - v_\mathrm{o}^2)\hat{k}_z^2] = 0,$$

giving

$$v_\mathrm{p}' = v_\mathrm{o}, \tag{1.135a}$$

$$v_\mathrm{p}'' = (v_\mathrm{o}^2 \cos^2\theta + v_\mathrm{e}^2 \sin^2\theta)^{1/2}, \tag{1.135b}$$

where θ is the angle between the optic axis and the direction of propagation. Thus, one of the waves in a uniaxial crystal propagates with a constant velocity v_o, irrespective of its direction of propagation. The normal surface for this wave is a sphere. This wave behaves much like a wave in an isotropic medium, hence the name ordinary wave given to this wave. The velocity of propagation of the other wave varies with the angle the propagation direction makes with the optic axis. This is the extraordinary wave. Its velocity equals the velocity of the ordinary wave v_o when propagating along the optic axis and v_e when propagating in a plane perpendicular to the optic axis. The normal surface of the extraordinary wave in a uniaxial crystal is an ellipsoid of revolution (spheroid), which touches the spherical normal surface of the ordinary wave at points on

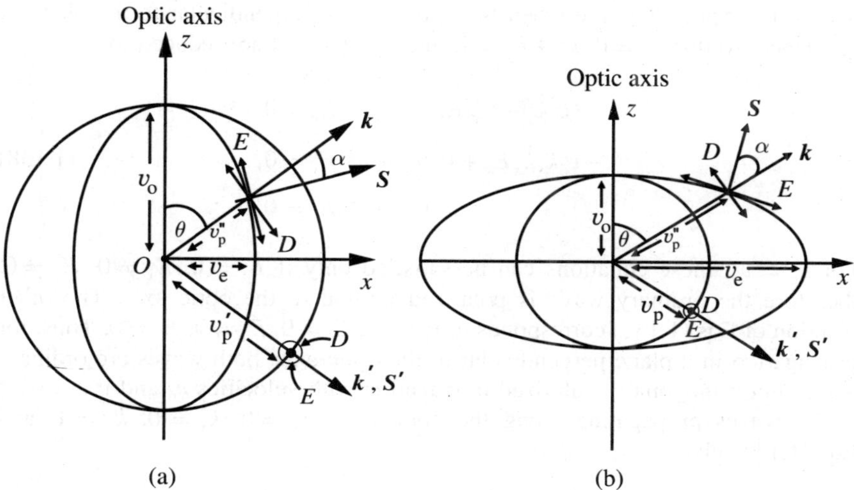

Fig. 1.27: Sections of normal surfaces for (a) positive uniaxial crystals ($v_o > v_e$) and (b) negative uniaxial crystals ($v_o < v_e$).

the optic axis. Sections of these surfaces in a plane containing the optic axis are shown in Fig. 1.27. A uniaxial crystal is called a positive uniaxial crystal if $v_o > v_e$ or $n_o < n_e$ and a negative uniaxial crystal if $v_o < v_e$ or $n_o > n_e$, where $n_o = c/v_o$ and $n_e = c/v_e$. An example of a positive uniaxial crystal is quartz with $n_o = 1.544$ and $n_e = 1.553$ for the sodium D lines. Calcite, on the other hand, is a negative uniaxial crystal with $n_o = 1.6583$ and $n_e = 1.4864$ for the sodium D lines.

To determine polarizations of the ordinary and extraordinary waves, we write Eq. (1.130) explicitly for each component of the electric field:

$$
\begin{aligned}
(v_x^2 - v_p^2)E_x - v_x^2\hat{k}_x(\hat{k}_xE_x + \hat{k}_yE_y + \hat{k}_zE_z) &= 0,\\
(v_y^2 - v_p^2)E_y - v_y^2\hat{k}_y(\hat{k}_xE_x + \hat{k}_yE_y + \hat{k}_zE_z) &= 0,\\
(v_z^2 - v_p^2)E_z - v_z^2\hat{k}_z(\hat{k}_xE_x + \hat{k}_yE_y + \hat{k}_zE_z) &= 0,
\end{aligned}
\tag{1.136}
$$

where in the present case $v_x = v_y = v_o$, and $v_z = v_e$, giving

$$
\begin{aligned}
[v_o^2(1-\hat{k}_x^2) - v_p^2]E_x - v_o^2\hat{k}_x\hat{k}_yE_y - v_o^2\hat{k}_x\hat{k}_zE_z &= 0,\\
-v_o^2\hat{k}_y\hat{k}_xE_x + [v_o^2(1-\hat{k}_y^2) - v_p^2]E_y - v_o^2\hat{k}_y\hat{k}_zE_z &= 0,\\
-v_e^2\hat{k}_z\hat{k}_xE_x - v_e^2\hat{k}_z\hat{k}_yE_y + [v_e^2(1-\hat{k}_z^2) - v_p^2]E_z &= 0.
\end{aligned}
\tag{1.137}
$$

We first consider the case when the optic axis is perpendicular to the plane of incidence, so that $\hat{k}_z = 0$, $\hat{k}_x^2 + \hat{k}_y^2 = 1$, and Eqs (1.137) are reduced to

$$\begin{aligned}(v_o^2\hat{k}_y^2 - v_p^2)E_x - v_o^2\hat{k}_x\hat{k}_y E_y &= 0,\\ -v_o^2\hat{k}_y\hat{k}_x E_x + (v_o^2\hat{k}_x^2 - v_p^2)E_y &= 0,\\ (v_e^2 - v_p^2)E_z &= 0.\end{aligned} \tag{1.138}$$

For $v_p = v_o$, these equations can be satisfied only if $E_z = 0$, $E_x \neq 0$, $E_y \neq 0$, therefore the ordinary wave is polarized normal to the optic axis. The other solution of Eqs (1.138) corresponds to $v_p = v_e$, $E_z \neq 0$, $E_x = 0$, $E_y = 0$. Thus, for propagation in a plane perpendicular to the optic axis, both waves are ordinary waves but orthogonally polarized propagating with velocities v_o and v_e.

For waves propagating along the optic axis, $\hat{k}_x = 0$, $\hat{k}_y = 0$, $\hat{k}_z = 1$, and Eqs (1.137) give

$$(v_o^2 - v_p^2)E_x = 0, \quad (v_o^2 - v_p^2)E_y = 0, \quad -v_p^2 E_z = 0,$$

with the only solution $v_p = v_o$, $E_z = 0$, $E_x \neq 0$, $E_y \neq 0$. Thus, both waves propagating along the optic axis are ordinary waves with v_o as their common velocity of propagation. The remaining cases covered by $0 < \hat{k}_z < 1$ can be exemplified by restricting the propagation vector to lie in the xz principal plane, so that $\hat{k}_y = 0$, giving

$$\begin{aligned}(v_o^2\hat{k}_z^2 - v_p^2)E_x - v_o^2\hat{k}_x\hat{k}_z E_z &= 0,\\ (v_o^2 - v_p^2)E_y &= 0,\\ -v_e^2\hat{k}_z\hat{k}_x E_x + (v_e^2\hat{k}_x^2 - v_p^2)E_z &= 0.\end{aligned} \tag{1.139}$$

For the ordinary wave with $v_p = v_o$, these equations can be satisfied only if $E_y \neq 0$, $E_x = 0$, $E_z = 0$, so that $\vec{D} = \epsilon_0 n_o^2 \vec{E}$, where n_o is the index of refraction for the ordinary wave. Therefore, the ordinary wave is polarized perpendicular to the plane containing the optic axis and the direction of propagation. In the present context, this plane is called the principal plane. The electric and displacement fields of the ordinary wave oscillate along the tangents to the spherical normal surface. Poynting vector in this case is in the direction of the propagation vector (see Fig. 1.27). For the extraordinary wave (velocity given by Eq. 1.135b), Eqs (1.139) require $E_y = 0$, $E_x \neq 0$, and $E_z \neq 0$ with the ratio

$$\frac{E_z}{E_x} = -\frac{v_e^2}{v_o^2}\frac{\hat{k}_x}{\hat{k}_z}.$$

Therefore, the extraordinary wave is polarized in the principal plane with polarization changing direction with the direction of the propagation vector. Since the $\vec{E}$ and $\vec{D}$ fields are not parallel in this case, the directions of the Poynting and propagation vectors differ as indicated in Fig. 1.27. The electric field $\vec{E}$ oscillates tangential to the normal surface and the displacement field $\vec{D}$ oscillates normal to the propagation vector.

1.10.4 Biaxial Crystals

All three principal dielectric constants are different in a biaxial crystal. For the sake of definiteness, let $\epsilon_z > \epsilon_y > \epsilon_x$, so that $v_z < v_y < v_x$. We can get a feel for the normal surface of a biaxial crystal by first considering its sections in the three coordinate planes of the principal axis system. The results obtained from Eqs (1.129b) and (1.136) are summarized below:

Case I: Propagation in the yz plane ($\hat{k}_x = 0$)

$$v'_{\text{p}} = v_x; \quad E_x \neq 0, \quad E_y = 0, \quad E_z = 0,$$
$$v''_{\text{p}} = (\hat{k}_y^2 v_z^2 + \hat{k}_z^2 v_y^2)^{1/2}; \quad E_x = 0, \quad E_y \neq 0, \quad E_z \neq 0,$$

Case II: Propagation in the xz plane ($\hat{k}_y = 0$)

$$v'_{\text{p}} = v_y; \quad E_y \neq 0, \quad E_x = 0, \quad E_z = 0,$$
$$v''_{\text{p}} = (\hat{k}_z^2 v_x^2 + \hat{k}_x^2 v_z^2)^{1/2}; \quad E_y = 0, \quad E_x \neq 0, \quad E_z \neq 0,$$

Case III: Propagation in the xy plane ($\hat{k}_z = 0$)

$$v'_{\text{p}} = v_z; \quad E_z \neq 0, \quad E_x = 0, \quad E_y = 0,$$
$$v''_{\text{p}} = (\hat{k}_x^2 v_y^2 + \hat{k}_y^2 v_x^2)^{1/2}; \quad E_z = 0, \quad E_x \neq 0, \quad E_y \neq 0.$$

Figure 1.28 shows sections of the normal surface in the principal coordinate planes. In each case, the section consists of a circle and an ellipse. For our choice of the relative magnitudes of the principal dielectric constants, the circle in the yz plane lies completely outside the ellipse (Fig. 1.28a) and in the xy plane, the circle lies completely inside the ellipse (Fig. 1.28c). The circle and the ellipse intersect at four points in the zx plane (Fig. 1.28b). The optic axes of a biaxial crystal, symmetrically inclined to the z-axis, pass through these points

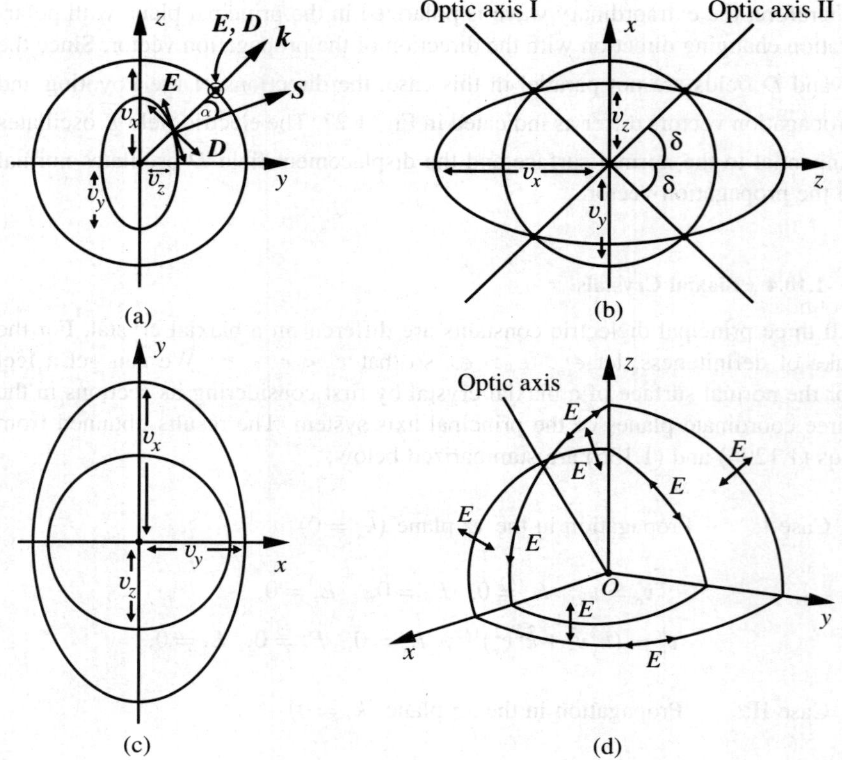

Fig. 1.28: Sections of the normal surface of a biaxial crystal in (a) yz, (b) zx, (c) xy planes; (d) normal surface of a biaxial crystal in one octant.

of interactions as shown in the figure. The angle δ between the z-axis and the optic axes can be obtained from Case II above, giving

$$\tan^2 \delta = \frac{v_x^2 - v_y^2}{v_y^2 - v_z^2}. \tag{1.140}$$

A positive biaxial crystal has $\delta < 45°$ and a negative biaxial crystal has $\delta > 45°$. For a uniaxial crystal, $\delta = 0$, and the two optic axes coincide with the z-axis. A view of the three-dimensional normal surface of a biaxial crystal in one octant is shown in Fig. 1.28d.

In summary, we can state that when wave propagation is restricted to the principal planes of a biaxial crystal, there is generally one ordinary and one extraordinary wave and for propagation along the principal axes, both waves are ordinary waves but with unequal velocities of propagation. It can be appreciated that for propagation in a biaxial crystal along directions not covered by the principal planes, both waves are extraordinary.

1.10.5 Double Refraction

We return to Section 1.7 on reflection and transmission of waves at a planar boundary, but this time the boundary is between isotropic and anisotropic media (see Fig. 1.7). We will not derive expressions for the reflection and transmission coefficients across such a boundary, but merely investigate the nature of the refraction process. The incident and refracted waves must satisfy Eq. (1.51c) in this case as well, requiring

$$\vec{k}_{\mathrm{i}} \cdot \vec{r}_{\mathrm{B}} = \vec{k}_{\mathrm{t}} \cdot \vec{r}_{\mathrm{B}}, \tag{1.51c}$$

where $\vec{k}_{\mathrm{i}}$ and $\vec{k}_{\mathrm{t}}$ are the propagation vectors of the incident and transmitted waves and $\vec{r}_{\mathrm{B}}$ is a vector in the boundary plane. Expressing $\vec{k}_{\mathrm{i}} = \frac{n}{c}\omega\hat{k}$ and $\vec{k}_{\mathrm{t}} = \frac{n_{\mathrm{t}}}{c}\omega\hat{k}_{\mathrm{t}}$, Eq. (1.51c) is equivalent to

$$(n\hat{k} - n_{\mathrm{t}}\hat{k}_{\mathrm{t}}) \cdot \vec{r}_{\mathrm{B}} = 0, \tag{1.141}$$

where n and n_{t} are the indices of refraction of the media on the two sides of the boundary. But since an anisotropic medium is characterized by two phase velocities $(v'_{\mathrm{p}}, v''_{\mathrm{p}})$ and hence two indices of refraction (n_1, n_2), Eq. (1.141) actually represents two equations:

$$(n\hat{k} - n_1\hat{k}_1) \cdot \vec{r}_{\mathrm{B}} = 0, \quad (n\hat{k} - n_2\hat{k}_2) \cdot \vec{r}_{\mathrm{B}} = 0. \tag{1.142}$$

Figure 1.29 shows the vectors $n\hat{k}$, $n_1\hat{k}_1$, and $n_2\hat{k}_2$ drawn from point O on the boundary. Equations (1.142) can be satisfied only if the tips of the vectors $n\hat{k}$, $n_1\hat{k}_1$, and $n_2\hat{k}_2$ lie on a line which is perpendicular to the plane of the boundary. This gives rise to two transmitted waves in the anisotropic medium, making angles θ_1 and θ_2 with the normal to the plane of the boundary, such that

$$n \sin\theta = n_1 \sin\theta_1, \quad n \sin\theta = n_2 \sin\theta_2. \tag{1.143}$$

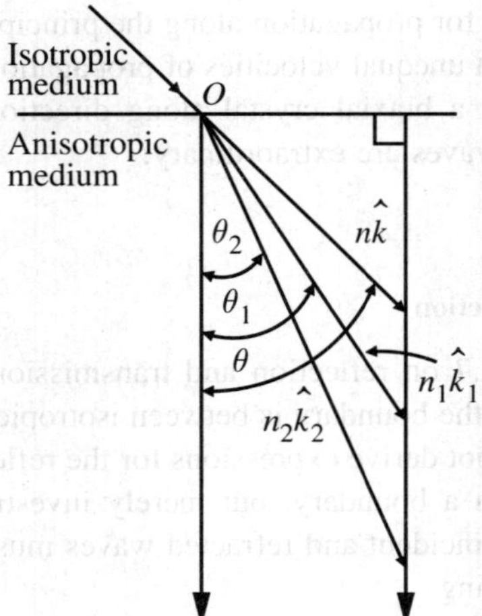

Fig. 1.29: Double refraction across a boundary between isotropic and anisotropic media.

These equations appear to be the usual expressions for the Snell's law. However, by expressing the indices of refraction in terms of the phase velocities, Eqs (1.143) can be expressed as

$$\frac{\sin\theta}{v} = \frac{\sin\theta_1}{v'_{\rm p}} = \frac{\sin\theta_2}{v''_{\rm p}}, \tag{1.144}$$

where v is the phase velocity in the isotropic medium. In uniaxial crystals and in the principal planes of the biaxial crystals, the phase velocity $v'_{\rm p}$ has been found to be independent of the direction of propagation. This corresponds to the ordinary wave for which the index of refraction n_1 is a constant and Snell's law holds. For the extraordinary wave, the phase velocity $v''_{\rm p}$ varies with the direction of propagation and Snell's law does not hold since n_2 is not a constant. For the transmitted waves in biaxial crystals in directions other than those lying in the principal planes, Snell's law does not hold for either of the waves since both waves are extraordinary in those directions. Double refraction in anisotropic media is also known as birefringence. Peculiar phenomenon of conical refraction takes place when transmitted wave in biaxial crystals travels along an optic axis. In that case, the elliptical section (Fig. 1.26) of the index ellipsoid perpendicular to the propagation direction $\vec{k}$ degenerates into a circle, giving infinitely many (and not just two as in Fig. 1.26) possible directions for the displacement field $\vec{D}$ and hence for the Poynting vector $\vec{S}$. As shown in Principles of Optics by Born and Wolf, the permitted directions of $\vec{S}$ lie along a cone which touches the optic axis.

1.10.6 Polarizing Prisms

There are a number of ways to produce polarized light. We have seen how incidence at Brewster angle (Section 1.7.1) on a singly refracting medium generates polarized light. Light scattered by molecules and small particles in directions orthogonal to the direction of the incident light is substantially polarized. Polarizing prisms exploit the phenomenon of double refraction in uniaxial crystals to produce polarized light. William Nicol developed the first polarizing prism, called the Nicol prism. Its sectional view is shown in Fig. 1.30a. The optic axis lies in the plane of the figure. The cleaved edges of a calcite crystal are inclined at 71° to each other. This angle is reduced to nearly 68° by grinding the sides. The crystal is then cut along the diagonal as shown, and the two halves are cemented together with a thin layer of canada balsam whose index of refraction ($n = 1.55$) lies between the indices n_o ($=1.6583$) and n_e ($=1.4864$) of calcite. The ordinary wave undergoes total internal reflection at the calcite–canada balsam interface,

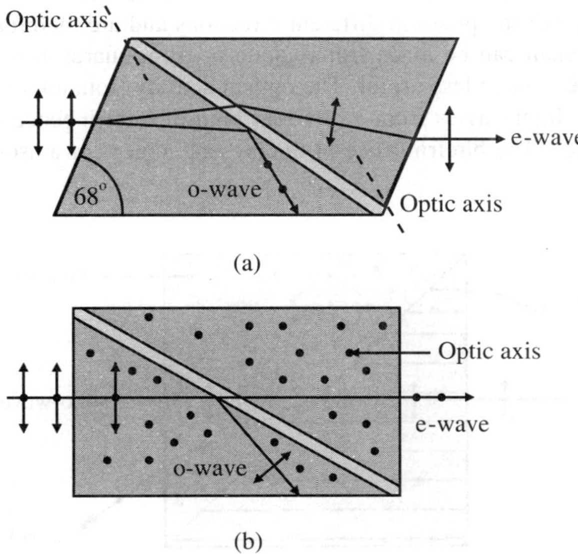

Fig. 1.30: Polarizing prisms; (a) Nicol prism, (b) Glan-Thompson prism.

but the extraordinary wave which is polarized in the plane containing the direction of propagation and the optic axis is substantially transmitted. The ordinary wave, after getting reflected, is absorbed at the blackened edge of the prism. The incident beam should be nearly parallel to the upper and lower edges of the prism. For large deviations (more than 10°−12°) from this direction, the ordinary and extraordinary waves may not get separated. Absorption of light by canada balsam restricts the use of Nicol prisms down to about 0.35 μm. To extend the use of the polarizing prisms to the ultraviolet, canada balsam should be replaced by air or UV transmitting oils. The lateral shift of the transmitted beam is another limitation of the Nicol prism. A Glan-Thompson prism (Fig. 1.30b) with perpendicular edges requires a large calcite crystal, but the transmitted wave comes out undeviated. The acceptance angle for this polarizing prism is much higher (≈30°). A Glan-Thompson air prism extends the spectral range of these polarizers down to about 0.21 μm. In the Rochon prism, the two halves of the prism are joined together with orthogonal orientations of the optic axis as shown in Fig. 1.31. The ordinary wave, polarized perpendicular to the section of the prism shown in the figure in the first half and in the plane of the figure in the second half, undergoes no refractive index change across the interface (sees n_o in both halves) and is therefore transmitted without any deviation. But the other wave is refracted at the interface because it behaves as an ordinary wave (polarized in the plane of the figure but perpendicular to the optic axis) in the first half and as an extraordinary wave (polarized along the optic axis) in the second half. As a result, the two waves exit the prism in different directions and are therefore separated. The Rochon prism can be made from calcite or from quartz, but quartz being optically active may be less useful. The optical activity (rotation of the plane of polarization of light) arises from a different kind of birefringence called circular birefringence. The birefringence in the present context of anisotropic media

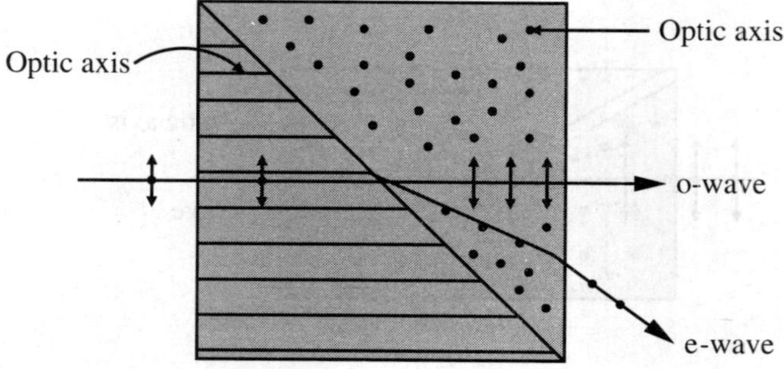

Fig. 1.31: The Rochon Prism.

may be called linear birefringence since refractive index change exists between linearly, but orthogonally polarized light waves. In optical activity, the refractive index change occurs between left and right circularly polarized light waves (see Section 3.1.2). Anisotropy can be induced in otherwise isotropic media such as glass, liquids, etc., by subjecting them to external disturbances in the forms of the electric, magnetic, and strain fields. The corresponding induced anisotropies are referred to as the electro-optic, the magneto-optic and the photo-elastic effects. We shall, however, not discuss these effects.

1.11 REFERENCES

1.1 Christopher C. Davis, Lasers and Electro-Optics: Fundamentals and Engineering, Cambridge University Press, Cambridge, 1996.

1.2 Peter W. Milonni and Joseph H. Eberly, Lasers, John Wiley & Sons, New York, 1991.

1.3 John M. Stone, Radiation and Optics, McGraw-Hill, New York, 1963.

1.4 A. L. Snyder and J. D. Love, 'The Goos – Hanchen shift', Appl. Opt. **15**, 236–8(1976).

1.5 Max Born and Emil Wolf, Principles of Optics, 7th ed., Cambridge University Press, Cambridge, 1999.

1.6 F. Abeles, Optics of thin films in Advanced Optical Techniques, Ed., A.C.S. Van Heel, North-Holland Publishing Co., Amsterdam, 1967.

1.7 Robert D. Guenther, Modern Optics, John Wiley & Sons, New York, 1990.

1.8 Miles V. Klein and Thomas E. Furtak, Optics, 2nd ed., John Wiley & Sons, New York, 1986.

1.9 Eugene Hecht, Optics, 4th ed., Addison-Wesley, Reading, 2001.

1.10 F. A. Jenkins and H. E. White, Fundamentals of Optics, 3rd ed., McGraw-Hill, New York, 1957.

1.11 S. G. Lipson, H. Lipson and D. S. Tannhauser, Optical Physics, 3rd ed., Cambridge University Press, Cambridge, 1995.

1.12 PROBLEMS

1.1 Two co-polarized plane electromagnetic waves with same frequency, amplitude and phase constant are propagating in opposite directions in free space. Find time averaged energy density and Poynting vector at a given point in space. Solve the problem using real and complex fields.

1.2 The spot size of a Gaussian TEM_{00} mode is $10\,\mu m$ at the beam waist. Plot the variations of the spot size $w(z)$ and radius of curvature $R(z)$ of the mode as a function of the axial distance from the beam waist ($z = 0$). At what distance from the beam waist, $R(z)$ has minimum value? What is the spot size at this point? Find the divergence angle and wavelength of the mode. Take $z_0 = 1$ mm.

1.3 A Gaussian TEM_{00} mode existing in a laser resonator has radii of curvatures of -5 m and $+8$ m at two points, 0.4 m apart. Find the positions of these points with respect to the beam waist ($z = 0$). Obtain the minimum spot size, Rayleigh range and divergence of the mode. Take $\lambda = 500$ nm.

1.4 Consider a monochromatic inhomogeneous wave (Fig. 1.5b) with real and imaginary parts of the propagation vector along the x- and z-directions, respectively. For the TE mode, let the electric field $\vec{E}$ be linearly polarized along the y-direction. Determine the magnitude and direction of the magnetic field $\vec{B}$ and comment on its state of polarization. Show that field $\vec{B}$ is not transverse to the real part of the propagation vector $\vec{k}$, but is transverse to the electric field $\vec{E}$ and complex propagation vector $\vec{\tilde{k}}$.

1.5 If in Problem 1.4, the real part of the propagation vector is also in the z-direction, the wave becomes homogeneous. Show that $\vec{B}$ is now linearly polarized if E is linearly polarized, but the two are not in phase. Find the phase difference between the $\vec{E}$ and $\vec{B}$ fields if the complex refractive index of the medium is $\tilde{n} = 1.30 + 7.11i$.

1.6 Work out the steps which lead to Eqs (1.59) and (1.62).

1.7 A monochromatic plane wave, travelling in air, falls on an air–glass ($n = 1.5$) interface at an angle of incidence of 60°. The electric field of the incident wave makes an angle of 45° with the normal to the plane of incidence. Determine the angle between the electric field of the reflected wave and the normal to the plane of incidence. Has the proportion of σ-polarization increased in the reflected wave?

1.8 Refer to Fig. 1.8 and determine the reflection losses suffered by σ-polarized light at the Brewster windows ($n = 1.5$) during one round trip between mirrors M_1 and M_2.

1.9 Disallowing total internal reflection, show that at an interface between two optically transparent ($\kappa = 0$) media,

$$r_\sigma + t_\sigma \neq 1, \quad r_\pi + t_\pi \neq 1 \text{ except when } \theta = \theta_B.$$

What is the significance of $r_\pi + t_\pi = 1$ for $\theta = \theta_B$?

1.10 Consider σ-polarized light incident at Brewster angle on a stack of N optically transparent glass slabs held parallel to each other with air gaps between the adjacent slabs. Find transmittance of the stack and plot its variation with the number of slabs in the stack. Take $n = 1.5$ for each slab. Repeat the calculation for π-polarized light. Comment on the difference in behavior in the two cases.

1.11 Calculate the angle of a Fresnel rhomb made from fused quartz with $n = 1.46$ so that the difference in phase between π- and σ-polarized light waves after two successive reflections in the rhomb is 90°.

1.12 Light is bent through 90° from two 45°–45°–90° prisms as shown in Fig. 1.32. The material of one of the prisms is glass with $n = 1.5$ and that of the other is MgF_2 with $n = 1.38$. Assuming the prisms to be perfectly transparent, find the amplitudes of the fields coming out of the prisms for the following two cases

(a) $\vec{E}_{\text{in}} = E_0 \hat{\sigma}\, \mathrm{e}^{\mathrm{i}(\vec{k}\cdot\vec{r}-\omega t)}$, (b) $\vec{E}_{\text{in}} = E_0 \hat{\pi}\, \mathrm{e}^{\mathrm{i}(\vec{k}\cdot\vec{r}-\omega t)}$,

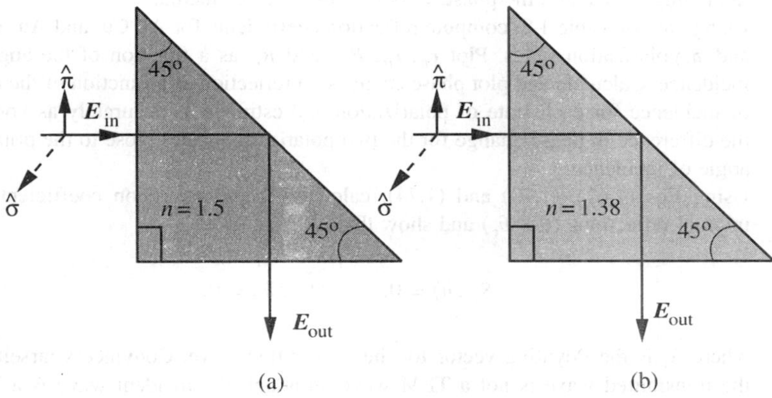

Fig. 1.32.

1.13 Consider internal reflection from glass ($n = 1.5$) to air. Find the angle(s) of incidence for which $2\psi_0 - 2\phi_0$ has maximum value, where the angles ϕ_0 and ψ_0 are defined in Eqs (1.79).

1.14 For the evanescent wave, find the time averaged components of the Poynting vector along and perpendicular to the interface between two optically transparent media when angle of incidence exceeds the critical angle. Incident light may be taken to be σ-polarized.

1.15 In an optical tunnelling experiment linearly polarized light, polarized in the plane of incidence, arrives at the first interface making an angle of 75° with the normal to the interface (Fig. 1.33). The thickness of the sandwiched medium is 1.5 times

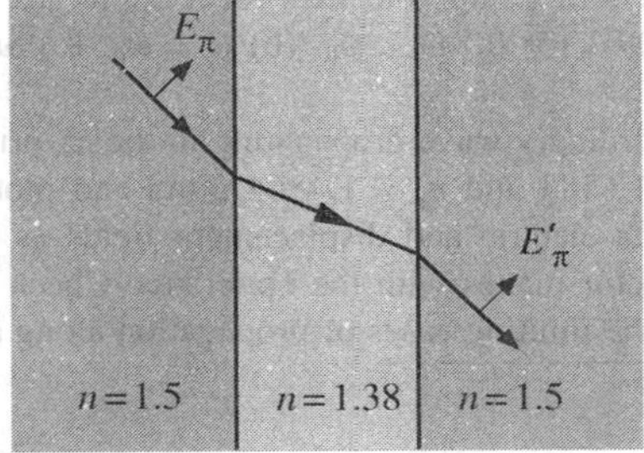

Fig. 1.33.

the penetration depth in that medium (i.e. when the second medium is unbounded on the right-hand side). You may assume all media to be perfectly transparent. Neglect multiple reflections in the sandwiched medium. Find transmittance of the tunnelling device and the phase velocities in the three media.

1.16 Using data of Table 1.2, compute reflection coefficients for Al, Cu, and Au for σ- and π-polarization states. Plot r_π, r_σ, R_π, and R_σ as a function of the angle of incidence. Calculate and plot phase changes on reflection as a function of the angle of incidence for each state of polarization and estimate as accurately as you can the difference in phase change for the two polarization states close to the principal angle of incidence.

1.17 Using Eqs (1.62), (1.73) and (1.74), calculate the transmission coefficients for internal reflections ($\theta > \theta_c$) and show that

$$\langle \vec{S}_t \,.\, \hat{n} \rangle = 0, \qquad \langle \vec{S}_t \,.\, \hat{\pi} \rangle \neq 0,$$

where $\vec{S}_t$ is the Poynting vector for the transmitted wave. Convince yourself that the transmitted wave is not a TEM wave, although the incident wave is a TEM wave.

1.18 A monochromatic plane wave of frequency ν is incident from air on a medium of complex index of refraction $\tilde{n} = 1.5 + 0.5i$ making an angle of 45° with the normal to the interface. Take $\nu = 6 \times 10^{14}$ Hz.

(a) Determine the angle of refraction, attenuation constant a_t, and wave number k_t in the second medium. State if the wave is homogeneous or inhomogeneous in the second medium.

(b) Calculate the magnitude and phase of the reflection coefficient if incident light is σ-polarized. What are the states of polarization of the $\vec{E}$ and $\vec{B}$ fields in the second medium?

1.19 A monochromatic plane wave travelling in air is reflected normally from a metallic film with complex index of refraction $\tilde{n} = 0.76 + 2.46i$. Find the resultant electric and magnetic fields in air. Are standing waves set up in air?

1.20 Calculate the phase and group velocities for a dilute gas with index of refraction given by Eq. (1.109a) for (a) $\omega < \omega_0$, (b) $\omega = \omega_0$, (c) $\omega = \omega_0 + \frac{\gamma}{4}$ and (d) $\omega = \omega_0 + \gamma$.

1.21 Consider the extraordinary wave propagating in the xz principal plane of a calcite crystal with $n_o = 1.6583$ and $n_e = 1.4864$. Find and plot the dependence of the angle α between its electric and displacement fields as a function of the angle the propagation vector makes with the optic axis. Check if you get the expected result ($\alpha = 0$) for the limiting cases of propagation along and perpendicular to the optic axis.

CHAPTER 2

Coherence of Light Waves

2.1 POLYCHROMATIC LIGHT

A number of monochromatic wave solutions of the wave equation were considered in Chapter 1. A monochromatic wave must exist for all times. Such a wave, if it does exist, must have seen the big-bang if it ever occurred and should see the doom's day if it comes! There are other unreal features of the monochromatic wave solutions. To establish even a small amplitude directed monochromatic wave, an infinite amount of energy must be expended. Needless to say that no source exists which gives strictly monochromatic light. Nevertheless, the monochromatic wave solutions of the wave equation are extremely useful to describe real light, which is polychromatic. A monochromatic wave has perfect coherence because its phase is completely defined at each and every point in space for all times. If the phase of a monochromatic wave at a space-time point $(\vec{r}_1, t_1)$ is known, then its phase at any arbitrary space-time point $(\vec{r}_2, t_2)$ can be precisely determined – in other words, the phases of a monochromatic wave are perfectly correlated. In the same spirit, the amplitude of a monochromatic wave is perfectly correlated. The extent to which the phase and amplitude correlations in time and space exist, determines the coherence properties of a light wave. A monochromatic plane wave

$$\vec{E}\,(\vec{r}, t) = \vec{E}_0\, \mathrm{e}^{\mathrm{i}(\vec{k}\cdot\vec{r} - \omega t + \phi_0)} \tag{2.1}$$

has amplitude $\vec{E}_0$ and phase constant ϕ_0 which are strictly independent of time and position.

Monochromatic waves are ideal single frequency waves and hence unrealizable. Practical light sources have spectral bandwidths varying from a fraction of a kHz for a good single mode laser to the broad spectrum of a black body radiator. All light fields are therefore polychromatic. This has to do with the inherent process of light emission. Thermal light is generated as a result of spontaneous emission from excited atoms and molecules radiating independently. Fourier decomposition[1] of thermal light contains waves with continuously distributed frequencies. Stimulated emission is the predominant mechanism of production of laser light which also contains a non-negligible component of the spontaneously emitted light restricting its bandwidth to a finite, albeit narrow spectral range. A scalar polychromatic light field can be Fourier decomposed:

$$E^{(r)}(t) = \int_{-\infty}^{+\infty} E(\nu)\mathrm{e}^{-\mathrm{i}2\pi\nu t}\mathrm{d}\nu, \tag{2.2}$$

where the real field $E^{(r)}(t)$ may represent a Cartesian component of the electric field vector of a light wave. Its space dependence has been suppressed. $E(\nu)\mathrm{d}(\nu)$ is the complex weighting factor for the waves with frequencies lying between ν and $\nu+\mathrm{d}\nu$. The Fourier decomposition (Eq. 2.2) necessarily involves positive as well as negative frequencies. However, by taking the inverse Fourier transform of Eq. (2.2) and making use of the fact that $E^{(r)}(t)$ is real, it can be shown that

$$E(-\nu) = E^*(\nu).$$

Therefore, all spectral information of $E^{(r)}(t)$ is contained in the positive frequencies. Accordingly, the Fourier decomposition of a polychromatic light field can be recast into a form that does not contain negative frequencies:

$$\begin{aligned} E^{(r)}(t) &= \int_0^{\infty} E(\nu)\mathrm{e}^{-\mathrm{i}2\pi\nu t}\mathrm{d}\nu + \int_{-\infty}^{0} E(\nu)\mathrm{e}^{-\mathrm{i}2\pi\nu t}\mathrm{d}\nu \\ &= \int_0^{\infty} E(\nu)\mathrm{e}^{-\mathrm{i}2\pi\nu t}\mathrm{d}\nu + \int_0^{\infty} E(-\nu)\mathrm{e}^{\mathrm{i}2\pi\nu t}\mathrm{d}\nu \\ &= \int_0^{\infty} E(\nu)\mathrm{e}^{-\mathrm{i}2\pi\nu t}\mathrm{d}\nu + \int_0^{\infty} E^*(\nu)\mathrm{e}^{\mathrm{i}2\pi\nu t}\mathrm{d}\nu \\ &= \int_0^{\infty} E(\nu)\mathrm{e}^{-\mathrm{i}2\pi\nu t}\mathrm{d}\nu + \mathrm{cc} \qquad (2.3a) \\ &= 2Re\int_0^{\infty} E(\nu)\mathrm{e}^{-\mathrm{i}2\pi\nu t}\mathrm{d}\nu \qquad (2.3b) \\ &= 2\int_0^{\infty} |E(\nu)|\cos(\phi(\nu) - 2\pi\nu t)\mathrm{d}\nu, \qquad (2.3c) \end{aligned}$$

where cc stands for complex conjugate and $E(\nu)$ has been expressed as

$$E(\nu) = |E(\nu)|\mathrm{e}^{\mathrm{i}\phi(\nu)}. \tag{2.4}$$

[1] Fourier transforms are discussed in Chapter 9.

The decomposition of polychromatic field now has only positive frequencies. We next define another real polychromatic field

$$E^{(i)}(t) = 2\int_0^{\infty} |E(\nu)| \sin(\phi(\nu) - 2\pi\nu t)\mathrm{d}\nu, \tag{2.5}$$

whose each spectral component is shifted in phase by 90° from the corresponding component of $E^{(r)}(t)$. The real functions $E^{(r)}(t)$ and $E^{(i)}(t)$ are related by the Hilbert transformation[2]:

$$E^{(i)}(t) = \frac{1}{\pi} P \int_{-\infty}^{+\infty} \frac{E^{(r)}(t')}{t' - t} \mathrm{d}t', \tag{2.6a}$$

$$E^{(r)}(t) = -\frac{1}{\pi} P \int_{-\infty}^{+\infty} \frac{E^{(i)}(t')}{t' - t} \mathrm{d}t', \tag{2.6b}$$

where P refers to the Cauchy principal value at $t' = t$. The complex polychromatic light field is defined as

$$E(t) = E^{(r)}(t) + \mathrm{i}E^{(i)}(t) \tag{2.7a}$$

$$= 2\int_0^{\infty} E(\nu)\mathrm{e}^{-\mathrm{i}2\pi\nu t}\mathrm{d}\nu, \tag{2.7b}$$

where

$$E(\nu) = \int_{-\infty}^{\infty} E^{(r)}(t)\mathrm{e}^{\mathrm{i}2\pi\nu t}\mathrm{d}t$$

is the inverse Fourier transform of $E^{(r)}(t)$. The complex light field $E(t)$ can be identified with the analytical signal $V(t)$ used in communication theory. The complex polychromatic light field $E(t)$ can be given an alternate description in terms of the envelope representation:

$$E(t) = A(t)\mathrm{e}^{-\mathrm{i}(2\pi\bar{\nu}t - \Phi(t))} \tag{2.8a}$$

$$= \{A(t)\mathrm{e}^{\mathrm{i}\Phi(t)}\}\mathrm{e}^{-\mathrm{i}2\pi\bar{\nu}t}, \tag{2.8b}$$

where the amplitude $A(t)$ and phase $\Phi(t)$ are time varying, and $\bar{\nu}$ is the mean frequency of polychromatic light. But, as we shall see later, such a representation of polychromatic light is not very useful, except when light possesses a narrow spectral bandwidth.

---

[2] P.M. Morse and H. Feshbach, Methods of Theoretical Physics.

2.1.1 Quasi-monochromatic Light

A source giving monochromatic light may be hard to find, but sources of light with relatively narrow frequency bandwidths are readily available. Conventional sodium, mercury, and cadmium lamps belong to this category of light sources. In addition, a narrow band interference filter used in conjunction with a polychromatic light source such as a tungsten–halogen lamp provides a convenient narrow band source. For quasi-monochromatic light,

$$\frac{\Delta\nu}{\bar{\nu}} \ll 1, \tag{2.9}$$

where $\bar{\nu}$ is the mean frequency and $\Delta\nu$ the frequency bandwidth of the source. A multi-mode laser is an excellent example of a quasi-monochromatic light source. A single mode laser must also be categorized as a quasi-monochromatic light source. We now show that the envelope representation (Eqs 2.8) can adequately describe quasi-monochromatic light. Re-arranging Eq. (2.8b) and making use of Eq. (2.7b), we have

$$\begin{aligned} A(t)\mathrm{e}^{\mathrm{i}\Phi(t)} &= E(t)\mathrm{e}^{\mathrm{i}2\pi\bar{\nu}t} \\ &= 2\int_0^{\infty} E(\nu)\mathrm{e}^{-\mathrm{i}2\pi(\nu-\bar{\nu})t}\mathrm{d}\nu \\ &= 2\int_{-\bar{\nu}}^{\infty} E(\bar{\nu}+\mu)\mathrm{e}^{-\mathrm{i}2\pi\mu t}\mathrm{d}\mu, \end{aligned} \tag{2.10}$$

where in view of Eq. (2.9), $\mu = \nu - \bar{\nu}$ is small $\approx \Delta\nu$. The time dependence of the product $A(t)\mathrm{e}^{\mathrm{i}\Phi(t)}$ comes via the exponential $\mathrm{e}^{-\mathrm{i}2\pi\mu t}$ which may not significantly differ from unity for quasi-monochromatic light with sufficiently narrow spectral bandwidth. In addition, $E(\bar{\nu}+\mu)$ is non-zero over a narrow range of frequencies in the neighborhood of the mean frequency $\bar{\nu}(\mu = 0)$. Therefore, the amplitude $A(t)$ and phase $\Phi(t)$ of the envelope representation of quasi-monochromatic light change slowly with time. This is precisely what the term quasi-monochromatic wave is supposed to imply. Later, we shall further sharpen the definition of a quasi-monochromatic wave. Slow variations of $A(t)$ and $\Phi(t)$ with time may imply the existence of correlations in the amplitude and phase of the electric field of quasi-monochromatic light at times t and $t+\tau$, if the time difference τ is not too large. On the other hand, for polychromatic light, $A(t)$ and $\Phi(t)$ vary so rapidly with time that the amplitude and phase of the wave lose any meaning.

2.2 PARTIALLY COHERENT LIGHT

Monochromatic light is perfectly coherent, but polychromatic light is not perfectly incoherent in the sense that no two space-time points exist with correlated phases. Perfect incoherence is just as unrealizable as perfect coherence. Light fields are partially coherent. Of course, over limited regions of space and time, coherence of light can closely approach either perfect coherence or perfect incoherence.

In the context of monochromatic light, we associated coherence with the presence of phase correlations at two space-time locations. However, the common usage of the term coherence is linked with the ability of light to produce interference effects. Within the scope of this interpretation, light is considered coherent if it can produce interference, and incoherent if it cannot. This definition of coherence suffers from a number of deficiencies. Undoubtedly, no interference is possible if light is not coherent, but the absence of interference may not necessarily imply incoherence of light. Furthermore, the interference effects when present may be well pronounced or may not be so well pronounced. Therefore, the term interference effects fails to provide a quantitative definition of coherence. The term *fringe visibility* introduced by Michelson may be more appropriate for a quantitative definition of coherence. Perfect coherence may correspond to 100% visibility and zero visibility may imply complete incoherence – in between we have the regime of the partially coherent light. The concept of the degree of coherence, to be introduced shortly, is intimately related to the fringe visibility when the fringes exist. However, the degree of coherence can be defined and hopefully measured as well even when the fringes do not exist. We are now referring to higher order coherence effects.

2.2.1 Spatial and Temporal Coherence

The concepts of spatial and temporal coherence are not fundamental to the description of coherent light, but they are helpful for an intuitive understanding of partially coherent light. As we shall see later, they represent two limiting cases of the general state of coherence of light fields. Temporal coherence is intimately related to the frequency bandwidth of a truncated wave train. Temporal coherence determines how far two points along the direction of propagation of a wave can be and still possess a definite phase relationship. For that reason, temporal coherence is also called longitudinal coherence. Michelson interferometer, which senses longitudinal path differences between the interfering waves, is ideally suited for investigating temporal coherence of light fields. Spatial coherence of light fields depends on the physical size of the light source. Light coming from a point source, which may be taken as a source with dimensions not exceeding the mean wavelength of the emitted light, possesses a high degree of spatial coherence, irrespective of the frequency bandwidth of the source. Commonly observed speckles with laser light reflect a high degree of spatial coherence of laser light despite the laser not being a point source. Light from a conventional extended source, on the other hand, has considerably reduced spatial coherence because different points on an extended source radiate independently and therefore are mutually incoherent. Light emanating from an extended source cannot be characterized by a definite state of spatial coherence. Spatial coherence of light from an extended source changes as light propagates. Star light will show little spatial coherence in the neighborhood of the star, but light from the same star will show on earth a high degree of spatial coherence. In fact, as we shall see later, large spatial coherence of star light on earth is a handicap in determining the angular size of a distant star. Sunlight approaches near perfect spatial coherence on earth over a patch of diameter 0.019 mm. We shall return to these considerations later in this chapter. Spatial coherence of light determines how far two points can lie in a plane transverse to the direction of propagation of light and still be correlated in phase. Spatial coherence of light can be investigated by interferometers of the type used by Young in his famous two-slit interference experiment. We now develop a mathematical framework to characterize the coherence of light fields.

2.3 COMPLEX COHERENCE FUNCTIONS

First-order coherence between scalar fields at two space-time points $(\vec{r}_1, t_1)$ and $(\vec{r}_2, t_2)$ is defined through the first-order complex coherence function [2.1]

$$\Gamma^{(1)}(\vec{r}_1, t_1; \vec{r}_2, t_2) = \langle E^*(\vec{r}_1, t_1) E(\vec{r}_2, t_2) \rangle. \tag{2.11}$$

Higher order coherence among scalar fields at many space-time points can be defined in a similar manner. The nth order complex coherence function

$$\begin{aligned} &\Gamma^{(n)}(\vec{r}_1, t_1, \vec{r}_2, t_2, \ldots, \vec{r}_n, t_n; \vec{r}_{n+1}, t_{n+1}, \ldots, \vec{r}_{2n}, t_{2n}) \\ &= \langle E^*(\vec{r}_1, t_1) E^*(\vec{r}_2, t_2) \cdots E^*(\vec{r}_n, t_n) E(\vec{r}_{n+1}, t_{n+1}) \cdots E(\vec{r}_{2n}, t_{2n}) \rangle \end{aligned} \tag{2.12}$$

correlates light fields at $2n$ space-time locations. The symbol $\langle\ \rangle$, as explained in the following subsection, indicates that some form of averaging of the field products is involved in the definition of the coherence functions. Interference of light is associated with the first-order coherence function $\Gamma^{(1)}(\vec{r}_1, t_1; \vec{r}_2, t_2)$. The absence of interference among co-polarized light fields implies absence of first-order coherence ($\Gamma^{(1)}(\vec{r}_1, t_1; \vec{r}_2, t_2) = 0$), and not absence of coherence to all orders. The first-order coherence function establishes phase correlation between light fields at two space-time points. If the points are spatially separated $(\vec{r}_1 \neq \vec{r}_2)$, the first-order complex coherence function is called the complex mutual coherence function, abbreviated as

$$\Gamma_{12}(t_1, t_2) = \langle E_1^*(t_1) E_2(t_2) \rangle. \tag{2.13}$$

The subscripts used with Γ_{12}, E_1, and E_2 refer to two spatially distinct locations. For spatially coincident points $(\vec{r}_1 = \vec{r}_2)$, first-order phase correlation is sought at two different times through the complex self coherence function

$$\Gamma^{(1)}(\vec{r}_1, t_1, t_2) = \langle E^*(\vec{r}_1, t_1)E(\vec{r}_1, t_2)\rangle, \tag{2.14a}$$

abbreviated as

$$\Gamma_{11}(t_1, t_2) = \langle E_1^*(t_1)E_1(t_2)\rangle. \tag{2.14b}$$

2.3.1 Stationary and Time-Averaged Fields

The coherence functions determine correlations among light fields at different times. For the present discussion, it is not important to know whether these correlations are sought at the same or at different spatial positions. It is convenient to assume that the origin of the time scale in the above definitions is not important for determining the average values of field correlations. It is only the time delay $\tau = t_2 - t_1$ between events which may be relevant. The coherence function should then have the same value for a given time delay τ, irrespective of the exact time at which a measurement is made. Light fields satisfying this requirement are known as stationary fields. Such fields are produced by sources which have attained steady-state operation. For stationary fields, self and mutual complex coherence functions can be expressed as

$$\Gamma_{11}(\tau) = \langle E_1(t+\tau)E_1^*(t)\rangle, \tag{2.15a}$$

$$\Gamma_{12}(\tau) = \langle E_1(t+\tau)E_2^*(t)\rangle, \tag{2.15b}$$

respectively. We must now specify the nature of the averaging process involved in these definitions. It should be realized that no instrument exists to measure instantaneous fields at optical frequencies. The averaging of the field correlations could be a time average done over a certain time T which is comparable or longer than the time needed to make a physical measurement. Accordingly, Eqs (2.15) may be expressed as

$$\Gamma_{11}(\tau) = \frac{1}{T}\int_{-T/2}^{+T/2} E_1(t+\tau)E_1^*(t)\mathrm{d}t, \tag{2.16a}$$

$$\Gamma_{12}(\tau) = \frac{1}{T}\int_{-T/2}^{+T/2} E_1(t+\tau)E_2^*(t)\mathrm{d}t. \tag{2.16b}$$

It is quite legitimate to ask whether the averaging process in Eqs (2.16) will yield unique answers if the same measurement is repeated over the same time or somewhat different averaging times. The answers for the repeated measurements are most likely to come out different for a number of reasons. The light fields may be changing for reasons beyond our control. There may be random changes in the refractive index of the medium in which light is propagating. Alternatively, we can say that light fields may be undergoing inherent random fluctuations. Such variations are commonly handled in statistical physics by the standard technique of ensemble averaging. In this technique, one averages a physical property over a large number of ensembles. All ensembles representing the same physical system are identical to each other in all respects, except for the fluctuations which may differ from ensemble to ensemble because there is no way to control them. Here, we make the additional assumption that light fields are ergodic so that an ensemble average yields the same result as the time average. For stationary and ergodic light fields, the coherence functions are expected to be independent of the origin of the time scale.

2.3.2 Intensity of Polychromatic Light

Except for a constant multiplying factor, the intensity of light at a given point is simply the self coherence function at that point with zero time delay, i.e.,

$$I(\vec{r}) = \left(\frac{1}{2}\epsilon_0 c\right)\langle E(\vec{r}, t)E^*(\vec{r}, t)\rangle = \left(\frac{1}{2}\epsilon_0 c\right)\Gamma_{11}(0). \tag{2.17}$$

The intensity of polychromatic light such as sunlight may be measured with a detector having a broad spectral response. We ask the question whether we can expect a definite result if the intensity of sunlight reaching Earth is measured. Let us evaluate the intensity of polychromatic light by averaging the self coherence function $\Gamma_{11}(0)$ over a finite time interval T. Using Eq. (2.7b), we obtain

$$\begin{aligned}
\frac{I}{\frac{1}{2}\epsilon_0 c} &= \Gamma_{11}(0) = \frac{1}{T}\int_{-T/2}^{+T/2} E(t)E^*(t)\mathrm{d}t \\
&= \frac{4}{T}\int_{-T/2}^{+T/2}\mathrm{d}t\int_0^{\infty}\!\!\int \mathrm{e}^{\mathrm{i}2\pi(\nu'-\nu)t}E(\nu)E^*(\nu')\mathrm{d}\nu\,\mathrm{d}\nu' \\
&= \frac{4}{T}\int_0^{\infty}\!\!\int \mathrm{d}\nu\,\mathrm{d}\nu' E(\nu)E^*(\nu')\int_{-T/2}^{+T/2}\mathrm{e}^{\mathrm{i}2\pi(\nu'-\nu)t}\mathrm{d}t \\
&= 4\int_0^{\infty}\!\!\int \mathrm{d}\nu\,\mathrm{d}\nu' E(\nu)E^*(\nu')\frac{\sin[\pi(\nu'-\nu)T]}{\pi(\nu'-\nu)T}.
\end{aligned} \tag{2.18}$$

For any two frequencies ν and ν' within the spectral bandwidth of polychromatic light, the dependence of the sinc function $\frac{\sin[\pi(\nu'-\nu)T]}{\pi(\nu'-\nu)T}$ on the averaging time T is sketched in Fig. 2.1. It is quite obvious that irrespective of the spectral composition of $E(\nu)$, the intensity of polychromatic light is going to change with the averaging time T. However, for very long averaging time, the sinc function has zero value except when $\nu' = \nu$, in which case the sinc function may be replaced by the Dirac delta function,[3] giving

$$\begin{aligned}\Gamma_{11}(0) &= 4\int\int_0^\infty \mathrm{d}\nu\mathrm{d}\nu' E(\nu)E^*(\nu')\delta(\nu'-\nu) \\ &= 4\int_0^\infty |E(\nu)|^2\mathrm{d}\nu \\ &= 4\int_0^\infty W(\nu)\mathrm{d}\nu\end{aligned} \tag{2.19a}$$

and

$$I = \left(\frac{1}{2}\epsilon_0 c\right) 4\int_0^\infty W(\nu)\mathrm{d}\nu, \tag{2.19b}$$

where $W(\nu) = |E(\nu)|^2$ is the spectral density function of polychromatic light. This result is the statement of Parseval's theorem (Eq. 9.46), to be discussed later. In the present context we note that for short observation times $(T \sim 1/(\nu' - \nu))$, interference among different frequency components of polychromatic light gives

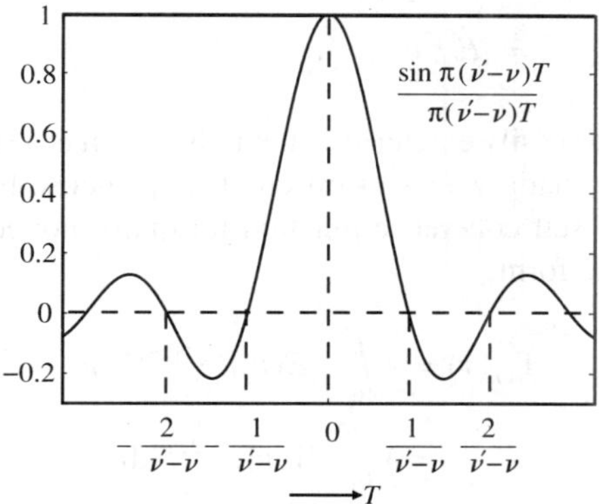

Fig. 2.1: The sinc function.

[3] Dirac delta function is discussed in Chapter 9.

rise to beats, making intensity of polychromatic light depend on the averaging time. However, for long averaging times ($T \gg 1/(\nu' - \nu)$), beats among different frequencies die out and interference among spectral components of the same frequency contribute to the intensity of polychromatic light. Accordingly, Eqs (2.16) must be modified to

$$\Gamma_{11}(\tau) = \lim_{T\to\infty} \frac{1}{T} \int_{-T/2}^{+T/2} E_1(t+\tau)E_1^*(t)\mathrm{d}t, \tag{2.20}$$

$$\Gamma_{12}(\tau) = \lim_{T\to\infty} \frac{1}{T} \int_{-T/2}^{+T/2} E_1(t+\tau)E_2^*(t)\mathrm{d}t. \tag{2.21}$$

The self and mutual coherence functions can be identified with the autocorrelation and crosscorrelation functions described in Chapter 9.

2.4 SELF COHERENCE

The complex self coherence function of a plane monochromatic light wave can be obtained by substituting Eq. (2.1) into Eq. (2.20), giving

$$\begin{aligned}\Gamma_{11}(\tau) &= \lim_{T\to\infty} \frac{1}{T} \int_{-T/2}^{+T/2} E_1(t+\tau)E_1^*(t)\mathrm{d}t \\ &= \lim_{T\to\infty} \frac{1}{T} \int_{-T/2}^{T/2} E_0E_0^*\mathrm{e}^{-\mathrm{i}2\pi\nu(t+\tau)}\mathrm{e}^{\mathrm{i}2\pi\nu t}\mathrm{d}t \\ &= |E_0|^2\mathrm{e}^{-\mathrm{i}2\pi\nu\tau}.\end{aligned} \tag{2.22}$$

This procedure can be easily extended to the light which is a superposition of any number of monochromatic waves of different frequencies. Following treatment of Section 2.3.2, the self coherence function for quasi-monochromatic light can be shown to have the form

$$\Gamma_{11}(\tau) = 4\int_0^\infty |E(\nu)|^2\mathrm{e}^{-\mathrm{i}2\pi\nu\tau}\mathrm{d}\nu \tag{2.23a}$$

$$= 4\int_0^\infty W(\nu)\mathrm{e}^{-\mathrm{i}2\pi\nu\tau}\mathrm{d}\nu. \tag{2.23b}$$

Multiplying both sides by $\mathrm{e}^{\mathrm{i}2\pi\bar{\nu}\tau}$, we obtain

$$\Gamma_{11}(\tau)\mathrm{e}^{\mathrm{i}2\pi\bar{\nu}\tau} = 4\int_0^\infty W(\nu)\mathrm{e}^{-\mathrm{i}2\pi(\nu-\bar{\nu})\tau}\mathrm{d}\nu. \tag{2.24}$$

For sufficiently narrow bandwidth of quasi-monochromatic light of mean frequency $\bar{\nu}$, the right-hand side and hence the left-hand side of Eq. (2.24) will have slow dependence on the time delay. Expressing,

$$\Gamma_{11}(\tau)\mathrm{e}^{\mathrm{i}2\pi\bar{\nu}\tau} = |\Gamma_{11}(\tau)|\mathrm{e}^{\mathrm{i}\Phi(\tau)}, \tag{2.25}$$

the complex self coherence function for quasi-monochromatic light takes the form

$$\Gamma_{11}(\tau) = |\Gamma_{11}(\tau)|\mathrm{e}^{\mathrm{i}(\Phi(\tau)-2\pi\bar{\nu}\tau)}, \tag{2.26}$$

where $|\Gamma_{11}(\tau)|$ and $\Phi(\tau)$ are necessarily slowly varying functions of the time delay. The fast τ-dependence of the complex self coherence function comes through the exponent $(-2\pi\bar{\nu}\tau)$. The slowly varying factors of $\Gamma_{11}(\tau)$ can be obtained by substituting Eq. (2.26) into Eq. (2.24), giving

$$|\Gamma_{11}(\tau)|\mathrm{e}^{\mathrm{i}\Phi(\tau)} = 4\int_0^\infty W(\nu)\mathrm{e}^{-\mathrm{i}2\pi(\nu-\bar{\nu})\tau}\mathrm{d}\nu. \tag{2.27}$$

In conclusion, the spectral density function of quasi-monochromatic light can be used to obtain the self coherence function or alternatively the spectral density function of quasi-monochromatic light can be determined from the self coherence function by inverting Eq. (2.23b), i.e.,

$$\begin{aligned} W(\nu) &= \frac{1}{4}\int_{-\infty}^{\infty} \Gamma_{11}(\tau)\mathrm{e}^{\mathrm{i}2\pi\nu\tau}\mathrm{d}\tau \quad \text{for } \nu \geq 0, \\ &= 0 \quad \text{for } \nu < 0. \end{aligned} \tag{2.28}$$

The normalized spectral density function is defined as

$$\begin{aligned} g(\nu) &= \frac{|E(\nu)|^2}{\int_0^\infty |E(\nu)|^2\mathrm{d}\nu} \quad \text{for } \nu > 0 \\ &= 0 \quad \text{for } \nu < 0. \end{aligned} \tag{2.29}$$

The self coherence function of polychromatic light can be obtained by exploiting the correspondence between the self coherence and autocorrelation functions, to which a reference has already been made. In the manner of the autocorrelation function (see Sections 9.5.1 and 9.7), the self coherence function may also be interpreted as the overlap integral of the complex polychromatic light field $E^*(t)$ with the shifted field $E(t+\tau)$. Unless the light field is well correlated in time, the overlap integral will be quite small. The amplitude and phase of completely incoherent light change so rapidly with time that even for short time delays, the positive and negative contributions to the overlap integral add upto zero. However, for zero time delay ($\tau = 0$), any field configuration exactly overlaps with itself. Therefore for completely incoherent light,

$$\Gamma_{11}(\tau) = 0 \quad \text{for} \ \tau \neq 0 \tag{2.30a}$$

$$= 1 \quad \text{for} \ \tau = 0. \tag{2.30b}$$

2.4.1 Complex Degree of Self Coherence

The complex degree of self coherence $\gamma(\tau)$ is defined as the ratio of the complex self coherence function $\Gamma_{11}(\tau)$ for an arbitrary time delay τ to its value for zero time delay, i.e.,

$$\gamma(\tau) = \frac{\Gamma_{11}(\tau)}{\Gamma_{11}(0)}. \tag{2.31}$$

For monochromatic light, Eq. (2.22) gives

$$\gamma(\tau) = \mathrm{e}^{-\mathrm{i}2\pi\nu\tau} \tag{2.32a}$$

with

$$|\gamma(\tau)| = 1, \tag{2.32b}$$

irrespective of the time delay. On the other hand, for completely incoherent light,

$$|\gamma(\tau)| = 0 \quad \text{for} \ \tau \neq 0. \tag{2.33}$$

The complex degree of self coherence for quasi-monochromatic light has the form

$$\gamma(\tau) = \frac{|\Gamma_{11}(\tau)|}{\Gamma_{11}(0)} \mathrm{e}^{\mathrm{i}(\Phi(\tau) - 2\pi\bar{\nu}\tau)}$$
$$= |\gamma(\tau)| \mathrm{e}^{\mathrm{i}(\Phi(\tau) - 2\pi\bar{\nu}\tau)}, \tag{2.34}$$

where $\Gamma_{11}(0)$, already identified with light intensity, has only a magnitude and no phase. The magnitude $|\gamma(\tau)|$ of the complex degree of self coherence will henceforth be referred as the degree of self coherence. For quasi-monochromatic light, it is a slowly varying function of the time delay and takes values between 0 and 1, i.e.,

$$0 < |\gamma(\tau)| < 1. \tag{2.35}$$

A reference was made for a possible connection between the degree of self coherence and visibility of interference fringes. We now show how the degree of self coherence $|\gamma(\tau)|$ and phase $\Phi(\tau)$ can be determined from an interference experiment using a Michelson interferometer. Figure 2.2 shows the basic configuration of a Michelson interferometer. Mirror M_1 is moveable and mirror M_2 is fixed. The 50–50 beam splitter BS, assumed thin for the present discussion, splits the incident beam of intensity I_0 into the reflected (1) and transmitted (2) beams of intensity $I_0/2$ each. After reflections from the mirrors M_1 and M_2, these beams are recombined by the beam splitter. The photodetector PD with a narrow aperture is kept in the region of overlap of the beams. Point P_0 is taken as a convenient reference point. The resultant scalar field at point P is

$$E(P, t) = \frac{1}{2}E(P_0, t_1) + \frac{1}{2}E(P_0, t_2), \tag{2.36a}$$

where $E(P_0, t_1)$ and $E(P_0, t_2)$ are the retarded fields at P_0 which reach point P at time t following the arms (1) and (2) of the interferometer, respectively; $t_1 = t - (l_0 + l + 2l_1)/c$ and $t_2 = t - (l_0 + l + 2l_2)/c$ are the times taken by the two waves to travel between the points P_0 and P. The factors of 1/2 appear in Eq. (2.36a), since the intensity of each beam reaching point P is quarter of the intensity of the incident beam. For a dielectric slab beam splitter, an additional phase change of π for beam (2) should be included because this beam undergoes

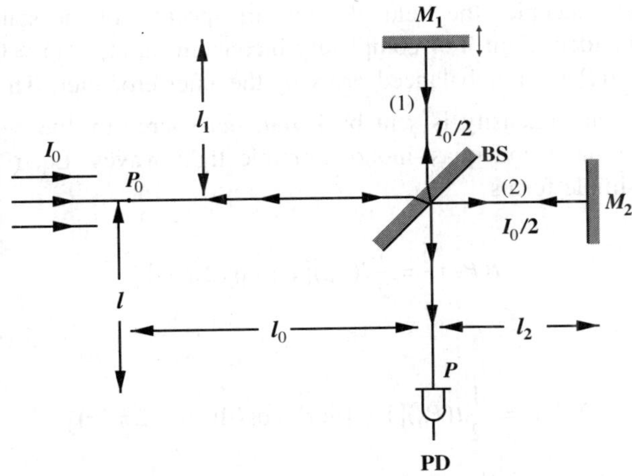

Fig. 2.2: The Michelson interferometer.

an external reflection at the beam splitter. For stationary fields, Eq. (2.36a) can be written as

$$E(P,t) = \frac{1}{2}E(P_0,t) + \frac{1}{2}E(P_0,t+\tau), \tag{2.36b}$$

where $\tau = t_2 - t_1 = 2(l_2 - l_1)/c$. The time-averaged intensity at point P is

$$I(P,\tau) = \left(\frac{1}{2}c\epsilon_0\right)\langle E(P,t)E^*(P,t)\rangle \tag{2.37a}$$

$$= \left(\frac{1}{2}c\epsilon_0\right)\langle\frac{1}{4}|E(P_0,t)|^2 + \frac{1}{4}|E(P_0,t+\tau)|^2 + \frac{1}{4}E^*(P_0,t)E(P_0,t+\tau) + \frac{1}{4}E(P_0,t)E^*(P_0,t+\tau)\rangle \tag{2.37b}$$

$$= \frac{1}{4}[2I(P_0) + c\epsilon_0 Re\langle E(P_0,t+\tau)E^*(P_0,t)\rangle] \tag{2.37c}$$

$$= \frac{1}{2}I(P_0)\left[1 + Re\left(\frac{\Gamma(\tau)}{\Gamma(0)}\right)\right] \tag{2.37d}$$

$$= \frac{1}{2}I(P_0)[1 + Re(\gamma(\tau))]. \tag{2.37e}$$

The real parts of the complex coherence function and complex degree of coherence can be obtained from intensity measurements of Michelson fringes as a function of the time delay τ. For the balanced arms ($\tau = 0$) of the interferometer, a bright fringe occupies the field of view, irrespective of the state of coherence of the incident light. For completely incoherent light, $\Gamma(\tau) = 0$ for $\tau \neq 0$, and $I(P) = \frac{1}{2}I(P_0)$ for unbalanced arms of the interferometer. The remaining 50% of the beam intensity is sent back into the source by the beam splitter. For monochromatic and quasi-monochromatic light waves, Eq. (2.37e) takes particularly simple forms

$$I(P,\tau) = \frac{1}{2}I(P_0)[1 + \cos 2\pi\bar{\nu}\tau] \tag{2.38a}$$

and

$$I(P,\tau) = \frac{1}{2}I(P_0)[1 + |\gamma(\tau)|\cos(\Phi(\tau) - 2\pi\bar{\nu}\tau)], \tag{2.38b}$$

respectively, where $|\gamma(\tau)|$ and $\Phi(\tau)$ are slowly varying functions of the time delay.

For completely or partially coherent light, interference fringes can be observed as the time delay, or equivalently, the path difference between the two arms of the interferometer is varied. The visibility of interference fringes is defined as

$$V(\tau) = \frac{I_{max} - I_{min}}{I_{max} + I_{min}}, \tag{2.39}$$

where I_{min} and I_{max} are the minimum and maximum intensities observed in the interference pattern. For monochromatic light, the fringe visibility like the degree of self coherence maintains unit value for any arbitrary time delay. Combining Eqs (2.34), (2.37e), and (2.39) gives

$$V(\tau) = |\gamma(\tau)|, \tag{2.40}$$

i.e., the visibility of Michelson fringes equals the degree of self coherence for monochromatic and quasi-monochromatic light waves. Furthermore, the fringe pattern for the quasi-monochromatic light is shifted with respect to the fringe pattern produced by monochromatic light (Eqs 2.38). The observed shift gives the phase $\Phi(\tau)$ of the quasi-monochromatic light.

We first consider quasi-monochromatic light having a single narrow spectral band with full width at half maximum (FWHM) of $\Delta\nu$ (Fig. 2.3a). The visibility

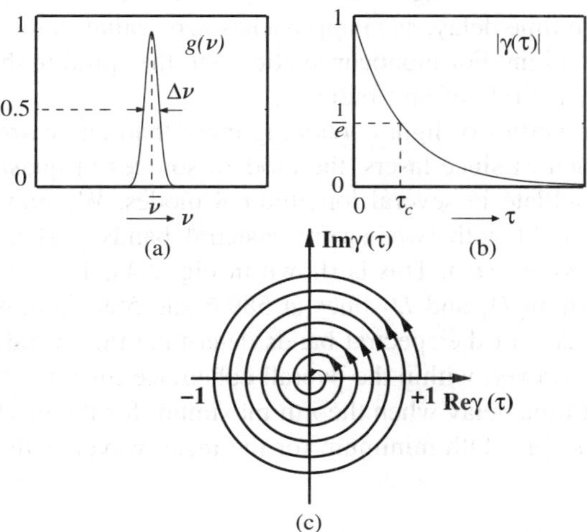

Fig. 2.3: Quasi-monochromatic light; (a) normalized spectral density function with one narrow band, (b) variation of degree of self coherence with time delay, (c) complex degree of self coherence in the complex plane.

of Michelson fringes (and hence the degree of self coherence) starts with unit value for the balanced arms of the interferometer and then falls off slowly for small $\Delta\nu$ as the path difference between the arms is increased (Fig. 2.3b).

The reduction in the visibility of the fringes is caused by the shifts in the fringe patterns produced by different frequency components (within the spectral bandwidth) with increasing path difference. The coherence time τ_c may be taken as the time during which the degree of self coherence falls to $1/e$ of its maximum value. The coherence length l_c of quasi-monochromatic light is

$$l_c = c\tau_c, \tag{2.41a}$$

where c is the velocity of light in a vacuum. The coherence time[4] τ_c has inverse dependence on the spectral bandwidth, i.e.,

$$\tau_c \sim \frac{1}{\Delta\nu} = \frac{\bar{\lambda}^2}{c\Delta\lambda}. \tag{2.41b}$$

This is a fairly general result (see Eq. 9.33). We shall not attempt its derivation here. The interested reader may refer to Born and Wolf [2.2] and Goodman [2.3]. For a source with a single narrow spectral band (Fig. 2.3a), the variation of the complex degree of self coherence with time delay is shown in the complex plane in Fig. 2.3c. It starts with unit value on the real axis and goes through circles of slowly diminishing radii with increasing time delay. Eventually for sufficiently large time delay, $\gamma(\tau)$ approaches zero value as the circle converges to a point at the origin. For monochromatic light, the spiral in the complex plane gets replaced by a circle of unit radius.

Coherence properties of light containing more than one narrow spectral band are of special interest since lasers, the modern sources of quasi-monochromatic light, usually oscillate in several longitudinal modes. We now consider quasi-monochromatic light with two narrow spectral bands peaked at wavelengths $\bar{\lambda}_1(=c/\bar{\nu}_1)$ and $\bar{\lambda}_2(=c/\bar{\nu}_2)$. This is shown in Fig. 2.4a. These bands may correspond to the sodium D_1 and D_2 lines at 589.6 and 589.0 nm, respectively. The widths $\Delta\nu_1$ and $\Delta\nu_2$ of the spectral bands determine the overall coherence time of the source. However, within the overall coherence time, the fringes disappear with increase in time delay when the nth maximum for the mean wavelength $\bar{\lambda}_1$ overlaps with the $(n+1)$th minimum for the mean wavelength $\bar{\lambda}_2$. With further

[4] A more rigorous definition of coherence time is:

$$\tau_c^2 = \frac{\int_{-\infty}^{+\infty} \tau^2 |\gamma(\tau)|^2 \mathrm{d}\tau}{\int_{-\infty}^{+\infty} |\gamma(\tau)|^2 \mathrm{d}\tau}.$$

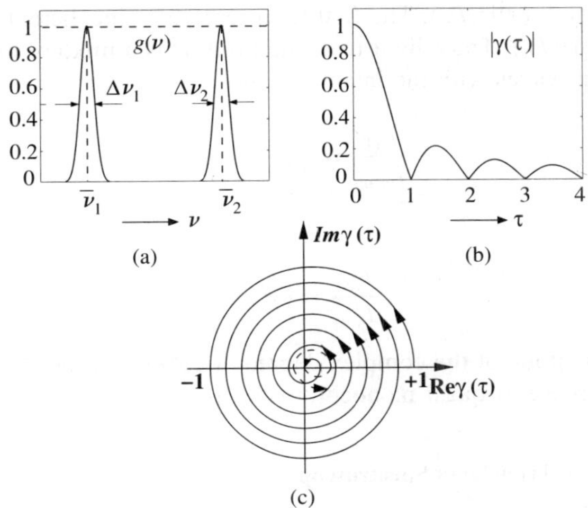

Fig. 2.4: Quasi-monochromatic light; (a) normalized spectral density function with two narrow bands, (b) variation of degree of self coherence with time delay, (c) complex degree of self coherence in the complex plane.

increase in the time delay, the maxima due to the two bands begin to come closer, leading to the re-emergence of the fringes. The next maximum of the visibility occurs when the mth maximum corresponding to the first band coincides with the $(m+1)$th maximum of the second band. The fringes appear and disappear repeatedly, but in successive cycles the fringe visibility gets reduced. The degree of coherence, like the visibility of fringes, goes through several cycles (Fig. 2.4b). The complex degree of self coherence initially spirals to the origin in the complex plane but in this case after acquiring zero value, it re-emerges and begins to spiral out reaching a maximum value smaller than the starting value. It may go through several such cycles (Fig. 2.4c). This discussion can be extended to a multi-mode laser with several longitudinal modes, oscillating simultaneously [2.4].

Before concluding this section, we demonstrate that $|\gamma(\tau)|$ has been appropriately termed as the degree of coherence, at least in the context of quasi-monochromatic light. Equation (2.38b) can be recast into the form

$$I(P, \tau) = (1 - |\gamma(\tau)|)\left(\frac{1}{2}I(P_0)\right) + |\gamma(\tau)|\left(\frac{1}{2}I(P_0)\right)[1 + \cos(\Phi(\tau) - 2\pi\bar{\nu}\tau)].$$

On comparing with Eq. (2.38a), we conclude that the second term in this equation represents interference produced by monochromatic and hence perfectly coherent light of intensity $|\gamma(\tau)|I(P_0)$. The first term represents incoherent light of intensity $(1-|\gamma(\tau)|)I(P_0)$. Thus, light reaching point P is a mixture of coherent and incoherent light waves with the intensity ratio

$$\frac{I_{\text{coh}}}{I_{\text{incoh}}} = \frac{|\gamma(\tau)|}{1-|\gamma(\tau)|}, \tag{2.42a}$$

or equivalently,

$$\frac{I_{\text{coh}}}{I_{\text{total}}} = |\gamma(\tau)|. \tag{2.42b}$$

Hence, the magnitude of the complex degree of coherence indeed represents the degree of coherence of quasi-monochromatic light.

2.4.2 Fourier Transform Spectroscopy

Generalizing Eq. (2.38a) for the output intensity distribution of a Michelson interferometer when light entering the interferometer is polychromatic (Eq. 2.19b) and not monochromatic, we have

$$I(\tau) = 4\left(\frac{1}{2}\epsilon_0 c\right)\int_0^\infty W(\nu)(1+\cos 2\pi\nu\tau)\mathrm{d}\nu. \tag{2.43}$$

The plots of Eq. (2.43), depicting the variation of intensity with the difference in path lengths between the arms of a Michelson interferometer, are called the interferograms. The maximum path difference is usually restricted due to practical considerations. For monochromatic light, the interferogram shows no loss of contrast ($I_{\max}/I_{\min}$) with increasing time delay (Fig. 2.5a). The contrast diminishes somewhat for quasi-monochromatic light (Fig. 2.5b). For incident light with broad spectral composition, significant intensity variations are seen for small time delays only (Fig. 2.5c). Rewriting Eq. (2.43),

$$\begin{aligned} I(\tau) &= 4\left(\frac{1}{2}\epsilon_0 c\right)\int_0^\infty W(\nu)\mathrm{d}\nu + 4\left(\frac{1}{2}\epsilon_0 c\right)\int_0^\infty W(\nu)\cos(2\pi\nu\tau)\mathrm{d}\nu \\ &= I_0 + \Delta I(\tau), \end{aligned}$$

where I_0 gives the total brightness of the source (Eq. 2.19b) and

$$\Delta I(\tau) = 4\left(\frac{1}{2}\epsilon_0 c\right)\int_0^\infty W(\nu)\cos(2\pi\nu\tau)\mathrm{d}\nu) \tag{2.44a}$$

$$= (\epsilon_0 c)\int_{-\infty}^{+\infty} W(\nu)\mathrm{e}^{-\mathrm{i}2\pi\nu\tau}\mathrm{d}\nu. \tag{2.44b}$$

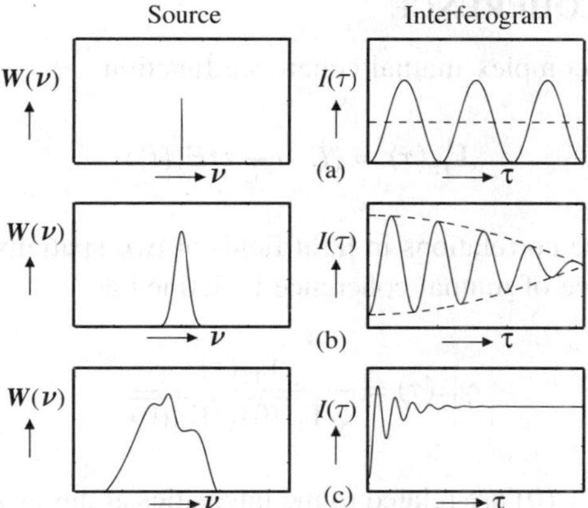

Fig. 2.5: $W(\nu)$ is the spectral density function of the source. Interferograms for monochromatic light (a), quasi-monochromatic light (b), broad band light (c).

The inverse Fourier transform of Eq. (2.44b) gives the spectral density function

$$W(\nu) = \left(\frac{1}{\epsilon_0 c}\right) \int_{-\infty}^{+\infty} \Delta I(\tau) e^{i2\pi\nu\tau} d\tau. \tag{2.45a}$$

Thus, the inverse Fourier transform of the oscillating part of the output intensity distribution of a Michelson interferometer gives the spectral distribution of the source. This is the underlying principle of the Fourier transform spectrometer which is particularly useful in the infrared region. The signal-to-noise ratio in Fourier transform spectroscopy is much higher because the intensity observed at the exit of the interferometer contains all frequency components of the source, and not just the one under investigation as in a dispersive instrument. Since $\Delta I(\tau)$ is a measured distribution and not an analytical function, its inverse Fourier transform can be calculated only numerically. In addition, intensity measurements beyond a certain maximum path difference ($d_{\max}$) are not possible. The spectral density function of the source obtained from a Fourier transform spectrometer may be expressed as

$$\begin{aligned} W(\nu) &= \left(\frac{1}{\epsilon_0 c}\right) \int_{-d_{\max}/c}^{d_{\max}/c} \Delta I(\tau) e^{i2\pi\nu\tau} d\tau \quad \text{for } \nu \geq 0 \\ &= 0 \qquad\qquad\qquad\qquad\qquad\qquad\qquad \text{for } \nu < 0. \end{aligned} \tag{2.45b}$$

The resolution of measurement can be increased by increasing the maximum path difference.

2.5 MUTUAL COHERENCE

We now consider complex mutual coherence function

$$\Gamma_{12}(\tau) = \langle E_1(t+\tau)E_2^*(t)\rangle$$

to investigate phase correlations in light fields at two spatially separated points. The complex degree of mutual coherence is defined as

$$\gamma_{12}(\tau) = \frac{\Gamma_{12}(\tau)}{\sqrt{\Gamma_{11}(0)}\sqrt{\Gamma_{22}(0)}}, \qquad (2.46)$$

where $\Gamma_{11}(0)$ and $\Gamma_{22}(0)$ are related to the intensities at the two points (Eq. 2.17). Mutual coherence of light fields can be investigated in Young's double slit type interference experiment shown schematically in Fig. 2.6. For the present discussion, the finite sizes of the source and slits are ignored. The resultant scalar field $E(P, t)$ at the observation point P is the superposition of the fields arriving from the two slits, i.e.,

$$\begin{aligned} E(P,t) &= E^{(1)}(P,t) + E^{(2)}(P,t) \\ &= K_1 E\left(\vec{r}_1, t - \frac{r_1'}{c}\right) + K_2 E\left(\vec{r}_2, t - \frac{r_2'}{c}\right), \end{aligned} \qquad (2.47)$$

where the fields at the observation point have been expressed in terms of the retarded fields at the locations of the slits. The proportionality constants K_1 and

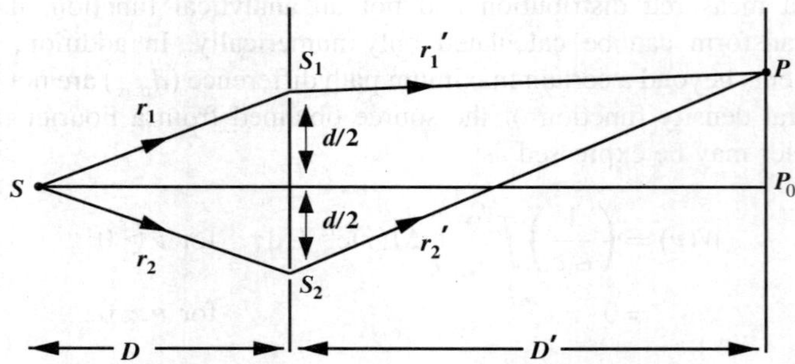

Fig. 2.6: Young's double slit arrangement. S is a point source.

K_2 can be obtained from the results of the diffraction theory (Eq. 7.21 with $\cos\theta = 1$ as applied to a point source):

$$E^{(1)}(P,t) = \frac{-\mathrm{i}a_0}{\lambda}\frac{\mathrm{e}^{\mathrm{i}kr_1}}{r_1 r_1'}\mathrm{e}^{\mathrm{i}(kr_1'-\omega t)} \tag{2.48a}$$

$$= \frac{-\mathrm{i}a_0}{\lambda r_1'}\frac{\mathrm{e}^{\mathrm{i}[kr_1-\omega(t-r_1'/c)]}}{r_1} \tag{2.48b}$$

$$= \frac{-\mathrm{i}a_0}{\lambda r_1'}E\left(S_1, t-\frac{r_1'}{c}\right), \tag{2.48c}$$

giving

$$K_1 = -\frac{\mathrm{i}a_0}{\lambda r_1'}.$$

Similarly, we can get

$$K_2 = -\frac{\mathrm{i}a_0}{\lambda r_2'},$$

where a_0 is the amplitude of the spherical wave at unit distance from the point source. The proportionality constants K_1 and K_2 are purely imaginary, so that the resultant intensity at the point of observation is

$$\begin{aligned} I(P,\tau) &= \left(\frac{1}{2}\epsilon_0 c\right)\left\langle \left\{E^{(1)}(P,t)+E^{(2)}(P,t)\right\}\left\{E^{(1)}(P,t)+E^{(2)}(P,t)\right\}^*\right\rangle \\ &= I^{(1)}(P)+I^{(2)}(P)+\frac{1}{2}\epsilon_0 c\left\langle E^{(1)}(P,t)E^{(2)*}(P,t)+\mathrm{cc}\right\rangle \\ &= I^{(1)}(P)+I^{(2)}(P)+\epsilon_0 c\times Re\left\langle K_1K_2^*E(\vec{r_1},t+\tau)E^*(\vec{r_2},t)\right\rangle \\ &= I^{(1)}(P)+I^{(2)}(P)+2\left(\frac{1}{2}\epsilon_0 c\right)|K_1||K_2|Re\Gamma_{12}(\tau), \end{aligned} \tag{2.49a}$$

where $\tau = (r_2' - r_1')/c$ and $\Gamma_{12}(\tau)$ is the complex mutual coherence function between the light fields at the positions of the slits. The intensity $I^{(1)}(P)$ is the intensity at point P when slit S_1 is open and slit S_2 is closed. The intensity

$I^{(2)}(P)$ corresponds to slit S_1 closed and slit S_2 open, and $I(P)$ is the intensity at P when both slits are open. Noting that

$$|K_1| = \left(\frac{I^{(1)}(P)}{I(\vec{r}_1)}\right)^{1/2},$$

$$|K_2| = \left(\frac{I^{(2)}(P)}{I(\vec{r}_2)}\right)^{1/2},$$

$$I(P,\tau) = I^{(1)}(P) + I^{(2)}(P) + 2\sqrt{I^{(1)}(P)I^{(2)}(P)}Re\frac{\Gamma_{12}(\tau)}{\sqrt{\Gamma_{11}(0)\Gamma_{22}(0)}}$$
$$= I^{(1)}(P) + I^{(2)}(P) + 2\sqrt{I^{(1)}(P)I^{(2)}(P)}Re[\gamma_{12}(\tau)]. \quad (2.49b)$$

For the observation point lying on the symmetry axis ($\tau = 0$),

$$I(P_0) = I^{(1)}(P_0) + I^{(2)}(P_0) + 2\sqrt{I^{(1)}(P_0)I^{(2)}(P_0)}Re[\gamma_{12}(0)], \quad (2.49c)$$

where

$$\gamma_{12}(0) = \frac{\Gamma_{12}(0)}{\sqrt{\Gamma_{11}(0)\Gamma_{22}(0)}} \quad (2.50)$$

gives the complex degree of mutual coherence between spatially shifted but temporally coincident points and

$$\Gamma_{12}(0) = \langle E_1(t)E_2^*(t)\rangle \quad (2.51a)$$

defines the mutual intensity

$$I_{12} = \left(\frac{1}{2}\epsilon_0 c\right)\Gamma_{12}(0) \quad (2.51b)$$

for the two slits. The mutual intensity function $\Gamma_{12}(0)$ is also called the complex spatial coherence function. The real part of the complex degree of mutual coherence can be expressed in terms of the measurable quantities:

$$Re[\gamma_{12}(\tau)] = \frac{I(P,\tau) - I^{(1)}(P) - I^{(2)}(P)}{2\sqrt{I^{(1)}(P)I^{(2)}(P)}}. \quad (2.52)$$

Schwarz's inequality[5] can be used to show that

$$|\gamma_{12}(\tau)| \le 1. \tag{2.53}$$

The equality sign holds for completely coherent light and inequality applies to partially coherent light.

2.5.1 Complex Degree of Mutual Coherence

The complex mutual coherence function for quasi-monochromatic light with mean frequency $\bar{\nu}$ can be defined with reference to Eq. (2.26) as

$$\Gamma_{12}(\tau) = |\Gamma_{12}(\tau)|e^{i(\alpha(\tau)-2\pi\bar{\nu}\tau)}, \tag{2.54}$$

where $|\Gamma_{12}(\tau)|$ and phase $\alpha(\tau)$ are expected to be slowly varying functions of the time delay τ. The complex degree of mutual coherence is given by

$$\gamma_{12}(\tau) = \frac{|\Gamma_{12}(\tau)|}{\sqrt{\Gamma_{11}(0)\Gamma_{22}(0)}}e^{i(\alpha(\tau)-2\pi\bar{\nu}\tau)} \tag{2.55a}$$

$$= |\gamma_{12}(\tau)|e^{i(\alpha(\tau)-2\pi\bar{\nu}\tau)}, \tag{2.55b}$$

where the degree of mutual coherence

$$|\gamma_{12}(\tau)| = \frac{|\Gamma_{12}(\tau)|}{\sqrt{\Gamma_{11}(0)\Gamma_{22}(0)}} \tag{2.56}$$

is also a slowly varying function of τ. Equation (2.49b) for the intensity in Young's experiment, performed with quasi-monochromatic light, takes the form

$$I(P,\tau) = I^{(1)}(P) + I^{(2)}(P) + 2|\gamma_{12}(\tau)|\sqrt{I^{(1)}(P)I^{(2)}(P)}\cos(\alpha(\tau) - 2\pi\bar{\nu}\tau). \tag{2.57}$$

For sufficiently narrow slits, large diffraction effects render $I^{(1)}(P)$ and $I^{(2)}(P)$ nearly independent of the time delay. The extremum values of the intensity distribution are

$$I_{\max}(P,\tau) = I^{(1)}(P) + I^{(2)}(P) + 2|\gamma_{12}(\tau)|\sqrt{I^{(1)}(P)I^{(2)}(P)}, \tag{2.58a}$$

---

[5] Schwarz's inequality theorem states

$$\int_{-\infty}^{+\infty} f(x)f^*(x)\mathrm{d}x \int_{-\infty}^{+\infty} g(x)g^*(x)\mathrm{d}x \ge \left|\int_{-\infty}^{+\infty} f^*(x)g(x)\mathrm{d}x\right|^2.$$

$$I_{\min}(P,\tau) = I^{(1)}(P) + I^{(2)}(P) - 2|\gamma_{12}(\tau)|\sqrt{I^{(1)}(P)I^{(2)}(P)}, \tag{2.58b}$$

giving, for the visibility of Young's fringes, the expression

$$V(\tau) = \frac{2\sqrt{I^{(1)}(P)I^{(2)}(P)}}{I^{(1)}(P) + I^{(2)}(P)}|\gamma_{12}(\tau)|. \tag{2.59}$$

The visibility of Young's fringes equals the degree of mutual coherence $|\gamma(\tau)|$ provided $I^{(1)}(P) = I^{(2)}(P)$.

The phase $\alpha(\tau)$ of the complex degree of mutual coherence can also be obtained from a careful analysis of Young's fringes. The phase $\alpha(\tau)$ appearing in Eq. (2.57) may be interpreted as some constant (as long as large changes in time delay are not involved) phase difference between the fields at the slits that one must take into account for quasi-monochromatic light as compared to monochromatic light. This merely shifts the center of the fringe pattern for quasi-monochromatic light as compared to the one for monochromatic light by an amount

$$\Delta x = \frac{D}{d}\bar{\lambda}\frac{\alpha(\tau)}{2\pi},$$

since a phase change of 2π radians shifts the fringe pattern by exactly one fringe. This shift of the center of the fringe pattern can be recognized and measured. It is therefore possible to obtain complete information on the complex degree of mutual coherence of quasi-monochromatic light from Young's interference experiment. As for self coherence, it can be shown by following the same argument that magnitude $|\gamma_{12}(\tau)|$ of the complex degree of mutual coherence indeed represents the degree of mutual coherence of quasi-monochromatic light.

We have characterized quasi-monochromatic light by the spectral bandwidth $\Delta\nu$ being much smaller than its mean frequency $\bar{\nu}$ (Eq. 2.9). We now impose an additional restriction on quasi-monochromatic light. Re-writing Eq. (2.23b) in the context of the mutual coherence function, we have

$$\Gamma_{12}(\tau) = 4\int_0^\infty W_{12}(\nu)\mathrm{e}^{-\mathrm{i}2\pi\nu\tau}\mathrm{d}\nu, \tag{2.60}$$

where the mutual spectral density function $W_{12}(\nu)$ is the inverse Fourier transform of the mutual coherence function $\Gamma_{12}(\tau)$, i.e.,

$$\begin{aligned} W_{12}(\nu) &= \frac{1}{4}\int_{-\infty}^{+\infty} \Gamma_{12}(\tau)\mathrm{e}^{\mathrm{i}2\pi\nu\tau}\mathrm{d}\tau \quad && \text{for } \nu \geq 0 \\ &= 0 && \text{for } \nu < 0. \end{aligned}$$

Combining Eqs (2.54) and (2.60) gives

$$|\Gamma_{12}(\tau)|e^{i\alpha(\tau)} = 4\int_0^\infty W_{12}(\nu)e^{-i2\pi(\nu-\bar{\nu})\tau}d\nu. \tag{2.61}$$

For time delays restricted to values much smaller than the coherence time, i.e., for

$$\tau \ll \frac{1}{\nu-\bar{\nu}}, \tag{2.62}$$

Eq. (2.61) can be approximated to

$$|\Gamma_{12}(\tau)|e^{i\alpha(\tau)} = 4\int_{-\bar{\nu}}^\infty W_{12}(\bar{\nu}+\mu)d\mu, \tag{2.63}$$

where as before $\mu = \nu - \bar{\nu}$. In this limit, the exponential in integral (2.61) takes nearly unit value in the frequency range over which $W_{12}(\nu)$ is non-zero. Consequently, in addition to Eq. (2.9), if quasi-monochromatic light satisfies Eq. (2.62), then the product $|\Gamma_{12}(\tau)|e^{i\alpha(\tau)}$ is not just slowly varying, but essentially independent of the time delay. We can therefore write

$$\begin{aligned} |\Gamma_{12}(\tau)|e^{i\alpha(\tau)} &= |\Gamma_{12}(0)|e^{i\alpha(0)} \\ &= \Gamma_{12}(0). \end{aligned} \tag{2.64}$$

With this assumption, Eqs (2.54) and (2.55b) can be approximated to

$$\Gamma_{12}(\tau) = \Gamma_{12}(0)e^{-i2\pi\bar{\nu}\tau} \tag{2.65a}$$

and

$$\gamma_{12}(\tau) = \gamma_{12}(0)e^{-i2\pi\bar{\nu}\tau} \tag{2.65b}$$

respectively, where

$$\begin{aligned} \gamma_{12}(0) &= \frac{\Gamma_{12}(0)}{\sqrt{\Gamma_{11}(0)\Gamma_{22}(0)}} \\ &= |\gamma_{12}(0)|e^{i\alpha(0)}. \end{aligned} \tag{2.66}$$

Quasi-monochromatic light satisfying these conditions is called coherent quasi-monochromatic light for the obvious similarity between Eqs (2.65a,b) and the corresponding equations for monochromatic light (Eqs 2.22 and 2.32a). However, the degree of mutual coherence $|\gamma_{12}(0)|$ remains less than one for quasi-monochromatic light. To satisfy Eq. (2.62), the observation point must be restricted to close proximity of the axial point P_0 (Fig. 2.6). For later use, we rewrite the above equations in the standard notation.

$$\Gamma_{12}(\tau) = J_{12}\mathrm{e}^{-\mathrm{i}2\pi\bar{\nu}\tau}, \tag{2.67a}$$

$$\gamma_{12}(\tau) = \mu_{12}\mathrm{e}^{-\mathrm{i}2\pi\bar{\nu}\tau}, \tag{2.67b}$$

where

$$J_{12} = \Gamma_{12}(0) = \langle E_1(t)E_2^*(t)\rangle = |\Gamma_{12}(0)|\mathrm{e}^{\mathrm{i}\alpha(0)}, \tag{2.68a}$$

$$\mu_{12} = \gamma_{12}(0) = \frac{J_{12}}{\sqrt{\Gamma_{11}(0)\Gamma_{22}(0)}} = |\gamma_{12}(0)|\mathrm{e}^{\mathrm{i}\alpha(0)}. \tag{2.68b}$$

2.5.2 Coherence of Light from an Extended Source

We have so far not paid any attention to the finite size of the source used in Young's experiment. Point sources are not only a practical impossibility, but often extended sources are preferred because of the enhancement of the overall irradiance level. An extended source can be treated as a collection of mutually incoherent point sources. To keep the discussion at an elementary level, but without losing the essential physical content of the argument, we consider here a linear source (line AC in Fig. 2.7). We further assume all points on the extended source to have identical emission characteristics such as the mean frequency of emission $\bar{\nu}$, the frequency bandwidth $\Delta\nu$, and the radiated power. Each point on the extended source produces an interference pattern on the screen which is identical to the interference pattern produced by any other point on the source, except for a spatial shift. The resultant intensity distribution on the screen is the superposition of the intensity distributions produced by different points lying on the source. The fringe pattern for the source point O lying on the optical axis is centered (zero path difference point) at O', also lying on the optical axis. The fringe pattern associated with the source point B is centered at B', where

$$x' = \frac{D'}{D}x.$$

This result comes from the path difference

$$\overline{BS}_2 - \overline{BS}_1 = \sqrt{D^2 + \left(\frac{d}{2} + x\right)^2} - \sqrt{D^2 + \left(\frac{d}{2} - x\right)^2}$$
$$\approx \frac{d}{D}x$$

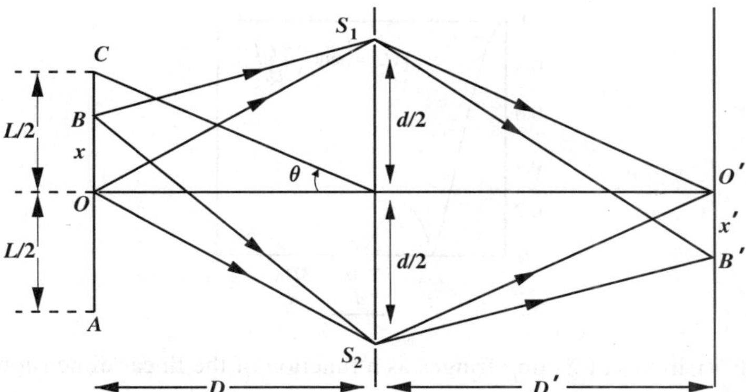

Fig. 2.7: Young's double slit interference experiment with an extended source.

and the fact that a path difference of one wavelength leads to a shift of exactly one fringe. The fringe separation on the screen for the mean wavelength $\bar{\lambda}$ is $D'\bar{\lambda}/d$. The shifts in the fringe patterns due to different point sources reduce the visibility of the fringes because the points of minimum intensity may no longer be points of zero intensity. For the interference pattern to be discernible, the shift between the interference patterns produced by points at either of the extreme ends and the middle of a symmetrically placed source of length L should be much less than half the fringe width, i.e.,

$$\frac{D'}{D}\frac{L}{2} < \frac{1}{2}\frac{D'}{d}\bar{\lambda},$$

or

$$\frac{d}{D}L < \bar{\lambda}. \tag{2.69}$$

This condition may appear too stringent for a laboratory experiment, but is easily met for the astronomical sources with large D. We leave it as an exercise to show that the fringe visibility for a linear source has the form

$$V(L) = \left|\operatorname{sinc}\left(\frac{\pi L d}{D\bar{\lambda}}\right)\right|. \tag{2.70}$$

Figure 2.8 shows the variation of the fringe visibility with the extent L of the linear source.

The visibility of fringes indeed falls to zero for $L = D\bar{\lambda}/d$, as expected. The fringes reappear with further increase in the length of the source, and the

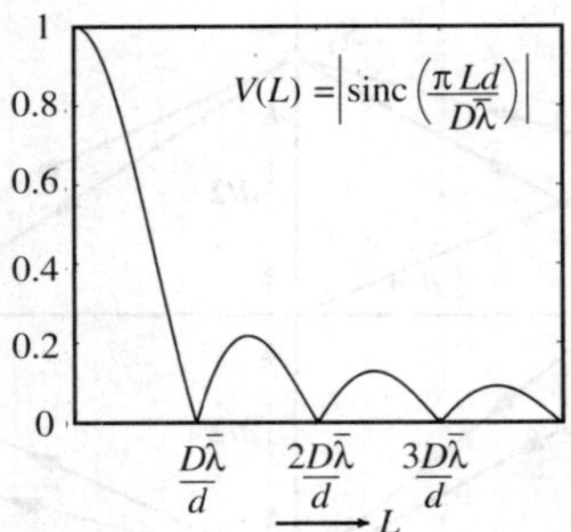

Fig. 2.8: Visibility of Young fringes as a function of the linear dimension of the source.

visibility of fringes shows periodic variations but with considerably reduced overall magnitude. Eventually, uniform illumination is established on the screen. Since the degree of mutual coherence $|\gamma_{12}(\tau)|$ is proportional to the visibility of Young's fringes, Fig. 2.8 may be taken to represent the behavior of the degree of mutual coherence as well. The sinc function is an important function which shows up in the analysis of many physical situations. We have already encountered it in this chapter. We shall see later that Fraunhofer diffraction from a slit of finite width is also described by a sinc function (Eq. 10.32a). At this point, we can naively ask if there is any link between the degree of coherence and Fraunhofer diffraction. This is actually the subject matter of Van Cittert–Zernike theorem. But before taking up this theorem, we describe how the visibility changes of Young's fringes can obtain the angular sizes and angular separations of stars.

2.5.3 Michelson Stellar Interferometer

The stars may be treated as point sources if their angular separations are much larger than their individual angular sizes. The shift between the interference patterns produced by two stars can be expressed as

$$\frac{d}{D}L = \Delta m\bar{\lambda}, \tag{2.71}$$

where Δm is the shift in the fringe order (not necessarily integral), L the distance between the stars treated as point sources, D the distance of the stars from earth, and d the distance between the slits in Young's two-slit arrangement. The stars are assumed identical, emitting quasi-monochromatic light with the same mean wavelength $\bar{\lambda}$. The visibility of the interference fringes remains unaffected if Δm is an integer, and fringes completely disappear if Δm is half integral. The first disappearance of fringes occurs for $\Delta m = \frac{1}{2}$, in which case, the angular separation of the stars is given by

$$\theta = \frac{L}{D} = \frac{\bar{\lambda}}{2d}. \tag{2.72}$$

Thus, the first disappearance of the fringes in an interferometric measurement determines the angle θ between the stars. The same method, in principle, can be used to measure the angular size of a star. However, the latter measurement is made difficult because the angles subtended by the stars on earth are extremely small, making it necessary to employ unmanageably large slit-separations. Michelson invented his famous stellar interferometer (Fig. 2.9) to circumvent this problem.

The slits S_1 and S_2 in this arrangement are fixed. For fixed D', the fringe separation $D'\bar{\lambda}/d$ on screen S remains unaffected by any other adjustment in the interferometer. On the other hand, the path difference between the waves arriving from the extremities of a star depends on the separation d' between the moveable mirrors M_1 and M_2, and not on slit separation d. For small separations between mirrors M_1 and M_2, the path difference between light waves arriving from the extremities of a star (or from two stars) is small ($\Delta m \ll 1/2$), giving good quality fringes on screen S. The mirror separation is then increased till the fringes disappear. This happens when the path difference $\theta d' = \bar{\lambda}/2$. In the original experiment at Mount Wilson observatory, slit separation d was kept at 114 cm and mirror separation could be increased upto to $d' = 6.1$ m to obtain the disappearance of fringes. The interferometer was mounted on the 100 in. reflecting telescope of the observatory. The first star studied by this interferometer was

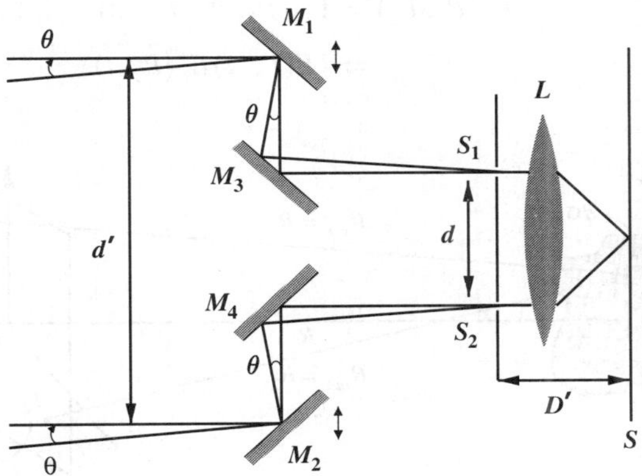

Fig. 2.9: Michelson stellar interferometer.

the orange looking star called Betelgeuse (α Orionis) subtending 0.047 arcsec on earth. It required $d' \approx 307$ cm at $\lambda = 570$ nm. The interferometric measurements not only give the angular sizes of the stars but can also provide useful information on the intensity distribution on the surface of a star, as we shall see in Section 2.6.

2.6 VAN CITTERT–ZERNIKE THEOREM

This theorem, originally proved by Van Cittert and later by Zernike, allows one to obtain the mutual coherence function and degree of mutual coherence on a surface, illuminated by an extended incoherent quasi-monochromatic source. We shall closely follow the treatment of Born and Wolf to prove the Van Cittert–Zernike theorem.

Figure 2.10 shows a two-dimensional incoherent quasi-monochromatic source σ and the observation plane xy, parallel to the source plane. These planes are separated by the distance R which is much larger than any dimension of the source and the distance between any two points in the plane of observation.

For sufficiently large R, light fields emanating from any point on the source can be expected to reach any two points such as the points P_1 and P_2 in the plane of observation with a time delay much smaller than the coherence time of the source. This assumption allows us to use the results obtained in Section 2.5.1. We may divide the two-dimensional source into infinitesimal area elements $d\sigma_m$, each smaller in dimension than the mean wavelength λ of the source. The complex mutual coherence function (Eq. 2.68a), also called the spatial coherence function (since $\tau = 0$), may be obtained by summing up contributions from each area element:

$$J_{12}(P_1, P_2) = \Gamma_{12}(P_1, P_2, \tau = 0) \tag{2.73a}$$

$$= \langle E(P_1, t)E^*(P_2, t)\rangle \tag{2.73b}$$

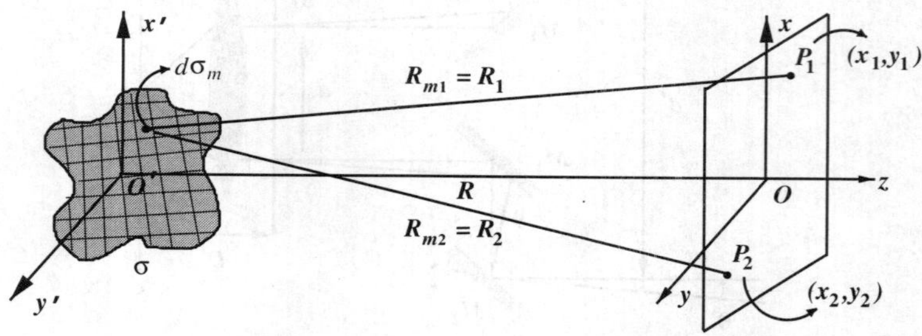

Fig. 2.10: Geometry for Van Cittert–Zernike theorem.

$$= \sum_m \sum_{m'} \langle E_{m,1}(t) E^*_{m',2}(t) \rangle \tag{2.73c}$$

$$= \sum_m \langle E_{m,1}(t) E^*_{m,2}(t) \rangle + \sum_m \sum_{m' \neq m} \langle E_{m,1}(t) E^*_{m',2}(t) \rangle \tag{2.73d}$$

$$= \sum_m \langle E_{m,1}(t) E^*_{m,2}(t) \rangle . \tag{2.73e}$$

The double sum in Eq. (2.73d), representing contributions from different area elements, vanishes for an incoherent quasi-monochromatic source. $E_{m,1}$ and $E_{m,2}$ are the scalar fields at points P_1 and P_2, respectively, due to the mth element of the source. Relating these fields to the fields in the source plane (Eq. 2.48c), we have

$$J_{12}(P_1, P_2) = \sum_m \left\langle \frac{A_m(t - R_{m1}/c) A^*_m(t - R_{m2}/c)}{R_{m1} R_{m2}} \mathrm{e}^{-\mathrm{i}2\pi\bar{\nu}(R_{m2} - R_{m1})/c} \right\rangle \tag{2.74a}$$

$$= \sum_m \frac{1}{R_{m1} R_{m2}} \langle A_m(t) A^*_m(t) \rangle \mathrm{e}^{-\mathrm{i}2\pi\bar{\nu}(R_{m2} - R_{m1})/c}, \tag{2.74b}$$

where the complex scalars $A_m(t)$ carry information on the amplitude and phase of the field in the source plane. Only the phase retardation effects have been retained in writing Eq. (2.74b). The amplitude retardation effects being insignificant under the present set of approximations are ignored. In the limit of the area element $d\sigma_m \to 0$, the sum in Eqs (2.74) can be replaced by the integral. Therefore,

$$\left(\frac{1}{2} \epsilon_0 c \right) J_{12}(P_1, P_2) = \int \int_\sigma \frac{I(x', y')}{R_1 R_2} \mathrm{e}^{-\mathrm{i}2\pi\bar{\nu}(R_2 - R_1)/c} \mathrm{d}x' \mathrm{d}y', \tag{2.75}$$

where $I(x', y')$ is the intensity distribution over the source plane. The complex degree of coherence (Eq. 2.68b) between point P_1 and P_2 is

$$\gamma_{12}(0) = \mu_{12}(P_1, P_2) = \frac{\int \int_\sigma \frac{I(x', y')}{R_1, R_2} \mathrm{e}^{-\mathrm{i}2\pi\bar{\nu}(R_2 - R_1)/c} \mathrm{d}x' \, \mathrm{d}y'}{\sqrt{I(P_1) I(P_2)}} \tag{2.76a}$$

$$= \frac{\mathrm{e}^{\mathrm{i}k\psi} \int \int_\sigma I(x', y') \mathrm{e}^{\frac{-\mathrm{i}2\pi}{\lambda}(px' + qy')} \mathrm{d}x' \, \mathrm{d}y'}{\int \int_\sigma I(x', y') \mathrm{d}x' \, \mathrm{d}y'}, \tag{2.76b}$$

where

$$I(P_1) = \frac{1}{2} \epsilon_0 c J_{11} = \int \int_\sigma \frac{I(x', y')}{R_1^2} \mathrm{d}x' \, \mathrm{d}y',$$

$$I(P_2) = \frac{1}{2} \epsilon_0 c J_{22} = \int \int_\sigma \frac{I(x', y')}{R_2^2} \mathrm{d}x' \, \mathrm{d}y',$$

$$R_1^2 = R^2 + (x_1 - x')^2 + (y_1 - y')^2,$$
$$R_2^2 = R^2 + (x_2 - x')^2 + (y_2 - y')^2,$$

so that

$$R_1 - R_2 \simeq \psi - (px' + qy'),$$

where

$$p = (x_1 - x_2)/R, \quad q = (y_1 - y_2)/R,$$

and

$$\psi = \frac{(x_1^2 + y_1^2) - (x_2^2 + y_2^2)}{2R}$$

represents the difference in the optical paths $\overline{O'P_2}$ and $\overline{O'P_1}$. For astronomical sources, this path difference is small and the exponential $e^{ik\psi}$ can be replaced by unity. In addition, since the source intensity distribution $I(x', y')$ is non-zero over a finite area only, the integration limits in Eq. (2.76b) can be extended from $-\infty$ to $+\infty$. Under these conditions, the degree of mutual coherence $|\gamma_{12}(0)|$ for a pair of points in the plane of observation, held parallel to a two-dimensional incoherent quasi-monochromatic source, is the normalized Fourier transform of the intensity distribution in the source plane calculated at the spatial frequencies

$$u = \frac{p}{\lambda} = \frac{(x_1 - x_2)}{R\lambda} \text{ and } v = \frac{q}{\lambda} = \frac{(y_1 - y_2)}{R\lambda},$$

provided the dimensions of the source and the distances between the observation points are restricted to values much smaller than the separation between the source and observation planes. This is the statement of the Van Cittert–Zernike theorem. The theorem as such does not relate the complex degree of mutual coherence with Fraunhofer diffraction because the latter as we shall see in Chapter 10 is described by the Fourier transform of the electric field distribution, and not by the Fourier transform of the intensity distribution. At this point, we exploit the mathematical similarity of Eq. (2.76b) with the normalized Fourier transform of the electric field distribution across a diffracting aperture. Equations (10.6a) and (10.9) for Fraunhofer diffraction from an aperture may be combined to give

$$\frac{F(u, v)}{F(0, 0)} = \frac{\iint\limits_{-\infty}^{\infty} E(x', y') e^{-i2\pi(ux' + vy')} dx'\, dy'}{\iint\limits_{-\infty}^{\infty} E(x', y') dx'\, dy'}, \tag{2.77}$$

where $E(x', y')$ is the field distribution over the aperture.

To establish an exact correspondence between the complex degree of mutual coherence (μ_{12}) of light emanating from a two-dimensional incoherent quasi-monochromatic source with Fraunhofer diffraction, (a) the source intensity distribution should be replaced by the field distribution over a hypothetical aperture having the exact shape and size of the two-dimensional quasi-monochromatic source, and (b) the aperture is illuminated by a spherical wave such that the diffraction pattern is centered at point P_2. Under these conditions, the normalized complex diffracted field at point P_1 gives the complex degree of mutual coherence between points P_1 and P_2.

2.6.1 Incoherent Quasi-monochromatic Source of Circular Cross-Section

We now apply Van Cittert–Zernike theorem to an incoherent quasi-monochromatic source of circular cross-section having uniform intensity distribution (Fig. 2.11). The source intensity distribution may be taken as

$$\begin{aligned} I(x', y') &= I_0 \quad \text{for } \sqrt{x'^2 + y'^2} \le a \\ &= 0 \quad \text{for } \sqrt{x'^2 + y'^2} > a, \end{aligned}$$

where a is the radius of the circle. The integrals appearing in Eq. (2.76b) can be solved for this intensity distribution to obtain the complex degree of mutual coherence between a moveable point $P_1(x_1, y_1)$ and a fixed point $P_2(x_2, y_2)$, lying in the plane of observation. Instead of solving the integrals, we make use of the Van Cittert–Zernike theorem. Equation (10.43) describes the Fraunhofer diffraction field distribution from a uniformly illuminated circular aperture of radius a.

To ensure exact correspondence with the Fraunhofer diffraction problem, the fixed point P_2 must coincide with the center of the diffraction pattern of the

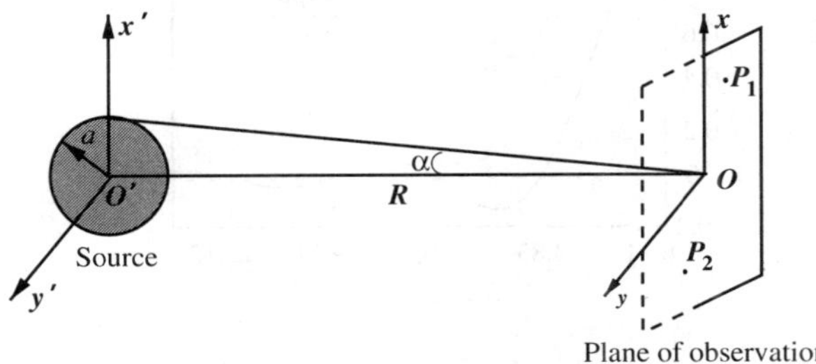

Fig. 2.11: Application of Van Cittert–Zernike theorem to a source of circular cross-section.

circular aperture. Accordingly, the complex degree of mutual coherence between points P_1 and P_2 can be expressed as

$$\mu_{12}(P_1, P_2) = e^{ik\psi} \frac{2J_1(2\pi\rho a)}{2\pi\rho a}, \tag{2.78}$$

where J_1, the Bessel function of the first rank, has real values (positive and negative, see Table B1 in Appendix B). The variable

$$\rho = \frac{\overline{P_1P_2}}{\bar{\lambda}R} = \frac{[(x_2 - x_1)^2 + (y_2 - y_1)^2]^{1/2}}{\bar{\lambda}R}$$

defines the geometrical conditions of the diffraction experiment. Comparing Eqs (2.68) and (2.78), we conclude that $\alpha(0)$ admits only zero and π values. Figure 2.12 shows the variation of the degree of mutual coherence. It starts with unit value when points P_1 and P_2 are coincident and then falls steadily as P_1 moves away from P_2, reaching zero value for $2\pi\rho a = 3.83$. With further increase in the distance between points P_1 and P_2, the degree of mutual coherence recovers but with reduced magnitude and negative sign, again falling to zero for $2\pi\rho a = 7.02$. It goes through cycles of positive ($\alpha(0) = 0$) and negative ($\alpha(0) = \pi$) values of diminishing magnitude. For negative values of the degree of mutual coherence, the fringe contrast is reversed, i.e., a bright fringe appears where otherwise one would expect a dark fringe and vice versa. Every time, the degree of mutual coherence goes through zero value, the fringes re-appear with reversed contrast. The first zero of the degree of coherence occurs when the observation point P_1 has moved a distance

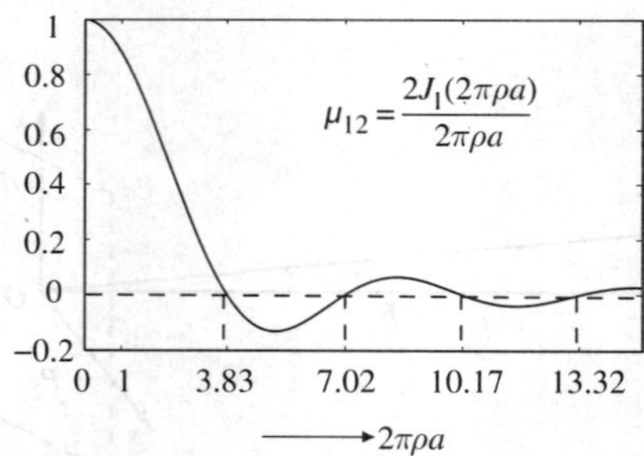

Fig. 2.12: Degree of mutual coherence produced by a quasi-monochromatic source of circular cross-section.

$$\overline{P_1P_2} = \frac{3.83}{2\pi}\frac{\bar{\lambda}}{\alpha} \tag{2.79a}$$

$$= 0.61\frac{\bar{\lambda}}{\alpha} \tag{2.79b}$$

away from the fixed point P_2, where $\alpha = a/R$ is the angular size of the source as viewed from the plane of observation.

2.6.2 Area of Coherence

We have seen that the degree of mutual coherence of light from an extended, distant incoherent quasi-monochromatic source decreases with increase in the distance between the points of observation. An area of high degree of coherence called the 'area of coherence' can be defined in the following manner. For a light source of circular cross-section and uniform irradiance over its surface, the region in the plane of observation covered by $2\pi\rho a$ values ranging from 0 to 1 may be considered as the area of coherence. The degree of mutual coherence over this region varies from 0.88 to 1. The separation between the farthest points for which the degree of mutual coherence is 88% or more can be calculated from the condition

$$\frac{2\pi}{\bar{\lambda}}\frac{a}{R}\overline{P_1P_2} = 1, \tag{2.80a}$$

giving

$$\begin{aligned}\overline{P_1P_2} &= \frac{1}{2\pi}\frac{\bar{\lambda}}{\alpha} \\ &= 0.16\bar{\lambda}/\alpha.\end{aligned} \tag{2.80b}$$

The distance $\overline{P_1P_2}$ (Fig. 2.11) is therefore the diameter of the area of coherence, also called the coherent patch. For a spherical light source such as a distant star, the coherent patch exists around any observation point on the surface of earth. Within that region, light from the distant star will show a high degree of mutual coherence and interference experiments can be performed with fringes of high contrast. A mask can be used to select the coherent patch as the source of illumination for an interference experiment. The diameter of the coherent patch on the surface of earth for light of mean wavelength $\bar{\lambda} = 550\,\text{nm}$ coming from the sun with $\alpha = 16'$ of an arc, assuming uniform illumination over its surface, is 0.019 mm. This is enough to successfully perform an interference experiment on earth with sunlight. Young's experiment was first performed with sunlight entering the room through a tiny hole in the wall. In the above example, the object intensity distribution has been assumed uniform. However, mutual coherence studies can provide some insight into the actual intensity distribution of a star.

2.7 INTENSITY CORRELATIONS

We have so far concentrated on first-order coherence which deals with phase correlations between light fields at two space-time points. The visibility of fringes produced in an interference experiment can provide complete information on first-order coherence. However, an interference experiment puts great demands on our experimental skills. The fluctuations in path lengths must be contained within the wavelength of light. We now describe a method based on amplitude correlations, as opposed to phase correlations, for the determination of the degree of coherence of light. This technique originally developed for radio frequency measurements was first applied in the optical regime in the mid-1950s by Hanbury Brown and Twiss. Intuitively, one can expect the changes in the amplitude of quasi-monochromatic light fields to be also correlated. The amplitude of a light wave, unlike its phase, is not too sensitive to external conditions. Appreciable changes in the amplitude of a light wave are not expected over distances which do not exceed its coherence length. Since amplitudes of light waves are not amenable to direct observation, we look for intensity correlations of the type

$$\begin{aligned}&\langle I(\vec{r}_1, t) I(\vec{r}_2, t+\tau)\rangle \\ &\quad = \left(\frac{1}{2}\epsilon_0 c\right)^2 \langle E(\vec{r}_1, t) E^*(\vec{r}_1, t) E(\vec{r}_2, t+\tau) E^*(\vec{r}_2, t+\tau)\rangle.\end{aligned} \tag{2.81}$$

The phase information is completely lost in the intensity correlations. The intensities $I(\vec{r}_1, t)$ and $I(\vec{r}_2, t+\tau)$ are short-time average intensities (Eq. 1.45) around the times t and $t+\tau$ at points $\vec{r}_1$ and $\vec{r}_2$, respectively. Short time in the present context means a few tens or a few hundreds of light periods. The long time average indicated by the symbol $\langle\,\rangle$ in Eq. (2.81) involves much longer times. Suppressing the space dependence, we define

$$I_1(t) = \langle I_1(t)\rangle + \Delta I_1(t), \tag{2.82a}$$

$$I_2(t+\tau) = \langle I_2(t+\tau)\rangle + \Delta I_2(t+\tau). \tag{2.82b}$$

It follows that the long time average fluctuations vanish, i.e.,

$$\langle \Delta I_1(t)\rangle = 0, \tag{2.83a}$$

$$\langle \Delta I_2(t+\tau)\rangle = 0, \tag{2.83b}$$

but the long time average of the product of fluctuations

$$\langle \Delta I_1(t)\Delta I_2(t+\tau)\rangle = \langle I_1(t)I_2(t+\tau)\rangle - \langle I_1(t)\rangle\langle I_2(t+\tau)\rangle \tag{2.84}$$

may not vanish. At this point, we would like to distinguish between the thermal or the incandescent light sources and the single mode laser sources. Thermal source is a generic name for sources involving a large number of independent optical oscillators which emit light through the process of spontaneous emission. Most light sources except lasers fall in this category. The dominant mode of light emission in a laser is the stimulated emission. For thermal sources, the intensity correlations can be expressed in terms of the degree of mutual coherence [2.5]:

$$\frac{\langle I_1(t)I_2(t+\tau)\rangle}{\langle I_1(t)\rangle\langle I_2(t+\tau)\rangle} = 1 + |\gamma_{12}(\tau)|^2. \tag{2.85a}$$

Expressing this result in terms of the correlation between the intensity fluctuations, we have

$$\frac{\langle \Delta I_1(t)\Delta I_2(t+\tau)\rangle}{\langle I_1(t)\rangle\langle I_2(t+\tau)\rangle} = |\gamma_{12}(\tau)|^2. \tag{2.85b}$$

It is therefore possible to determine the degree of mutual coherence of quasi-monochromatic thermal light from a measurement of its intensity correlations. Interferometers based on intensity correlations, also called intensity correlators, have the advantage that much larger path differences can be introduced without any detrimental effect on the quality of measurement. Angular sizes of stars down to 5×10^{-4} arcsec have been measured by this technique. Being inherently insensitive to phase modulations, the performance of intensity correlators is not adversely affected by atmospheric turbulence. In comparison, conventional interferometers are highly sensitive to atmospheric conditions.

2.7.1 Hanbury Brown and Twiss Experiment

Figure 2.13 shows the arrangement used by Hanbury Brown and Twiss to measure intensity–intensity correlations. A collimated beam from a mercury arc lamp was split and made to fall on two photomultiplier tubes. The current produced in each photomultiplier tube has a d.c. component representing the long time average beam intensity $\langle I(t)\rangle$ incident on it and a time varying part which corresponds to the fluctuations $\Delta I(t)$ over the average intensity. The amplifiers remove the d.c. components and amplify only the time-varying components. Any desired time delay can be introduced electronically in any of the arms. The fluctuating signals with appropriate time delays are multiplied in the correlator and

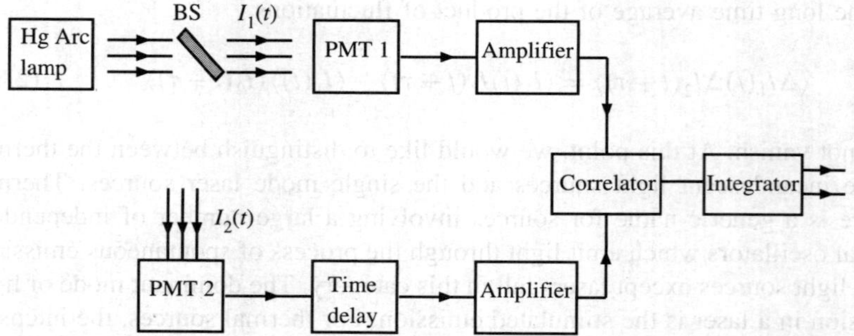

Fig. 2.13: Schematic of Hanbury Brown and Twiss experiment to measure intensity–intensity correlations.

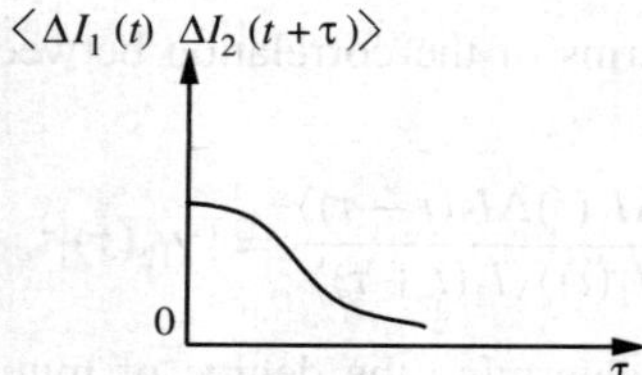

Fig. 2.14: Correlations in intensity fluctuations in Hg arc light in Hanbury Brown and Twiss experiment.

time averaged by the integrator circuit. The output of the integrator is proportional to the correlations between the intensity fluctuations $\langle \Delta I_1(t)\Delta I_2(t+\tau)\rangle$. Brown and Twiss found a positive correlation between the intensity fluctuations for small values of the time delay (Fig. 2.14).

The arrangement of Fig. 2.13 measures the temporal coherence of light reaching the beam splitter (BS). However, a slight modification in which the photomultiplier tubes PMT1 and PMT2 receive light directly from the source (and not through the beam splitter) can measure the spatial coherence of incident light at the locations of the photomultiplier tubes. For astronomical measurements, the photomultipliers are kept at the foci of large concave mirrors which are appropriately oriented to receive light from a particular star.

2.7.2 Photon Statistics

The positive correlation observed in the Brown–Twiss experiment shows that for small time delays, the intensity fluctuations of thermal light are indeed correlated. To understand how the intensity correlations may arise, we dwell briefly on how the optical signals are detected. Fast photomultiplier tubes used as light detectors can have response times of a nanosecond or less. Other fast photodetectors are the P–I–N and avalanche photodiodes. These detectors, of course, cannot follow instantaneous intensity variations of optical fields, but changes in intensity on the scale of the coherence time can be detected. The basic mechanism of light detection is the emission of electrons when light falls on the cathode of a photomultiplier tube. The dynode chain between the cathode and anode can multiply the electron number by a factor, as high as 10^9, enabling the photomultiplier tube to detect a single incident photon. However, an incident photon may not always succeed in releasing a photoelectron from the cathode of the tube. The quantum efficiency for the release of a photoelectron varies from cathode to cathode. It is, however, expected that the statistics of the photoelectrons emitted in a certain time T reflects the statistics of photons incident on the photocathode. For a light beam of constant intensity (Fig. 2.15a), the probability of n photoelectrons being emitted by the cathode in time T is given by the Poisson distribution [2.5]

$$P_n(T) = \frac{(\bar{n})^n \bar{e}^{\bar{n}}}{n!} \tag{2.86a}$$

with variance (mean square deviation)

$$\sigma^2 = \langle(\Delta n)^2\rangle = \langle(n-\bar{n})^2\rangle = \bar{n}. \tag{2.86b}$$

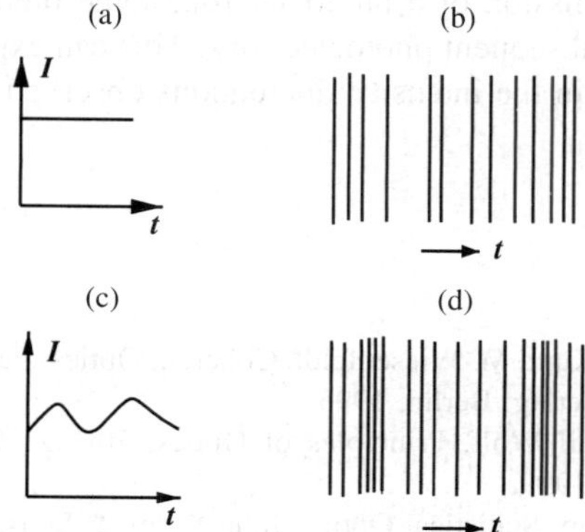

Fig. 2.15: (a) Constant intensity source. (b) Random time sequence of photoelectrons emitted by a constant intensity source. (c) A thermal source with random intensity fluctuations. (d) Bunching tendency in the time sequence of photoelectron emission from a thermal source.

Here, $\bar{n}$ is the average number of photoelectrons produced and counted in time T. A thermal source with intensity averaged over a time much longer than the coherence time ($t \gg \tau_c$) and a single mode laser are examples of sources with minimal intensity fluctuations. Figure 2.15b shows a random time sequence of emission of the photoelectrons for a source of constant intensity. A thermal source exhibits random intensity fluctuations (Fig. 2.15c). The probability of counting n photoelectrons in time T under these conditions has the distribution

$$P(n, T) = \frac{(\bar{n})^n}{(1+\bar{n})^{n+1}} \tag{2.87a}$$

with variance

$$\sigma^2 = \bar{n}^2 + \bar{n}. \tag{2.87b}$$

This is the Bose–Einstein distribution with a variance which always exceeds the variance of the Poisson distribution. Thus a thermal source and a laser source having exactly the same degree of first-order coherence and same average photon number can be distinguished by the variance in the distribution of photoelectrons produced by them.

For a constant intensity source, the photoelectron emission is a completely random process, and an experiment of the Brown and Twiss type carried out with such a source will reveal no intensity correlations. But the photoelectrons produced by a thermal source with random intensity fluctuations show the bunching tendency (Fig. 2.15d). The bunching of photoelectrons can be interpreted to imply that after the emission of a photoelectron, some prediction can be made for the release of the subsequent photoelectrons. This can explain the appearance of positive correlation in the intensity fluctuations observed by Hanbury Brown and Twiss.

2.8 REFERENCES

2.1 W. Lauterborn, T. Kurz, M. Wiesenfeldt, Coherent Optics: Fundamentals and applications, Springer-Verlag, Berlin, 1995.

2.2 Max Born and Emil Wolf, Principles of Optics, 7th ed., Cambridge University Press, Cambridge, 1999.

2.3 Joseph W. Goodman, Statistical Optics, John Wiley & Sons, New York, 1985.

2.4 K. D. Rao, R. S. Gurjar, Bipin Bihari, G. R. Kumar and K. K. Sharma, Appl. Phys. Lett. **60**, 3108–3110 (1992).

2.5 Christopher C. Davis, Lasers and Electro-Optics: Fundamentals and Engineering, Cambridge University Press, Cambridge, 1996.

2.6 Jan Perina, Coherence of Light, D. Reidel Publishing Company, Dordrecht, 1985.

2.7 Arvind S. Marathay, Elements of Optical Coherence Theory, John Wiley & sons, New York, 1982.

2.8 Leonard Mandel and Emil Wolf, Optical Coherence and Quantum Optics, Cambridge University Press, Cambridge, 1995.

2.9 PROBLEMS

2.1 Find the frequency spectra ($E(\nu)$) of the triangular and rectangular pulse waves:

$$\text{Triangle function: } \Lambda(t) = 1 - \left|\frac{t}{t_0}\right| \quad \text{for } -t_0 \le t \le t_0$$
$$= 0 \quad \text{otherwise.}$$
$$\text{Rectangle function: } \mathrm{rect}(t) = 1 \quad \text{for } -t_0 \le t \le t_0$$
$$= 0 \quad \text{otherwise.}$$

2.2 Find the envelope representations of the pulse waves of Problem 2.1.

2.3 The self coherence function of a Gaussian wave with complex field

$$E(t) = \frac{E_0}{\sqrt{2\pi\sigma}}\, \mathrm{e}^{-t^2/2\sigma^2}\, \mathrm{e}^{-\mathrm{i}2\pi\bar{\nu}t}$$

is defined as

$$\Gamma_{11}(\tau) = \int_{-\infty}^{+\infty} E^*(t)E(t+\tau)\,\mathrm{d}t,$$

where σ characterizes the frequency width and $\bar{\nu}$ the mean frequency of the wave. Show that the complex degree of coherence of a Gaussian wave is described by a Gaussian function. Find its coherence time and normalized spectral density function.

2.4 Consider an ideal laser oscillating in five longitudinal modes of frequencies $\nu = \nu_0$, $\nu_0 \pm \Delta\nu$, $\nu_0 \pm 2\Delta\nu$, where ν_0 is the mean frequency of oscillation and $\Delta\nu(=c/2L$, L is mirror separation and c is velocity of light) is the mode separation. Each longitudinal mode may be represented by a delta function. Find complex degree of coherence, degree of coherence, phase $\Phi(\tau)$ of the complex degree of coherence, and coherence time of the laser radiation.

2.5 Emission lines in a low pressure gas discharge are primarily Doppler broadened with the normalized spectral density function

$$g(\nu) = \frac{2}{\delta\nu_D}\sqrt{\frac{\ln 2}{\pi}}\exp\left[-4\left(\frac{\nu-\bar{\nu}}{\delta\nu_D}\right)^2 \ln 2\right],$$

where $\delta\nu_D = \frac{2\bar{\nu}}{c}\left(\frac{2kT}{m}\ln 2\right)^{1/2}$, m is mass of the atom or the molecule as the case may be. For the 632.8 nm line of Ne, $\delta\nu_D = 1500$ MHz and for the 10.6 μm line of CO_2, $\delta\nu_D = 61$ MHz at 400 K. Find degrees of self coherence, phase $\Phi(\tau)$ of the complex degrees of coherence, and the coherence times for the above transitions.

2.6 Spectral lines in a high pressure discharge are primarily collision broadened with normalized spectral density function

$$g(\nu) = \frac{1}{\pi} \frac{\Delta\nu/2}{(\nu - \bar{\nu})^2 + \left(\frac{\Delta\nu}{2}\right)^2},$$

where $\bar{\nu}$ is the mean frequency of emission and $\Delta\nu$ is the FWHM. Find an expression for the coherence time of the light emitted in a high pressure gas discharge.

2.7 One of the most monochromatic atomic transitions is the red line ($\lambda = 6348\,\text{A}°$) of cadmium with $\Delta\lambda$(FWHM) $= 0.013\,\text{A}°$. The red light ($\lambda = 6348\,\text{A}°$) coming from a cadmium lamp through an opening of negligible dimensions illuminates the double slit in a Young's interference experiment with slit separation of 2 mm. The interference fringes are observed on a screen held 2 m behind the slits. The slits are at a distance of 20 cm from the lamp opening.

(a) Find the number of fringes observed on the screen.
(b) Keeping the slit separation fixed, lamp opening is gradually increased. Find the lamp openings for the first two disappearances of the fringes.
(c) For a fixed lamp opening (radius = 0.1 mm), the slit separation is gradually increased. Find the slit separations for the first two disappearances of fringes.

2.8 Derive Eq. (2.70) for the visibility of Young's fringes for a linear source of length L.

2.9 For Young's interference experiment, find an expression for the normalized spectral density function of light at a point on the observation screen, assuming identical normalized spectral density functions at the slits.

2.10 It is desired to illuminate a circular aperture of radius 0.5 mm coherently in a diffraction experiment performed with sodium light of mean wavelength 589.3 nm. The sodium lamp is kept in an enclosure with a small opening. Find the diameter of the lamp opening if the aperture is kept 1 m away from the opening.

2.11 Find the smallest angular diameter of a star that can be measured with an optical intensity correlator having mirror separation of 200 m. The mean wavelength of light emitted by the star may be taken as 500 nm.

2.12 For the rectangular pulse wave of Problem 2.1, find the degree of coherence and the phase $\Phi(\tau)$.

2.13 Interference with a quasi-monochromatic linear source of length l held a distance h above the mirror M is obtained on the screen S at distance D from the source (Fig. 2.16). Describe the changes in the visibility of fringes as a function of x. Find x_1 for the first disappearance of fringes. Obtain a numerical estimate of x_1 for reasonable values of h, l, D, and the mean wavelength.

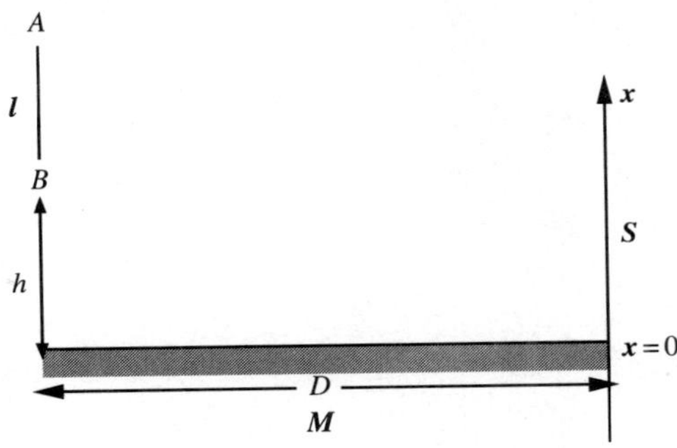

Fig. 2.16.

CHAPTER 3

Polarization of Light Waves

3.1 STATES OF POLARIZATION

Consider a monochromatic plane wave

$$\vec{E}\,(\vec{r}, t) = \vec{E}_0\ \mathrm{e}^{\mathrm{i}(kz-\omega t)}, \tag{3.1a}$$

$$\vec{B}\,(\vec{r}, t) = \vec{B}_0\ \mathrm{e}^{\mathrm{i}(kz-\omega t)}, \tag{3.1b}$$

propagating in the positive z-direction in an isotropic medium. The amplitude vectors $\vec{E}_0$ and $\vec{B}_0$ are in general complex. The direction of the electric field amplitude $\vec{E}_0$, quite arbitrarily but in accordance with the common usage, is taken to represent the state of polarization of light. For light propagating in free space and in other non-absorbing isotropic media, the polarization state is completely described by the transverse components of its electric field. Accordingly, Eq. (3.1a) can be expressed as

$$\vec{E}\,(x, y, z, t) = E_x\hat{i} + E_y\hat{j} \tag{3.2a}$$

$$= (E_{0x}\hat{i} + E_{0y}\hat{j})\,\mathrm{e}^{\mathrm{i}(kz-\omega t)}. \tag{3.2b}$$

For definiteness, the x and y axes in the transverse plane are taken along the horizontal and vertical directions, respectively. It may not be out of place to mention at this point that the phase of a monochromatic plane wave is arbitrarily chosen to be $(kz - \omega t)$ and not $(\omega t - kz)$. This minor detail needs to be stated because the terms like 'phase advance' and 'phase lag' to be used later are dependent on this choice.

3.1.1 Linear Polarization

Light is linearly polarized if the field components E_x and E_y oscillate in phase or 180° out of phase. This is ensured if E_{0x} and E_{0y} are real. The field components

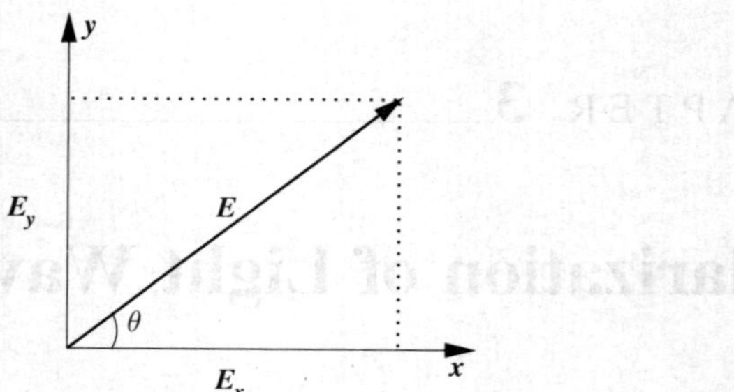

Fig. 3.1: Linearly polarized light.

attain extremum values at the same time. A wave is horizontally polarized (E_{H}) if E_y is identically zero and vertically polarized (E_{V}) when E_x vanishes. The general state of linear polarization (E_θ) occurs when E_x and E_y are both non-zero. The direction of polarization of the wave then makes an angle θ with the x-direction, where $\theta = \tan^{-1}\left(E_{0y}/E_{0x}\right)$. This is shown in Fig. 3.1.

As time changes, the tip of the electric vector at a given point oscillates along a fixed line (hence the name, linear polarization) in the transverse plane with a period $T = 2\pi/\omega$. At other points along the direction of propagation, the electric vectors oscillate in exactly the same manner along parallel lines which lie in a plane containing the direction of propagation (Fig. 3.2a). Alternatively, one

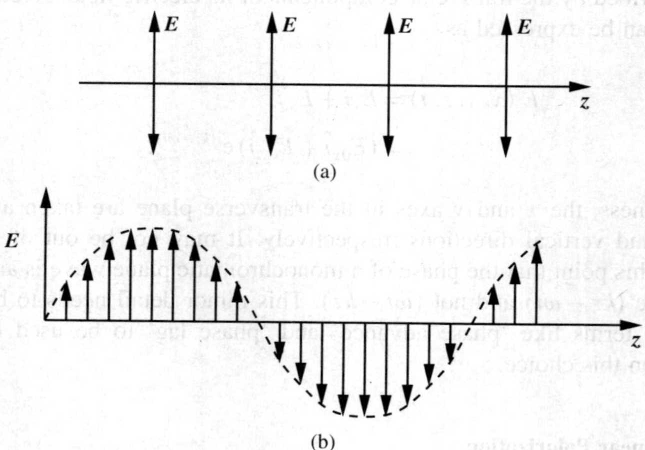

Fig. 3.2: Linearly polarized light; (a) tips of electric field vectors oscillate along parallel lines in a fixed plane, (b) instantaneous distribution of electric field vectors.

can imagine taking a snap shot of the electric vectors. The snap shot will reveal electric vectors distributed sinusoidally along the direction of propagation in a plane which contains the direction of propagation (Fig. 3.2b). For that reason, a linearly polarized wave is also called a plane-polarized wave. It should, however, be understood that the above visualization is only through thought experiments since no detector exists to follow the rapidly changing light fields.

3.1.2 Elliptical and Circular Polarizations

For complex E_{0x} and E_{0y}, the oscillations of the field components along the horizontal and vertical directions are generally not in phase, and we can write

$$E_x = \varepsilon_x \mathrm{e}^{\mathrm{i}(kz-\omega t+\phi_x)}, \tag{3.3a}$$

$$E_y = \varepsilon_y \mathrm{e}^{\mathrm{i}(kz-\omega t+\phi_y)}, \tag{3.3b}$$

where the amplitudes ε_x and ε_y are now real. For plane-polarized light,

$$\phi_y - \phi_x = 0, \pm\pi \tag{3.4}$$

so that

$$\frac{E_y}{E_x} = \frac{\varepsilon_y}{\varepsilon_x} \quad \text{for } \phi_y = \phi_x, \tag{3.5a}$$

$$\frac{E_y}{E_x} = -\frac{\varepsilon_y}{\varepsilon_x} \quad \text{for } \phi_y = \phi_x \pm \pi. \tag{3.5b}$$

The proportionality of the field components $[E_y = \pm(\varepsilon_y/\varepsilon_x)E_x]$ is an essential requirement for the wave to be linearly polarized. When the field components along the horizontal and vertical directions do not oscillate in phase or exactly out of phase, the tip of the electric vector in general traces an ellipse in the transverse plane, called the polarization ellipse. The ellipticity and orientation of this ellipse depend on the amplitude ratio $\varepsilon_y/\varepsilon_x$ and the phase difference $(\phi_y - \phi_x)$. Eliminating $(kz - \omega t)$ from the real fields

$$E_x = \varepsilon_x \cos(kz - \omega t + \phi_x), \tag{3.6a}$$

$$E_y = \varepsilon_y \cos(kz - \omega t + \phi_y), \tag{3.6b}$$

we obtain

$$\left(\frac{E_y}{\varepsilon_y}\right)^2 + \left(\frac{E_x}{\varepsilon_x}\right)^2 - 2\left(\frac{E_y}{\varepsilon_y}\right)\left(\frac{E_x}{\varepsilon_x}\right)\cos\phi_0 = \sin^2\phi_0, \tag{3.7}$$

where $\phi_0 = \phi_y - \phi_x$. This is the general equation of an ellipse with its principal axes rotated with respect to the horizontal and vertical directions. For $\phi_0 = \pm(m+\frac{1}{2})\pi$, where m is an integer, Eq. (3.7) reduces to

$$\left(\frac{E_y}{\varepsilon_y}\right)^2 + \left(\frac{E_x}{\varepsilon_x}\right)^2 = 1. \tag{3.8}$$

The polarization ellipse, in this case, is symmetrically oriented with respect to the coordinates axes (Fig. 3.3a). For $\varepsilon_x = \varepsilon_y$ and $\phi_0 = \pm(m+\frac{1}{2})\pi$, the polarization ellipse degenerates into a circle (Fig. 3.3b). Linear polarization is obtained for $\phi_0 = 0, \pm\pi$ (Fig. 3.3c,d). For phase differences other than the multiples of $\pi/2$ and π, light is elliptically polarized with the polarization ellipse asymmetrically oriented with respect to the horizontal and vertical directions. The major axis of the ellipse makes an angle ψ with the horizontal direction (Fig. 3.3e). The polarization ellipse is contained in a rectangle of sides $2\varepsilon_x$ and $2\varepsilon_y$ parallel to

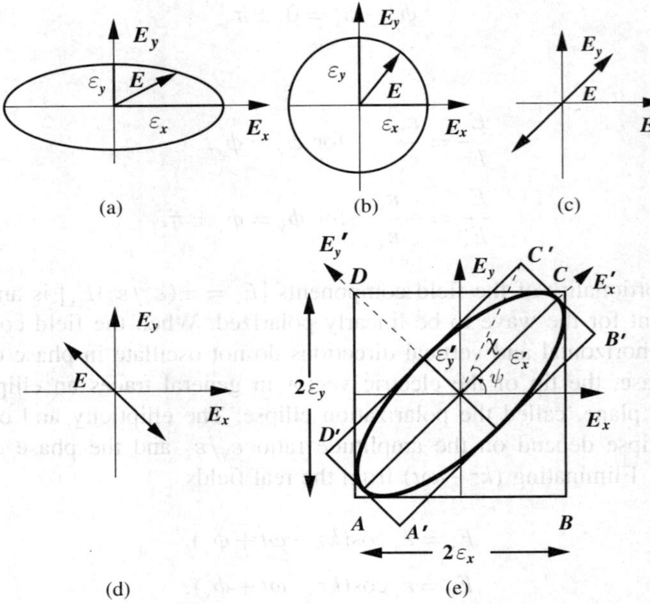

Fig. 3.3: States of polarization of a plane wave; (a) elliptical polarization with major and minor axes along horizontal and vertical directions, (b) circular polarization, (c) linear polarization along a line with positive slope, (d) linear polarization along a line with negative slope, (e) general state of elliptical polarization.

the horizontal and vertical axes, respectively. This ellipse is also contained in another rectangle of sides $2\varepsilon'_x$ and $2\varepsilon'_y$, where $2\varepsilon'_x$ and $2\varepsilon'_y$ are the lengths of the major and minor axes of the polarization ellipse, respectively. The angles χ and ψ in Fig. 3.3e give the ellipticity and orientation of the polarization ellipse, respectively.

3.1.3 Helicity of Light Waves

The electric vector of the elliptically polarized light rotates with its tip tracing an ellipse in the transverse plane. The same ellipse can be traced by clockwise or counter-clockwise rotation of the electric vector. This gives rise to two states of helicity for the elliptically polarized light. We need to define unambiguously the terms 'clockwise' and 'counter-clockwise' rotations in the present context. To fix this nomenclature, we take $\phi_0 = \phi_y - \phi_x = \pm\pi/2$, although the argument holds for any ϕ_0. Equations (3.6) now become

$$E_x = \varepsilon_x \cos(kz_0 - \omega t),$$

$$E_y = \mp\varepsilon_y \sin(kz_0 - \omega t),$$

where the $(-)$ and $(+)$ signs correspond to $\phi_0 = +\pi/2$ and $\phi_0 = -\pi/2$, respectively, and z_0 is any given point on the z-axis. Table 3.1 lists values of E_x and E_y at some specified times within a period of oscillation. The initial time t_0 is chosen to make the initial phase $kz_0 - \omega t_0 = 0$.

Figure 3.4 shows the corresponding polarization ellipses. It is seen that for $\phi_0 = +\pi/2$, the ellipse is traced in the counter-clockwise direction as seen from above against the direction $(+z)$ of propagation of light. This represents left elliptically polarized light or light with negative helicity (Fig. 3.4a). For $\phi_0 = -\pi/2$,

Table 3.1. Values of E_x and E_y for $\phi_0 = \pi/2$ and $-\pi/2$.

t	$\phi_0 = +\pi/2$		$\phi_0 = -\pi/2$	
	E_x	E_y	E_x	E_y
t_0	$+\varepsilon_x$	0	$+\varepsilon_x$	0
$t_0 + \frac{\pi}{2\omega}$	0	$+\varepsilon_y$	0	$-\varepsilon_y$
$t_0 + \frac{\pi}{\omega}$	$-\varepsilon_x$	0	$-\varepsilon_x$	0
$t_0 + \frac{3\pi}{2\omega}$	0	$-\varepsilon_y$	0	$+\varepsilon_y$

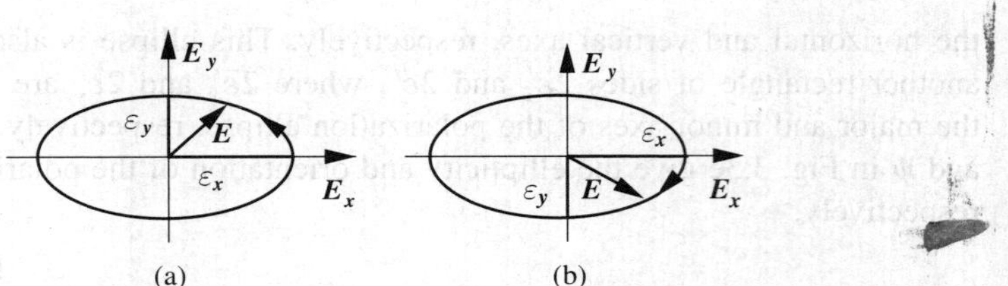

Fig. 3.4: Polarization ellipse; (a) left elliptical polarization ($\phi_0 = +\pi/2$), (b) right elliptical polarization ($\phi_0 = -\pi/2$).

the electric vector appears to rotate clockwise as seen against the direction of propagation. This corresponds to right elliptically polarized light or light with positive helicity (Fig. 3.4b). The helicity of the circularly polarized light is defined in a similar manner. There is no special reason to call light with electric vector rotating in the clockwise (counter-clockwise) direction as right (left) elliptically polarized light. This nomenclature is, however, generally preferred.

For $\phi_0 = +\pi/2$, the field component E_x leads E_y since E_x reaches its maximum value one quarter of a period before E_y reaches its maximum value (Fig. 3.5a). A similar argument shows that E_x lags behind E_y for $\phi_0 = -\pi/2$ (Fig. 3.5b).

It must be stated once again that the terms leading and lagging of the fields in the present context is linked to our choice $(kz - \omega t)$ to represent the phase of a plane wave. Some authors use $(\omega t - kz)$ for the phase of a plane wave, in which case the terminologies will be just the opposite.

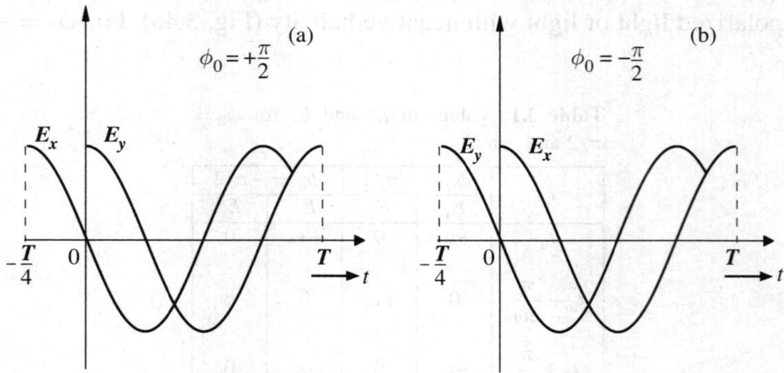

Fig. 3.5: Horizontal component of electric field E_x (a) leads the vertical component E_y for $\phi_0 = +\pi/2$ and (b) lags behind the vertical component E_y for $\phi_0 = -\pi/2$.

3.2 THE POLARIZATION ELLIPSE

The most general form of the polarization ellipse is shown in Fig. 3.3e. The angle of inclination of this ellipse will be shown to be given by

$$\tan 2\psi = \frac{2\varepsilon_x \varepsilon_y \cos\phi_0}{\varepsilon_x^2 - \varepsilon_y^2}. \tag{3.9}$$

For arbitrary ϕ_0, the ellipse is not symmetrical about the horizontal and vertical axes, but is obviously symmetrical about its principal axes ε'_x and ε'_y. Equation (3.7) when referred to the principal axes of the ellipse is transformed to

$$\left(\frac{E'_x}{\varepsilon'_x}\right)^2 + \left(\frac{E'_y}{\varepsilon'_y}\right)^2 = 1,$$

where

$$E'_x = \varepsilon'_x \cos(kz - \omega t + \phi'_x),$$
$$E'_y = \varepsilon'_y \cos(kz - \omega t + \phi'_y).$$

Here, ε'_x and ε'_y are, respectively, the semi-major and semi-minor axes of the polarization ellipse and $\phi'_y - \phi'_x = \pm\pi/2$. Therefore, we can write

$$E'_x = \varepsilon'_x \cos(kz - \omega t + \phi'_0), \quad E'_y = \mp\varepsilon'_y \sin(kz - \omega t + \phi'_0). \tag{3.10}$$

The $(\mp)$ signs correspond to $\phi'_y - \phi'_x = \pm\pi/2$. The components of the electric field in the two coordinate systems are related:

$$E'_x = E_x \cos\psi + E_y \sin\psi, \tag{3.11a}$$

$$E'_y = -E_x \sin\psi + E_y \cos\psi. \tag{3.11b}$$

Substituting Eqs (3.6) with $\phi_x = 0$, $\phi_y = \phi_0$ and Eqs (3.10) into Eqs (3.11), we obtain

$$\begin{aligned}\varepsilon'_x \cos\phi'_0 \cos(kz - \omega t) - \varepsilon'_x \sin\phi'_0 \sin(kz - \omega t) &= [\varepsilon_x \cos\psi + \varepsilon_y \sin\psi \cos\phi_0] \cos(kz - \omega t)\\ &\quad - \varepsilon_y \sin\psi \sin\phi_0 \sin(kz - \omega t),\end{aligned}$$

$$\mp\varepsilon'_y \sin\phi'_0 \cos(kz-\omega t) \mp \varepsilon'_y \cos\phi'_0 \sin(kz-\omega t)$$
$$=[-\varepsilon_x \sin\psi + \varepsilon_y \cos\psi \cos\phi_0]\cos(kz-\omega t)$$
$$-\,\varepsilon_y \cos\psi \sin\phi_0 \sin(kz-\omega t).$$

For these equalities to hold for all t and z, following conditions must be satisfied:

$$\varepsilon'_x \cos\phi'_0 = \varepsilon_x \cos\psi + \varepsilon_y \sin\psi \cos\phi_0, \tag{3.12a}$$

$$\varepsilon'_x \sin\phi'_0 = \varepsilon_y \sin\psi \sin\phi_0, \tag{3.12b}$$

$$\mp\varepsilon'_y \sin\phi'_0 = -\varepsilon_x \sin\psi + \varepsilon_y \cos\psi \cos\phi_0, \tag{3.12c}$$

$$\mp\varepsilon'_y \cos\phi'_0 = -\varepsilon_y \cos\psi \sin\phi_0. \tag{3.12d}$$

Multiplying Eq. (3.12a) with Eq. (3.12c) and Eq. (3.12b) with Eq. (3.12d), we get

$$\mp\varepsilon'_x\varepsilon'_y \sin\phi'_0 \cos\phi'_0 = (\varepsilon_x \cos\psi + \varepsilon_y \sin\psi \cos\phi_0) \times (-\varepsilon_x \sin\psi + \varepsilon_y \cos\psi \cos\phi_0)$$
$$= \varepsilon_x\varepsilon_y \cos\phi_0 \cos 2\psi + (\varepsilon_y^2 \cos^2\phi_0 - \varepsilon_x^2)\sin\psi\cos\psi \tag{3.13a}$$

$$\mp\varepsilon'_x\varepsilon'_y \sin\phi'_0 \cos\phi'_0 = -\varepsilon_y^2 \sin^2\phi_0 \sin\psi\cos\psi. \tag{3.13b}$$

The desired result (Eq. 3.9) can be obtained by subtracting Eq. (3.13b) from Eq. (3.13a), giving

$$\tan 2\psi = \frac{2\varepsilon_x\varepsilon_y \cos\phi_0}{\varepsilon_x^2 - \varepsilon_y^2}.$$

Squaring and adding Eqs (3.12a) and (3.12d) gives

$$\varepsilon_x'^2 + \varepsilon_y'^2 = \varepsilon_x^2 + \varepsilon_y^2. \tag{3.14a}$$

Further, by adding the product of Eq. (3.12a) with Eq. (3.12d) to the product of Eq. (3.12b) with Eq. (3.12c), we obtain

$$\mp\varepsilon'_x\varepsilon'_y = \varepsilon_x\varepsilon_y \sin\phi_0. \tag{3.14b}$$

Combining Eqs (3.14a) and (3.14b), one gets

$$\mp\frac{\varepsilon'_x\varepsilon'_y}{\varepsilon_x'^2 + \varepsilon_y'^2} = \frac{\varepsilon_x\varepsilon_y \sin\phi_0}{\varepsilon_x^2 + \varepsilon_y^2}, \tag{3.15a}$$

which is equivalent to

$$\sin(2\chi) = \sin(2\alpha)\sin\phi_0, \tag{3.15b}$$

where

$$\tan\alpha = \frac{\varepsilon_y}{\varepsilon_x}, \quad \tan\chi = \mp\frac{\varepsilon'_y}{\varepsilon'_x}. \tag{3.16}$$

The negative sign in Eqs (3.14b) and (3.15a) corresponds to clockwise $(-\frac{\pi}{2} \le \phi_0 \le 0)$ and positive sign to counter-clockwise $(0 \le \phi_0 \le \frac{\pi}{2})$ rotations of the electric vector. The ellipticity angle χ carries information on the ellipticity and sense of rotation of the polarization ellipse. We shall return to these relations when we introduce Stokes parameters later in the chapter. For completely polarized light, orientation, ellipticity, and sense of rotation of the polarization ellipse show no variation with time.

3.3 MATRIX REPRESENTATION OF POLARIZATION STATES

As described in Section 3.2, the polarization state of a monochromatic plane wave propagating in a transparent isotropic medium is completely determined if the magnitudes and phases of the horizontal and vertical components of its electric field are known. Several matrix representations of the polarization state of a plane wave are in vogue. Matrix approach to describe the polarization state of light is quite natural since the components of a light field after a polarizing device are linearly related to its components before it entered the device. Therefore, the polarization changing characteristics of a device can be represented by a matrix. The matrix approach is particularly useful in optics in general. This should not be construed to imply that nonlinear effects in optics are rare. On the contrary, with the advent of lasers, nonlinear optical effects can be observed rather easily.

3.3.1 The Jones Vectors

Jones column vectors are useful to describe the polarization behavior of coherent light. The matrix form of Eqs (3.3) is

$$\begin{bmatrix} E_x \\ E_y \end{bmatrix} = \begin{bmatrix} \varepsilon_x e^{i\phi_x} \\ \varepsilon_y e^{i\phi_y} \end{bmatrix} e^{i(kz-\omega t)}, \tag{3.17}$$

where the two component column (complex) vector on the right-hand side, which completely specifies the amplitude and phase of the light field and hence its state of polarization, is called the Jones vector. Two mutually coherent waves of the same frequency having Jones vectors

$$\begin{bmatrix} E_{0x}^{(1)} \\ E_{0y}^{(1)} \end{bmatrix} = \begin{bmatrix} \varepsilon_x^{(1)} e^{i\phi_x(1)} \\ \varepsilon_y^{(1)} e^{i\phi_y(1)} \end{bmatrix}$$

and

$$\begin{bmatrix} E_{0x}^{(2)} \\ E_{0y}^{(2)} \end{bmatrix} = \begin{bmatrix} \varepsilon_x^{(2)} e^{i\phi_x(2)} \\ \varepsilon_y^{(2)} e^{i\phi_y(2)} \end{bmatrix}$$

can be superimposed to generate a wave with the state of polarization described by the Jones vector

$$\begin{bmatrix} E_{0x} \\ E_{0y} \end{bmatrix} = \begin{bmatrix} \varepsilon_x^{(1)} e^{i\phi_x(1)} + \varepsilon_x^{(2)} e^{i\phi_x(2)} \\ \varepsilon_y^{(1)} e^{i\phi_y(1)} + \varepsilon_y^{(2)} e^{i\phi_y(2)} \end{bmatrix}. \tag{3.18}$$

The above definition of Jones vector is precise, but perhaps a bit too elaborate. It can be simplified, but at some cost to the information it carries. This may not matter if the Jones vector is being used merely to label the polarization state of light.

First, we note that only the phase difference $\phi_0 = \phi_y - \phi_x$, and not the actual phases ϕ_x and ϕ_y are needed to determine the polarization state of a wave. Accordingly, the Jones vector can be written as

$$\begin{bmatrix} E_{0x} \\ E_{0y} \end{bmatrix} = e^{i\phi_x} \begin{bmatrix} \varepsilon_x \\ \varepsilon_y e^{i\phi_0} \end{bmatrix}. \tag{3.19a}$$

The common phase factor $e^{i\phi_x}$ may be suppressed without losing any information on the state of polarization of the wave, but this cannot be done if interference of this wave with another wave is contemplated. The Jones vector can be normalized by requiring

$$E_{0x}E_{0x}^* + E_{0y}E_{0y}^* = 1.$$

Ignoring the phase factor $e^{i\phi_x}$ in Eq. (3.19a), the normalized Jones vector can be put in the form

$$\begin{bmatrix} E_{0x} \\ E_{0y} \end{bmatrix} = \begin{bmatrix} \cos\theta \\ \sin\theta e^{i\phi_0} \end{bmatrix}, \tag{3.19b}$$

where

$$\cos\theta = \frac{\varepsilon_x}{\sqrt{\varepsilon_x^2 + \varepsilon_y^2}}, \quad \sin\theta = \frac{\varepsilon_y}{\sqrt{\varepsilon_x^2 + \varepsilon_y^2}}$$

We are now ready to write Jones vectors for different states of polarization of light.

3.3.1.1 Linearly Polarized Light

Linearly polarized light is characterized by the horizontal and vertical components of the electric field oscillating in phase ($\phi_0 = 0$) or out of phase ($\phi_0 = \pm\pi$). The Jones vector for plane polarized light therefore has the general form

$$E_{(\theta)} = \begin{bmatrix} E_{0x} \\ E_{0y} \end{bmatrix} = \begin{bmatrix} \cos\theta \\ \sin\theta \end{bmatrix}, \tag{3.20}$$

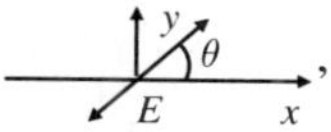

where the electric vector makes an angle θ with the horizontal direction. As special cases of plane polarized light, the Jones vectors for the horizontally and vertically polarized waves are

$$E_{(\mathrm{H})} = \begin{bmatrix} 1 \\ 0 \end{bmatrix}, \tag{3.21a}$$

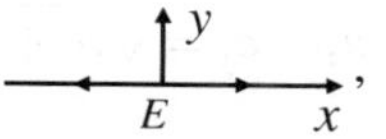

$$E_{(\mathrm{V})} = \begin{bmatrix} 0 \\ 1 \end{bmatrix}, \tag{3.21b}$$

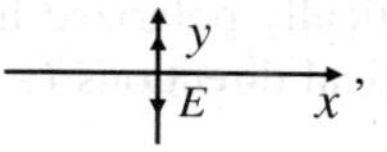

respectively. For light polarized at (+45°) to the horizontal direction, the normalized Jones vector has the form:

$$E_{(+45^\circ)} = \frac{1}{\sqrt{2}} \begin{bmatrix} 1 \\ 1 \end{bmatrix}. \tag{3.21c}$$

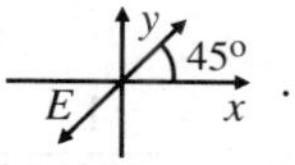

3.3.1.2 Circularly Polarized Light

Normalized Jones vectors for right ($\epsilon_x = \epsilon_y$, $\phi_0 = -\pi/2$) and left ($\epsilon_x = \epsilon_y$, $\phi_0 = +\pi/2$) circular polarizations are

$$E_{(\mathrm{RCP})} = \frac{1}{\sqrt{2}} \begin{bmatrix} 1 \\ -\mathrm{i} \end{bmatrix}, \tag{3.22a}$$

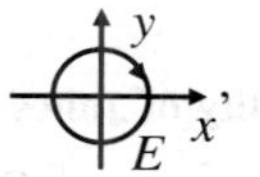

$$E_{(\mathrm{LCP})} = \frac{1}{\sqrt{2}} \begin{bmatrix} 1 \\ +\mathrm{i} \end{bmatrix}, \tag{3.22b}$$

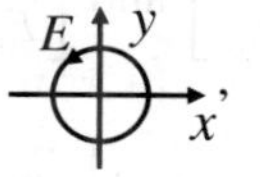

respectively.

3.3.1.3 Elliptically Polarized Light

Elliptically polarized light is described by an arbitrary value of ϕ_0 and no constraint on the relative magnitudes of ε_x and ε_y. The Jones vectors for the right and left elliptical polarizations have the general form

$$E_{(\mathrm{REP})} = \frac{1}{\sqrt{a^2+b^2+c^2}}\begin{bmatrix} a \\ b-\mathrm{i}c \end{bmatrix}, \tag{3.23a}$$

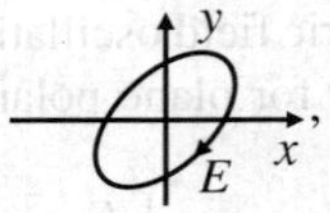

$$E_{(\mathrm{LEP})} = \frac{1}{\sqrt{a^2+b^2+c^2}}\begin{bmatrix} a \\ b+\mathrm{i}c \end{bmatrix}, \tag{3.23b}$$

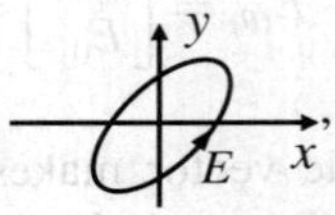

respectively, where

$$\varepsilon_x = a, \quad \varepsilon_y = \sqrt{b^2+c^2}, \quad \phi_0 = \mp\tan^{-1}\frac{c}{b}.$$

Jones vectors for elliptically polarized light with principal axes coinciding with the horizontal and vertical directions ($\varepsilon_x \neq \varepsilon_y$, $\phi_0 = \pm\pi/2$) are

$$E_{(\mathrm{REP})} = \frac{1}{\sqrt{a^2+b^2}}\begin{bmatrix} a \\ -\mathrm{i}b \end{bmatrix}, \tag{3.23c}$$

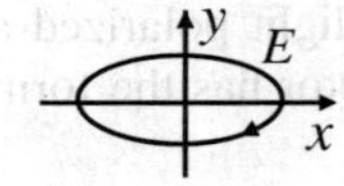

$$E_{(\mathrm{LEP})} = \frac{1}{\sqrt{a^2+b^2}}\begin{bmatrix} a \\ \mathrm{i}b \end{bmatrix}, \tag{3.23d}$$

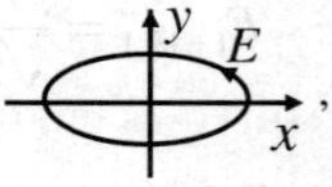

where

$$\varepsilon_x = a, \quad \varepsilon_y = b, \quad \phi_0 = \mp\frac{\pi}{2}.$$

3.3.1.4 Orthogonality of Jones Vectors

The Jones vectors $\begin{bmatrix} E_{0x} \\ E_{0y} \end{bmatrix}$ and $\begin{bmatrix} E'_{0x} \\ E'_{0y} \end{bmatrix}$ are orthogonal if the matrix product

$$\begin{bmatrix} E^*_{0x} & E^*_{0y} \end{bmatrix}\begin{bmatrix} E'_{0x} \\ E'_{0y} \end{bmatrix} = E^*_{0x}\ E'_{0x} + E^*_{0y}E'_{0y} = 0, \tag{3.24}$$

where the elements of the row vector $[E_{0x}^* \ E_{0y}^*]$ are complex conjugate of the elements of the Jones vector $\begin{bmatrix} E_{0x} \\ E_{0y} \end{bmatrix}$. Jones vectors representing the horizontal and vertical polarization states satisfy this condition and therefore constitute a pair of orthogonal polarization states. Similarly, the right and left circular polarization states are also orthogonal to each other. Orthogonal elliptical polarization states also exist. For example, the Jones vectors

$$(1/5)\begin{bmatrix} 3 \\ 4\mathrm{i} \end{bmatrix}, \quad (1/5)\begin{bmatrix} 4 \\ -3\mathrm{i} \end{bmatrix}$$

represent an orthogonal pair of elliptically polarized states. In fact, there are infinite pairs of orthogonal polarization states – all elliptically polarized, except the horizontal–vertical and ±45° linear polarization pairs and the pair representing the right and left circular polarizations. Any pair of orthonormal polarization states forms a complete set in the same sense as the orthonormal eigenfunctions of the Schrodinger equation form a complete set. Any arbitrary state of polarization can be expressed as a linear combination of the polarization states belonging to any pair of orthogonal polarization states. For example, the right circular polarization state can be expressed as a linear combination of the horizontal and vertical polarization states with appropriate coefficients:

$$\frac{1}{\sqrt{2}}\begin{bmatrix} 1 \\ -\mathrm{i} \end{bmatrix} = \frac{1}{\sqrt{2}}\begin{bmatrix} 1 \\ 0 \end{bmatrix} - \frac{\mathrm{i}}{\sqrt{2}}\begin{bmatrix} 0 \\ 1 \end{bmatrix}.$$

Furthermore, we note that the sum of any number of Jones vectors is a Jones vector. In other words, superposition of different states of polarization in the Jones scheme must always lead to a state of definite polarization. For example, the addition of right and left circular polarization states leads to the horizontal polarization state of twice the amplitude of either of the circular polarization states, i.e.,

$$\frac{1}{\sqrt{2}}\begin{bmatrix} 1 \\ -\mathrm{i} \end{bmatrix} + \frac{1}{\sqrt{2}}\begin{bmatrix} 1 \\ \mathrm{i} \end{bmatrix} = \frac{1}{\sqrt{2}}\begin{bmatrix} 2 \\ 0 \end{bmatrix} = \sqrt{2}\begin{bmatrix} 1 \\ 0 \end{bmatrix}.$$

It therefore follows that the Jones scheme of labeling polarization states cannot describe unpolarized light. This is a serious limitation of the Jones scheme since natural light is substantially unpolarized.

At this stage, we wish to refer to another aspect of Jones vectors. The use of the plane waves in the present discussion restricts the classification of the polarization states in terms of the Jones vectors to only monochromatic or completely coherent light with ε_x, ε_y, and ϕ_0 possessing no time dependence. Real light sources, at best, are quasi-monochromatic. The amplitude and phase of quasi-monochromatic light fluctuate with time. One may then ask if Jones scheme of classification of the polarization states can ever describe real light. But as mentioned in Chapter 2, a quasi-monochromatic wave behaves like a coherent wave for times much shorter than the coherence time of the wave. In that limit, the description of the polarization states of quasi-monochromatic light in terms of the Jones vectors becomes valid.

3.3.2 Jones Matrices for Linear Optical Devices

Polarizing devices include linear polarizers, phase retarders, and polarization rotators. A linear polarizer has a preferred direction, called the transmission axis of the polarizer. It transmits plane polarized light with minimum (maximum) loss when its transmission axis is oriented along (orthogonal to) the direction of oscillation of the incident light field. An ideal linear polarizer transmits light polarized parallel to its transmission axis with no loss at all, and completely blocks light if polarized perpendicular to this direction. For an angle θ between the transmission axis of the polarizer and the polarization direction of the incident light, the transmitted field and intensity are

$$E = E_0 \cos\theta, \quad I = I_0 \cos^2\theta,$$

respectively. This is the statement of *Malus Law*. Practical polarizers fail to meet these stringent requirements. The extinction ratio of a polarizer is the ratio of the maximum ($\theta = 0$) and minimum ($\theta = 90°$) intensities transmitted by the polarizer. With this definition, the extinction ratio is greater than one. Some authors prefer the reciprocal of this ratio for the extinction ratio. Two types of polarizers exist. The dichroic polarizers, such as the polaroid sheets, have low extinction ratio of the order of 10^3. A polaroid sheet has electrons free to move in response to the incident light field along only one direction. This is the direction of low transmission of the polaroid sheet. The electrons cannot absorb light polarized perpendicular to this direction. This is the transmission direction of the sheet. The other type of polarizers exploit double refraction in anisotropic crystals as described in Section 1.10.5. An anisotropic crystal gives rise to two refracted waves with orthogonal states of polarization. These are the ordinary and extraordinary waves. These waves can be physically separated, yielding a much higher extinction ratio (10^7 or so). Nicol and Glan-Thompson prisms, described in Section 1.10.6, are examples of such devices.

A phase retarder is a device which introduces a desired amount of phase difference between orthogonally polarized, co-propagating light waves. The phase retarders make use of the difference in the index of refraction (birefringence) for orthogonal states of polarization in an anisotropic medium.

3.3.2.1 Linear Polarizers

The action of a linear polarizer in transforming the state of polarization of a plane wave can be described by the matrix equation

$$\begin{bmatrix} \cos\theta' \\ \sin\theta' \end{bmatrix} = \begin{bmatrix} a_{11} & a_{12} \\ a_{21} & a_{22} \end{bmatrix} \begin{bmatrix} \cos\theta \\ \sin\theta \end{bmatrix}, \tag{3.25}$$

where the 2×2 matrix $\begin{bmatrix} a_{11} & a_{12} \\ a_{21} & a_{22} \end{bmatrix}$ represents the nature of the linear transformation performed by the polarizer. The transformation matrix $\begin{bmatrix} a_{11} & a_{12} \\ a_{21} & a_{22} \end{bmatrix}$ is real since a linear polarizer changes only the amplitude and not the phase of the light field passing through it. The elements of this matrix can be obtained in a straightforward manner. We illustrate this procedure by taking a few specific examples. Let us first consider the action of a polarizer with transmission axis oriented in the horizontal direction. Such a polarizer will transmit horizontally polarized light unchanged and in the ideal case will completely block light with vertical state of polarization. Accordingly,

$$\begin{bmatrix} a_{11} & a_{12} \\ a_{21} & a_{22} \end{bmatrix} \begin{bmatrix} 1 \\ 0 \end{bmatrix} = \begin{bmatrix} 1 \\ 0 \end{bmatrix},$$

and

$$\begin{bmatrix} a_{11} & a_{12} \\ a_{21} & a_{22} \end{bmatrix} \begin{bmatrix} 0 \\ 1 \end{bmatrix} = \begin{bmatrix} 0 \\ 0 \end{bmatrix}.$$

These equations yield

$$a_{11} = 1, \quad a_{12} = a_{21} = a_{22} = 0.$$

Therefore, the matrix representing the action of a linear polarizer with horizontal transmission axis is

$$M_{(\mathrm{H})} = \begin{bmatrix} 1 & 0 \\ 0 & 0 \end{bmatrix}. \tag{3.26a}$$

Similarly, it can be shown that the matrix

$$M_{(\mathrm{V})} = \begin{bmatrix} 0 & 0 \\ 0 & 1 \end{bmatrix} \tag{3.26b}$$

represents the action of a linear polarizer with transmission axis along the vertical direction. A little more effort shows that the matrix representing the action of a linear polarizer with transmission axis oriented at +45° to the horizontal direction has the form

$$M_{(+45°)} = \frac{1}{2}\begin{bmatrix} 1 & 1 \\ 1 & 1 \end{bmatrix}. \tag{3.26c}$$

This result can be derived by solving the following matrix equations:

$$\begin{bmatrix} a_{11} & a_{12} \\ a_{21} & a_{22} \end{bmatrix}\begin{bmatrix} \frac{1}{\sqrt{2}} \\ \frac{1}{\sqrt{2}} \end{bmatrix} = \frac{1}{\sqrt{2}}\begin{bmatrix} 1 \\ 1 \end{bmatrix},$$

$$\begin{bmatrix} a_{11} & a_{12} \\ a_{21} & a_{22} \end{bmatrix}\begin{bmatrix} \frac{1}{\sqrt{2}} \\ -\frac{1}{\sqrt{2}} \end{bmatrix} = \begin{bmatrix} 0 \\ 0 \end{bmatrix}.$$

We leave it to the reader to prove that the matrix

$$M_{(\theta)} = \begin{bmatrix} \cos^2\theta & \cos\theta\sin\theta \\ \cos\theta\sin\theta & \sin^2\theta \end{bmatrix} \tag{3.27}$$

represents the action of a linear polarizer with transmission axis oriented at an angle θ to the horizontal direction.

3.3.2.2 Phase Retarders

The phase retarders, as mentioned earlier, make use of the birefringence property of anisotropic media. The index of refraction of an appropriately cut uniaxial crystal has maximum and minimum values along orthogonal directions called the slow axis (SA) and the fast axis (FA), respectively. Figure 3.6 shows incident wave polarized at an angle θ with respect to the slow axis taken along the horizontal direction. Inside the crystal, the wave can be imagined to consist of two component waves – one polarized along the slow axis and the other along the fast axis. The wave polarized along the fast axis moves faster (inside the retarder) than the one polarized along the slow axis. The two waves, however, propagate along the same direction albeit with different wave numbers ($k = \omega/v$). This introduces a phase difference of magnitude

$$\begin{aligned}\phi_0 = \phi_y - \phi_x &= (k_2 - k_1)d \\ &= \frac{2\pi}{\lambda_v}(n_2 - n_1)d\end{aligned} \tag{3.28}$$

after traversing a thickness d inside the crystal. Here, n_1 and n_2 are the indices of refraction for light polarized along the fast and slow axes, respectively, and λ_v is the wavelength of light in a vacuum. The thickness of the phase retarder must not

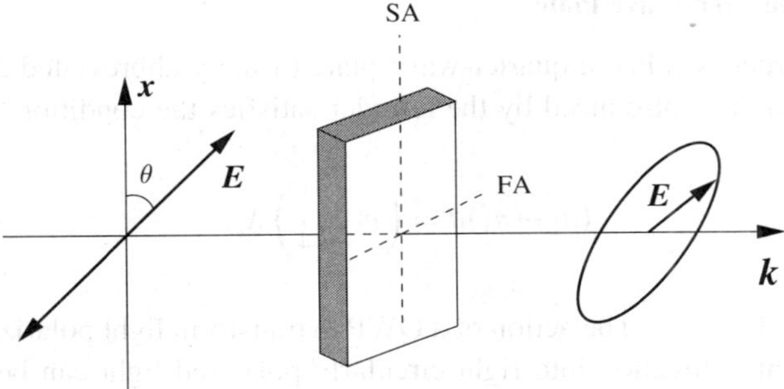

Fig. 3.6: Action of a phase retarder, SA and FA are slow and fast axes of the phase retarder.

exceed the coherence length of the light wave. The phase difference introduced by the phase retarder transforms a plane polarized wave into an elliptically polarized wave with circular and linear polarizations as special cases, depending on the thickness d of the phase retarder and angle θ between the polarization direction of the incident light and the slow axis of the phase retarder. The phase retarder changes only the phase, and not the amplitude of the wave. When the slow and fast axes of the phase retarder are oriented along the horizontal and vertical directions, respectively, the matrix representing the action of the phase retarder has non-zero elements along the diagonal only. Accordingly,

$$M(0) = \begin{bmatrix} e^{i\phi_x} & 0 \\ 0 & e^{i\phi_y} \end{bmatrix}. \tag{3.29a}$$

When the slow axis of the phase retarder makes an angle θ with the horizontal direction, the transformation matrix of the phase retarder is given by the similarity transformation

$$M(\theta) = R(-\theta)M(0)R(\theta), \tag{3.29b}$$

where

$$R(\theta) = \begin{bmatrix} \cos\theta & \sin\theta \\ -\sin\theta & \cos\theta \end{bmatrix}$$

represents the rotation matrix for the transformation of axes.

3.3.2.3 Quarter-Wave Plate

A phase retarder is called a quarter-wave plate (usually abbreviated as QWP) if the path difference introduced by the retarder satisfies the condition

$$(n_2 - n_1)d = \left(m + \frac{1}{4}\right)\lambda_v, \tag{3.30}$$

where $m = 0, 1, 2, \ldots$. The action of a QWP to transform light polarized at +45° to the horizontal direction into right circularly polarized light can be described by the matrix equation

$$\begin{aligned}\frac{1}{\sqrt{2}}\begin{bmatrix}1\\-\mathrm{i}\end{bmatrix} &= \frac{1}{\sqrt{2}}\begin{bmatrix}\mathrm{e}^{\mathrm{i}\phi_x} & 0\\0 & \mathrm{e}^{\mathrm{i}\phi_y}\end{bmatrix}\begin{bmatrix}1\\1\end{bmatrix}\\ &= \frac{1}{\sqrt{2}}\mathrm{e}^{\mathrm{i}\psi_0}\begin{bmatrix}\mathrm{e}^{\mathrm{i}(\phi_x-\psi_0)} & 0\\0 & \mathrm{e}^{\mathrm{i}(\phi_y-\psi_0)}\end{bmatrix}\begin{bmatrix}1\\1\end{bmatrix}.\end{aligned} \tag{3.31}$$

This matrix equation can be satisfied by choosing $\phi_x - \psi_0 = 0$ and $\phi_y - \psi_0 = -\pi/2$, so that

$$\phi_y - \phi_x = \frac{2\pi}{\lambda_v}(n_2 - n_1)d = -\frac{\pi}{2}.$$

This action of the QWP is described by the matrix

$$M(\mathrm{QWP})_{\mathrm{SAH}} = \mathrm{e}^{\mathrm{i}\psi_0}\begin{bmatrix}1 & 0\\0 & -\mathrm{i}\end{bmatrix}, \tag{3.31a}$$

where the subscript SAH indicates the slow axis of the QWP being horizontal ($n_1 > n_2$). Similarly, it can be shown that a QWP with its slow axis vertical ($\phi_y - \phi_x = +\pi/2$) converts +45°-polarized light into left circularly polarized light, and this action of the QWP is represented by the matrix

$$M(\mathrm{QWP})_{\mathrm{SAV}} = \mathrm{e}^{\mathrm{i}\psi_0}\begin{bmatrix}1 & 0\\0 & +\mathrm{i}\end{bmatrix}, \tag{3.31b}$$

where the subscript SAV stands for the slow axis being vertical. Notice, there is an arbitrariness to the extent of a constant phase ψ_0 in defining these matrices. This constant phase is usually ignored.

3.3.2.4 Half-Wave Plate

A phase retarder acts as a half-wave plate (HWP) if it introduces a path difference of

$$(n_2 - n_1)d = \left(m + \frac{1}{2}\right)\lambda_v$$

between the co-propagating waves with orthogonal states of polarization, where $m = 0, 1, 2, \ldots$. The action of a HWP with the slow axis horizontal or vertical is described by the matrix

$$M = e^{i\psi_0}\begin{bmatrix} 1 & 0 \\ 0 & -1 \end{bmatrix}. \tag{3.31c}$$

It can be seen that a HWP simply rotates the plane of polarization of linearly polarized light. This is particularly useful in changing the state of polarization of laser light. Strictly speaking, a phase retarder of fixed thickness acts as a QWP or a HWP for the selected wavelength only. Variable thickness phase retarders in the form of compensators can be used at different wavelengths. In Babinet's compensator, a quartz wedge is slid against another wedge of the same material to change the thickness of the phase retarder.

The state of polarization of a light wave can be modified by introducing in its path any number of polarization-changing elements in succession. The final state of polarization $\begin{bmatrix} E'_x \\ E'_y \end{bmatrix}$ of the wave is related to its initial state $\begin{bmatrix} E_x \\ E_y \end{bmatrix}$ by the matrix equation

$$\begin{bmatrix} E'_x \\ E'_y \end{bmatrix} = (M_N M_{N-1} \cdots M_2 M_1)\begin{bmatrix} E_x \\ E_y \end{bmatrix}, \tag{3.32}$$

where M_1 and M_N are, respectively, the matrices representing the actions of the first and last optical elements that the wave encounters in its path. The transformation matrices (Eqs 3.27 and 3.29) are unitary, so that

$$MM^\dagger = \begin{bmatrix} M_{11} & M_{12} \\ M_{21} & M_{22} \end{bmatrix}\begin{bmatrix} M_{11}^* & M_{21}^* \\ M_{12}^* & M_{22}^* \end{bmatrix} = \begin{bmatrix} 1 & 0 \\ 0 & 1 \end{bmatrix},$$

where matrix $M^\dagger$ is the Hermitian conjugate of matrix M, representing the action of a linear polarizer or that of a phase retarder.

3.4 THE STOKES PARAMETERS

Jones vectors discussed in Section 3.3 provide an adequate description of the states of polarization of completely polarized light. Unpolarized light, however, cannot be characterized in terms of the Jones vectors. Completely polarized light with no component of unpolarized light is an idealization similar to the perfectly monochromatic light possessing absolutely no frequency spread. In fact, a monochromatic wave is completely polarized. Light from practical sources, being either unpolarized or partially polarized, cannot be described by the Jones vectors. Furthermore, light fields (electric fields in the present case) in terms of which the Jones vectors are defined are not directly observable. It may be argued that a description of the state of polarization of light in terms of measurable quantities such as the light irradiance should be preferred. However, such a description cannot account for interference effects associated with coherent light. Therefore, the descriptions of the states of polarization in terms of the field and intensity of light may complement each other to treat real light.

At a given point in space, the instantaneous Stokes parameters of a plane wave propagating in the z-direction are defined as

$$S_0(t) = \left(\frac{1}{2}\epsilon_0 nc\right)\left[|E_x(t)|^2 + |E_y(t)|^2\right], \tag{3.33a}$$

$$S_1(t) = \left(\frac{1}{2}\epsilon_0 nc\right)\left[|E_x(t)|^2 - |E_y(t)|^2\right], \tag{3.33b}$$

$$\begin{aligned} S_2(t) &= \left(\frac{1}{2}\epsilon_0 nc\right)\left[\frac{1}{2}\{|E_x(t) + E_y(t)|^2 - |E_x(t) - E_y(t)|^2\}\right] \\ &= \left(\frac{1}{2}\epsilon_0 nc\right)\left[E_x(t)E_y^*(t) + E_x^*(t)E_y(t)\right], \end{aligned} \tag{3.33c}$$

$$\begin{aligned} S_3(t) &= \left(\frac{1}{2}\epsilon_0 nc\right)\left[\frac{1}{2}\{|E_x(t) + \mathrm{i}E_y(t)|^2 - |E_x(t) - \mathrm{i}E_y(t)|^2\}\right] \\ &= \left(\frac{1}{2}\epsilon_0 nc\right)\left[-iE_x(t)E_y^*(t) + \mathrm{i}E_x^*(t)E_y(t)\right], \end{aligned} \tag{3.33d}$$

where $E_x(t)$ and $E_y(t)$ are the complex instantaneous Cartesian components of the electric field. The Stokes parameters S_0, S_1, S_2, S_3 have the dimensions of irradiance. However, the prefactors $(\frac{1}{2}\epsilon_0 nc)$ are usually not explicitly written in these definitions. We shall also not carry these factors any further. With Eqs (3.3), the Stokes parameters can be recast as below:

$$S_0(t) = \varepsilon_x^2(t) + \varepsilon_y^2(t), \tag{3.34a}$$

$$S_1(t) = \varepsilon_x^2(t) - \varepsilon_y^2(t), \tag{3.34b}$$

$$S_2(t) = 2\varepsilon_x(t)\varepsilon_y(t)\cos\phi_0(t), \tag{3.34c}$$

$$\begin{aligned} S_3(t) &= -2\varepsilon_x(t)\varepsilon_y(t)\sin\phi_0(t) \\ &= 2\varepsilon_x(t)\varepsilon_y(t)\sin(-\phi_0(t)), \end{aligned} \tag{3.34d}$$

where $\phi_0(t) = \phi_y(t) - \phi_x(t)$. As discussed earlier, negative values of $\phi_0(t)$ in the interval $-\pi/2 \leq \phi_0 \leq 0$ correspond to right elliptical polarization and positive values of ϕ_0 $(0 \leq \phi_0 \leq \pi/2)$ refer to left elliptical polarization. Therefore $S_3(t)$ is positive for right elliptically polarized light and negative for left elliptically polarized light. The Stokes column matrix $\begin{bmatrix} S_0 \\ S_1 \\ S_2 \\ S_3 \end{bmatrix}$, also called the Stokes vector, carries complete information on the intensity and state of polarization of a plane wave. The Stokes parameters may be normalized by dividing each parameter by S_0, which amounts to considering a light beam of unit irradiance.

3.4.1 Monochromatic Light

For monochromatic light, the amplitude and phase factors in Eqs (3.34) are time independent and the Stokes parameters satisfy the condition

$$S_0^2 = S_1^2 + S_2^2 + S_3^2. \tag{3.35}$$

Consequently for monochromatic light, only three of the four Stokes parameters are independent. Normalized Stokes parameters and Jones vectors for different states of polarization are given in Table 3.2.

The Stokes parameters can be expressed in terms of the observables of a light beam. The parameter S_0 measures intensity of the beam in units of $(\frac{1}{2}\epsilon_0 nc)$. The parameter S_1 gives the extent by which the intensity of horizontal polarization exceeds the intensity of vertical polarization in the beam. The parameter S_2 determines the excess of the intensity of +45°-polarization over the intensity of −45°-polarization, and finally the parameter S_3 estimates the excess of the intensity of right circularly polarized light over the intensity of left circularly polarized light. All these parameters can be easily measured. The first three parameters (S_0, S_1, S_2) can be obtained by intensity measurement with a detector such as a photodiode in conjunction with a linear polarizer, used in different orientations. Accordingly, we can write

$$S_0 = I(0°, 0°) + I(90°, 0°), \tag{3.36a}$$

$$S_1 = I(0°, 0°) - I(90°, 0°), \tag{3.36b}$$

$$S_2 = I(45°, 0°) - I(-45°, 0°), \tag{3.36c}$$

Table 3.2. The Jones and Stokes vectors for different states of polarization.

State of polarization	Jones vector	Stokes vector
Horizontal polarization	$\begin{bmatrix}1\\0\end{bmatrix}$	$\begin{bmatrix}1\\1\\0\\0\end{bmatrix}$
Vertical polarization	$\begin{bmatrix}0\\1\end{bmatrix}$	$\begin{bmatrix}1\\-1\\0\\0\end{bmatrix}$
±45° polarization	$\frac{1}{\sqrt{2}}\begin{bmatrix}1\\\pm1\end{bmatrix}$	$\begin{bmatrix}1\\0\\\pm1\\0\end{bmatrix}$
General state of linear polarization	$\begin{bmatrix}\cos\theta\\\sin\theta\end{bmatrix}$	$\begin{bmatrix}1\\\cos 2\theta\\\sin 2\theta\\0\end{bmatrix}$
Right circular polarization	$\frac{1}{\sqrt{2}}\begin{bmatrix}1\\-i\end{bmatrix}$	$\begin{bmatrix}1\\0\\0\\1\end{bmatrix}$
Left circular polarization	$\frac{1}{\sqrt{2}}\begin{bmatrix}1\\+i\end{bmatrix}$	$\begin{bmatrix}1\\0\\0\\-1\end{bmatrix}$

where $I(\theta, \phi)$ is the measured intensity of the beam when the transmission axis of the polarizer makes an angle θ with the horizontal direction, and $\phi = \phi_y - \phi_x$ is the phase retardation introduced by the phase retarder. Of course, in the above measurements, the phase retarder is absent. The measurement of the fourth Stokes parameter requires a linear polarizer and a quarter wave plate:

$$S_3 = I(45°, -90°) - I(45°, 90°). \tag{3.36d}$$

3.4.2 Quasi-monochromatic Light

Monochromatic light is characterized by constant values of ε_x, ε_y, and ϕ_0. For polychromatic and quasi-monochromatic light, these quantities, however, change with time. For changing amplitude and phase factors, the concept of the polarization ellipse characterizing the state of polarization of light may no longer be valid because the ellipticity and orientation of the polarization ellipse may fluctuate randomly. However, the fluctuations in the amplitude and phase of quasi-monochromatic light with sufficiently narrow spectral bandwidth are relatively slow, but not entirely insignificant on the time scale needed to make a measurement. It is then necessary to take an ensemble average which under certain conditions (Section 2.3.1) can be replaced by the time average. The Stokes parameters for quasi-monochromatic light can be obtained by replacing instantaneous intensities in Eqs (3.33) by their time averaged values. Accordingly, for quasi-monochromatic light,

$$\begin{aligned} S_0 &= \langle E_x(t)E_x^*(t)\rangle + \langle E_y(t)E_y^*(t)\rangle \\ &= \langle \varepsilon_x^2(t)\rangle + \langle \varepsilon_y^2(t)\rangle, \end{aligned} \tag{3.37a}$$

$$\begin{aligned} S_1 &= \langle E_x(t)E_x^*(t)\rangle - \langle E_y(t)E_y^*(t)\rangle \\ &= \langle \varepsilon_x^2(t)\rangle - \langle \varepsilon_y^2(t)\rangle, \end{aligned} \tag{3.37b}$$

$$\begin{aligned} S_2 &= \langle E_x(t)E_y^*(t)\rangle + \langle E_x^*(t)E_y(t)\rangle \\ &= 2\langle \varepsilon_x(t)\varepsilon_y(t)\cos\phi_0(t)\rangle, \end{aligned} \tag{3.37c}$$

$$\begin{aligned} S_3 &= \langle -\mathrm{i}E_x(t)E_y^*(t) + \mathrm{i}E_x^*(t)E_y(t)\rangle \\ &= 2\langle \varepsilon_x(t)\varepsilon_y(t)\sin(-\phi_0(t)\rangle. \end{aligned} \tag{3.37d}$$

For quasi-monochromatic light, the time averaged Stokes parameters are not expected to change appreciably, and one may still be able to define the state of polarization of quasi- monochromatic light. Obviously quasi-monochromatic light is not completely polarized because that would require its polarization ellipse to be absolutely stationary. At the same time quasi-monochromatic light is not completely unpolarized either because slow changes in the orientation and ellipticity may not wash away the polarization ellipse altogether. Such light is called partially polarized light. The concept of partially polarized light is similar to the concept of partially coherent light discussed in Chapter 2. Schwarz's inequality (see footnote 5 in Chapter 2) requires the Stokes parameters for partially polarized light to satisfy the condition

$$S_0^2 \geq S_1^2 + S_2^2 + S_3^2, \tag{3.38}$$

where the equality sign holds for completely polarized light and the greater than sign is applicable to partially polarized light.

3.4.3 Completely Unpolarized Light

The concept of polarization ellipse is not applicable to completely unpolarized light because its amplitude and phase undergo rapid changes with time. Furthermore, the intensity of completely unpolarized light is not sensitive to the orientation of a linear polarizer or a phase retarder kept in its path. This allows us to draw the following conclusions:

$$\langle \varepsilon_x^2(t)\rangle = \langle \varepsilon_y^2(t)\rangle,$$
$$\langle \cos\phi_0(t)\rangle = 0,$$
$$\langle \sin\phi_0(t)\rangle = 0.$$

Therefore, for completely unpolarized light,

$$\begin{aligned}\langle E_x(t)E_x^*(t)\rangle + \langle E_y(t)E_y^*(t)\rangle &= S_0,\\ \langle E_x(t)E_x^*(t)\rangle - \langle E_y(t)E_y^*(t)\rangle &= 0,\\ \langle E_x(t)E_y^*(t)\rangle &= -\langle E_x^*(t)E_y(t)\rangle,\end{aligned}$$

giving

$$\langle E_x(t)E_x^*(t)\rangle = \langle E_y(t)E_y^*(t)\rangle = \frac{S_0}{2}, \tag{3.39a}$$
$$\langle E_x(t)E_y^*(t)\rangle = \langle E_x^*(t)E_y(t)\rangle = 0. \tag{3.39b}$$

The completely unpolarized light is characterized by its intensity alone with the Stokes vector

$$\begin{bmatrix} S_0 \\ S_1 \\ S_2 \\ S_3 \end{bmatrix}_{\text{unpol}} = \begin{bmatrix} S_0 \\ 0 \\ 0 \\ 0 \end{bmatrix}. \tag{3.40}$$

The inequality Eq. (3.38) takes the form

$$S_0^2 = 2\langle \varepsilon_x^2(t)\rangle = 2\langle \varepsilon_y^2(t)\rangle \geq 0$$

for completely unpolarized light. Equation (3.39b) implies that the orthogonal components of unpolarized light are completely uncorrelated. Accordingly, orthogonal components of completely unpolarized if brought to the same state of polarization, fail to interfere. This is one of the laws enunciated by Fresnel and Arago on interference of light waves.

We observe that unlike the Jones vectors, the Stokes vectors representing the horizontal and vertical polarization states add up to the Stokes vector of unpolarized light of twice the intensity of either state of polarization, i.e.,

$$\begin{bmatrix} 1 \\ 1 \\ 0 \\ 0 \end{bmatrix} + \begin{bmatrix} 1 \\ -1 \\ 0 \\ 0 \end{bmatrix} = \begin{bmatrix} 2 \\ 0 \\ 0 \\ 0 \end{bmatrix} = 2 \begin{bmatrix} 1 \\ 0 \\ 0 \\ 0 \end{bmatrix} . \tag{3.41}$$

This, of course, requires that the fields representing the horizontal and vertical polarizations are mutually incoherent since we have added their intensities and not the amplitudes. The above statement applies to mutually incoherent right and left circularly polarized light fields as well. So that

$$\begin{bmatrix} 1 \\ 0 \\ 0 \\ 1 \end{bmatrix} + \begin{bmatrix} 1 \\ 0 \\ 0 \\ -1 \end{bmatrix} = 2 \begin{bmatrix} 1 \\ 0 \\ 0 \\ 0 \end{bmatrix} .$$

These results can be generalized. An equal mixture of orthogonal but mutually incoherent polarization states produces unpolarized light in the Stokes representation. The converse of this statement also holds. The Stokes parameters permit the representation of unpolarized light in terms of an infinite set of orthogonal polarization states of mutually incoherent light fields. This is in contrast to the Jones scheme, where no combination of Jones vectors can describe unpolarized light.

3.4.4 Mixture of Mutually Incoherent Light Fields

We have seen how the addition of Stokes vectors representing orthogonal but mutually incoherent light fields gives rise to unpolarized light. The addition of Stokes vectors is a general feature not restricted to orthogonal states of polarization only. The Stokes parameters of a mixture of two or more mutually incoherent light fields can be shown to be given by the sum of the corresponding Stokes parameters of the individual light fields, i.e.,

$$\begin{aligned} S_0 &= S_0^{(1)} + S_0^{(2)} + \cdots , \\ S_1 &= S_1^{(1)} + S_1^{(2)} + \cdots , \\ S_2 &= S_2^{(1)} + S_2^{(2)} + \cdots , \\ S_3 &= S_3^{(1)} + S_3^{(2)} + \cdots . \end{aligned} \tag{3.42}$$

These results can be obtained in a straightforward manner by extending Eqs (3.33) to include a mixture of mutually incoherent light fields satisfying the condition

$$\langle E^{(i)}(t)E^{(j)}(t)\rangle = 0.$$

Partially polarized light can be treated as an incoherent mixture of completely polarized and completely unpolarized light fields described by the Stokes vector $\begin{bmatrix} (\mathrm{p}) \\ S_0 \\ S_1 \\ S_2 \\ S_3 \end{bmatrix}$ and $\begin{bmatrix} (\mathrm{u}) \\ S_0' \\ 0 \\ 0 \\ 0 \end{bmatrix}$, respectively, i.e.,

$$\begin{bmatrix} S_0 + S_0' \\ S_1 \\ S_2 \\ S_3 \end{bmatrix} = \begin{bmatrix} (\mathrm{p}) \\ S_0 \\ S_1 \\ S_2 \\ S_3 \end{bmatrix} \begin{matrix} \\ + \\ + \\ + \\ + \end{matrix} \begin{bmatrix} (\mathrm{u}) \\ S_0' \\ 0 \\ 0 \\ 0 \end{bmatrix}, \tag{3.43}$$

where the superscripts (p) and (u) refer to completely polarized and completely unpolarized components, respectively. Equation (3.43) can be expressed in an equivalent form

$$\begin{bmatrix} S_0 \\ S_1 \\ S_2 \\ S_3 \end{bmatrix} = (1-P)\begin{bmatrix} S_0 \\ 0 \\ 0 \\ 0 \end{bmatrix} + \begin{bmatrix} PS_0 \\ S_1 \\ S_2 \\ S_3 \end{bmatrix}, \tag{3.44}$$

where P represents the *degree of polarization* satisfying the condition

$$0 \le P \le 1. \tag{3.45}$$

Light is completely polarized for $P = 1$, completely unpolarized for $P = 0$, and partially polarized for intermediate values of P. The degree of polarization of light is the ratio of the intensity of the completely polarized light to its total intensity, i.e.,

$$P = \frac{S_0^{(\mathrm{p})}}{S_0^{(\mathrm{p})} + S_0^{(\mathrm{u})}} = \frac{(S_1^2 + S_2^2 + S_3^2)^{1/2}}{S_0}. \tag{3.46}$$

Expression (3.44) is not the only possible decomposition of partially polarized light. As for the completely unpolarized light, infinite equivalent decompositions of partially polarized light in terms of orthogonal but mutually incoherent polarization states exist,

$$\begin{bmatrix} S_0 \\ S_1 \\ S_2 \\ S_3 \end{bmatrix} = \frac{1+P}{2P}\begin{bmatrix} PS_0 \\ S_1 \\ S_2 \\ S_3 \end{bmatrix} + \frac{1-P}{2P}\begin{bmatrix} PS_0 \\ -S_1 \\ -S_2 \\ -S_3 \end{bmatrix}. \tag{3.47}$$

We note in passing that Stokes parameters cannot describe superposition of mutually coherent light fields.

3.4.5 Geometrical Interpretation of Stokes Parameters

The Stokes parameters of completely polarized light can be expressed in a form that makes S_1, S_2, S_3 appear as the Cartesian components of S_0, treated as a polar vector (Fig. 3.7).

The parameter S_2 can be expressed as

$$S_2 = 2\varepsilon_x\varepsilon_y \cos\phi_0 = (\varepsilon_x^2 - \varepsilon_y^2)\frac{2\varepsilon_x\varepsilon_y}{\varepsilon_x^2 - \varepsilon_y^2}\cos\phi_0 = S_1 \tan 2\psi, \tag{3.48a}$$

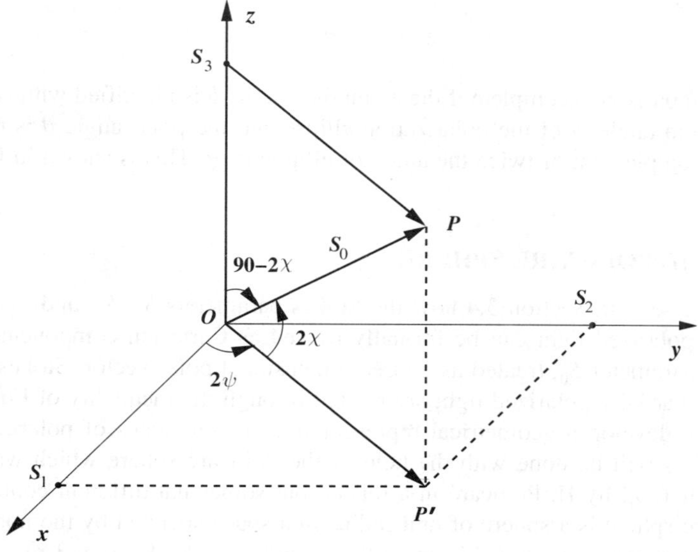

Fig. 3.7: Stokes parameters S_1, S_2, S_3 as Cartesian components of Stokes parameter S_0 for perfectly polarized light.

where $\tan 2\psi$ has already been defined (Eq. 3.9). Similarly, the parameter S_3 may be written as

$$S_3 = 2\varepsilon_x\varepsilon_y \sin(-\phi_0) = 2S_0 \frac{\varepsilon_x}{\sqrt{\varepsilon_x^2+\varepsilon_y^2}} \frac{\varepsilon_y}{\sqrt{\varepsilon_x^2+\varepsilon_y^2}} \sin(-\phi_0)$$

$$= S_0 \sin 2\alpha \sin(-\phi_0) = S_0 \sin 2\chi. \tag{3.48b}$$

The angles α and χ have been defined in Eq. (3.16). Substituting Eqs (3.48) into Eq. (3.35) and solving for S_1 and S_2 gives

$$S_1 = S_0 \cos 2\chi \cos 2\psi = S_0 \sin(90 - 2\chi) \cos 2\psi, \tag{3.49a}$$

$$S_2 = S_0 \cos 2\chi \sin 2\psi = S_0 \sin(90 - 2\chi) \sin 2\psi, \tag{3.49b}$$

$$S_3 = S_0 \sin 2\chi = S_0 \cos(90 - 2\chi). \tag{3.49c}$$

The above equations bear close resemblance to the relationships among the Cartesian and spherical polar components of the position vector:

$$x = r \sin\theta \cos\phi,$$

$$y = r \sin\theta \sin\phi,$$

$$z = r\cos\theta.$$

This comparison is complete if the azimuthal angle ϕ is identified with twice the inclination angle ψ of the polarization ellipse and the polar angle θ is replaced by the complement of twice the angle of ellipticity χ. This is shown in Fig. 3.7.

3.5 THE POINCARÉ SPHERE

We have seen in Section 3.4 how the Stokes parameters S_1, S_2, and S_3 of completely polarized light can be formally treated as Cartesian components of the Stokes parameter S_0, treated as a three-dimensional polar vector. Stokes parameters of partially polarized light are related through the inequality of Eq. (3.38). We now develop a geometrical representation for the states of polarization of light. This will be done with the help of the Poincaré sphere which was introduced in 1892 by H. Poincaré in a related but somewhat different context. The Poincaré sphere is a sphere of unit radius in a space spanned by the normalized Stokes parameters $\sigma_1 = S_1/S_0$, $\sigma_2 = S_2/S_0$, and $\sigma_3 = S_3/S_0$ (Fig. 3.8).

It follows from the construction that each point on the surface of the Poincaré sphere represents a unique state of polarization (S_1, S_2, S_3) and vice versa. A point

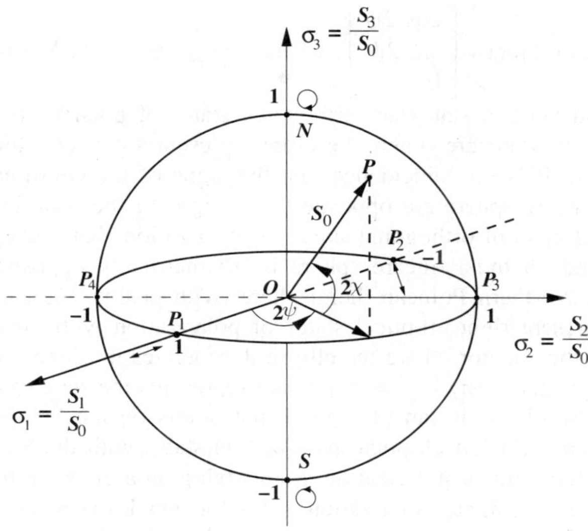

Fig. 3.8: Representation of states of polarization of perfectly polarized light on the Poincaré sphere of unit radius, N is north pole, S is south pole.

such as P on the Poincaré sphere can be located in terms of the angles of longitude (2ψ) and latitude (2χ), where angle ψ gives the orientation of the polarization ellipse with respect to the reference axes and χ determines the ellipticity of the polarization ellipse (Fig. 3.3e) and the sense of rotation of the electric vector. A point on the Poincaré sphere with coordinates $(\sigma_1, \sigma_2, \sigma_3)$ represents the most general (elliptical) state of polarization of completely polarized light. Points on the equator (zero latitude) with $\chi = 0$ and hence $\sigma_3 = 0$ represent all possible states of linearly polarized light.

The horizontal state of polarization is represented by point P_1 with coordinates $\begin{bmatrix} 1 \\ 0 \\ 0 \end{bmatrix}$ on the Poincaré sphere. This is the point of intersection of the increasing direction of the S_1/S_0 axis with the Poincaré sphere. Vertical polarization corresponds to point P_2 on the Poincaré sphere with coordinates $\begin{bmatrix} -1 \\ 0 \\ 0 \end{bmatrix}$. Points P_3 and P_4 represent $\pm 45°$-polarization states, respectively. The remaining states of linear polarization are represented by points on the equator of the Poincaré sphere with coordinates $\begin{bmatrix} \cos 2\psi \\ \sin 2\psi \\ 0 \end{bmatrix}$, where $-\pi \leq 2\psi \leq +\pi$. We recall that the horizontal and vertical states are orthogonal states of polarization. The points P_1 and P_2 on the Poincaré sphere therefore represent a pair of orthogonal states of polarization. It is no coincidence that the signs of the coordinates of point P_2 on the Poincaré sphere are opposite to the signs of the coordinates of point P_1. In fact, all pairs of orthogonal states of polarization share this property and are represented on the Poincaré sphere by diametrically opposite points. All points on the Northern Poincaré hemisphere (with positive S_3 and hence negative ϕ_0) represent right elliptical states of polarization with the exception of the points on the equator where the ellipse degenerates into lines and the North pole ($\phi_0 = -\pi/2$, $\alpha = \pi/4$, $\varepsilon_x = \varepsilon_y$) which represents the state of right circular polarization. Similarly, it can be argued that points on the Southern Poincaré hemisphere represent left elliptical polarization states with the South pole representing the left circular polarization. Points lying on a given latitude (constant 2χ) represent all elliptical polarization states for which the polarization ellipse maintains its shape but the orientation of its major axis with respect to the horizontal direction takes all possible values. Putting it differently, a given latitude represents all polarization states generated by the rotation of the polarization ellipse of a definite ellipticity about the direction of propagation of the wave. A similar statement can be made for points lying on a given longitude (meridian). In this case the orientation of the polarization ellipse with respect to the horizontal direction does not change, but the aspect ratio $(\varepsilon_y/\varepsilon_x)$ goes through all values between zero and infinity. Partially polarized light can be represented by a point inside the Poincaré sphere such that the distance $\left(\frac{S_1^2+S_2^2+S_3^2}{S_0^2}\right)^{1/2}$ of the point from the center of the Poincaré sphere gives the degree of polarization P. The center of the Poincaré sphere represents completely unpolarized light. In conclusion, it can be said that all possible states of polarization of light can be envisioned on or within the surface of the Poincaré sphere.

3.6 MUELLER MATRICES

We have described polarization states of completely or partially polarized light in terms of the Stokes vectors. The state of polarization of light can be changed by interposing polarizing elements in its path. The action of a polarizing element can be described by the matrix equation

$$\begin{bmatrix} S_0' \\ S_1' \\ S_2' \\ S_3' \end{bmatrix} = \begin{bmatrix} M_{11} & M_{12} & M_{13} & M_{14} \\ M_{21} & M_{22} & M_{23} & M_{24} \\ M_{31} & M_{32} & M_{33} & M_{34} \\ M_{41} & M_{42} & M_{43} & M_{44} \end{bmatrix} \begin{bmatrix} S_0 \\ S_1 \\ S_2 \\ S_3 \end{bmatrix}, \tag{3.50}$$

where $\begin{bmatrix} S_0 \\ S_1 \\ S_2 \\ S_3 \end{bmatrix}$ and $\begin{bmatrix} S'_0 \\ S'_1 \\ S'_2 \\ S'_3 \end{bmatrix}$ are the initial and final Stokes vectors, respectively, of completely or partially polarized light. The 4×4 transformation matrix M is called the Mueller matrix. We now develop Mueller matrices for linear polarizers and phase retarders.

3.6.1 Linear Polarizer

Figure 3.9 shows an ideal linear polarizer LP with transmission axis making an angle θ with the horizontal direction.

Matrix (3.27) can be used to express the components of the field emerging from the polarizer in terms of the field components of the incident field:

$$E'_x = (\cos^2\theta)E_x + (\cos\theta\sin\theta)E_y,$$
$$E'_y = (\cos\theta\sin\theta)E_x + (\sin^2\theta)E_y.$$

On substituting these expressions in Eqs (3.33), following relationships among the Stokes parameters of the emergent and incident light fields can be obtained:

$$S'_0 = E'_x E'^*_x + E'_y E'^*_y = \frac{1}{2}[S_0 + S_1\cos 2\theta + S_2\sin 2\theta],$$
$$S'_1 = E'_x E'^*_x - E'_y E'^*_y = \frac{1}{2}\left[S_0\cos 2\theta + S_1\cos^2 2\theta + S_2\cos 2\theta\sin 2\theta\right],$$
$$S'_2 = E'_x E'^*_y + E'^*_x E'_y = \frac{1}{2}\left[S_0\sin 2\theta + S_1\cos 2\theta\sin 2\theta + S_2\sin^2(2\theta)\right],$$
$$S'_3 = \mathrm{i}\left[-E'_x E'^*_y + E'^*_x E'_y\right] = 0.$$

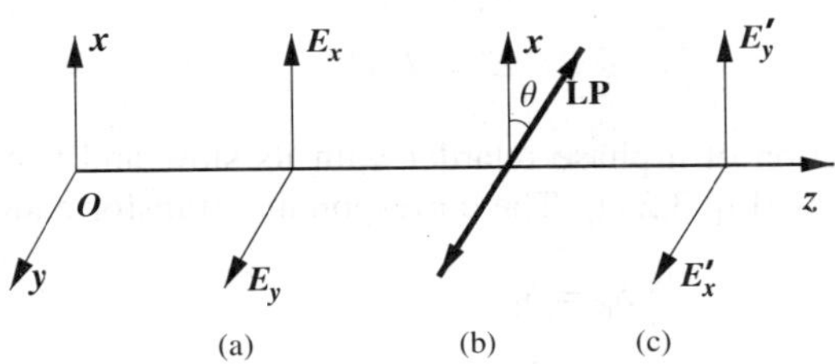

Fig. 3.9: Action of a linear polarizer (LP); (a) field components of incident light, (b) linear polarizer with transmission axis making an angle θ with the horizontal direction, (c) field components of emergent light.

Expressing these results in the matrix form, we have

$$\begin{bmatrix} S_0' \\ S_1' \\ S_2' \\ S_3' \end{bmatrix} = M(\theta) \begin{bmatrix} S_0 \\ S_1 \\ S_2 \\ S_3 \end{bmatrix}, \tag{3.51}$$

where the matrix

$$M(\theta) = \frac{1}{2} \begin{bmatrix} 1 & \cos 2\theta & \sin 2\theta & 0 \\ \cos 2\theta & \cos^2 2\theta & \cos 2\theta \sin 2\theta & 0 \\ \sin 2\theta & \cos 2\theta \sin 2\theta & \sin^2 2\theta & 0 \\ 0 & 0 & 0 & 0 \end{bmatrix} \tag{3.52a}$$

is the Mueller matrix representing the action of an ideal linear polarizer oriented at an angle θ with respect to the horizontal direction. Mueller matrices for some specific values of angle θ are given below.

$$M(0^\circ) = \frac{1}{2} \begin{bmatrix} 1 & 1 & 0 & 0 \\ 1 & 1 & 0 & 0 \\ 0 & 0 & 0 & 0 \\ 0 & 0 & 0 & 0 \end{bmatrix}, \tag{3.52b}$$

$$M(90^\circ) = \frac{1}{2} \begin{bmatrix} 1 & -1 & 0 & 0 \\ -1 & 1 & 0 & 0 \\ 0 & 0 & 0 & 0 \\ 0 & 0 & 0 & 0 \end{bmatrix}. \tag{3.52c}$$

3.6.2 Phase Retarder

The transformation

$$E_x' = E_x e^{i\phi_x},$$
$$E_y' = E_y e^{i\phi_y}$$

describes the action of a phase retarder with its slow and fast axes coinciding with the x, y axes (Eq. 3.29a). The corresponding transformation

$$\begin{aligned} S_0' &= S_0, \\ S_1' &= S_1, \\ S_2' &= S_2 \cos\phi_0 - S_3 \sin\phi_0, \\ S_3' &= S_2 \sin\phi_0 + S_3 \cos\phi_0, \end{aligned} \tag{3.53}$$

of the Stokes parameters yields

$$M_{(\mathrm{PR})} = \begin{bmatrix} 1 & 0 & 0 & 0 \\ 0 & 1 & 0 & 0 \\ 0 & 0 & \cos\phi_0 & -\sin\phi_0 \\ 0 & 0 & \sin\phi_0 & \cos\phi_0 \end{bmatrix} \tag{3.54a}$$

as the Mueller matrix for the phase retarder. The Mueller matrices for the quarter ($\phi_0 = \pm 90°$) and half ($\phi_0 = \pm 180°$) wave plates are

$$M_{(\mathrm{QWP})} = \begin{bmatrix} 1 & 0 & 0 & 0 \\ 0 & 1 & 0 & 0 \\ 0 & 0 & 0 & \mp 1 \\ 0 & 0 & \pm 1 & 0 \end{bmatrix}, \tag{3.54b}$$

$$M_{(\mathrm{HWP})} = \begin{bmatrix} 1 & 0 & 0 & 0 \\ 0 & 1 & 0 & 0 \\ 0 & 0 & -1 & 0 \\ 0 & 0 & 0 & -1 \end{bmatrix}, \tag{3.54c}$$

respectively.

3.7 THE COHERENCY MATRIX

There is yet another scheme to describe the states of polarization of light, completely or partially polarized. This scheme is based on Wolf's 2×2 coherency matrix

$$J = \begin{bmatrix} J_{xx} & J_{xy} \\ J_{yx} & J_{yy} \end{bmatrix}. \tag{3.55}$$

Following Born and Wolf, the elements of the coherency matrix defined in terms of the time averaged field products are

$$J_{xx} = \langle E_x(t) E_x^*(t) \rangle, \tag{3.56a}$$

$$J_{xy} = \langle E_x(t) E_y^*(t) \rangle, \tag{3.56b}$$

$$J_{yx} = \langle E_y(t) E_x^*(t) \rangle, \tag{3.56c}$$

$$J_{yy} = \langle E_y(t) E_y^*(t) \rangle. \tag{3.56d}$$

A comparison of Eqs (3.37) and (3.56) gives

$$J_{xx} = \frac{1}{2}(S_0 + S_1), \tag{3.57a}$$

$$J_{xy} = \frac{1}{2}(S_2 - iS_3), \tag{3.57b}$$

$$J_{yx} = \frac{1}{2}(S_2 + iS_3), \tag{3.57c}$$

$$J_{yy} = \frac{1}{2}(S_0 - S_1). \tag{3.57d}$$

For horizontally polarized light, $J_{xx} = S_0$, $J_{xy} = 0$, $J_{yx} = 0$, $J_{yy} = 0$, so that the coherency matrix for the horizontally polarized light of unit irradiance takes the form

$$J_{(\mathrm{H})} = \begin{bmatrix} 1 & 0 \\ 0 & 0 \end{bmatrix}. \tag{3.58a}$$

The coherency matrices for some other states of polarization are given below:

$$J_{(\pm 45°)} = \frac{1}{2}\begin{bmatrix} 1 & \pm 1 \\ \pm 1 & 1 \end{bmatrix}, \tag{3.58b}$$

$$J_{(\mathrm{V})} = \begin{bmatrix} 0 & 0 \\ 0 & 1 \end{bmatrix}, \tag{3.58c}$$

$$J_{(\mathrm{RCP})} = \frac{1}{2}\begin{bmatrix} 1 & \mathrm{i} \\ -\mathrm{i} & 1 \end{bmatrix}, \tag{3.58d}$$

$$J_{(\mathrm{LCP})} = \frac{1}{2}\begin{bmatrix} 1 & -\mathrm{i} \\ \mathrm{i} & 1 \end{bmatrix}. \tag{3.58e}$$

For completely unpolarized light with

$$|E_x|^2 = |E_y|^2 = S_0/2, \quad S_1 = S_2 = S_3 = 0,$$

the coherency matrix for unit light irradiance is

$$J_{(\mathrm{un})} = \frac{1}{2}\begin{bmatrix} 1 & 0 \\ 0 & 1 \end{bmatrix}. \tag{3.58f}$$

The coherency matrix approach is capable of describing the states of polarization of partially polarized light and of light which may be a mixture of incoherent light fields.

3.8 PANCHARATNAM THEOREM

During his investigations on how interfering beams with non-orthogonal states of polarization can have the same phase, Pancharatnam at the age of 22 proved a remarkable theorem called the Pancharatnam theorem [3.8]. If the state of polarization of a light beam is changed in a cyclic manner so that at the end of the cycle the light beam is once again in its initial state of polarization, then according to this theorem, the light wave may pick up an additional phase during the cycle which is not accounted for by the path differences, if any, involved in the process. This phase called Pancharatnam–Berry phase is purely geometrical in nature. The actual change in the phase depends on the intermediate states of polarization that the light beam is made to go through. Pancharatnam theorem can be best illustrated with reference to the Poincaré sphere (Fig. 3.10). We recall that each point on the surface of the Poincaré sphere represents a unique state of polarization of completely polarized light. Consider a closed path C such as the path $ABDA$ traced on the surface of the Poincaré sphere. The light beam returns to its original state of polarization represented by point A after undergoing changes in its polarization indicated by the path. On return to the initial state of polarization, the phase of the light wave changes by an amount equal to half the solid angle subtended by the closed path (the spherical triangle ABD in the present example) at the center of the Poincaré sphere. If the cyclic changes are made along a path that subtends zero solid angle at the center, the light beam undergoes no phase change. The phase change predicted by Pancharatnam has been verified by Pancharatnam himself and by others. For more details, the reader is referred to Fundamentals of Polarized light by Brosseau [3.3].

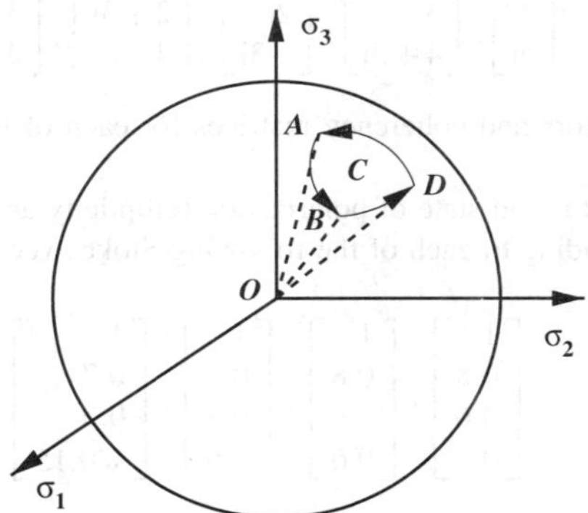

Fig. 3.10: Poincaré Sphere and Pancharatnam Theorem.

3.9 REFERENCES

3.1 Max Born and Emil Wolf, Principles of Optics, 7th ed., Cambridge University Press, Cambridge, 1999.
3.2 Edward Collett, Polarized Light-Fundamentals and Applications, Marcel Dekker, Inc., New York, 1993.
3.3 Christian Brosseau, Fundamentals of Polarized Light, A Statistical Optics Approach, John Wiley & Sons, Inc., New York, 1998.
3.4 Jan Perina, Coherence of Light, D. Reidel Publishing Company, Dordrecht, 1985.
3.5 M.V. Klein and T.E. Furtak, Optics, 2nd ed., John Wiley, New York, 1986.
3.6 Frank L. Pedrotti and S. J. Leno S. Pedrotti, Introduction to Optics, 2nd ed., Prentice-Hall, New Jersey, 1993.
3.7 Eugene Hecht, Optics, 4th ed., Addison-Wesley, Reading, 2001.
3.8 S. Pancharatnam, Proc. Indian Acad. Sci. **A44**, 247(1956).

3.10 PROBLEMS

3.1 Describe the states of polarization of the following waves:

(a) $\vec{E} = \hat{i}E_0\cos(kz - \omega t) \mp \hat{j}E_0\sin(kz - \omega t \mp \pi/4)$
(b) $\vec{E} = \hat{i}E_0\cos(kz - \omega t + \pi/4) \mp \hat{j}E_0\sin(kz - \omega t \mp \pi/4)$
(c) $\vec{E} = \hat{i}E_0\cos(kz - \omega t + \pi/8) \pm \hat{j}E_0\sin(kz - \omega t \mp \pi/8)$
(d) $\vec{E} = \hat{i}E_0\cos(kz - \omega t) + \hat{j}2E_0\cos(kz - \omega t - \pi/6)$.

3.2 Use Eqs (3.19b) and (3.34) to write the Jones and Stokes vectors for the waves given in Problem 3.1.

3.3 Find the orientation and ellipticity of the polarization ellipse for each of the following Jones vectors:

$$\begin{bmatrix} 2 \\ 5i \end{bmatrix}, \begin{bmatrix} 3 \\ 4+5i \end{bmatrix}, \begin{bmatrix} 2i \\ -3i \end{bmatrix}, \begin{bmatrix} 2+3i \\ 4 \end{bmatrix}, \begin{bmatrix} 3i \\ 2 \end{bmatrix}.$$

3.4 Obtain Stokes vectors and coherency matrices for each of the Jones vectors given in Problem 3.3.

3.5 Find the Jones vector and state of polarization (ellipticity and orientation, wherever relevant) corresponding to each of the following Stokes vectors:

$$\begin{bmatrix} 1 \\ 0.8 \\ 0.6 \\ 0 \end{bmatrix}, \begin{bmatrix} 1 \\ 0.8 \\ 0 \\ 0.6 \end{bmatrix}, \begin{bmatrix} 1 \\ 0 \\ 0.8 \\ 0.6 \end{bmatrix}, \begin{bmatrix} 1 \\ 0.7 \\ 0.6 \\ \sqrt{0.15} \end{bmatrix}.$$

3.6 (a) Interpret the results of the following experiments in which the intensities of two light beams are measured after introducing linear polarizers and phase retarders in different orientations in the paths of the beams. Find the degree and state of polarization of each beam.

	Beam I	Beam II
$I(0°, 0°) + I(90°, 0°)$	1	1
$I(0°, 0°) - I(90°, 0°)$	0.8	0.8
$I(45°, 0°) - I(-45°, 0°)$	0.59	0.6
$I(45°, -90°) - I(45°, 90°)$	0.1	0.0

(b) Express the Stokes vector of each beam in terms of the Stokes vectors of completely polarized but mutually incoherent light fields.

3.7 Horizontally polarized light passes through two ideal linear polarizers with transmission directions making angles of θ and $-\theta$ with the horizontal direction. Find polarization state of the emergent light and its intensity as a function of θ. For what values of θ, no light comes from the second polarizer?

3.8 Right circularly polarized light of unit intensity passes through a quarter wave plate with slow axis making an angle of 30° with the horizontal direction and a one-eighth wave plate with slow axis horizontal. Find the intensity of light transmitted by the device. Determine the state of polarization of light just after the quarter wave plate and after it exits the one-eighth wave plate.

3.9 Find the intensity and polarization state of linearly polarized light polarized at 45° to the horizontal direction after passing through a quarter-wave plate with slow axis horizontal, followed by a half-wave plate with slow axis at 45° to the horizontal direction. Take the initial intensity of the light beam to be one unit.

3.10 Suggest and demonstrate by calculations an arrangement to convert left circularly polarized light into right circularly polarized light.

CHAPTER 4

Geometrical Optics

4.1 INTRODUCTION

Image formation by optical instruments is critically dependent on the wave nature of light. In fact, image formation and processing based on the wave theory of light is the subject matter of a chapter, later in this book. However, a great deal about the working and performance (resolving power is one exception) of optical instruments can be learnt without a direct reference to the wave theory. This is a consequence of the wavelength of light being much smaller than the dimensions of components used in optical imaging. Careful observations are needed to discern effects associated with the wave nature of light. The diffraction of light, a direct manifestation of its wave nature, is characterized by diffraction angles of the order of λ/a, where a represents the nominal size of the diffracting object and λ the wavelength of light. For light fields, λ/a amounts to just a few arc seconds for objects of macroscopic dimensions. These are small angles, but not so small to remain undetected even by an unaided eye. Geometrical optics holds in the limit $\lambda/a \to 0$. In this limit ($a \to \infty$), light propagation in a homogeneous medium is rectilinear. The laws of geometrical optics can be deduced from Fermat's principle. We may state this principle by requiring that the optical path length $\int_1^2 n(s)\mathrm{d}s$ of the path taken by light between two points be an extremum, i.e.,

$$\delta \int_1^2 n(s)\mathrm{d}s = 0, \tag{4.1}$$

where $\mathrm{d}s$ is an element of the path in a medium of refractive index $n(s)$. Equivalently, it may be stated that between two points light propagates along a stationary path, implying that all paths in its neighborhood have very nearly equal optical path lengths. Light does not always take the shortest path. Figure 4.1 is helpful in appreciating this point. The figure shows sections of a flat mirror (a), an elliptical mirror with foci at F_1 and F_2 (b), and a curved mirror (c), all having a common normal at A. Consider light starting from F_1 and reaching F_2 after undergoing reflections from the three mirrors. For the elliptical mirror,

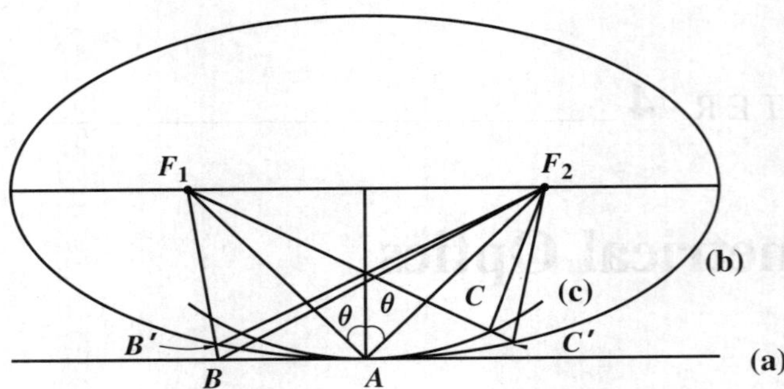

Fig. 4.1: (a) Length of the path F_1AF_2 between points F_1 and F_2 is least for flat mirror, (b) same as for any other path for elliptical mirror, and (c) maximum for curved mirror.

light can take any of the infinitely many paths of exactly the same path length. For the flat mirror, path F_1AF_2 has the least path length because any other path such as F_1BF_2 is longer than the corresponding path $F_1B'F_2$ involving the elliptical mirror. On the other hand, for the curved mirror (c), path F_1AF_2 has the maximum path length because any other path like F_1CF_2 is clearly shorter than the corresponding path $F_1C'F_2$ for the elliptical mirror. Snell's law

$$n_1 \sin\theta_1 = n_2 \sin\theta_2$$

and laws of reflection already derived from Maxwell's equations in Chapter 1 can be deduced from Fermat's principle as well.

4.1.1 Paraxial Approximation

The concept of light rays is extremely useful in geometrical optics. Rays are hypothetical lines somehow describing the rectilinear motion of light. For a plane wave propagating in an isotropic medium, rays are parallel to the propagation vector $\vec{k}$. A ray can be made more specific if it is associated with the direction of energy propagation at a given point in the medium or if it represents the normal to the wavefront at a given point. These two directions, as explained in Section 1.10, differ in an anisotropic medium but we shall ignore such details in the present context. The rays proceed undeviated in a homogeneous medium. Deviation in the direction of a ray occurs as a result of refraction and reflection at an interface between two media. It is possible to trace the path of a ray in an optical system by employing Snell's law at each interface encountered within the optical system. But this is a cumbersome procedure when a large number

Table 4.1. Deviations from the paraxial approximation.

$\theta°$	θ^{rad}	$\sin\theta$	$\tan\theta$	$\cos\theta$
1	0.017 45	0.017 45	0.017 45	0.999 8
5	0.087 30	0.087 16	0.087 49	0.996 2
10	0.174 5	0.173 7	0.176 3	0.985
20	0.349 0	0.342 0	0.364 0	0.94

of interfaces are involved. These complications can be considerably reduced if the small angle approximation is made. However, in a real optical system, large angles are always involved and often desirable as well. Deviations from the small angle approximation lead to geometrical aberrations to be taken up in Chapter 5. Gaussian optics or the first-order optics deals with light rays with angles of incidence, reflection, and refraction at an interface, which satisfy the conditions

$$\tan\theta \approx \sin\theta \approx \theta, \quad \cos\theta \approx 1, \tag{4.2}$$

where angle θ is in radians. This is the paraxial approximation of geometrical optics. This approximation is not as restrictive as it may appear at first sight. Table 4.1 shows that the paraxial approximation holds to within 1% for angles upto 5°, and even at angles as high as 20°, the error introduced by the paraxial approximation may not exceed 5–6%. In this approximation, Snell's law simplifies to

$$n_1\theta_1 = n_2\theta_2. \tag{4.3}$$

4.2 RAY MATRIX APPROACH TO GAUSSIAN OPTICS

Having linearized Snell's law (Eq. 4.3), a matrix representation for the transformation of a ray within a centered optical system seems most appropriate.[1] A centered optical system possesses rotational symmetry about the optical axis, usually taken as the z-axis of the Cartesian coordinate system. A *meridional ray* is a ray which intersects the optical axis and remains confined to a single plane as it makes its way through the optical system. This is the plane containing the ray and the optical axis. The non-meridional rays, more often called the *skew rays* do not meet the optical axis. We shall exclude such rays from the present

[1] Matrix representation for ray transformation in an optical system with the exact form of Snell's law is also possible [4.1, 4.2].

discussion. Within the paraxial approximation, the skew rays do not provide any additional information in analyzing the performance of an optical system. This may not hold when the paraxial approximation is relaxed as we shall find in Chapter 5. With meridional rays, image formation by an optical system is confined to two dimensions. With the z-axis taken along the optical axis, we choose the xz-plane to describe the transformation of a ray in an optical system (Fig. 4.2). A ray at a given point in a homogeneous medium confined to this plane can be identified by the height x of the point above the optical axis, the angle α the ray makes with the optical axis, and the refractive index n of the medium around this point. This analysis can be extended to a stratified medium with position-dependent index of refraction. The height x and the product $n\alpha$ are usually chosen to describe the transformation of a ray. Before we proceed any further, it is desirable to fix our sign convention because some of the quantities describing the transformation of a ray may change sign as the ray traverses the optical system. Several sign conventions exist. Our sign convention is based on the Cartesian sign convention.

Sign Convention

1. A ray in an optical system is assumed to travel from left to right. We shall later describe how a ray travelling from right to left can be handled.
2. The height x of a point on a ray is taken positive if the point lies above the z-axis and negative if it is below the z-axis.
3. The ray angle α is positive if the ray can be obtained by a counter-clockwise rotation of the z-axis. Thus, angle α is positive if the ray has up-slope and negative if it has down-slope. The angles of incidence and

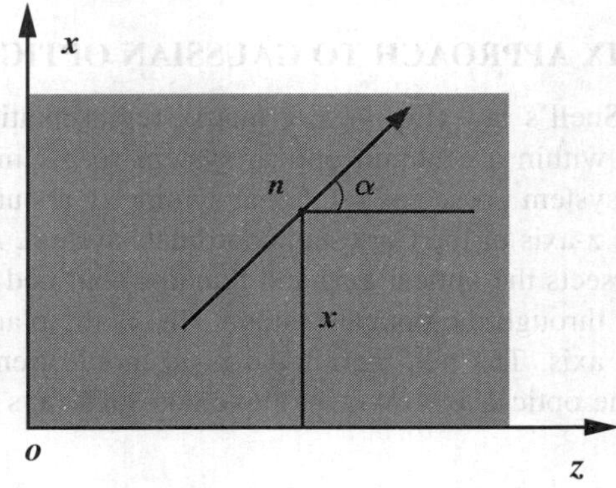

Fig. 4.2: The coordinates of a meridional ray.

refraction follow the same sign convention, except that the normal to the surface replaces the z-axis to decide the sense of rotation.

4. Horizontal distances are positive if measured from left to right and negative if measured from right to left.

At this point we can also mention, as a matter of general notation, that a ray will be identified with unprimed quantities before and with primed quantities after each interface.

4.2.1 The Lens Matrix

The passage of a meridional ray through a thick biconvex lens is shown in Fig. 4.3. The lens with center C has thickness t_1 between its vertices V_1 and V_2. The thickness of the lens and curvatures of its surfaces are exaggerated for clarity of drawing. In the paraxial approximation (ray incidence close to vertex V_1), the sagitta (distance V_1O_1) is small and lens thickness same for all rays. The horizontal distances in the object space (left of vertex V_1) and image space (right of vertex V_2) are measured from V_1 and V_2, respectively. The figure shows a ray arriving at point P_1 on the left interface with coordinates $(n_1\alpha_1, x_1)$ just before incidence. The ray coordinates just after crossing the first interface are $(n_1'\alpha_1', x_1')$. The lens surfaces are assumed spherical with radii R_1 and R_2 and centers C_1 and C_2. The angles of incidence and refraction (θ_1 and θ_1') at the first interface are both positive as per our sign convention. The refracted ray is incident on the right interface at point P_2. The ray coordinates just before and just

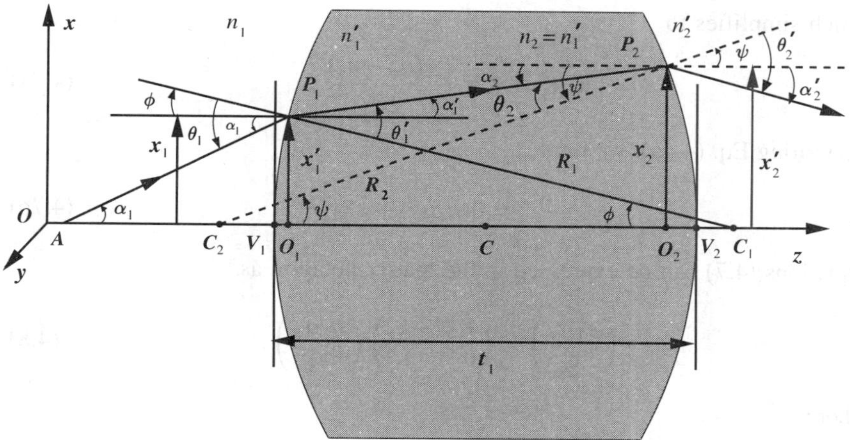

Fig. 4.3: Passage of a meridional ray through a thick lens.

after the right interface are $(n_2\alpha_2, x_2)$ and $(n'_2\alpha'_2, x'_2)$, respectively. Assuming sharp boundaries between the media, refraction at each interface changes the direction of the ray, leaving the ray height unmodified. Accordingly,

$$x'_1 = x_1, \tag{4.4a}$$

$$x'_2 = x_2. \tag{4.4b}$$

For the angles at the first interface, we have

$$|\theta_1| = |\alpha_1| + |\phi|, \tag{4.5}$$

where angle ϕ being negative by our sign convention is written as $\phi = -x'_1/R_1$ since x'_1 and R_1 are both positive. The radius R_1 of the first surface of the lens is to be measured from vertex V_1. Angle α_1 is positive since the incident ray has been chosen with up-slope. We can therefore drop the magnitude signs in Eq. (4.5) and write

$$\theta_1 = \alpha_1 - \phi. \tag{4.6a}$$

Similarly

$$\theta'_1 = \alpha'_1 - \phi. \tag{4.6b}$$

Substituting Eqs (4.6) into Eq. (4.3), we obtain

$$n'_1(\alpha'_1 - \phi) = n_1(\alpha_1 - \phi),$$

which simplifies to

$$n'_1\alpha'_1 = n_1\alpha_1 - \frac{(n'_1 - n_1)}{R_1}x_1. \tag{4.7a}$$

Re-writing Eq. (4.4a), we have

$$x'_1 = 0(n_1\alpha_1) + x_1. \tag{4.7b}$$

Equations (4.7) can be expressed in the matrix notation as

$$\begin{pmatrix} n'_1\alpha'_1 \\ x'_1 \end{pmatrix} = \begin{pmatrix} 1 & -k_1 \\ 0 & 1 \end{pmatrix} \begin{pmatrix} n_1\alpha_1 \\ x_1 \end{pmatrix}, \tag{4.8}$$

where

$$k_1 = \frac{n'_1 - n_1}{R_1}. \tag{4.9}$$

The column matrices $\begin{pmatrix} n_1\alpha_1 \\ x_1 \end{pmatrix}$ and $\begin{pmatrix} n_1'\alpha_1' \\ x_1' \end{pmatrix}$ identify the incident and refracted rays, respectively, at the front surface of the lens. The 2×2 unimodular refraction matrix

$$\mathcal{R}_1 = \begin{pmatrix} 1 & -k_1 \\ 0 & 1 \end{pmatrix} \tag{4.10}$$

describes refraction at the front surface of the lens. The transformation of the ray between the front and back surfaces of the lens is a translation operation described by the equations

$$\begin{aligned} n_2\alpha_2 &= n_1'\alpha_1' + 0(x_1'), \\ x_2 &= \alpha_1' t_1 + x_1' \\ &= \left(\frac{t_1}{n_1'}\right) n_1'\alpha_1' + x_1'. \end{aligned}$$

The matrix form of these equations is

$$\begin{pmatrix} n_2\alpha_2 \\ x_2 \end{pmatrix} = \begin{pmatrix} 1 & 0 \\ \frac{t_1}{n_1'} & 1 \end{pmatrix} \begin{pmatrix} n_1'\alpha_1' \\ x_1' \end{pmatrix}. \tag{4.11}$$

The column matrix $\begin{pmatrix} n_2\alpha_2 \\ x_2 \end{pmatrix}$ identifies the refracted ray just before the second interface. For consistency of notation, we have introduced n_2 for the index of refraction of the lens material just in front of the back surface of the lens. Of course, $n_2 = n_1'$ in the present case.

The unimodular translation matrix

$$\mathcal{T}_{21} = \begin{pmatrix} 1 & 0 \\ \frac{t_1}{n_1'} & 1 \end{pmatrix} \tag{4.12}$$

describes translation of the ray between the front and back surfaces of the thick lens. Reduced thickness t_1/n_1' and not the actual lens thickness t_1 appears in the translation matrix because of our choice $n\alpha$ (and not α) as the angular coordinate of the ray. This choice has the advantage that the refraction and translation matrices are unimodular. For a thin lens ($t_1 = 0$), the translation matrix is the unit matrix

$$\mathcal{T}_{21}(t_1 = 0) = \begin{pmatrix} 1 & 0 \\ 0 & 1 \end{pmatrix}. \tag{4.13}$$

The angles at the back surface of the lens satisfy the following relationships:

$$-\theta_2 = -\alpha_2 + \psi = -\alpha_2 - \frac{x_2}{R_2}, \tag{4.14a}$$

$$-\theta_2' = -\alpha_2' + \psi = -\alpha_2' - \frac{x_2}{R_2}, \tag{4.14b}$$

where α_2 and x_2 are positive by our sign convention but $\theta_2, \theta_2', \alpha_2'$, and R_2 (measured from V_2) are negative. It should be realized that Eqs (4.14) actually represent relationships among the magnitudes of the angles in the spirit of Eq. (4.5). The need for the sign conventions in geometrical optics arises precisely for these reasons. The geometrical relationships among angles (and also among distances) are relationships among their magnitudes. If the magnitude symbols are not to be carried over everywhere, the use of sign conventions becomes imperative. Applying Snell's law

$$n_2'\theta_2' = n_2\theta_2$$

at the back surface of the lens gives

$$n_2'\alpha_2' = n_2\alpha_2 - \frac{n_2' - n_2}{R_2}x_2. \tag{4.15a}$$

Also

$$x_2' = 0(n_2\alpha_2) + x_2. \tag{4.15b}$$

The matrix form of Eqs (4.15) is

$$\begin{pmatrix} n_2'\alpha_2' \\ x_2' \end{pmatrix} = \begin{pmatrix} 1 & -k_2 \\ 0 & 1 \end{pmatrix} \begin{pmatrix} n_2\alpha_2 \\ x_2 \end{pmatrix}, \tag{4.16}$$

where the column matrix $\begin{pmatrix} n_2'\alpha_2' \\ x_2' \end{pmatrix}$ identifies the ray emerging from the back surface of the lens, and

$$k_2 = \frac{n_2' - n_2}{R_2} = \frac{n_2' - n_1'}{R_2}. \tag{4.17}$$

The 2×2 unimodular matrix

$$\mathcal{R}_2 = \begin{pmatrix} 1 & -k_2 \\ 0 & 1 \end{pmatrix} \tag{4.18}$$

describes refraction at the back surface of the lens. The complete ray transformation caused by a lens of thickness t_1 is given by the matrix equation

$$\begin{pmatrix} n_2'\alpha_2' \\ x_2' \end{pmatrix} = \mathcal{R}_2\mathcal{T}_{21}\mathcal{R}_1 \begin{pmatrix} n_1\alpha_1 \\ x_1 \end{pmatrix}, \tag{4.19}$$

where the unimodular 2×2 product matrix

$$\mathcal{L}_{V_2V_1} = \mathcal{R}_2\mathcal{T}_{21}\mathcal{R}_1 \tag{4.20}$$

representing the ray transformation produced by a thick lens is called the lens matrix or the system matrix. The order of the matrix product in Eq. (4.20) is from right to left because the incident ray is first transformed by the front surface (on the left) of the lens. The ray transformation by a combination of lenses can be expressed in terms of the product of matrices describing the refraction and translation operations within the optical system in the manner of Eq. (4.20). The matrix representing the action of the first lens encountered by the ray appears on the extreme right position. Attention must be paid to the signs of the radii of curvatures of the surfaces encountered in the optical system. The lens matrix (Eq. 4.20) can be worked out to yield

$$\mathcal{L}_{V_2V_1} = \begin{pmatrix} 1 - k_2\frac{t_1}{n_1'} & -k_1 - k_2 + k_1k_2\frac{t_1}{n_1'} \\ \frac{t_1}{n_1'} & 1 - k_1\frac{t_1}{n_1'} \end{pmatrix}. \tag{4.21}$$

For light passing at small angles through a flat dielectric slab with parallel faces $(k_1 = k_2 = 0)$, the ray transformation

$$\begin{pmatrix} n_2'\alpha_2' \\ x_2' \end{pmatrix} = \begin{pmatrix} 1 & 0 \\ \frac{t_1}{n_1'} & 1 \end{pmatrix} \begin{pmatrix} n_1\alpha_1 \\ x_1 \end{pmatrix}$$

gives

$$n_2'\alpha_2' = n_1\alpha_1,$$
$$x_2' = \left(\frac{t_1}{n_1'}\right) n_1\alpha_1 + x_1.$$

The emergent ray is parallel $(\alpha_2' = \alpha_1)$ to the incident ray if the media on the two sides of the slab have equal indices of refraction, but it suffers a lateral displacement $(x_2' - x_1 = \frac{t_1}{n_1'} n_1\alpha_1)$, which is independent of the index of refraction of the medium of emergence. For a thin lens, the lens matrix simplifies to

$$\mathcal{L}_{V_2V_1}(t_1 = 0) = \begin{pmatrix} 1 & -k_1 - k_2 \\ 0 & 1 \end{pmatrix}, \tag{4.22}$$

where

$$k_1 + k_2 = \frac{n_1' - n_1}{R_1} + \frac{n_2' - n_1'}{R_2}. \tag{4.23}$$

For a thin lens of a material of refractive index n $(=n_1')$ kept in air $(n_1 = n_2' = 1)$,

$$k_1 + k_2 = (n-1)\left(\frac{1}{R_1} - \frac{1}{R_2}\right) \tag{4.24}$$

is to be recognized as the power (P) of the thin lens in air. Accordingly, the thin lens matrix can be expressed as

$$\mathcal{L}_{V_2V_1}(t_1 = 0) = \begin{pmatrix} 1 & -P \\ 0 & 1 \end{pmatrix}. \tag{4.25}$$

In practice, a lens is considered thin if the radii of curvatures of its surfaces and the object and image distances from the lens are much greater than the thickness of the lens. A high power (short focal length) lens has to be necessarily thick. Expressing Eq. (4.24) in terms of the focal length of a thin lens in air, we have the lens maker's formula:

$$P = \frac{1}{f} = (n-1)\left(\frac{1}{R_1} - \frac{1}{R_2}\right). \tag{4.26}$$

The unit of refractive power of a lens is a Diopter when its focal length is expressed in meters. A lens with $f = +5\,\text{cm}$ is rated to have a power of +20 Diopters (usually abbreviated as +20 D). Equation (4.23) gives the power of a thin lens in the general case when the indices of refraction of the media on the two sides of the lens are different. At this stage, it may be tempting to identify the top right element $-k_1 - k_2 + \frac{t_1}{n_1'} k_1 k_2$ of the thick lens matrix (Eq. 4.21) with the negative of the power of the thick lens. This in fact is true, but it needs to be proved. We note that the thin lens matrix has unit elements along the diagonal and its lower left element is zero. We now explore the possibility of transforming the thick lens matrix to the form of the thin lens matrix. The lens matrix (Eq. 4.21) was obtained by considering the transformation of a ray between the vertical planes passing through the vertices of the thick lens. We now show that the thick lens matrix referred to its principal planes formally resembles the thin lens matrix. This brings us to the discussion of the cardinal points of a lens.

4.2.2 Cardinal Points of a Lens

An ideally thin $(t_1 = 0)$ lens is characterized by its center and its front and back focal points, also called the primary and secondary focal points. The vertices V_1

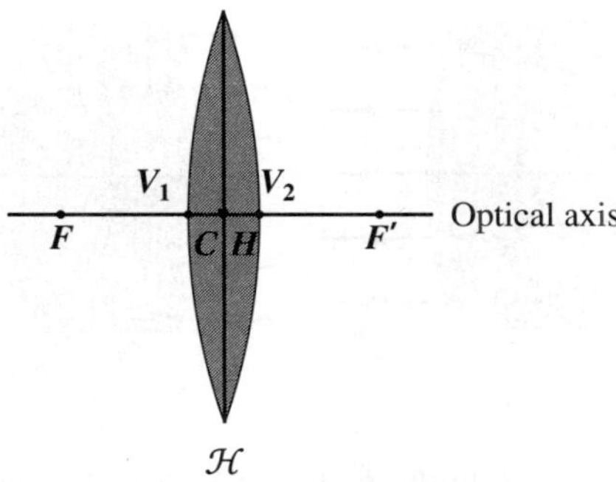

Fig. 4.4: Principal point H of a thin lens coincides with its center.

and V_2 of a thin lens coincide with the center of the lens (Fig. 4.4). One may also think of a plane perpendicular to the optical axis of the lens and passing through its center. In the limit of the lens being ideally thin, the two refracting surfaces overlap with this plane. One can then imagine the entire refraction process taking place in this plane. This plane may be called the principal plane $\mathcal{H}$. The intersection of this plane with the optical axis gives the principal point H, which also coincides with the center of the thin lens. The rays diverging from the primary (front) focal point F become parallel as they emerge from the lens (Fig. 4.5a) and a bundle of rays incident parallel to the optical axis converges to the secondary (back) focal point F' (Fig. 4.5b). For a thick lens, the primary and secondary focal points F and F' are defined in exactly the same manner as for a thin lens. The planes perpendicular to the optical axis and passing through the primary and secondary focal points are called the primary ($\mathcal{F}$) and secondary ($\mathcal{F}'$) focal planes, respectively (Fig. 4.6). The primary principal surface S of a thick lens is the surface of intersection of the rays starting from the primary focal

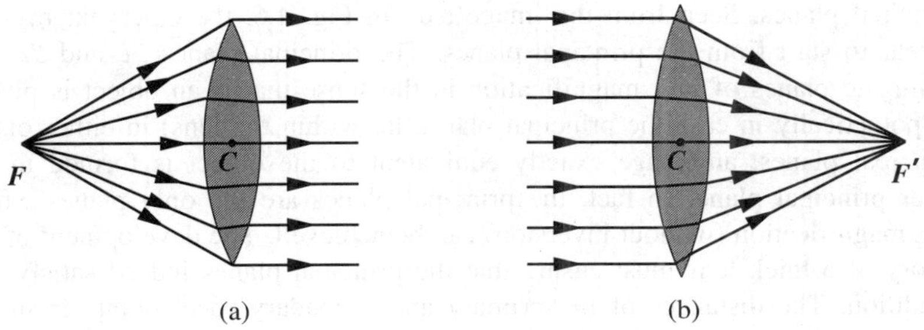

Fig. 4.5: (a) Primary and (b) secondary focal points of a thin lens.

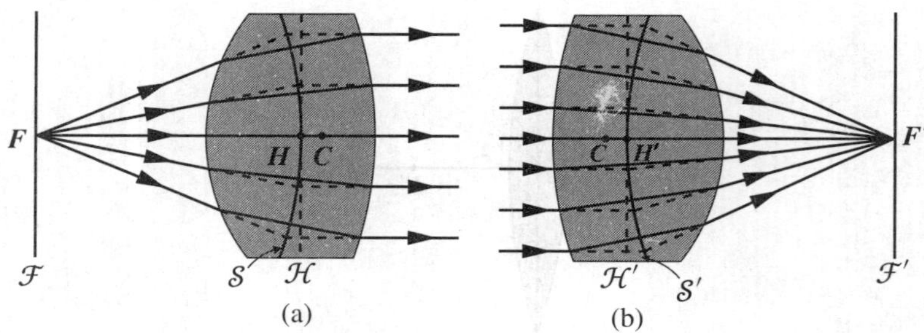

Fig. 4.6: (a) Primary focal point F, primary principal point H, and primary principal plane $\mathcal{H}$ and (b) secondary focal point F', secondary principal point H', and secondary principal plane $\mathcal{H}'$ of a thick convex lens.

point F of the lens and the emergent parallel rays when extended to intersect each other (Fig. 4.6a). This surface is in general curved but the portion of this surface near the optical axis (paraxial approximation) constitutes the primary principal plane $\mathcal{H}$ of a thick lens. The primary principal point H is the point of intersection of the primary principal plane with the optical axis. The secondary focal point F', the secondary principal surface S', the secondary principal plane $\mathcal{H}'$, and the secondary principal point H' are likewise defined in Fig. 4.6b with reference to a bundle of incident rays parallel to the optical axis. The principal planes may lie inside or outside a thick lens, depending on the curvatures of its surfaces and its thickness. The two principal planes of a thick lens merge into one plane for a thin lens. For a convex or a positive lens, the primary focal point F lies on the left of the lens (Figs 4.5a and 4.6a) and the secondary focal point F' lies on the right of the lens (Figs 4.5b and 4.6b). The situation is just the opposite for a concave (also called negative) lens (Fig. 4.7).

For mathematical convenience, we may consider the refraction not to take place at the front and back surfaces of a lens but at its primary and secondary principal planes. Seen from the image side in Fig. 4.6, the emergent rays do appear to start from the principal planes. The principal planes $\mathcal{H}$ and $\mathcal{H}'$ are conjugate planes of unit magnification in the sense that if an object is placed (hypothetically in case the principal planes lie within the lens) in either of the principal planes, an image exactly equivalent to the object is formed in the other principal plane. In fact, the principal planes are the only planes where unit magnification (without inversion) can be achieved. The development of the theory of a thick lens must ensure that the principal planes indeed satisfy this condition. The distances of the primary and secondary focal points from the left and right vertices of the lens are denoted as the primary and secondary focal lengths f_1 and f_2, respectively, and when referred to the primary and

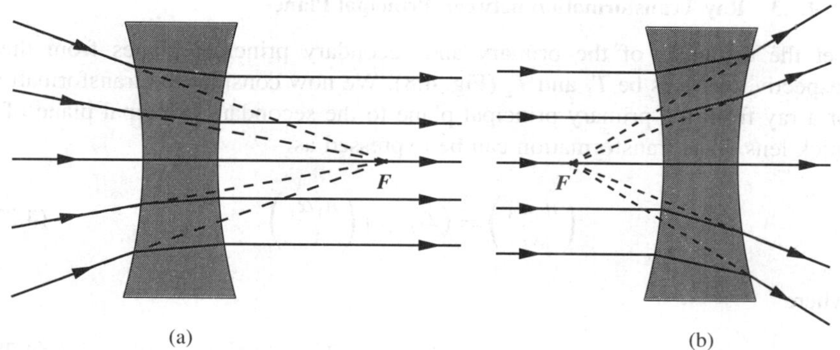

Fig. 4.7: (a) Primary and (b) secondary focal points of a concave lens.

secondary principal planes, they will be denoted as f and f', respectively. By our sign convention, the primary focal length of a convex lens is negative and its secondary focal length is positive whereas just the opposite holds for a concave lens. In normal use, focal length of a lens implies its secondary focal length which is positive for a convex lens and negative for a concave lens.

The four cardinal points consisting of two focal points (F, F') and two principal points (H, H') suffice for the purpose of ray tracing through a thick lens surrounded by the same medium on both sides. However, as we shall see later, additional cardinal points (called nodal points) are useful for ray tracing when media on the two sides of the lens have different indices of refraction. This, for example, is the case for the cornea of an eye with air on one side and aqueous humor on the other (see Fig. 4.31). The nodal points are points on the optical axis having unit angular magnification. They coincide with the principal points when the index of refraction is same on both sides of the lens.

The cardinal points of a positive lens or of a complete optical system can be easily determined. The focal points can be located by keeping a mirror behind the lens so that the object and its image coincide at the focal point. Similarly, the focal lengths f and f' $(=-f)$ can be obtained by applying Newton's equation (Eq. 4.58)

$$(u-f)(v-f')=ff'$$

to any pair of conjugate planes, where $(u-f)$ and $(v-f')$ are the object and image distances from the primary and secondary focal planes, respectively. Knowing the focal lengths and positions of the focal planes, the positions of the principal planes can be determined.

4.2.3 Ray Transformation between Principal Planes

Let the distances of the primary and secondary principal planes from their respective vertices be T_1 and T_2 (Fig. 4.8). We now consider the transformation of a ray from the primary principal plane to the secondary principal plane of a thick lens. This transformation can be expressed as

$$\begin{pmatrix} n_3\alpha_3 \\ x_3 \end{pmatrix} = (\mathcal{L}_{\mathcal{H}'\mathcal{H}}) \begin{pmatrix} n_1\alpha_1 \\ x_1 \end{pmatrix}, \tag{4.27}$$

where

$$\mathcal{L}_{\mathcal{H}'\mathcal{H}} = \mathcal{T}_{\mathcal{H}'V'}\mathcal{L}_{V'V}\mathcal{T}_{V\mathcal{H}}. \tag{4.28}$$

The translation matrices between the principal planes and the corresponding planes through the vertices of the lens are

$$\mathcal{T}_{V\mathcal{H}} = \begin{pmatrix} 1 & 0 \\ \frac{-T_1}{n_1} & 1 \end{pmatrix}, \tag{4.29a}$$

$$\mathcal{T}_{\mathcal{H}'V'} = \begin{pmatrix} 1 & 0 \\ \frac{T_2}{n_3} & 1 \end{pmatrix}, \tag{4.29b}$$

where $(-T_1)$ and T_2 are assumed positive. If, on the other hand, T_1 turns out to be positive for a given situation, the primary principal plane lies on the right

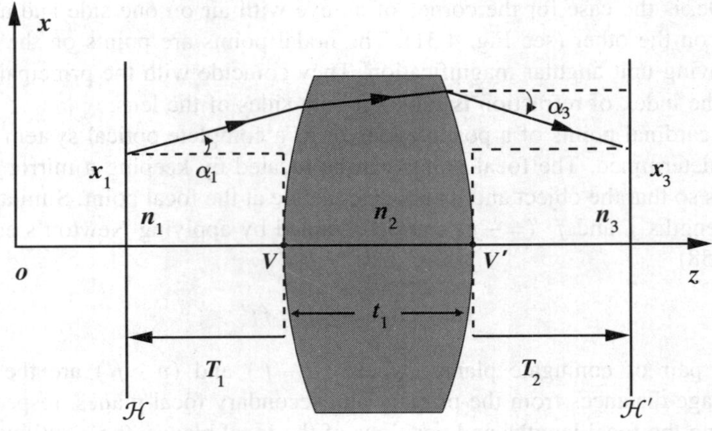

Fig. 4.8: Ray transformation between principal planes of a thick lens.

of vertex V. Similar considerations apply to T_2 as well. With Eqs (4.29), the product matrix (Eq. 4.28) takes the form

$$\mathcal{L}_{\mathcal{H}'\mathcal{H}} = \begin{pmatrix} 1 & 0 \\ \frac{T_2}{n_3} & 1 \end{pmatrix} \begin{pmatrix} a_{11} & a_{12} \\ a_{21} & a_{22} \end{pmatrix} \begin{pmatrix} 1 & 0 \\ \frac{-T_1}{n_1} & 1 \end{pmatrix}$$
$$= \begin{pmatrix} a_{11} - \frac{T_1}{n_1} a_{12} & a_{12} \\ \frac{T_2}{n_3}\left(a_{11} - \frac{T_1}{n_1} a_{12}\right) + a_{21} - \frac{T_1}{n_1} a_{22} & a_{22} + \frac{T_2}{n_3} a_{12} \end{pmatrix}. \tag{4.30}$$

Here, the lens matrix (Eq. 4.21) has been abbreviated as

$$\begin{pmatrix} 1 - \frac{t_1}{n_1'} k_2 & -k_1 - k_2 + \frac{t_1}{n_1'} k_1 k_2 \\ \frac{t_1}{n_1'} & 1 - \frac{t_1}{n_1'} k_1 \end{pmatrix} = \begin{pmatrix} a_{11} & \mathrm{a}_{12} \\ a_{21} & \mathrm{a}_{22} \end{pmatrix}. \tag{4.31}$$

Combining Eqs (4.27) and (4.30), we have

$$x_3 = \left[\frac{T_2}{n_3}\left(a_{11} - \frac{T_1}{n_1} a_{12}\right) + a_{21} - \frac{T_1}{n_1} a_{22}\right] n_1 \alpha_1 + \left(a_{22} + \frac{T_2}{n_3} a_{12}\right) x_1, \tag{4.32a}$$

$$n_3 \alpha_3 = \left(a_{11} - \frac{T_1}{n_1} a_{12}\right) n_1 \alpha_1 + a_{12} x_1. \tag{4.32b}$$

The principal planes are planes of unit linear magnification ($x_3/x_1 = 1$), irrespective of angle α_1 the ray makes with the optical axis. Hence, we must have

$$\frac{T_2}{n_3}\left(a_{11} - \frac{T_1}{n_1} a_{12}\right) + a_{21} - \frac{T_1}{n_1} a_{22} = 0, \tag{4.33a}$$

and

$$a_{22} + \frac{T_2}{n_3} a_{12} = 1. \tag{4.33b}$$

Equation (4.33b) locates the secondary principal plane at

$$T_2 = \frac{n_3}{a_{12}}(1 - a_{22}). \tag{4.34a}$$

Furthermore, since the determinant of the matrix $\mathcal{L}_{\mathcal{H}'\mathcal{H}}$ must be unity, its upper left element must also have unit value. This locates the primary principal plane at

$$T_1 = \frac{n_1}{a_{12}}(a_{11} - 1). \tag{4.34b}$$

The lens transformation matrix (Eq. 4.30) between the principal planes then simplifies to

$$\mathcal{L}_{\mathcal{H}'\mathcal{H}} = \begin{pmatrix} 1 & a_{12} \\ 0 & 1 \end{pmatrix}. \tag{4.35}$$

This has exactly the form of the thin lens matrix (Eq. 4.25), so that the power of a thick lens is

$$\begin{aligned} P_{\mathrm{L}} &= -a_{12} \\ &= k_1 + k_2 - \frac{t_1}{n_1'} k_1 k_2 \\ &= \frac{n_2 - n_1}{R_1} + \frac{n_3 - n_2}{R_2} - \left(\frac{n_2 - n_1}{R_1}\right)\left(\frac{n_3 - n_2}{R_2}\right)\frac{t_1}{n_2}. \end{aligned} \tag{4.36}$$

The power of a lens of thickness t_1 and refractive index n ($= n_1' = n_2$) with air on both sides ($n_1 = n_3 = 1$) is

$$P_{\mathrm{L}} = (n-1)\left[\frac{1}{R_1} - \frac{1}{R_2} + \frac{n-1}{n}\frac{t_1}{R_1 R_2}\right]. \tag{4.37}$$

This is the lens maker's formula for a thick lens. The thick lens matrix can be put in the standard thin lens form

$$\mathcal{L}_{\mathcal{H}'\mathcal{H}} = \begin{pmatrix} 1 & -P_{\mathrm{L}} \\ 0 & 1 \end{pmatrix}, \tag{4.38}$$

where P_{L} is the power of the thick lens. The fact that all rays starting from a given point on the primary principal plane end up at one point on the secondary principal plane implies that these planes are indeed conjugate planes, and Eq. (4.33a) is actually a statement of the relationship between the object distance T_1 and the image distance T_2 (from their respective vertices). A rearrangement of Eq. (4.33a) gives

$$\frac{n_3 a_{22}}{T_2} - \frac{n_1 a_{11}}{T_1} - \frac{n_1 n_3 a_{21}}{T_1 T_2} = -a_{12} = P_{\mathrm{L}}. \tag{4.39}$$

The not-so-simple form of this relationship between the object and image distances reinforces the fact that the planes passing through the vertices of a thick lens are not the most convenient reference planes to describe image formation by

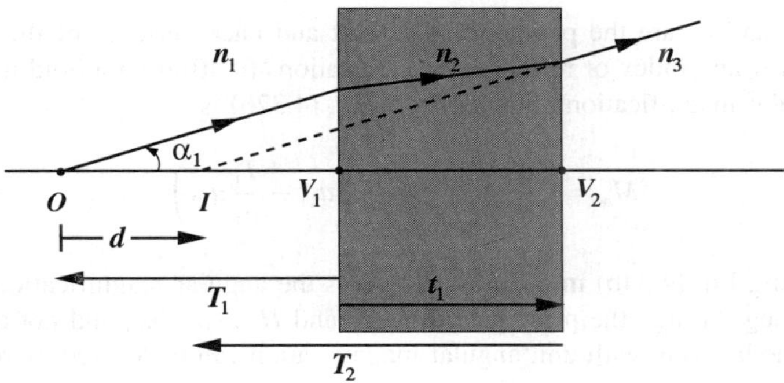

Fig. 4.9: Image formation by a transparent slab. Negative T_2 implies virtual image on left of V_2.

a thick lens. However, Eq. (4.39) becomes particularly simple for a transparent block with flat and parallel surfaces (Fig. 4.9), giving

$$\frac{T_2}{n_3} = \frac{T_1}{n_1} - \frac{t_1}{n_1'}.$$

This equation locates the image of an object formed by a transparent block. For $T_1 = 0$, $T_2 = -n_3 \frac{t_1}{n_1'}$ gives the usual result

$$\frac{\text{Apparent depth}}{\text{Real depth}} = \frac{n_3}{n_1'}.$$

For $T_1 \neq 0$ and $n_1 = n_3$, the image displacement is given by

$$\begin{aligned} d &= |T_1| + t_1 - |T_2| \\ &= t_1 \left(1 - \frac{n_1}{n_1'}\right). \end{aligned}$$

Now that the element a_{12} of the thick lens matrix has been recognized as the negative of the power of the lens, the distances T_1 and T_2 of the principal planes from their respective vertices can be expressed in terms of the refractive parameters of the lens:

$$T_1 = \frac{n_1}{n_2}\frac{k_2}{P_L} t_1, \tag{4.40a}$$

$$T_2 = -\frac{n_3}{n_2}\frac{k_1}{P_L} t_1, \tag{4.40b}$$

where k_1 and k_2 are the powers of the front and back surfaces of the lens (of thickness t_1 and index of refraction n_2). Equations (4.40) do not hold if $P_L = 0$. The angular magnification obtained from Eq. (4.32b) is

$$M_\alpha = \left(\frac{\alpha_3}{\alpha_1}\right)_{x_1=0} = \frac{n_1}{n_3}\left(a_{11} - \frac{T_1}{n_1}a_{12}\right). \tag{4.41}$$

Substituting Eq. (4.34b) into Eq. (4.41) gives the angular magnification for the rays passing through the principal points H and H' as n_1/n_3, and not one. The primary nodal point with unit angular magnification can be located by requiring

$$\left(\frac{\alpha_3}{\alpha_1}\right)_{x_1=0} = 1, \tag{4.42}$$

giving

$$T_1^N = \frac{n_1}{a_{12}}\left(a_{11} - \frac{n_3}{n_1}\right). \tag{4.43a}$$

The position of the secondary nodal point can be obtained from Eq. (4.33a) by replacing T_1 and T_2 by T_1^N and T_2^N, respectively, giving

$$T_2^N = \frac{n_3}{a_{12}}\left(\frac{n_1}{n_3} - a_{22}\right). \tag{4.43b}$$

As a consequence of unit angular magnification, the incident and emergent rays directed towards or away from the nodal points are parallel. Intersection of these rays (upon extension) with the optical axis gives the positions of the nodal points (Fig. 4.10). Like the principal points, the nodal points can lie within the lens or

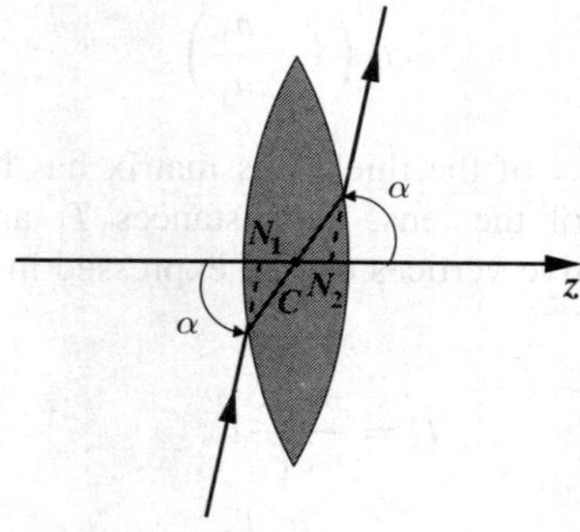

Fig. 4.10: Incident and emergent rays passing through the nodal points (after extension) are parallel to each other.

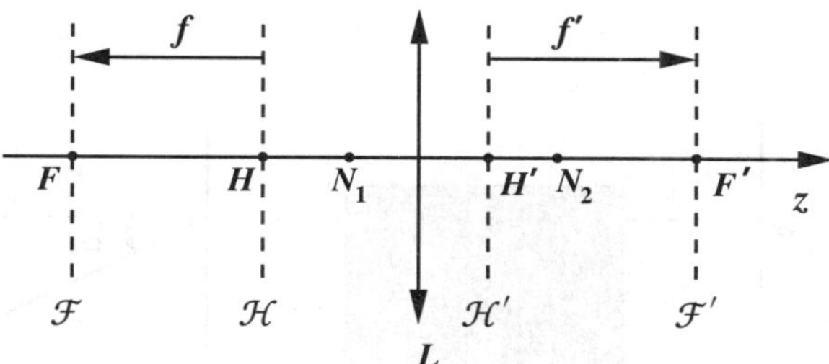

Fig. 4.11: Cardinal points of a thick lens L; focal points (F, F'), principal points (H, H'), nodal points (N_1, N_2).

outside it. Figure 4.11 shows the six cardinal points of a thick lens (symbolically represented by $\updownarrow$).

4.2.4 Ray Matrix for Image Formation

With the simple form of the thick lens matrix between its principal planes at our disposal, image formation by a thick lens or by an optical system (Fig. 4.12) can be handled rather easily. As for a single lens, the principal planes of a complete optical system are conjugate planes with unit linear magnification. The ray matrix between the principal planes of an optical system has exactly the form of the ray matrix of a thick lens between its principal planes. We merely need to replace the power P_{L} of the lens in Eq. (4.38) by the power P_{sys} of the optical system. The lens matrix $\mathcal{L}_{V'V}$ in Eq. (4.28) is replaced by the product of the matrices representing the ray transformation between the left vertex of the first element and the right vertex of the last element of the optical system. For separations, if any, between successive elements, translation matrices of the type described by Eq. (4.12) need to be incorporated. The ray matrix for image formation by an optical system can be obtained by simply replacing T_1 and T_2 by $T_1 + u$ and $T_2 + v$, in Eq. (4.30), where u and v are the object and image distances from the primary and secondary principal planes of the optical system, respectively. However, it is much easier to develop the object–image matrix in terms of the system matrix between its principal planes:

$$\mathcal{L}_{IO} = \mathcal{T}_{I\mathcal{H}'}\mathcal{L}_{\mathcal{H}'\mathcal{H}}\mathcal{T}_{\mathcal{H}O} \tag{4.44a}$$

$$= \begin{pmatrix} 1 & 0 \\ \frac{v}{n_3} & 1 \end{pmatrix} \begin{pmatrix} 1 & -P_{\mathrm{sys}} \\ 0 & 1 \end{pmatrix} \begin{pmatrix} 1 & 0 \\ \frac{-u}{n_1} & 1 \end{pmatrix} \tag{4.44b}$$

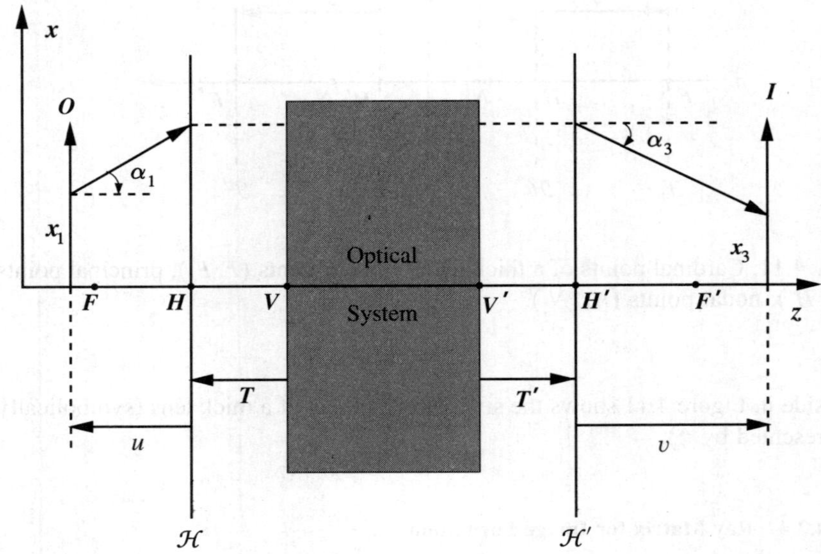

Fig. 4.12: Transformation of a meridional ray between the object (O) and image (I) planes of an optical system.

$$= \begin{pmatrix} 1 + \dfrac{u}{n_1} P_{\text{sys}} & -P_{\text{sys}} \\ \dfrac{v}{n_3}\left(1 + \dfrac{u}{n_1} P_{\text{sys}}\right) - \dfrac{u}{n_1} & 1 - \dfrac{v}{n_3} P_{\text{sys}} \end{pmatrix}. \tag{4.44c}$$

We remind the reader once again that by our sign convention, u is negative and v is positive in Eqs (4.44) if the image is formed on the right of the principal plane $\mathcal{H}'$. Here, P_{sys} is the power of the optical system as a whole and is obtained from the negative of the top right element of the system matrix calculated between its principal planes. The transformation of a ray from the object point to the image point, described by the matrix equation

$$\begin{pmatrix} n_3 \alpha_3 \\ x_3 \end{pmatrix} = \begin{pmatrix} 1 + \dfrac{u}{n_1} P_{\text{sys}} & -P_{\text{sys}} \\ \dfrac{v}{n_3}\left(1 + \dfrac{u}{n_1} P_{\text{sys}}\right) - \dfrac{u}{n_1} & 1 - \dfrac{v}{n_3} P_{\text{sys}} \end{pmatrix} \begin{pmatrix} n_1 \alpha_1 \\ x_1 \end{pmatrix}, \tag{4.45}$$

gives

$$n_3 \alpha_3 = \left(1 + \frac{u}{n_1} P_{\text{sys}}\right) n_1 \alpha_1 - P_{\text{sys}} x_1, \tag{4.46a}$$

$$x_3 = \left[\frac{v}{n_3}\left(1+\frac{u}{n_1}P_{\text{sys}}\right)-\frac{u}{n_1}\right]n_1\alpha_1+\left(1-\frac{v}{n_3}P_{\text{sys}}\right)x_1. \tag{4.46b}$$

The angular magnification of the image is

$$M_\alpha = \left(\frac{\alpha_3}{\alpha_1}\right)_{x_1=0} = \frac{n_1}{n_3}\left(1+\frac{u}{n_1}P_{\text{sys}}\right). \tag{4.47a}$$

For a sharp image of the object in the image plane, the coefficient of $(n_1\alpha_1)$ in Eq. (4.46b) must be identically zero, giving the lateral (linear) image magnification as

$$M_x = \frac{x_3}{x_1} = 1 - \frac{v}{n_3}P_{\text{sys}}. \tag{4.47b}$$

With Eqs (4.47), the object–image matrix for an optical system takes the form

$$\mathcal{L}_{\text{IO}} = \begin{pmatrix} \frac{n_3}{n_1}M_\alpha & -P_{\text{sys}} \\ 0 & M_x \end{pmatrix}. \tag{4.48}$$

Since this must also be a unimodular matrix, we obtain the well-known result

$$M_\alpha M_x = \frac{n_1}{n_3} \tag{4.49}$$

for the product of the angular and lateral magnifications, known as the Smith–Helmholtz formula. The object–image matrix can be equivalently expressed as

$$\mathcal{L}_{\text{IO}} = \begin{pmatrix} 1/M_x & -P_{\text{sys}} \\ 0 & M_x \end{pmatrix}. \tag{4.50}$$

4.2.4.1 Object–Image Distance Relation

As stated above, a sharp image of an object is possible only if the coefficient of $n_1\alpha_1$ in Eq. (4.46b) vanishes, i.e., if

$$\frac{v}{n_3} - \frac{u}{n_1} + \frac{vuP_{\text{sys}}}{n_1 n_3} = 0. \tag{4.51a}$$

Dividing by $(uv)/(n_1n_3)$ and rearranging terms, we obtain

$$\frac{n_3}{v} - \frac{n_1}{u} = P_{\text{sys}}. \tag{4.51b}$$

This is the standard object–image distance relationship for a thin lens. It is usually expressed not in terms of the power but in terms of the focal length of the lens. In the present formulation of image formation, Eq. (4.51b) is applicable to a thick lens as well as to any multi-element optical system. The object and image planes constitute a pair of conjugate planes.

The object distance u and image distance v in the context of a thick lens are measured from its principal planes and not from its vertices. For an optical system, they are to be measured from the primary and secondary principal planes of the optical system as a whole. Combining Eqs (4.47b) and (4.51b) gives the lateral magnification

$$M_x = \frac{n_1}{n_3}\frac{v}{u}. \tag{4.52a}$$

For an object lying in the primary focal plane of an optical system, the image moves to infinity ($v = \infty$), so that

$$\lim_{v\to\infty} u = f = -\frac{n_1}{P_{\text{sys}}}, \tag{4.52b}$$

where the primary focal length f is the distance between the primary focal plane $\mathcal{F}$ and the primary principal plane $\mathcal{H}$ of the optical system. If, on the other hand, the incident rays are parallel ($u = \infty$), the image is formed in the secondary focal plane $\mathcal{F}'$ with the image distance from the secondary principal plane $\mathcal{H}'$ given by

$$\lim_{u\to\infty} v = f' = \frac{n_3}{P_{\text{sys}}}, \tag{4.52c}$$

where f' is the secondary focal length of the lens or of the optical system as the case may be. Accordingly, Eq. (4.51b) can be put in the more familiar form

$$\frac{n_3}{v} - \frac{n_1}{u} = -\frac{n_1}{f} = \frac{n_3}{f'}. \tag{4.53}$$

For an optical system with an overall positive power, the primary and secondary focal lengths f and f' take negative and positive values, respectively. The situation is reversed for an optical system with negative power. We can put the object–image matrix (Eq. 4.44c) in yet another form involving the secondary focal length f' of the optical system

$$\mathcal{L}_{\text{IO}} = \begin{pmatrix} 1/M_x & -n_3/f' \\ 0 & M_x \end{pmatrix}. \tag{4.54}$$

The primary and secondary focal lengths (defined with respect to the principal planes) f and f' for a thick lens have same magnitude. However, the primary and secondary focal lengths

$$f_1 = f_V = f + T_1, \tag{4.55a}$$

$$f_2 = f'_{V'} = f' + T_2, \tag{4.55b}$$

measured with respect to the vertices may not have the same magnitude if the principal planes of a thick lens are asymmetrically located. Re-arranging Eq. (4.53) gives

$$\frac{1}{v/n_3} = \frac{1}{u/n_1} + \frac{1}{f'/n_3}, \tag{4.56}$$

where $1/(v/n_3)$ and $1/(u/n_1)$ represent the image and object vergences, respectively. The vergence is related to the curvature of the wavefront. In air, $1/u$ is the curvature of the spherical wavefront emanating from the point object and reaching the primary principal plane and $1/v$ is the curvature of the wavefront in the secondary principal plane which converges to form the point image of a point object. The lens (or the optical system) changes the curvature of the incident wavefront by an amount equal to its power. It follows that all rays forming a sharp image have exactly equal path lengths between the object and image points. This is consistent with Fermat's principle. Another useful form of Eq. (4.53) can be obtained by noting that under image forming conditions, the product of the diagonal elements of the object–image matrix (Eq. 4.44c) must have unit value, i.e.,

$$\left(1 + \frac{u}{n_1} P_{\text{sys}}\right)\left(1 - \frac{v}{n_3} P_{\text{sys}}\right) = 1. \tag{4.57}$$

Substituting Eqs (4.52) into Eq. (4.57) gives

$$(u - f)(v - f') = ff'. \tag{4.58a}$$

This is exactly like the Newton's equation for image formation by a thin lens. A more familiar form of this equation is

$$XX' = ff', \tag{4.58b}$$

where $X = u - f$ and $X' = v - f'$. This form of the object–image relationship is useful to visualize the changes in the position of the image as the object

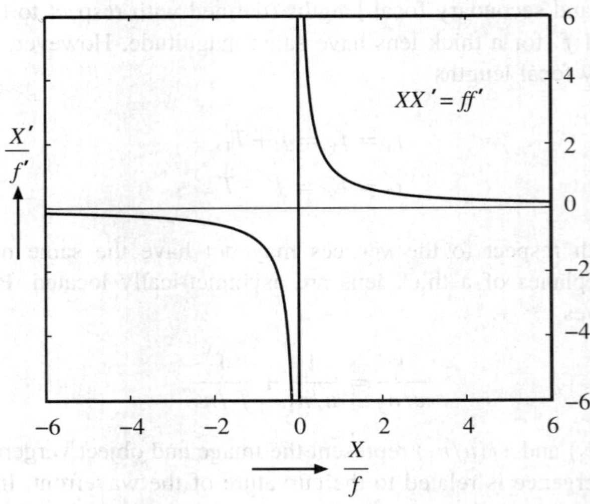

Fig. 4.13: Variation of normalized image distance with normalized object distance.

position is changed. Figure 4.13 shows the dependence of the normalized image distance (X'/f') on the normalized object distance (X/f). For a convex lens with negative f, X/f remains positive as long as $X(=u-f)$ remains negative, i.e., the object remains to the left of the primary focal plane. For unit normalized object distance ($u = 2f$), the normalized image distance is also one ($v = 2f'$). When the object approaches the primary focal point ($X = 0$), the image moves to the extreme right position ($X' = +\infty$). This behavior is shown by the hyperbola in the first quadrant. In this quadrant, the image is real, inverted and diminished in size for $X/f > 1$ and enlarged for $X/f < 1$. When the object moves to the right of the primary focal point, X/f and hence X'/f' becomes negative (third quadrant). Since f' is positive for a convex lens, X' becomes negative. This is the regime in which an erect, magnified but a virtual image is formed on the left-hand side of the lens. This situation continues till the object approaches the primary principal plane. For $u = 0$, $X/f = X'/f' = -1$ and $v = 0$. Beyond this point, $X/f < -1$ and the object lies on the right of the primary principal plane of the lens, or in other words, the object has become virtual. A virtual object corresponds to the incidence of converging (rather than diverging or parallel) rays on the lens (Fig. 4.14). We leave it to the reader to interpret Fig. 4.13 for a concave lens. The longitudinal magnification of an optical system defined as

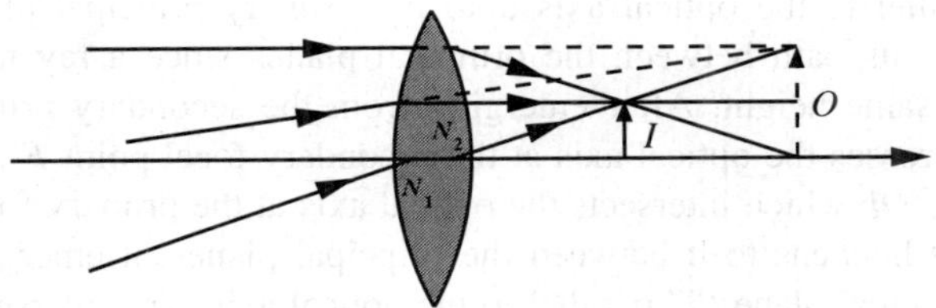

Fig. 4.14: Converging rays incident on a lens are equivalent to a virtual object (O) on the right of the lens.

the ratio of the longitudinal shift in the image position to the longitudinal shift in the object position, obtained from Eq. (4.53), is

$$M_l = \lim_{\Delta u \to 0} \frac{\Delta v}{\Delta u} = \frac{n_1}{n_3}\frac{v^2}{u^2}. \tag{4.59}$$

4.2.5 Ray Tracing

The introduction of the principal planes greatly simplifies the task of ray tracing through an optical system. It is of course necessary to first construct the system matrix between the vertices of the first and last interfaces of the optical system. This would be the equivalent of the system matrix $\begin{pmatrix} a_{11} & a_{12} \\ a_{21} & a_{22} \end{pmatrix}$ of a thick lens (Eq. 4.31). The top right element of the system matrix gives the negative of the power of the optical system. The positions of the principal, nodal, and focal points of the optical system can be obtained from Eqs (4.34), (4.43), and (4.52), respectively. Figure 4.15 depicts an optical system and a linear object placed in front of its primary focal plane. A ray (Oa) from point O on the object

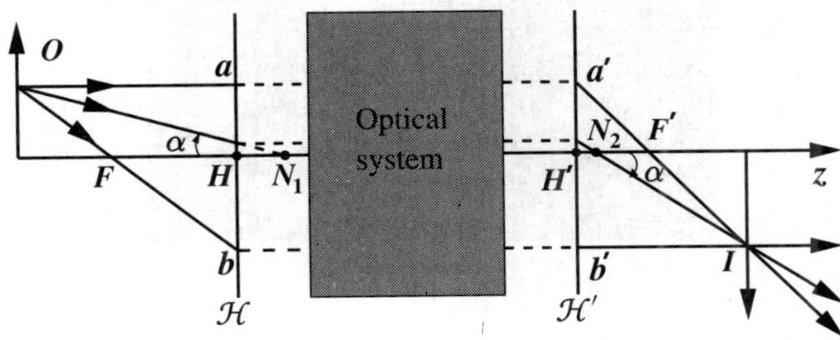

Fig. 4.15: Ray tracing through an optical system in the paraxial approximation.

is drawn parallel to the optical axis upto the primary principal plane $\mathcal{H}$. We need not trace its path between the principal planes since a ray touches both planes at the same height. After emerging from the secondary principal plane $\mathcal{H}'$, this ray crosses the optical axis at the secondary focal point F'. We choose the second ray Ob which intersects the optical axis at the primary focal point F. Ignoring what happens to it between the principal planes, it emerges from the secondary principal plane $\mathcal{H}'$ parallel to the optical axis. The intersection of the rays $Oaa'F'$ and Obb' on extension gives the image point I. To make sure that the ray tracing has been done correctly, a third ray from point O directed towards the primary nodal point N_1 is drawn making an angle α with the optical axis. This ray comes out from the secondary nodal point N_2, making the same angle α with the optical axis. If this ray also passes through the image point I, the ray tracing has been done correctly. Figure 4.15 has been drawn for an optical system with positive power. Alternatively, the ray tracing can be handled numerically. The object–image matrix (Eq. 4.44c) and the ray parameters $(n_3\alpha_3, x_3)$ in the image space can be calculated with a computer. With this technique, the rays can be traced in the object and image spaces and also within the optical system.

4.2.6 Ray Matrix for Reflection

We have developed the ray matrix formalism for refraction and translation of a ray on the assumption that a ray always travels from left to right. A mirror reverses the direction of propagation of a ray. We now bring reflection at an interface within the framework of the ray matrix approach. Figure 4.16 shows

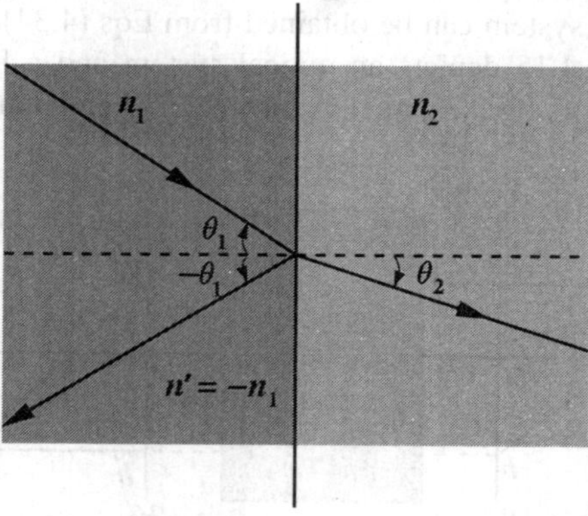

Fig. 4.16: Reflection at an interface is equivalent to refraction from a medium of refractive index n to a medium of refractive index $-n$.

reflection and refraction at an interface between media of refractive indices n_1 and n_2.

According to Snell's law

$$n_1 \sin\theta_1 = n_2 \sin\theta_2.$$

Replacing n_2 by $(-n_1)$, we get

$$n_1 \sin\theta_1 = -n_1 \sin\theta_2,$$

which for acute angles can be satisfied only if

$$\theta_2 = -\theta_1.$$

But this is exactly the condition for reflection $(\theta' = -\theta_1)$. Hence, reflection at a plane or a spherical interface may be mathematically treated as refraction from a medium of refractive index n to a medium of refractive index $-n$. Furthermore, whenever a ray travels from right to left, the index of refraction n of the medium is replaced by $-n$. With this rather unphysical but mathematically sound manipulation, the ray matrix approach can be applied to catadioptric systems involving refracting and reflecting elements. It should be understood that a ray having undergone a reflection at an interface continues to travel in media with negative refractive indices even after undergoing refractions at subsequent interfaces unless, of course, it suffers another reflection which once again reverses its direction of propagation and hence the sign of the refractive index.

With this interpretation, the refraction matrix

$$\mathcal{R} = \begin{pmatrix} 1 & -\frac{n_1' - n_1}{R} \\ 0 & 1 \end{pmatrix}$$

can represent reflection provided n_1' is replaced by $-n_1$, giving

$$\mathcal{R}' = \begin{pmatrix} 1 & \frac{2n_1}{R} \\ 0 & 1 \end{pmatrix} \tag{4.60}$$

as the reflection matrix, where R is positive for a convex mirror (Fig. 4.17a) and negative for a concave mirror (Fig. 4.17b). The power of a mirror remains unchanged if the mirror is turned around. For example in Fig. 4.17b, the power of the concave mirror is

$$P = \frac{n' - n_1}{R} = \frac{-n_1 - n_1}{R} = -\frac{2n_1}{R},$$

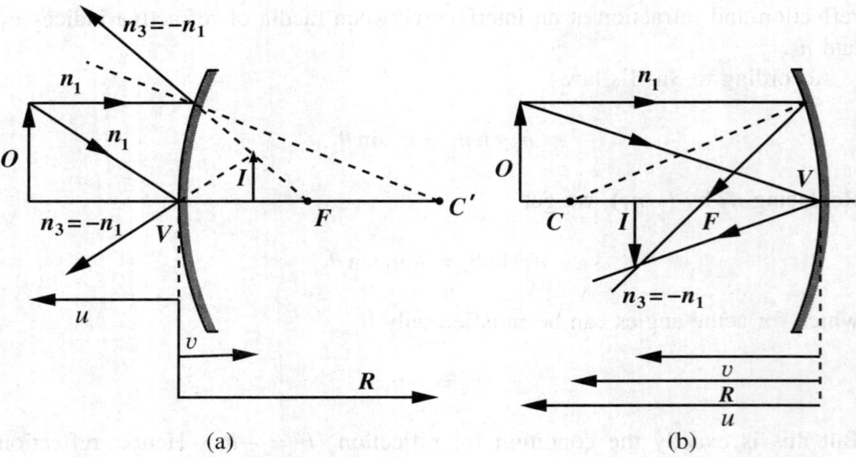

Fig. 4.17: Image formation by mirrors; (a) a convex mirror forms an erect, virtual and diminished image, (b) a concave mirror forms a real, inverted (if object to the left of F) or a virtual, erect and magnified image (if object to the right of F).

where R is negative, so that its power is positive. If this mirror is turned around, then light is incident from right to left so that n_1 must be replaced by $-n_1$ and $n' = n_1$, giving $P = 2n_1/R$, where R is now positive and the power of the mirror remains positive. The ray transformation from the object to the image plane for a mirror is given by the matrix equation

$$\begin{pmatrix} n_3\alpha_3 \\ x_3 \end{pmatrix} = \begin{pmatrix} 1 & 0 \\ \frac{v}{n_3} & 1 \end{pmatrix} \begin{pmatrix} 1 & \frac{2n_1}{R} \\ 0 & 1 \end{pmatrix} \begin{pmatrix} 1 & 0 \\ \frac{-u}{n_1} & 1 \end{pmatrix} \begin{pmatrix} n_1\alpha_1 \\ x_1 \end{pmatrix}$$

$$= \begin{pmatrix} 1 - \dfrac{2u}{R} & \dfrac{2n_1}{R} \\ \dfrac{v}{n_3} - \dfrac{2uv}{n_3 R} - \dfrac{u}{n_1} & \dfrac{v}{n_3}\dfrac{2n_1}{R} + 1 \end{pmatrix} \begin{pmatrix} n_1\alpha_1 \\ x_1 \end{pmatrix}.$$

For a sharp image,

$$\frac{v}{n_3} - \frac{2uv}{n_3 R} - \frac{u}{n_1} = 0.$$

Rearranging this equation and using $n_3 = -n_1$ gives

$$\frac{1}{v} + \frac{1}{u} = \frac{1}{f'}, \tag{4.61a}$$

where $f' = \lim_{u\to\infty} v = R/2$. A difference of sign in Eqs (4.51b) and (4.61a) with the $1/u$ term be noted. With $n_3 = -n_1$, Eq. (4.52a) gives

$$M_x = -\frac{v}{u} \tag{4.61b}$$

as the lateral magnification produced by a mirror.

4.3 OPTICAL SYSTEMS

Optical systems use real optical elements with machining and material deficiencies. It may not be possible to mathematically model these and other imperfections present in an optical system. Furthermore, the paraxial approximation which lies at the core of the matrix formulation of the preceding section may not be fully satisfied during the actual use of an optical system. Deviations from the paraxial approximation lead to geometrical aberrations (spherical aberration, coma, astigmatism, etc.), which degrade the quality of the image formed by an optical system. These deviations, at least in principle, can be handled mathematically, but the computations can be quite long and tedious. In addition, we must take note of the fact that the index of refraction of the lens material changes with the wavelength, thus separating colors of white light in the image plane. This is the chromatic aberration. The effects of these and other aberrations are usually minimized by replacing a single lens by a suitable combination of lenses or by optimizing the radii of curvatures of the lenses (lens bending). Furthermore, diffraction of light puts a fundamental limit to the sharpness of optical images. Notwithstanding the fundamental role of diffraction in image formation, particularly in determining the resolving capability of optical systems, it is still useful to describe image formation by optical instruments within the paraxial approximation. In what follows, we shall analyze a few simple optical systems within this approximation, beginning with the simplest optical systems using just a single lens.

Before taking up specific examples, we briefly digress on the role of apertures and stops in determining image brightness and field of view of optical instruments.

4.3.1 Apertures and Stops

The rims of the lenses present in an optical system restrict the light cone and hence the brightness of the image, formed by the optical system. In addition, stops are deliberately introduced either outside or within the optical system to minimize aberrations. To identify the aperture which ultimately limits the cone of the light rays emanating from an on-axis object and making its way through

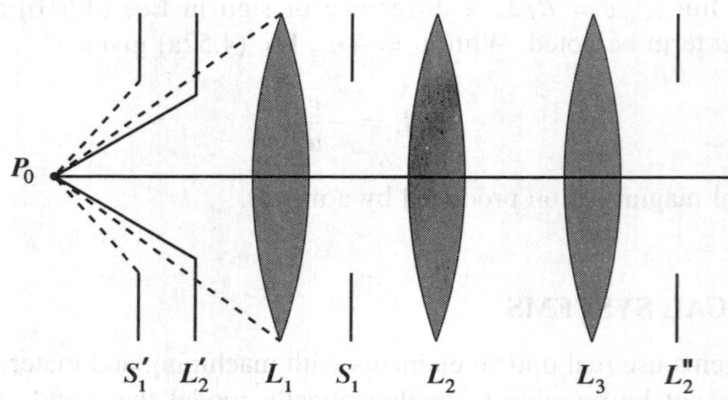

Fig. 4.18a: Optical system consisting of lenses L_1, L_2, L_3, and aperture S_1. Lens L_2 acts as the aperture stop. Its images L_2' and L_2'' formed by L_1 and L_3 are the entrance and exit pupils, respectively.

the optical system, each aperture or stop present in the optical system is imaged in the object space by the lenses which lie on the object side of it (Fig. 4.18a). The aperture image which subtends the smallest angle at the axial object is the *entrance pupil* and the physical aperture which gives rise to this image (real or virtual) is the *Aperture Stop* or the *limiting iris*. The image of the aperture stop in the image space formed by the lenses which lie on the image side of it is called the *exit pupil*. In Fig. 4.18a, L_2 is the aperture stop since its image L_2' (entrance pupil) formed by L_1 subtends the smallest angle at the axial point P_0. The exit pupil L_2'' is the image of L_2 formed by L_3. It follows that the entrance and exit pupils are images of each other.

The field of view of an optical system determines its ability to form an unobstructed image of an extended object. The aperture responsible for restricting the field of view of an optical system is called the *Field Stop*. The concept of the chief rays, also called the principal rays, is useful in determining which aperture in the optical system acts as the field stop. A *chief ray* (CR) is a ray from an off-axis object point which after passing through the center of the entrance pupil emerges from the optical system through the center of the exit pupil. The field stop determines the chief rays starting from the farthest off-axis points in the object plane (Fig. 4.18b). The image of the field stop, called the entrance window, formed in the object space by the lenses preceding it subtends the smallest angle at the center of the entrance pupil as compared to images of other apertures in the object space. This angle defines the *angular field of view* of the optical system in the object space. The object points lying within the entrance window are imaged with equal brightness (if the object illumination is uniform) but points outside the entrance window are partially or wholly obstructed by the field stop. This is known as *vignetting*.

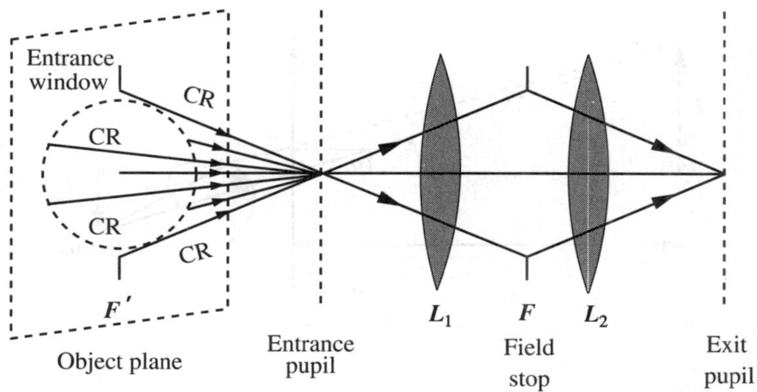

Fig. 4.18b: Optical system consisting of lenses L_1, L_2, and aperture F. The cone of the farthest chief rays passing through the center of the entrance pupil determines the field of view in the object space. Aperture F is the field stop.

4.3.2 Single Lens Magnifier

Image formation by a lens, kept in air, is described by the lens equation

$$\frac{1}{v}-\frac{1}{u}=P_{\mathrm{L}}=\frac{1}{f'},$$

where f' is the secondary focal length of the lens. A single lens magnifier is a short focal length converging lens which makes an erect and magnified image of a near object. The object is held within, but close to the focal distance from the lens (Fig. 4.19a). Accordingly, the image distance

$$v=\frac{f'}{u+f'}u \tag{4.62}$$

is negative and greater in magnitude than u. The image lies on the left of the primary focal plane. The eye usually held just behind the lens converts this virtual image into a real, inverted image on its retina. The relevant magnification in the present context is the ratio of the retinal image sizes with and without the lens. The retinal image size increases as the object is brought closer to the eye. However, the eye has to use its accommodating power to get sharp images of closer objects. The eye is most comfortable (zero accommodation) to see distant objects. The least distance of distinct vision (L) is the object distance from the eye, below which the eye fails to make a sharp image of the object. The point at the least distance of distinct vision is called the near point of the eye. The

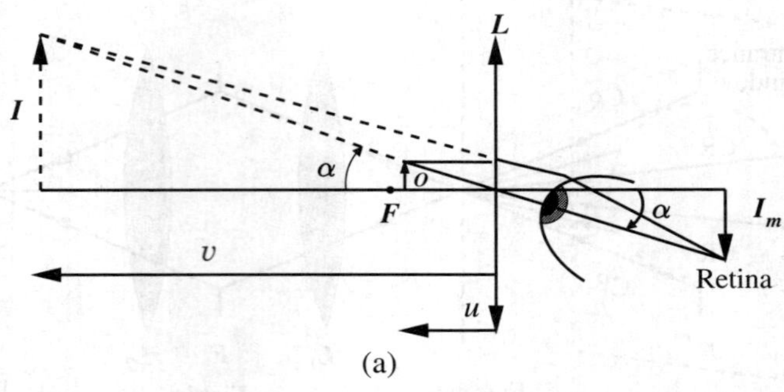

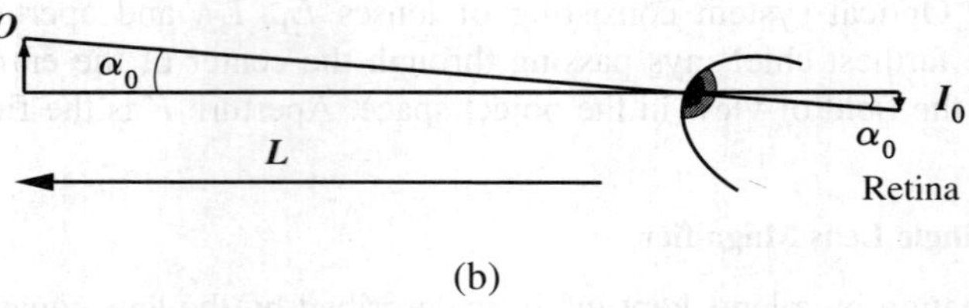

Fig. 4.19: (a) Single lens magnifier-object within the focal distance, image at the near point of the eye, (b) object at the near point of the eye.

magnifying lens allows the object to be kept well within the near point of the eye while maintaining the sharpness of the enlarged retinal image. The magnifying power of a single lens magnifier is therefore defined as the ratio of the retinal image sizes with and without the lens, the object being held at the least distance of distinct vision in the latter case (Fig. 4.19b).

The magnifying power or equivalently the angular magnification of a single lens magnifier is given by

$$M = \frac{I_m}{I_0} = \frac{\alpha}{\alpha_0}, \tag{4.63}$$

where α is the angle subtended at the eye by the virtual image I (I_m is the retinal image size under these conditions) and α_0 is the angle the same object (of size O) subtends at the eye when kept at the least distance of distinct vision (I_0 is the corresponding retinal image size). Figure 4.19 gives for an eye held just behind the lens,

$$\alpha = \frac{O}{u} = \frac{I}{v}, \quad \alpha_0 = \frac{O}{L}. \tag{4.64}$$

As per our sign convention, u, v, and L are negative. Accordingly,

$$M = \frac{I}{O}\frac{L}{v} = M_x\frac{L}{v} = \left(1 - \frac{v}{f'}\right)\frac{L}{v}$$
$$= \left(1 + \frac{|L|}{f'}\right) = 1 + |L|P_L, \tag{4.65a}$$

which is the usual expression for the lateral magnification of a lens with the restriction that the virtual image formed by the lens is located at the least distance of distinct vision of the eye ($v = L$) and the eye is kept just behind the lens. The eye is not relaxed when it receives diverging rays (Fig. 4.19a). For the eye to receive parallel rays, the object must be kept in the front focal plane of the lens (Fig. 4.20). Now, the relaxed eye can be kept anywhere behind the lens. With $\alpha = O/f$ in this arrangement, the magnifying power

$$M = \frac{L}{f} = \frac{|L|}{f'} = |L|P_{\mathrm{L}} \tag{4.65b}$$

is reduced by one unit. It can be seen that Eq. (4.65b) also holds when the eye in Fig. 4.19a is located in the secondary focal plane of the magnifier. The magnification is then independent of the exact location of the object as long as the object lies within the primary focal distance of the magnifier. This is known as the Badal principle.

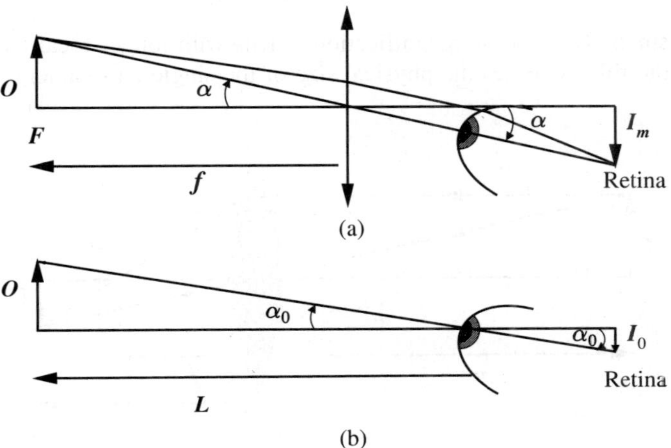

Fig. 4.20: (a) A single lens magnifier with object at the focal distance, (b) object at the near point of the eye.

There is some arbitrariness in the definition of the magnifying power of a lens magnifier. The least distance of distinct vision varies from person to person. For children, the near point can be as close as 10 cm, and for people above 50, the near point can be quite far (50 cm or more). To remove this arbitrariness, the magnifying power of a lens is usually defined for $|L| = 25\,\text{cm}$ which is the least distance of distinct vision for most young people. With this choice, a lens of power P has magnifying power ($M = |L|P$) of $P/4$ so that a $+20\,\text{D}$ lens has $5\times$ magnification. The magnifying power of a single lens can be increased by reducing its focal length, but a short focal length lens must necessarily have surfaces with small radii of curvatures. Excessive bending of rays at these surfaces runs the risk of not adhering to the paraxial approximation.

4.3.3 Single Lens Camera

A single lens magnifier makes a virtual image which is erect and enlarged. In a camera, on the other hand, one is interested in obtaining a real image of the object, usually a few meters away from the camera. This makes the object vergence $(1/u)$ negligibly small compared to the power of the lens (focal length $\approx$ a few cms). The photographic film therefore must be kept close to the secondary focal plane of the camera lens (Fig. 4.21). The distant objects are sharply focused on the film, but the near objects get focused somewhat behind the film. Slight movement of the lens away from the film allows for sharp focusing of near objects. The lateral magnification (in air)

$$M_x = 1 - \frac{v}{f'} = \frac{v}{u} \simeq \frac{f'}{u} \tag{4.66}$$

is rather small. To increase magnification, a lens with longer focal length must be used, but this increases the physical size of the single lens camera.

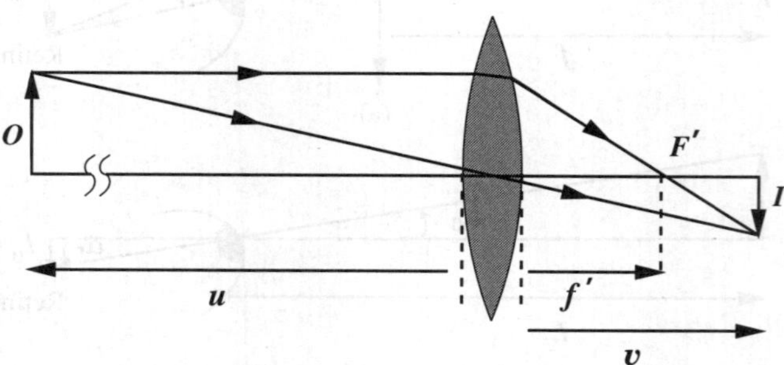

Fig. 4.21: Single lens camera; image is formed close to the back focal plane.

Image irradiance in a camera increases with the aperture area of the lens and decreases with the image area, the latter being proportional to the square of the focal length of the lens (Eq. 4.66). The ratio D/f is called the relative aperture, where D is the diameter of the lens aperture. The f-number of a camera is the inverse of its relative aperture, i.e.,

$$f\text{-number} = f/\text{number} = \frac{f}{D}.$$

The lens aperture is controlled by the iris kept in front of the lens. A camera lens with 50 mm focal length and maximum aperture diameter of 12.5 mm has f-number of 4, usually written as $f/4$.

4.3.4 Two-Lens Optical Systems

We first consider a general two-lens system kept in air (Fig. 4.22). Lenses L_1 and L_2 have powers P_1 and P_2, respectively. The primary and secondary principal planes of lens L_1 are $\mathcal{H}_1$ and $\mathcal{H}_1'$. The planes $\mathcal{H}_2$ and $\mathcal{H}_2'$ are the principal planes of lens L_2. The distances T and T' locate the primary and secondary principal planes ($\mathcal{H}$ and $\mathcal{H}'$) of the composite two-lens system with respect to the planes $\mathcal{H}_1$ and $\mathcal{H}_2'$, respectively. The separation between the lenses is represented by the distance d between the secondary principal plane of the first lens and the primary principal plane of the second lens.

The complete two-lens system matrix between its principal planes $\mathcal{H}$ and $\mathcal{H}'$ is

$$\mathcal{L}_{\mathcal{H}'\mathcal{H}} = \begin{pmatrix} 1 & 0 \\ T' & 1 \end{pmatrix} \begin{pmatrix} 1 & -P_2 \\ 0 & 1 \end{pmatrix} \begin{pmatrix} 1 & 0 \\ d & 1 \end{pmatrix} \begin{pmatrix} 1 & -P_1 \\ 0 & 1 \end{pmatrix} \begin{pmatrix} 1 & 0 \\ -T & 1 \end{pmatrix}. \tag{4.67}$$

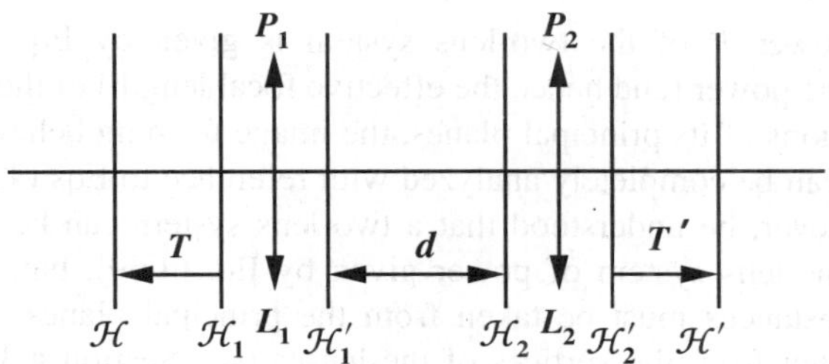

Fig. 4.22: Two-lens optical system. $\mathcal{H}$ and $\mathcal{H}'$ are the primary and secondary principal planes of the two-lens system.

It is really not necessary to work out this matrix product since the location of the principal planes $\mathcal{H}$ and $\mathcal{H}'$ can be obtained from Eqs (4.40). However, this multiplication is rather easy and we go through it as an illustration.

$$\mathcal{L}_{\mathcal{H}'\mathcal{H}} = \begin{pmatrix} 1+P_1T+P_2T-P_1P_2Td-P_2d & -P_1-P_2+P_1P_2d \\ \{T'+P_1TT'-P_2T'd-P_1P_2TT'd & \{1-P_1T'-P_2T' \\ \quad +P_2TT'+d+P_1Td-T\} & \quad +P_1P_2T'd-P_1d\} \end{pmatrix}. \tag{4.68}$$

The upper right element of this matrix gives the power of the two-lens combination, i.e.,

$$P = P_1 + P_2 - P_1P_2d. \tag{4.69}$$

Furthermore, this matrix must have unit elements along the diagonal since the principal planes are conjugate planes with unit magnification. Accordingly, we obtain

$$T = \frac{P_2d}{P}, \tag{4.70a}$$

$$T' = -\frac{P_1d}{P}. \tag{4.70b}$$

The object–image relationship between the principal planes requires the lower left element of the matrix to vanish identically. Hence,

$$TT'(P_1+P_2-P_1P_2d)+T'(1-P_2d)-T(1-P_1d)+d=0. \tag{4.71}$$

The two-lens system matrix (Eq. 4.68) then takes the simple form

$$\mathcal{L}_{\mathcal{H}'\mathcal{H}} = \begin{pmatrix} 1 & -P \\ 0 & 1 \end{pmatrix}, \tag{4.72}$$

where the power P of the two-lens system is given by Eq. (4.69). Having determined the power (and hence the effective focal length) of the optical system and the positions of its principal planes, the image forming behavior of the two-lens system can be completely analyzed with reference to Eqs (4.47) and (4.53). It must, however, be understood that a two-lens system can be replaced by an equivalent one-lens system of power given by Eq. (4.69), but now the object and image distances must be taken from the principal planes of the two-lens system, and not from the vertices of the lenses (see Section 4.3.7). Depending on the actual powers P_1, P_2 of the lenses and the separation d between them, the two-lens system can be put to a variety of uses such as a two-lens eye-piece, a microscope, a telescope, a two-lens camera, etc. We briefly discuss some of these applications.

4.3.5 The Microscope

A compound microscope uses two converging lenses (Fig. 4.23). The short focal length lens L_1 facing the object is called the objective and lens L_2 in front of the eye is called the eye-piece. The objective makes a real, inverted, and enlarged image of the object behind the primary focal plane of the eye-piece. This image acts as the object for the eye-piece which makes an enlarged, erect, and virtual image of this object just as in a single lens magnifier.

The distance d between the secondary principal plane of the first lens and the primary principal plane of the second lens is given by

$$d = f_1' + l - f_2 = f_1' + l + f_2', \tag{4.73}$$

where l (usually 16 cm) is the distance between the secondary focal plane of the first lens and the primary focal plane of the second lens. The power and hence the secondary focal length of the microscope can be obtained from Eq. (4.69), giving

$$\begin{aligned} P = \frac{1}{f'} &= \frac{1}{f_1'} + \frac{1}{f_2'} - \frac{f_1' + f_2' + l}{f_1' f_2'} \\ &= -\frac{l}{f_1' f_2'}. \end{aligned} \tag{4.74}$$

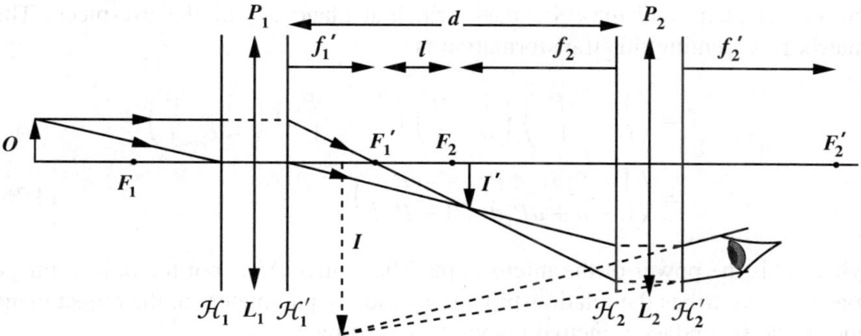

Fig. 4.23: Ray diagram for a compound microscope with final image at the near point of the eye.

The overall power of the microscope is negative ($f' = -\frac{5}{16}$ cm for $f_1' = 1$ cm, $f_2' = 5$ cm, $l = 16$ cm). Equation (4.65a) gives the magnifying power of the microscope as

$$M = 1 - \left(\frac{l}{f_1'}\right)\left(\frac{|L|}{f_2'}\right). \tag{4.75}$$

For the above example, the magnifying power of the microscope is −79. The negative sign indicates that a microscope produces an inverted image. To see this image, the eye must be kept not just behind the eye-piece but near the exit pupil which coincides with the image of the objective formed by the eye-piece, assuming the objective acts as the aperture stop as well as the entrance pupil.

The eye-piece can cause vignetting because it acts as the field stop. To avoid vignetting, an additional lens called the *field lens* is introduced a little behind the plane of the intermediate image I', where it has practically no effect on the magnifying power of the microscope. The field lens if kept in the plane of the intermediate image may distort the final image due to dust particles settling on it. The field lens is chosen to produce the image of the objective (entrance pupil) just behind the eye-piece. The pencil of emerging rays now passes through the central portion of the eye-piece, thus preventing any vignetting there. The introduction of the field lens reduces vignetting at the eye-piece, but it also reduces the eye relief since eye must now be kept close to the eye-piece. In addition, the field lens itself can cause some vignetting.

The case when the real image formed by the objective lies in the primary focal plane of the eye-piece needs special attention because in this case all rays starting from a given point on the object come out parallel from the eye-piece (Fig. 4.24). To obtain the magnifying power of a microscope under relaxed viewing, we construct the matrix representing the ray transformation between the object plane and the secondary principal plane $\mathcal{H}_2'$ of the eye-piece. The matrix representing this transformation is

$$\begin{aligned}\mathcal{M} &= \begin{pmatrix} 1 & -P_2 \\ 0 & 1 \end{pmatrix}\begin{pmatrix} 1 & 0 \\ d & 1 \end{pmatrix}\begin{pmatrix} 1 & -P_1 \\ 0 & 1 \end{pmatrix}\begin{pmatrix} 1 & 0 \\ -u & 1 \end{pmatrix} \\ &= \begin{pmatrix} 1 - P_2 d + uP & -P \\ d - u + uP_1 d & 1 - P_1 d \end{pmatrix},\end{aligned} \tag{4.76}$$

where P is the power of the microscope. The matrix $\mathcal{M}$ is not the object–image matrix. It describes the relationship among the ray parameters in the object plane and in the secondary principal plane of the eye-piece, i.e.,

$$\begin{pmatrix} n_3\alpha_3 \\ x_3 \end{pmatrix} = \begin{pmatrix} 1 - P_2 d + uP & -P \\ d - u + uP_1 d & 1 - P_1 d \end{pmatrix}\begin{pmatrix} n_1\alpha_1 \\ x_1 \end{pmatrix}, \tag{4.77}$$

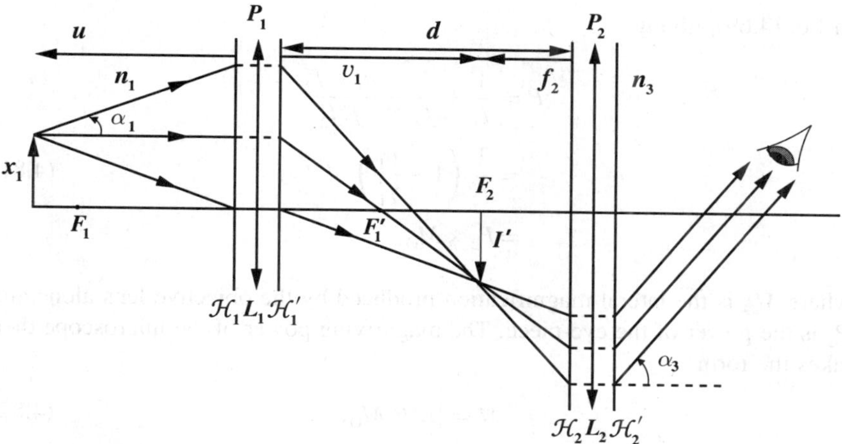

Fig. 4.24: Ray diagram for a compound microscope set for relaxed viewing.

giving

$$n_3\alpha_3 = (1 - P_2 d + uP)n_1\alpha_1 - Px_1.$$

However, the rays emerge from the eye-piece as a parallel beam. Therefore angle α_3 cannot depend on the ray angle α_1 in the object space. This can be ensured if

$$1 - P_2 d + uP = 0,$$

so that

$$\alpha_3 = -\frac{P}{n_3}x_1. \tag{4.78a}$$

Direct viewing of the object at the least distance of distinct vision (Fig. 4.19b) gives

$$\alpha_0 = \frac{x_1}{-|L|}. \tag{4.78b}$$

The magnifying power of the microscope under these conditions ($n_3 = 1$) is

$$M = \frac{\alpha_3}{\alpha_0} = |L|P. \tag{4.79}$$

The effective power of the microscope can be obtained by substituting

$$d = v_1 - f_2 = v_1 + f_2' \tag{4.80}$$

in Eq. (4.69), giving

$$\begin{aligned} P &= \frac{1}{f_1'} + \frac{1}{f_2'} - \frac{v_1 + f_2'}{f_1' f_2'} \\ &= \frac{1}{f_2'}\left(1 - \frac{v_1}{f_1'}\right) \\ &= P_2 \times M_{\mathrm{O}}, \end{aligned} \tag{4.81}$$

where M_{O} is the lateral magnification produced by the objective lens alone and P_2 is the power of the eye-piece. The magnifying power of the microscope then takes the form

$$M = |L| P_2 M_{\mathrm{O}}, \tag{4.82}$$

where $|L|P_2$ is the magnifying power of the eye-piece (Eq. 4.65b). Thus, the magnifying power of a microscope adjusted for relaxed viewing (image at infinity) is the product of the lateral magnification of the objective and the angular magnification of the eye-piece.

To reduce the chromatic and geometrical aberrations (primarily coma and spherical aberrations) of a microscope, suitable combinations of lenses replace its objective and eye-piece. A high magnification microscope objective makes use of the aplanatic points of a spherical surface (see Section 5.2) and the eye-piece usually consists of two lenses – the field lens and the eye-lens, a certain distance apart (see Section 5.6).

Figure 4.25 shows a part of the microscope objective consisting of a plano-convex lens and a meniscus lens. The latter is an asymmetrical lens whose both centers of curvatures lie on the same side of the lens. A small biological sample P kept under a thin cover glass is illuminated from below. It is desirable that the largest cone of light originating from the sample enters the microscope. With air between the cover glass and the plano-convex lens (Fig. 4.25a), angle θ of the light cone entering the microscope is determined by

$$n_{\mathrm{g}} \sin\theta = 1 \sin\theta_1,$$

where n_{g} is the index of refraction of the cover glass. Refraction at the upper surface of the cover glass increases the angular divergence of the rays reaching the microscope objective ($\theta_1 > \theta$). In Fig. 4.25b, a transparent liquid of index of refraction n_1, very close to the index of refraction of the cover glass, fills the gap. The cone of light now given by

$$n_{\mathrm{g}} \sin\theta' = n_1 \sin\theta_2$$

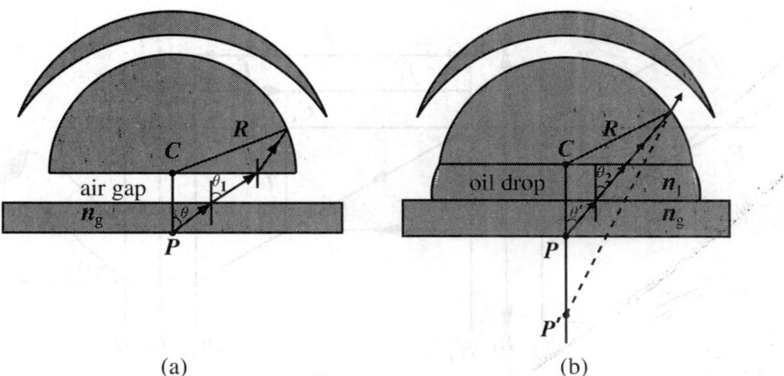

Fig. 4.25: Oil immersion microscope objective; object P lies below the cover glass. (a) Air gap between the cover glass and hemispherical lens, (b) oil drop between the cover glass and hemispherical lens. Points P and P' are aplanatic points of the spherical surface of the plano-convex lens.

reaching the microscope objective is considerably increased ($\theta' > \theta$). This is the oil-immersion technique of increasing the numerical aperture ($\text{NA} = n \sin\theta$) of a microscope. The object P and its virtual image P' are located at the aplanatic points of the spherical surface of the convex lens (see Section 5.2). The divergence of the rays can be further reduced by pushing the virtual image formed by the meniscus lens farther away along the line PP', while the imaging still takes place between the aplanatic points of the surfaces.

4.3.6 The Telescope

Like a microscope, a telescope also consists of an objective and an eye-piece. A microscope is used to get a magnified view of a near object. A telescope, on the other hand, is used to see distant objects – astronomical or terrestrial. Rays from a distant object arrive at the objective of the telescope as a parallel beam making a small angle with its optical axis. If the eye-piece is adjusted for relaxed viewing, the rays leave the eye-piece also as a parallel beam, making a relatively larger angle with the optical axis. A telescope used under these conditions is called an afocal telescope since it possesses zero net power. It behaves like a dielectric slab in the sense that a parallel beam comes out as a parallel beam, but unlike for a slab with parallel faces, the incident and emergent beams are not parallel. A two-lens Keplerian telescope, also called an astronomical telescope, employs positive lenses in a manner that the secondary focal plane of the objective coincides with the primary focal plane of the eye-piece (Fig. 4.26a). The Galilean or the

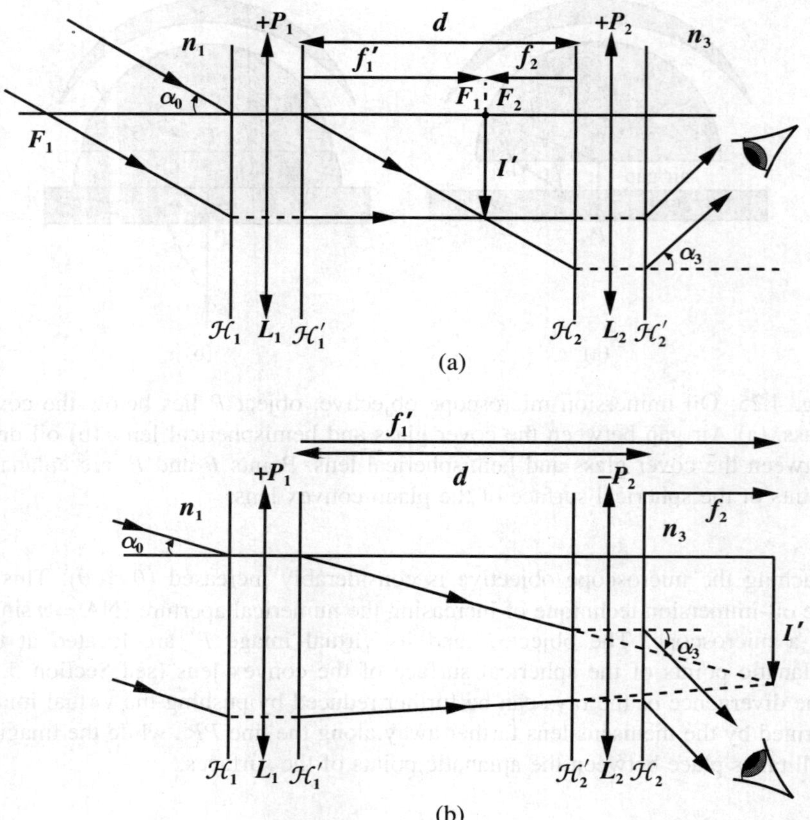

Fig. 4.26: Ray diagram for (a) a two-lens Keplerian telescope, (b) a two-lens Galilean telescope.

terrestrial telescope uses a positive objective lens and a negative eye-piece lens (Fig. 4.26b). Once again, the secondary focal plane of the objective and primary focal plane of the eye-piece coincide. In both cases, the outgoing rays leave as parallel beams.

The separation between the lenses taken as the distance between the secondary principal plane of the objective and the primary principal plane of the eye-piece is given by

$$d = f_1' - f_2 = f_1' + f_2',$$

where f_2 is negative and f_2' is positive for the Keplerian telescope and just the opposite holds for the Galelian telescope. Accordingly, the power of the telescope is zero in both cases, i.e.,

$$\begin{aligned} P &= P_1 + P_2 - P_1 P_2 d \\ &= \frac{1}{f_1'} + \frac{1}{f_2'} - \frac{f_1' + f_2'}{f_1' f_2'} \\ &= 0. \end{aligned} \tag{4.83}$$

The principal planes of an afocal telescope move out to infinity (Eqs 4.70). It is therefore not very useful to construct the ray matrix for an afocal telescope between its principal planes. Instead, we construct the ray matrix for the transformation between the primary principal plane of the objective and the secondary principal plane of the eye-piece:

$$\begin{aligned} \mathcal{L}_{\mathcal{H}_2'\mathcal{H}_1} &= \begin{pmatrix} 1 & -P_2 \\ 0 & 1 \end{pmatrix} \begin{pmatrix} 1 & 0 \\ f_1' + f_2' & 1 \end{pmatrix} \begin{pmatrix} 1 & -P_1 \\ 0 & 1 \end{pmatrix} \\ &= \begin{pmatrix} \frac{-f_1'}{f_2'} & 0 \\ f_1' + f_2' & -\frac{f_2'}{f_1'} \end{pmatrix}. \end{aligned} \tag{4.84}$$

The angular magnification produced by the telescope between the above planes can be obtained from the matrix equation

$$\begin{pmatrix} n_3\alpha_3 \\ x_3 \end{pmatrix} = \begin{pmatrix} \frac{-f_1'}{f_2'} & 0 \\ f_1' + f_2' & -\frac{f_2'}{f_1'} \end{pmatrix} \begin{pmatrix} n_1\alpha_0 \\ x_1 \end{pmatrix},$$

giving

$$M_\alpha = \frac{\alpha_3}{\alpha_0} = -\frac{n_1}{n_3}\frac{f_1'}{f_2'}. \tag{4.85}$$

So that

$$\mathcal{L}_{\mathcal{H}_2'\mathcal{H}_1} = \begin{pmatrix} -\frac{n_3 M_\alpha}{n_1} & 0 \\ f_1' + f_2' & -\frac{n_1}{n_3 M_\alpha} \end{pmatrix}. \tag{4.86}$$

A Keplerian telescope has negative angular magnification (f_1' and f_2' are both positive) and a Galelian telescope has positive angular magnification (f_2' is negative).

The object–image relationship for an afocal telescope for viewing relatively near objects can be obtained from the two-lens system matrix (Eq. 4.68) by

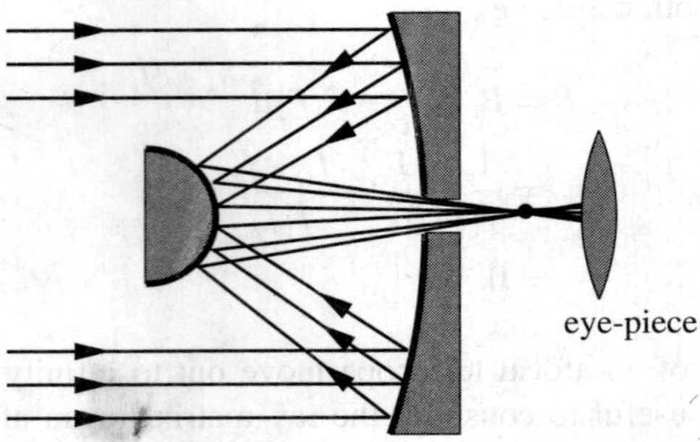

Fig. 4.27: Cassegrain telescope with hyperboloidal mirrors.

treating T and T' not as the distances of the principal planes but as the object and image distances (u, v) from the first and last vertices of the telescope, respectively. Equation (4.71) gives the image distance as

$$v = \frac{u(1-P_1 d)}{1-P_2 d} - \frac{d}{1-P_2 d}$$
$$= u\left(\frac{f_2'}{f_1'}\right)^2 + f_2'\left(1+\frac{f_2'}{f_1'}\right)$$

with lateral magnification $M_x = -f_2'/f_1'$. An afocal telescope used in reverse (light entering from the side of the eye-piece) acts as a beam expander, often used to expand laser beams (see Section 11.3.1.1).

Astronomical telescopes generally use mirrors and not lenses since good quality lenses with large apertures are difficult to make. In addition, mirrors are free from chromatic aberration. A typical reflecting telescope (Cassegrain) employing hyperboloidal mirrors is shown in Fig. 4.27.

4.3.7 Telephoto Lens

A long focal length lens increases image magnification in a single lens camera. However, to keep the physical dimensions of the camera small, low power lens must not increase the distance of the image plane from the lens. A multi-element telephoto lens can meet these apparently conflicting requirements for imaging distant objects. We illustrate this by considering a two-element telephoto lens. The first lens is usually a weakly converging lens of focal length f_1', followed by a diverging lens of focal length f_2', a distance d apart such that $f_1' > d > f_1' + f_2'$, where f_2' is negative. To keep the analysis simple, lenses are assumed thin.

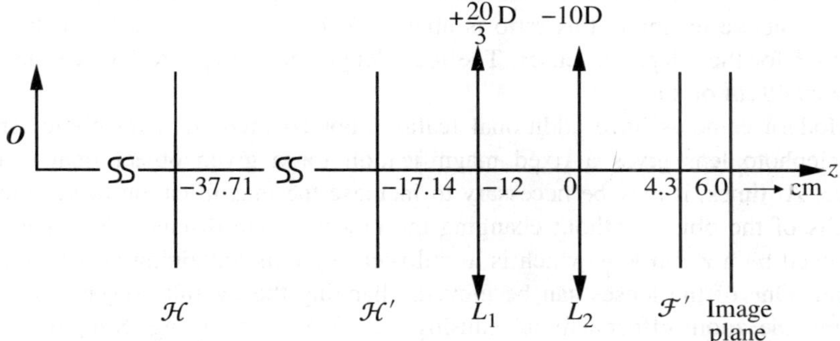

Fig. 4.28: Two-element telephoto lens.

Figure 4.28 shows a $(+20/3)$ D converging lens kept 12 cm in front of a -10 D diverging lens. The power of the combination is

$$P = P_1 + P_2 - P_1 P_2 d = +\frac{14}{3} \text{D}.$$

The positive power of the combination ensures that a real image of a distant object is formed. The primary and secondary focal lengths of the lens combination, measured from their respective principal planes, are $-150/7$ and $+150/7$ cm, respectively. Equations (4.70) determine the positions of the principal planes at $T = -180/7$ cm and $T' = -120/7$ cm. Thus, both principal planes of the telephoto lens have been pushed out of the camera to its left. The positions of the pertinent planes of the telephoto lens are shown in the figure. All distances are measured with respect to the back lens.

The principal planes $\mathcal{H}$ and $\mathcal{H}'$ of the telephoto lens lie at 37.71 and 17.14 cm to the left of the back lens. The secondary focal plane $\mathcal{F}'$ of the combination lies only 4.3 cm to the right of the back lens. The object has been taken 3.25 m to the left of the back lens. The image plane lies 23.1 cm to the right of the principal plane $\mathcal{H}'$ and just 6 cm behind the back lens. With the photographic film kept in the image plane, the long dimension of the camera for this lens combination goes to 18 cm. The lateral magnification produced by this telephoto lens is

$$M_x = 1 - \frac{v}{f'} = -0.08.$$

This should be compared with -0.02 magnification of the single lens camera of 6 cm focal length and object distance of 3 m. The telephoto effect is the ratio of the focal length of the telephoto lens to its overall length which is the distance between the first lens and the secondary focal plane (F') of the telephoto lens. For the above example, this ratio is about 1.3. Usually this ratio lies between 2 and 3 for the telephoto lenses. The focal length of a telephoto lens can be as high as 40 cm or so.

Modern cameras have additional features not covered by a telephoto lens. A telephoto lens gives a fixed magnification for a given object–image distance. At times, it may be necessary to increase the magnification to see more details of the object without changing the object–image distance. This can be achieved by a zoom lens which is a multi-lens system containing at least three lenses. One of the lenses can be moved, changing the overall power and producing the zoom effect without causing significant defocusing. Simple zoom configurations will be taken up as problems at the end of the chapter (Problem 4.7). The paraxial approximation is usually invalidated in the normal use of a camera. Modern cameras have additional features to minimize image aberrations, associated with large angles. Tessar is one such lens configuration (see Problem 4.6).

4.4 OPTICS OF A LASER CAVITY

We now consider an optical system in which the direction of propagation of a ray changes by reflection, and not by refraction as in earlier examples. In a laser, the active medium, for example an appropriate mixture of helium and neon gases in a He–Ne laser is kept in a cylindrical cavity with highly reflecting mirrors at the two ends. Light emitted by the excited atoms or molecules goes back and forth between the mirrors repeatedly and gets amplified in the process. Here, our intention is not to introduce laser concepts to the reader, but to show how the ray matrix approach can be applied to light propagation in a laser cavity. Diffraction effects are ignored. Figure 4.29 shows a cylindrical laser cavity of length L enclosed between spherical mirrors M_1 and M_2, where n is the index of refraction of the medium filling the cavity. Consider a ray starting from point A on mirror M_1 and returning back to point C after undergoing a reflection at point B of mirror M_2. This ray completes one round trip after getting reflected at point C. The ray angles are exaggerated for clarity but are expected to be small enough to satisfy the paraxial approximation. The translation of the ray from mirror M_1 to M_2 along the path AB is described by the ray matrix

$$\mathcal{T}_{21} = \begin{pmatrix} 1 & 0 \\ \frac{L}{n} & 1 \end{pmatrix}, \tag{4.87}$$

and the reflection at B by the matrix

$$\mathcal{R}_2' = \begin{pmatrix} 1 & -\frac{n'-n}{R_1'} \\ 0 & 1 \end{pmatrix} = \begin{pmatrix} 1 & -\frac{(-n-n)}{-R_2} \\ 0 & 1 \end{pmatrix}$$
$$= \begin{pmatrix} 1 & -\frac{2n}{R_2} \\ 0 & 1 \end{pmatrix}, \tag{4.88}$$

where R_1' being negative by our sign convention has been replaced by $-R_2$. R_2 is positive and has the same magnitude as R_1'. Here, reflection has been treated as refraction from a medium of refractive index n to a medium of refractive index $n' = -n$ (see Section 4.2.6). The ray matrix describing the translation from B to C has the form

$$\mathcal{T}_{12} = \begin{pmatrix} 1 & 0 \\ \frac{-L}{-n} & 1 \end{pmatrix} = \begin{pmatrix} 1 & 0 \\ \frac{L}{n} & 1 \end{pmatrix}. \tag{4.89}$$

This translation is subsequent to the reflection from mirror M_2 and therefore the reflected ray has been assumed to travel in a medium of refractive index $-n$. Furthermore, for the return trip, the translation is to be measured from vertex V_2 and hence the negative sign with L. The subsequent reflection at mirror M_1 is

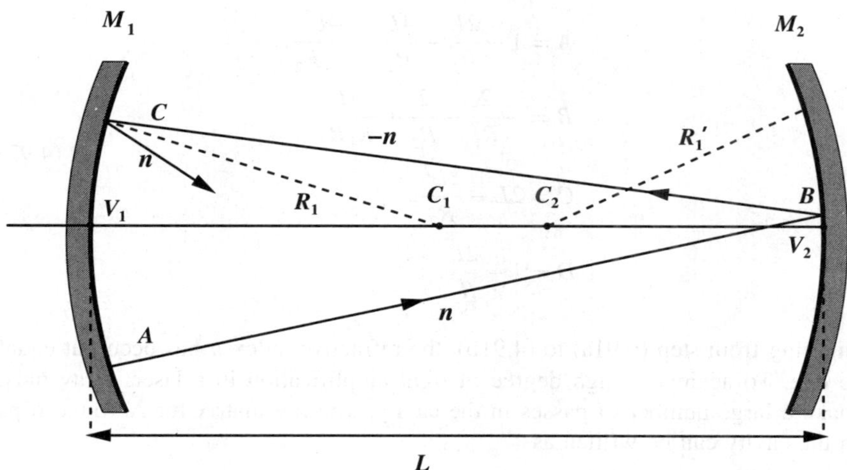

Fig. 4.29: Ray transformation in a cylindrical laser cavity of length L; mirrors M_1 and M_2 have radii of curvatures of R_1 and R_1'.

to be treated as refraction from a medium of refractive index $(-n)$ to one with refractive index $(+n)$ and is described by the matrix

$$\mathcal{R}_1' = \begin{pmatrix} 1 & -\frac{n-(-n)}{R_1} \\ 0 & 1 \end{pmatrix} = \begin{pmatrix} 1 & -\frac{2n}{R_1} \\ 0 & 1 \end{pmatrix}, \tag{4.90}$$

where R_1 is positive. In Fig. 4.29, M_1 and M_2 are both concave mirrors with positive powers. If M_1 and M_2 happen to be convex mirrors, then R_1 and R_2 will be negative in the present notation. The matrix representing the ray transformation for one complete round trip in the cavity is the product matrix

$$\mathcal{M} = \mathcal{R}_1'\mathcal{T}_{12}\mathcal{R}_2'\mathcal{T}_{21}$$

$$= \begin{pmatrix} 1 & -\frac{2n}{R_1} \\ 0 & 1 \end{pmatrix}\begin{pmatrix} 1 & 0 \\ \frac{L}{n} & 1 \end{pmatrix}\begin{pmatrix} 1 & -\frac{2n}{R_2} \\ 0 & 1 \end{pmatrix}\begin{pmatrix} 1 & 0 \\ \frac{L}{n} & 1 \end{pmatrix} \tag{4.91a}$$

$$= \begin{pmatrix} 1 - \frac{2L}{R_2} - \frac{4L}{R_1} + \frac{4L^2}{R_1R_2} & -\frac{2}{R_1} - \frac{2}{R_2} + \frac{4L}{R_1R_2} \\ 2L - \frac{2L^2}{R_2} & 1 - \frac{2L}{R_2} \end{pmatrix} \tag{4.91b}$$

$$= \begin{pmatrix} A & B \\ C & D \end{pmatrix}, \tag{4.91c}$$

where

$$\begin{aligned} A &= 1 - \frac{2L}{R_2} - \frac{4L}{R_1} + \frac{4L^2}{R_1R_2}, \\ B &= -\frac{2}{R_1} - \frac{2}{R_2} + \frac{4L}{R_1R_2}, \\ C &= 2L - \frac{2L^2}{R_2}, \\ D &= 1 - \frac{2L}{R_2}. \end{aligned} \tag{4.92}$$

In going from step (4.91a) to (4.91b), the refractive index n has been put equal to one. To achieve a high degree of light amplification in a laser, a ray must make a large number of passes in the cavity. The ray matrix for N round trips in the cavity can be written as

$$M^N = \begin{pmatrix} A & B \\ C & D \end{pmatrix}^N. \tag{4.93}$$

For large enough N, evaluation of this matrix is a tedious task. We can obtain an analytical expression for the N-trip matrix by assuming the trace of the $ABCD$ matrix to satisfy the condition

$$-2 \leq A + D \leq +2, \tag{4.94}$$

in which case, we can write

$$A + D = 2\cos\theta \tag{4.95}$$

We can now make use of the Sylvester's theorem, according to which

$$\begin{pmatrix} A & B \\ C & D \end{pmatrix}^N = \frac{1}{\sin\theta}\begin{bmatrix} A\sin N\theta - \sin(N-1)\theta & B\sin N\theta \\ C\sin N\theta & D\sin N\theta - \sin(N-1)\theta \end{bmatrix}. \tag{4.96}$$

The theorem can be proved by the method of induction. It obviously holds for $N = 1$. The ray transformation for N round trips inside the cavity satisfies the matrix equation

$$\begin{pmatrix} n_1'\alpha_1' \\ x_1' \end{pmatrix} = \frac{1}{\sin\theta}\begin{bmatrix} A\sin N\theta - \sin(N-1)\theta & B\sin N\theta \\ C\sin N\theta & D\sin N\theta - \sin(N-1)\theta \end{bmatrix}\begin{pmatrix} n_1\alpha_1 \\ x_1 \end{pmatrix}. \tag{4.97}$$

The ray coordinate

$$x_1' = \frac{1}{\sin\theta}\left[(C\sin N\theta)n_1\alpha_1 + \{D\sin N\theta - \sin(N-1)\theta\}x_1\right] \tag{4.98}$$

after making N round trips in the cavity oscillates and therefore remains finite as long as Eq. (4.94) is satisfied. This leads to the confinement of the ray within the cavity after N round trips. A laser cavity satisfying this condition constitutes a stable resonator. Accordingly, a stable resonator must satisfy

$$\begin{aligned}
&-2 \le 2 - \frac{4L}{R_1} - \frac{4L}{R_2} + \frac{4L^2}{R_1 R_2} \le 2 \\
&\to -1 \le 1 - \frac{2L}{R_1} - \frac{2L}{R_2} + \frac{2L^2}{R_1 R_2} \le 1 \\
&\to -2 \le -\frac{2L}{R_1} - \frac{2L}{R_2} + \frac{2L^2}{R_1 R_2} \le 0 \\
&\to -1 \le -\frac{L}{R_1} - \frac{L}{R_2} + \frac{L^2}{R_1 R_2} \le 0 \qquad (4.99) \\
&\to 0 \le 1 - \frac{L}{R_1} - \frac{L}{R_2} + \frac{L^2}{R_1 R_2} \le 1 \\
&\to 0 \le \left(1 - \frac{L}{R_1}\right)\left(1 - \frac{L}{R_2}\right) \le 1 \\
&\to 0 \le g_1 g_2 \le 1,
\end{aligned}$$

where

$$g_1 = 1 - \frac{L}{R_1}, \quad g_2 = 1 - \frac{L}{R_2}. \tag{4.100}$$

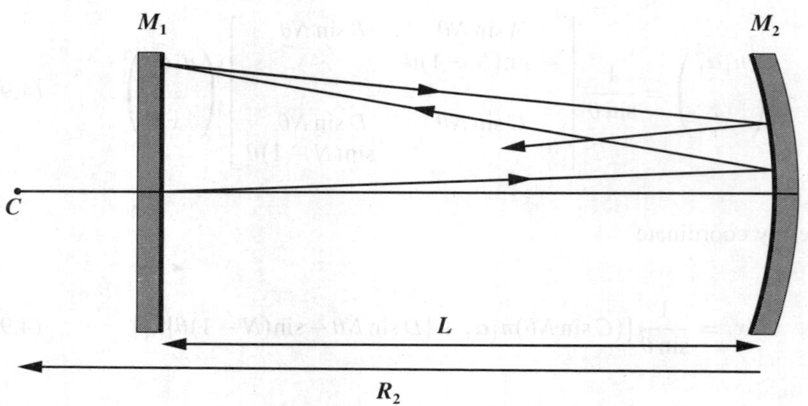

Fig. 4.30: Laser cavity with $R_1 = \infty$, $R_2 > L$.

Therefore for a stable resonator, the product $g_1 \ g_2$ must lie between 0 and 1. The resonator becomes unstable, i.e., the rays do not remain confined to the resonator after N round trips if Eq. (4.99) is not satisfied. A He–Ne laser cavity (Fig. 4.30) with $R_1 = \infty$ (flat mirror), $R_2 > L$ has $g_1 = 1$, $g_2 = 1 - \frac{L}{R_2} < 1$ (but >0), making the cavity a stable resonator. Note that in our notation, R_1 and R_2 are both positive for a cavity using concave mirrors. If any of the cavity mirrors is convex, the corresponding radius of curvature must be taken with a negative sign.

4.5 OPTICS OF THE HUMAN EYE

The human eye closely resembles a spherical ball of diameter in the range of 22–24 mm. Light enters the eye through the cornea consisting of a transparent tissue of refractive index 1.376. The cornea is about 12 mm in diameter and nearly 0.6 mm thick at the center with hardly any trace of blood. The air–cornea interface provides nearly three-fourths of eye's refractive power as maximum refractive index change ($n = 1$ to $n = 1.376$) occurs at this interface. Immediately behind the cornea is the anterior chamber filled with the fluid called the aqueous humor with an index of refraction of 1.336. The cornea–aqueous interface with a rather small ($\Delta n = 0.040$) refractive index change across it does not contribute much towards the power of the eye. Submerged in the aqueous humor is the iris which controls the opening of the aperture (called the pupil) through which light enters the rest of the eye. The color of the pigment around the iris determines the color of the eye. The pupil can open up to 8 mm in dim light and for bright light the pupil opening can be as small as 2 mm. After passing through the pupil, light enters the crystalline lens which not only provides additional power, but is also responsible for the entire accommodating power of the eye. Its shape and size changes during accommodation under the control of the ciliary muscles (see Fig. 4.31). Under relaxed viewing of distant objects, the front surface of the eye lens is flatter than its back surface. For seeing nearer objects, the front surface bulges out, reducing its radius of curvature and the focal length. Accommodation is the ability of the eye to reduce the focal length of the crystalline lens while seeing near objects. The crystalline lens, made of several layers of tissue is nearly 4 mm thick and 9 mm in diameter. The index of refraction near the center of the lens is 1.406, and 1.386 near its periphery as if nature knew how to correct for the spherical aberration (see Section 5.5.1). The crystalline lens is followed by the posterior chamber filled with vitreous humor of very nearly the same index of refraction as the aqueous humor. The aqueous–lens and lens–vitreous interfaces provide the remaining refractive power of the eye. After passing through the lens and vitreous humor, light makes its way to the retina at the back of the eye. Retina is the seat of millions of photo receptors in the form of rods and cones.

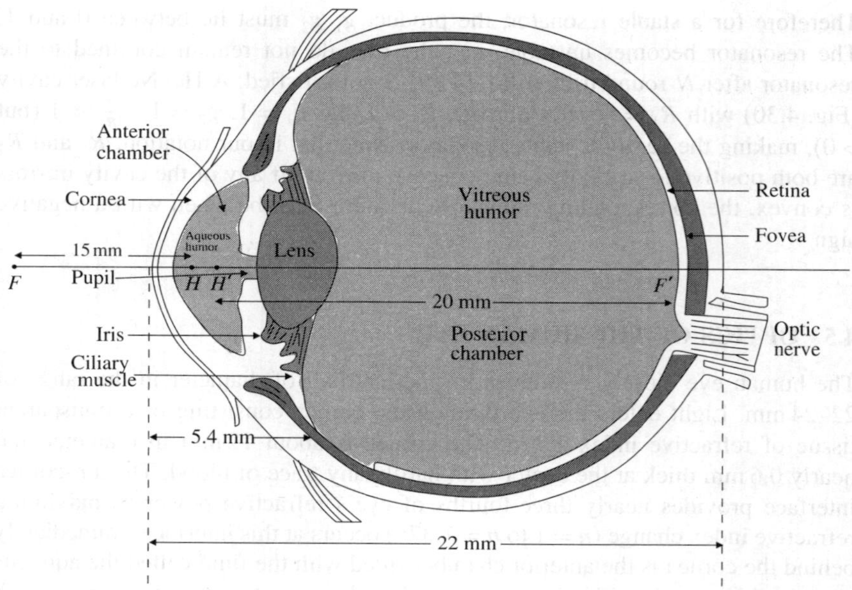

Fig. 4.31: Horizontal section of a human eye – a model representation.

The rods and cones are unevenly distributed – rods being more numerous near the periphery of the retina and cones dominate the central portion of the retina. The rods, nearly 2 μm in diameter, function like a black and white film, unable to distinguish between colors. The rods possess high photo-sensitivity and are active in dim light. The rods are capable of detecting a single light photon. The rods get easily saturated and become inactive during bright light such as the day light. In comparison, the cones (nearly 6 μm in diameter) can distinguish colors but require bright light illumination. The information collected by the rods and cones is transmitted to the brain by the optic nerve. At the root of the optic nerve, the retina is devoid of the rods and cones. This spot is called the blind spot. The Fovea, consisting of only the cones, lies near the center of the retina. Foveal vision is used for distinguishing very fine details as, for example, during reading and viewing distant objects.

Eyes vary from person to person. Several models of the eye exist and they differ somewhat from each other. Figure 4.31 is one model representation of the horizontal section of the eye. The distances given in the figure may not exactly match with actual distances in the eye, but they adequately describe the image forming properties of the eye. The figure shows that the primary and secondary focal lengths of the eye are quite different. The primary focal length is shown to be 15 mm and the secondary focal length is 20 mm. This has to do with the substantial difference in the refractive indices of the media (air and aqueous) on the two sides of the cornea. The representative primary focal length of the eye may be taken approximately as 17 mm for a relaxed eye and 14 mm for a fully accommodated eye. The power of the cornea is +43 D and the crystalline lens if kept in air would have power of +19 D. A standard eye has +58.6 D power when viewing distant objects. Visual acuity concerns the resolving capability of the eye. A 6/6 eye can resolve details up to 1 arcmin.

4.5.1 Defects of the Human Eye

An eye with its secondary focal plane coincident with the retina is called the normal or the *emmetropic eye*. An eye for which this does not happen is called the *ametropic eye*. An ametropic eye is *myopic* if the secondary focal plane of the eye lies in front of the retina. A myopic eye would obviously have difficulty in seeing distant objects because they get focused in front of the retina. However, myopic eye has no difficulty in seeing near objects because they are imaged on the retina or close to it with no or little eye accommodation. In fact, a myopic eye has an advantage in seeing near objects because its near point (located at the least distance of distinct vision) can be considerably closer than for an emmetropic eye. This abnormality of the eye can be corrected by the use of spectacles fitted with negative lenses which reduce the overall power of the eyes. The increased focal length of the eye–spectacle combination brings the secondary focal plane in coincidence with the retina. The myopic defect arises because the eye happens to be a bit too long along its axis. Normal eyesight of a myopic eye can be restored in a surgical intervention called *radial keratotomy*. The cornea of the eye is given appropriate cuts either with a surgical knife or with a laser. Upon healing, the cornea tends to flatten, thus reducing the power of the eye. Similarly, in some cases, the eye ball is somewhat smaller so that the secondary focal plane of the eye lies behind the retina. This is the *hyperopic* condition or far-sightedness of the eye. To bring the images of distant objects on the retina, the eye makes use of its accommodating power. A far-sighted person can see distant objects but only with eye accommodation and the accompanied strain. The eye accommodation is insufficient for a far-sighted person to see near objects clearly. The near-point has moved farther away. The hyperopia (also called *hypermetropia*) of the eye can be corrected by using spectacles with converging lenses. The secondary focal point moves back to overlap with the retina. *Presbyopia* is the gradual loss of eye accommodation which sets in adults beyond the age of 40. Spectacles fitted with bifocal lenses (one for seeing near objects and the other for seeing distant objects) provide the necessary compensation for presbyopia.

In addition, an eye can suffer from an abnormality condition called *Astigmatism*. This is a fairly common defect caused by an uneven cornea. Ideally, the cornea possesses rotational symmetry. However, it may happen that different portions of the cornea have different radii of curvatures and hence different powers. This asymmetry leads to blurring of the images on the retina. Regular astigmatism occurs when the directions along which the power of the cornea has maximum and minimum values are orthogonal to each other. This abnormality can be corrected by the use of cylindrical lenses which have zero power in the direction of the axis of the cylinder. The cylindrical lens is usually ground on the back of the spherical lens used to correct other defects of the eye. For more details on the functioning of the human eye, the reader is referred to *Geometric, Physical, and Visual Optics* by Michael P. Keating [4.3].

4.6 CYLINDRICAL LENS

A cylindrical rod of a transparent material acts as an equiconvex cylindrical lens if light enters the rod through its curved surface. A cylindrical lens has two perpendicular meridians. The meridian, parallel to the axis of the cylinder having flat cross-section is the axis meridian (Fig. 4.32a). This meridian has zero refractive power. The meridian with circular cross-section, perpendicular to the axis meridian, is the power meridian. Lensing action takes place only in the power meridian. In the paraxial approximation, a plane incident wavefront becomes cylindrical on exiting the lens, converging to a line on its axis. Figure 4.32b shows the point object O in front of a plano–convex cylindrical lens with vertical

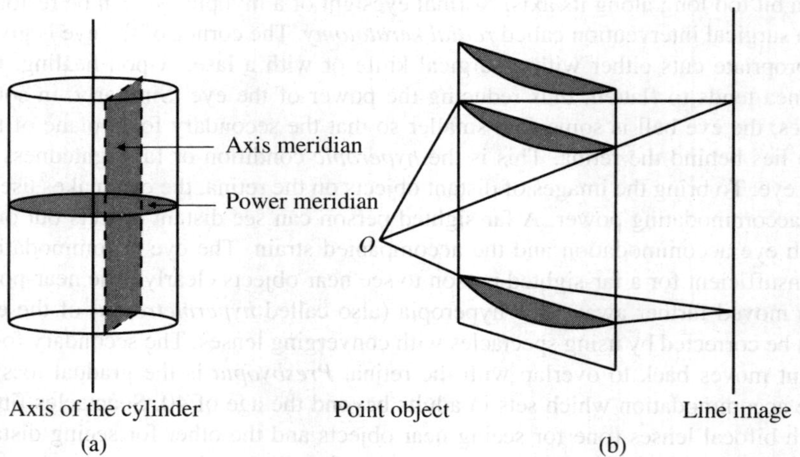

Fig. 4.32: (a) Equiconvex cylindrical lens, (b) plano–convex cylindrical lens with vertical axis meridian. Each horizontal segment of the lens forms a point image of the point object in its horizontal plane. The image is a vertical line.

axis meridian. The paraxial image of the point is a vertical line. To understand the formation of the line image, the lens may be divided into thin horizontal segments. The power meridian being horizontal in this case, each horizontal segment of the lens converges the rays (incident on it) horizontally to form a point image in its horizontal plane. The net result is a vertical line image, parallel to the axis meridian, but produced by the power meridian. Equation (4.101)

$$P = (n-1)\left(\frac{1}{R_1} - \frac{1}{R_2}\right) \tag{4.101}$$

for the power of a spherical lens in air is applicable to the cylindrical lens as well provided it is understood that the lensing action takes place only in the power meridian.

4.7 REFERENCES

4.1 Edward L. O'Neill, Introduction to Statistical Optics, Addison-Wesley Publishing Company, Inc., Reading, 1963.

4.2 Allen Nussbaum and Richard A. Phillips, Contemporary Optics for Scientists and Engineers, Prentice-Hall, Inc., Englewood Cliffs, New Jersey, 1976.

4.3 Michael P. Keating, Geometric, Physical, and Visual Optics, Butterworths, Boston, 1988.

4.4 A. Gerrad and J. M. Burch, Introduction to Matrix Methods in Optics, Dover Publications, Inc., New York, 1994.

4.5 Miles V. Klein and Thomas E. Furtak, Optics, 2nd ed., John Wiley & Sons, New York, 1986.

4.6 Pantazis Mouroulis and John Macdonald, Geometrical Optics and Optical design, Oxford University Press, New York, 1997.

4.7 Eugene Hecht, Optics, 4th ed., Addison-Wesley, Reading, 2001.

4.8 Frank L. Pedrotti, S. J. Leno and S. Pedrotti, Introduction to Optics, 2nd ed., Prentice-Hall, New Jersey, 1993.

4.8 PROBLEMS

4.1 A transparent rod of length 20 cm and index of refraction 1.5 has polished end surfaces of radii of curvatures of 10 and −10 cm. Find the position and nature of the image of a small axial object kept at a distance of 20 cm from the left vertex of the rod.

4.2 Two identical thin convex lenses, each of focal length 10 cm, are 25 cm apart. Find the position of the image of a distant axial object by considering the image formed by the first lens as the object for the second, and also by considering a single lens which is equivalent to the above two-lens combination.

4.3 A concave lens of focal length -20 cm lies 6 cm behind a convex lens of focal length $+10$ cm. Locate the cardinal planes of this combination of lenses. An object lies 28.75 cm in front of the convex lens. Find the position and lateral magnification of the final image. Comment on the use of this lens combination as a telephoto lens.

4.4 Two small objects lie on the axis of a transparent cylindrical rod of length 10 cm and index of refraction 1.56. The rod has flat, polished end surfaces. One object is stuck to the front surface of the rod and the other is kept 2 cm in front of it as shown in Fig. 4.33. Use the paraxial ray matrix approach to locate the images of the objects. Interpret your results in terms of the real and apparent depths.

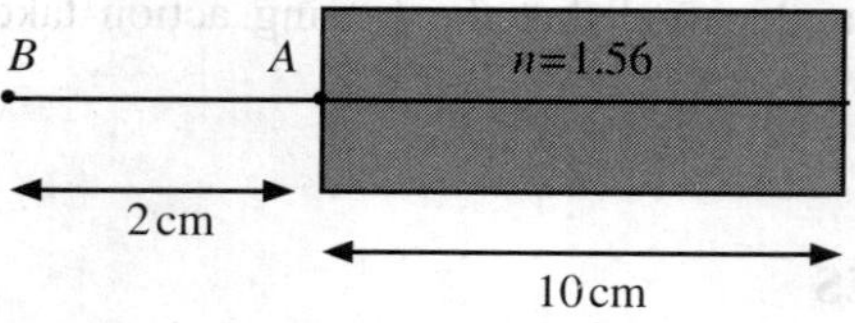

Fig. 4.33.

4.5 A small object lies in front of a transparent ball of radius R and index of refraction n as shown in Fig. 4.34. Consider light entering the ball at small angles only. On reaching the back surface of the ball, light is partly reflected and partly transmitted. Find the restriction on the index of refraction n if the image formed by the reflected light is to be at the position of the object. What should be the object distance for this to happen? Trace the path of rays. Find image magnification and check if the Smith–Helmholtz formula (Eq. 4.49) holds. Consider the special case of $n = 2$. Such round particles are used as retro-reflectors in highway signs.

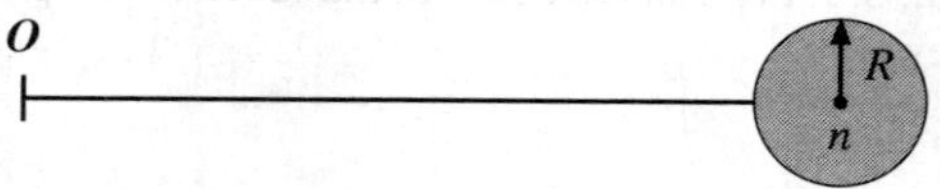

Fig. 4.34.

4.6 Find the positions of the principal and focal planes of a lens combination with parameters given in the following table (taken from Ref. 4.1). This lens combination, called Tessar, is used in cameras. The first column gives the radii of curvatures of the surfaces from left to right. The second and third columns give the indices of refraction before and after an interface. The last column gives the separations among the interfaces. All distances are in cm.

R	n	n'	t
1.628	1.0000	1.6116	0.357
−27.57	1.6116	1.000	0.189
−3.457	1.0000	1.6053	0.081
1.582	1.6053	1.0000	0.325
∞	1.0000	1.5123	0.217
1.920	1.5123	1.6116	0.396
−2.400	1.6116	1.000	

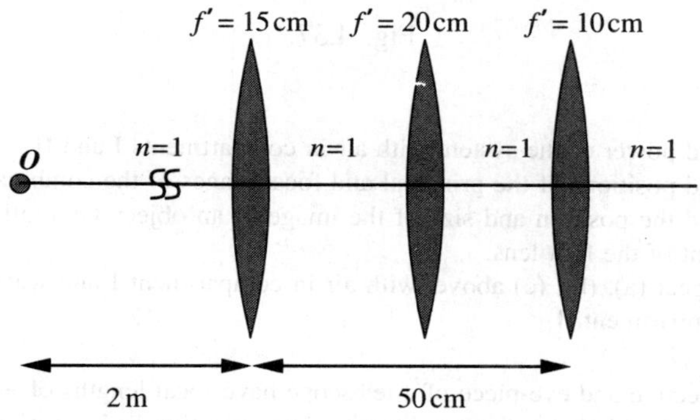

Fig. 4.35.

4.7 Consider three positive, thin lenses of focal lengths 15, 20, and 10 cm, arranged as shown in Fig. 4.35. The first and third lenses are 50 cm apart and occupy fixed positions. An object lies 2 m in front of the first lens. Find changes in lateral magnification and object–image distance as the middle lens is moved between the fixed lenses (zooming effect). You may use analytical or numerical approach.

4.8 Locate the principal and focal planes of the following lens combination (Fig. 4.36, Ramsden eye-piece). The index of refraction of the material of the lenses is 1.52. $R_1 = \infty$, $R_2 = -2.1$ cm, $R_3 = 1.9$ cm, $R_4 = \infty$.

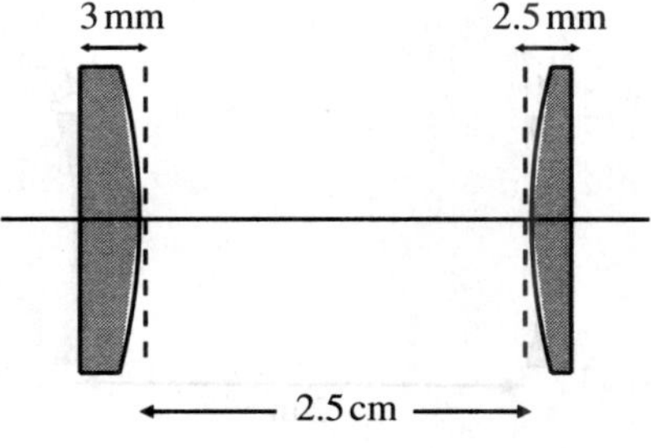

Fig. 4.36.

4.9 Consider the combination of three lenses as shown in Fig. 4.37. The radii of curvatures of the surfaces from left to right are 10, −10, 15, −15, 10, −10 cm. The index of refraction of the material of the lenses is 1.5.

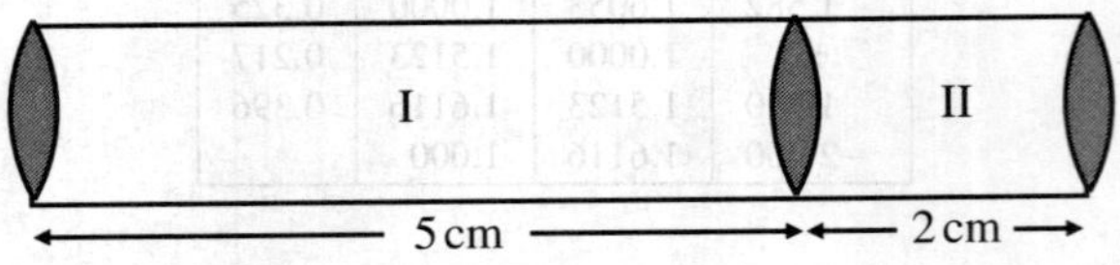

Fig. 4.37.

(a) Find power of the system with air in compartments I and II.
(b) Find positions of the principal and focal planes of the combination.
(c) Find the position and size of the image of an object 1 cm tall, kept 30 cm in front of the first lens.
(d) Repeat (a), (b), (c) above, with air in compartment I and water ($n = 4/3$) in compartment II.

4.10 The objective and eye-piece of a telescope have focal lengths of +20 and +2 cm, respectively. Find the distance between the objective and eye-piece if the image of an object 10 m away from the objective is to be observed at the distance of distinct vision (25 cm). Find the power, the lateral and angular magnifications of the telescope under the above conditions.

4.11 A He–Ne laser cavity consists of two identical concave mirrors, separated by 34 cm. The radius of curvature of each mirror is 10 m. Show that the field configuration inside the cavity reproduces itself after 12 round trips.

4.12 Consider a laser cavity consisting of a concave mirror and a convex mirror, separated by 2 m as shown in Fig. 4.38. Given $|R_1| = |R_2| = 2$ m, where R_1 and R_2 are the radii of curvatures of the concave and convex mirrors, respectively. Obtain the matrix representing the ray transformation for one complete round trip in the cavity. Is this cavity stable or unstable?

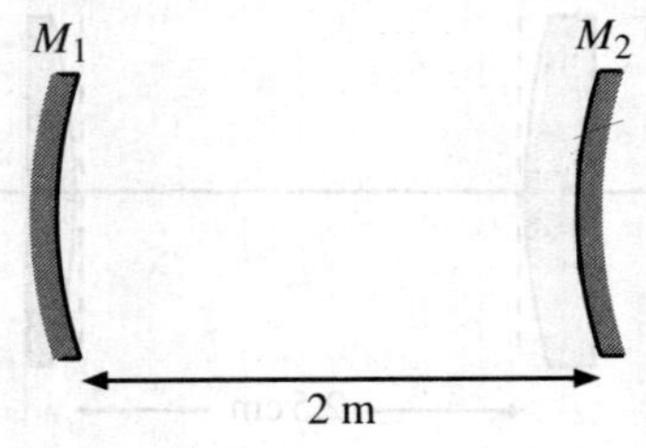

Fig. 4.38.

CHAPTER 5

Lens Aberrations

5.1 STIGMATIC IMAGE

The image of a point object formed by an imaging system consisting of a single lens or a combination of lenses is never a point image for a variety of reasons. No imaging system can transfer the entire spherical wavefront (emanating from the point object) from the object space to the image space. As a consequence, the image of a point object, necessarily consists of the Fraunhofer diffraction pattern of the wavefront-obstructing aperture of the optical system.[1] For an optical system with an axis of symmetry, this pattern consists of the Airy disk surrounded by concentric rings. The need to consider diffraction effects in image formation arises only when the size of the geometrical image of a point object can be reduced to the size of the Airy disk.

Geometrical optics leads to a point image of a point object only in the paraxial approximation (Fig. 5.1). It is assumed here that all rays emanating from the point object O and reaching the lens (or a more general optical system) arrive at a unique image point I after passing through the lens. In the language of wave optics, the incident diverging spherical wavefront A centered at O must be transformed by the lens into another spherical wavefront B converging at the image point I. Such an image is called a stigmatic or a sharp image. In addition, a perfect imaging system images a line perpendicular to the optical axis in the object plane as a line perpendicular to the optical axis in the image plane. The term perfect imaging system here refers only to the geometrical similarity between the object and its image, and need not imply a perfect image in an absolute sense. Stigmatic imaging by a lens is possible only if the lens possesses a unique focal length and a unique transverse magnification when monochromatic light illuminates the object. This happens only for the paraxial rays, putting severe restrictions on the angles the rays make with the optical axis. Non-paraxial rays which are always present in any imaging system produce distorted images. Furthermore, chromatic aberration occurs when object is illuminated

[1] See the paragraph just before Section 10.2.

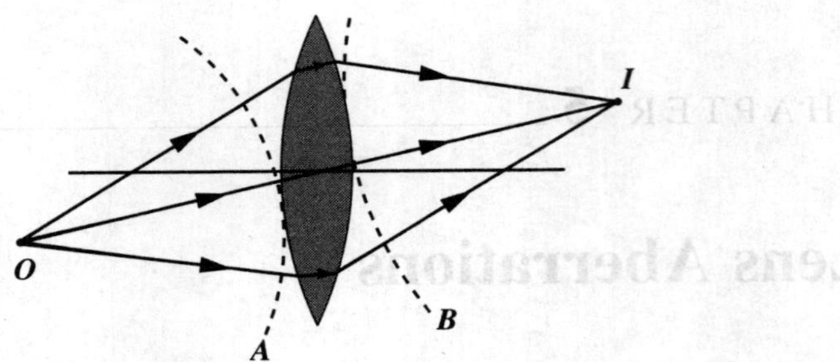

Fig. 5.1: Point image of a point object in paraxial approximation. *A* is a diverging spherical wavefront in object space and *B* is a converging spherical wavefront in image space.

with polychromatic light. The lens no longer has a unique focal length even for the paraxial rays because the index of refraction of the material of the lens changes with wavelength.

5.2 APLANATIC POINTS

Most imaging systems fail to produce stigmatic images. A lens of finite aperture can be divided into infinitesimally narrow concentric zones about its axis (Fig. 5.2). The focal length and transverse magnification of the lens varies from zone to zone. This is an inherent limitation of the spherical surface. One immediate consequence of this variation is the absence of a unique position of the image of a point object formed by a spherical surface. The image is no longer stigmatic, and the notion of the image plane becomes somewhat vague. Rays

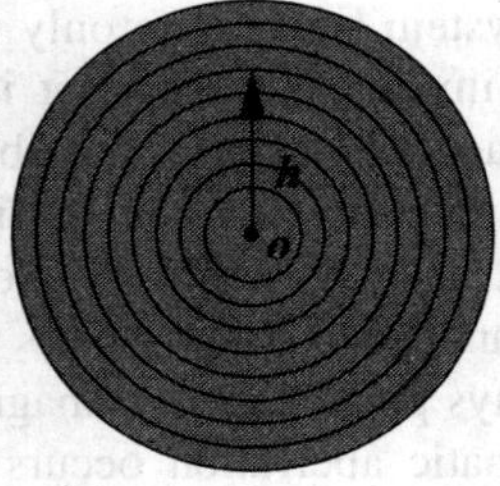

Fig. 5.2: Concentric zones of a lens. The axis of the lens points normal to the plane of the paper.

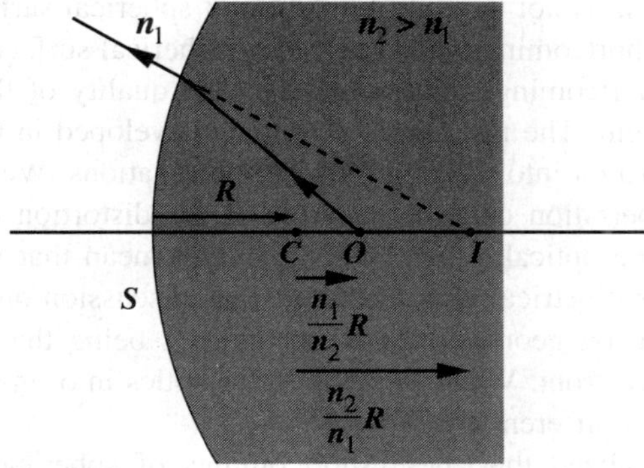

Fig. 5.3: Aplanatic points (O and I) of the spherical surface S.

from a parallel incident beam passing through different zones are focused at different distances from the lens or putting it differently, the wavefront emerging from the lens is no longer spherical. Special aspherical surfaces and lenses can be prepared so that the optical path lengths for all rays from a fixed object position to a fixed image position are exactly equal. Aspherical refracting surfaces were first studied by Descartes and are known as the *Cartesian ovals*. They are also known as *aplanatic surfaces* and the corresponding object and image points are called the *aplanatic points*. Aspherical surfaces are most useful when the object distances do not change appreciably.

It was Huygens who first showed the existence of aplanatic points for spherical surfaces. This is shown in Fig. 5.3. All rays starting from point O after leaving the spherical surface S appear to originate from I. The aplanatic points lie $(n_1/n_2)R$ and $(n_2/n_1)R$ distances away from the center of curvature of the spherical surface, where R is its radius of curvature. As described in Section 4.3.5, this property of spherical surfaces is utilized in the oil-immersion objectives of microscopes. Excellent quality aspheric lenses are available, but they are difficult to grind and therefore are more expensive. No wonder spherical lenses continue to be used extensively.

5.3 IMAGE FORMATION WITH NON-PARAXIAL RAYS

In Chapter 4, optical systems were analyzed within the paraxial approximation. Aperture stops must be used, especially for imaging near objects, so that only low angle rays reach the optical system. This may not be always possible or even desirable. The use of large aperture optical elements may be unavoidable. Lack of a unique focal length of a large aperture spherical lens, commonly known as spherical aberration, is not the only limitation of spherical surfaces. There are a number of other shortcomings (aberrations) of spherical surfaces which we now take up. These shortcomings adversely affect the quality of the image formed by an optical system. The ray matrix technique developed in Chapter 4 can be extended to get insight into the origin of these aberrations. We, however, prefer to develop the aberration concept in terms of the distortion of the wavefront passing through the optical system. This does not mean that we are no longer in the regime of geometrical optics. The ensuing discussion on aberrations is in fact entirely based on geometrical optics; the rays being the directions of the normals to the wavefront. We shall bring wave optics into image formation but at a later stage in a different chapter.

It should be realized that these shortcomings of spherical surfaces called aberrations are not because of any defect in grinding, centering, or assembling of spherical lenses or because of any material inhomogeneities, but because a spherical surface inherently transforms an incident spherical wavefront into an aspherical or an aberrated wavefront which cannot form a stigmatic image. More precisely, the term 'geometrical aberrations' refers to the deviations in the actual image formed by a lens or a combination of lenses with mathematically precise spherical surfaces from the image formed by the paraxial rays. Powerful ray tracing programs exist which can simulate image formation by optical systems in two and three dimensions. One then optimizes the quality of the image by parameterizing the radii of the optical surfaces, their separations, positions of stops, indices of refraction of the lens materials, etc. The final image is then compared with the paraxial image to identify the residual aberrations. This will take us deeper into the design methodology of optical systems which is not what concerns us at the moment. Here, we wish to focus our attention on the origin of geometrical aberrations by following the conventional approach which provides a reasonable insight into the performance of optical systems. In the process, we shall hopefully learn how to minimize the aberrations. For the present discussion, the paraxial approximation is relaxed to the next higher order by replacing the sines and cosines of the ray angles by $(\alpha - \alpha^3/3!)$ and $(1 - \alpha^2/2!)$, respectively. These aberrations were classified as primary aberrations by Seidel who first made a systematic study of geometrical aberrations. In literature, they are variously referred as *Seidel aberrations*, or *first-order aberrations* (because they correspond to first-order correction to the paraxial image), or *third-order aberrations* (because of the presence of the α^3 term), or *fourth-order aberrations* because of the appearance of the fourth-order terms involving the lens aperture (or its equivalent) and the off-axis object or image distances in the aberration function. To avoid repeated use of the term spherical surfaces, we shall discuss geometrical aberrations in the context of a lens, but these aberrations exist for spherical mirrors as well.

5.3.1 Tangential and Sagittal Planes

We begin by defining the terms which describe monochromatic aberrations of a lens. For an on-axis point object, the cone of rays incident on the lens has complete rotational symmetry about the optical axis. All these rays lie in *meridional planes*. A meridional plane is any plane containing the optical axis. The image of an on-axis point object produced by a lens of finite aperture is a light patch which retains the rotational symmetry. For off-axis objects, the rotational symmetry about the optical axis is lost, in particular, the cone of rays incident on the lens lacks this symmetry. However, there is still a plane of symmetry called the *tangential plane*. This is the meridional plane containing the point object and its paraxial image. It is generally defined as the plane containing the optical axis and the chief ray (CR). The latter, as defined earlier, is a ray which starts from an off-axis point object and passes through the center of the exit pupil (see Section 4.3). The exit pupil has been defined in Section 4.3.1, but in the context of a thin lens, it may be taken as a plane perpendicular to the optical axis and passing through the center of the lens. Without loss of generality, the point object may be taken on the y-axis of the Cartesian coordinate system with the optical axis being designated as the z-axis. With this choice of axes, the tangential plane is the vertical plane yz. The rays emanating from an off-axis point object and lying in the tangential plane are called the *tangential rays* (Fig. 5.4).

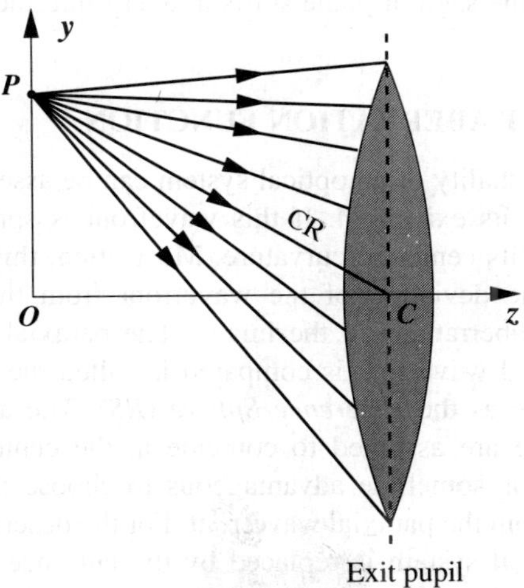

Fig. 5.4: Tangential rays lie in the plane containing the chief ray (CR) and the axis of the lens.

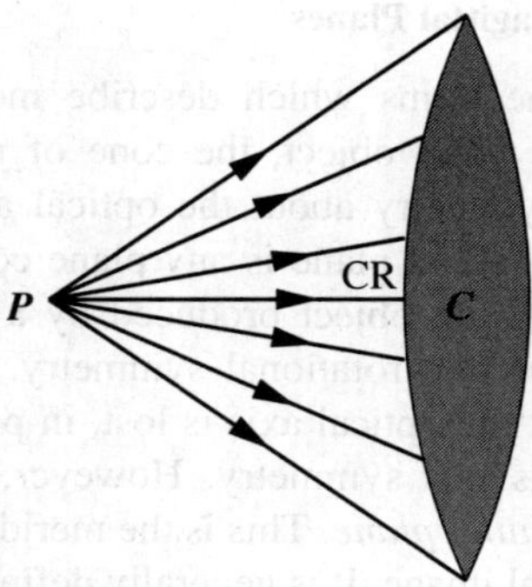

Fig. 5.5: Sagittal rays. Except for the chief ray (CR), sagittal rays are non-meridional.

The plane containing the chief ray and perpendicular to the tangential plane is called the sagittal plane. The only meridional ray in the sagittal plane is the chief ray. Except for this, the rays in the sagittal plane are non-meridional or skew rays (Fig. 5.5). The rays lying in the tangential and sagittal planes constitute only a small subset of the incident cone originating from an off-axis object point. These two planes cannot provide complete image description, but they do play special role in image formation. We shall see later a deeper mathematical basis to single out these two planes. There is a single tangential plane for any multi-element optical system, but the sagittal plane shifts at every interface due to refraction.

5.4 WAVEFRONT ABERRATION FUNCTION

The image forming quality of an optical system can be assessed from the nature of the wavefront in its exit pupil. If this wavefront is spherical, the image is stigmatic located at its center of curvature. Most often, this wavefront deviates from sphericity. The deviation of the wavefront from the paraxial spherical wavefront leads to aberrations in the image. The paraxial spherical wavefront with which the actual wavefront is compared is called the *Reference Spherical Wavefront* or simply as the *Reference Sphere* (*RS*). The actual wavefront and the reference sphere are assumed to coincide at the center of the exit pupil. As we shall see, it is sometime advantageous to choose the reference sphere, somewhat shifted from the paraxial wavefront. For the description of geometrical aberrations, an optical system is replaced by the entrance and exit pupils (the apertures A and B) with centers at E and E', respectively (Fig. 5.6). SS is the spherical wavefront incident at the entrance pupil, RS and $S'S'$ are, respectively, the intersections of the reference sphere and actual wavefront with the tangential

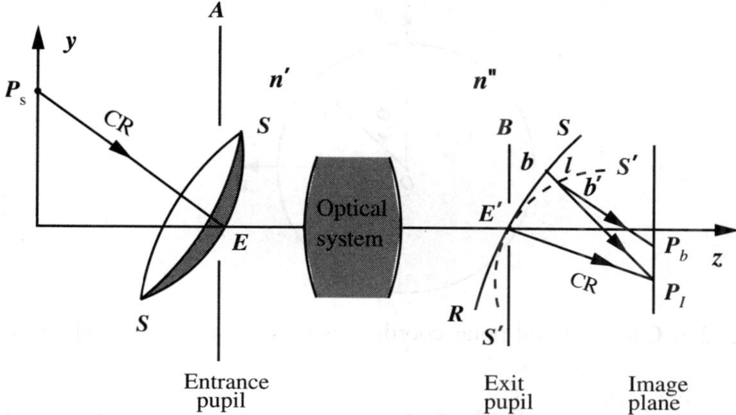

Fig. 5.6: P_I is paraxial image of P_s. SS is the incident spherical wavefront in the entrance pupil, RS and $S'S'$ are sections of the reference sphere and actual wavefront in the tangential plane at the exit pupil.

plane at the exit pupil, $b'P_b$ is the ray starting from point b' on the actual wavefront and meeting the paraxial image plane at P_b, bb' is the directed distance along the ray bP_I (passing through point b') between the actual wavefront and reference sphere, where P_I is the paraxial image of P_s. The corresponding phase change is $(2\pi/\lambda)bb'$. The wavefront aberration function W is defined as the optical path length corresponding to the directed distance $bb'(= l)$, i.e.,

$$W(l) = n''l, \tag{5.1}$$

where n'' is the index of refraction of the medium in the region of the exit pupil. For a precision optical system such as a telescope, the directed distance l must not exceed a fraction of the wavelength of light. Here, we make a subtle distinction between the plane of the exit pupil and the actual wavefront. As can be seen from Fig. 5.6, the two do not coincide. Their separations is, however, exaggerated for clarity of drawing. We should consider points on the wavefront which in the spirit of Huygen's wavelets actually generate the subsequent wavefronts and hence the image. This requires point-to-point shifting of the origin along the optical axis. To avoid these complications, we scan the exit pupil to generate the aberration function.

In principle, the aberrated wavefront and hence the aberration function can be generated via the ray tracing, but we take here a phenomenological approach and express the aberration function as a power series expansion in terms of the coordinates of a point in the exit pupil. Figure 5.7 shows the Cartesian and polar

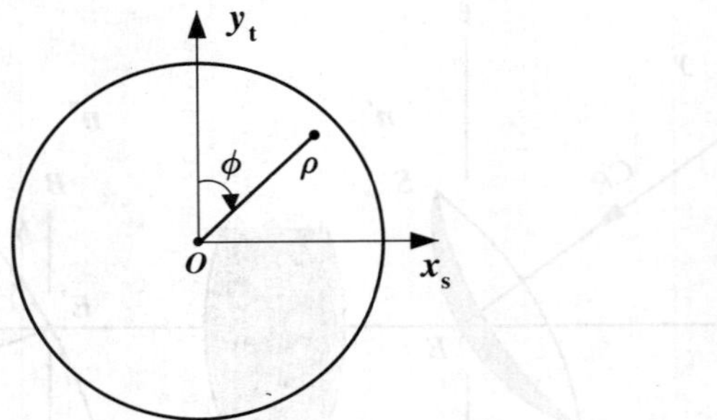

Fig. 5.7: Cartesian and polar coordinates in the plane of the exit pupil.

coordinates in the exit pupil. The Cartesian coordinate axes x_s and y_t are chosen along the intersections of the sagittal and tangential planes, respectively, with the plane of the exit pupil. It is more convenient to choose the azimuthal angle ϕ as the angle between the polar variable ρ and the y_t-axis. The Cartesian and polar coordinates are normalized so that at the edge of the exit pupil $x_t = 1$, $y_t = 1$, and $\rho = 1$. The wavefront aberration function $W(l)$ varies with the position of a point in the exit pupil and must also vary with the position of the point object in the object plane. The off-axis object distance is denoted by the normalized variable r so that $r = 1$ at the edge of the field of view in the object plane (see Section 4.3.1). The variable r can represent the position of the paraxial image as well since there is one to one correspondence between the object point and its paraxial image. For small wavefront aberration, a power series expansion of the aberration function in terms of ρ, $\cos\phi$, and r may be valid. The choice of the variable $\cos\phi$ ensures

$$W(-\phi) = W(\phi),$$

consistent with the requirement that the tangential plane be a plane of symmetry. In addition, for $r = 0$ (on-axis object), full rotational symmetry about the optical axis should be restored. Therefore, terms such as $\cos^n\phi$ and $\rho^n \cos^m\phi$ which do not involve the variable r and lack rotational symmetry cannot appear in the power series expansion. We also note that if the object is shifted below the optical axis ($r \to -r$), the tangential plane remains unchanged. Figure 5.8 shows two positions ($+r$) and ($-r$) of the object and the intersections $S'S'$ and $S''S''$ of the corresponding aberrated wavefronts in the tangential plane at the exit pupil. It then follows that the wavefront aberration function at the corresponding points such as the points A and B must be equal. This suggests that if r is changed to $-r$, and ρ to $-\rho$, leaving ϕ unchanged, the aberration function W remains

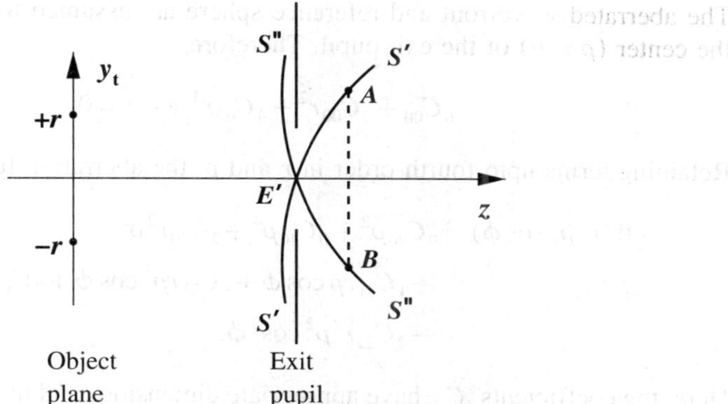

Fig. 5.8: Section of the aberrated wavefront in the tangential plane at the exit pupil changes from $S'S'$ to $S''S''$ as object position is changed from $+r$ to $-r$.

unchanged. This can be ensured if the terms involving powers of the product of all three variables satisfy

$$\rho^m r^n \cos^k \phi = (-\rho)^m (-r)^n \cos^k \phi.$$

All these requirements are met if the aberration function W is expanded as products of the powers of r^2, ρ^2, $r\rho\cos\phi$. Guenther [5.1] has given a simple argument for choosing this set of variables. The optical system has rotational symmetry about the optical axis. Treating r and ρ as vectors, their simultaneous rotation about the optical axis cannot change the aberration function. Accordingly the aberration function must be defined in terms of the scalars $\vec{r} \cdot \vec{r}$, $\vec{\rho} \cdot \vec{\rho}$, and $\vec{r} \cdot \vec{\rho} = r\rho\cos\phi$. The aberration function may therefore be expressed as

$$\begin{aligned} W(r, \rho, \cos\phi) = {}& {}_0C_{00} + {}_2C_{00}r^2 + {}_4C_{00}r^4 + {}_6C_{00}r^6 + \cdots \\ & + {}_0C_{20}\rho^2 + {}_0C_{40}\rho^4 + {}_0C_{60}\rho^6 + \cdots \\ & + {}_1C_{11}r\rho\cos\phi + {}_2C_{22}r^2\rho^2\cos^2\phi + \cdots \\ & + {}_2C_{20}r^2\rho^2 + {}_4C_{40}r^4\rho^4 + \cdots \\ & + {}_3C_{11}r^3\rho\cos\phi + \cdots \\ & + {}_1C_{31}r\rho^3\cos\phi + \ldots \end{aligned} \tag{5.2}$$

The aberrated wavefront and reference sphere are assumed to exactly match at the center ($\rho = 0$) of the exit pupil. Therefore,

$$_0C_{00} + {}_2C_{00}r^2 + {}_4C_{00}r^4 + \cdots = 0.$$

Retaining terms upto fourth-order in r and ρ, the aberration function becomes

$$\begin{aligned} W(r, \rho, \cos\phi) = {}& {}_0C_{20}\rho^2 + {}_0C_{40}\rho^4 + {}_2C_{20}r^2\rho^2 \\ & + {}_1C_{11}r\rho\cos\phi + {}_1C_{31}r\rho^3\cos\phi + {}_3C_{11}r^3\rho\cos\phi \\ & + {}_2C_{22}r^2\rho^2\cos^2\phi. \end{aligned} \tag{5.3}$$

Here, the coefficients $_iC_{jk}$ have appropriate dimensions and have been so labeled that i, j, k yield the powers of r, ρ, $\cos\phi$ in that order. The aberration function can be further simplified if the center of the reference sphere is suitably shifted axially and/or transversely with respect to the paraxial image point.

5.4.1 Ray Deviations

Departure of the wavefront (at the exit pupil) from sphericity gives rise to a spread-out image in place of a point image for a spherical wavefront. The ray aberration is the distance in the paraxial image plane by which a ray misses the paraxial image (Fig. 5.9). This has two consequences. Firstly, the image is a patch of light in any image plane. Secondly, the rays meeting within the light patch have non-zero optical path differences among them. As a result, the image irradiance is considerably reduced as compared to the paraxial image, where all rays meet in phase.

The shape and size of the light patch in any image plane can be obtained from the aberration function (Eq. 5.3). Figure 5.9 shows the rays from points A and B lying on the reference sphere (RS) and meeting at the paraxial image point I_P. A' and B' are the corresponding points on the aberrated wavefront with directed path lengths $AA' = l$ and $BB' = l + \Delta l$, respectively. It is seen from the figure that the ray starting from point A' along the normal to the aberrated wavefront ($S'S'$) crosses the image plane at point A''. The ray deviation along y'' in the paraxial image plane is approximately given by

$$\Delta y'' = R\Delta\theta = R\frac{\partial l}{\partial y_t} = \frac{R}{n''}\frac{\partial W}{\partial y_t}, \tag{5.4a}$$

where R is the distance between the exit pupil and image plane. Similarly, the deviation in the x'' direction is

$$\Delta x'' = \frac{R}{n''}\frac{\partial W}{\partial x_s}. \tag{5.4b}$$

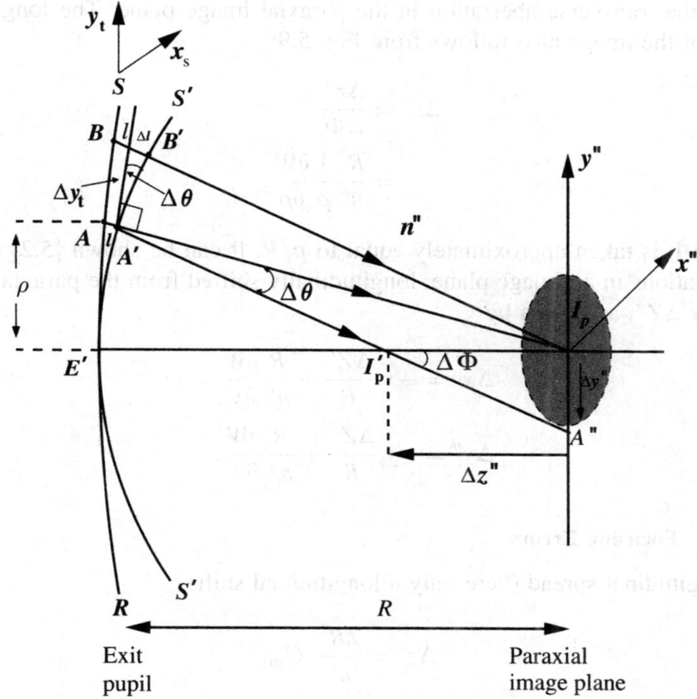

Fig. 5.9: Ray deviations in the paraxial image plane. *RS* and *S′S′* are sections of the reference sphere and aberrated wavefront in the tangential plane.

The spreads in $\Delta x''$ and $\Delta y''$ values determine the size and shape of the image of a point object in the paraxial image plane. Expressing these deviations in the polar coordinates, we have

$$\Delta y'' = \frac{R}{n''}\left[\cos\phi\frac{\partial W}{\partial\rho} - \frac{\sin\phi}{\rho}\frac{\partial W}{\partial\phi}\right], \tag{5.4c}$$

$$\Delta x'' = \frac{R}{n''}\left[\sin\phi\frac{\partial W}{\partial\rho} + \frac{\cos\phi}{\rho}\frac{\partial W}{\partial\phi}\right]. \tag{5.4d}$$

The radius of the light patch (assuming $\frac{\partial W}{\partial\phi} = 0$) in the paraxial image plane is

$$\Delta r'' = \left[(\Delta x'')^2 + (\Delta y'')^2\right]^{1/2} = \frac{R}{n''}\frac{\partial W}{\partial\rho}. \tag{5.4e}$$

This is the transverse aberration in the paraxial image plane. The longitudinal spread of the image also follows from Fig. 5.9:

$$\begin{aligned}\Delta z'' &= \frac{\Delta r''}{\Delta \Phi} \\ &= \frac{R^2}{n''}\frac{1}{\rho}\frac{\partial W}{\partial \rho},\end{aligned} \tag{5.5}$$

where $\Delta\Phi$ is taken approximately equal to ρ/R. It can be shown [5.2] that the ray deviations in an image plane, longitudinally shifted from the paraxial image plane by $\Delta Z''$, are given by

$$\Delta x'' = -x_s\frac{\Delta Z''}{R} + \frac{R}{n''}\frac{\partial W}{\partial x_s}, \tag{5.6a}$$

$$\Delta y'' = -y_t\frac{\Delta Z''}{R} + \frac{R}{n''}\frac{\partial W}{\partial y_t}. \tag{5.6b}$$

5.4.2 Focusing Errors

The longitudinal spread (here only a longitudinal shift)

$$\Delta z'' = \frac{2R^2}{n''}{}_0C_{20} \tag{5.7}$$

obtained from the first term (${}_0C_{20}\rho^2$) of the aberration function is independent of the position of a point in the exit pupil. Therefore, the wavefront in the exit pupil with aberration given by only the first term of Eq. (5.3) is actually spherical giving a stigmatic image in front of the paraxial image for positive ${}_0C_{20}$, in conformity with Eqs (5.6) which yield

$$\Delta x'' = \Delta y'' = 0$$

for $\Delta Z'' = \Delta z'' = \frac{2R^2}{n''}{}_0C_{20}$. This term therefore represents image defocusing, and not an aberration of the image (Fig. 5.10).

Similarly, the fourth term

$${}_1C_{11}r\rho\cos\phi = {}_1C_{11}ry_t$$

in Eq. (5.3) gives

$$\Delta x'' = 0,$$

$$\Delta y'' = \frac{R}{n''}{}_1C_{11}r$$

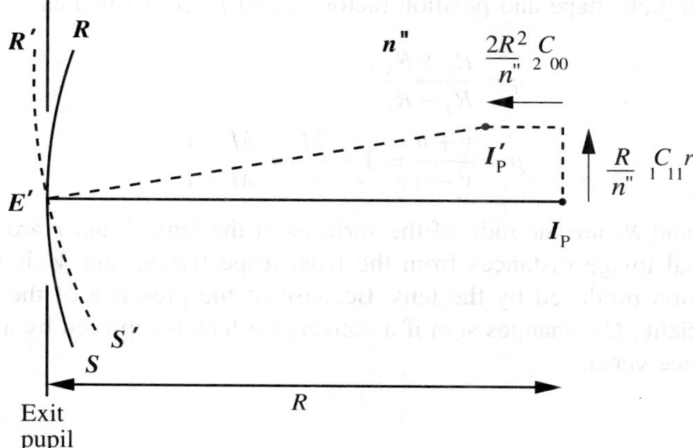

Fig. 5.10: RS is the section of the paraxial reference sphere centered at I_P. $R'S'$ is the section of the new reference sphere centered at I'_P.

in the paraxial image plane. Once again, this term also does not represent an image aberration since it is independent of the coordinates of a point in the exit pupil. The image is stigmatic and lies in the paraxial image plane. It is merely shifted in the transverse direction (Fig. 5.10). For a suitably shifted reference sphere ($R'S'$ in Fig. 5.10), the relevant aberration function is obtained by dropping the first and fourth terms in Eq. (5.3), giving

$$W(r, \rho, \cos\phi) = {}_0C_{40}\rho^4 + {}_1C_{31}r\rho^3\cos\phi + {}_2C_{22}r^2\rho^2\cos^2\phi + {}_2C_{20}r^2\rho^2 + {}_3C_{11}r^3\rho\cos\phi. \tag{5.8}$$

The terms in the aberration function (Eq. 5.8) have been arranged in increasing powers of r – the off-axis object distance. Each term in this expression represents a particular kind of primary aberration. The coefficients ${}_iC_{jk}$ can in principle be calculated. Born and Wolf [5.3] have given a general derivation of these coefficients. For a thin lens of paraxial focal length f and refractive index n, Klein and Furtak [5.4] give

$${}_0C_{40} = -\frac{1}{32f^3}\frac{1}{n(n-1)}\left[\frac{n+2}{n-1}q^2 + 4(n+1)pq + (3n+2)(n-1)p^2 + \frac{n^3}{n-1}\right]. \tag{5.9}$$

The Coddington shape and position factors q and p are defined as

$$q = \frac{R_2 + R_1}{R_2 - R_1}, \tag{5.10}$$

$$p = \frac{v+u}{v-u} = 1 - \frac{2f}{v} = \frac{M+1}{M-1}, \tag{5.11}$$

where R_1 and R_2 are the radii of the surfaces of the lens, u and v are the object and paraxial image distances from the lens, respectively, and M is the lateral magnification produced by the lens. Because of the presence of the f^3 factor, the coefficient ${}_0C_{40}$ changes sign if a converging lens is replaced by a diverging lens and vice versa.

5.5 PRIMARY ABERRATIONS

The five terms appearing in Eq. (5.8) represent five primary aberrations – spherical aberration, coma, astigmatism, Petzval curvature, and distortion in that order. These aberrations should be applicable to aspherical surfaces also as long as the axis of symmetry is retained. To get insight into the nature of primary aberrations, we consider each term in Eq. (5.8) separately. This amounts to assuming that all other aberrations, except the one under consideration, have somehow been eliminated.

5.5.1 Spherical Aberration

Historically, the first term

$$W_s = {}_0C_{40}\rho^4 \tag{5.12}$$

in the aberration function has been associated with the primary spherical aberration. Higher even powers of ρ lead to higher order spherical aberration. Since Eq. (5.12) does not involve the off-axis object distance r, this is the only aberration which is common to on- and off-axis object positions. All other aberrations are absent when the object lies on the optical axis. Figure 5.11 shows the variation of the spherical aberration function in the plane of the exit pupil.

Equation (5.12) can be re-written as

$$W_s = ({}_0C_{40}\rho^2)\rho^2. \tag{5.13}$$

Ignoring for the moment the ρ dependence of the multiplying factor within the brackets, the ρ^2 dependence of W_s reminds us of the longitudinal shift of the paraxial image (Section 5.4.2), but since the bracketed factor also involves ρ,

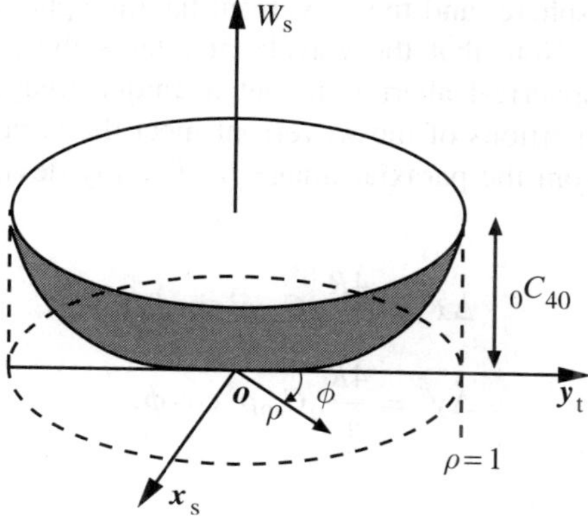

Fig. 5.11: Spherical aberration function in the plane of exit pupil.

the longitudinal shift increases with increasing ρ. Accordingly for positive ${}_0C_{40}$, the marginal rays (originating from the extremities of the exit pupil) are focused closest to the exit pupil and the paraxial rays farthest from it. This is shown in Fig. 5.12, where AA, RS, and AW are, respectively, the intersections of the exit

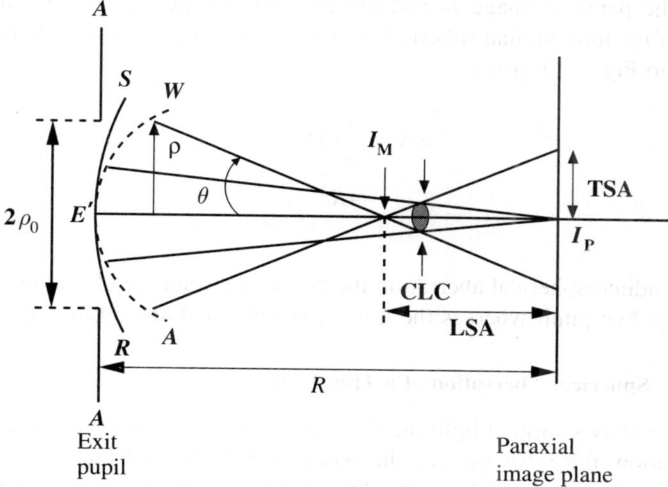

Fig. 5.12: Spherical aberration for an on-axis point object; TSA is transverse spherical aberration, LSA is longitudinal spherical aberration, CLC is the circle of least confusion.

pupil, the reference sphere, and the wavefront having spherical aberration with the tangential plane. Note that the wavefront retains the rotational symmetry in the presence of spherical aberration, but a unique image point is missing. Rays from different portions of the wavefront meet the paraxial image plane at different distances from the paraxial image $I_{\rm P}$. The ray deviations in this plane are

$$\Delta x'' = \frac{4R}{n''}\,{}_0C_{40}\rho^3 \sin\phi, \tag{5.14a}$$

$$\Delta y'' = \frac{4R}{n''}\,{}_0C_{40}\rho^3 \cos\phi, \tag{5.14b}$$

so that

$$(\Delta x'')^2 + (\Delta y'')^2 = \left(\frac{4R}{n''}\,{}_0C_{40}\rho^3\right)^2. \tag{5.15}$$

The patch in the paraxial image plane is a circle of radius $\frac{4R}{n''}\,{}_0C_{40}\rho^3$. The spread of the light patch in this plane is called the transverse spherical aberration (TSA). Its size decreases as the image plane is moved towards the exit pupil. It goes through a minimum size, called the circle of least confusion (CLC), and then increases again. The image is not localized at a unique distance from the exit pupil, giving rise to the longitudinal spherical aberration (LSA). The separation between the paraxial image $I_{\rm P}$ and marginal ray image $I_{\rm M}$ may be taken as a measure of the longitudinal spherical aberration. A rough estimate, obtained with reference to Fig. 5.12, gives

$$\begin{aligned} \text{LSA} &= \frac{R}{\rho}(\text{TSA}) \\ &= \frac{4R^2}{n''}\,{}_0C_{40}\rho^2. \end{aligned} \tag{5.16}$$

The longitudinal spherical aberration increases as the square of the distance of a point in the exit pupil whereas the transverse spherical aberration varies as ρ^3.

5.5.1.1 Spherical Aberration of a Thin Lens

Figure 5.13 shows parallel light incident on thin spherical lenses. In the paraxial approximation, the refracted rays lie within a well-defined cone whose vertex coincides with the paraxial image. The cones formed by rays refracted from different zones of a large aperture lens do not have a common vertex. The surface generated by the envelopes of these cones is called the *Caustic Surface*. We note that the marginal rays from a convex (concave) lens converge to

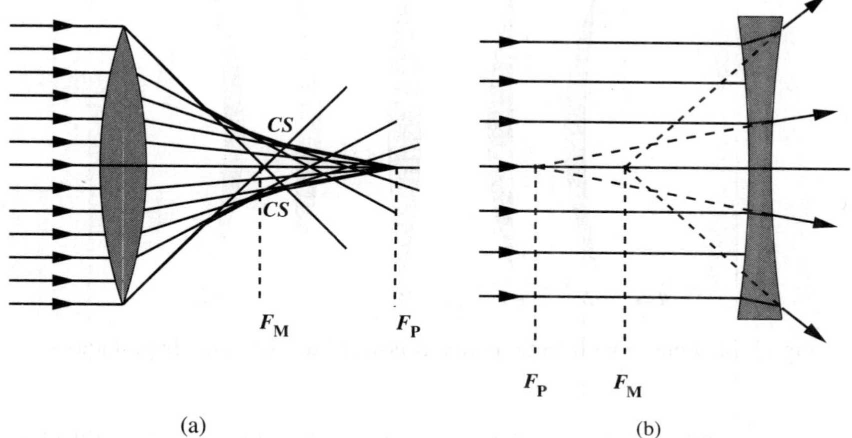

Fig. 5.13: Spherical aberration for (a) thin convex lens and (b) thin concave lens. F_M and F_P are the marginal and paraxial focal points. *CS*, sections of the caustic surface.

(appear to diverge from) a point which is closer to the lens. A convex lens converges the marginal rays more strongly than the paraxial rays. The spherical aberration in this case is positive, the paraxial focal length f_p being larger than the marginal focal length f_m. Positive spherical aberration is also known as under-corrected spherical aberration. The concave lens, on the other hand, diverges marginal rays more strongly in comparison to paraxial rays. The concave lens has negative ($f_p < f_m$) or over-corrected spherical aberration. A proper choice of the radii of curvatures of the lens surfaces (the shape factor), but without a change in the focal length (i.e. different $\frac{1}{R_1}$ and $\frac{1}{R_2}$ but same $(\frac{1}{R_1} - \frac{1}{R_2})$) can minimize the spherical aberration of a thin lens. This is known as lens bending (Fig. 5.14).

The change in the image distance with the zone radius (h) of a thin lens in air can be expressed as

$$\begin{aligned}\text{LSA} &= v - v_h = 4v^2h^2|_0C_{40}| \\ &= \frac{h^2}{8f^3}\frac{v^2}{n(n-1)}\left[\frac{n+2}{n-1}q^2 + 4(n+1)pq + (3n+2)(n-1)p^2 + \frac{n^3}{n-1}\right].\end{aligned} \tag{5.17}$$

Here, v is the paraxial image distance from the lens and v_h the corresponding distance of the image formed by the zone of radius h (Fig. 5.2), f the paraxial

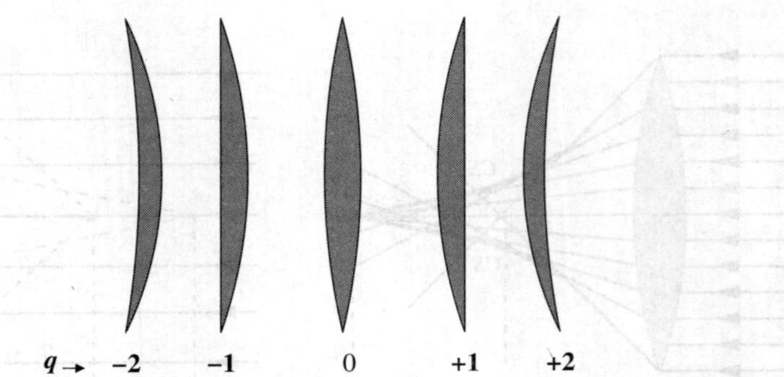

Fig. 5.14: Lenses with same paraxial power but different shape factors.

focal length of the thin lens, and n the refractive index of the material of the lens. The shape factor q and position factor p are as defined in Eqs (5.10) and (5.11). For a given object–image distance, i.e., for a given value of the position factor p, one can reduce the spherical aberration by a proper choice of the shape factor. For example, for parallel incident light, a plano-convex lens with convex side facing the incident beam is the best choice for reduced spherical aberration, and just the opposite orientation of the lens achieves minimum spherical aberration if the emergent beam has to come out as a parallel beam. Turning the lenses around can considerably increase the spherical aberration. An equi-convex lens works best when the object and image distances are nearly equal. A thumb rule to reduce the spherical aberration of a lens is to equalize the ray deviations across its two surfaces.

Because of the f^3 dependence of spherical aberration on the paraxial focal length, a suitable combination of positive and negative lenses can eliminate the primary spherical aberration. However, higher order spherical aberration may still persist.

5.5.2 Coma

The aberration function in the presence of primary coma alone is

$$\begin{aligned} W_c &= {}_1C_{31} r\rho^3 \cos\phi \\ &= {}_1C_{31} r y_t (x_s^2 + y_t^2). \end{aligned} \tag{5.18}$$

Higher order coma involves terms with higher odd powers of $\cos\phi$. Due to the presence of the first power of the off-axis object distance r in Eq. (5.18), coma is the first aberration that one encounters as the object is taken to off-axis positions. We can rewrite the coma aberration function as

$$W_c = {}_1C_{31}\rho^2(r\rho\cos\phi). \tag{5.19}$$

The factor $r\rho\cos\phi$ suggests that the primary coma produces a transverse shift $\frac{R}{n''}r_1c_{31}\rho^2$ (see Section 5.4.2) of the paraxial image. However, because of the additional ρ^2 factor in the coma aberration function, this transverse shift increases with the radius of a ring in the exit pupil. Accordingly, primary coma may be associated with the change in the transverse magnification of the lens from zone to zone.

The variation of the aberration function W_c in the plane of the exit pupil is sketched in Fig. 5.15. The wavefront experiences largest deviation from the reference sphere in the tangential plane ($\phi = 0, \pi$) and coincides with the reference sphere in the sagittal plane ($W_c = 0$ for $\phi = \pi/2, 3\pi/2$). Sections of the reference sphere and wavefront with primary coma in the plane of the exit pupil are shown in Fig. 5.16.

Unlike for the spherical aberration, the coma aberrated wavefront is asymmetrically oriented about the reference sphere. The ray deviations from the paraxial image are

$$\Delta x'' = \frac{R}{n''}{}_1C_{31}r\rho^2\sin 2\phi, \tag{5.20a}$$

$$\Delta y'' = \frac{R}{n''}{}_1C_{31}r\rho^2(2+\cos 2\phi). \tag{5.20b}$$

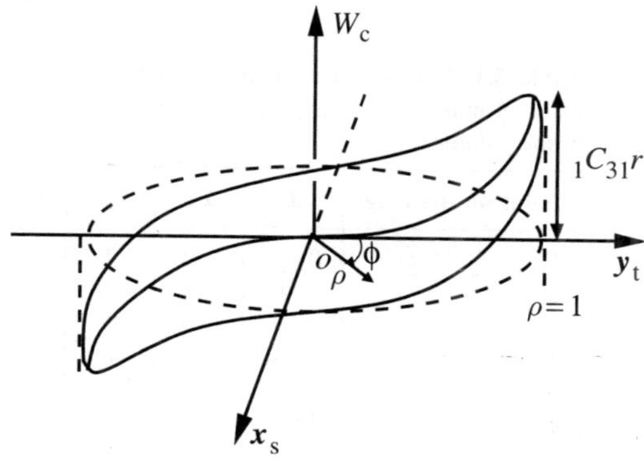

Fig. 5.15: Aberration function representing primary coma.

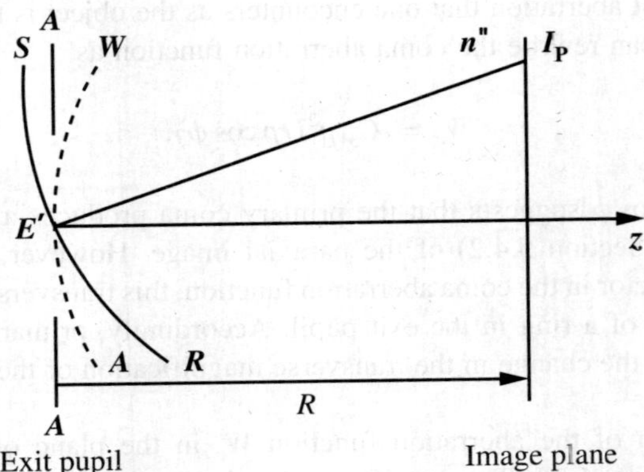

Fig. 5.16: Sections of the reference sphere (*RS*) and wavefront (*AW*) with primary coma in the plane of the exit pupil.

The deviations (from the paraxial image) of the rays starting from points lying on a ring of radius ρ in the exit pupil (Fig. 5.17a) are listed in Table 5.1 in units of $(R/n'')_1 C_{31} r\rho^2$. These deviations are plotted in Fig. (5.17b).

The figure shows that the image of an off-axis point generated by each ring in the exit pupil is a circle in the paraxial image plane. Rays leaving a ring from diametrically opposite points generate a single image point. For example, points (1, 5) lying in the tangential plane give rise to the image at the top of the circle and points (3, 7) lying in the sagittal plane generate the lowest point of the circle, and so on. It is seen that the circle in the image plane is traced twice over as the azimuthal angle in the exit pupil is changed from 0 to 2π. Thus for a fixed value of ρ, the rays from an off-axis point trace a circle of radius

Table 5.1. Ray deviations in the paraxial image plane in units of $\frac{R}{n''}{}_1 C_{31} r\rho^2$ in the presence of primary coma.

Point on the ring	ϕ	$\Delta x''$	$\Delta y''$
1	0	0	3
2	$\pi/4$	1	2
3	$\pi/2$	0	1
4	$3\pi/4$	-1	2
5	π	0	3
6	$5\pi/4$	1	2
7	$3\pi/2$	0	1
8	$7\pi/4$	-1	2

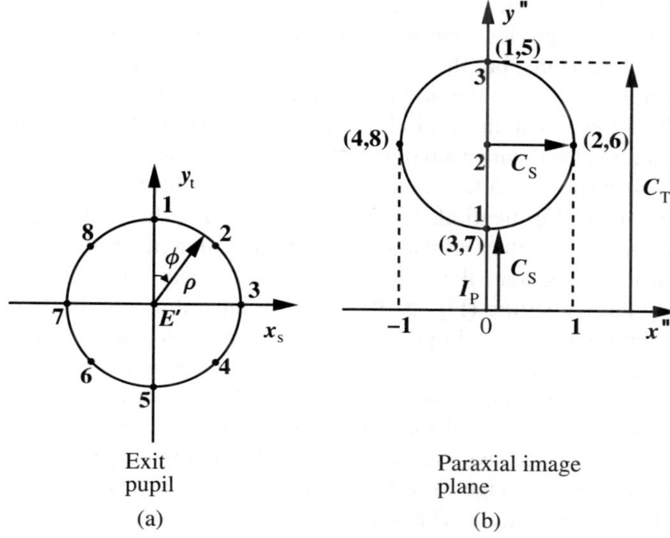

Fig. 5.17: (a) A concentric ring of radius ρ in the plane of the exit pupil with marked points from 1 to 8. (b) The image of an off-axis point object formed by each ring in the exit pupil is a circle in the paraxial image plane; C_S is sagittal coma and C_T is tangential coma.

$(R/n'')_1C_{31}r\rho^2$. The center of the circle is displaced a distance $2_1C_{31}(R/n'')r\rho^2$ from the paraxial image along the y''-axis. To see this more clearly, Eqs (5.20a) and (5.20b) can be combined to yield

$$(\Delta x'')^2 + \left(\Delta y'' - \frac{2R}{n''}{}_1C_{31}r\rho^2\right)^2 = \left(\frac{R}{n''}{}_1C_{31}r\rho^2\right)^2, \tag{5.20c}$$

which represents a circle of radius $(R/n'')_1C_{31}r\rho^2$ centered at the point $2(R/n'')_1C_{31}r\rho^2$ on the y'' axis in the paraxial image plane. We note that the wavefront coincides with the reference sphere in the sagittal plane ($W_c = 0$ for $\phi = \pi/2,\ 3\pi/2$), but the sagittal image does not coincide with the paraxial image. The rays or the normals to the wavefront in the sagittal plane do not coincide with the radial lines of the reference sphere because of the tilt of the wavefront in the perpendicular direction (along the y_t-axis). The tangential coma C_T and sagittal coma C_s shown in Fig. (5.17b) have values of $3_1C_{31}(R/n'')r\rho^2$ and ${}_1C_{31}(R/n'')r\rho^2$, respectively.

Furthermore, we note that the radius of the circular image (comatic circle) and the distance of the center of this circle from the paraxial image have ρ^2

dependence on the location of the ring in the exit pupil. Thus, the image plane contains a series of circles (one for each ring in the exit pupil) with increasing radii and displacements, but the centers of these circles always lie on the y''-axis which is parallel to the y_t-axis in the exit pupil (Fig. 5.18).

It can be shown that these circles are bounded between common tangents making an angle of 60° with each other. These tangents meet at the paraxial image point. This aberration is called coma because the overall image of a point has the shape of a comet. We mentioned in the beginning that the changing transverse magnification of the zones is responsible for the coma aberration. This can be appreciated if we consider the image of a distant object formed by a thin lens of relatively large aperture (Fig. 5.19). Here we have drawn only the tangential rays. The marginal rays (1, 1) give the farthest image I_M and image I_P formed by the paraxial rays is closest to the optical axis. In this case, the marginal rays experience the largest transverse magnification. This is an example of positive coma. The coma is negative if magnification is least for the marginal rays. The tangential rays such as rays (1, 1) in Fig. 5.19 passing through a given zone of the lens give point image of a point object. In fact, this point image lies on the top of the comatic circle. The remaining rays (other than tangential) passing through this zone of the lens fill the remaining image points on the comatic circle. The primary coma can be eliminated if same transverse magnification can be ensured for all zones.

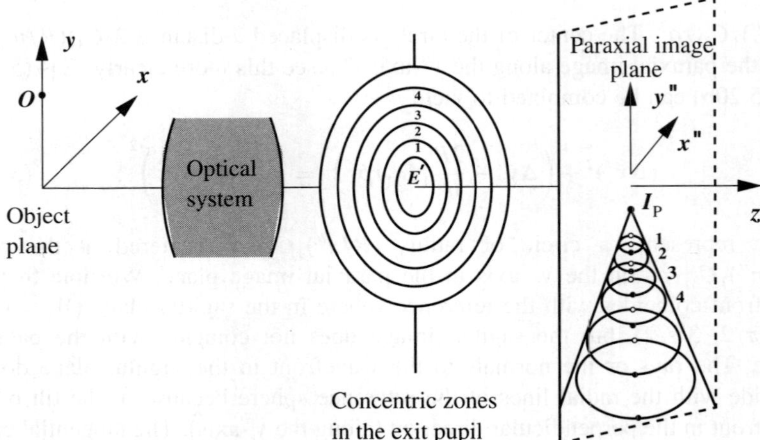

Fig. 5.18: Optical system with primary coma; image of an off-axis point formed by each zone of the exit pupil is a circle. Solid dots in the paraxial image plane represent tangential images and hollow dots are sagittal images.

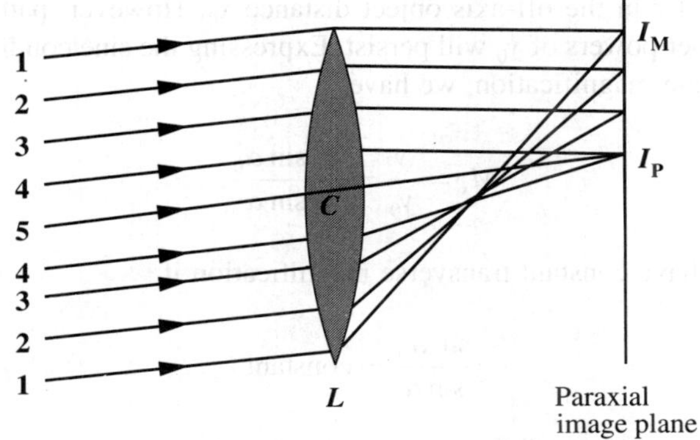

Fig. 5.19: A thin lens showing positive coma.

5.5.2.1 The Sine Condition

Consider a single lens image forming system of Fig. 5.20. Let O and I lying on the optical axis be a pair of conjugate points of the lens, for which the spherical aberration has been removed. A stigmatic image I' of an off-axis point object O' which is not too far from the optical axis can also be obtained provided the lens satisfies the Abbe sine condition

$$n_0 y_0 \sin \alpha_0 = n y \sin \alpha \tag{5.21}$$

for arbitrary angle α_0, not necessarily restricted to the paraxial approximation, where α_0 and α are the angles a ray makes with the optical axis in the object and image spaces with indices of refraction n_0 and n, respectively, and y_0 and y are the off-axis object and image distances. It can be shown that if the sine condition is satisfied, all optical paths between the points O' and I' are equal to

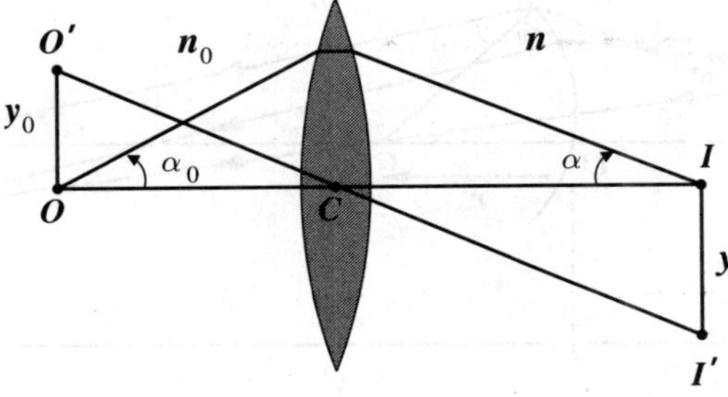

Fig. 5.20: Geometry for sine condition.

within first order in the off-axis object distance y_0. However, path differences involving higher powers of y_0 will persist. Expressing the sine condition in terms of the transverse magnification, we have

$$M_x = \frac{y}{y_0} = \frac{n_0 \sin \alpha_0}{n \sin \alpha}.$$

The lens will have constant transverse magnification if

$$\frac{\sin \alpha_0}{\sin \alpha} = \text{constant}$$

for all α_0. Since this condition must be satisfied by paraxial rays as well, the sine condition can also be expressed as

$$\frac{\sin \alpha_0}{\alpha_0} = \frac{\sin \alpha}{\alpha}.$$

We give here a simple derivation of the sine condition for a spherical interface. Figure 5.21 shows the formation of a stigmatic image y of a linear object y_0. Applying the sine law to the triangles BAC and ACB', we have

$$\frac{BC}{\sin \phi} = \frac{AC}{\sin \alpha_0}, \tag{5.22a}$$

$$\frac{AC}{\sin \alpha} = \frac{CB'}{\sin \theta}. \tag{5.22b}$$

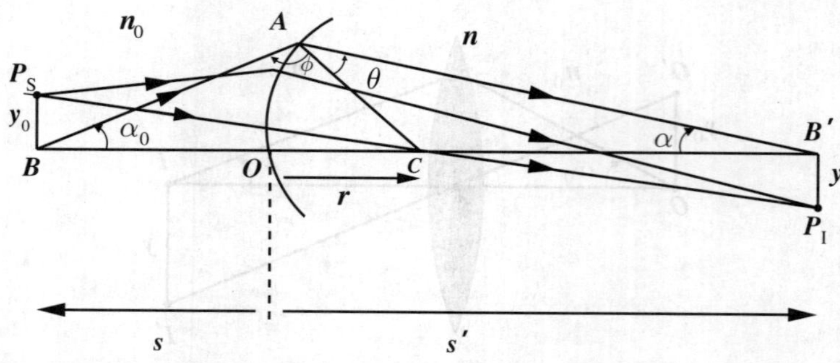

Fig. 5.21: Stigmatic image formed by a spherical surface.

These results can be re-expressed as

$$\frac{s+r}{\sin\phi} = \frac{r}{\sin\alpha_0}, \tag{5.22c}$$

$$\frac{r}{\sin\alpha} = \frac{s'-r}{\sin\theta}. \tag{5.22d}$$

Substituting values of $\sin\phi$ and $\sin\theta$ into Snell's law

$$n_0 \sin\phi = n \sin\theta$$

gives

$$\frac{y}{y_0} = \frac{s'-r}{s+r} = \frac{n_0 \sin\alpha_0}{n \sin\alpha}, \tag{5.23}$$

which is the statement of the sine condition. It is interesting to note that the sine condition which applies to image formation of off-axis points involves the angles which the rays make with the optical axis. It is usually not possible to design lenses completely satisfying the sine condition. Proper bending of lenses (and hence a suitable choice of the principal planes) can minimize the disagreement.

A lens is said to be aplanatic for a pair of conjugate points if spherical aberration and primary coma are absent. Such a lens is usually aspherical. In practical systems, spherical aberration and primary coma can be considerably reduced by suitably bending spherical lenses. The lens shape which gives minimum spherical aberration also gives small coma. Meniscus lenses, with radii of curvatures having the same sign, are particularly useful in this respect.

5.5.3 Astigmatism

The third term

$$W_a = {}_2C_{22} r^2 \rho^2 \cos^2\phi \tag{5.24}$$

in the aberration function gives rise to primary astigmatism. This aberration has square dependence on the off-axis object distance r. The next term in Eq. (5.8) also has r^2 dependence. Some authors prefer to discuss these two terms together. We shall, however, discuss them separately. We mention in passing that the astigmatism of the eye discussed in Chapter 4 arises because its cornea deviates from sphericity, resulting in different focusing behavior of the eye in different directions. Here, we are discussing astigmatism produced by spherical surfaces. As already mentioned, the wavefront in the exit pupil is not spherical in the presence of aberrations. Non-spherical surfaces possess an interesting property.

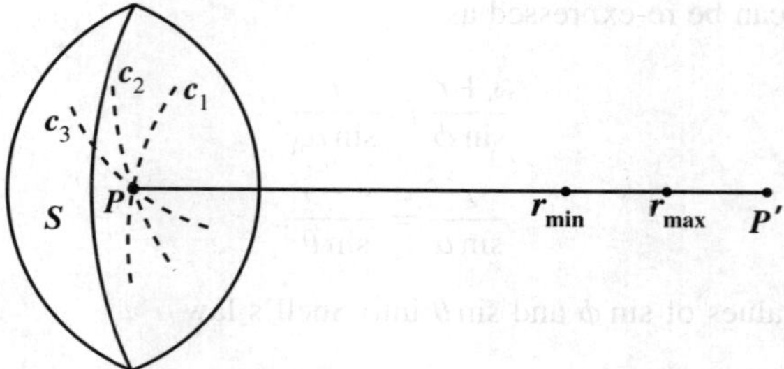

Fig. 5.22: Distribution of the radii of curvatures of an aspherical surface.

Figure 5.22 shows an aspherical wavefront S. PP' is the ray which emerges from point P of this wavefront. By definition, the ray PP' coincides with the normal to the wavefront at point P.

A plane containing the line PP' when rotated about PP' generates arcs c_1, c_2, c_3, etc., as its successive intersections on the wavefront. The radii of curvatures of these arcs lying on the aspherical wavefront and intersecting each other at P are different. However, the centers of curvatures of these arcs lie on the line PP'. The arcs of intersection and hence the planes containing the arcs with minimum and maximum radii of curvature are orthogonal to each other. These planes may be associated with the tangential and sagittal planes defined in Section 5.3.1.

The variation of the aberration function W_a in the exit pupil is shown in Fig. 5.23. As for coma, this aberration function also vanishes in the sagittal plane. But unlike for coma, W_a does not change sign with the azimuthal angle. The sections of the reference sphere (RS), and wavefront (AW) with primary astigmatism in the tangential plane are shown in Fig. (5.24). The wavefront possesses 180° rotational symmetry about the chief ray which should be reflected

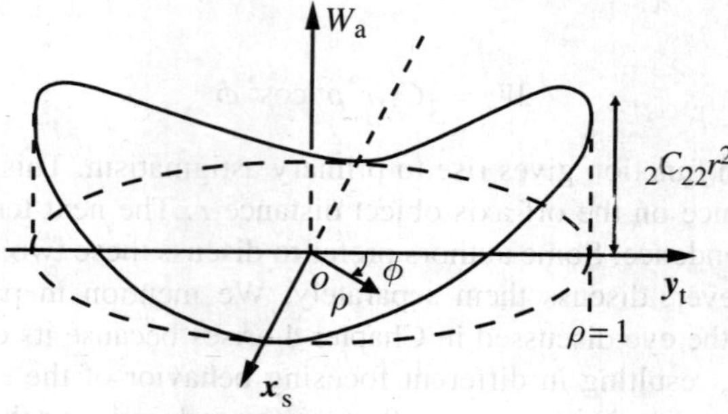

Fig. 5.23: Aberration function for primary astigmatism in the plane of the exit pupil.

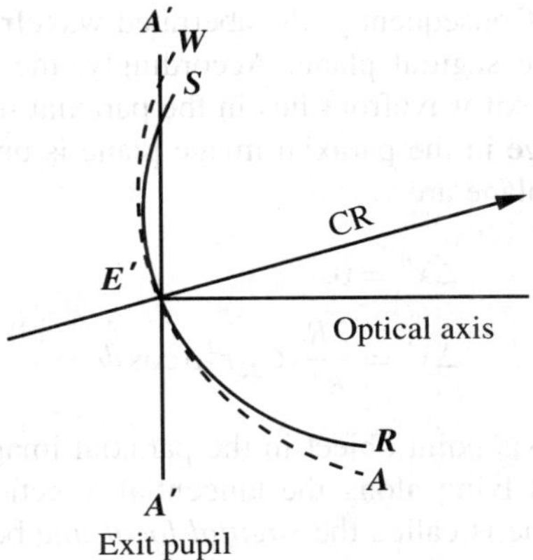

Fig. 5.24: Sections of the reference sphere (RS) and wavefront with astigmatic aberration (AW) in the tangential plane. CR is the chief ray.

in the image formed by an optical system with primary astigmatism. The coma-aberrated image lacks this symmetry. The function

$$W_a(\phi = 0, \pi) = {}_2C_{22}\rho^2 r^2$$

represents astigmatism in the tangential plane. It follows from the argument of Section 5.4.2 that the image formed by the tangential section of the wavefront lies a distance $2\frac{R^2}{n''}{}_2C_{22}r^2$ in front of the paraxial image plane. The ray deviations

$$\begin{aligned}\Delta x'' &= -\frac{2R}{n''}{}_2C_{22}r^2 x_s \\ &= -\frac{2R}{n''}{}_2C_{22}r^2\rho\sin\phi,\end{aligned} \tag{5.25a}$$

$$\Delta y'' = 0, \tag{5.25b}$$

in this shifted plane, obtained from Eqs (5.6) and (5.24), occur only along the sagittal direction (horizontal) and vary linearly with the radius of a concentric ring in the exit pupil. For a given ring, it varies from $-\frac{2R}{n''}{}_2C_{22}r^2\rho$ for $\phi = \pi/2$ to $+\frac{2R}{n''}{}_2C_{22}r^2\rho$ for $\phi = -\pi/2$. Thus the image of an off-axis point object in this longitudinally shifted image plane is a line of length $\frac{4R}{n''}{}_2C_{22}r^2$ lying in the sagittal plane. We have taken $\rho = 1$ at the extremities of the exit pupil. This line image is called the *tangential focal line* because it is formed by the tangential rays. The tangential focal line, of course, lies in the sagittal plane. The aberration function (Eq. 5.24) representing astigmatism vanishes in the sagittal plane ($\phi = \pi/2, \frac{3}{2}\pi$). Consequently, the aberrated wavefront coincides with the reference sphere in the sagittal plane. Accordingly, the image formed by the sagittal section of the exit wavefront lies in the paraxial image plane. This does not mean that the image in the paraxial image plane is unaberrated. In fact, the ray deviations in this plane are

$$\Delta x'' = 0, \tag{5.26a}$$

$$\Delta y'' = \frac{2R}{n''} {}_2C_{22} r^2 \rho \cos\phi. \tag{5.26b}$$

The image of an off-axis point object in the paraxial image plane is also a line of length $\frac{4R}{n''} {}_2C_{22} r^2$ but lying along the tangential direction. The line image in the paraxial image plane is called the *sagittal focal line* because it is formed by the sagittal rays. For image planes between these two extreme positions, the ray deviations along x'' and y'' directions are non- zero, and the image of an off-axis point object is in general an ellipse.

The concept of fans of rays is useful to visualize astigmatic aberration. The cone of rays emanating from an off-axis point object can be divided into the tangential and sagittal fans of rays. The tangential fans include those rays which intersect the entrance and exit pupils along lines parallel to the tangential plane (vertical line *aa* and those parallel to it in Fig. 5.25). The sagittal fans of rays intersect the entrance and exit pupils along lines parallel to the sagittal plane (lines *bb* and those parallel to it in Fig. 5.25). The reader is advised to pay full

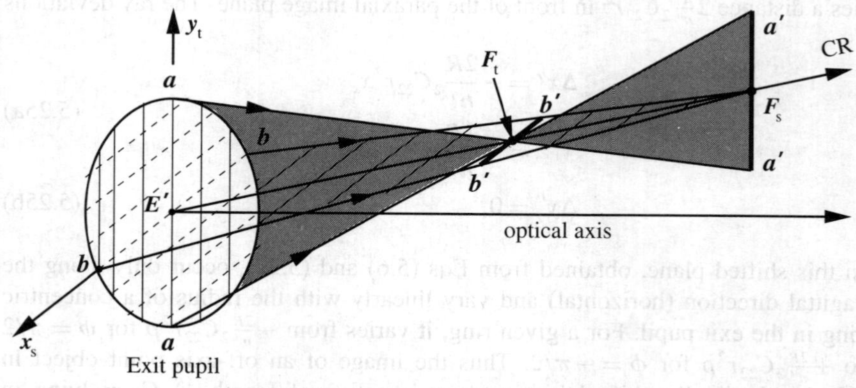

Fig. 5.25: Astigmatic aberration; E' is the center of the exit pupil, tangential fan containing CR is shaded and sagittal fan containing CR is crossed with horizontal lines, F_t and F_s are foci of these two fans, $b'b'$ is tangential focal line (horizontal) and $a'a'$ is sagittal focal line (vertical).

attention to the following discussion to avoid getting lost in the terminology which might otherwise appear confusing.

The tangential fan which contains the chief ray is shaded in Fig. 5.25. Only the marginal rays (aa') of this fan are drawn. The rays in this particular tangential fan converge at the tangential focus F_t and continue to diverge beyond this point. The remaining tangential fans converge along the horizontal focal line $b'b'$ with the tangential focus F_t at its center. This focal line has already been defined as the tangential focal line, though it lies in the sagittal plane in the horizontal direction. The sagittal fan containing the CR and bounded by the marginal rays bb' is shaded with horizontal lines. This sagittal fan converges at the sagittal focus F_s, but before focusing at F_s this fan gives the horizontal line image which exactly coincides with the tangential focal line $b'b'$. Similarly the tangential fan aa proceeds beyond its focus F_t to give a vertical line image $a'a'$. The vertical line $a'a'$ also happens to be the locus of the foci of all sagittal fans and for this reason it is called the *sagittal focal line*, but lying in the tangential (vertical) plane. The focal points F_t and F_s lying on the chief ray are the centers of curvatures of orthogonal arcs on the wavefront (possessing primary astigmatism) with the minimum and maximum radii of curvature, to which a reference was made in the beginning of this section. Thus, the aberration function W_a gives rise to two orthogonal line images of an off-axis point which lie along the tangential and sagittal focal lines. The tangential fans which lie in vertical planes give rise to a horizontal (lying in the sagittal plane) line image $b'b'$, and the sagittal fans give rise to a vertical line image $a'a'$ which lies in the tangential plane. The tangential focal line is also called the primary image and the sagittal focal line as the secondary image. Between these focal lines, the cross-section of the light patch is elliptical, except at the half-way point where it is circular. This is the circle of least confusion. Figure 5.25 should not mislead the reader to wrongly conclude that the tangential and sagittal focal lines pass through the optical axis. These line images are the horizontal and vertical lines around the chief ray (and not about the optical axis) which starts from the off-axis point object and passes through the center of the exit pupil.

The appearance of two separated line images of an off-axis point object in orthogonal directions leads to some interesting image distortions. From the preceding discussion, it follows that the image of a vertical line will appear sharply focused along the sagittal focal line – this line being in the tangential plane is parallel to the line object. On the other hand, the image in the vertical plane containing the tangential focal line will be blurred horizontally because each point of the vertical line is imaged as a horizontal line in this plane. By the same argument, concentric circles in the object plane will be sharply focused in the vertical plane containing the tangential focal line, but will carry radial distortions in the vertical plane containing the sagittal focal line. These distortions are dramatically manifested in the image of a spoked wheel (Fig. 5.26).

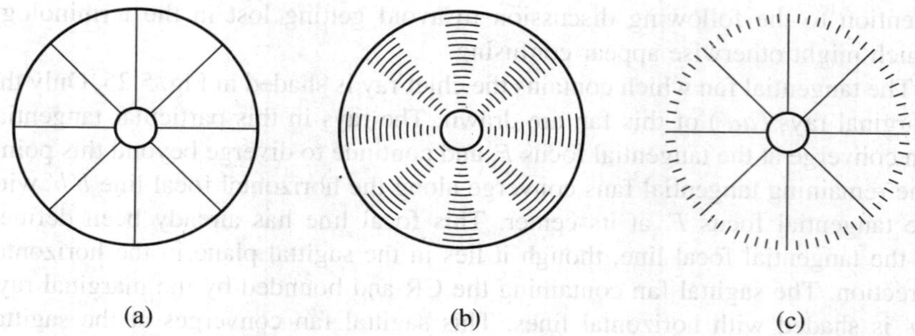

Fig. 5.26: Image distortion by astigmatism; (a) spoked wheel with a small hub is the object, (b) rim of the wheel is sharply focused but the spokes are horizontally defocused in the tangential image plane, (c) spokes are sharply focused but the rim has radial distortion in the sagittal image plane.

The rim of the wheel appears sharp in the tangential (primary) image and the spokes are imaged sharply in the sagittal (secondary) image. The hub of the wheel remains sharp in both images because being small, it satisfies the paraxial image conditions. The horizontal distortions of the spokes increasing radially outward in the tangential image and the radial distortion of the rim in the sagittal image should be noted.

5.5.4 Field Curvature

The next term

$$W_{\text{fc}} = {}_2C_{20}r^2\rho^2 \tag{5.27}$$

in the aberration function representing the field curvature is sketched in Fig. 5.27. The ρ^2 dependence implies a longitudinal shift of the paraxial image which increases quadratically with the off-axis object distance r. Thus, the image in the presence of this aberration is stigmatic, but lies on a spherical surface. The name 'field curvature' is derived from the fact that the image of a flat surface becomes curved.

The field curvature and astigmatism represent qualitatively different aberrations despite some similarity in their aberration functions. A point image of a point object exists for the former, but not for the latter. The field curvature aberration function does not depend on the azimuthal angle ϕ whereas astigmatism has its characteristic ϕ dependence. In the absence of astigmatism (${}_2C_{22} = 0$), the image curvature is called Petzval field curvature (the curve PP in Fig. 5.28 is a section of the Petzval surface). The Petzval surface of an optical system

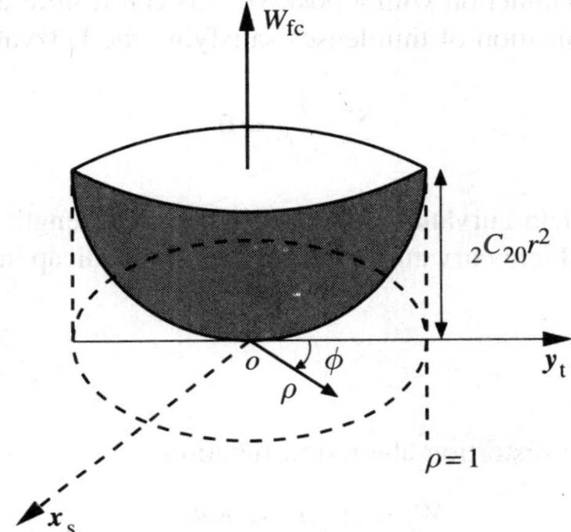

Fig. 5.27: Aberration function representing field curvature.

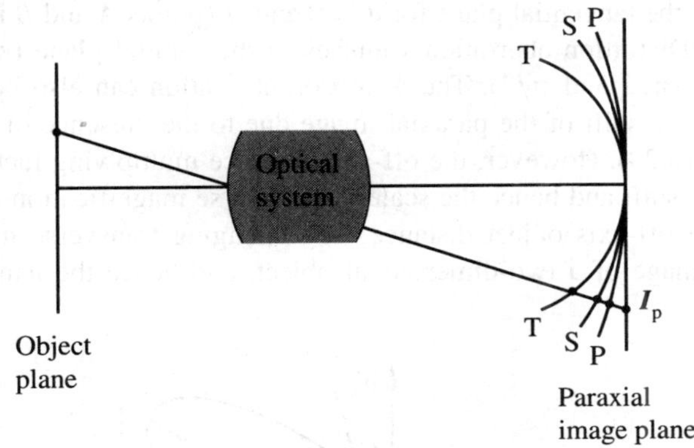

Fig. 5.28: Image surfaces as modified by astigmatism and field curvature; Petzval (PP), sagittal (SS), tangential (TT).

is not affected by lens bending or by changing distance between the lenses. In the presence of astigmatism, the Petzval surface is replaced by the sagittal and tangential surfaces (sections SS and TT in Fig. 5.28). A point on the tangential image surface at a given height always lies three times farther from the Petzval image surface as compared to the corresponding point on the sagittal image surface. A positive lens bends the Petzval image surface towards the exit pupil and a negative lens has just the opposite effect. Thus, a negative lens called *field flattener* used in conjunction with a positive lens can restore the flat image of a flat object. A combination of thin lenses satisfying the Petzval condition

$$\sum_i \frac{1}{n_i f_i} = 0 \tag{5.28}$$

can eliminate the field curvature. Here, f_i is the focal length of the ith lens of refractive index n_i. Field curvature can be a serious handicap in image-projecting systems.

5.5.5 Distortion

The variation of the distortion aberration function

$$\begin{aligned} W_{\mathrm{d}} &= {}_3C_{11} r^3 \rho \cos\phi \\ &= {}_3C_{11} r^2 (r\rho\cos\phi) \end{aligned} \tag{5.29}$$

in the exit pupil is shown in Fig. 5.29. Maximum positive and negative aberrations occur in the tangential plane for $\phi = 0$ and π (points A and B in Fig. 5.29), respectively. Distortion aberration vanishes in the sagittal plane (points C and D with $\phi = -\pi/2$ and $\pi/2$). The distortion aberration can also be interpreted as the transverse shift of the paraxial image due to the presence of the $r\rho\cos\phi$ factor in Eq. (5.29). However, the off-axis distance multiplying factor r^2 makes the transverse shift and hence the scale of transverse magnification of the image vary with the off-axis object distance. The changing transverse magnification distorts the image of a two-dimensional object, and hence the name distortion

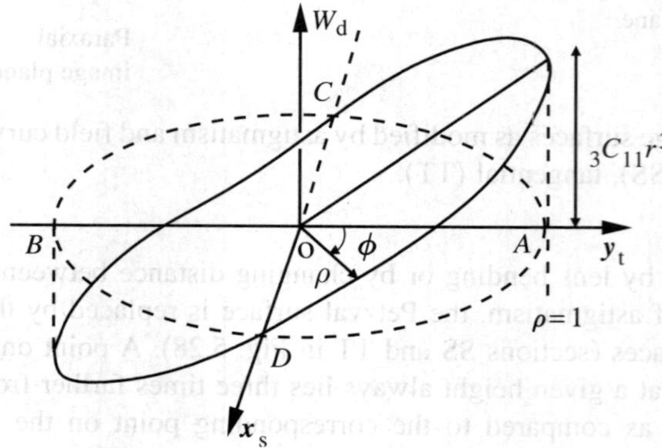

Fig. 5.29: Distortion aberration function in the plane of the exit pupil.

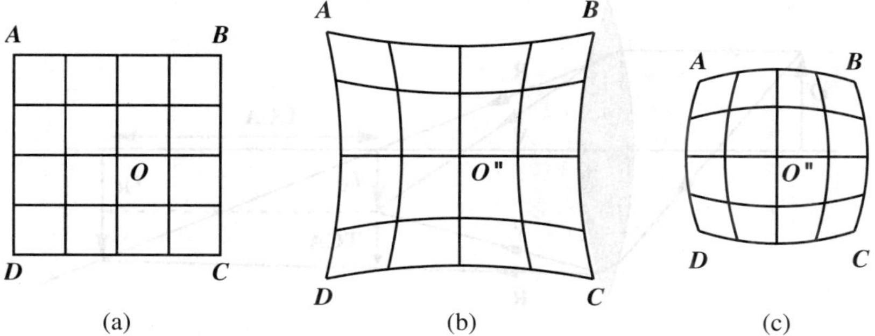

Fig. 5.30: (a) A square mesh placed in the object plane, (b) pin-cushion distortion due to positive ${}_3C_{11}$, (c) barrel-shaped distortion due to negative ${}_3C_{11}$.

given to this aberration. The image is, however, stigmatic since the transverse shift depends on the off-axis object distance and not on the location of a point in the exit pupil (see Section 5.4.2).

The ray deviations in the paraxial image plane due to the distortion aberration are

$$\Delta x'' = 0, \tag{5.30a}$$

$$\Delta y'' = \frac{R}{n''}\,{}_3C_{11} r^3. \tag{5.30b}$$

We consider an object in the form of a square mesh kept in the object plane (Fig. 5.30a). Because of the r^3 dependence on the off-axis object distance, the image of a square mesh develops a pin-cushion distortion for positive ${}_3C_{11}$ (Fig. 5.30b) and a barrel-like distortion for negative ${}_3C_{11}$ (Fig. 5.30c). The mesh lines which pass through the optical axis appear as lines (elongated or shortened depending on the sign of ${}_3C_{11}$) in the image, but all other lines pick up curvature in the image. A thin lens shows negligible distortion for any object distance but thick lenses show pin-cushion and barrel-like distortions, depending on the sign of ${}_3C_{11}$.

5.6 CHROMATIC ABERRATION

The index of refraction of optically transparent media decreases with increasing wavelength of light (see Figure 1.21). This gives rise to longitudinal and transverse chromatic aberrations (separation of colors) in the image formed by a lens with white light (Fig. 5.31). The decrease in the index of refraction is quite

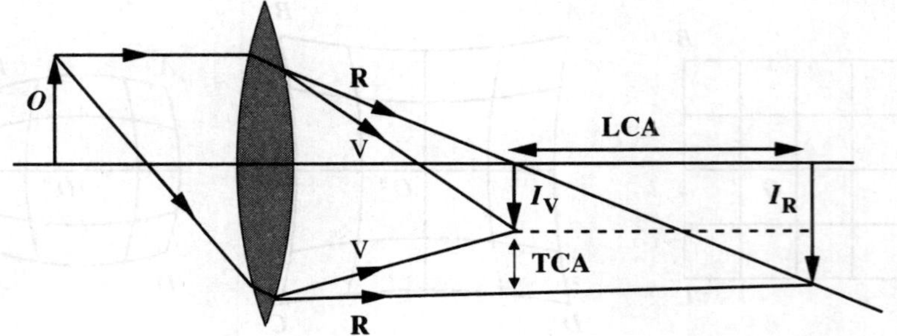

Fig. 5.31: Longitudinal (LCA) and transverse (TCA) chromatic aberrations of a lens; I_V and I_R are the images of object O, produced by violet and red colors of white light. Images produced by remaining colors lie in between.

small, but enough to make the chromatic aberration of a lens comparable to its geometrical aberrations. For a thin lens with

$$\frac{1}{f} = (n-1)\left(\frac{1}{R_1} - \frac{1}{R_2}\right),$$

the dispersive power w is defined as

$$\frac{1}{w} = \frac{\delta f}{f} = \frac{\delta n}{n-1}, \tag{5.31a}$$

where δf is the change in the focal length of the lens corresponding to a change δn in the index of refraction for the extreme wavelengths (red and blue) in the visible spectrum and n is the index of refraction at the mean wavelength (yellow). So that

$$\frac{1}{w} = \frac{n_B - n_R}{n_Y - 1}, \tag{5.31b}$$

where n_B, n_Y, n_R are the indices of refraction at blue, yellow, and red lines (see Section 1.8). A single lens will always have different focal lengths for different colors ($\delta f = \frac{f}{w} \neq 0$) but two thin lenses, held together or held apart, can have the same focal length for blue and red lines (no dispersion). This happens for two thin lenses made from flint and crown glasses, cemented together, when

$$\frac{w_1}{f_1} + \frac{w_2}{f_2} = 0, \tag{5.32}$$

where

$$w_1 = \frac{n_Y^f - 1}{n_B^f - n_R^f}, \tag{5.33a}$$

$$w_2 = \frac{n_Y^c - 1}{n_B^c - n_R^c} \tag{5.33b}$$

are the dispersive powers of the flint and crown glass lenses, respectively, and f_1 and f_2 are their focal lengths for the yellow line. Since the dispersive powers of the flint and crown glasses are positive but different, the achromatic combination should consist of a positive lens and a negative lens, cemented together. The radii of curvatures of the individual lenses are still available for reducing geometrical aberrations. The reciprocal of the dispersive power is called Abbe number which is usually supplied by the glass manufacturers. The dispersive power in the context of white light is defined in terms of the Fraunhofer F, D, and C lines with wavelengths $\lambda_F = 486.1\,\text{nm}$, $\lambda_D = 589.3\,\text{nm}$, and $\lambda_C = 656.3\,\text{nm}$ in the blue, yellow, and red regions, respectively.

For two lenses of the same material, a distance d apart,

$$\frac{1}{f} = \frac{1}{f_1} + \frac{1}{f_2} - \frac{d}{f_1 f_2},$$

so that

$$\frac{\delta f}{f^2} = \frac{\delta f_1}{f_1^2} + \frac{\delta f_2}{f_2^2} - \frac{d}{f_2 f_1^2}\delta f_1 - \frac{d}{f_1 f_2^2}\delta f_2,$$

where

$$\frac{\delta f_1}{f_1} = \frac{\delta f_2}{f_2} = \frac{1}{w}.$$

For this lens combination to be achromatic ($\delta f = 0$),

$$\frac{1}{f_1} + \frac{1}{f_2} - \frac{2d}{f_1 f_2} = 0,$$

giving

$$d = \frac{1}{2}(f_1 + f_2). \tag{5.34}$$

Huygens eye-piece used in microscopes has two lenses made from the same material separated by a distance equal to their mean focal length. With chromatic aberration eliminated, the radii of curvatures of individual lenses can be chosen to minimize geometrical aberrations of the eye-piece.

5.7 REFERENCES

5.1 Robert D. Guenther, Modern Optics, John Wiley & Sons, New York, 1990.
5.2 Edward L. O' Neill, Introduction to Statistical Optics, Addison-Wesley Publishing Company, Inc., Reading, 1963.
5.3 Max Born and Emil Wolf, Principles of Optics, 7th ed., Cambridge University Press, Cambridge, 1999.
5.4 Miles V. Klein and Thomas E. Furtak, Optics, 2nd ed., John Wiley & Sons, New York, 1986.
5.5 F. A. Jenkins and H. E. White, Fundamentals of Optics, 3rd ed., McGraw-Hill, New York, 1957.
5.6 Pantazis Mouroulis and John Macdonald, Geometrical Optics and Optical Design, Oxford University Press, New York, 1997.

5.8 PROBLEMS

5.1 A thin equiconvex lens of diameter 1 cm has focal length 20 cm in air. The index of refraction of the material of the lens is 1.5.

(a) Find the maximum value of the aberration function for the primary spherical aberration, expressed in terms of the mean wavelength of white light ($\bar{\lambda} =$ 550 nm) if the object lies 1 m in front of the lens.
(b) Find the transverse spherical aberrations in the paraxial image planes for the object distances of 25 and 40 cm. What are the corresponding longitudinal spherical aberrations? Comment on your results.

5.2 Light from a He–Ne laser, lasing at 632.8 nm, falls normally on a plano-convex lens ($n = 1.5$) of diameter 1 cm and focal length 30 cm in air. The radius of the laser beam is 1 mm. Compare the transverse spherical aberrations in the back focal plane of the lens when light falls on (a) the plane surface, (b) the curved surface of the lens.

5.3 Find the optimum radii of curvatures of a thin lens ($n = 1.5$) of focal length 20 cm in air for use with object distance of about 50 cm to have minimum spherical aberration. What is the residual transverse spherical aberration if the diameter of the lens is 1 cm? Now turn the lens around and find the new transverse spherical aberration.

5.4 Find the radius of the largest comatic circle for the thin lens of Problem 5.3 which has been optimized for minimum spherical aberration. Take the object distance from the optical axis as 1.0 cm. You may use

$$_1C_{31} = \frac{1}{4f^2v}\left[\frac{2n+1}{n}p + \frac{n+1}{n(n-1)}q\right],$$

where v and f are the paraxial image distance and paraxial focal length, respectively, n is the index of refraction, p and q are the Coddington position and shape factors, respectively.

5.5 Convince yourself by taking a few representative values of the index of refraction n that for a thin lens, the condition for minimum spherical aberration is not much different from the condition for zero comatic aberration (${}_1C_{31} = 0$).

CHAPTER 6

Interference of Light Waves

6.1 INTERFERENCE

When two or more light waves cross each other, the resultant field, given by the superposition principle, is the vector sum of the fields associated with the individual waves, i.e.,

$$\vec{E}(\vec{r}, t) = \sum_i \vec{E}_i(\vec{r}, t), \tag{6.1}$$

where $\vec{E}_i(\vec{r}, t)$ is the electric field associated with the ith wave. Here, we have considered superposition of the electric fields since, as was first shown by Wiener, most optical detectors including the human eye are influenced primarily by the electric field of the light waves. Needless to state that the superposition principle applies to magnetic fields as well:

$$\vec{B}(\vec{r}, t) = \sum_i \vec{B}_i(\vec{r}, t).$$

The superposition principle permits the resultant irradiance $I(\vec{r}, t)$ at a given point to differ from the sum of the irradiances of the individual waves when present alone, i.e., superposition principle for the intensities may not always hold. When

$$I(\vec{r}, t) \neq \sum_i I_i(\vec{r}, t), \tag{6.2}$$

the light waves are said to have interfered with each other. The waves, after interfering, continue to move forward unaltered, except for a phase retardation in a lossless medium which bears no relationship, whatsoever, to the fact that interference among the waves has taken place in the region of their overlap. As has already been mentioned in Chapter 2, only mutually coherent waves can interfere but the lack of interference does not necessarily imply incoherence of the interfering waves. Arago and Fresnel had concluded that orthogonally polarized coherent light waves do not interfere.

6.2 TWO-WAVE INTERFERENCE

Interference between two monochromatic waves of the same frequency gives rise to a spatially stationary distribution of time averaged intensities. Interference among monochromatic waves with widely different frequencies can hardly be observed. However, two monochromatic waves with a small frequency difference give rise to a moving interference pattern, which under suitable conditions can be observed (see Fig. 1.23). For two-wave interference in vacuum, average resultant intensity at a given point can be obtained from Eq. (1.46):

$$I = \left(\frac{1}{2}\epsilon_0 c\right) \langle(\vec{E}_1 + \vec{E}_2)\cdot(\vec{E}_1^* + \vec{E}_2^*)\rangle$$

$$= I_1 + I_2 + \epsilon_0 c Re\,\langle \vec{E}_1 \cdot \vec{E}_2^*\rangle, \tag{6.3}$$

where $\vec{E}_1$ and $\vec{E}_2$ are the complex fields associated with the two waves. The symbol $\langle\rangle$ represents time averaging for ergodic fields. The averaging time must be sufficiently large. For light waves with orthogonal states of polarization,

$$\langle \vec{E}_1 \cdot \vec{E}_2^* \rangle = 0 \tag{6.4}$$

and the resultant intensity is the sum of the intensities of the two waves, in agreement with our earlier statement that cross-polarized waves do not interfere. For co-polarized light waves of the same frequency,

$$Re\langle \vec{E}_1 \cdot \vec{E}_2^* \rangle = Re\langle E_1 E_2^* \rangle$$

$$= |E_1||E_2| \cos\delta, \tag{6.5}$$

where δ is the phase difference with which the waves arrive at the point of interference. The phase difference δ, arising due to a difference in the path lengths travelled by the interfering waves, is

$$\delta = \frac{2\pi}{\lambda_v} \times \text{(optical path difference)}$$

$$= 2\pi\nu\tau, \tag{6.6}$$

where λ_v is wavelength of light in a vacuum and τ is the difference in the path lengths divided by the velocity of light in the medium. Equations (6.4) and (6.5) together can handle interference among waves with arbitrary states of polarization. The resultant intensity

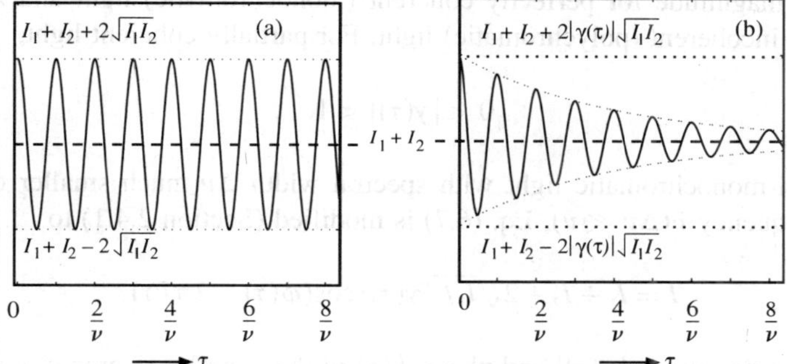

Fig. 6.1: Intensity variation in two-wave interference produced by (a) monochromatic source, (b) quasi-monochromatic source with one narrow spectral band.

$$\begin{aligned} I(\delta) &= I_1 + I_2 + 2\sqrt{I_1 I_2}\cos\delta \\ &= I_1 + I_2 + 2\sqrt{I_1 I_2}\cos 2\pi\nu\tau \end{aligned} \tag{6.7}$$

for two-wave interference goes through maximum and minimum values (Fig. 6.1a) for

$$\delta = 2m\pi \tag{6.8a}$$

and

$$\delta = (2m+1)\pi, \tag{6.8b}$$

respectively, where $m = 0, 1, 2, \ldots$. The extremum values of the resultant intensity distribution remain unchanged, however, large a difference in the paths is introduced between monochromatic interfering waves. For monochromatic waves of equal amplitudes, the interference minima have zero intensity and the visibility of interference fringes defined as

$$V(\tau) = \frac{I_{\max} - I_{\min}}{I_{\max} + I_{\min}} \tag{6.9}$$

attains the maximum value of one.

The mathematical framework needed to extend these results to quasi-monochromatic and polychromatic light fields has already been described in Chapter 2. The complex degree of coherence $\gamma(\tau)$, introduced in Chapter 2, has unit magnitude for perfectly coherent (monochromatic) light and zero for perfectly incoherent (polychromatic) light. For partially coherent light,

$$0 < |\gamma(\tau)| < 1. \tag{6.10}$$

For quasi-monochromatic light with spectral width $\Delta\nu$ much smaller than the mean frequency $\bar{\nu}(\Delta\nu \ll \bar{\nu})$, Eq. (6.7) is modified (Section 2.4.1) to

$$I = I_1 + I_2 + 2\sqrt{I_1 I_2}|\gamma(\tau)|\cos(\phi(\tau) - 2\pi\bar{\nu}\tau), \tag{6.11}$$

where the magnitude $|\gamma(\tau)|$ and phase $\phi(\tau)$ of the complex degree of coherence do not change appreciably over a limited range of values of the time delay. Accordingly, interference between two quasi-monochromatic light waves can be described in exactly the same manner as interference between two monochromatic light waves provided the time delays are restricted to values much smaller than the characteristic coherence time τ_c which is of the order of $\frac{1}{\Delta\nu}$.

Notwithstanding what has just been said, there are qualitative differences between the interference effects produced by monochromatic and quasi-monochromatic light fields. No doubt, Eqs (6.8) locate the maxima and minima of the resultant intensity distribution in both cases. However, since the magnitude $|\gamma(\tau)|$ of the complex degree of coherence is less than unity for quasi-monochromatic light, the intensity changes between the minimum and maximum values are less marked, leading to a reduction in the visibility of the interference fringes. Beyond a certain time delay for quasi-monochromatic light, the maxima and minima of the intensity distribution can hardly be distinguished and the visibility of fringes becomes zero (Fig. 6.1b). This happens because the fringe patterns due to different wavelengths within the spectral bandwidth of quasi-monochromatic light are somewhat displaced from each other. For zero path difference, the intensity maxima for all wavelengths overlap exactly and for small path differences, the fringes due to different wavelengths are nearly coincident but for large path differences, the fringe patterns due to different wavelengths are sufficiently displaced from each other to produce uniform intensity distribution. This statement can be made a little more rigorous. Equation (6.8a) can be equivalently expressed in terms of the path difference

$$\mathcal{L} = m\bar{\lambda} \tag{6.12}$$

for the mth order maximum corresponding to the mean wavelength $\bar{\lambda}$. With wavelength spread $\Delta\lambda$ about the mean wavelength, the condition

$$\mathcal{L} = (m - \epsilon)(\bar{\lambda} + \Delta\lambda) \tag{6.13}$$

may also be simultaneously satisfied, where ϵ is the change (integral or fractional) in the order of the maximum for the wavelength $\bar{\lambda} + \Delta\lambda$ with respect to the order of the maximum for the mean wavelength $\bar{\lambda}$. For the overall fringe pattern to remain discernible, $\epsilon \ll 1$. Combining Eqs (6.12) and (6.13) and neglecting the product $\epsilon\Delta\lambda$ gives

$$\epsilon = m/(\bar{\lambda}/\Delta\lambda) \tag{6.14a}$$

or equivalently,

$$\epsilon = \mathcal{L}/((\bar{\lambda})^2/\Delta\lambda). \tag{6.14b}$$

To have good quality fringes ($\epsilon \ll 1$) with quasi-monochromatic light of mean wavelength $\bar{\lambda}$ and wavelength spread $\Delta\lambda$, the order m of the fringe for the mean wavelength should be much smaller than the ratio $\bar{\lambda}/\Delta\lambda$. This condition can be better stated by requiring that for good quality interference fringes with quasi-monochromatic light, the difference in path lengths ($\mathcal{L}$) between the interfering beams should be much smaller than the ratio $\bar{\lambda}^2/\Delta\lambda$, which represents the coherence length of quasi-monochromatic light (Eqs 2.41).

The visibility of the fringes produced by quasi-monochromatic light possessing two narrow spectral bands goes through cycles of maximum and minimum values. Eventually, for sufficiently large path difference, the intensity distribution becomes uniform (Fig. 6.2). The interference fringes due to the two spectral

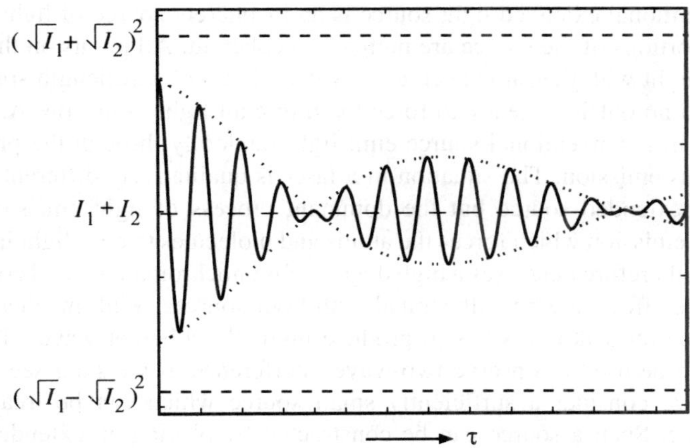

Fig. 6.2: Intensity variation in two-wave interference produced by a quasi-monochromatic source with two narrow spectral bands.

bands with mean wavelengths $\bar{\lambda}_1$ and $\bar{\lambda}_2$ coincide, leading to a high visibility of the fringes, whenever the path difference $\mathcal{L}$ satisfies the condition

$$\mathcal{L} = m_1\bar{\lambda}_1 = (m_1+n)\bar{\lambda}_2,$$

where m_1 and n are integers. The visibility of the fringes becomes zero for the first time when the mth maximum due to $\bar{\lambda}_1$ overlaps with the $(m+1)$th minimum due to $\bar{\lambda}_2$. For further study on the interference produced by quasi-monochromatic light, the reader is advised to consult references cited at the end of Chapter 2. We may mention in passing that a laser is a good source of quasi-monochromatic light. A small laboratory He–Ne laser with visible radiation at 632.8 nm has an extremely small spread in wavelength, of the order of 10^{-5} nm, giving $\bar{\lambda}/\Delta\lambda$ of the order of 10^7 and coherence length $(\bar{\lambda})^2/\Delta\lambda$ of few tens of meters. However, a He–Ne laser usually oscillates simultaneously in several longitudinal modes separated typically by 10^{-4} nm in wavelength. This gives rise to pulsation of visibility of fringes with path difference as mentioned earlier.

We now describe experimental schemes to observe two-wave interference. Throughout this discussion, it will be assumed that the maximum path difference between the interfering waves is well within the coherence length of the quasi-monochromatic light field. With this assumption, an explicit reference to the degree of coherence may not be necessary. The magnitude of the degree of coherence is assumed not to change appreciably over the path differences to be encountered. Two quasi-monochromatic light waves with a certain degree of mutual coherence can produce discernible interference effects. A sodium lamp used in an undergraduate laboratory is quite adequate for this purpose. Any conventional extended light source is an incoherent source of light because different portions of the source are mutually incoherent. All points on the source may emit light with the same average wavelength $\bar{\lambda}$ and wavelength spread $\Delta\lambda$, but there is no outside agency to force them to emit light in unison. Atoms and molecules in a conventional source emit light randomly through the process of spontaneous emission. The situation in a laser is qualitatively different. A laser is also an extended source but the dominant process of light emission is the stimulated emission which forces the atoms and molecules to emit light in unison. Laser light therefore possesses a high degree of monochromaticity and coherence. Interference effects are best illustrated with laser sources. With incoherent light sources, one must devise ways to produce mutually coherent waves. Extended sources can be used to observe two-wave interference as we shall see later but for now, we consider a sufficiently small source which can be treated as a point source. Such a source can be constructed by placing an extended quasi-monochromatic light source inside a dark enclosure with a small hole. This tiny hole, through which light escapes from the enclosure, acts as a point source if its dimensions are sufficiently small. Mutually coherent quasi-monochromatic waves can be obtained from a 'point source' in two ways. In the wavefront division approach, the spherical wavefront emanating from the point source is split and then recombined after introducing an appropriate path difference. This is what happens in Young's two slit arrangement described in Section 2.5. Alternatively, the amplitude of the incident wave is split at an interface between two media (division of amplitude), as in Michelson interferometer (Section 2.4.1), to generate two waves which interfere upon recombination.

6.2.1 Interference by Division of Wavefront

Some of the standard arrangements used to observe two-wave interference by division of the wavefront are shown in Fig. 6.3. The narrow slits S_1 and S_2 in Young's double slit arrangement (Fig. 6.3a) intercept portions of the spherical wavefront and act as real mutually coherent point sources, diffracting light in the forward direction. Interference among the diffracted waves can be observed anywhere in the region of overlap (shaded portion) behind the plane of the

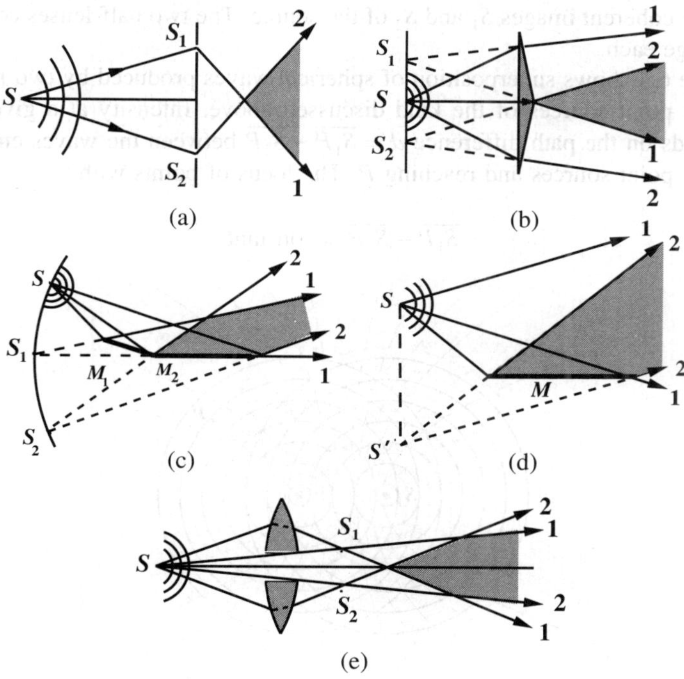

Fig. 6.3: Two-wave interference; (a) Young's two-slit arrangement, (b) Fresnel's biprism, (c) Fresnel's two mirrors, (d) Loyd's mirror, (e) Billet's split lens.

slits. Historically, the interference produced in Young's double slit experiment was not accepted as a conclusive proof of the wave nature of light because it was thought that the fringes in Young's experiment could arise due to some unexplained interaction of light with the edges of the slits. Fresnel's biprism arrangement (Fig. 6.3b), however, established the wave nature of light beyond any doubt. Fresnel's biprism consists of two small angle (a few degrees) prisms juxtaposed in a manner that the incident spherical wavefront is split by the two prisms. The split wavefronts travel in different directions, eventually overlap and produce interference. S_1 and S_2 act as virtual but mutually coherent point sources. Figure 6.3c shows the two-mirror arrangement, also devised by Fresnel. Here, the portions of the spherical wavefront reflected by the two mirrors overlap to produce interference. The source images S_1 and S_2, formed by the two mirrors, are virtual but mutually coherent. In Lloyd's single mirror arrangement (Fig. 6.3d), interference is produced by the portion of the wavefront reflected by the mirror and the portion which propagates directly to the region of superposition. In this case, the point source S and its virtual image S' act as mutually coherent point sources. Figure 6.3e shows Billet's split- lens arrangement to produce two real, mutually coherent images S_1 and S_2 of the source. The two half-lenses contribute one image each.

Figure 6.4 shows superposition of spherical waves produced by two mutually coherent point sources of the kind discussed above. Intensity at a given point P depends on the path difference $d = \overline{S_1P} - \overline{S_2P}$ between the waves emanating from the point sources and reaching P. The locus of points with

$$\overline{S_1P} - \overline{S_2P} = \text{constant} \tag{6.15}$$

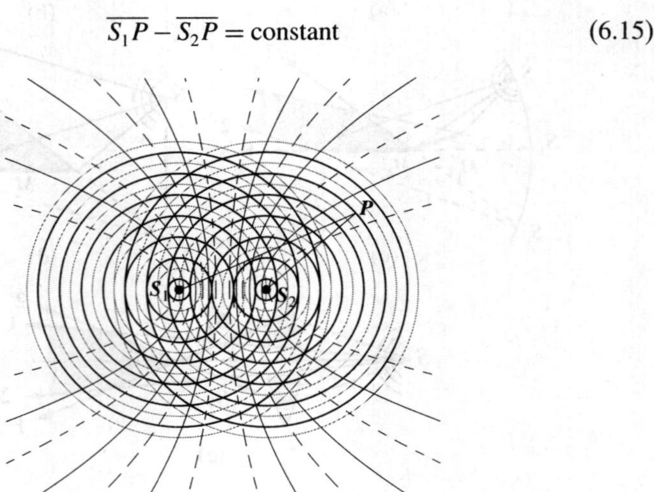

Fig. 6.4: Hyperbolic fringes due to two mutually coherent point sources.

is a hyperbola with S_1 and S_2 as its foci. The contours of the interference fringes in a plane are hyperbolic and the fringes in space are along the hyperboloids of revolution. However, sufficiently far away from the point sources, the fringes appear nearly straight in any given plane of observation (see Photo 10.4). Fringes produced by these methods lie everywhere in the region where the two waves overlap. These fringes are therefore called non-localized fringes.

6.2.2 Interference by Division of Amplitude

In the preceding section, we considered two-wave interference when different portions of the wavefront are made to propagate in different directions and then recombined. Now, we discuss two-wave interference when a quasi-monochromatic wave is incident on a thin transparent film (Fig. 6.5). The wave is partly reflected and partly transmitted at each interface. Amplitudes of successively reflected and transmitted waves diminish rapidly for films of low reflectivity. The amplitude transmission coefficient for passage of the wave from the medium of refractive index n_1 to the medium of refractive index n_2 is t and t' is the corresponding amplitude transmission coefficient for passage in the reverse direction. The amplitude reflection coefficients for the external and internal reflections are r and $r'(= -r)$, respectively. For sufficiently small r ($r^2 \ll 1$), only two waves need to be considered in reflection as well as in transmission, leading to two-wave interference. The amplitudes of the first two

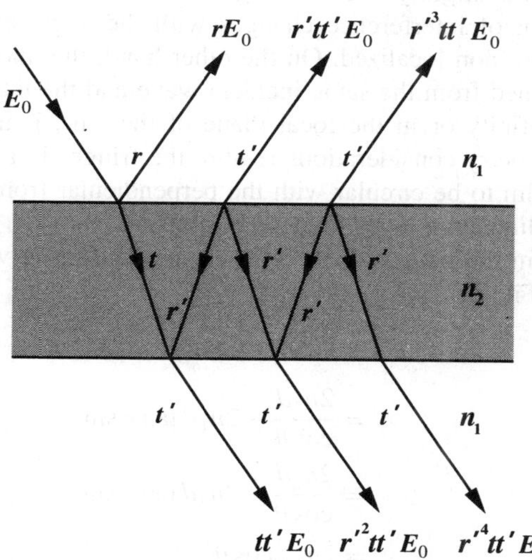

Fig. 6.5: Reflection and transmission across a thin film.

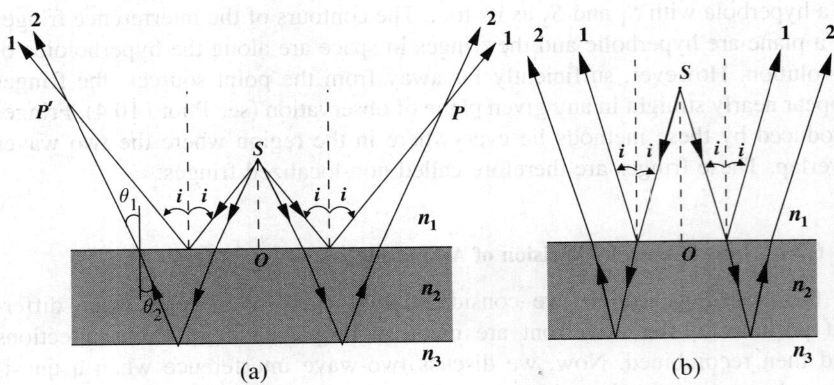

Fig. 6.6: Two-wave interference in reflected light from a thin film; (a) non-localized fringes, (b) fringes localized at infinity.

waves in reflection are comparable, but those in transmission differ considerably. As a result, interference fringes in reflected light have higher visibility than those in transmitted light. Figure 6.6 shows two possible ways to obtain two-wave interference in reflected light with the division of amplitude.

S is a point source. One of the interfering waves is reflected from the front surface and the other from the back surface of the transparent film. In Fig. 6.6a, two waves incident at slightly different angles interfere at a finite distance from the film. The point of interference changes with the angle of incidence. The fringes are therefore non-localized. On the other hand, the interfering waves in Fig. 6.6b are obtained from the same incident wave and the interference fringes are localized at infinity or in the focal plane of the lens, if used to focus the parallel rays. Symmetry considerations require the fringes in a plane parallel to the plane of the film to be circular with the perpendicular from the source S to the plane of the film acting as the axis of symmetry.

The difference in the path lengths between the interfering waves, calculated with reference to Fig. 6.7, is

$$\begin{aligned}\text{Path Diff} &= n_2(AD+DB) - n_1 AC \\ &= \frac{2n_2 d}{\cos\theta} - 2n_1 d \tan\theta \sin i \\ &= \frac{2n_2 d}{\cos\theta} - 2n_2 d \tan\theta \sin\theta \\ &= 2n_2 d \cos\theta \\ &= 2d(n_2^2 - n_1^2 \sin^2 i)^{1/2},\end{aligned} \tag{6.16}$$

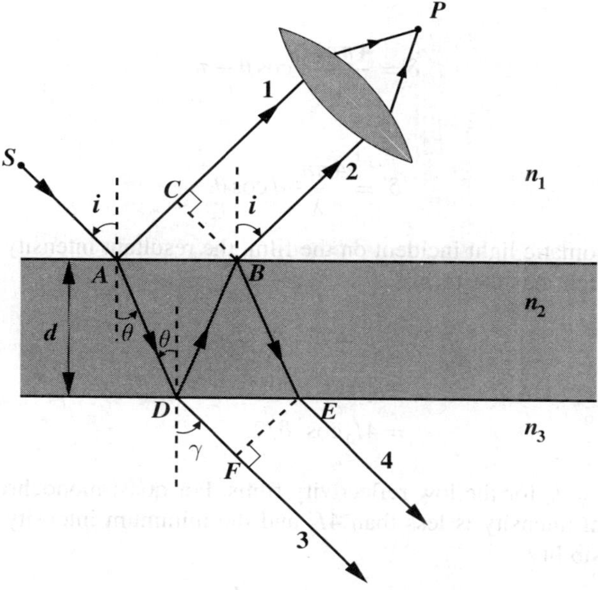

Fig. 6.7: Localized fringes produced by a thin film.

where d is the film thickness and i and θ are the angles of incidence and refraction, respectively, at the first interface.

The phase difference between reflected waves (1) and (2) is

$$\delta = \frac{4\pi}{\bar{\lambda}} n_2 d \cos\theta + \phi_0, \tag{6.17}$$

where $\bar{\lambda}$ is mean wavelength of the quasi-monochromatic light in vacuum. The phase constant $\phi_0 = 0$ or $\pm\pi$ takes care of the phase change on reflection, depending on the relative values of the indices of refraction n_1, n_2, and n_3. The phase difference for the transmitted waves (3) and (4) can likewise be shown to be given by

$$\begin{aligned} \delta' &= \frac{4\pi}{\bar{\lambda}} n_2 d \cos\theta + \psi_0 \\ &= \frac{4\pi}{\bar{\lambda}} d(n_2^2 - n_3^2 \sin^2\gamma)^{1/2} + \psi_0, \end{aligned} \tag{6.18}$$

where ψ_0 is zero if $\phi_0 = \pm\pi$ and vice versa and γ is the angle of emergence in the third medium. Here, we take $\phi_0 = -\pi(n_2 > n_1, n_3)$. Accordingly, we can write,

$$\delta = \frac{4\pi n_2}{\bar{\lambda}} d\cos\theta - \pi \tag{6.19}$$

and

$$\delta' = \frac{4\pi n_2}{\bar{\lambda}} d\cos\theta. \tag{6.20}$$

For monochromatic light incident on the film, the resultant intensity distribution in reflected light has the form

$$\begin{aligned} I(\delta) &= I_1 + I_2 + 2\sqrt{I_1 I_2}\cos\delta \\ &= 2I_0(1+\cos\delta) \\ &= 4I_0\cos^2\delta/2, \end{aligned} \tag{6.21}$$

since $I_1 \approx I_2 = I_0$ for the low reflectivity films. For quasi-monochromatic light, the maximum intensity is less than $4I_0$ and the minimum intensity is not quite zero. The visibility

$$V(\delta) = \frac{I_{max} - I_{min}}{I_{max} + I_{min}} \tag{6.22}$$

of the interference fringes in reflected light is good, but always less than one. The visibility of the fringes in transmitted light is low because of unequal amplitudes of the interfering waves. The conditions for the maxima and minima of intensity distribution in reflected light, for the above choice of the indices of refraction, are

$$n_2 d\cos\theta = (2m+1)\bar{\lambda}/4 \tag{6.23}$$

and

$$n_2 d\cos\theta = 2m\bar{\lambda}/4, \tag{6.24}$$

respectively, where $m = 0, 1, 2, \ldots$. These fringes are called fringes of constant inclination because for a fringe of a given order, the angle of incidence has a definite value. The fringe separation decreases with increase in film thickness, making it difficult to observe interference from thick films.

6.2.3 Testing Flatness of Surfaces

Non-localized fringes of the kind described in Fig. 6.6a can be used to determine the deviation from exact parallelism between the faces of a transparent plate [6.8].

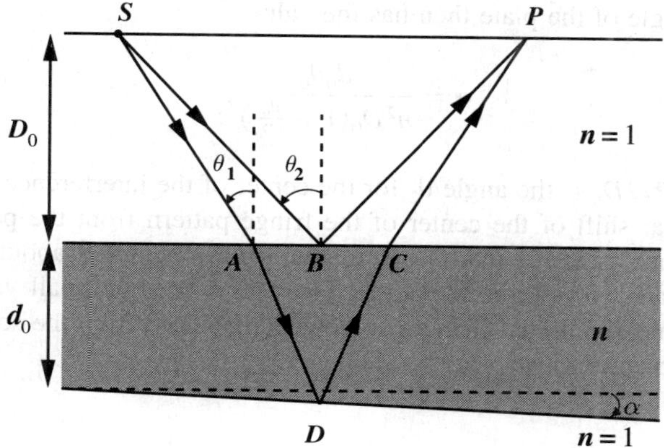

Fig. 6.8: Non-localized fringes from a wedge shaped plate.

Figure 6.8 shows a quasi-monochromatic point source S kept in front of a transparent plate of nominal thickness d_0 and wedge angle α. The plate thickness must be well within the coherence length of the light source. A low power He–Ne laser with its beam made slightly divergent with a convex lens is an excellent substitute for the point source. Non-localized fringes in reflected light can be observed anywhere in front of the plate. Here, we choose the plane of observation which contains the point source S and is parallel to the front surface of the test plate. The figure shows two rays incident at angles θ_1 and θ_2 and meeting at point P in the plane of observation after one of them gets reflected from the front surface and the other from the back surface of the test plate. Angles θ_1 and θ_2, in the small angle approximation, satisfy the relation

$$\theta_1 = \frac{\theta_2}{1 + \frac{d_0}{nD_0}} - n\alpha, \tag{6.25}$$

where n is the index of refraction of the plate kept at a distance D_0 from the point source. The point P acts as the center of the fringe pattern if the path difference

$$\Delta = SA + n(AD + DC) + CP - SB - BP$$

has an extremum value. After considerable trigonometric manipulation, the extremum condition in the small angle approximation gives

$$2n\alpha\left(1 - \frac{d_0^2}{n^2 D_0^2}\right) - 2\frac{\theta_1 d_0}{nD_0}\left(1 + \frac{d_0}{nD_0}\right) = 0. \tag{6.26}$$

The wedge angle of the plate then has the value

$$\alpha = \frac{d_0\theta_0}{n^2 D_0(1+\frac{d_0}{nD_0})}, \tag{6.27}$$

where $\theta_0 = SP/2D_0$ is the angle θ_2 for the center of the interference pattern and SP is the linear shift of the center of the fringe pattern from the point source. The interference pattern consists of circular fringes centered about the source point for a plate with perfectly parallel faces ($\alpha = 0$). For small values of the wedge angle, nearly circular fringes somewhat displaced from the source can be seen (see Problem 6.8).

6.3 INTERFERENCE WITH EXTENDED SOURCES

If the point source in Fig. 6.7 is replaced by an extended source, good quality interference fringes localized at infinity or in the focal plane of the converging lens can still be observed. This happens because the path difference between the interfering waves is dependent only on the film thickness and angle of incidence, and not on the exact location of the point source (Eq. 6.16). Waves emanating from different points of the extended source, arriving at the film of constant thickness at the same angle of incidence, emerge from the film as a parallel beam and are brought to a common focus by the lens (lens not shown in Fig. 6.9). Interference, however, takes place between the waves originating from the same point on the extended source. The resultant intensity is additive for waves originating from different points of the extended source and reaching a given point in the plane

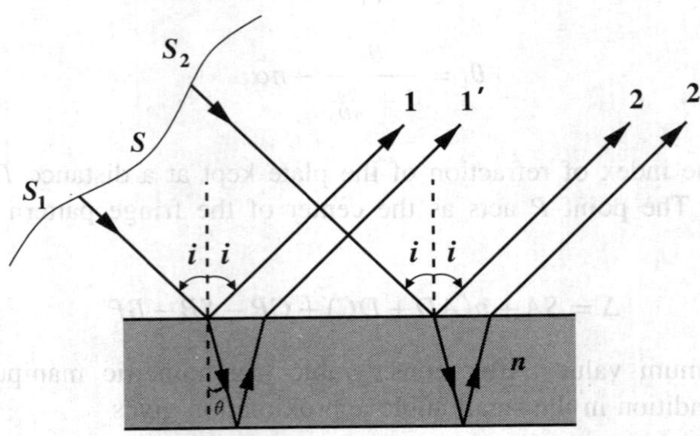

Fig. 6.9: Fringes localized at infinity for an extended source; S_1 and S_2 are two points on the extended source S.

of observation. In this case, the fringe visibility for the extended source is as good as for a point source, but the fringes are much brighter. We state without proof that for an extended source, non-localized fringes are generally difficult to observe. This can be appreciated with reference to Fig. 6.6a. Waves starting from different points of the extended source reach any observation point (like P) at a finite distance from the film with different angles of incidence and hence with different phases. This should lead to uniform illumination.

6.3.1 Haidinger Fringes

It was mentioned in Section 6.2.2 that good quality fringes are difficult to obtain from thick films. The best chance of observing interference from a thick film is when light falls on the film at or near normal incidence. Fringes observed from thick films with light from extended sources falling at near normal incidence are called Haidinger fringes after the name of the Austrian physicist Wilhelm Karl Haidinger. Figure 6.10 shows a possible arrangement to observe Haidinger fringes. S is an extended source. The beam splitter BS is oriented to ensure near-normal incidence on the film F of thickness d. Haidinger fringes produced by this arrangement are circular if the lens L is kept parallel to the film. It should

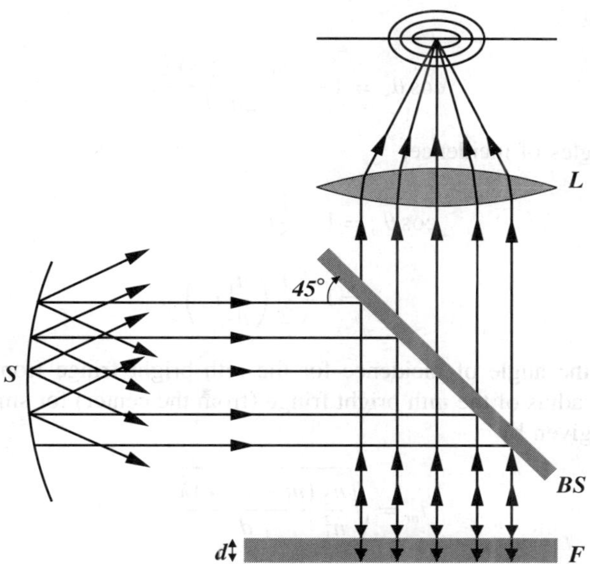

Fig. 6.10: Arrangement to produce Haidinger fringes from a dielectric film; S is an extended source, BS is a beam splitter.

be noted that the highest order Haidinger fringe occurs for normal incidence (Eq. 6.16) and lies at the center of the interference pattern. However, the central fringe need not always be bright. The order of a Haidinger fringe decreases with increasing angle of incidence. Let the order of the fringe at the center ($i = 0$) of the interference pattern be m_0 (not necessarily an integer), so that

$$n_2 d = (2m_0 + 1)\bar{\lambda}/4. \tag{6.28}$$

If m_0 is not an integer, then the first bright fringe corresponds to an integral order $(m_0 - \epsilon)$, where ϵ is a fraction less than one. Referring to Fig. 6.9, the first bright fringe closest to the center of the interference pattern satisfies the condition

$$n_2 d \cos\theta_1 = [2(m_0 - \epsilon) + 1]\,\bar{\lambda}/4.$$

For the mth bright fringe from the center of the interference pattern,

$$\begin{aligned} n_2 d \cos\theta_m &= [2(m_0 - m + 1 - \epsilon) + 1]\,\bar{\lambda}/4 \\ &= (2m_0 + 1)\bar{\lambda}/4 - 2(m - 1 + \epsilon)\bar{\lambda}/4. \end{aligned} \tag{6.29}$$

The angular size of this fringe can be obtained by combining Eqs (6.28) and (6.29), giving

$$\cos\theta_m = 1 - \frac{(m - 1 + \epsilon)\bar{\lambda}}{2n_2 d}. \tag{6.30}$$

For small angles of incidence,

$$\begin{aligned} \cos\theta_m &= 1 - \frac{1}{2}\theta_m^2 \\ &= 1 - \frac{1}{2}\left(\frac{n_1}{n_2} i_m\right)^2, \end{aligned}$$

where i_m is the angle of incidence for the mth bright fringe from the center. The angular radius of the mth bright fringe (from the center) for small angles of incidence is given by

$$i_m = \sqrt{\frac{n_2}{n_1^2}\frac{(m - 1 + \epsilon)\bar{\lambda}}{d}}. \tag{6.31}$$

The angular radius of a Haidinger fringe decreases inversely as the square root of the film thickness. We shall encounter these fringes, when we discuss the Fabry–Perot interferometer.

6.3.2 Fizeau Fringes

We now closely examine our earlier statement that non-localized fringes can be observed with a point source, but not with an extended source. Consider two waves (1 and 2 in Fig. 6.11) starting from point S_1 on the extended source S and crossing each other at point P at a finite distance from film F after one wave undergoes reflection at the front surface and the other at the back surface of the film. The exact intensity at P due to point S_1 alone depends on the phase difference with which these waves arrive at this point. There can be many points (S_2 is one such point) on the extended source from which similar pairs of waves after getting reflected from different portions of the film may cross each other at point P. The resultant intensity at P will include all such contributions. The calculation of the path difference between the waves (such as the waves 1 and 2 in Fig. 6.11) starting from a given point on the extended source and crossing each other at an arbitrary distance from the film after reflection from the front and back surfaces of the film is somewhat tedious as observed in Section 6.2.3. However, if the source and point of observation are far from a sufficiently thin film, the situation cannot be much different from the one discussed when the waves emerge from the film in parallel directions (Fig. 6.7). As a first approximation, we may use Eq. (6.16) to describe this path difference. To generalize the problem, we may also allow changes in the thickness of the film from point to point. Thus, the crucial factor determining the phase difference and hence the intensity at point P is still going to be the product $n_2 d \cos\theta$. But now the film thickness d and angle θ may be different for waves starting from different points on the source and reaching point P. This situation is markedly different from the one for the Haidinger fringes. In that case, the phase difference between the interfering waves at a given point of observation was exactly the same, irrespective of the location of the point on the extended source. But in the present case, this phase difference varies with the position of a point on the extended source. This should lead to uniform illumination, and

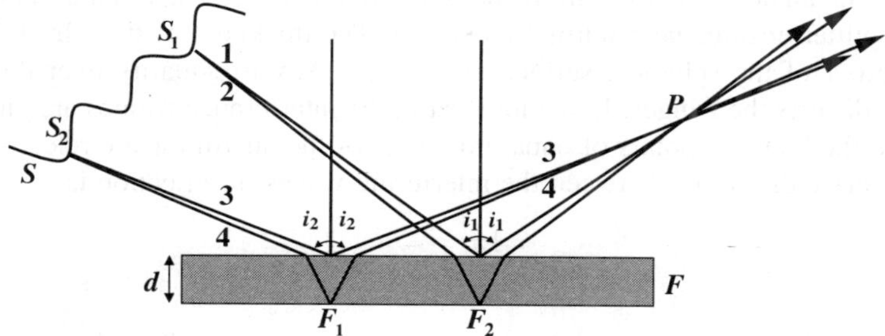

Fig. 6.11: Non-localized fringes with an extended source.

not a distinct interference pattern unless we can ensure that maximum change in phase among the interfering waves emanating from different points on the extended source can be made quite small (much less than π). One way to meet this requirement is to bring the point of observation P closer to the film. This in turn brings points F_1 and F_2 on the film closer to each other and the likely variation in the film thickness is minimized. It also restricts the number of points on the source which can contribute to the intensity at this point. For a point of observation located on the film itself, the film thickness is essentially fixed. The point of observation can be moved close to or right on the film if the eye or the microscope used to observe the fringes is focused near the film. The changes in the angular factor ($\cos\theta$) can be further restricted by reducing the entrance aperture of the microscope and by restricting angle θ to values close to zero. Interference fringes localized on or close to the film observed under these conditions with an extended source are called Fizeau fringes. These are fringes of equal thickness. These fringes are useful for testing the flatness of a surface by keeping the test plate on top of a standard flat surface. Because of the unevenness of the test surface, an air film is trapped between the two surfaces. The contours of fringes in reflection or in transmission mark points of equal air gaps between the surfaces. Between two consecutive contour lines, the air gap changes by $\lambda/2$. For perfectly flat surfaces, light reflected or transmitted by the air gap will have uniform intensity distribution.

6.3.3 Newton's Rings

Newton's rings provide an example of fringes of equal thickness. These are two-wave interference fringes formed when monochromatic or nearly monochromatic light falls on an air film bounded between a plano-convex lens and a flat surface as shown in Fig. 6.12. The collimated light beam after reflection from the beam splitter BS is incident on the plano-convex lens L. Fringes localized near the lower surface of the lens are formed by interference between waves reflected from the top and bottom of the air film. These are Fizeau fringes and can be seen by the unaided eye or with the help of a microscope. The orientation of the beam splitter ensures near normal incidence. The thickness of the film follows the contour of the spherical surface of the lens. Any irregularity over the lens surface distorts the fringes. In the ideal case, the interference fringes are circular because the locus of points of equal thickness of the air film is a circle.

The phase difference between the interfering waves in reflection is

$$\delta = \frac{4\pi}{\lambda} d(x) - \pi, \tag{6.32}$$

where $d(x)$ is the thickness of the film at a distance x from the point of contact of the lens with the flat surface. The phase difference π appears in Eq. (6.32)

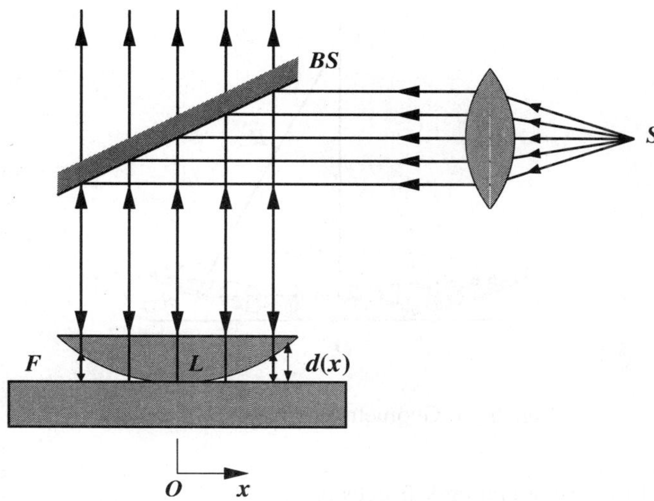

Fig. 6.12: Arrangement to observe Newton's rings. F is a block with flat top surface.

since one of the interfering waves suffers an internal reflection whereas the other undergoes an external reflection. The bright fringes appear at

$$d(x) = (2m+1)\bar{\lambda}/4 \tag{6.33}$$

and the dark fringes are located at

$$d(x) = 2m\bar{\lambda}/4. \tag{6.34}$$

The center of the fringe pattern in reflected light is dark since the film thickness is zero at the point of contact. Interference fringes seen in transmitted light are complementary to those seen in reflected light. The radii of Newton's rings can be obtained with reference to Fig. 6.13:

$$R^2 = x^2 + \{R - d(x)\}^2.$$

For small $d(x)$, we can neglect $(d(x))^2$, giving

$$x = \sqrt{2Rd(x)}.$$

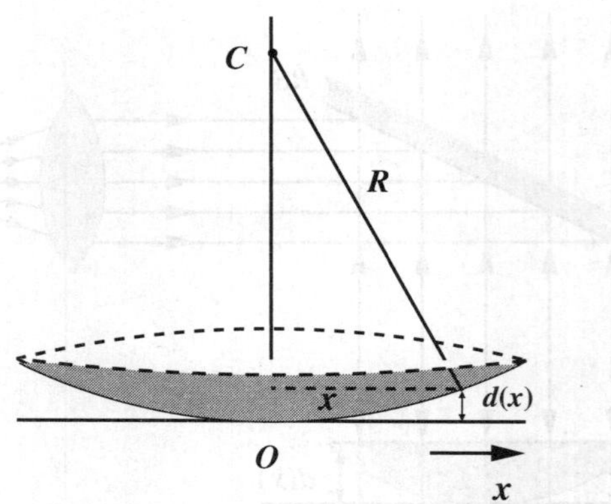

Fig. 6.13: Geometry for Newton's rings.

The radii of the bright and dark fringes are

$$x_\mathrm{b} = \sqrt{(2m+1)R\bar{\lambda}/2} \tag{6.35}$$

and

$$x_\mathrm{d} = \sqrt{mR\bar{\lambda}}, \tag{6.36}$$

respectively, where m takes values of $0, 1, 2, \ldots$ Like the Haidinger fringes, Newton's rings are also circular, but the two differ at the fundamental level. The center of the Haidinger fringe pattern is occupied by the fringe of the highest order which may be bright, dark, or may have any intermediate intensity. The center of the Newton's ring pattern in reflected light always has a dark fringe of the lowest order. It is somewhat puzzling why these fringes are named after Newton since Newton was not a believer of the wave theory of light.

6.3.4 Straight Fringes

Fringes of equal thickness can also be observed from a wedge-shaped air film bounded between two flat surfaces (Fig. 6.14). We can also have a wedge-shaped film of a transparent medium. The fringes are straight and localized on the film itself. For a small angle wedge, the film thickness is given by

$$d(x) = \alpha x, \tag{6.37}$$

where α is the wedge angle and x is the horizontal distance of a point on the wedge from the point of contact of the surfaces. As in Newton's rings, the lowest

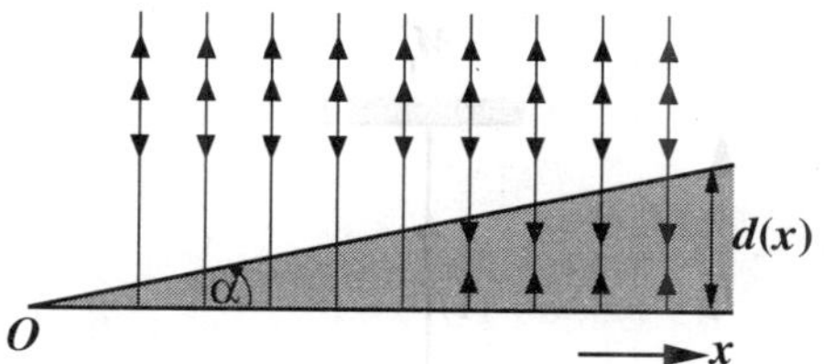

Fig. 6.14: A wedge angled film produces localized straight fringes.

order fringe is dark. The appearance of the bright and dark (straight) fringes is still described by Eqs (6.33) and (6.34), respectively. The mth bright fringe is located at

$$x_{\mathrm{b}} = \frac{(2m+1)}{\alpha}\bar{\lambda}/4, \tag{6.38}$$

and the mth dark fringe appears at

$$x_{\mathrm{d}} = \frac{(2m)}{\alpha}\bar{\lambda}/4. \tag{6.39}$$

6.4 TWO-WAVE INTERFEROMETERS

A number of two-wave interferometers exist with myriad applications in optics, metrology, plasma diagnostics, and other related fields. Most of these interferometers are variants of the historic Michelson interferometer. The rudiments of this interferometer were discussed in Section 2.4.1. Here, we dwell on the formation and nature of the interference fringes in a Michelson interferometer. This will be followed by a brief discussion on other commonly used interferometers.

6.4.1 Michelson Interferometer

Figure 6.15 shows the basic configuration of a Michelson interferometer. A light beam from the extended source S is split equally by the 50–50 beam-splitter BS kept with the reflecting coating away from the source. A small source kept in front of a ground glass plate or a collimating lens acts as a convenient extended source. The orientations of mirrors M_1 and M_2 can be controlled precisely. Mirror M_2 usually has a fixed position. The distance of mirror M_1 from the beam splitter can be adjusted with a fine pitch screw. The beam splitter is oriented at 45° to the mirrors. The source, as mentioned, is an extended one, sending light beams in different directions but for illustration we concentrate on one such beam. The

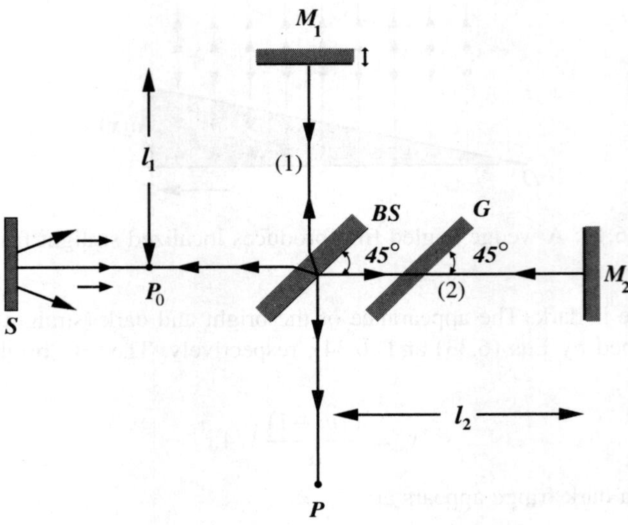

Fig. 6.15: Michelson interferometer; S is an extended source, BS is a 50–50 beam splitter, G is the compensating plate, mirror M_1 is moveable and mirror M_2 is fixed.

split beam (1) traverses the beam splitter BS thrice before combining with beam (2) which traverses the beam splitter only once. For sources with low temporal coherence such as the mercury and sodium discharge lamps, it is necessary to use the compensating plate G which is identical to the beam splitter plate, but without the reflecting coating on it. It is kept in the path of the second beam parallel to the beam splitter. The compensating plate is unnecessary when the interferometer is used with a laser source, but is absolutely unavoidable with a white light source. The fringes produced by interference between the two beams can be visually observed with an unaided eye or with a telescope. The intensity distribution of the interference pattern can be recorded with a photodiode.

The nature of the fringes formed in a Michelson interferometer can be better analyzed with the help of Fig. 6.16, where M_2' is the virtual image of mirror M_2 formed by the beam splitter. Similarly, the extended source S has also been brought in line with the direction of observation. The observed fringes can be interpreted as two-wave interference fringes formed by an air film bounded between mirror M_1 and the virtual image M_2' of mirror M_2. In replacing mirror M_2 by its virtual image M_2', due attention should be paid to phase changes, if any, produced by reflections from the beam splitter. The bounding surfaces M_1 and M_2' of the air film will be exactly parallel if the optically flat mirrors M_1 and

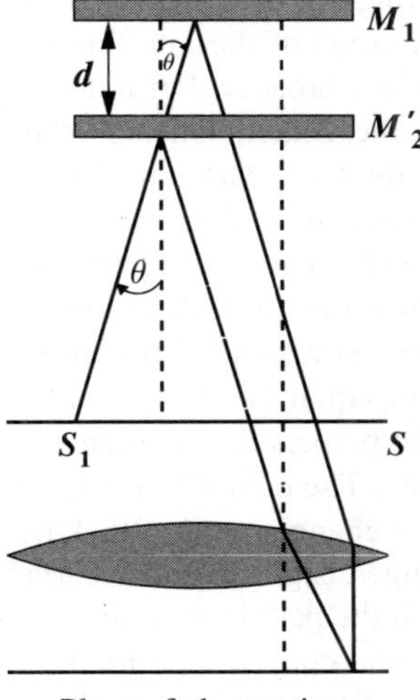

Plane of observation

Fig. 6.16: Air film equivalence of Michelson interferometer.

M_2 are oriented exactly perpendicular to each other. The film thickness d equals the distance mismatch $(l_1 - l_2)$ between the two arms of the interferometer. This arrangement is exactly equivalent to the one used to observe Haidinger fringes from a thick film (see Figs 6.7 and 6.10). Fringes localized at infinity can be seen with a telescope. Alternatively, the fringes can be observed in the focal plane of a converging lens as shown in Fig. 6.16. The symmetry of the optical arrangement gives rise to circular fringes with the center of the fringe pattern lying on the optical axis. Equations (6.23) and (6.24) locate the bright and dark fringes of the Michelson interferometer provided it is assumed that the differential phase change introduced by the beam splitter in the two beams is π radians. This is strictly not true since the 50–50 beam-splitter is not just a transparent plate.

For a perfectly collimated beam incident normally on the mirrors, the entire field of view will have uniform illumination-maximum, minimum, or any value in between, depending on the exact thickness of the air film. This is the underlying principle of the Twyman–Green interferometer used for testing optical elements. Circular fringes of equal inclination can be observed with a somewhat divergent light beam incident on the interferometer. With $n_1 = 1, n_2 = n$, Eq. (6.30) gives the angular radius of the mth bright fringe from the center as

$$\theta_m = \sqrt{\frac{(m - 1 + \epsilon)\bar{\lambda}}{nd}}, \tag{6.40}$$

where $d = (l_1 - l_2)$. The fringe at the center has the highest order. As the path difference between the two arms of the interferometer is decreased, the fringes appear to move in and become broader. For a decrease in d by $\lambda/2$, the highest order fringe disappears at the center. On the other hand, the fringes become sharp and move out as the mirror separation is increased. A new fringe appears at the center for every increase of $\lambda/2$ in the mirror separation. When the two arms of the Michelson interferometer are perfectly balanced ($d = 0$) and the mirrors are exactly perpendicular to each other, the central fringe expands to fill the entire field of view. For small differences in the path lengths of the two arms, straight fringes of equal thickness can be seen when mirrors M_1 and M_2 deviate slightly from the perpendicular orientation. The air film between the mirrors is now wedge shaped. The path difference between the interfering beams now varies primarily due to changes in the thickness of the wedge, giving rise to straight fringes. The fringes begin to show curvature with increasing wedge angle because the changes in the path lengths due to the inclination factor ($\cos\theta$) can no longer be ignored. The convex side of the curved fringes is always on the apex side of the wedge. The visibility of Michelson fringes, obtained with a 50–50 beam splitter and quasi-monochromatic light of degree of coherence $|\gamma(\tau)|$, is (see Eq. 2.40)

$$V(\delta) = |\gamma(\tau)|, \tag{6.41}$$

where $\delta = 2\pi\bar{\nu}\tau = \frac{4\pi}{\lambda}(l_2 - l_1)$. The fringe visibility starts with unit value for the balanced arms of the interferometer and then decreases slowly with increasing path difference. For monochromatic light, the visibility of the fringes is independent of the path difference.

6.4.1.1 Alignment of the Michelson Interferometer

To align the interferometer, its two arms are made equal to within a few mm using an ordinary scale. The lens or the ground glass plate between the point source and the interferometer is then removed (alternatively a sharp pin is kept between the ground glass plate and the beam splitter). Two images of the point source (or of the pin), one formed by the mirror in each arm, can be seen through the beam splitter even without a telescope. These images are brought to coincidence by adjusting the coarse tilting screws on the fixed mirror (M_2). The mirrors M_1 and M_2 are now nearly perpendicular to each other. A fringe pattern can be seen if the lens (or the ground glass plate) is restored. Since the mirrors are not exactly perpendicular to each other, the fringes are localized. Hence, at this stage the eyes should be focused in the neighborhood of mirror M_1. The fine tilting screws on the fixed mirror are now adjusted to obtain circular fringes with the center of the fringe pattern in the middle of the field of view. When this happens, the mirrors M_1 and M_2 are in exact perpendicular orientation.

The fringes at this stage will usually be quite thin and sharp. The position of the moveable mirror is now adjusted with the fine pitched screw to equalize the lengths of the two arms of the interferometer. During this adjustment, the fringes in the field of view should become broad and fewer in number. The arms are nearly balanced when no more than a few fringes cover the entire field of view. The arm lengths are exactly equal if the central fringe fills the entire field of view. The central fringe is not necessarily dark since the 50–50 beam splitter usually does not introduce a phase difference of exactly π radians between the two arms of the interferometer. If a lens is used, ensure that a slightly divergent beam falls on the beam splitter.

6.4.1.2 White Light Fringes

To produce interference with white light, the path difference between the interfering waves must not exceed a few wavelengths of light, making it necessary to use the compensating plate. This condition can be achieved first with the quasi-monochromatic source in place as mentioned above (only one or two circular fringes filling the entire field of view). It will be convenient to work with straight fringes at this stage. They can be obtained by a slight misalignment of the mirrors. The white light source may now be introduced. It will help to retain the quasi-monochromatic source as well so that fringes due to both the sources can be seen simultaneously. With white light, the central fringe corresponding to exactly zero path difference for all wavelengths will show no color, but the remaining few fringes visible with white light will be colored. In fact, the observation of the achromatic white light fringe is taken as an indication of the two arms of the Michelson interferometer being exactly balanced. This fact has been exploited with great success in the calibration of the standard meter with a Michelson interferometer.

The index of refraction of a thin transparent plate of known thickness t can be measured by introducing it in the fixed arm of the interferometer and counting the number of fringes crossing the field of view. The counting can be accomplished with the help of white light fringes. The interferometer must be set to see straight fringes with monochromatic light and white light simultaneously before the plate is inserted, which results in the displacement of fringes in the field of view. The path length of the moveable arm is varied till the white light fringes re-appear in the field of view. The index of refraction of the plate can be obtained from

$$n-1 = \frac{\Delta m \lambda}{2t},$$

where Δm is the number of monochromatic fringes counted between the two appearances of the white light fringes.

6.4.1.3 Calibration of the Standard Meter

The split-beams in the Michelson interferometer can be widely separated from each other so that any desired path difference can be introduced between them. This makes the Michelson interferometer an extremely versatile tool in optical research and testing. The coherence length of the source and the ability to count a large number of fringes crossing the field of view are the only limitations. These limitations pose no real problem with the present day technology. A laser can have coherence length of several hundred meters and electronic devices can count any number of fringes. However, Michelson used the discharge lamps for calibrating the standard meter in terms of the optical wavelengths. The coherence lengths of these sources are much smaller than a meter. To get over these problems, Michelson used an ingenious device. He used nine intermediate standards of increasing lengths called etalons. Each intermediate standard was nearly twice in length of the one immediately preceding it. The longest etalon used by him was nearly 10 cm long. It was necessary to count the fringes, crossing the field of view, when the mirror was being displaced over the length of the smallest etalon. White light fringes were used to ascertain the equality of the lengths of the two arms of the interferometer. Care had to be exercised to standardize the ambient conditions since the wavelength in air could change with change in the ambient conditions. The standard meter consists of 1,553,163.5 wavelengths of the red line of Cd ($\lambda = 6438.4722$). It was concluded that the wavelength of the red line of Cd is $\lambda = 6438.4696$ A° in dry atmosphere at 15° C and a pressure of 760 mm Hg. Subsequently (1960), the meter was expressed in terms of the orange-red line of krypton ($^{86}Kr_{36}$) of wavelength 6057.8021 A°. The standard meter being equivalent to 1,650,763.73 wavelengths of this spectral line of Krypton. The precision of measurement permitted the detection of a displacement of less than 1/100 of a fringe. This is less than the widths of the lines engraved on the bar of platinum–iridium alloy kept at 0° C in Paris as an International Prototype Meter.

At this stage, it is pertinent to recall that the Michelson interferometer has played an important role in the development of the electromagnetic theory of light. In the last quarter of the nineteenth century, it was being conjectured that light waves require a material medium to propagate. This medium was given the name aether and was assigned some peculiar properties. It was supposed to fill the entire space. The celebrated Michelson–Morley experiment proved conclusively that such a medium does not exist and that light can propagate just as well in empty space.

6.4.2 Twyman–Green Interferometer

The Twyman–Green interferometer is one of the many variants of the Michelson interferometer. It is particularly useful for testing optical elements such as lenses, prisms, flats, etc. The field of view of a Michelson interferometer carries uniform illumination if perfectly collimated light falls on the beam-splitter at 45° when the mirrors are oriented exactly perpendicular to each other.

Twyman–Green interferometer makes use of this property of the Michelson interferometer (Fig. 6.17). A well-corrected lens L_1 collimates light from the point source S on to the beam splitter BS. The optical element to be tested is kept in one of the arms of the interferometer. This arm terminates with a distortion-free spherical convex mirror M for testing lenses or with a flat mirror while testing flat surfaces of prisms, cubes, optical flats, etc. For lens testing, the center of curvature of the convex mirror coincides with the back focal point of the test lens. If the lens is perfect with no aberrations at all, the plane wavefront returning from it is exactly orthogonal to the plane wavefront returning from mirror M_1, and the field of view is uniformly illuminated. If, on the other hand, the lens suffers from some aberration, the wavefront is distorted in the double passage through the lens and a fringe pattern characteristic of the nature of

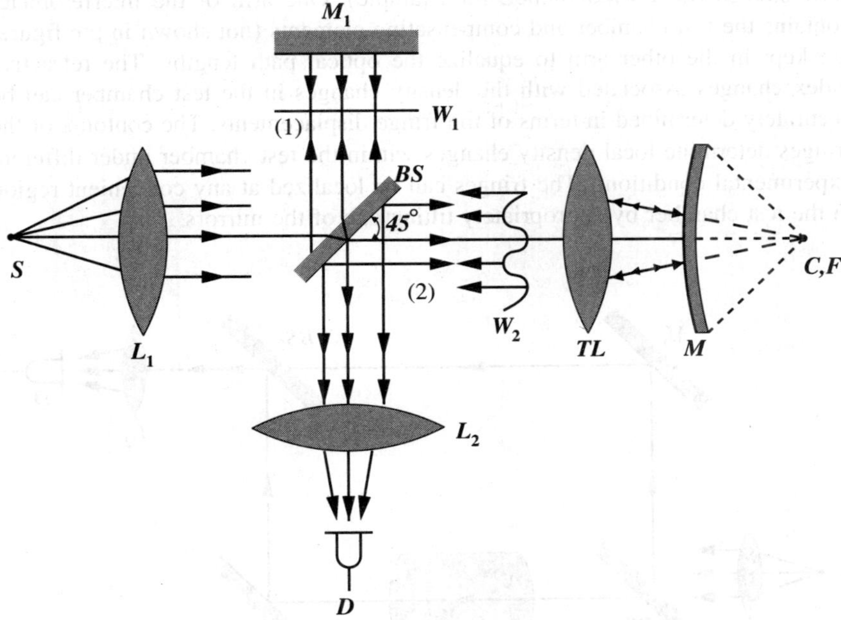

Fig. 6.17: Twyman–Green interferometer; L_1 is collimating lens, L_2 is focusing lens, TL is the test lens, M is spherical convex mirror, BS is beam splitter, W_1 is a plane wavefront in arm (1) and W_2 is the distorted wavefront in arm (2), D is the detector.

the aberration appears. The fringe contours can be marked on the test element. Alternatively, point-to-point aberrations of the test element can be determined by photographic or electronic recording of the fringe contours, and subsequently corrected. A laser source can be used for its enhanced coherence and brightness.

6.4.3 Mach–Zehnder Interferometer

In the Michelson and Twyman–Green interferometers, the same beam splitter is used to first split the incident beam and then to combine the split beams after introducing the desired path difference between them. The Mach–Zehnder interferometer, on the other hand, uses two beam splitters – one for splitting the incident beam and the other for combining the split-beams (Fig. 6.18). Mirrors M_1 and M_2 steer the beams appropriately. The centers of the beam splitters and mirrors lie on the corners of a parallelogram. The split-beams travel widely separated paths before they are combined by the second beam splitter. This interferometer is particularly useful for plasma diagnostics and gas flow studies (in a wind tunnel, for example). One arm of the interferometer contains the test chamber and compensating elements (not shown in the figure) are kept in the other arm to equalize the optical path lengths. The refractive index changes associated with the density changes in the test chamber can be accurately determined in terms of the fringe displacements. The contours of the fringes determine local density changes within the test chamber under different experimental conditions. The fringes can be localized at any convenient region in the test chamber by appropriately tilting one of the mirrors.

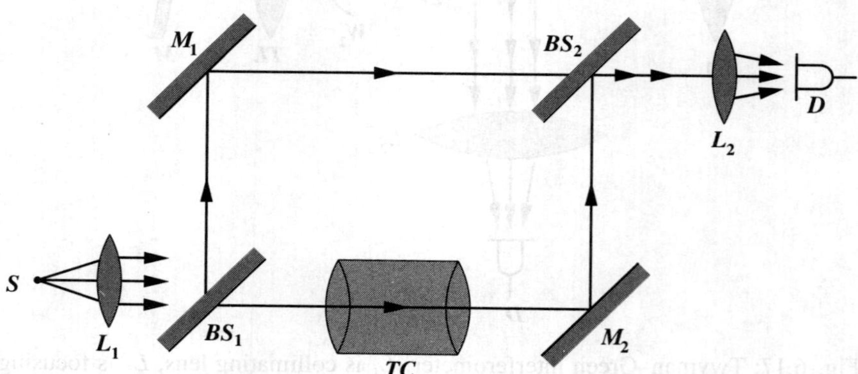

Fig. 6.18: Mach–Zehnder interferometer; BS_1 and BS_2 are beam splitters, M_1 and M_2 are mirrors, TC is test chamber, D is detector.

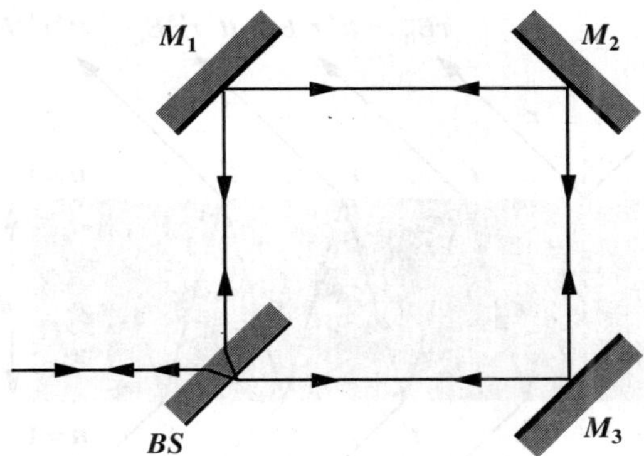

Fig. 6.19: Sagnac interferometer.

6.4.4 Sagnac Interferometer

The Sagnac interferometer differs from the interferometers discussed, so far, in that the interfering beams travel along a common closed path, albeit in opposite directions. The closed path can involve three, four, or more optical elements. Figure 6.19 shows the optical configuration of a four-element Sagnac interferometer. It consists of one beam splitter and three steering mirrors. When the beam splitter BS and mirrors M_1 and M_3 are exactly parallel and the mirror M_2 in the exact perpendicular orientation, the trajectories of the counter-propagating beams coincide and no difference in the path lengths can be introduced between the two beams by putting an object in the path of the beams. However, a path difference in the beams can be introduced by tilting one of the mirrors, resulting in the appearance of the interference fringes. The Sagnac interferometer is primarily used to measure rotational speeds. The rotation of the interferometer support about its axis introduces phase difference, between the counter-propagating beams, which is proportional to the speed of rotation. The speed of rotation can be obtained from the resulting fringe displacement. However, the phase shift introduced is quite small unless the overall length through which light passes can be significantly increased by using optical fiber to construct the interferometer. A laser-gyro using a ring laser is one such modern device to measure rotational speeds of systems.

6.5 MULTI-WAVE INTERFERENCE

We have so far considered two-wave interference which is characterized by a sinusoidal variation of light intensity with phase difference between the interfering waves. We now consider multi-wave interference. A diffraction grating

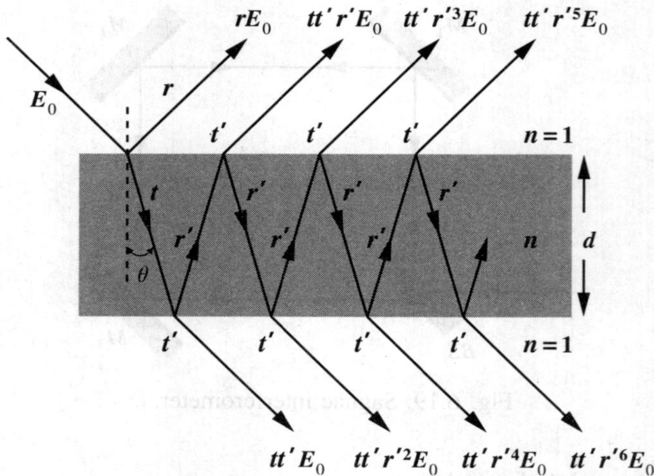

Fig. 6.20: Multiple internal reflections in a high reflectivity film.

produces multi-wave interference (see Section 10.5). Multi-wave interference can also be produced by multiple internal reflections within a thin transparent film of high reflection coefficient (Fig. 6.20).

Tables 6.1 and 6.2 list amplitudes of the first few waves in reflection and transmission for a glass film with $r = 0.20$, a film of antimony sulphide (a high reflectance material of index of refraction 3.0) with $r = 0.50$, and a multi-layer dielectric film used as end mirrors in laser cavities with $r = 0.99$.

These tables show that with successively diminishing amplitudes, interference effects for low reflectivity films are adequately described by two-wave interference. For films of sufficiently high reflectivity, the amplitudes of successive waves fall off rather slowly, leading to multi-wave interference. It will be shown that despite the large difference in the amplitudes of the first and successive waves, the intensity minima in light reflected from high reflectivity films have nearly zero intensities. We shall also find interference effects among

Table 6.1. Amplitudes of successive waves in reflected light ($E_0 = 1$).

Successive reflected wave	Amplitude		
	(r = 0.20)	**(r = 0.50)**	**(r = 0.99)**
1	0.20	0.50	0.99
2	0.192	0.375	0.0197
3	7.7×10^{-3}	0.093	0.0193
4	3.1×10^{-4}	0.023	0.0189
5	1.2×10^{-5}	0.0058	0.0185

Table 6.2. Amplitudes of successive waves in transmitted light ($E_0 = 1$).

Successive transmitted wave	Amplitude		
	(r = 0.2)	**(r = 0.50)**	**(r = 0.99)**
1	0.96	0.75	0.0199
2	0.038	0.1875	0.0195
3	1.5×10^{-3}	0.0469	0.0191
4	6.1×10^{-5}	0.0117	0.0187

multiply reflected waves markedly different from those associated with two-wave interference discussed so far. For the intermediate case of $r = 0.50$, the successive amplitudes do not decrease as rapidly, but the amplitude becomes vanishingly small after a few reflections.

The phase difference between any two successive waves is

$$\delta = \bar{k}\Delta, \tag{6.42}$$

where $\bar{k}$ $(=2\pi/\bar{\lambda})$ is the mean vacuum wavenumber of light incident on the film and

$$\Delta = 2nd\cos\theta \tag{6.43}$$

is the optical path difference between the successive waves (Eq. 6.16). For a film with flat and parallel surfaces, interference fringes can be observed at infinity or in the focal plane of a converging lens. The path difference between the first and last among the interfering waves in multi-wave interference must not exceed the coherence length of light used to illuminate the film.

6.5.1 Intensity Distribution in Multi-wave Interference

For the present discussion, incident light may be assumed to be polarized perpendicular to the plane of incidence. The resultant amplitude of the transmitted wave can be written as

$$\begin{aligned} E_t &= E_0 tt' \,\mathrm{e}^{\mathrm{i}\bar{k}\Delta'}\left[1 + r'^2\,\mathrm{e}^{\mathrm{i}\bar{k}\Delta} + r'^4\,\mathrm{e}^{\mathrm{i}2\bar{k}\Delta} + \cdots + r'^{2n}\,\mathrm{e}^{\mathrm{i}n\bar{k}\Delta} + \cdots\right] \\ &= \frac{E_0 tt'\,\mathrm{e}^{\mathrm{i}\bar{k}\Delta'}}{1 - r'^2\,\mathrm{e}^{\mathrm{i}\bar{k}\Delta}}, \end{aligned} \tag{6.44}$$

where Δ' determines the phase of the first transmitted wave (see Fig. 6.20). Here, we have assumed infinitely many interfering waves in the transmitted light.

This poses no serious problem since the amplitudes of the multiply reflected waves must eventually become vanishingly small. The intensity distribution of the transmitted light is

$$\begin{aligned} I_\mathrm{t} &= \left(\frac{1}{2}\epsilon_0 c\right) E_\mathrm{t} E_\mathrm{t}^* \\ &= I_0 \frac{|tt'|^2}{(1-r'^2\,\mathrm{e}^{\mathrm{i}\bar{k}\Delta})(1-r'^2\,\mathrm{e}^{-\mathrm{i}\bar{k}\Delta})} \\ &= I_0 \frac{|tt'|^2}{1+r'^4-2r'^2\cos(\bar{k}\Delta)} \\ &= I_0 \frac{|tt'|^2}{(1-r'^2)^2+4r'^2\sin^2(\bar{k}\Delta/2)}. \end{aligned} \tag{6.45}$$

In this derivation, real reflection coefficients are assumed. Accordingly, angle θ for the internal reflections must be less than the critical angle. For non-absorbing media, the principle of reversibility (Fig. 6.21) requires

$$r^2 + tt' = 1, \qquad r' = -r. \tag{6.46}$$

These results can be obtained from Fresnel's relations as well. The transmitted intensity distribution then becomes

$$I_\mathrm{t} = I_0 \frac{(1-r^2)^2}{(1-r^2)^2+4r^2\sin^2(\bar{k}\Delta/2)} = I_0 \frac{1}{1+F(r)\sin^2(\bar{k}\Delta/2)}, \tag{6.47}$$

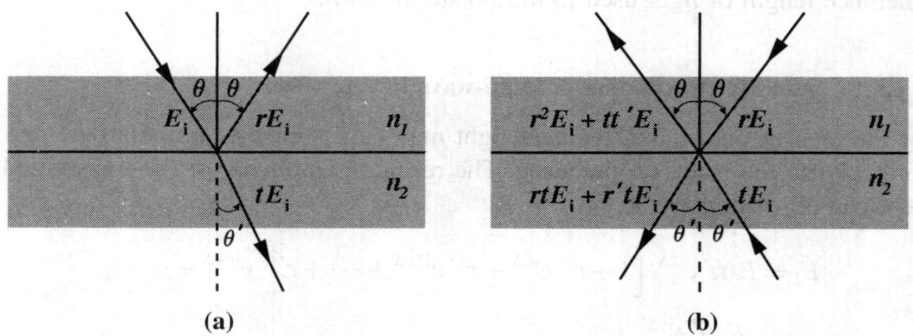

Fig. 6.21: Principle of reversibility across an interface between non-absorbing media; (a) incident field E_i gives rise to reflected field rE_i and transmitted field tE_i, (b) Incident fields tE_i and rE_i generate the fields $(r^2+tt')\,E_\mathrm{i}$ and $(r+r')tE_\mathrm{i}$.

where

$$F(r) = \frac{4r^2}{(1-r^2)^2} = \frac{4R}{(1-R)^2} \tag{6.48}$$

and $R = r'^2 = r^2$. The film transmittance function

$$T = \frac{I_t}{I_0} = \frac{1}{1 + F(r)\sin^2(\bar{k}\Delta/2)}, \tag{6.49}$$

known as the Airy function or the Airy Formula is plotted in Fig. 6.22 for a few representative values of the reflection coefficient. The transmission peaks with

$$\left(\frac{I_t}{I_0}\right)_{\text{max}} = 1 \quad \text{for } \bar{k}\Delta = 2m\pi \tag{6.50}$$

are characterized by unit transmittance, irrespective of the value of the reflection coefficient. Here m takes integral values 0, 1, 2, ... The minimum film transmittance

$$\left(\frac{I_t}{I_0}\right)_{\text{min}} = \frac{1}{1+F(r)} \quad \text{for } \bar{k}\Delta = (2m+1)\pi \tag{6.51}$$

is, however, dependent on the reflection coefficient of the film. For films of low reflection coefficient, it is not much below one and the visibility of the interference fringes is low. For films of sufficiently high reflection coefficient, the denominator of the Airy function becomes quite large even for slight deviation from the maximal condition ($\bar{k}\Delta = 2m\pi$). Accordingly, the film transmittance

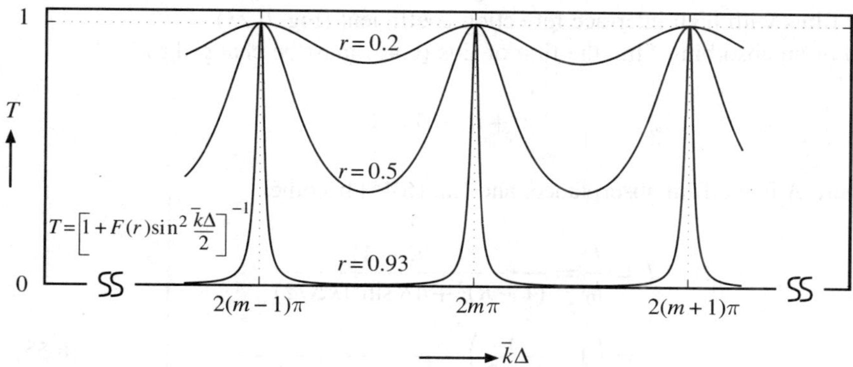

Fig. 6.22: Changes in film transmittance with phase difference between successive interfering waves for $r = 0.2, 0.5, 0.93$.

falls abruptly as soon as one moves away from the transmission peaks. This gives rise to extremely sharp and bright fringes separated by broad regions of almost complete darkness in the transmitted light. The slow decrease of the amplitudes of multiply reflected waves from high reflectivity films gives rise to an intensity distribution which differs non-trivially from the sinusoidal distribution found in two-wave interference. The intensity distribution for multi-wave interference in reflected light is complementary to the intensity distribution in transmitted light. Therefore for non-absorbing films,

$$\mathcal{R} = \frac{I_r}{I_0} = 1 - \frac{I_t}{I_0} = \frac{F(r)\sin^2(\bar{k}\Delta/2)}{1+F(r)\sin^2(\bar{k}\Delta/2)}. \tag{6.52}$$

Maximum reflectance

$$\mathcal{R}_{\max} = \frac{F(r)}{1+F(r)} \quad \text{for } \bar{k}\Delta = (2m+1)\pi \tag{6.53}$$

remains less than one, except when $F(r)$ approaches infinity ($r \to 1$). This is in contrast to the transmission maxima with unit transmittance, irrespective of the value of the reflection coefficient. The reflectance of a film with large $F(r)$ is not very sensitive to changes in the phase difference, except when

$$\bar{k}\Delta = 2m\pi. \tag{6.54}$$

This condition locates the minima of the intensity distribution in reflected light. Narrow dark fringes among broad regions of brightness appear in reflected light for films with high interface reflection coefficient (Fig. 6.23).

For an absorbing film, the first of Eqs (6.46) must be changed to

$$r^2 + tt' + A = 1,$$

where A is the film absorptance, and Eq. (6.45) becomes

$$\begin{aligned} T = \frac{I_t}{I_0} &= \frac{(1-R-A)^2}{(1-R)^2 + 4R\sin^2(\bar{k}\Delta/2)} \\ &= \left(1 - \frac{A}{1-R}\right)^2 \frac{1}{1+F(r)\sin^2(\bar{k}\Delta/2)} \\ &= \frac{T_{\max}}{1+F(r)\sin^2(\bar{k}\Delta/2)}, \end{aligned} \tag{6.55}$$

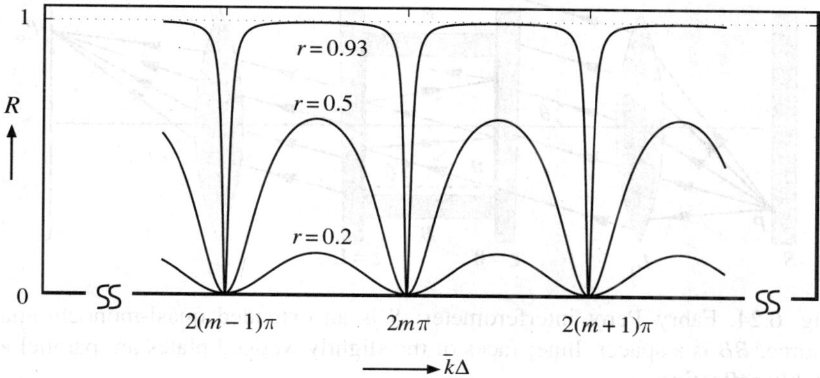

Fig. 6.23: Changes in film reflectance with phase difference between successive interfering waves for $r = 0.2, 0.5, 0.93$.

where the peak transmittance

$$T_{\max} = \left(1 - \frac{A}{1-R}\right)^2 \tag{6.56}$$

is less than one for an absorbing film. The reduction in the maximum transmittance can be quite substantial even for the weakly absorbing films because the factor $(1 - R)$ can be quite small for the highly reflecting films. The absorption losses in the dielectric films include scattering from material inhomogeneities whereas metallic films possess intrinsic absorption losses.

6.6 FABRY–PEROT INTERFEROMETER

High contrast $(I_{\max}/I_{\min})$ of interference fringes in light transmitted by high reflectivity films is exploited in Fabry–Perot interferometer – a device of unmatched spectral resolution among conventional spectroscopic instruments. A Fabry–Perot interferometer in its simplest form consists of two identical glass or quartz plates with highly reflecting coatings on sides facing each other (Fig. 6.24). In the interferometric version of the device, the plate separation is adjustable. A Fabry–Perot etalon has fixed plate separation. An optically finished hollow invar cylinder, called the spacer, maintains the plate separation. Adjustable fine pitch screws ensure parallelism of the inner surfaces of the plates. The outer surfaces of the plates are slightly wedged to prevent undesirable multiple reflections. An extended source is used for illumination with or without the converging lens

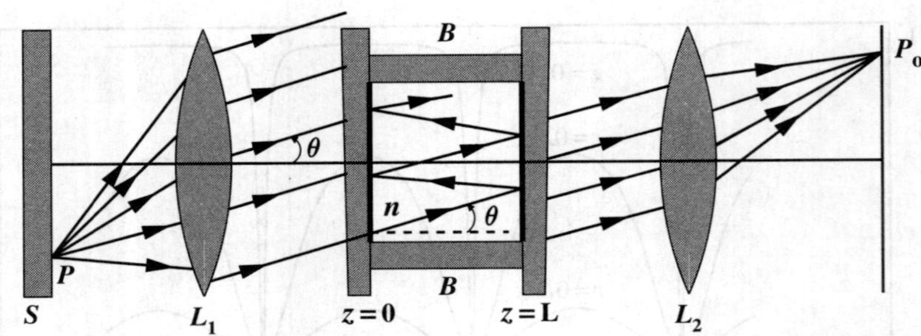

Fig. 6.24: Fabry–Perot interferometer; S is an extended quasi-monochromatic source, BB is a spacer. Inner faces of the slightly wedged plates are parallel and highly reflecting.

L_1. A large number of plane waves enter the interferometer making different angles with the optical axis of the interferometer. The figure shows one such plane wave. Multiple reflections within the interferometer give rise to a large number of waves in the transmitted light which are brought to a common focus by the second lens L_2. The condition for the appearance of intensity maxima in transmitted light is same as for two-wave interference, namely,

$$\frac{4\pi n}{\lambda} L \cos\theta = 2\pi m. \tag{6.57}$$

Here, we have ignored any phase change on reflection. We need not take explicit cognizance of this phase change as long as it remains independent of the wavelength and angle of incidence. Further, we note that the condition for maximum intensity (6.57) depends only on the angle of incidence (or equivalently on angle θ), and not on the exact location of the point on the extended source. Therefore, in the absence of the converging lens L_1, all waves emanating from different points of the extended source but travelling in the same direction reinforce each other. However, different points on the extended source are mutually incoherent, and hence the emergent waves after multiple reflections within the interferometer but originating from a single point on the source are the only waves which can interfere. For light waves starting from different points of the source but in parallel directions and converging to the same point in the focal plane of lens L_2, it is the intensities and not the amplitudes which add up.

The normalized transmittance of the Fabry–Perot interferometer obtained from Eq. (6.55) is

$$\left(\frac{I_t}{I_0}\right)_n = \frac{I_t/I_0}{(1-\frac{A}{1-R})^2} = \frac{1}{1+F(r)\sin^2(\bar{k}\Delta/2)}. \tag{6.58}$$

Bright fringes in the light transmitted by the Fabry–Perot interferometer are extremely sharp. These are fringes of equal inclination, with the highest order fringe at the center of the pattern (Haidinger fringes). The fringes are circular for an interferometer possessing an axis of symmetry. Equation (6.40) gives the angular radius of the mth bright fringe from the center. The arrangement of Fig. 6.24 with fixed separation between the plates is a Fabry–Perot etalon[1] and not exactly a Fabry–Perot interferometer, as mentioned earlier. However, the same arrangement can be used as an interferometer if the path difference

$$\Delta = 2nL\cos\theta$$

between the successively reflected waves can be changed. This can be done by changing the plate separation L. However, parallelism between the plates during displacement may be difficult to ensure. Alternatively, the incidence angle could be changed. The better option is to change the refractive index n by changing the pressure of the gas filling the space between the plates.

6.6.1 Widths of Transmission Peaks

Consider a Fabry–Perot interferometer with plate separation L. For convenience, we take $\theta = 0$ so that $\bar{k}\Delta = 2n\bar{k}L$. We now calculate the wave number and frequency spreads of the light exiting the interferometer when wave number of the light entering the interferometer is changed. Figure 6.25 shows a typical

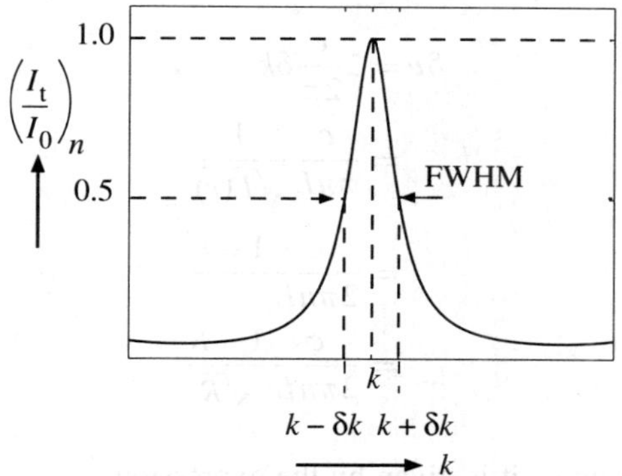

Fig. 6.25: Transmission profile of a Fabry–Perot interferometer.

[1] A well-polished transparent plate with parallel faces is also an etalon.

transmission profile of a Fabry–Perot interferometer with peak transmission at $n\bar{k}L = m\pi$. Let $(\bar{k} - \delta k)$ and $(\bar{k} + \delta k)$ be the wave numbers of the points on the transmission peak with 50% of the maximum transmission. For these points, Eq. (6.58) gives

$$\frac{1}{2} = \frac{1}{1 + F(r)\sin^2(m\pi \pm nL\delta k)},$$

requiring

$$F(r)\sin^2(\pm nL\delta k) = 1. \tag{6.59}$$

For large $F(r)$, δk is given by

$$\delta k = \frac{1}{nL}\frac{1}{\sqrt{F(r)}}.$$

The full width at half the maximum (FWHM) of the transmission peak of the interferometer is defined as

$$\text{FWHM} = 2\delta k = \frac{2}{nL}\frac{1}{\sqrt{F(r)}}. \tag{6.60a}$$

The FWHM in frequency units is

$$\begin{aligned}\delta\nu &= 2\frac{c}{2\pi}\delta k \\ &= \frac{c}{\pi nL}\frac{1}{\sqrt{F(r)}} \\ &= \frac{c}{2\pi nL}\frac{1-r^2}{r} \\ &= \frac{c}{2\pi nL}\frac{1-R}{\sqrt{R}}\end{aligned} \tag{6.60b}$$

and in wavelength units, it is given by the expression

$$\delta\lambda = \frac{\bar{\lambda}^2}{2\pi nL}\frac{1-R}{\sqrt{R}}. \tag{6.60c}$$

Some representative values of the FWHM of the Fabry–Perot transmission peaks are given below:

$$\begin{aligned}\delta\nu &= 10\,\text{MHz} \quad \text{for } r = 0.99 \text{ and } L = 10\,\text{cm},\\ &= 10\,\text{MHz} \quad \text{for } r = 0.9999 \text{ and } L = 1\,\text{mm},\\ &= 1\,\text{MHz} \quad \text{for } r = 0.9999 \text{ and } L = 1\,\text{cm}.\end{aligned}$$

The spectral widths of the transmission peaks can be reduced by increasing the film reflectivity and plate separation. However, as we shall see shortly, increasing the plate separation reduces the useful spectral range of the interferometer.

6.6.2 Fabry–Perot Interferometer as a Spectrometer

A spectrometer is an instrument which can determine the wavelength distribution of a light source. A Fabry–Perot interferometer can be used as a spectrometer, albeit within a narrow spectral range. However, within its limited spectral range, it provides an extremely high degree of precision. If the transmission of a Fabry–Perot interferometer with highly reflecting plates is recorded as a function of the source frequency, high transmission will be found at certain frequencies and practically no transmission for intermediate frequencies. Figure 6.26 shows this behavior. For the sake of convenience, we have taken $\theta = 0$. The frequencies and wavelengths of the transmission peaks are (Eq. 6.57)

$$\nu_m = m\frac{c}{2nL}, \tag{6.61a}$$

$$\lambda_m = \frac{2nL}{m}, \tag{6.61b}$$

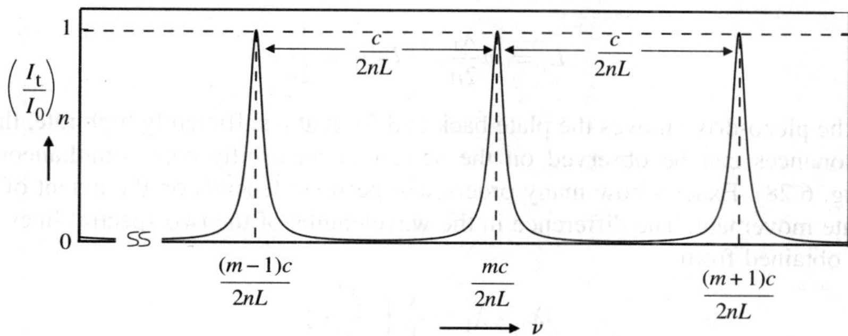

Fig. 6.26: Normalized transmittance of a Fabry–Perot interferometer as a function of the source frequency.

respectively. The frequency and wavelength separations between successive transmission peaks are

$$\Delta\nu = \frac{c}{2nL}, \tag{6.61c}$$

$$\Delta\lambda = \frac{\lambda^2}{2nL}, \tag{6.61d}$$

respectively, where n is the index of refraction of the medium between the plates of the interferometer. Re-writing Eq. (6.61b) as

$$L = m\left(\frac{1}{2}\frac{\lambda_m}{n}\right) = (m+1)\left(\frac{1}{2}\frac{\lambda_{m+1}}{n}\right) = (m+2)\left(\frac{1}{2}\frac{\lambda_{m+2}}{n}\right) = \cdots, \tag{6.62}$$

reveals that a Fabry–Perot interferometer transmits all those wavelengths, with minimum or no attenuation, for which the plate separation is an integral multiple of half wavelengths in the medium filling the Fabry–Perot interferometer. It is therefore possible to obtain the spectral distribution of the source by changing the plate separation in a continuous manner. A piezo-drive can be used to move one of the plates while keeping the other plate in a fixed position. However, for an unambiguous determination of the wavelength distribution of the source, the permitted range of displacements of the plate is extremely small. To see this, imagine the Fabry–Perot interferometer being illuminated by a source with a single, narrow emission line centered at wavelength λ_1. Depending on the range covered by the piezo drive, the interferometer will show transmission maxima whenever the plate separation equals an integral multiple of $\lambda_1/2n$ (Fig. 6.27).

Now, suppose that the source emission is peaked at two very close-lying wavelengths λ_1 and λ_2, and the spectral width of each line is much smaller than their wavelength separation. The interferometer will now show two very close transmission peaks or resonances for each order m at plate separations of

$$L_1 = m\frac{\lambda_1}{2n}, \quad L_2 = m\frac{\lambda_2}{2n}.$$

If the piezo-drive moves the plate back and forth at a sufficiently high rate, these resonances can be observed on the screen of an oscilloscope simultaneously (Fig. 6.28). Exactly how many orders will be seen depends on the extent of the plate movement. The difference in the wavelengths of the two spectral lines can be obtained from

$$\lambda_2 - \lambda_1 = \frac{x}{X}\left(\frac{\lambda^2}{2nL}\right),$$

where x is the separation on the screen between the transmission peaks for λ_1 and λ_2 in a given order, and X is the separation between consecutive transmission

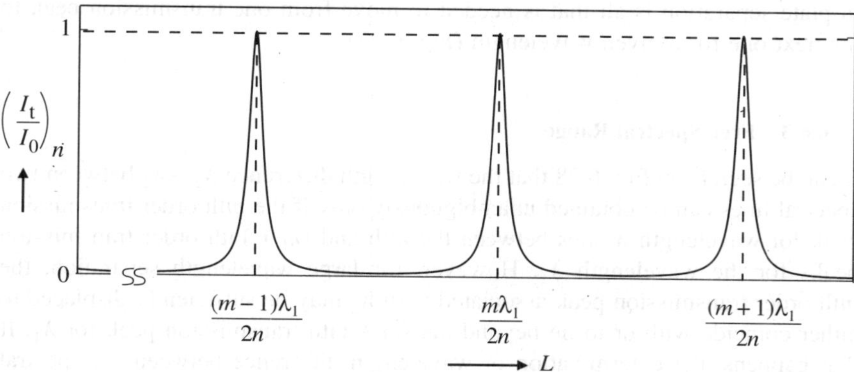

Fig. 6.27: Change in normalized transmittance of a Fabry–Perot interferometer with plate separation. Source contains a single, narrow spectral line centered at λ_1.

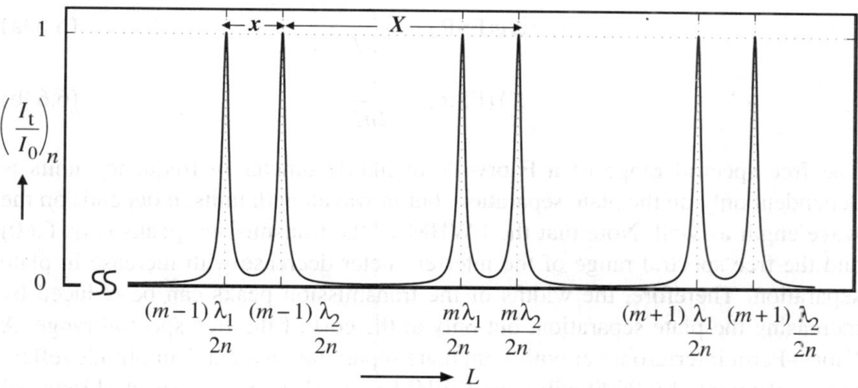

Fig. 6.28: Change in transmittance of a Fabry–Perot interferometer with plate separation when source emission has two close spectral lines λ_1 and λ_2.

peaks for wavelength λ_1 or λ_2. As mentioned earlier, $\lambda^2/2nL$ is the wavelength interval between successive transmission peaks for either wavelength, where λ is the average of λ_1 and λ_2 and L is the nominal separation between the plates of the interferometer during this scan. The change in the plate separation, needed to observe the transmission peaks associated with the two wavelengths in the same order, is a very small fraction of the wavelength since a change of $\lambda/2n$

in plate separation is all that is needed to move from one transmission peak to the next one for a given wavelength (Fig. 6.27).

6.6.3 Free Spectral Range

It can be seen from Fig. 6.28 that the wavelength difference $\lambda_2 - \lambda_1$ between two spectral lines can be obtained unambiguously only if the mth order transmission peak for wavelength λ_2 lies between the mth and $(m+1)$th order transmission peaks for the wavelength λ_1. However, for large wavelength separation, the mth order transmission peak associated with λ_2 may be sufficiently displaced to either coincide with or to lie beyond the $(m+1)$th transmission peak for λ_1. If that happens, the determination of wavelength difference between the spectral lines becomes uncertain. This puts a limit to the useful spectral range of the interferometer. Clearly, the useful spectral range cannot exceed the frequency or wavelength interval between successive transmission peaks. Equations (6.61c) and (6.61d) therefore define the free spectral range (FSR) of the Fabry–Perot interferometer in frequency and wavelength units, respectively, i.e.,

$$\Delta\nu(\text{FSR}) = \frac{c}{2nL}, \tag{6.63a}$$

$$\Delta\lambda(\text{FSR}) = \frac{\lambda^2}{2nL}. \tag{6.63b}$$

The free spectral range of a Fabry–Perot interferometer in frequency units is dependent only on the plate separation, but in wavelength units, it depends on the wavelength as well. Note that the FWHM of the transmission peaks (Eqs 6.60) and the free spectral range of the interferometer decrease with increase in plate separation. Therefore, the widths of the transmission peaks can be reduced by increasing the plate separation, but only at the cost of the free spectral range. A Fabry–Perot interferometer with 1 cm plate separation in air and amplitude reflection coefficient of 0.9999 will have FWHM of 1 MHz and free spectral range of 15 GHz which at 500 nm corresponds to a free spectral range of only 0.125 Å. This, indeed, is a very small spectral range for spectroscopic measurements. Therefore, the Fabry–Perot interferometer finds use only in high-resolution spectroscopy where one is interested in finding frequency or wavelength differences between very close spectral lines. A useful parameter to characterize the high-resolution capability of a Fabry–Perot interferometer is its finesse ($\mathcal{F}$), defined as the ratio of the free spectral range to the FWHM of the transmission peaks, i.e.,

$$\mathcal{F} = \frac{\Delta\nu}{\delta\nu} = \frac{\Delta\lambda}{\delta\lambda} = \frac{\pi r}{1-r^2}. \tag{6.64}$$

A finesse of 1000 requires $r \sim 0.9998$. Optical surfaces with finesse as high as 10 000 are commercially available.

6.6.4 Spectral Resolution

Spectral resolution of an instrument is the closest wavelength (or frequency) separation between two spectral lines that it can resolve. However, there is a certain degree of arbitrariness as to when the two spectral lines are considered to be resolved. This has led to several resolution criteria. Rayleigh's criterion of resolution is one such criterion (see Section 10.5.3), commonly used in diffraction studies. A slightly different criterion for resolution is used in the present context because the minimum transmittance (Eq. 6.51) in a Fabry–Perot interferometer can be quite small, but difficult to pinpoint. The Rayleigh criterion makes use of the minimum or the zero intensity point. But as we shall find, the two criteria yield almost identical results. Two close spectral lines of equal intensity are considered just resolved by a Fabry–Perot interferometer if the 50% normalized transmittance points on the transmission peaks due to the two spectral lines in a given order coincide as shown in Fig. 6.29. The dip (saddle point), with transmittance of nearly 0.81 of the maximum transmittance of the combined profile, appearing in the middle is taken as a guide for the resolution of spectral

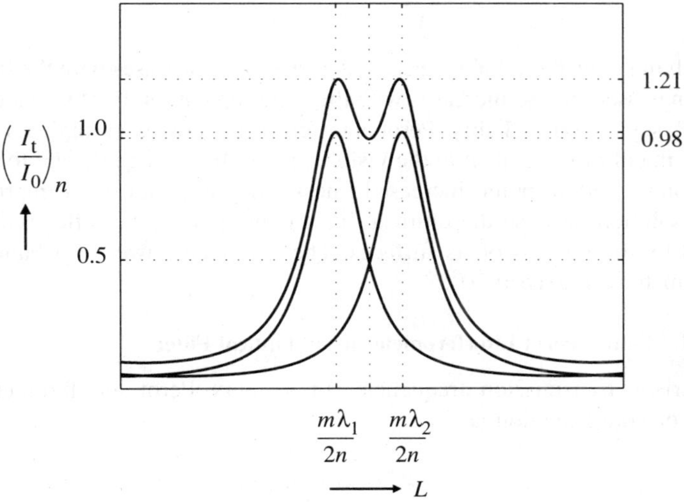

Fig. 6.29: Resolution criterion for a Fabry–Perot interferometer ($F(r) = 20$); The peaks are separated by FWHM of each. Dip height is nearly 0.81 times the maximum height of the combined profile.

lines.[2] This criterion can be slightly rephrased. Two spectral lines with identical spectral profiles are considered just resolved by a Fabry–Perot interferometer if their transmission peaks are separated by the FWHM of each spectral line. Therefore, the smallest frequency interval (resolution limit) that can be resolved by a Fabry–Perot interferometer by this criterion is

$$\delta\nu = \text{FWHM} = \frac{c}{2\pi nL}\frac{1-r^2}{r} = \frac{c/2nL}{\mathcal{F}}, \tag{6.65a}$$

where $\mathcal{F}$ is the finesse of the interferometer. The smallest wavelength interval that a Fabry–Perot interferometer can resolve is

$$\delta\lambda = \frac{\lambda^2}{2\pi nL}\frac{1-r^2}{r} = \frac{\lambda^2/2nL}{\mathcal{F}}. \tag{6.65b}$$

In either case, the resolution limit is the ratio of the FSR and finesse of the interferometer. The *Resolving Power (RP)* of an instrument is defined as the ratio of the mean wavelength of the spectral lines to the smallest resolvable wavelength interval between them, i.e.,

$$\text{RP} = \frac{\bar{\lambda}}{\delta\lambda} = \frac{\bar{\nu}}{\delta\nu} = \frac{2\pi nL}{\lambda}\frac{r}{1-r^2} \tag{6.66a}$$

$$= \frac{2nL}{\lambda}\mathcal{F}. \tag{6.66b}$$

The resolving power of a Fabry–Perot interferometer increases with the finesse of the coatings used. It also increases with the plate separation. For the same finesse and plate separation, a Fabry–Perot interferometer possesses higher resolving power in the ultra-violet than in the visible region. It may be relevant to mention that beyond a certain point, increased finesse may not lead to an improvement in the resolution because the ultimate limit is not put by the reflectivity of the film, but by the flatness of its surfaces. The resolving power of a Fabry–Perot interferometer can exceed 10^9.

6.6.4.1 Fabry–Perot Interferometer as an Optical Filter

Characteristic transmission frequencies of a Fabry–Perot interferometer with minimal or no attenuation are

$$\nu_m = m\frac{c}{2nL},$$

[2] In Rayleigh's criterion of resolution, the intensity at the saddle point is $8/\pi^2$ times the maximum intensity in the combined distribution.

where m is an integer. For a high finesse interferometer, the spectral widths of the transmission peaks can be extremely narrow. Light at intermediate frequencies is not able to make its way through the interferometer. Thus, a Fabry–Perot interferometer may be called a multi-pass optical filter. However, for macroscopic plate separations of the interferometer, there is hardly any filtering because the transmission peaks at these plate separations are spectrally very close. To act as a narrow band optical filter, a Fabry–Perot interferometer must have plate separation of no more than a few wavelengths of light. The typical order $m = (2/\lambda)nL$ of a transmission maximum of a Fabry–Perot interferometer at optical wavelengths is quite high ($\sim 10^5$ for $n = 1$, $L = 1\,\text{cm}$) and the wavelength and frequency differences between successive orders are quite small. However, for L of the order of the wavelength of light, the transmission maximum order m is a small integer and the inter-order separation becomes large. For $L = \lambda_0/2$, where λ_0 is some specific wavelength of interest, the order of a transmission peak in air can be expressed as

$$m = \frac{\lambda_0}{\lambda}.$$

A Fabry–Perot interferometer with plate separation $\lambda_0/2$ has zero transmission for $\lambda > \lambda_0$ because then m becomes non-integral. The transmission peaks occur at $\lambda = \lambda_0, \lambda_0/2, \lambda_0/3, \ldots$. The wavelength intervals between the successive transmission peaks are now so large that for most experimental situations, the Fabry–Perot interferometer has only one transmission peak of interest. This is exactly what is needed for optical filtering. Figure 6.30 is drawn for $\lambda_0 = 500\,\text{nm}$. The $m = 1$ transmission peak occurs at 500 nm and the second ($m = 2$)

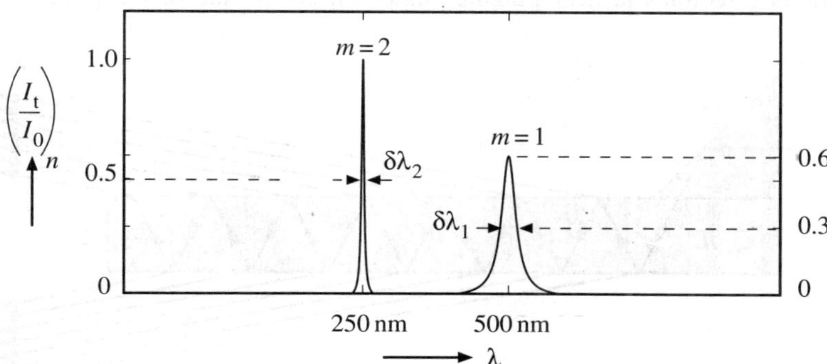

Fig. 6.30: Fabry–Perot interferometer with $L = 250\,\text{nm}$ as a narrow band optical filter.

transmission peak lies in the ultra-violet ($\lambda = 250\,\text{nm}$) and is four times narrower than the first-order transmission peak. The transmission bandwidth

$$\delta\lambda = \frac{\lambda^2}{2\pi nL}\frac{1-R}{\sqrt{R}}$$

of the filter around the mean wavelength λ can be made as small as desired by a proper choice of the film reflectivity. However, increasing the film reflectivity reduces the peak transmission (Eq. 6.56) of the filter. These filters are called interference filters since interference among the multiply reflected waves is responsible for the filtering action. Interference filters with bandwidths of few tens of angstroms are readily available.

6.7 LUMMER–GEHRCKE PLATE

High-Resolution Fabry–Perot interferometers require highly reflecting coatings. The absorption and scattering losses in the optical coatings reduce the transmittance of the interferometer. Another approach to get high reflectivity at an interface is to exploit the internal reflections at incident angles very close to, but below the critical angle. At critical and above critical angles, total internal reflection makes the reflection coefficient complex and of unit magnitude. However, just below the critical angle, the reflection coefficient is real and sufficiently high (Section 1.7.3). The Lummer–Gehrcke (LG) interferometer makes use of this property of internal reflections. It consists of a glass or a quartz plate, a few mm thick, several mm in width, and a few tens of cm in length (Fig. 6.31). A prism of appropriate apex angle is optically bonded to one end of the plate to obtain the desired angle of incidence for the internal reflections. Multiple internal reflections within the LG plate give rise to waves propagating in parallel directions at near grazing angles on either side of the plate. These

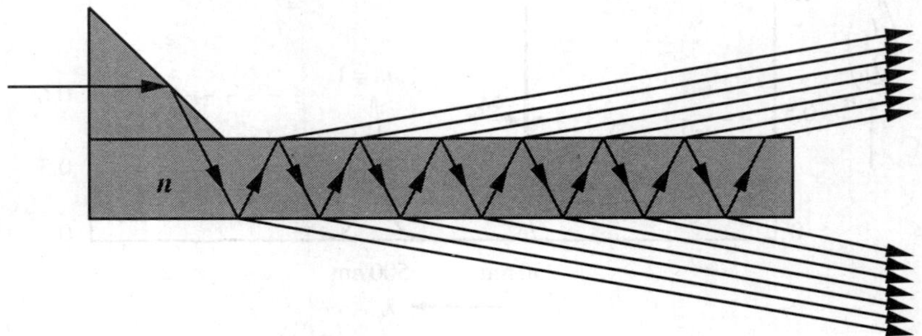

Fig. 6.31: Lummer–Gehrcke plate.

waves can be focused with a lens just as in a Fabry–Perot interferometer. The Lummer–Gehrcke plates have been quite useful in the study of fine structure of spectral lines in the ultraviolet region.

6.8 THIN OPTICAL COATINGS

Path differences among the multiply reflected interfering waves in a film must not exceed the coherence length of the source. This puts some restriction on the thickness of the film. However, for the present discussion, a film is considered thin if its thickness is comparable to the wavelength of light. The top portion of a soap film in a vertical frame may be thin enough to be categorized as a thin film in the present context. In this section we shall deal with films which appear as coatings on a substrate. These films are generally prepared by evaporation in a vacuum chamber (pressure $= 10^{-6}$–10^{-11} torr). The material to be evaporated can be heated by passing current through it (for metal films) or by an electron gun, or by laser ablation. A number of techniques exist to monitor and control the thickness of the film as it grows. A quartz thickness monitor senses changes in the frequency of vibration of a quartz strip due to changes in the mass during deposition. The reflectance and transmittance of the film can also be used for monitoring its thickness during growth. Among the numerous applications of thin optical films, mention may be made to anti-reflection (AR) coatings, high reflectance (HR) mirrors, beam splitters, interference filters, phase retarders, and dichroic mirrors (reflecting and transmitting wavelengths selectively). The films used for most of these applications are multi-layer coatings. Here, we shall consider only the dielectric coatings. They are superior to metal films in many respects.

6.8.1 Single Layer Optical Coatings

We consider a non-absorbing thin film of index of refraction n_1 and thickness t_1 coated on a non-absorbing substrate (assumed semi-infinite) of refractive index n_s (Fig. 6.32). Let a quasi-monochromatic plane wave of amplitude E_0 and mean wavelength λ in vacuum be incident on the film from a semi-infinite medium of index of refraction n_0. The wave undergoes multiple reflections in the film. The incident angle is assumed small so that the reflection and transmission coefficients remain real. The resultant amplitude of the reflected wave is given by the geometric series:

$$\begin{aligned} E_r &= E_0[r_1 + tt'r_2 e^{i\phi} + tt'r_1' r_2^2 e^{i2\phi} + tt'r_1'^2 r_2^3 e^{i3\phi} + \cdots] \\ &= E_0[r_1 + tt'r_2 e^{i\phi}\{1 + r_1' r_2 e^{i\phi} + (r_1' r_2)^2 e^{i2\phi} + \cdots\}] \\ &= E_0\left[r_1 + \frac{r_2(1 - r_1^2)e^{i\phi}}{1 - r_1' r_2 e^{i\phi}}\right], \end{aligned} \tag{6.67}$$

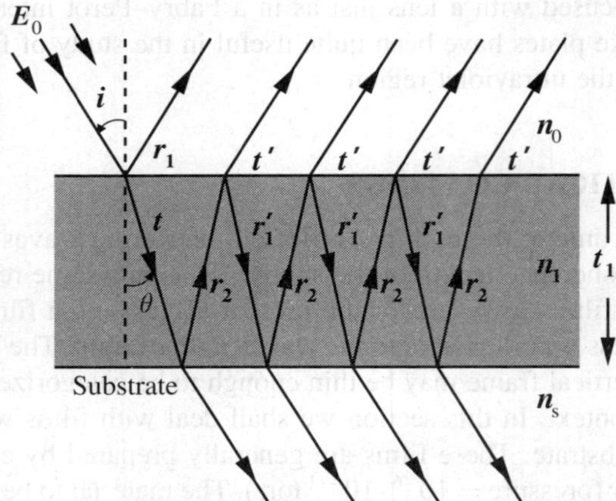

Fig. 6.32: Multiple reflections in a single layer optical coating.

where

$$\phi = \frac{4\pi}{\lambda} n_1 t_1 \cos\theta, \tag{6.68}$$

$$tt' = 1 - r_1^2. \tag{6.46a}$$

Replacing r_1' by $-r_1$,

$$\begin{aligned}\frac{E_r}{E_0} &= r_1 + \frac{r_2(1-r_1^2)e^{i\phi}}{1+r_1 r_2 e^{i\phi}} \\ &= \frac{r_1 + r_2 e^{i\phi}}{1+r_1 r_2 e^{i\phi}}.\end{aligned} \tag{6.69}$$

The film reflectance is

$$\begin{aligned}\mathcal{R} = \frac{I_r}{I_0} &= \frac{(r_1 + r_2 e^{i\phi})(r_1 + r_2 e^{-i\phi})}{(1+r_1 r_2 e^{i\phi})(1+r_1 r_2 e^{-i\phi})} \\ &= \frac{r_1^2 + r_2^2 + 2r_1 r_2 \cos\phi}{1 + r_1^2 r_2^2 + 2r_1 r_2 \cos\phi}.\end{aligned} \tag{6.70}$$

The transmittance of a non-absorbing film is obtained as

$$T = \frac{I_t}{I_0} = 1 - \mathcal{R} = \frac{(1-r_1^2)(1-r_2^2)}{1 + r_1^2 r_2^2 + 2r_1 r_2 \cos\phi}. \tag{6.71}$$

At normal incidence and $\phi = \pi$ radians, the film reflectance takes the form

$$\begin{aligned}\mathcal{R} &= \frac{(r_1 - r_2)^2}{(1 - r_1 r_2)^2} \\ &= \frac{(n_1^2 - n_0 n_s)^2}{(n_1^2 + n_0 n_s)^2},\end{aligned} \tag{6.72}$$

where

$$r_1 = \frac{n_0 - n_1}{n_0 + n_1},$$
$$r_2 = \frac{n_1 - n_s}{n_1 + n_s}.$$

The choice of the phase angle

$$\phi = \frac{4\pi}{\bar{\lambda}} n_1 t_1 \cos\theta = \pi \tag{6.73}$$

is a particularly useful one, as we shall see later. For $\theta = 0$, it makes the film thickness

$$t_1 = \frac{1}{4}\frac{\bar{\lambda}}{n_1} \tag{6.74}$$

equal to quarter of the mean wavelength in the film.

The reflectivity of a single layer quarter wave optical coating can vary between wide limits, depending on the indices of refraction of the film and the media surrounding it. Table 6.3 gives indices of refraction of materials, commonly used for optical coatings. A glass substrate ($n_s = 1.5$) coated with a quarter-wave film of antimony sulphide ($n = 3.0$) with reflectance $\mathcal{R} = 0.5$ can be used as a 50–50 beam splitter in the near infrared region. This is about the maximum reflectivity in this spectral region that can be obtained from a single layer coated glass substrate. The SiO ($n = 2.0$) quarter-wave coated glass jewelry can reflect upto 20% of the incident light (slightly higher than 17% reflectivity of natural diamond). These are examples of high-reflectance single layer coatings. Single layer coatings can also be used as anti-reflection (AR) coatings to reduce the reflection losses. The reflectance (Eq. 6.72) of a single layer quarter-wave coating becomes zero if

$$n_1^2 = n_0 n_s. \tag{6.75}$$

This requires a quarter wave coating of a material of index of refraction of about 1.22 to eliminate reflection from a glass ($n_s = 1.50$) substrate. Unfortunately,

Table 6.3. Dielectric materials for thin film coatings.

Material	Refractive index	Spectral region
Cryolite ($AlF_3 \cdot 3NaF$)	1.33	visible
Lithium Fluoride (LiF)	1.36	visible
Magnesium Fluoride (MgF_2)	1.38	visible
Cerium Fluoride	1.63	visible
Aluminum Oxide (Al_2O_3)	1.76	visible
Silicon Oxide (SiO)	2.0	visible
Zinc Sulphide (ZnS)	2.3	visible
Rutile (TiO_2)	2.6	visible
Antimony Sulphide (Sb_2S_3)	3.0	1 μm
Germanium (Ge)	4.0	2 μm
Tellurium (Te)	5.0	4 μm

there is no good material with refractive index close to this value. The usual choice for AR coating of glass substrates is either cryolite ($AlF_3 \cdot 3NaF$) with $n = 1.33$ or magnesium fluoride (MgF_2) with $n = 1.38$. The latter, being more durable, is preferred. A quarter-wave film of MgF_2 on glass substrate cuts down its reflectivity from 4 to nearly 1.2%. This reduction is not insignificant. It brings substantial improvement in the performance of optical instruments. For example, reflection loss for a camera with four lenses is reduced from nearly 32% down to about 4% if each of the lenses is given a quarter-wave MgF_2 coating. This leads to not only brighter images but removes the haziness caused by light reflected from the surfaces of the lens.

Equation (6.73) can be satisfied for only one particular wavelength for a film of a given refractive index. Therefore, an optical coating can act as a quarter-wave coating for that particular wavelength only. To see the spectral behavior of single layer coatings, we re-write Eq. (6.73) as

$$\phi = \pi \frac{\lambda_0}{\bar{\lambda}}, \tag{6.76}$$

where $\lambda_0 = 4n_1 t_1 \cos\theta$. With this change of notation, Eq. (6.70) becomes

$$\mathcal{R}(\bar{\lambda}) = \frac{r_1^2 + r_2^2 + 2r_1 r_2 \cos(\pi\lambda_0/\bar{\lambda})}{1 + r_1^2 r_2^2 + 2r_1 r_2 \cos(\pi\lambda_0/\bar{\lambda})}. \tag{6.77}$$

The film reflectance shows periodic dependence on $1/\lambda$ (Fig. 6.33). We distinguish two cases:

HR coatings: $n_1^2 > n_0 n_s$,
AR coatings: $n_1^2 = n_0 n_s$.

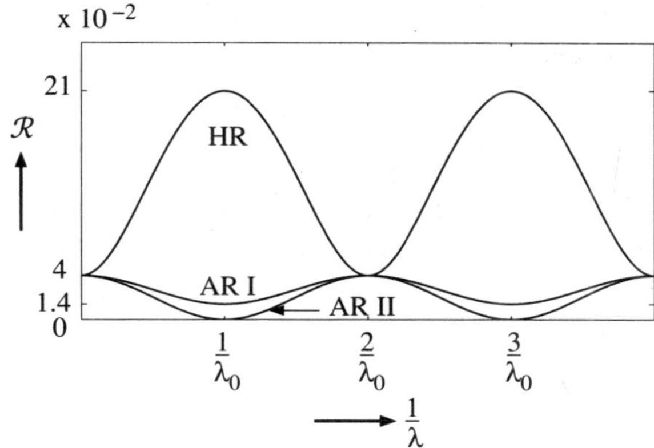

Fig. 6.33: Reflectivity of single layer HR and AR coatings on glass substrate ($n_s = 1.5$); HR ($n_1 = 2$), ARI ($n_1 = 1.38$), AR II ($n_1 = \sqrt{1.5}$).

The upper curve in Fig. 6.33 shows the wavelength dependence of the reflectance of an HR coating ($n_0 = 1.0, n_1 = 2, n_s = 1.5$) and the lower curve ARI refers to the performance of an AR coating with $n_0 = 1.0$, $n_s = 1.5$ (glass) and $n_1 = 1.38$ (MgF_2). The lower curve ARII corresponds to a hypothetical AR coating with $n_0 = 1.0$, $n_s = 1.5$, $n_1 = \sqrt{1.5}$. Maximum reflectance of single layer HR coatings and minimum reflectance of single layer AR coatings occur at $\bar{\lambda} = \lambda_0,\ \lambda_0/3,\ \lambda_0/5,\ \lambda_0/6,\ \ldots$. Minimum reflectance of single layer HR coatings and maximum reflectance of single layer AR coatings occur at $\lambda = \infty$, $\lambda_0/2,\ \lambda_0/4, \ldots$. The reflectivity in the latter case is simply the reflectivity of the substrate in the absence of the coating. Needless to state that the single layer coatings lack broad spectral features.

6.8.2 Multi-layer Optical Coatings

To further reduce the reflectance of AR coatings and to enhance the reflectance of HR coatings, multi-layer thin film coatings are employed. As we shall find, multi-layer coatings can be designed to possess broad spectral features as well. The earlier approach of adding amplitudes of the multiply reflected waves in each film will be too cumbersome when applied to multi-layer coatings. We now outline an alternate procedure to calculate the reflectance and transmittance of a single non-absorbing film and then generalize it to a stack of N films.

The multiply reflected waves travel in two directions inside the film. All waves propagating in either direction can be combined to yield two homogeneous waves

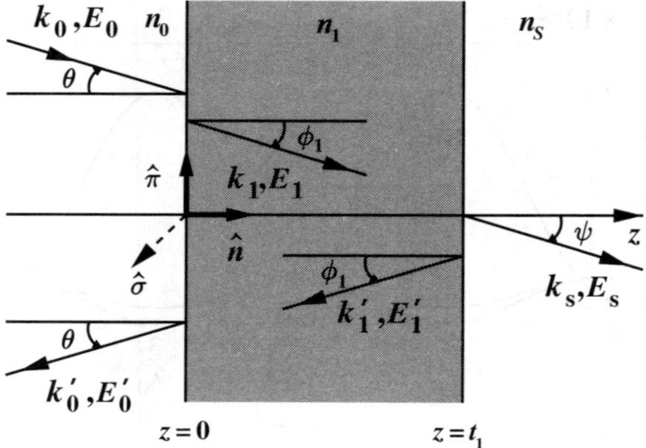

Fig. 6.34: Homogeneous waves for a single layer optical coating.

at every point of the film. In the new approach we deal with these resultant waves only. Similarly, two homogeneous waves exist in the semi-infinite medium in front of the film, but only one wave propagating away from the second interface exists in the substrate. Figure 6.34 shows the propagation vectors of these waves. The unprimed amplitudes and propagation vectors refer to the resultant waves propagating from left to right and the primed quantities refer to those travelling from right to left. The boundary conditions at the two interfaces determine the amplitudes of the resultant waves in each medium. The electric fields of the resultant waves in the three media are:

Medium I ($n = n_0$):

$$\vec{E}_i = \vec{E}_0 \, e^{i(\vec{k}_0 \cdot \vec{r} - \bar{\omega} t)},$$
$$\vec{E}_r = \vec{E}'_0 \, e^{i(\vec{k}'_0 \cdot \vec{r} - \bar{\omega} t)}. \tag{6.78a}$$

Medium II ($n = n_1$):

$$\vec{E}_t = \vec{E}_1 \, e^{i(\vec{k}_1 \cdot \vec{r} - \bar{\omega} t)},$$
$$\vec{E}_r = \vec{E}'_1 \, e^{i(\vec{k}'_1 \cdot \vec{r} - \bar{\omega} t)}. \tag{6.78b}$$

Medium III ($n = n_s$),

$$\vec{E}_t = \vec{E}_s \, e^{i(\vec{k}_s \cdot \vec{r} - \bar{\omega} t)}. \tag{6.78c}$$

Applying the boundary conditions (Eqs 1.60a and 1.61b with $a_t = 0$) at the first interface ($z = 0$) for π-polarized fields, we have

$$E_{0\pi} + E'_{0\pi} = E_{1\pi} + E'_{1\pi}, \tag{6.79a}$$

$$\frac{k_0}{\cos\theta}(E_{0\pi} - E'_{0\pi}) = \frac{k_1}{\cos\phi_1}(E_{1\pi} - E'_{1\pi}). \tag{6.79b}$$

For σ-polarized fields, the corresponding restrictions are

$$E_{0\sigma} + E'_{0\sigma} = E_{1\sigma} + E'_{1\sigma}, \tag{6.80a}$$

$$(k_0 \cos\theta)(E_{0\sigma} - E'_{0\sigma}) = (k_1 \cos\phi_1)(E_{1\sigma} - E'_{1\sigma}), \tag{6.80b}$$

where θ and ϕ_1 are the angles of incidence and refraction, respectively, at the first interface. For non-absorbing media,

$$k'_0 = k_0 = n_0\frac{2\pi}{\bar{\lambda}}, \quad k'_1 = k_1 = n_1\frac{2\pi}{\bar{\lambda}}, \quad k_s = n_s\frac{2\pi}{\bar{\lambda}},$$

where $\bar{\lambda}$ is the mean wavelength of quasi-monochromatic light in vacuum. Equations (6.79) and (6.80) can be combined into two equations:

$$E_0 + E'_0 = E_1 + E'_1, \tag{6.81a}$$

$$y_0(E_0 - E'_0) = y_1(E_1 - E'_1), \tag{6.81b}$$

where $y_0 = n_0/\cos\theta$, $y_1 = n_1/\cos\phi_1$ for π-polarized fields and $y_0 = n_0\cos\theta$, $y_1 = n_1\cos\phi_1$ for σ-polarized fields.

Similarly, applying boundary conditions at the second interface ($z = t_1$), we have

$$E_1 e^{i\beta_1 t_1} + E'_1 e^{-i\beta_1 t_1} = E_s e^{i\beta_s t_1} = E_t, \tag{6.82a}$$

$$y_1(E_1 e^{i\beta_1 t_1} - E'_1 e^{-i\beta_1 t_1}) = y_s E_s e^{i\beta_s t_1} = y_s E_t, \tag{6.82b}$$

where

$$y_s = n_s/\cos\psi \quad \text{for } \pi\text{-polarized field,}$$
$$= n_s\cos\psi \quad \text{for } \sigma\text{-polarized field,}$$
$$\beta_1 = k_1\cos\phi_1,$$
$$\beta_s = k_s\cos\psi.$$

Here, ψ is the angle of refraction in the third medium. Equations (6.82) give

$$E_1 = \left(1 + \frac{y_s}{y_1}\right) \frac{e^{-i\beta_1 t_1}}{2} E_t, \tag{6.83a}$$

$$E_1' = \left(1 - \frac{y_s}{y_1}\right) \frac{e^{i\beta_1 t_1}}{2} E_t. \tag{6.83b}$$

Substituting these expressions in Eqs (6.81), we obtain

$$\begin{aligned} E_0 + E_0' &= \left[\left(1 + \frac{y_s}{y_1}\right) \frac{e^{-i\beta_1 t_1}}{2} + \left(1 - \frac{y_s}{y_1}\right) \frac{e^{i\beta_1 t_1}}{2}\right] E_t \\ &= \left[\cos\beta_1 t_1 - \left(\frac{y_s}{y_1}\right) i \sin\beta_1 t_1\right] E_t \end{aligned} \tag{6.84a}$$

and

$$\begin{aligned} y_0(E_0 - E_0') &= y_1[(1 + \frac{y_s}{y_1}) \frac{e^{-i\beta_1 t_1}}{2} - (1 - \frac{y_s}{y_1}) \frac{e^{i\beta_1 t_1}}{2}] E_t \\ &= [-i y_1 \sin\beta_1 t_1 + y_s \cos\beta_1 t_1] E_t. \end{aligned} \tag{6.84b}$$

Expressing Eqs (6.84) in the matrix form, we have

$$\begin{pmatrix} E_0 + E_0' \\ y_0(E_0 - E_0') \end{pmatrix} = \begin{pmatrix} \cos\beta_1 t_1 & \frac{-i}{y_1} \sin\beta_1 t_1 \\ -i y_1 \sin\beta_1 t_1 & \cos\beta_1 t_1 \end{pmatrix} \begin{pmatrix} E_t \\ y_s E_t \end{pmatrix}. \tag{6.85}$$

The 2×2 matrix in Eq. (6.85) with unit determinant, characterizing the action of the single-layer coating, connects the fields in the substrate with those in the medium of incidence. Equation (6.85) can be expressed in terms of the reflection ($r = E_0'/E_0$) and transmission ($t = E_t/E_0$) coefficients:

$$\begin{pmatrix} 1 + r \\ y_0(1 - r) \end{pmatrix} = \begin{pmatrix} \cos\beta_1 t_1 & \frac{-i}{y_1} \sin\beta_1 t_1 \\ -i y_1 \sin\beta_1 t_1 & \cos\beta_1 t_1 \end{pmatrix} \begin{pmatrix} t \\ y_s t \end{pmatrix}. \tag{6.86}$$

Solution of this matrix equation yields,

$$r = \frac{y_1(y_0 - y_s)\cos\beta_1 t_1 - i(y_0 y_s - y_1^2)\sin\beta_1 t_1}{y_1(y_0 + y_s)\cos\beta_1 t_1 - i(y_0 y_s + y_1^2)\sin\beta_1 t_1}, \tag{6.87}$$

$$t = \frac{2 y_0 y_1}{y_1(y_0 + y_s)\cos\beta_1 t_1 - i(y_0 y_s + y_1^2)\sin\beta_1 t_1}. \tag{6.88}$$

For normal incidence, $y_0 = n_0$, $y_1 = n_1$, $y_s = n_s$ for either state of polarization, and Eqs (6.87) and (6.88) simplify to

$$r = \frac{n_1(n_0 - n_s)\cos(\frac{2\pi}{\bar{\lambda}}n_1t_1) - i(n_0n_s - n_1^2)\sin(\frac{2\pi}{\bar{\lambda}}n_1t_1)}{n_1(n_0 + n_s)\cos(\frac{2\pi}{\bar{\lambda}}n_1t_1) - i(n_0n_s + n_1^2)\sin(\frac{2\pi}{\bar{\lambda}}n_1t_1)}, \tag{6.89a}$$

$$t = \frac{2n_0n_1}{n_1(n_0 + n_s)\cos(\frac{2\pi}{\bar{\lambda}}n_1t_1) - i(n_0n_s + n_1^2)\sin(\frac{2\pi}{\bar{\lambda}}n_1t_1)}, \tag{6.89b}$$

respectively. The reflectance of the quarter-wave film with $(2\pi/\bar{\lambda})n_1t_1 = \pi/2$ takes the form

$$\mathcal{R} = r^2 = \left(\frac{n_0n_s - n_1^2}{n_0n_s + n_1^2}\right)^2,$$

which is exactly the result (Eq. 6.72), obtained earlier by considering multiple reflections in the film.

6.8.2.1 Extension to Multi-layer Coatings

We first consider a stack of two optical coatings (Fig. 6.35). Application of the boundary conditions at the three interfaces ($z = 0, t_1, t_1 + t_2$) yields the following results:

$$E_0 + E_0' = E_1 + E_1', \tag{6.90a}$$

$$y_0(E_0 - E_0') = y_1(E_1 - E_1'), \tag{6.90b}$$

$$E_1 e^{i\beta_1 t_1} + E_1' e^{-i\beta_1 t_1} = E_2 e^{i\beta_2 t_1} + E_2' e^{-i\beta_2 t_1}, \tag{6.90c}$$

$$y_1(E_1 e^{i\beta_1 t_1} - E_1' e^{-i\beta_1 t_1}) = y_2(E_2 e^{i\beta_2 t_1} - E_2' e^{-i\beta_2 t_1}), \tag{6.90d}$$

$$E_2 e^{i\beta_2(t_1+t_2)} + E_2' e^{-i\beta_2(t_1+t_2)} = E_t, \tag{6.90e}$$

$$y_2(E_2 e^{i\beta_2(t_1+t_2)} - E_2' e^{-i\beta_2(t_1+t_2)}) = y_s E_t, \tag{6.90f}$$

where $\beta_2 = k_2 \cos\phi_2$, and y_2 is defined in the manner of y_1 for the second layer. Starting with Eqs (6.90c)–(6.90f) and following the treatment of the single layer coating, the field amplitudes in the first layer can be expressed in terms of the field amplitudes in the substrate:

$$\begin{pmatrix} E_1 e^{i\beta_1 t_1} + E_1' e^{-i\beta_1 t_1} \\ y_1(E_1 e^{i\beta_1 t_1} - E_1' e^{-i\beta_1 t_1}) \end{pmatrix} = \begin{pmatrix} \cos\beta_2 t_2 & \frac{-i}{y_2}\sin\beta_2 t_2 \\ -iy_2 \sin\beta_2 t_2 & \cos\beta_2 t_2 \end{pmatrix} \begin{pmatrix} E_t \\ y_s E_t \end{pmatrix} \tag{6.91}$$

where the 2×2 matrix on the right-hand side represents the action of the second layer. The field amplitudes E_1 and E_1' obtained from this equation can

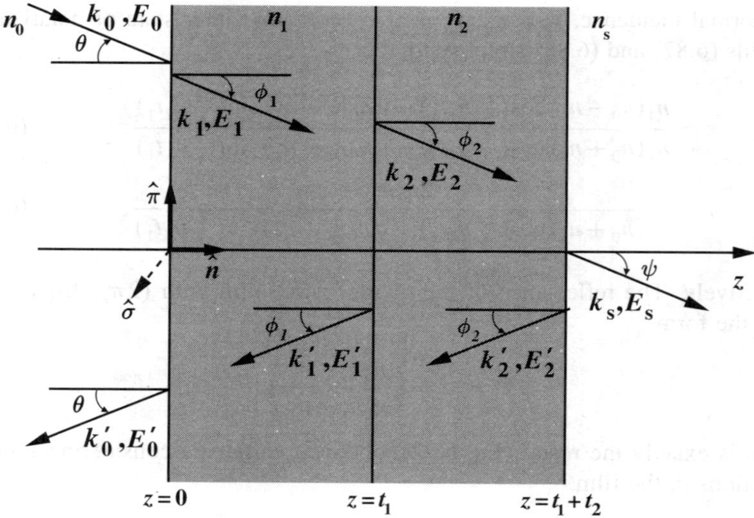

Fig. 6.35: Homogeneous waves for a two layer stack.

be substituted in Eqs (6.90a) and (6.90b) to obtain the field amplitudes in the first medium. Alternatively, we can extend Eq. (6.85) to yield

$$\begin{pmatrix} E_0 + E_0' \\ y_0(E_0 - E_0') \end{pmatrix} = \begin{pmatrix} \cos\beta_1 t_1 & \frac{-i}{y_1}\sin\beta_1 t_1 \\ -iy_1 \sin\beta_1 t_1 & \cos\beta_1 t_1 \end{pmatrix} \times \begin{pmatrix} E_1 e^{i\beta_1 t_1} + E_1' e^{-i\beta_1 t_1} \\ y_1(E_1 e^{i\beta_1 t_1} - E_1' e^{-i\beta_1 t_1}) \end{pmatrix}. \tag{6.92}$$

Combining Eqs (6.91) and (6.92), we obtain the desired result

$$\begin{pmatrix} E_0 + E_0' \\ y_0(E_0 - E_0') \end{pmatrix} = \begin{pmatrix} \cos\beta_1 t_1 & \frac{-i}{y_1}\sin\beta_1 t_1 \\ -iy_1 \sin\beta_1 t_1 & \cos\beta_1 t_1 \end{pmatrix} \times \begin{pmatrix} \cos\beta_2 t_2 & \frac{-i}{y_2}\sin\beta_2 t_2 \\ -iy_2 \sin\beta_2 t_2 & \cos\beta_2 t_2 \end{pmatrix} \begin{pmatrix} E_t \\ y_s E_t \end{pmatrix}. \tag{6.93}$$

This matrix equation has the obvious generalization for N layers (Fig. 6.36):

$$\begin{pmatrix} E_0 + E_0' \\ y_0(E_0 - E_0') \end{pmatrix} = M_1 M_2 \cdots M_j \cdots M_N \begin{pmatrix} E_t \\ y_s E_t \end{pmatrix}, \tag{6.94}$$

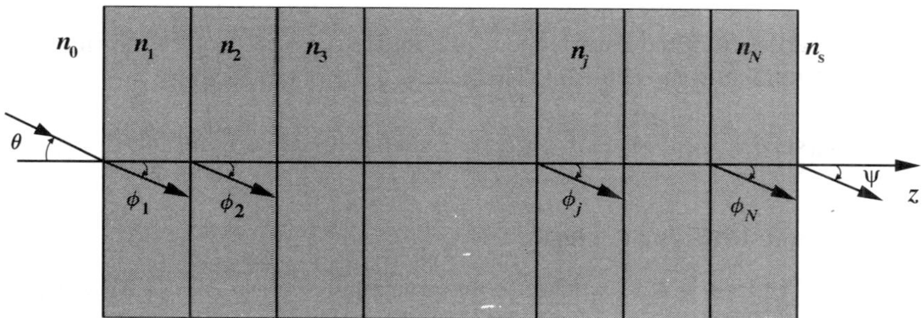

Fig. 6.36: N layer stack; ϕ_j and n_j are the angle of refraction and index of refraction of the jth layer.

where

$$M_j = \begin{pmatrix} \cos\beta_j t_j & \frac{-i}{y_j}\sin\beta_j t_j \\ -iy_j \sin\beta_j t_j & \cos\beta_j t_j \end{pmatrix}$$

is the matrix representing the action of the jth layer of thickness t_j and $\beta_j = n_j(2\pi/\lambda)\cos\phi_j$ in the process of wave propagation through an N layer stack. The order of multiplication of the matrices must be taken note of. The matrix for the last (Nth) layer operates on the fields in the substrate. The product matrix M, being a 2×2 matrix, can be expressed as

$$\begin{aligned} M &= M_1 \cdot M_2 \cdot M_3 \cdots M_j \cdots M_N \\ &= \begin{pmatrix} M_{11} & M_{12} \\ M_{21} & M_{22} \end{pmatrix}, \end{aligned} \tag{6.95}$$

so that Eq. (6.94) has the equivalent form

$$\begin{pmatrix} 1+r \\ y_0(1-r) \end{pmatrix} = \begin{pmatrix} M_{11} & M_{12} \\ M_{21} & M_{22} \end{pmatrix} \begin{pmatrix} t \\ y_s t \end{pmatrix}. \tag{6.96}$$

The amplitude reflection and transmission coefficients of the N-layer stack are

$$r = \frac{y_0 M_{11} + y_0 y_s M_{12} - M_{21} - y_s M_{22}}{y_0 M_{11} + y_0 y_s M_{12} + M_{21} + y_s M_{22}}, \tag{6.97a}$$

$$t = \frac{2y_0}{y_0 M_{11} + y_0 y_s M_{12} + M_{21} + y_s M_{22}}, \tag{6.97b}$$

respectively. The coefficients $y_0, y_1, \ldots, y_N, y_s$ can be calculated for either state of polarization from the knowledge of the indices of refraction of the films and angles of refraction in each film. The latter can be obtained from

$$n_0 \sin\theta = n_1 \sin\phi_1 = n_2 \sin\phi_2 = \cdots = n_N \sin\phi_N = n_s \sin\psi. \tag{6.98}$$

6.8.3 Anti-Reflection Coatings

A single $MgF_2(n = 1.38)$ quarter-wave coating on glass $(n = 1.5)$ substrate reduces its reflectance at normal incidence from 4 to nearly 1.2%. This reduction in reflectance takes place at one particular wavelength. The reflectance increases on either side of this wavelength (Fig. 6.33). To improve the performance of multi-layer AR coatings, we have more variables at our disposal in the forms of the thickness and index of refraction of each of the layers. Computer simulations can be carried out to select optimum combinations of thin film coatings to achieve low reflectance over the desired spectral range. Two quarter-wave coatings with materials of high and low indices of refraction can give zero reflectance at two-wavelengths, but reduction in reflectance in the spectral range between the two-wavelengths is rather small. A three-layer coating is more effective in reducing reflectance over a broad spectral range.

Figure 6.37 shows a sequence of three layers on light flint glass substrate [6.4]. The reflectance of this combination over most of the visible spectrum is less than 0.03% (Fig. 6.38) as compared to 4% reflectance of an air–glass interface and 1.2% reflectance of a MgF_2 coated glass substrate. The AR coatings usually have no more than three or four layers and show only marginal degradation in performance for deviations from normal incidence.

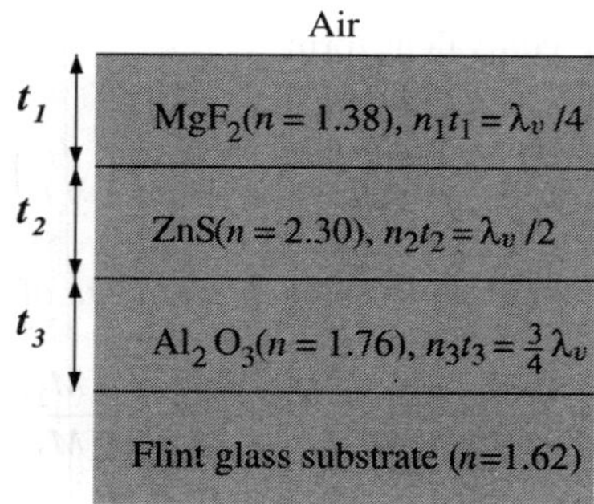

Fig. 6.37: A three layer AR coating.

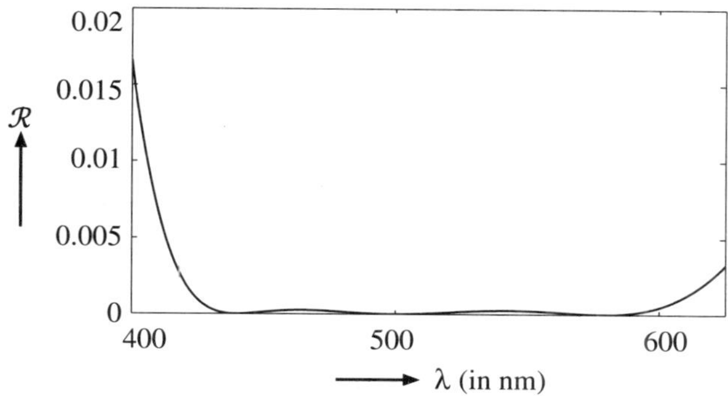

Fig. 6.38: Reflectivity of the three layer AR coating of Fig. 6.37.

6.8.4 High Reflectance Coatings

Laser and Fabry–Perot resonators require high reflectivities that are unattainable from metallic films which also suffer from high absorption losses. The all-dielectric-multilayer coatings can achieve high reflectivities with minimal scattering and absorption losses. However, a large number of dielectric layers must be used to obtain reflectivities of 0.99 or higher. High reflectance coatings usually consist of alternate quarter-wave layers of materials with high and low indices of refraction ($n_H t_H = n_L t_L = \frac{\lambda_v}{4}$), as shown in Fig. 6.39.

Films of ZnS ($n = 2.30$) and MgF_2($n = 1.38$) are often used in HR coatings but other choices also exist (see Table 6.3). The transformation matrix for a stack of N pairs of quarter-wave layers of high and low refractive index materials can be expressed in the form

$$M = (M_H M_L)^N,$$

n_0 n_H n_L n_H n_L n_H n_L n_H n_L n_s

Fig. 6.39: Stack of alternate high and low refractive index quarter-wave layers for high reflectance applications.

where

$$M_H = \begin{pmatrix} \cos\beta_H t_H & \frac{-i}{y_H}\sin\beta_H t_H \\ -iy_H \sin\beta_H t_H & \cos\beta_H t_H \end{pmatrix},$$

$$M_L = \begin{pmatrix} \cos\beta_L t_L & \frac{-i}{y_L}\sin\beta_L t_L \\ -iy_L \sin\beta_L t_L & \cos\beta_L t_L \end{pmatrix}.$$

Therefore,

$$\begin{aligned} M &= \left[\begin{pmatrix} 0 & \frac{-i}{y_H} \\ -iy_H & 0 \end{pmatrix}\begin{pmatrix} 0 & \frac{-i}{y_L} \\ -iy_L & 0 \end{pmatrix}\right]^N \\ &= \begin{pmatrix} \left(\frac{-y_L}{y_H}\right)^N & 0 \\ 0 & \left(\frac{-y_H}{y_L}\right)^N \end{pmatrix}, \end{aligned} \tag{6.99}$$

where we have assumed normal incidence, and

$$\beta_H t_H = \frac{2\pi}{\bar{\lambda}_v} n_H t_H = \pi/2 \quad \text{for } \bar{\lambda}_v = \lambda_0,$$

$$\beta_L t_L = \frac{2\pi}{\bar{\lambda}_v} n_L t_L = \pi/2 \quad \text{for } \bar{\lambda}_v = \lambda_0,$$

giving the reflectance of the stack as

$$\mathcal{R} = r^2 = \left[\frac{n_s\left(\frac{-n_H}{n_L}\right)^{2N} - n_0}{n_s\left(\frac{-n_H}{n_L}\right)^{2N} + n_0}\right]^2. \tag{6.100}$$

The reflectance approaches unity as the number of pairs in the stack becomes large ($N \to \infty$). For eight alternate layers ($N = 4$) of ZnS and MgF_2 on a glass substrate ($n_s = 1.5$), Eq. (6.100) predicts reflectance of about 0.96, and 0.999 for a stack of 16 such layers. The above analysis has ignored scattering losses which are always present in dielectric optical coatings. The reflectivity of the stack increases with the number of layers in the stack and the spectral bandwidth of high reflectance increases with the n_H/n_L ratio. Multi-layer broad band high reflectance dielectric mirrors are now readily available.

6.8.5 Narrow Band Interference Filters

A Fabry–Perot interferometer with plate separation $L = \lambda_0/2$ was shown to possess transmission peaks at λ_0, $\frac{1}{2}\lambda_0$, $\frac{1}{3}\lambda_0, \ldots$. With such large separations in

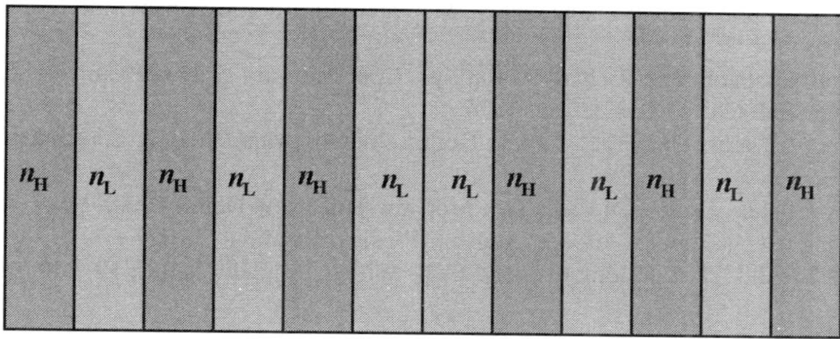

Fig. 6.40: An all-dielectric multi-layer interference filter. Alternate layers are high and low index quarter-wave layers. Middle two layers have same index of refraction.

the transmission wavelengths, optical filtering can be achieved quite easily as mentioned earlier. The spectral band-widths of the transmission peaks can be reduced by increasing the finesse of the Fabry–Perot interferometer. The peak transmission

$$T_{\text{max}} = \left(1 - \frac{A}{1-R}\right)^2$$

of a Fabry–Perot interferometer with silver coating ($R = 0.95$, $A = 0.04$) is only 4% as compared to 100% transmission of non-absorbing films. A mere 4% absorption loss in the silver film is enough to reduce the peak transmittance of the Fabry–Perot interferometer from 100 to 4%. On the other hand, transmission losses in all-dielectric-multilayer coatings are much less. For a nominal size dielectric multi-layer stack with $R = 0.983$, absorption loss ($A = 0.005$) can be an order of magnitude less than for the silver films. Peak transmittance of a Fabry–Perot interferometer with dielectric HR coatings can be higher than 50%. A typical configuration of a narrow band, high transmission interference filter employing quarter-wave optical coatings of high and low index materials is shown in Fig. 6.40. The two quarter-wave films in the middle of the stack with same index of refraction constitute the half-wavelength spacer of the Fabry–Perot etalon.

6.9 REFERENCES

6.1 F. Jenkins and H. White, Fundamental of Optics, 3rd ed., McGraw-Hill, New York, 1957.

6.2 Max Born and Emil Wolf, Principles of Optics, 7th ed., Cambridge University Press, Cambridge, 1999.

6.3 John M Stone, Radiation and Optics, McGraw-Hill Book Company, Inc., New York, 1963.
6.4 Allen Nussbaum and Richard A. Phillips; Contemporary Optics, Prentice-Hall, Inc., Englewood Cliffs, New Jersey, 1976.
6.5 Miles V. Klein, Thomas E. Furtak, Optics, 2nd ed., John Wiley & Sons, New York, 1986.
6.6 Ajoy Ghatak, Optics, 2nd ed., Tata McGraw-Hill, New Delhi, 1992.
6.7 Eugene Hecht, Optics, 4th ed., Addison-Wesley, Reading, 2001.
6.8 J. H. Wasilik, T. V. Blomquist, and C. S. Willett, Applied Optics, **10**, 2107 (1971).

6.10 PROBLEMS

6.1 Two-wave interference is produced by light from a source emitting frequencies ν_1 and ν_2 with equal amplitudes. Plot the resultant intensity distribution and visibility of interference fringes as a function of the time delay τ. How will your results change if amplitude of one wave is half the amplitude of the other?

6.2 Two-wave interference is studied with a source of degree of coherence described by the Gaussian function $\gamma(\tau) = e^{(-\tau^2/2\sigma^2)}$, where σ is real, and τ is the time delay between the interfering waves. Plot the resultant intensity distribution and visibility of interference fringes as a function of the time delay. Be sure to consider time delays beyond the coherence time τ_c which may be defined as the time in which the visibility of fringes falls to $1/e$ of its maximum value.

6.3 Consider two narrow slits 1.5 mm apart, symmetrically placed behind a small source giving light of wavelength 632.8 nm. The interference pattern is observed on a screen 2 m behind the plane of the slits.

(a) A thin glass plate ($n = 1.50$) of thickness 1.5×10^{-2} cm is placed behind one of the slits. Find the number of fringes crossing the center of the observation screen and the displacement of the central fringe due to the introduction of the glass plate.

(b) Find the visibility of interference fringes if one slit was twice as wide as the other.

(c) Now suppose the monochromatic source is replaced by a white light source. Identify the wavelengths in the spectrum of white light which will produce dark fringes 2 mm away from the center of the interference pattern.

6.4 White light falls normally on a thin oil film ($n = 1.25$) of thickness 1×10^{-3} cm. Determine the wavelengths which will be seen in the reflected light.

6.5 Haidinger fringes with an extended source giving light of wavelength 546.1 nm are observed in air from a film of thickness 0.500 mm and index of refraction 1.500. What is the order of the fringe at the center? Find the angular radius of the 5th bright fringe from the center.

6.6 The beam splitter of the Michelson interferometer (Fig. 6.15) is illuminated with the D_1 and D_2 lines of sodium having mean wavelengths of 589.6 and 589.0 nm, respectively. The visibility of the interference fringes goes through several cycles of decreasing and increasing values as the path difference between the two arms of the interferometer is increased. Find the path length mismatches of the arms when the visibility of fringes has minimum value for the first time and maximum value for the first time (excluding the one for the balanced arms of the interferometer). What are the orders of the overlapping fringes for the two wavelengths in each case?

6.7 Fringes of equal thickness are observed from a wedge of a material of index of refraction 2.0. The wedge of dimensions shown in Fig. 6.41 is illuminated normally with filtered mercury light containing the wavelengths 577 and 579 nm. Find the maximum number of bright fringes that can be observed for each wavelength. Locate the position(s) on the wedge where the visibility of the fringes is maximum.

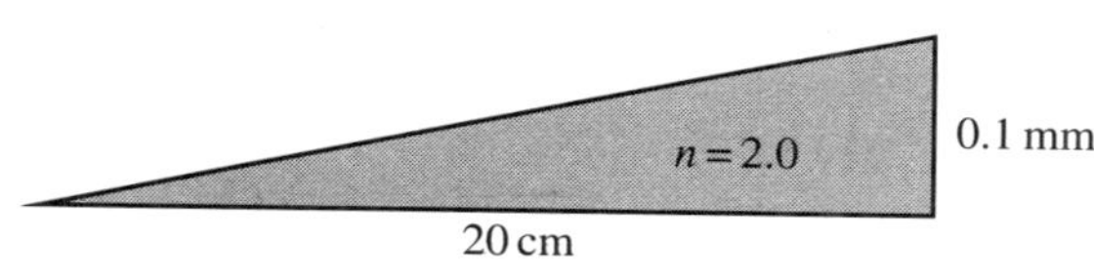

Fig. 6.41

6.8 Non-localized interference fringes from a polished but slightly wedged plate ($n = 1.5$) of nominal thickness 1 mm are observed in a plane which is parallel to the front surface of the plate and lies 10 cm in front of it. A point source emitting light of 632.8 nm is suitably positioned in this plane. The center of nearly circular fringes in this plane is found displaced from the source by 5 cm. Determine the wedge angle of the plate.

6.9 The two arms of the Michelson interferometer are initially balanced with white light fringes. The white light source is then replaced by a He–Ne laser emitting light at 632.8 nm. When a thin plate of crown glass of index of refraction 1.525 is introduced in one arm of the interferometer, 100 bright fringes cross the field of view. Find the thickness of the plate. With the crown glass plate in position, find the angular radii of the 20th bright and dark fringes.

6.10 Plot the Airy function $T = 1/(1 + F(r)\sin^2(\bar{k}\Delta/2))$ as a function of $\bar{k}\Delta$ for a non-absorbing film of thickness 1mm with amplitude reflection coefficient $r = 0.95$ and obtain the FWHM (full width at half maximum) of the transmission peaks and finesse of the film. Find the maximum transmittances of the films with $r = 0.95$ and absorptance $A = 0.04$, 0.004.

6.11 A Fabry–Perot interferometer is required to resolve the longitudinal modes of a He–Ne laser emitting 632.8 nm radiation. The inter-mode separation of the He–Ne laser is 300 MHz. What minimum plate separation is required if the reflectivity of its plates $R = 0.99$? What is the free spectral range of the interferometer in frequency and wavelength units in this spectral range? What is the highest order of the fringes produced by the interferometer?

6.12 A quarter-wave film of ZnS ($n = 2.3$) for the wavelength $\lambda_0 = 500$ nm in vacuum is deposited on a fused quartz substrate ($n = 1.46$). What is the thickness of the film? Plot the reflectance of the coated substrate for the wavelength interval between 400 and 600 nm for light incidence from vacuum at 0° and 45°.

6.13 Taking $\lambda_v = 500$ nm, calculate and plot the reflectance of the three layer AR coating of Fig. 6.37 between the spectral interval 400–600 nm by taking a few representative wavelengths.

6.14 Equation (6.100) for the reflectance of a stack of alternate quarter-wave layers of high and low refractive index materials neglects absorption and scattering losses. Within this approximation, find the number of pairs of ZnS ($n = 2.3$) and MgF_2 ($n = 1.38$) quarter-wave layers needed to achieve reflectance $\mathcal{R} = 0.999$.

6.15 An interference filter consisting of multi-layer coatings of dielectric materials (Fig. 6.40) has reflectance $\mathcal{R} = 0.983$ and absorptance $A = 0.005$. Find its maximum transmittance and the FWHM of its transmission peaks at 488.0 nm.

CHAPTER 7

Diffraction of Light

7.1 INTRODUCTION

The presence of dark and bright bands near the edges of geometric shadows of objects was reported by Francesco Maria Grimaldi (1618–1663) in his book, published 2 years after his death. This observation was not consistent with the corpuscular theory of light being propounded by Sir Issac Newton (1642–1727). Grimaldi called the phenomenon of bending of light across edges as diffraction. He and Robert Hooke (1635–1703), independently, proposed the wave hypothesis of light. Diffraction of light takes place when an obstacle comes in its path, but it can be easily missed since the extent of light bending ($\theta \sim \frac{\lambda}{a} \sim 10^{-5}$) is rather small. In fact, the apparent absence of bending of light across corners and edges was taken as an evidence against the wave theory and in favor of the corpuscular theory of light. Diffraction is a universal wave phenomenon, vanishing only in the limit of zero wavelength. Diffraction makes sound audible behind edges of buildings and structures.

Light fields can induce currents in the obstacle material and these currents in turn can produce additional electromagnetic fields. Diffraction of light should therefore be described in terms of Maxwell's equations. In fact, Thomas Young (1773–1829) who demonstrated diffraction of light in his celebrated two-slit interference experiment (1802) had initially proposed this approach to describe diffraction. However, handling diffraction with Maxwell's equations is too horrendous a task. Sommerfeld was the first to exactly solve the problem of diffraction of a plane wave by a semi-infinite thin infinitely conducting plate (1896). This approach has been further extended by Smythe, Rubinowicz, Maggi, Wolf, and others. Rigorous solutions of this kind for the commonly employed diffracting geometries are difficult to obtain. To describe diffraction of light, Fresnel (1788–1827) extended Huygens' hypothesis of wave propagation to include the possibility of interference among Huygens' secondary wavelets. Kirchhoff (1824–1887) developed a rigorous theory of diffraction, but his theory also ignores the vector nature of light fields. Nevertheless, the results of his theory have withstood substantial experimental scrutiny.

7.2 HUYGENS' PRINCIPLE

Christian Huygens (1629–1695), a contemporary of Newton but a strong proponent of the wave theory of light, treated every point on an unobstructed wavefront as a secondary source of spherical wavelets which propagate with medium-dependent velocities in the forward directions. The envelope of these wavelets at a later time gives the new position of the wavefront (Fig. 7.1a).

Huygens' approach was merely graphical and made no reference to the phases and amplitudes of the secondary wavelets. However, quantitative laws of reflection and refraction at an infinite interface can be obtained on the basis of this principle. Since Huygens confined himself to the task of constructing the wavefront from its position at an earlier time, interference among the secondary wavelets played no role in this construction. Actually, Huygens was not concerned with diffraction at all. He was trying to explain the observed phenomenon of double refraction on the basis of the wave theory of light. It was much later that Fresnel, taking a clue from Young's interference experiment, explicitly stated the possibility of interference among Huygens' secondary wavelets. Figure 7.1a shows Huygens' construction. The radius of each wavelet drawn in Fig. 7.1a is $v\Delta t$, where Δt is the time taken by the wavefront to travel from its previous

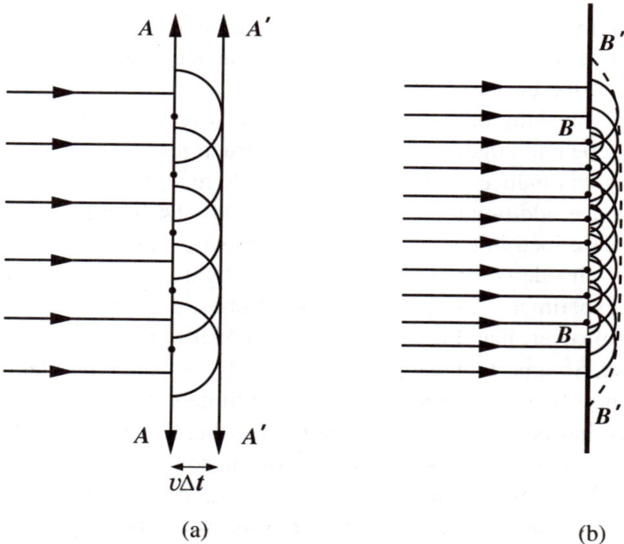

Fig. 7.1: (a) Huygens' construction; AA is an unobstructed plane wavefront. $A'A'$ is wavefront at a later time. (b) Fresnel's extension; BB is an obstructed wavefront. Subsequent wavefront $B'B'$ shows bending of light near the edges.

position to the present position with velocity v. Figure 7.1b is Fresnel's extension to an obstructed wavefront, leading to wave propagation in the shadow region.

7.3 HUYGENS–FRESNEL THEORY

Fresnel developed a mathematical theory of light diffraction based on Huygens' concept of secondary wavelets, but allowing the possibility of interference among these wavelets. Figure 7.2 shows the diffraction geometry. P_s may be taken as a monochromatic point source and P_o is the point of observation. The figure shows a section of the spherical wavefront reaching aperture $\sum$. Each point on the unobstructed portion of the wavefront in the plane of the aperture becomes Huygens' source of secondary wavelets. The net scalar field at the point of observation is the superposition of the fields produced by all such sources:

$$E(P_o) = \iint_{\Sigma} a_0 \frac{e^{ikr'}}{r'} K(\theta) \frac{e^{ikr''}}{r''} \, dS. \tag{7.1}$$

The factor $(a_0 \frac{e^{ikr'}}{r'})$ represents the field incident on the aperture, where a_0 is the amplitude of the spherical wave at unit distance from the source. The factor $e^{ikr''}/r''$ represents Huygens' spherical wavelet, with unit amplitude at unit distance, emanating from any given point of the aperture. Integration over the clear portion of the aperture automatically takes into account interference among the secondary wavelets. To ensure the absence of backward propagation of the secondary wavelets, Fresnel introduced a direction-dependent factor $K(\theta)$, with dimension of inverse length, which takes maximum value in the forward direction and null value for propagation back to the source. Fresnel developed the

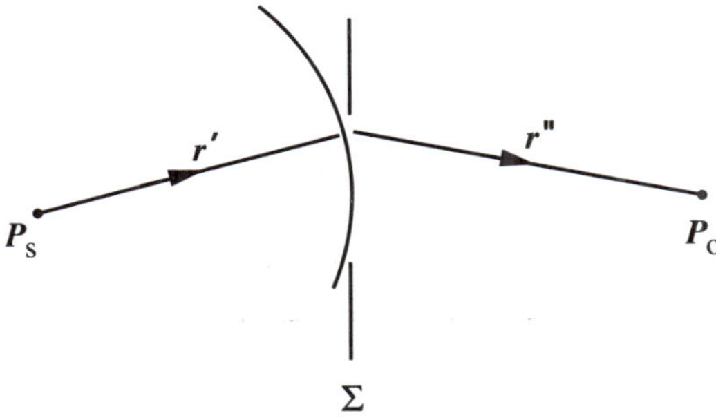

Fig. 7.2: Diffraction by an aperture.

concept of Fresnel zones to establish the consistency of Huygens–Fresnel theory with known facts about the propagation of spherical waves in free space. For details, the interested reader is referred to *Principles of Optics* by Born and Wolf.

7.4 KIRCHHOFF'S DIFFRACTION THEORY

The basic diffraction problem is to obtain the light field when an obstacle or an aperture of arbitrary shape is introduced between the source and point of observation. Here, the term aperture is used in the general sense. It includes the possibility when only the phase of the wavefront is modified, as for example with a transparent block of variable thickness or with a lens placed in the path of the light. Apart from its well-known focusing action, a lens diffracts the light waves. Even if all geometrical aberrations of a lens are eliminated, diffraction by the lens, as we shall see in a later chapter, does not permit a point image of a point object. The term *diffraction-limited optics* is used when diffraction, and not the geometrical aberrations of a lens, determines the ultimate quality of an optical image. Figure 7.3 shows the diffracting aperture $\sum$ between the point source P_s and point of observation P_o. The diffracted light field satisfies the homogeneous wave equation

$$\nabla^2 \vec{E}(\vec{r}, t) - \frac{1}{v^2} \frac{\partial^2}{\partial t^2} \vec{E}(\vec{r}, t) = 0 \tag{7.2}$$

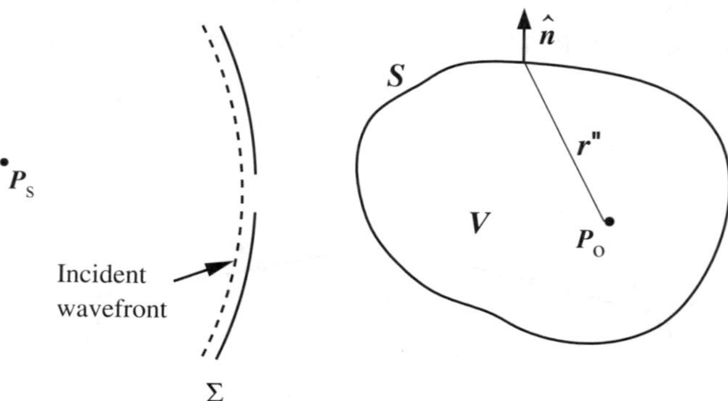

Fig. 7.3: Point source P_s in front of diffracting aperture $\sum$. Point of observation P_o is surrounded by an arbitrary surface S enclosing volume V. Unit vector $\hat{n}$ is along the outward normal to surface S.

in the source-free volume V bounded by the closed surface S. Instead of solving the vector wave equation, Kirchhoff chose to solve the corresponding scalar wave equation

$$\nabla^2 E(\vec{r}, t) - \frac{1}{v^2}\frac{\partial^2}{\partial t^2}E(\vec{r}, t) = 0. \tag{7.3}$$

In doing so, polarization effects in diffraction are ignored. Ordinarily, this may not be a serious limitation of the scalar theory of light diffraction except when the size of the diffracting aperture is not much larger than the wavelength of light. This is because the boundary conditions at an edge of the aperture are different for light waves polarized parallel and perpendicular to the plane of the edge. Nevertheless, it is hoped that the solutions of the scalar wave equation can describe light diffraction in most practical situations, irrespective of the state of polarization of light. Clearly, vector $\vec{E}$ cannot be replaced by $\hat{n}E$ (where $\hat{n}$ is some convenient unit vector) without running the risk of violating the divergence requirement ($\nabla\cdot \vec{E} = 0$) in the source-free space. However, E could represent any one component of the vector field $\vec{E}$. For the quasi-monochromatic light field

$$E(\vec{r}, t) = E(\vec{r})\mathrm{e}^{-\mathrm{i}\omega t} \tag{7.4}$$

of mean frequency ω, the complex spatial field $E(\vec{r})$ is the solution of the Helmholtz equation

$$(\nabla^2 + k^2)E(\vec{r}) = 0, \tag{7.5}$$

where $k^2 = \omega^2/c^2$. Let $\psi(\vec{r})$ be some other scalar field, also satisfying the Helmholtz equation. The fields $E(\vec{r})$ and $\psi(\vec{r})$ and their first and second partial derivatives are assumed finite and continuous within the volume V and also on all points on the surface S bounding this volume. Application of Gauss' theorem to the vectors $\psi\nabla E$ and $E\nabla\psi$ leads to the Green's theorem:

$$\oiint_S (E\nabla\psi - \psi\nabla E)\cdot \mathrm{d}\vec{S} = \iiint_V (E\nabla^2\psi - \psi\nabla^2 E)\mathrm{d}V, \tag{7.6}$$

where the integration on the left-hand side is over the closed surface S. The right-hand side of Eq. (7.6) is identically zero since the scalar fields E and ψ satisfy Eq. (7.5). Hence,

$$\oiint_S [E(\nabla\psi)\cdot\hat{n} - \psi(\nabla E)\cdot\hat{n}]\,\mathrm{d}S = 0, \tag{7.7}$$

where the area element $d\vec{S} = \hat{n}dS$. The unit vector $\hat{n}$ is along the outward (or inward, if chosen consistently) normal at a given point on the closed surface S. Since ψ is an arbitrary field satisfying Eq. (7.5), let it represent the spherical wave (suppressing the temporal factor $e^{-i\omega t}$)

$$\psi(r'') = \frac{e^{ikr''}}{r''} \tag{7.8}$$

propagating outward from the point of observation P_o with unit amplitude at unit distance. The validity of Green's theorem is then assured everywhere, except at point P_o. To get over this difficulty ($\psi \to \infty$), we exclude point P_o from the domain of applicability of Greens' theorem by surrounding it with a small spherical surface S' of radius ϵ, centered at P_o (Fig. 7.4).

The integration in Eq. (7.6) is now confined to the volume bounded between the surfaces S and S'. Accordingly, Eq. (7.7) can be written as

$$\begin{aligned}\oiint_S [E(\nabla\psi)\cdot\hat{n} - \psi(\nabla E)\cdot\hat{n}]\, dS \\ + \oiint_{S'} [E(\nabla\psi)\cdot\hat{n} - \psi(\nabla E)\cdot\hat{n}]\, dS' = 0,\end{aligned} \tag{7.9}$$

where

$$\begin{aligned}\nabla\psi\cdot\hat{n} &= \frac{\partial\psi}{\partial r''}\cos(\hat{r''}, \hat{n}) \\ &= \left(\frac{ik}{r''} - \frac{1}{r''^2}\right) e^{ikr''}\cos(\hat{r''}, \hat{n}).\end{aligned} \tag{7.10}$$

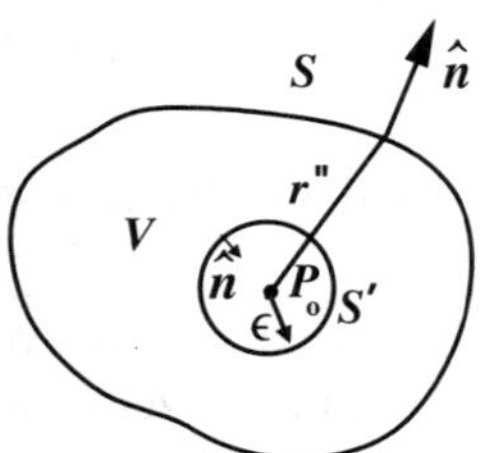

Fig. 7.4: Point of observation P_o is surrounded by a spherical surface S' of infinitesimally small radius ϵ. Green's theorem is applied in the space between surfaces S and S'.

This result holds for all points lying on S and S'. For points on S', $\cos(\hat{r''}, \hat{n}) = -1$ and $r'' = \epsilon$. Substituting Eq. (7.10) into Eq. (7.9), we have

$$\oiint_S [E(\nabla\psi)\cdot\hat{n} - \psi(\nabla E)\cdot\hat{n}]\,\mathrm{d}S = -\oiint_{S'} [-E\left(\frac{ik}{\epsilon} - \frac{1}{\epsilon^2}\right)e^{ik\epsilon} - \frac{\mathrm{e}^{ik\epsilon}}{\epsilon}(\nabla E)\cdot\hat{n}]\epsilon^2 \sin\theta\,\mathrm{d}\theta\,\mathrm{d}\phi, \tag{7.11}$$

where $\epsilon^2 \sin\theta \mathrm{d}\theta \mathrm{d}\phi$ is an area element on the spherical surface S'. In the limit $\epsilon \to 0$, the field at the observation point P_o approaches the field on the surface S'. Therefore, the right-hand side of Eq. (7.11) takes the value $-4\pi E(P_o)$, giving,

$$E(P_o) = -\frac{1}{4\pi}\oiint_S [E(\nabla\psi)\cdot\hat{n} - \psi(\nabla E)\cdot\hat{n}]\,\mathrm{d}S, \tag{7.12}$$

where ψ and $\nabla\psi$ are known and E is the field at any point on the closed surface S. This result is known as Kirchhoff's integral theorem. It reduces the problem of obtaining the field at a point due to an obstructed wavefront to solving the integral (7.12) over an arbitrarily chosen closed surface S, enclosing the point in question but excluding the sources. This, of course, requires the knowledge of the scalar field E and its normal derivative at every point on the chosen surface. Any convenient surface which facilitates the evaluation of the integral is good enough. This is quite different from the usual superposition approach where fields from all source points are added. Furthermore, the choice of the scalar field ψ is quite arbitrary. In fact, major criticism of Kirchhoff's theory arises from the over-specification of the boundary conditions. It should be enough to specify either E or $(\nabla E).\hat{n}$ on the bounding surface. However, with Kirchhoff's choice of ψ, both E and its normal derivative must be known on the surface S.

7.4.1 Kirchhoff's Boundary Conditions

Kirchhoff's diffraction integral in its present form does not appear to have any connection with the Huygens–Fresnel description of diffraction. The latter description would have required integration over the aperture to systematically incorporate contributions from the secondary wavelets emanating from the unobstructed portion of the wavefront. Instead, Eq. (7.12) involves integration over an arbitrary surface which may not even include the aperture plane. We shall now provide the missing link in the two descriptions. Consider a monochromatic point source P_s in front of a plane aperture as shown in Fig. 7.5. The dimensions of the aperture are assumed much smaller in comparison to the distances of the source and point of observation from the aperture. The infinite aperture screen

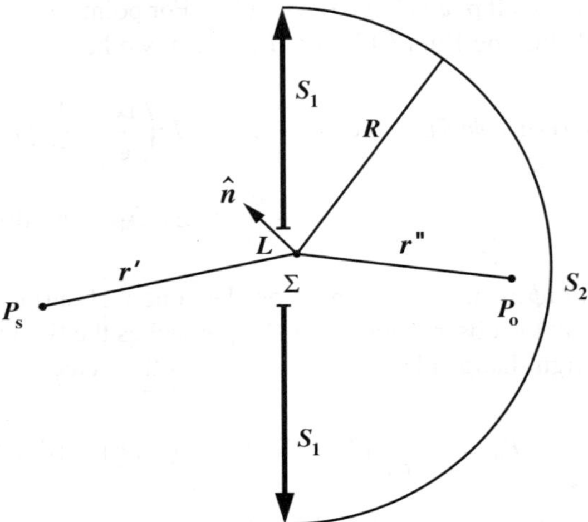

Fig. 7.5: Geometry for Kirchhoff's boundary conditions; L is a point within the aperture $\sum$, $\hat{n}$ is unit vector normal to the plane of the aperture.

is opaque, except for the portion $\sum$. The diffraction zone lies on the right of the aperture screen.

The integral in Eq. (7.12) may be solved over the closed surface consisting of the clear aperture $\sum$, the plane surface S_1 immediately behind the opaque portion of the aperture screen and the hemispherical surface S_2 of sufficiently large radius R. To proceed further, we need to know E and $\nabla E \cdot \hat{n}$ on this closed surface. Kirchhoff assumed the following boundary conditions:

$$\begin{aligned} E &= E_{\text{in}} \quad \text{on aperture} \textstyle\sum, \\ &= 0 \quad \text{on } S_1 \text{ and } S_2, \end{aligned} \tag{7.13a}$$

$$\begin{aligned} (\nabla E).\hat{n} &= (\nabla E_{\text{in}}) \cdot \hat{n} \quad \text{on aperture} \textstyle\sum, \\ &= 0 \quad \text{on } S_1 \text{ and } S_2. \end{aligned} \tag{7.13b}$$

Here, E_{in} stands for the field incident on the aperture. Kirchhoff's boundary conditions require the field E and its normal derivative on aperture $\sum$ to have the values which would be there if the aperture screen was removed but the source remained in its position. The field and its normal derivative are assumed to vanish on the remaining portions of the closed surface. This calls for some justification. The induced currents in the aperture material will certainly modify the field and its normal derivative at least for points close to the edges of the aperture. Kirchhoff neglected these modifications, perhaps under the implicit assumption that these modifications may be confined to distances no more than a few wavelengths from the edges, whereas aperture $\sum$ is assumed much larger on that scale. The screen S_1 is assumed to be completely opaque, so no field reaches the back side of the screen. Several arguments can be offered for the null field and its normal derivative on the hemispherical surface S_2. Here is one such argument. Radiation emitted by a polychromatic or a quasi-monochromatic light source never reaches the surface S_2, infinite distance away or alternatively one can rely on the Sommerfeld radiation condition

$$\lim_{R\to\infty} R[(\nabla E)\cdot\hat{n} - \mathrm{i}kE] = 0$$

for the field and its normal derivative to vanish on the hemispherical surface S_2 if there exists only an outgoing spherical wave in that region. We may also mention that Sommerfeld dealt with the problem concerning Kirchhoff's boundary conditions as well. He expressed the scalar field ψ in terms of two spherical waves

$$\psi_{\pm} = \frac{\mathrm{e}^{\mathrm{i}kr''}}{r''} \pm \frac{\mathrm{e}^{\mathrm{i}kr''_0}}{r''_0}, \tag{7.14}$$

where r''_0 is measured from the mirror image of the observation point with respect to the aperture plane. Nevertheless, Eq. (7.12) is extensively used in diffraction studies. Perhaps, one could interpret Kirchhoff's integral not as a boundary value problem but merely as an integral with known values of the field and its normal derivative at each point of the surface.

7.4.2 Fresnel–Kirchhoff Diffraction Formula

The field E and its normal derivative on the aperture, obtained from Kirchhoff's boundary conditions, are

$$E_{\mathrm{in}} = a_0 \frac{\mathrm{e}^{\mathrm{i}kr'}}{r'} \tag{7.15a}$$

and

$$(\nabla E_{\mathrm{in}})\cdot\hat{n} = a_0\left(\mathrm{i}k - \frac{1}{r'}\right)\frac{\mathrm{e}^{\mathrm{i}kr'}}{r'}\cos(\hat{r}', \hat{n}), \tag{7.15b}$$

respectively, where r' specifies the position of a point in the aperture with respect to the point source, a_0 is the amplitude of the spherical wave at unit distance from the source and $\hat{n}$ is the outward unit normal to the aperture (see Fig. 7.5). Substituting Eqs (7.10) and (7.15) into Eq. (7.12), we obtain

$$E(P_o) = -\frac{1}{4\pi}\iint_{\Sigma}\left[a_0\frac{e^{ikr'}}{r'}\left(ik-\frac{1}{r''}\right)\frac{e^{ikr''}}{r''}\cos(\hat{r''},\hat{n})\right]dS$$
$$+\frac{1}{4\pi}\iint_{\Sigma}\left[a_0\frac{e^{ikr''}}{r''}\left(ik-\frac{1}{r'}\right)\frac{e^{ikr'}}{r'}\cos(\hat{r'},\hat{n})\right]dS. \quad (7.16)$$

We now state the crucial assumption of Kirchhoff's theory of light diffraction. The distances of the source and observation points from any point in the aperture are much larger than the wavelength ($\lambda = 2\pi/k$) of light, i.e.,

$$r' \gg \lambda, \quad r'' \gg \lambda. \quad (7.17)$$

This condition can be satisfied for light waves, but not necessarily for all scalar fields. Hence, the following results of Kirchhoff's theory may not hold for scalar fields, not satisfying this condition. With the above assumption, Eq. (7.16) can be written in several equivalent forms of the Fresnel–Kirchhoff diffraction formula:

$$E(P_o) = -\frac{a_0}{2\pi}(ik)\iint_{\Sigma}\left[\frac{\cos(\hat{r''},\hat{n})-\cos(\hat{r'},\hat{n})}{2}\right]\frac{e^{ik(r'+r'')}}{r'r''}dS \quad (7.18a)$$

$$= -\frac{ia_0}{\lambda}\iint_{\Sigma}Q(\hat{r'},\hat{r''},\hat{n})\frac{e^{ik(r'+r'')}}{r'r''}dS \quad (7.18b)$$

$$= \iint_{\Sigma}\left(a_0\frac{e^{ikr'}}{r'}\right)Q(\hat{r'},\hat{r''},\hat{n})\left(\frac{e^{-i\frac{\pi}{2}}}{\lambda}\frac{e^{ikr''}}{r''}\right)dS, \quad (7.18c)$$

where the obliquity factor $Q(\hat{r'},\hat{r''},\hat{n})$ denoted simply as Q for subsequent use is defined as

$$Q = \frac{1}{2}\left[\cos(\hat{r''},\hat{n})-\cos(\hat{r'},\hat{n})\right]. \quad (7.19)$$

We first note that the Fresnel–Kirchhoff diffraction formula represents a superposition integral, adding elemental contributions from different portions of the aperture just as in the Huygens–Fresnel approach. Spherical waves of the type $e^{ikr''}/r''$, emanating from every point of the aperture with well-defined amplitudes and phases, propagate into the diffraction zone. These waves can be identified with the Huygens' secondary wavelets and represent diffraction in the sense that the aperture does not merely control the incident wavefront going through it (that is what the geometrical optics would have required), it somehow has become a source radiating in all directions. The obliquity factor Q controls the extent of diffraction in different directions. In particular, it forbids wave propagation in the backward direction ($Q=0$ when $\hat{r''}=\hat{r'}$). The clear portion of the aperture becoming a source of radiation is intriguing but this is exactly what the Huygens–Fresnel theory postulates. Kirchhoff's formulation goes beyond and exactly specifies the amplitudes and phases of the secondary wavelets. From the form (7.18c) of the Fresnel–Kirchhoff diffraction formula, the amplitude of a secondary wavelet may be taken as $1/\lambda$, where λ is the wavelength of light, and its phase may be taken to lead the phase of the incident wave by 90°. Interference effects among the secondary wavelets are automatically included because as the aperture is scanned in the process of integration, the phase factor $\mathrm{e}^{\mathrm{i}k(r'+r'')}$ changes. In fact, k is so large ($\sim 10^5\,\mathrm{cm}^{-1}$) for the light fields and phase $k(r'+r'')$ changes so rapidly that the secondary sources lying in a small region of the aperture in the neighborhood of the point of intersection of the line joining the source and point of observation with the plane of the aperture are the primary contributors to the diffraction integral. The path lengths $(r'+r'')$ between the source and point of observation through these points on the aperture are nearly equal. This is the stationarity argument which will be extensively exploited in later chapters. Rapid changes in the phases tend to nullify contributions from the remaining portions of the aperture. One may surmise that diffraction is indeed a small perturbation over geometrical optics. This also provides a partial justification for neglecting the edge effects in Kirchhoff's diffraction theory. It may also imply that the exact shape of the aperture may not be that important to interpret diffraction results. This point, however, cannot be over-emphasized. These considerations suggest that if angle $(\hat{r''}, \hat{n})=\theta$, then angle $(\hat{r'}, \hat{n})\approx\pi-\theta$, so that the obliquity factor can be approximated to

$$Q=\cos\theta, \tag{7.20}$$

where θ is the angle the line joining the source and point of observation makes with the normal to the aperture (Fig. 7.6). Furthermore, since θ remains constant for a given point of observation, Eq. (7.18b) simplifies to

$$E(P_\mathrm{o})=-\frac{\mathrm{i}a_0}{\lambda}\cos\theta\iint_\Sigma\frac{\mathrm{e}^{\mathrm{i}k(r'+r'')}}{r'r''}\mathrm{d}S. \tag{7.21}$$

Equations (7.18) and (7.21) demonstrate the interchangeability of the source and point of observation in a diffraction experiment. This is the statement of the reciprocity theorem.

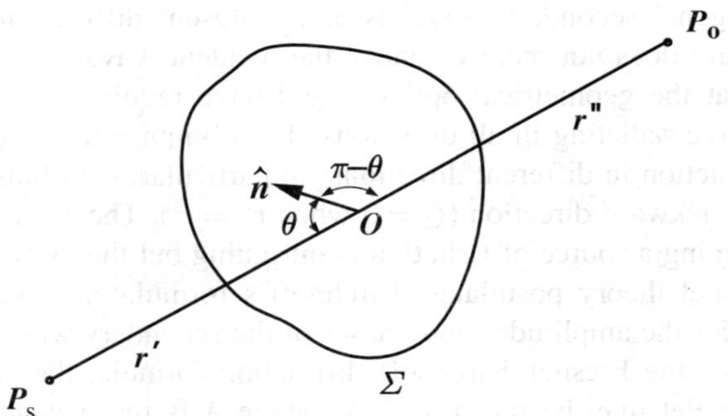

Fig. 7.6: Primary contribution to Kirchhoff's diffraction integral comes from portion of the aperture close to the point of intersection (O) of the line joining the point source and point of observation with the plane of the aperture.

With the obliquity factor Q replaced by a constant ($\cos\theta$), the information on the spatial extent of the aperture is contained in the sum $(r' + r'')$ in the phase factor and in the product $r'r''$ in the amplitude factor. Under the usual conditions of diffraction, the changes in r' and r'', as the aperture is scanned during integration, do not significantly change the amplitude factor $1/r'r''$ and we may replace it by the constant factor $1/R'_0R''_0$ (see Fig. 7.7). The sum $(r'+r'')$ also does not change much but as mentioned earlier, the phase $k(r'+r'')$ may change quite substantially. It is therefore essential to pay due attention to the changes in $(r'+r'')$. Figure 7.7 shows the geometry of the diffraction process.

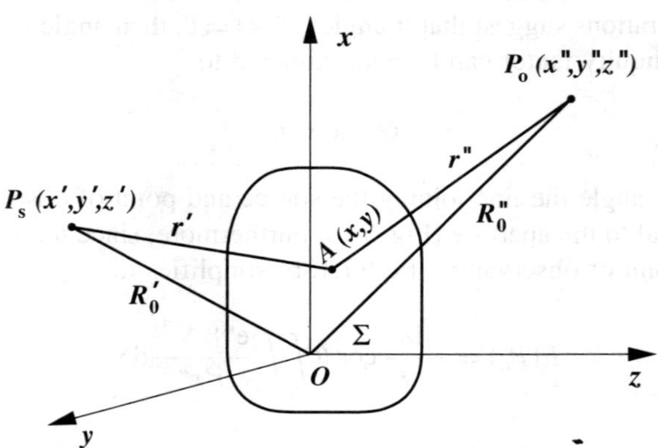

Fig. 7.7: Diffraction configuration; P_s is a monochromatic point source, P_o is the point of observation, A is a point in aperture $\sum$.

The position coordinates of the point source P_s and point of observation P_o are (x', y', z') and (x'', y'', z''), respectively. The origin of the coordinates lies in the plane of the aperture taken as the xy plane. A is a point in the aperture with position coordinates $(x, y, 0)$. From Fig. 7.7, we obtain

$$\begin{aligned} r' &= \left[(x-x')^2+(y-y')^2+(z')^2\right]^{1/2} \\ &= \left[R_0'^2-2(xx'+yy')+x^2+y^2\right]^{1/2} \\ &= R_0'\left[1-2\frac{xx'+yy'}{R_0'^2}+\frac{x^2+y^2}{R_0'^2}\right]^{1/2} \\ &= R_0'\left[1-\frac{xx'+yy'}{R_0'^2}+\frac{x^2+y^2}{2R_0'^2}-\frac{(xx'+yy')^2}{2R_0'^4}\right], \end{aligned} \tag{7.22}$$

where

$$R_0'^2 = x'^2+y'^2+z'^2. \tag{7.23}$$

Binomial expansion has been used in the penultimate step. Terms of order $(x^2/R_0'^2)^2$, $(y^2/R_0'^2)^2$, and higher have been neglected in the expansion. Similarly, we can write

$$r'' = R_0''\left[1-\frac{xx''+yy''}{R_0''^2}+\frac{x^2+y^2}{2R_0''^2}-\frac{(xx''+yy'')^2}{2R_0''^4}\right], \tag{7.24}$$

where

$$R_0''^2 = x''^2+y''^2+z''^2.$$

Combining Eqs (7.22) and (7.24),

$$\begin{aligned} r'+r'' = {}& (R_0'+R_0'')-x\left(\frac{x'}{R_0'}+\frac{x''}{R_0''}\right)-y\left(\frac{y'}{R_0'}+\frac{y''}{R_0''}\right) \\ &+\frac{1}{2}(x^2+y^2)\left(\frac{1}{R_0'}+\frac{1}{R_0''}\right)-\frac{1}{2R_0'}\left(\frac{xx'}{R_0'}+\frac{yy'}{R_0'}\right)^2 \\ &-\frac{1}{2R_0''}\left(\frac{xx''}{R_0''}+\frac{yy''}{R_0''}\right)^2 \end{aligned} \tag{7.25a}$$

$$\begin{aligned} ={}& (R_0'+R_0'')+x(l'-l'')+y(m'-m'')+\frac{1}{2}(x^2+y^2) \\ &\times\left(\frac{1}{R_0'}+\frac{1}{R_0''}\right)-\frac{1}{2R_0'}(xl'+ym')^2-\frac{1}{2R_0''}(xl''+ym'')^2, \end{aligned} \tag{7.25b}$$

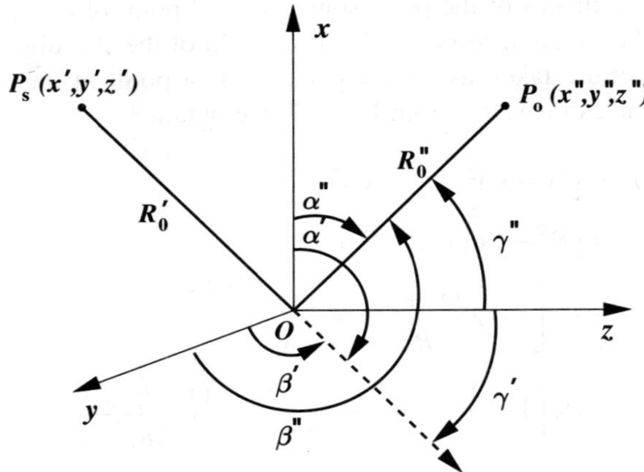

Fig. 7.8: Angles defining orientations of source and point of observation with respect to an origin lying in the plane of aperture.

where the direction cosines (l', m', n') and (l'', m'', n'') of the directions of propagation of the incident and diffracted waves are defined below with reference to Fig. 7.8:

$$l' = \cos\alpha' = -x'/R'_0, \tag{7.26a}$$

$$m' = \cos\beta' = -y'/R'_0, \tag{7.26b}$$

$$n' = \cos\gamma', \tag{7.26c}$$

$$l'' = \cos\alpha'' = x''/R''_0, \tag{7.26d}$$

$$m'' = \cos\beta'' = y''/R''_0, \tag{7.26e}$$

$$n'' = \cos\gamma''. \tag{7.26f}$$

The negative signs in the definitions of l' and m' make α' and β' greater than 90° for positive values of x' and y'.

The diffraction integral (Eq. 7.21) now takes the form

$$E(P_o) = -\frac{\mathrm{i}a_0}{\lambda}\cos\theta\frac{\mathrm{e}^{\mathrm{i}k(R'_0+R''_0)}}{R'_0R''_0}\iint\limits_{\Sigma} t(x, y)\mathrm{e}^{\mathrm{i}k\xi(x,y)}\,\mathrm{d}x\,\mathrm{d}y, \tag{7.27}$$

where

$$\xi(x, y) = x(l' - l'') + y(m' - m'') + \frac{1}{2}(x^2 + y^2)\left(\frac{1}{R_0'} + \frac{1}{R_0''}\right)$$
$$- \frac{1}{2R_0'}(xl' + ym')^2 - \frac{1}{2R_0''}(xl'' + ym'')^2 \tag{7.28}$$

and $t(x, y)$ is the transmission function of the aperture to be defined later.

7.5 REGIMES OF DIFFRACTION

Approximation (7.17) used to obtain the Fresnel–Kirchhoff diffraction formula restricts distances of the source and point of observation from the diffracting aperture to values much larger than the wavelength of light. Therefore, diffraction in the immediate neighborhood of the aperture cannot be investigated through this formalism. The diffraction zone which can be investigated with the diffraction integral (7.27) is further constrained by the binomial expansion used to obtain Eq. (7.22), which is justified only if

$$\frac{p^4}{R_0^3} \ll \lambda, \tag{7.29}$$

where p stands for the x and y coordinates of a point in the aperture and R_0 stands for R_0' and R_0'' (see Fig. 7.7). Taking for illustration, $p^4/R_0^3 = \lambda/100$, $p = 1\,\text{mm}$, $\lambda = 5 \times 10^{-5}\,\text{cm}$, gives $R_0 = 6\,\text{cm}$. Therefore, under these conditions, the source and observation points can be as close as a few centimeters from the aperture. The condition $p^4/R_0^3 = \lambda/100$ corresponds to a phase change of the order of a degree due to the first neglected term in the binomial expansion. Within this approximation, only the linear and quadratic phase factors need to be retained in the diffraction integral. This is the regime of Fresnel or the near-field diffraction characterized by a relatively large size aperture and large but not necessarily too large distances of the source and point of observation from the aperture. In Fresnel diffraction, the stationarity condition is satisfied over only a portion of the aperture as shown in Fig. 7.9.

Far-field or Fraunhofer diffraction occurs if the phase introduced by the quadratic factor is much less than 2π radians. This requires

$$\frac{p^2}{R_0} \ll \lambda. \tag{7.30}$$

To get a feel for the numbers in a Fraunhofer diffraction experiment, we may quantify Eq. (7.30) as $p^2/R_0 = \lambda/100$. For the earlier example of $p = 1\,\text{mm}$,

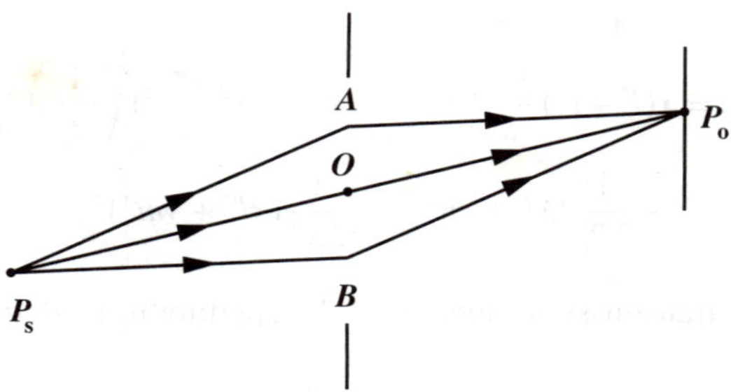

Fig. 7.9: In Fresnel diffraction, only a part of the aperture is covered by optical paths of nearly equal lengths.

$\lambda = 5 \times 10^{-5}$ cm, R_0 is 200 m – an unmanageable distance for a laboratory experiment. For Fraunhofer diffraction, the path length $(r' + r'')$ between the source and point of observation has linear dependence on the position coordinates of a point in the aperture. This condition is met for plane wavefronts reaching and leaving the aperture as shown in Fig. 7.10 for the incident wavefront. In this case, the path lengths between the source and point of observation passing through two points in the aperture separated by a distance x differ by $x \sin \alpha$, where α is the inclination of the incident wavefront with the plane of the aperture. To observe Fraunhofer diffraction, the aperture is kept small and the source and observation points are located far away from the aperture so that the stationarity condition is satisfied over most of the aperture (Fig. 7.11).

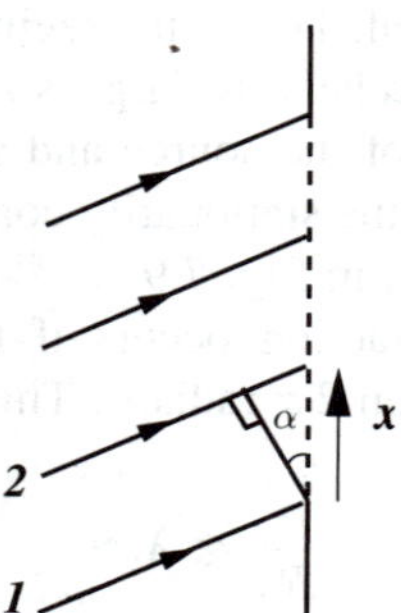

Fig. 7.10: Fraunhofer diffraction is realized with plane wavefronts reaching and leaving the aperture.

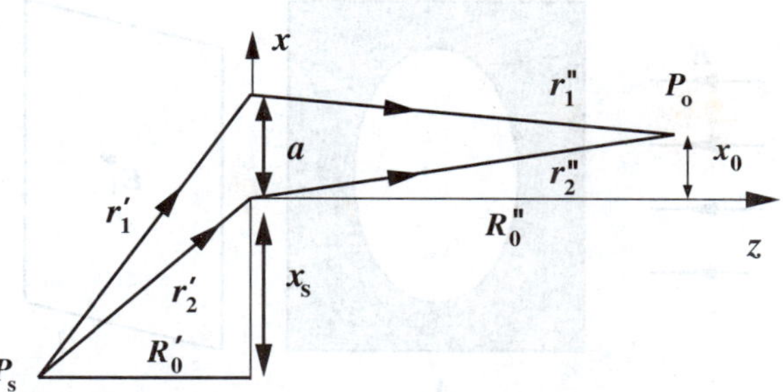

Fig. 7.11: In Fraunhofer diffraction, most of aperture is covered by optical paths of nearly equal lengths.

The path difference Δ for the extreme portions of the aperture is

$$\begin{aligned}\Delta &= (r_1' + r_1'') - (r_2' + r_2'') \\ &= R_0'\left[1 + \frac{(a+x_s)^2}{R_0'^2}\right]^{1/2} + R_0''\left[1 + \frac{(a-x_0)^2}{R_0''^2}\right]^{1/2} \\ &\quad - R_0'\left[1 + \frac{x_s^2}{R_0'^2}\right]^{1/2} - R_0''\left[1 + \frac{x_0^2}{R_0''^2}\right]^{1/2}. \\ &= a\left(\frac{x_s}{R_0'} - \frac{x_0}{R_0''}\right) + \frac{a^2}{2}\left(\frac{1}{R_0'} + \frac{1}{R_0''}\right) + \cdots,\end{aligned} \tag{7.31}$$

where a characterizes the dimensions of the aperture. To keep path difference Δ to within a fraction of a wavelength of light to satisfy the stationarity condition over the entire aperture, the source and observation points need to be moved very far (optical infinity). Fraunhofer regime is more easily realized with the use of lenses.

7.6 BABINET'S PRINCIPLE

Fresnel–Kirchhoff diffraction formula demonstrates an interesting feature recognized as Babinet's principle. We note that the integration in Eq. (7.27) is to be carried over the clear portion of the aperture screen. The field at the observation point does not change if this integral is expressed as a sum of any number of integrals as long as the areas covered by the individual integrals add upto the original aperture area.

Consider the apertures shown in Fig. 7.12. The clear portions of apertures A_1 and A_2 together cover the entire xy plane. The apertures A_1 and A_2 are

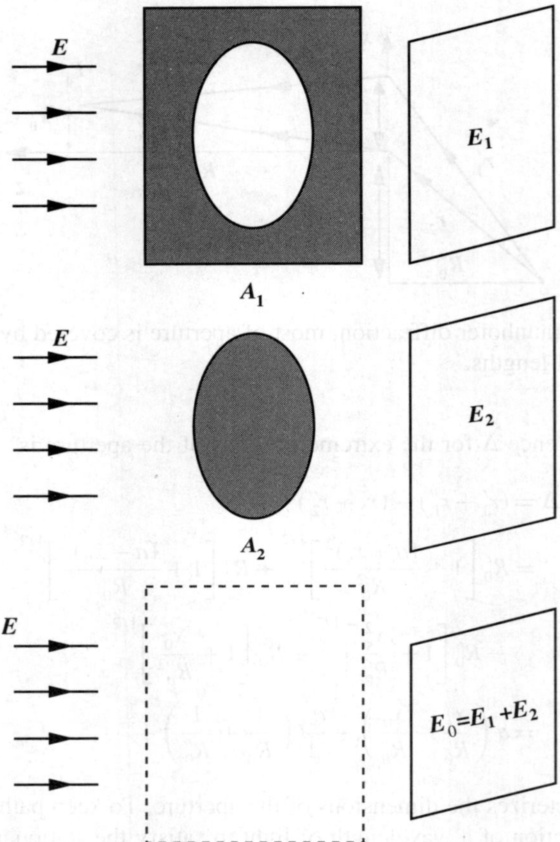

Fig. 7.12: Apertures A_1 and A_2 are complementary if clear portion of A_1 equals opaque portion of A_2 and vice versa.

considered complementary to each other if the clear portions of aperture A_1 exactly correspond to the opaque portions of aperture A_2 and vice versa. We can therefore write

$$E_0(P_o) = E_1(P_o) + E_2(P_o), \tag{7.32}$$

where E_1 is the field at the observation point P_o when only aperture A_1 is present and E_2 is the field at the same point P_o when only aperture A_2 is present, and E_0 is the field at P_o in the absence of both apertures. The quasi-monochromatic source remains in position during these measurements. We can re-write Eq. (7.32) as

$$E_1(P_o) = E_0(P_o) - E_2(P_o)$$

or as

$$E_2(P_o) = E_0(P_o) - E_1(P_o).$$

Equation (7.32) or its equivalent forms constitute the statement of the Babinet's principle. It allows us to express diffraction effects of an aperture in terms of the diffraction effects of its complementary aperture. To appreciate the complementary nature of the apertures, we consider a few special cases. We first consider an observation point of zero intensity in the absence of apertures A_1 and A_2. With $E_0(P_o) = 0$,

$$E_1(P_o) = -E_2(P_o),$$

and

$$I_1(P_o) = I_2(P_o).$$

Thus at points of zero field in the absence of any aperture, the complementary apertures give rise to identical irradiance, but phase-reversed fields. This situation occurs, for example, in the image plane of an optical system beyond the sharp image. If, on the other hand, the observation point is chosen at the dark fringe of aperture A_1 $[E_1(P_o) = 0]$, then

$$E_2(P_o) = E_0(P_o). \tag{7.33}$$

Thus, the field due to an aperture exactly equals the field in the absence of any aperture at points of zero field of its complementary aperture. These aspects of Kirchhoff's theory can be readily verified. Babinet's principle, being a characteristic of the diffraction integral, is applicable to Fresnel as well as Fraunhofer diffractions. However, its manifestations are mostly found in Fraunhofer diffraction. This is because in Fresnel diffraction, there are no points of zero field in the absence of apertures. On the other hand, in the image plane of an optical system (Fraunhofer diffraction regime), zero field exists beyond the image area.

7.7 REFERENCES

7.1 Max Born and Emil Wolf, Principles of Optics, 7th ed., Cambridge University Press, Cambridge, 1999.

7.2 Robert D. Guenther, Modern Optics, John Wiley & Sons, New York, 1990.

7.8 PROBLEMS

7.1 Use Huygens' principle to obtain the laws of reflection and refraction of light across an infinite interface between two media.

7.2 Using the scalar function ψ of Eq. (7.14), obtain a modified form of the Fresnel–Kirchhoff diffraction formula.

7.3 Show that the obliquity factor defined in Eq. (7.19) is consistent with the reciprocity statement.

7.4 Find a value for the nominal size of the diffracting aperture if Fresnel approximation is to be valid for distances of the order of 100 wavelengths of light from the aperture.

7.5 What typical size of an aperture is needed to perform a good quality Fraunhofer diffraction experiment in the laboratory without a lens? Specify the corresponding distances of the source and point of observation from the aperture.

CHAPTER **8**

Fresnel Diffraction

8.1 NEAR-FIELD DIFFRACTION

Near-field diffraction can be divided into two broad categories – diffraction very close to the aperture and diffraction relatively farther away from the aperture. Diffraction within a distance of a few wavelengths of light from the aperture will not be discussed here. But this is an important distance regime in which the resolution of a microscope can be extended beyond the usual limit of one wavelength or so (see Section 11.7.1). Certain object details are simply not available at far off points. They are lost on the way. Diffraction in the immediate proximity of an object is difficult to investigate because the basic assumption (Eq. 7.17) of Kirchhoff's formalism may not hold and, in addition, it may not be easy to delink the source and detector in this distance regime. Fresnel diffraction refers to the case of diffraction relatively farther away and can be described by the diffraction integral in its present form (Eq. 7.27). However, evaluation of the diffraction integral is made difficult by the presence of the linear and quadratic phase factors. It is possible to eliminate the linear phase factor by a proper choice of the origin of coordinates. Figure 8.1 shows the diffracting aperture $\sum$ lying in the xy plane behind the point source P_s. P_o is the point of observation. The origin O is chosen to be the point of intersection of the line joining the point source and point of observation with the plane of the aperture. The x-axis is taken along the projection of the line P_sOP_o in the plane of the aperture.

In this coordinate system, the position coordinates of the point source and point of observation are (x', y', z') and (x'', y'', z''), respectively. Accordingly, Eqs (7.26), with reference to Fig. 7.8, give

$$l' = -\frac{x'}{R_0'} = \sin\theta = \frac{x''}{R_0''} = l'', \tag{8.1a}$$

$$m' = -\frac{y'}{R_0'} = 0 = \frac{y''}{R_0''} = m'', \tag{8.1b}$$

$$n'' = n' = \cos\theta, \tag{8.1c}$$

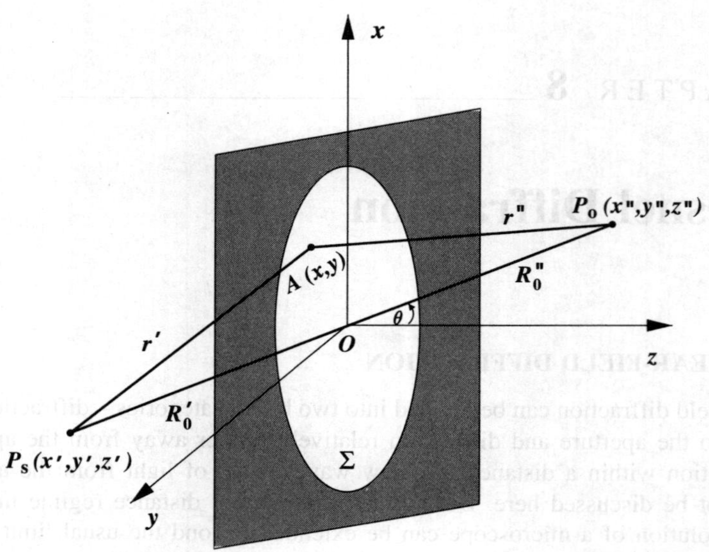

Fig. 8.1: Geometry for Fresnel diffraction; P_s is a point source, P_o is point of observation, A is a point in the aperture lying in the xy plane. Origin O is the point of intersection of the line joining the point source and point of observation with the plane of aperture.

where θ is the angle the line P_sOP_o, lying in the xz plane, makes with the z-axis. With this choice of the coordinate system, the linear phase term vanishes and the diffraction integral (Eq. 7.27) takes the simpler form

$$E(P_o) = -\frac{\mathrm{i}a_0}{\lambda}\cos\theta\,\frac{\mathrm{e}^{\mathrm{i}k(R_0'+R_0'')}}{R_0'R_0''}\iint_{\Sigma} t(x,y)\,\mathrm{e}^{\mathrm{i}\frac{\pi}{\lambda}\left(\frac{1}{R_0'}+\frac{1}{R_0''}\right)(x^2\cos^2\theta+y^2)}\,\mathrm{d}x\,\mathrm{d}y, \qquad (8.2)$$

where $t(x, y)$ represents the amplitude transmission function of the aperture and a_0 is the amplitude of the incident spherical wave at unit distance from the source. In writing Eq. (8.2), the terms $(x^2/R_0')(x'/R_0')^2$ and $(x^2/R_0'')(x''/R_0'')^2$ in Eq. (7.28) have been neglected in comparison to x^2/R_0' and x^2/R_0'' because for typical diffraction geometries $x'^2/R_0'^2 \ll 1$, $x''^2/R_0''^2 \ll 1$. Accordingly, angle θ in Fig. 8.1 is rather small.

The diffraction integral can be transformed to the form of Eq. (8.2) even when the aperture is illuminated by a plane wave provided the origin is chosen at the foot of the perpendicular drawn from the point of observation to the plane of the aperture. Under conditions of Fresnel diffraction (Eq. 7.29), the quadratic phase term in the diffraction integral introduces a phase change which is usually in excess of 2π radians. Therefore, for Fresnel diffraction,

$$\frac{p^2}{R_0} > \lambda, \tag{8.3}$$

where p stands for the x, y coordinates of a point in the aperture and R_0 represents R_0', R_0'' in Eq. (8.2). Defining

$$u = \sqrt{\frac{2}{\lambda}\left(\frac{1}{R_0'} + \frac{1}{R_0''}\right)}\, x \cos\theta, \tag{8.4a}$$

$$v = \sqrt{\frac{2}{\lambda}\left(\frac{1}{R_0'} + \frac{1}{R_0''}\right)}\, y, \tag{8.4b}$$

the diffraction integral can be re-written as

$$E(P_o) = \frac{a_0 e^{ik(R_0'+R_0'')}}{R_0' + R_0''} \iint_{\Sigma} \left(-\frac{i}{2}\right) t(x, y)\, e^{i\frac{\pi}{2}(u^2+v^2)}\, du\, dv. \tag{8.5}$$

The pre-factor in Eq. (8.5) is exactly the field of the unobstructed spherical wave originating from the point source and reaching the point of observation. The integral in Eq. (8.5) therefore represents the modification in amplitude and phase, of the unobstructed spherical wave, caused by the presence of the aperture.

It may appear inconvenient to link the origin of the coordinate system with the point of observation. Nevertheless, this choice simplifies the diffraction integral considerably. Additional justification for this choice of the origin comes from the stationarity argument of Section 7.4.2, according to which, major contribution to the diffraction integral comes from points of the aperture which lie close to the chosen origin. We now consider some specific examples of Fresnel diffraction.

8.2 RECTANGULAR APERTURE

Figure 8.2 shows a rectangular aperture of height a and width b. The line joining the point source P_s and observation point P_o intersects the aperture at O which is taken as the origin of the coordinates. The center C of the aperture

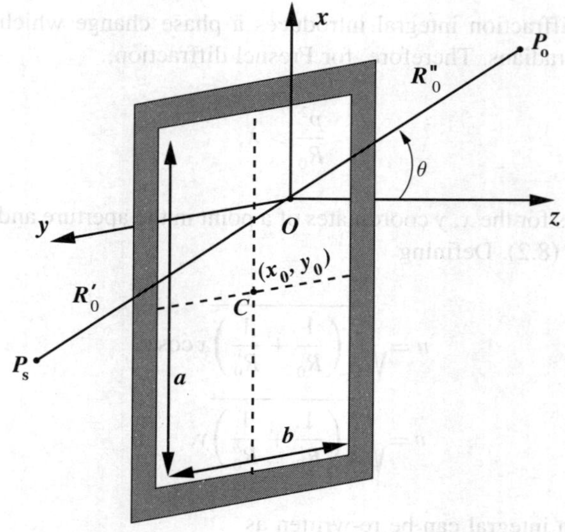

Fig. 8.2: Geometry for Fresnel diffraction from a rectangular aperture; C is the center of the aperture.

has position coordinates (x_0, y_0) with respect to the origin O. The aperture function is

$$\begin{aligned} t(x, y) &= 1 \quad \text{for} \quad x_0 - \frac{a}{2} \le x \le x_0 + \frac{a}{2}, \\ &\qquad\qquad y_0 - \frac{b}{2} \le y \le y_0 + \frac{b}{2}, \\ &= 0 \quad \text{otherwise.} \end{aligned} \tag{8.6}$$

The field at P_o is

$$E(P_o) = \frac{a_0 e^{ik(R'_0 + R''_0)}}{R'_0 + R''_0} \left(-\frac{i}{2}\right) \left[\int_{u_1}^{u_2} e^{i\frac{\pi}{2}u^2}\, du \int_{v_1}^{v_2} e^{i\frac{\pi}{2}v^2}\, dv \right], \tag{8.7}$$

where the integration limits are given by

$$u_1 = \sqrt{\frac{2}{\lambda}\left(\frac{1}{R'_0} + \frac{1}{R''_0}\right)}(x_0 - a/2), \tag{8.8a}$$

$$u_2 = \sqrt{\frac{2}{\lambda}\left(\frac{1}{R'_0} + \frac{1}{R''_0}\right)}(x_0 + a/2), \tag{8.8b}$$

$$v_1 = \sqrt{\frac{2}{\lambda}\left(\frac{1}{R'_0} + \frac{1}{R''_0}\right)}(y_0 - b/2), \tag{8.8c}$$

$$v_2 = \sqrt{\frac{2}{\lambda}\left(\frac{1}{R'_0} + \frac{1}{R''_0}\right)}(y_0 + b/2). \tag{8.8d}$$

Without introducing much error, the obliquity factor ($\cos\theta$) has been taken as one. The complex integrals in Eq. (8.7) can be expressed in terms of the Fresnel integrals, defined as

$$C(w) = \int_0^w \cos\left(\frac{\pi}{2}q^2\right) \mathrm{d}q, \tag{8.9a}$$

$$S(w) = \int_0^w \sin\left(\frac{\pi}{2}q^2\right) \mathrm{d}q. \tag{8.9b}$$

Table A1 (Appendix A) gives values of the Fresnel integrals for w lying between 0 and 7.7. Some of the properties of the Fresnel integrals are given below:

$$C(0) = S(0) = 0, \tag{8.10a}$$

$$C(-\infty) = S(-\infty) = -1/2, \tag{8.10b}$$

$$C(+\infty) = S(+\infty) = +1/2, \tag{8.10c}$$

$$C(-w) = -C(w), \tag{8.10d}$$

$$S(-w) = -S(w). \tag{8.10e}$$

Equation (8.7), when expressed in terms of the Fresnel integrals, takes the form

$$E(P_o) = \frac{a_0 \mathrm{e}^{\mathrm{i}k(R'_0+R''_0)}}{R'_0 + R''_0}\left(-\frac{\mathrm{i}}{2}\right)[C(u_2) - C(u_1) + \mathrm{i}\{S(u_2) - S(u_1)\}] \\ \times [C(v_2) - C(v_1) + \mathrm{i}\{S(v_2) - S(v_1)\}], \tag{8.11}$$

giving the intensity at the point of observation as

$$I(P_o) = \left(\frac{1}{2}\epsilon_0 c\right) E(P_o)E^*(P_o) \\ = \frac{I_0}{4}\left[\{C(u_2) - C(u_1)\}^2 + \{S(u_2) - S(u_1)\}^2\right] \\ \times \left[\{C(v_2) - C(v_1)\}^2 + \{S(v_2) - S(v_1)\}^2\right], \tag{8.12}$$

where

$$I_0 = \frac{1}{2}\epsilon_0 c \frac{a_0^2}{(R_0' + R_0'')^2}$$

is the unobstructed (in the absence of aperture) intensity at P_o.

For the center of the Fresnel diffraction pattern, the origin O coincides with the center of the aperture ($x_0 = 0, y_0 = 0$), so that

$$u_2 = -u_1 = \sqrt{\frac{2}{\lambda}\left(\frac{1}{R_0'} + \frac{1}{R_0''}\right)}\frac{a}{2} \tag{8.13a}$$

and

$$v_2 = -v_1 = \sqrt{\frac{2}{\lambda}\left(\frac{1}{R_0'} + \frac{1}{R_0''}\right)}\frac{b}{2}. \tag{8.13b}$$

Accordingly, the intensity at the center of the diffraction pattern is

$$I(P_c) = 4I_0[\{C(u_2)\}^2 + \{S(u_2)\}^2][\{C(v_2)\}^2 + \{S(v_2)\}^2]. \tag{8.14}$$

For known values of R_0', R_0'', a, b, and λ, values of the Fresnel integrals can be obtained from the tables. To find intensity at any other point in the plane of observation, the origin will have to be relocated as mentioned earlier. The limits of integration (Eqs 8.8) will change because of the change in the coordinates (x_0, y_0) of the center of the aperture with respect to the new origin. This process can be repeated to generate the field at any point in the plane of observation. There is, however, an elegant graphical procedure devised by the French scientist Marie Alfred Cornu to obtain Fresnel diffraction intensities for the rectangular apertures. It makes use of a geometrical construction, known as the Cornu spiral.

8.2.1 The Cornu Spiral

Table A1 (Appendix A) reveals that the Fresnel integrals take a rather small range of values. A graphical representation of $C(w)$ as a function of $S(w)$ or vice versa for a large range of values of w is possible. Such a plot in the complex plane with $C(w)$ along the real axis and $S(w)$ along the imaginary axis generates a spiral in the first and third quadrants, called the Cornu spiral (Fig. 8.3).

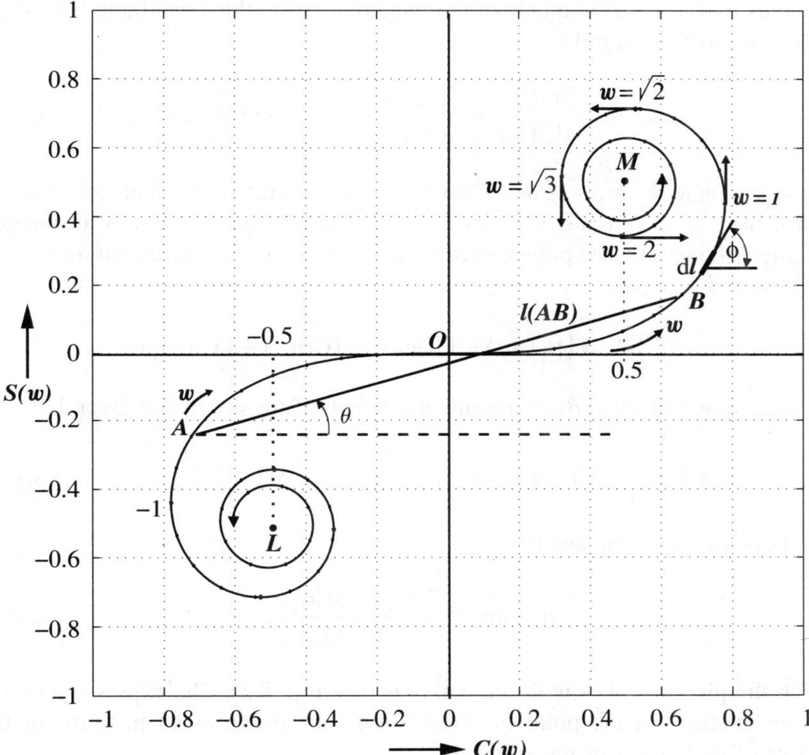

Fig. 8.3: The Cornu spiral.

The spiral passes through the origin O and asymptotically approaches the points $L(-\frac{1}{2}, -\frac{1}{2})$ and $M(+\frac{1}{2}, +\frac{1}{2})$ for w approaching $-\infty$ and $+\infty$, respectively. The points L and M are sometimes called the eyes of the Cornu spiral. A differential element of the length of the arc of the spiral is

$$\begin{aligned} \mathrm{d}l &= \left[(\mathrm{d}S(w))^2 + (\mathrm{d}C(w))^2\right]^{1/2} \\ &= \left[\sin^2\left(\frac{\pi}{2}w^2\right) + \cos^2\left(\frac{\pi}{2}w^2\right)\right]^{1/2} \mathrm{d}w \\ &= \mathrm{d}w. \end{aligned} \tag{8.15}$$

Therefore w, in either direction from the origin, is a measure of the length of an arc of the spiral. Points on the spiral can be labeled by the values of w. We take

w as positive in the first quadrant and negative in the third quadrant. The slope at any point of the spiral is

$$\tan\phi = \frac{dS(w)}{dC(w)} = \frac{\sin(\pi w^2/2)}{\cos(\pi w^2/2)} = \tan(\pi w^2/2). \tag{8.16}$$

The slope angle ϕ varies as w^2. The horizontal and vertical tangents to the spiral appear at $w = \pm\sqrt{2n}$ and $w = \pm\sqrt{2n+1}$, respectively, where n is an integer. The line joining any two points on the spiral represents a complex number called the Phasor, i.e.,

$$\text{Ph}(AB) = [\{C(w_B) + iS(w_B)\} - \{C(w_A) + iS(w_A)\}]. \tag{8.17}$$

The magnitude of Ph(AB) represents the length of the chord AB given by

$$l(AB) = \left[\{C(w_B) - C(w_A)\}^2 + \{S(w_B) - S(w_A)\}^2\right]^{1/2} \tag{8.18a}$$

and its phase gives the angle

$$\theta = \tan^{-1}\frac{S(w_B) - S(w_A)}{C(w_B) - C(w_A)}, \tag{8.18b}$$

which the phasor makes with the real axis (see Fig. 8.3). The expression (8.12) for the intensity at the point of observation can be expressed in terms of the lengths of the chords of the spiral, i.e.,

$$I(P_o) = \frac{I_0}{4} l_1^2(u_1, u_2) l_2^2(v_1, v_2). \tag{8.19}$$

To find the intensity at any point in the plane of observation, one first locates the appropriate origin in the plane of the aperture, as described in Section 8.1. The coordinates (x_0, y_0) of the center of the aperture with respect to this origin determine the limits of integration u_1, u_2, v_1, and v_2. The points $w = u_1, u_2, v_1$, and v_2 are then marked on the same Cornu spiral and the chord lengths $l_1(u_1, u_2)$ and $l_2(v_1, v_2)$ may be measured with a scale to obtain the intensity at the point of observation. The use of the Cornu spiral is particularly convenient since w is a dimensionless quantity.

8.2.2 Narrow Slit

A rectangular aperture becomes a narrow slit if one of its sides is allowed to extend indefinitely and the other made small (Fig. 8.4).

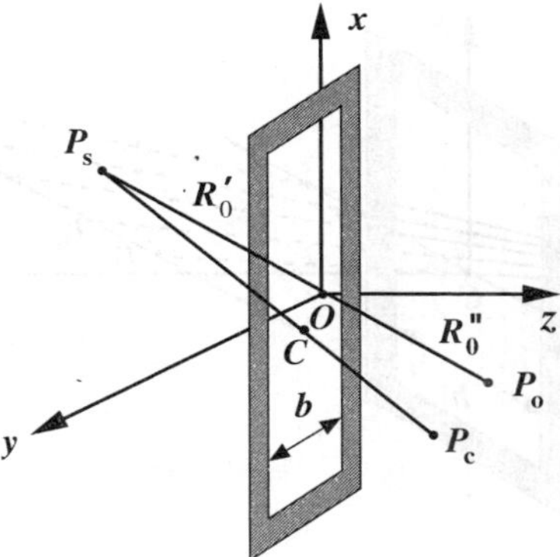

Fig. 8.4: Geometry for Fresnel diffraction from a long, narrow slit.

With $\pm a/2 = \pm\infty$, Eq. (8.12) reduces to

$$I(P_o) = \frac{I_0}{2}\left[\{C(w_2) - C(w_1)\}^2 + \{S(w_2) - S(w_1)\}^2\right], \tag{8.20}$$

where

$$w_1 = \sqrt{\frac{2}{\lambda}\left(\frac{1}{R_0'} + \frac{1}{R_0''}\right)}(y_0 - b/2), \tag{8.21a}$$

$$w_2 = \sqrt{\frac{2}{\lambda}\left(\frac{1}{R_0'} + \frac{1}{R_0''}\right)}(y_0 + b/2). \tag{8.21b}$$

Here, y_0 locates the center of the slit with respect to the chosen origin O. The intensity at the center of the diffraction pattern ($y_0 = 0$) is

$$I(P_c) = 2I_0\left[\{C(w_2)\}^2 + \{S(w_2)\}^2\right]. \tag{8.22}$$

The origin in this case coincides with the center of the slit. For an infinitely long slit, no intensity changes should occur if the observation point is shifted parallel to the length of the slit, but the intensity changes as the observation point is shifted in the perpendicular direction. The origin moves from C to E as the observation point is moved anti-parallel to the y-axis from the center of the diffraction pattern P_c to P_e along the line GH (Fig. 8.5). The origin lies at the edge of the slit for the observation point P_b and in the opaque portion of the aperture screen for observations in the geometric shadow of the aperture.

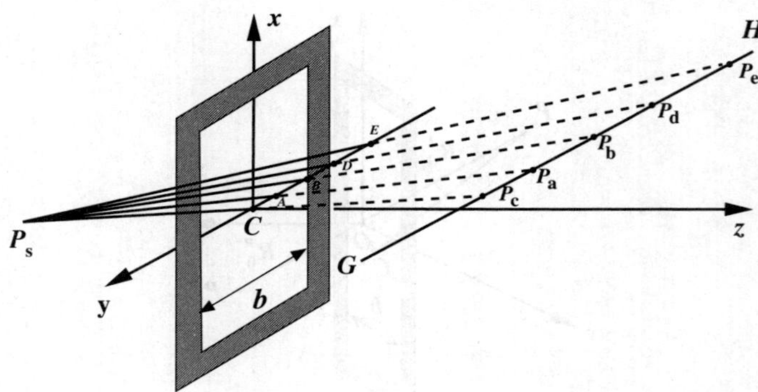

Fig. 8.5: Fresnel Diffraction from a narrow slit; as point of observation is shifted from P_c to P_e, the origin shifts from C to E.

The intensity at the edge of the geometric shadow can be obtained from Eq. (8.20) with

$$w_1 = 0 \text{ and } w_2 = \sqrt{\frac{2}{\lambda}\left(\frac{1}{R_0'} + \frac{1}{R_0''}\right)}\, b.$$

For points within the geometric shadow, the integration limits are

$$w_1 = \sqrt{\frac{2}{\lambda}\left(\frac{1}{R_0'} + \frac{1}{R_0''}\right)}\, d$$

and

$$w_2 = \sqrt{\frac{2}{\lambda}\left(\frac{1}{R_0'} + \frac{1}{R_0''}\right)}\,(d+b),$$

where d is the displacement of the origin along the y-axis with respect to the edge of the slit. Similar statements can be made when observations are made in the geometric shadow on the other side of the slit. The midpoint w_0 and the arc length Δw between the limiting points w_1 and w_2 on the spiral are defined as

$$w_0 = \frac{w_1 + w_2}{2} = \sqrt{\frac{2}{\lambda}\left(\frac{1}{R_0'} + \frac{1}{R_0''}\right)}\, y_0 \qquad (8.23)$$

and

$$\Delta w = w_2 - w_1 = \sqrt{\frac{2}{\lambda}\left(\frac{1}{R_0'} + \frac{1}{R_0''}\right)}b, \tag{8.24}$$

respectively. The arc length Δw, determined by the parameters of the Fresnel diffraction (R_0', R_0'', b, λ), does not change with the point of observation. The midpoint w_0 of the arc, however, changes with the point of observation. Equation (8.20) can be rewritten as

$$I(P_o) = \frac{I_0}{2} l^2(w_0, \Delta w), \tag{8.25}$$

where $l(w_0, \Delta w)$ represents the length of the chord of the arc of length Δw centered at point w_0 on the Cornu spiral. Different observation points are explored by simply sliding this arc of fixed length along the spiral and measuring the corresponding chord lengths. To illustrate this procedure, we take $\Delta w = 1.0$. This may correspond to, for example, $R_0' = R_0'' = 8\,\text{m}$, $b = 1.0\,\text{mm}$, and $\lambda = 500\,\text{nm}$. This choice of the distances and the aperture size may be more typical of Fraunhofer than Fresnel diffraction. We have chosen these numbers to emphasize the fact that no clear demarcation exists between the two diffraction regimes. The center of the diffraction pattern corresponds to positioning of this arc (arc *AB* in Fig. 8.6) symmetrically on the Cornu spiral with its midpoint coinciding with the origin *O*. As the point of observation moves away from the center of the diffraction pattern towards point P_d and beyond (see Fig. 8.5), the y-coordinate of the center of the aperture and hence w_0 changes from zero to positive values. This represents the movement of the arc *AB* of length Δw up the spiral toward point

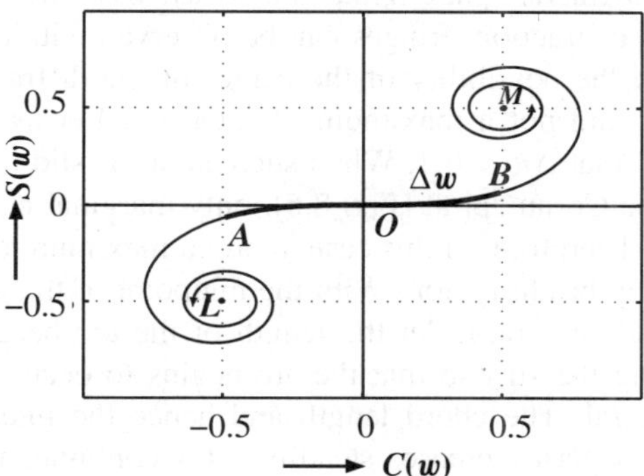

Fig. 8.6: Use of Cornu spiral to obtain intensity distribution in Fresnel diffraction from a narrow slit.

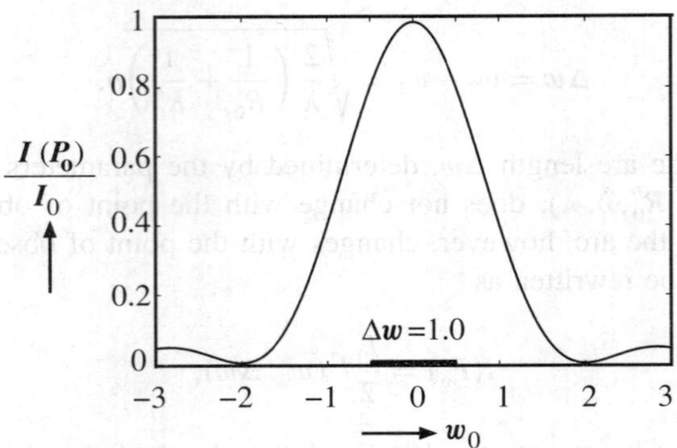

Fig. 8.7: Normalized intensity distribution of Fresnel diffraction from a narrow slit. Dark line on abscissa marks geometrically bright region. A change in w_0 represents a shift of point of observation.

M. The chord length $l(w_0, \Delta w)$ first decreases, resulting in fall in the intensity as one moves away from the center of the diffraction pattern. However, continued climb up the spiral is accompanied by the chord length going through successive maximum and minimum values as the arc slides over the sharply bending portions of the spiral. The resulting intensity changes are shown in Fig. 8.7.

8.2.2.1 Intensity Variations in the Geometrically Bright Region

Figure 8.7 shows that for $\Delta w = 1.0$, the intensity at the center of the diffraction pattern, which is also the center of the geometrically bright region, is maximum. The center of the diffraction pattern may not always have the maximum intensity. In fact, in Fresnel diffraction, fringes can be observed within the geometrically bright region with the possibility of the center of the diffraction pattern being a local minimum, and not a maximum of intensity. Let us begin with a very small slit width so that $\Delta w = 0.1$. When such an arc is slid in the neighborhood of the origin of the Cornu spiral (Fig. 8.6), only marginal changes in the chord length take place. Therefore, in this case, a broad maximum occurs at the center of the geometrically bright region. With the midpoint of the arc coinciding with the origin of the Cornu spiral, let the length of the arc be gradually increased (by further opening the slit) so that the arc begins to occupy larger and larger portions of the spiral. The chord length and hence the intensity at the center of the diffraction pattern increases steadily. This continues till the arc touches points A and B of the spiral, as shown in Fig. 8.8. Further increase in the arc length decreases the length of the chord and hence the intensity at the center of the diffraction pattern. The chord length reaches its minimum value when

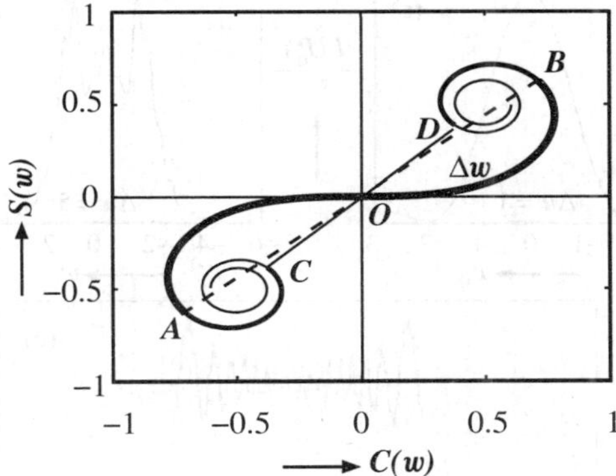

Fig. 8.8: Changes in chord length with increasing arc length Δw; arc length AB gives maximum intensity and arc length CD gives minimum intensity at the center of geometrically bright portion.

the arc Δw has increased in length to occupy the spiral between the points C and D. The intensity in the middle of the geometrically bright portion is minimum for this particular value of the slit width. A fringe pattern appears within the geometrically bright portion in the plane of observation. Figure 8.9 shows calculated intensity variations for three values of the slit width.

A change in w_0 in these figures indicates a shift of the point of observation parallel to the shorter edge of the slit. As we shall see in Chapter 10, Fig. 8.9a resembles the intensity profile of Fraunhofer diffraction from a narrow slit, whereas Fig. 8.9b,c shows typical intensity variations in Fresnel diffraction from a slit. We see here a transition between the Fraunhofer and Fresnel diffraction regimes. The thick portions of the abscissas in these figures indicate the arc lengths Δw, demarcating the geometrical limits of the bright portions in the plane of observation. For large slit widths (Fig. 8.9c), Fresnel diffraction is primarily confined to the geometrically bright region with little irradiance in the geometric shadow. Distinct fringes for a wide slit can be seen around the edges of the slit only. It should be noted that as wavelength λ decreases, the arc length Δw increases for fixed values of R'_0, R''_0 and b. Therefore for a given geometry of Fresnel diffraction, a larger portion of the Cornu spiral is covered at shorter wavelengths. In the limit of $\lambda \to 0$, the arc length Δw covers the entire spiral from L to M. The chord length now takes a fixed value of $\sqrt{2}$, irrespective of the position of the observation point. We are now in the regime of geometrical optics and fringes disappear altogether. Note that an infinitely wide slit also gives rise to an arc which completely covers the Cornu spiral and once again the chord length becomes $\sqrt{2}$. This is as it should be since the removal of the slit screen

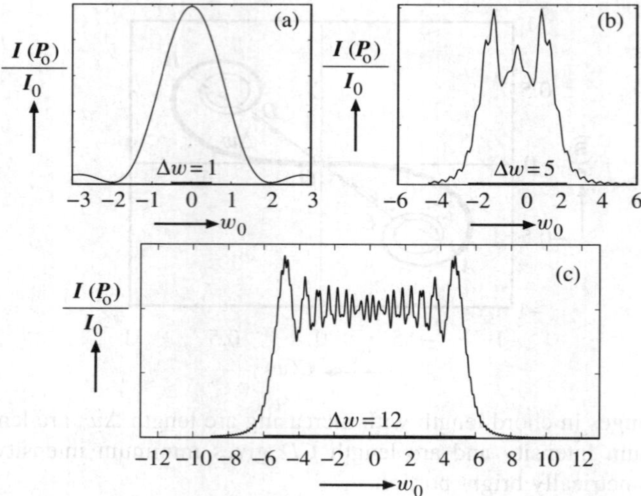

Fig. 8.9: Normalized intensity distributions of Fresnel diffraction from a slit. Thick lines on abscissas indicate geometrically bright regions. Changes in Δw indicate changes in slit width.

should restore the unobstructed intensity distribution. This may appear somewhat intriguing since the derivation of the diffraction integral assumes small aperture dimensions. Fresnel diffraction from 0.23 mm wide slit recorded with 514.5 nm line of an Argon ion laser is shown in Photo 8.1.

Photo 8.1: Fresnel diffraction from a slit of width 0.23 mm recorded with 514.5 nm line of an Argon ion laser.

8.2.3 Straight Edge

Figure 8.10 shows a semi-infinite opaque screen lying in the xy plane, with the diffracting edge held parallel to the y-axis. The aperture function for the straight edge is

$$\begin{aligned} t(x, y) &= 1 \qquad \text{for } -\infty \le y \le +\infty, \\ &\qquad\qquad x_1 \le x \le +\infty, \\ &= 0 \qquad \text{otherwise}, \end{aligned} \tag{8.26}$$

where x_1 changes with the point of observation (see Fig. 8.10). For the straight edge, Eq. (8.12) reduces to

$$I(P_o) = \frac{I_0}{2}\left[\left\{\frac{1}{2} - C(w_1)\right\}^2 + \left\{\frac{1}{2} - S(w_1)\right\}^2\right], \tag{8.27}$$

where

$$w_1 = \sqrt{\frac{2}{\lambda}\left(\frac{1}{R'_0} + \frac{1}{R''_0}\right)}\, x_1.$$

In terms of the Cornu spiral, the upper end of the arc extends upto point M whereas the lower end of the arc takes position on the Cornu spiral, depending on the value of x_1 (Fig. 8.11).

The intensity at point P_c just opposite to the diffracting edge ($x_1 = 0$) is

$$I(P_c) = \frac{I_0}{4}. \tag{8.28}$$

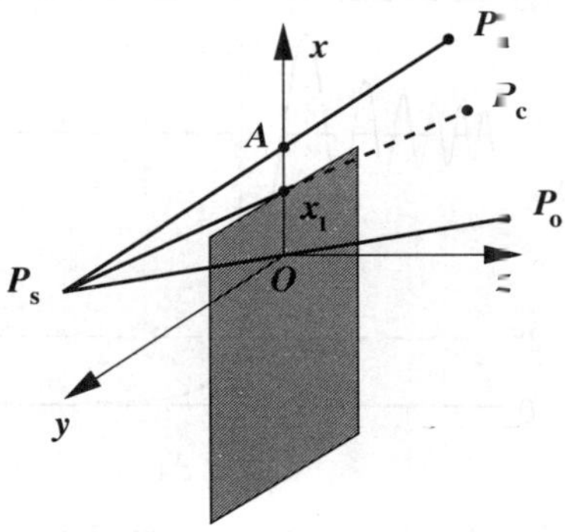

Fig. 8.10: Fresnel diffraction from a straight edge.

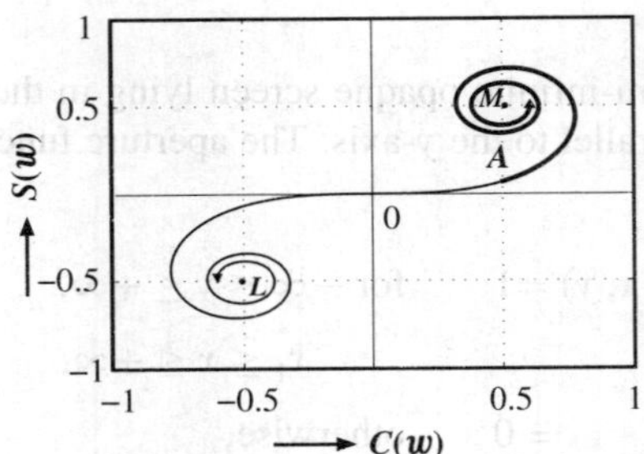

Fig. 8.11: Fresnel diffraction from a straight edge can be described by up or down movement of lower end of arc whose upper end is fixed at M. This figure corresponds to the observation point P_o lying in the shadow region.

This is the expected result. With exactly half of the incident spherical wavefront obstructed by the diffracting screen, the field is reduced to half its un-obstructed value. As we move up into the geometrically bright portion in the plane of observation, the lower end of the arc moves down the spiral, whereas the upper end remains glued to the upper eye of the spiral. For example, for the observation point P_a (Fig. 8.10), the origin lies at A so that a little more than half the wavefront contributes toward diffraction. As the observation point keeps moving up, the lower end of the arc begins to curl around the lower half of the spiral and the intensity goes through extremum values. We therefore encounter straight fringes in the geometrically bright portion. On the other hand, as the shadow region is explored (point P_o, for example, in Fig. 8.10), the free end of the arc moves up the spiral from the origin and the chord length decreases monotonically. The intensity in the geometric shadow therefore falls steadily, as shown in Fig. 8.12.

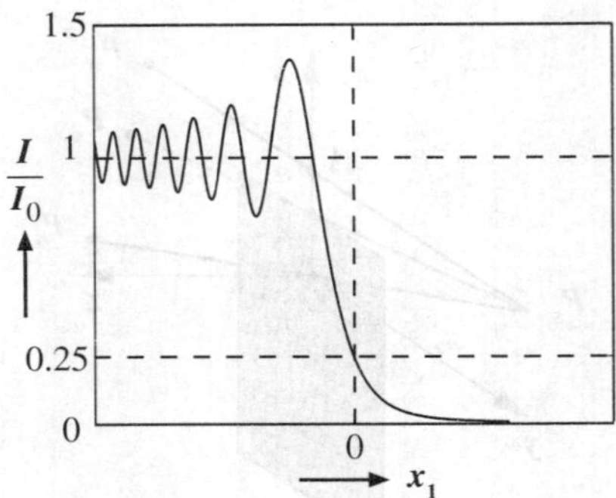

Fig. 8.12: Normalized intensity variation of Fresnel diffraction from a straight edge. Intensity decreases monotonically in the shadow region (positive x_1).

Photo 8.2: Fresnel diffraction from a straight edge recorded with 514.5 nm line of an Argon ion laser.

We should ponder over these results since our general theory of diffraction assumes aperture dimensions much smaller than the distances of the source and point of observation from the aperture. The aperture of the present example is semi-infinite in extent.

Photograph 8.2 shows Fresnel diffraction from a straight edge recorded with 514.5 nm line of an Argon ion laser.

8.2.4 Rectangular Obstacle

We next consider a long, narrow, opaque strip of width b lying in the xy plane, with the long edge running parallel to the x-axis (Fig. 8.13).

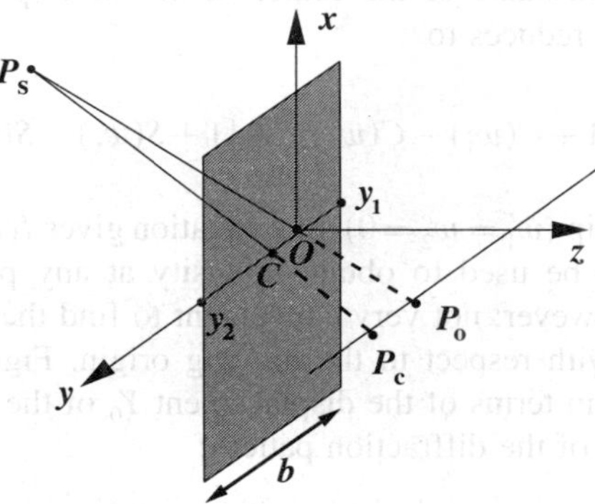

Fig. 8.13: Fresnel diffraction from a long, opaque rectangular strip.

The diffracting aperture in this case is the entire xy plane, except for the portion occupied by the opaque strip. The aperture function for the rectangular strip is

$$\begin{aligned} t(x, y) &= 1 \quad \text{for} -\infty \leq x \leq +\infty, \\ &\qquad -\infty \leq y \leq y_1, \\ &\qquad y_2 \leq y \leq +\infty, \\ &= 0 \quad \text{otherwise}, \end{aligned} \tag{8.29}$$

where y_1 and y_2 vary with the point of observation. Equation (8.12), now takes the form

$$\begin{aligned} I(P_o) = \frac{I_0}{2}[\{C(w_1') - C(w_1) + C(w_2) - C(w_2')\}^2 \\ + \{S(w_1') - S(w_1) + S(w_2) - S(w_2')\}^2], \end{aligned} \tag{8.30}$$

where

$$w_1 = -\infty,$$

$$w_2 = +\infty,$$

$$w_1' = \sqrt{\frac{2}{\lambda}\left(\frac{1}{R_0'} + \frac{1}{R_0''}\right)}(y_0 - b/2), \tag{8.31}$$

$$w_2' = \sqrt{\frac{2}{\lambda}\left(\frac{1}{R_0'} + \frac{1}{R_0''}\right)}(y_0 + b/2).$$

Here, y_0 is the y-coordinate of the center of the strip (point C in Fig. 8.13). Equation (8.30) then reduces to

$$I(P_o) = \frac{I_0}{2}[\{1 + C(w_1') - C(w_2')\}^2 + \{1 + S(w_1') - S(w_2')\}^2]. \tag{8.32}$$

On removal of the strip ($w_1' = w_2' = 0$), this equation gives $I(P_o) = I_0$, as expected. Equation (8.32) can be used to obtain intensity at any point in the plane of observation. It is, however, not very convenient to find the coordinate y_0 of the center of the strip with respect to the moving origin. Figure 8.14 shows how y_0 can be expressed in terms of the displacement Y_0 of the point of observation from the center (P_c) of the diffraction pattern:

$$y_0 = -\frac{R_0'}{R_0' + R_0''}Y_0. \tag{8.33}$$

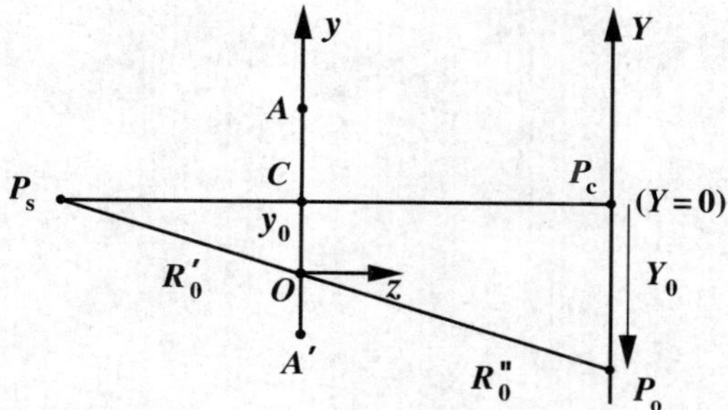

Fig. 8.14: AA' represents width of the rectangular opaque strip, y_0 locates the center of the strip with respect to the moving origin O. P_c is center of the diffraction pattern in the plane of observation.

Now all measurements can be made in the plane of observation with respect to a fixed origin (P_c).

It is quite instructive to see how the Cornu spiral can be used to obtain quantitative information on Fresnel diffraction from a rectangular obstacle. For a given point of observation, Fig. 8.15 shows the portion AB of the Cornu spiral which is to be excluded due to the presence of the obstacle. The contribution of the lower part of the spiral ($-\infty \leq w \leq w_1$) is given by the phasor $\vec{l}_{LA}$ and that of the upper part ($w_2 \leq w \leq +\infty$) by the phasor $\vec{l}_{BM}$, giving the resultant intensity at the point of observation as

$$I(P_o) = \frac{I_0}{2}\left|\vec{l}_{LA} + \vec{l}_{BM}\right|^2. \tag{8.34}$$

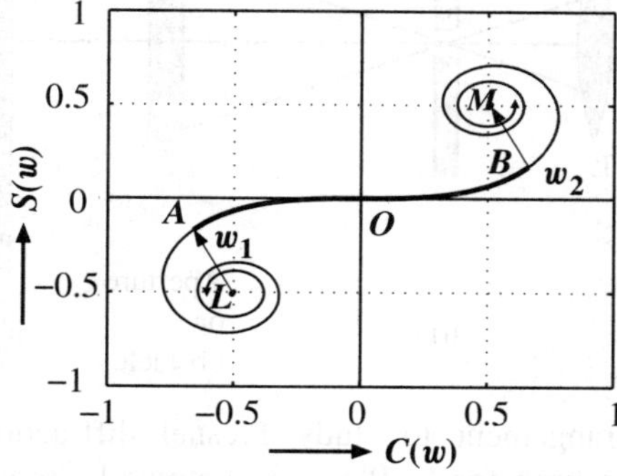

Fig. 8.15: Use of Cornu spiral to describe Fresnel diffraction from an opaque strip.

Photo 8.3: Fresnel diffraction from a wire of diameter 0.12 mm recorded with 514.5 nm line of an Argon ion laser. Bright fringe in the geometric shadow of the wire can be seen.

We have put the vector sign over the phasors since they can be added as vectors.

The magnitudes and phase angles of the phasors can be obtained from the Cornu spiral as explained in Section 8.2.1. The intensity at the symmetric point behind the opaque strip will not be zero, unless it is so wide that points A and B approach the eyes of the spiral. Photograph 8.3 shows straight fringes appearing

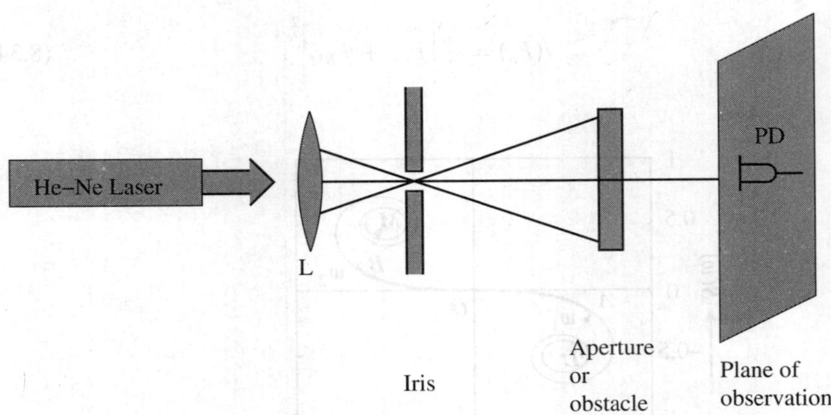

Fig. 8.16: Experimental arrangement to study Fresnel diffraction. A 10× microscope objective can be used for L. PD is a photodiode, mounted on an $x-y$ translator.

in the Fresnel diffraction of a wire of diameter 0.12 mm, taken with 514.5 nm line of an Argon ion laser. The bright fringe in the middle of the geometric shadow of the wire can be clearly seen.

Before we move on to the next topic, we note that the intensity distributions of Fresnel diffraction (Eqs 8.25 and 8.34) for a slit and an opaque strip, having same widths, are different. This should not be interpreted as a violation of Babinet's principle. In fact these results are entirely consistent with it (see Problem 8.4). The complementary apertures give same intensity distributions only in regions which are dark in the absence of any aperture.

Figure 8.16 shows a simple experimental arrangement to study Fresnel diffraction from apertures and obstacles. The intensity measurements can be done with a photo-detector (PD) or a CCD camera.

8.3 CIRCULAR APERTURE

For the rectangular diffracting apertures discussed in Section 8.2, it was possible to drop the linear phase factor from the diffraction integral by introducing a moveable origin in the aperture plane. This procedure is not very helpful in the context of circular apertures. We therefore restrict our discussion of Fresnel diffraction from a circular aperture when the source and observation points lie on the symmetry axis of the aperture (Fig. 8.17).

We begin by writing the diffraction integral in the form (Eq.7.18b)

$$E(P_o) = -\frac{ia_0}{\lambda}\iint_{\Sigma} t(x, y)Q\frac{e^{ik(r'+r'')}}{r'r''}\,dS, \tag{8.35}$$

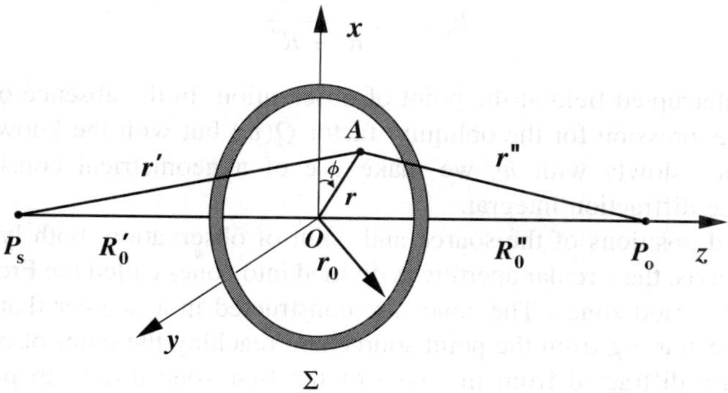

Fig. 8.17: Geometry for Fresnel diffraction from a circular aperture. The source and observation points lie on the symmetry axis.

where Q is the obliquity factor. The aperture function $t(x, y)$ has unit value over the aperture and zero outside it. For an on-axis observation point, the direction cosines l', l'', m'; m'' (Eq. 7.26) are identically zero and (Eq. 7.25b) reduces to

$$r' + r'' = R'_0 + R''_0 + \frac{1}{2}\left(\frac{1}{R'_0} + \frac{1}{R''_0}\right)(x^2 + y^2). \tag{8.36}$$

The diffraction integral can then be expressed as

$$E(P_o) = -\frac{ia_0}{\lambda}\frac{e^{ik(R'_0+R''_0)}}{R_0 R''_0}\int_{r=0}^{r_0}\int_{\phi=0}^{2\pi} Q(r)\, e^{i\frac{\pi}{\lambda}\left(\frac{1}{R'_0}+\frac{1}{R''_0}\right)r^2}\, r\, dr\, d\phi, \tag{8.37}$$

where r_0 is the radius of the circular aperture. Introducing

$$w = \frac{2}{\lambda}\left(\frac{1}{R'_0} + \frac{1}{R''_0}\right) r^2, \tag{8.38}$$

Eq. (8.37) becomes

$$E(P_o) = -i\frac{\pi}{2} E_0 \int_0^{w'} Q(w) e^{i\frac{\pi}{2}w} dw, \tag{8.39}$$

where

$$w' = \frac{2}{\lambda}\left(\frac{1}{R'_0} + \frac{1}{R''_0}\right) r_0^2 \tag{8.40}$$

and

$$E_0 = a_0 \frac{e^{ik(R'_0+R''_0)}}{R'_0 + R''_0} \tag{8.41}$$

is the uninterrupted field at the point of observation. In the absence of a simple analytical expression for the obliquity factor $Q(w)$ but with the knowledge that $Q(w)$ varies slowly with w, we make use of a geometrical construction to evaluate the diffraction integral.

For fixed positions of the source and point of observation, both lying on the symmetry axis, the circular aperture is divided into zones called the Fresnel zones or the half-period zones. The zones are constructed in a manner that the phase of the wave starting from the point source and reaching the point of observation after getting diffracted from the edge of the first zone differs in phase by π radians from the phase of the wave travelling straight from the source to the point of observation. Furthermore, the phases of the waves getting diffracted from the outer edges of any two successive zones and reaching the point of

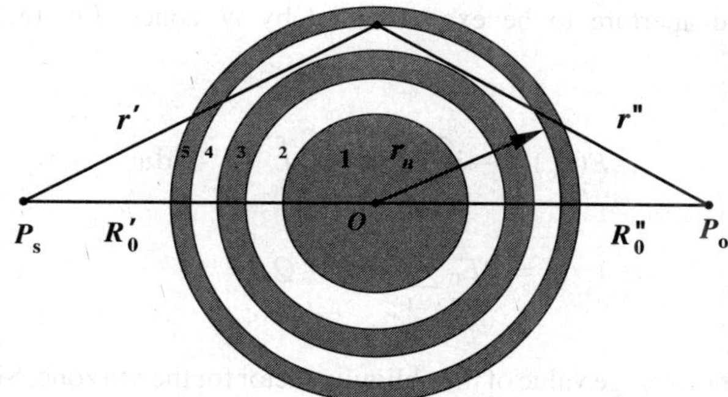

Fig. 8.18: Fresnel's half period zones.

observation also differ by π radians. The Fresnel zones are shown schematically in Fig. 8.18. The nth zone of radius r_n satisfies the condition

$$r' + r'' - R'_0 - R''_0 = \frac{n\lambda}{2}. \tag{8.42}$$

Neglecting terms of order

$$\left(\frac{r_n}{R'_0}\right)^4, \text{ and } \left(\frac{r_n}{R''_0}\right)^4,$$

and higher, we have

$$r' - R'_0 = \frac{r_n^2}{2R'_0}, \tag{8.43a}$$

$$r'' - R''_0 = \frac{r_n^2}{2R''_0}, \tag{8.43b}$$

so that

$$r_n^2 = \frac{n\lambda}{\left(\frac{1}{R'_0} + \frac{1}{R''_0}\right)}. \tag{8.44}$$

To be precise, r_n is the radius of the outer edge of the nth zone. Within the above approximation, the zones so constructed are equal area zones. Furthermore, we note that

$$w_n = \frac{2}{\lambda}\left(\frac{1}{R'_0} + \frac{1}{R''_0}\right) r_n^2 \tag{8.45a}$$

$$= 2n. \tag{8.45b}$$

Assuming the aperture to be exactly filled by N zones, Eq. (8.39) may be written as

$$E(P_o) = -\mathrm{i}\frac{\pi}{2} E_0 \sum_{n=1}^{N} Q_n \int_{w_{n-1}}^{w_n} \mathrm{e}^{\mathrm{i}\frac{\pi}{2}w}\,\mathrm{d}w \tag{8.46a}$$

$$= 2E_0 \sum_{n=1}^{N} (-1)^{n+1} Q_n, \tag{8.46b}$$

where Q_n is the average value of the obliquity factor for the nth zone. Since changes in the obliquity factor from zone to zone are small, the contributions to the resultant field $E(P_o)$ from successive zones have very nearly equal magnitudes, but opposite signs. This is the whole purpose of constructing the Fresnel zones. For even N, Eq. (8.46b) can be written as

$$E(P_o) = 2E_0[Q_1 - Q_2 + Q_3 - Q_4 + \cdots + Q_{N-1} - Q_N] \tag{8.47a}$$

$$= 2E_0\left[Q_1 - \frac{Q_2}{2} - \left(\frac{Q_2}{2} + \frac{Q_4}{2} - Q_3\right) - \left(\frac{Q_4}{2} + \frac{Q_6}{2} - Q_5\right) - \cdots - \left(\frac{Q_{N-2}}{2} + \frac{Q_N}{2} - Q_{N-1}\right) - \frac{Q_N}{2}\right]. \tag{8.47b}$$

For small changes in the obliquity factor from zone to zone, as mentioned earlier, the bracketed quantities in Eq. (8.47b) are vanishingly small. Therefore, for even N,

$$E(P_o) \approx 2E_0\left[\frac{Q_1}{2} - \frac{Q_N}{2}\right]. \tag{8.48}$$

Similarly for odd N,

$$\begin{aligned} E(P_o) &= 2E_0[Q_1 - Q_2 + Q_3 - Q_4 + \cdots - Q_{N-1} + Q_N] \\ &= 2E_0\left[\frac{Q_1}{2} + \left(\frac{Q_1}{2} + \frac{Q_3}{2} - Q_2\right) + \left(\frac{Q_3}{2} + \frac{Q_5}{2} - Q_4\right) \cdots + \left(\frac{Q_{N-2}}{2} + \frac{Q_N}{2} - Q_{N-1}\right) + \frac{Q_N}{2}\right] \\ &\approx 2E_0\left[\frac{Q_1}{2} + \frac{Q_N}{2}\right]. \end{aligned} \tag{8.49}$$

For a sufficiently large aperture, the obliquity factor Q_N for the last zone is vanishingly small as the angles the vectors $\vec{r'}$ and $\vec{r''}$ make with the normal to the aperture plane approach 90°. So that, $E(P_o) = E_0$, as expected.

However, for a small aperture at a suitable distance from the source, it is quite possible that for a particular point of observation, the first zone itself may exactly fill the aperture, in which case the field becomes twice as large as the uninterrupted field and the intensity four times the uninterrupted intensity. This is the point of maximum intensity for Fresnel diffraction from a circular aperture. This happens, for example for $r_0 = 0.9\,\text{mm}$, $R_0' = R_0'' = 3.2\,\text{m}$, and $\lambda = 500\,\text{nm}$. On the other hand, for some other point of observation on the optical axis, somewhat closer to the aperture, the same aperture may accommodate exactly two zones. The intensity at that point is nearly zero because the contributions from the two zones are nearly equal in magnitude but opposite in sign. This is shown in Photo 8.4 for a circular aperture of 0.33 mm diameter recorded with 514.5 nm line of an Argon ion laser. As the observation point moves still closer to the aperture, the zone radii decrease and the number of zones covering the aperture increases. The intensity distribution goes through maximum and minimum values as the number of zones completely filling the aperture takes odd and even values, respectively. A similar behavior can be expected if the size of the circular aperture is increased and intensity changes are observed at a fixed point on the optical axis. Increasing the aperture size for fixed positions of the source and observation points amounts to adding more zones in the aperture.

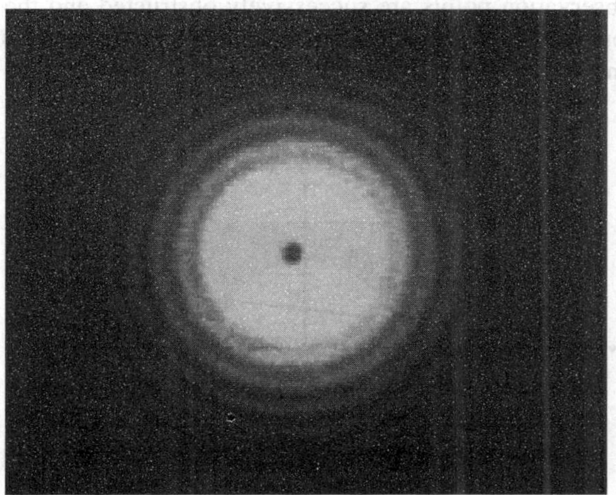

Photo 8.4: Fresnel diffraction from a circular aperture of diameter 0.33 mm recorded with 514.5 nm line of an Argon ion laser. The aperture contains two Fresnel zones, making the center of the diffraction pattern dark.

For a given point of observation, the aperture may not contain an exact number of Fresnel zones. The contribution of the incomplete zone, near the edge of the aperture, can be evaluated from the integral

$$\Delta E(P_o) = -i\frac{\pi}{2}E_0 Q_n \int_{w_{n-1}}^{w_{n-1}+\Delta w} e^{i\frac{\pi}{2}w}\, dw. \tag{8.50}$$

8.3.1 Irradiance at Off-Axial Points

The calculation of the intensity distribution of Fresnel diffraction from a circular aperture at off-axial points is considerably more difficult [8.4] and will not be attempted here. The new origin O', for an off-axial point of observation P_o, is the point of intersection of the line P_sP_o with the plane of the aperture (Fig. 8.19). The rotational symmetry is now lost. To get some feel of what to expect, we construct Fresnel zones but now with respect to point O' which no longer coincides with the center of the aperture. As seen from the off-axial points, only the innermost few zones appear unobstructed. In Fig. 8.20, only the first two zones as seen from P_o are fully inside the aperture. The third and higher zones are partially obstructed. The obstruction is caused by the opaque portion of the aperture screen. A partially obstructed zone makes only a partial contribution to the field at an off-axial observation point. As the observation point is moved perpendicular to the symmetry axis, the irradiance goes through extremum values. The half-period zones which lie wholly within the aperture for the on-axis observation points are successively obstructed and the zones which do not contribute toward on-axis irradiance begin to contribute for off-axis points of observations.

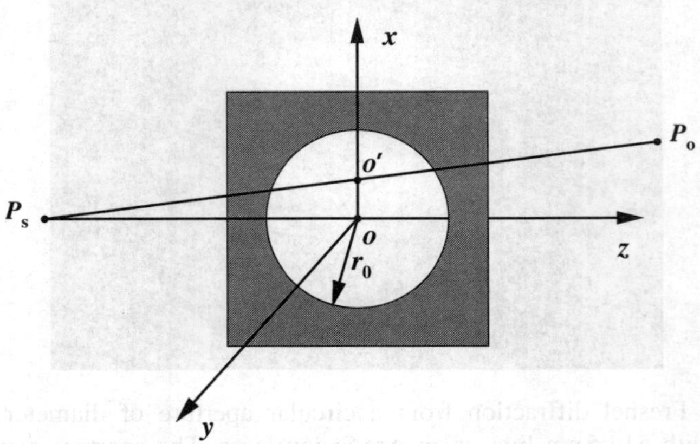

Fig. 8.19: Geometry for off-axis Fresnel diffraction from a circular aperture.

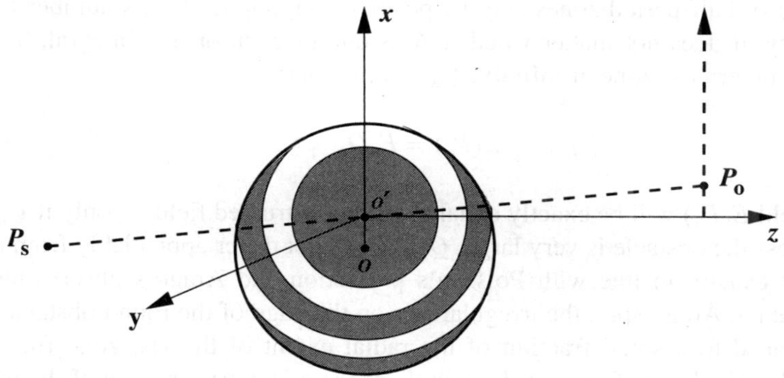

Fig. 8.20: Partially obstructed zones for off-axial observation point.

8.3.2 The Arago Bright Spot

If a circular obstacle is used in place of a circular aperture to observe Fresnel diffraction, then a bright spot appears within the geometric shadow, unless one is too close to the obstacle. This was actually a conclusion drawn by Poisson based on Fresnel's wave theory and verified experimentally by Arago.[1] The intensity of the bright spot is nearly equal to the unobstructed intensity at that point. This can be understood in terms of the half-period zones which can be constructed in exactly the same manner as for the circular aperture. For a given point of observation on the optical axis, let the circular obstacle contain exactly *m* Fresnel zones. It does not matter if *m* is odd or even because these zones do not contribute anything to the field. The diffracted field at this axial point due to the zones, lying outside the circular obstacle, is

$$E(P_o) = 2E_0 \left[\frac{Q_{m+1}}{2} \mp \frac{Q_N}{2} \right], \tag{8.51}$$

where we have included contributions from all zones beyond the edge of the obstacle in the manner of Eqs (8.48) and (8.49). The minus sign in Eq. (8.51) applies if the space beyond the edge of the obstacle contains exactly an even

[1] Augustin Jean Fresnel submitted, at the age of 30, an essay on the wave theory of light to the French Academy. The expert Committee included Simeon D. Poisson and D.F.J. Arago, among others. Poisson used Fresnel's theory and predicted the appearance of a bright spot in the geometric shadow of a round object. This, Poisson thought was absurd enough to reject Fresnel's essay, but Arago went ahead and performed the experiment and observed the bright spot exactly as predicted by Poisson. Fresnel was awarded the first prize.

number of half-period zones and the positive sign applies if this number is odd. Actually, it does not matter whether N is odd or even or non-integral, because for the outermost zone at infinity, $Q_N = 0$, giving

$$E(P_o) = E_0 Q_{m+1}. \tag{8.52}$$

The field $E(P_o)$ will be exactly equal to the unobstructed field E_0 only if $Q_{m+1} = 1$. Unless the obstacle is very large, Q_{m+1} does not differ appreciably from unity. This is exactly in line with Poisson's prediction and Arago's observation. To observe the Arago spot, the irregularities on the edge of the round obstacle must be reduced to a small fraction of the radial extent of the last zone filling the obstacle. The bright fringe in the middle of the geometric shadow of the wire in Photo 8.3 appears precisely for the same reason as the Arago bright spot for a circular obstacle.

8.4 THE ZONE PLATE

Fresnel half-period zones are defined for fixed positions of the source and point of observation, both lying on the symmetry axis of the circular aperture. A zone plate is an image-forming device, much like a lens, but based on the concept of Fresnel half-period zones. We begin by re-writing Eq. (8.44) in the form

$$\frac{1}{R_0''} + \frac{1}{R_0'} = \frac{n\lambda}{r_n^2}, \tag{8.53}$$

where r_n is the radius of the outer edge of the nth Fresnel zone and R_0' and R_0'' are the distances of the source and point of observation from the circular aperture, respectively. For fixed positions of the source and point of observation, the radii of successive zones increase as the square root of successive integers. The irradiance at any point of observation is rather low since the fields contributed by the neighboring zones are out of phase with each other. Maximum irradiance is achieved when the circular aperture contains exactly one Fresnel zone. Even under these conditions, the irradiance level is quite low because the solid angle subtended by the aperture at the source is rather small. The irradiance level can be enhanced substantially if the circular aperture is made large and alternate zones are somehow blocked so that the remaining zones contribute in phase. Consider a situation where for a given point of observation, a circular aperture contains exactly 40 Fresnel zones. The resultant field with alternate zones blocked, is

$$E(P_o) = 2E_0 [Q_1 + Q_3 + Q_5 + \cdots + Q_{39}]. \tag{8.54}$$

Fig. 8.21: A zone plate. Alternate zones are blocked.

Assuming all obliquity factors to have nearly unit magnitude, the resultant amplitude is now nearly 40 times the unobstructed amplitude and the resultant intensity 1600 times the unobstructed intensity. Such a device with alternate Fresnel zones blocked is called a *zone plate* (Fig. 8.21). Irradiance level can be increased even further if the alternate zones are not blocked, but are enhanced or retarded in phase by π radians with respect to the neighboring zones. For the previous example of an aperture containing exactly 40 Fresnel zones, the intensity at the point of observation can now reach 6400 times the unobstructed intensity. We might as well call this point of observation, so much brighter than the surrounding points, as the image of the point source.

The image-forming action of a zone plate can be appreciated, at least in a formal sense, by comparing Eq. (8.53) with the lens formula

$$\frac{1}{v} - \frac{1}{u} = \frac{1}{f}. \tag{4.51b}$$

This comparison can be made exact if it is realized that to be consistent with the sign convention of geometrical optics, R_0' in Fig. 8.18 must be measured from O and not from P_s. The primary focal length of the zone plate is

$$f_0 = \frac{r_n^2}{n\lambda} = \frac{r_1^2}{\lambda} = \frac{r_2^2}{2\lambda} = \cdots, \tag{8.55}$$

where r_1, r_2, and r_n are the radii of the outer edges of the first, second, and nth Fresnel zones, respectively. At optical frequencies, the primary focal length f_0 of a zone plate is rather long. To use a zone plate as a lens, let the object be placed at a distance R_0' in front of the zone plate. The image formed at the distance R_0'' (obtained from Eq. (8.53) with primary focal length f_0) behind the aperture is the primary image. A zone plate is capable of generating several real and virtual images, simultaneously. For the primary image, each zone marked on the zone plate contains exactly one Fersnel zone. As the observation point is moved from the primary image towards the zone plate, the radii of the Fresnel zones decrease and there are positions between the primary image and the zone plate, where each zone marked on the zone plate contains exactly 3, 5, 7, . . . , $(2n+1)$ Fresnel zones. These are the secondary real images of the object, corresponding to the secondary focal lengths $f_0/3$, $f_0/5$, $f_0/7$, etc. of the zone plate. The virtual images lie between the zone plate and the source. These are points on the optical axis for which the effective Fresnel zone distributions in the zone plate are exactly the same as for the corresponding real secondary images, but now the zone plate has focal lengths of $-f_0/3$, $-f_0/5$, $-f_0/7$, etc. The virtual images arise from the waves diffracted by the zone plate which diverge, rather than converge as shown in Fig. 8.22.

Whereas the primary image formed by a zone plate can be quite intense, the secondary images have considerably reduced brightness. To see this, we consider the first secondary image for which the zone plate has an effective focal length of $f_0/3$. For this image point as the observation point, each zone marked on the zone plate accommodates three Fresnel zones. However, the effective

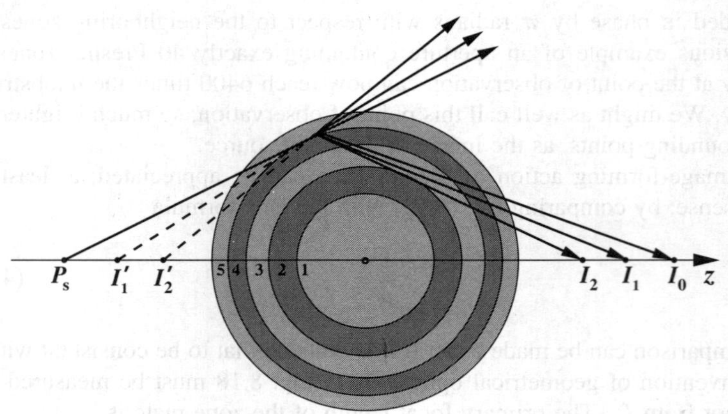

Fig. 8.22: Imaging action of a zone plate; I_0, I_1, I_2 are real images and I_1', I_2' are virtual images of P_s. I_0 is the primary image.

contribution toward image brightness is due to only one of these zones, the other two zones nearly cancel each other's contributions. Thus, the field for the first secondary image is reduced by a factor of three and the intensity by a factor of nine as compared, respectively, to the field and intensity of the primary image. Similar statements can be made for the remaining secondary images. Between successive images, there are points of minimum intensity corresponding to even number of Fresnel zones filling each marked zone of the zone plate.

A zone plate acts as a highly chromatic lens because its focal length is wavelength dependent (Eq. 8.55). On the other hand, the lensing action of the zone plate is not dependent on the refractive properties of the medium of the zone plate. Fresnel zone plates can be extremely useful as focusing devices for X-rays and in other regions of the electromagnetic spectrum where suitable refractive materials are difficult to find.

8.5 PIN-HOLE CAMERA

A pin-hole camera is a lensless device for taking clear images of distant and stationary objects. In Section 8.4, we have seen how a circular aperture can act as an image-forming device. The image intensity depends critically on the number of Fresnel zones filling the aperture. The intensity becomes maximum when the aperture contains exactly one Fresnel zone. Under these conditions, the radius of the circular aperture is

$$r = \left(\frac{\lambda}{\frac{1}{R'_0} + \frac{1}{R''_0}} \right)^{1/2}, \tag{8.56}$$

where R'_0 and R''_0 are the object and image distances from the aperture, respectively.

A pin-hole camera, essentially, consists of a box with a small hole on one side and a photographic film on the opposite side. Inverted images of the objects in front of the camera are formed on the photographic film. The pertinent dimensions of the camera are the size of the hole and the distance between the hole and the film. For distant objects, Eq. (8.56) can be approximated to

$$r = \sqrt{R''_0 \lambda}, \tag{8.57}$$

where R''_0 is the distance between the pin-hole and the film. For viewing distant objects with $R''_0 = 30\,\text{cm}$, the radius of the pin-hole is nearly 0.4 mm at 500 nm. It is indeed a very small camera aperture, requiring extra long exposure times. A more detailed analysis of the pin-hole camera suggests a slightly higher value for the hole radius [8.5]. A camera with hole radius significantly larger than the one given by Eq. (8.57) leads to unacceptably blurred images. In fact, for larger holes, the image tends to get the shape of the hole, and not that of the object.

Before we move on to Fraunhofer diffraction, it is desirable to have some working knowledge of the Fourier transforms because of their repeated use in Fraunhofer diffraction. Chapter 9 is therefore devoted to the Fourier transforms.

8.6 REFERENCES

8.1 Eugene Hecht, Optics, 4th ed., Addison-Wesley, Reading, 2001.

8.2 Miles V. Klein and Thomas E. Furtak, Optics, 2nd ed., John Wiley & Sons, New York, 1986.

8.3 Robert D. Guenther, Modern Optics, John Wily & Sons, New York, 1990.

8.4 D. S. Burch – Fresnel diffraction by a circular aperture; Am. J. Phys. **53**, 255–260 (1985).

8.5 Kazuo Sayanagi, Pinhole Imagery, J. Opt. Soc. Am. **57**, 1091–1099 (1967).

8.7 PROBLEMS

8.1 A point source of monochromatic radiation ($\lambda = 500\,\text{nm}$) lies on the axis of a $1\,\text{mm} \times 2\,\text{mm}$ rectangular aperture. The source is 25 cm in front of the aperture and the plane of observation, parallel to the plane of the aperture, is 50 cm behind it.

(a) Calculate $p^2/R_0\lambda$, and see if inequality (8.3) holds.

(b) Find the irradiance, normalized to the unobstructed irradiance, at the center of the plane of observation.

(c) Using the Cornu spiral of Fig. 8.3 and the symmetry of the diffracting aperture, determine as accurately as you can the position and normalized irradiance of the first dark fringe of the diffraction pattern in the plane of observation. You may prefer a computational approach.

8.2 The beam of a He–Ne laser, emitting 632.8 nm radiation, is focused by a short focal length lens. The focal point of the lens lies on the line passing through the midpoint of a long slit and perpendicular to its plane. The slit is 0.5 mm wide and lies 20 cm behind the focal point of the lens and 20 cm in front of the plane of observation which is parallel to the plane of the slit.

(a) Find the normalized irradiance at the center of the plane of observation and state if it is more or less than the irradiances at the neighboring points in the plane of observation.

(b) Find the normalized irradiance at a point in the plane of observation, 2 mm displaced from the optical axis in the direction of the width of the slit. Does this point lie within or outside the geometric shadow of the slit?

8.3 Answer parts (a) and (b) of Problem 8.2 after removing the focusing lens and assuming that the He–Ne laser produces a plane wave which falls normally on the slit.

8.4 Consider Fresnel diffractions from a long slit and a long, opaque strip, each of width 1 mm. The point source ($\lambda = 500$ nm) is 15 cm in front of the slit/strip and the plane of observation is 25 cm behind the slit/strip. Find, in each case, the normalized irradiance at the center of the diffraction pattern. Explain how your results are consistent with Babinet's principle.

8.5 Consider Fresnel diffraction from a semi-infinite opaque screen with a straight edge (Fig. 8.10) for $R_0' = 30$ cm and $\lambda = 550$ nm. The observation plane, parallel to the plane of the screen lies 50 cm behind it. Using the Cornu spiral of Fig. 8.3, find in the plane of observation, the positions of the first two maxima and the minimum between them. In each case, obtain the irradiance, normalized to the unobstructed irradiance.

8.6 Fresnel diffraction is observed from two long, parallel slits, 0.5 mm apart as shown in Fig. 8.23. Each slit is 0.1 mm wide. Point source S of monochromatic light of wavelength 500 nm lies on the optical axis 10 cm in front of the plane of the slits. Find the irradiance, normalized to the unobstructed irradiance at a point lying on the optical axis, 40 cm behind the plane of the slits.

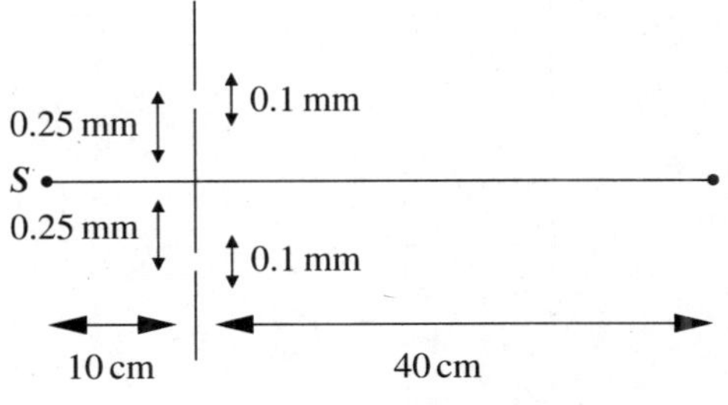

Fig. 8.23.

8.7 An annular circular aperture of inner radius 2.00 mm is illuminated by an axial point source of monochromatic light of wavelength 500 nm. The source lies 4 m in front of the aperture. It is found that the point of maximum irradiance lies on the optical axis, 4 m behind the aperture. Find the outer radius of the annular aperture and the number of zones filling the inner opaque portion of the annular aperture.

8.8 Consider Fresnel diffraction from a circular aperture of radius 0.4 mm kept 50 cm behind an axial point source of monochromatic radiation of wavelength 600 nm.

(a) Find the normalized irradiance at an axial point, 50 cm behind the circular aperture.
(b) Find maximum distance of the plane of observation (parallel to the plane of the aperture) from the aperture so that a diffraction pattern with a minimum at the center can be seen.

(c) Find positions of the five strongest maxima of intensity and the minima between them on the axis of the aperture. Obtain their relative intensities.

(d) Compare your results of part (c) with those obtained from Eq. (8.39) by assuming the obliquity factor of a constant value of one.

8.9 A zone plate with alternate zones blocked is used to obtain a real image of a small axial object kept 20 cm in front of the zone plate. The desired image magnification is 5. It is further desired that the image irradiance be 900 times the unobstructed irradiance at the image point. Find the smallest diameter of the zone plate. Is this a practical device? Take $\lambda = 632.8\,\text{nm}$.

8.10 Find the smallest diameter of the zone plate if the image in Problem 8.9 is not the primary image, but the first secondary real image. Comment on the primary image under this condition.

8.11 A zone plate with alternate zones blocked has primary focal length of 50 cm when a He–Ne laser is used as the source of radiation ($\lambda = 632.8\,\text{nm}$). Find the diameter of the zone plate if it has exactly 24 dark and 25 clear half-period zones. Find positions of the primary and first secondary real images of a small axial object kept 75 cm in front of the zone plate.

CHAPTER 9

The Fourier Transform

9.1 INTRODUCTION

Fourier transforms are extensively used in optics. Two-dimensional Fourier transforms in spatial coordinates are particularly useful in Fraunhofer diffraction, optical image formation, and processing. In this chapter, we introduce Fourier series and Fourier transforms with some typical examples. Important properties of the Fourier transforms will be derived. This will be followed by a discussion on the convolution and correlation of functions. The concepts developed in this chapter will be applied in the succeeding chapters. The technique of expressing a complicated function in terms of simpler functions provides a means to tackle many of the complex problems of science and engineering. A number of mathematicians, Euler, Dirichlet, Fourier to name a few have made seminal contributions in this development. It was J. B. J. Fourier who first applied the series expansion, now called the Fourier series, to solve the problem of heat flow in one dimension. Stated simply, this technique allows one to express any periodic function satisfying certain conditions of continuity, etc., in terms of an infinite series called the Fourier series, and a function which is not periodic in terms of an integral called the Fourier transform. We shall concentrate primarily on Fourier transforms in spatial coordinates because of their relevance to Fourier optics. In Chapter 2, Fourier transforms in time domain were used to describe polychromatic light.

9.2 THE FOURIER SERIES

We begin by considering a single valued one-dimensional periodic function

$$f(x+\Lambda) = f(x) \quad \text{for } -\infty \leq x \leq +\infty \tag{9.1}$$

with period Λ and possessing a finite number of points of ordinary discontinuity and a finite number of maxima and minima within its period. Furthermore, $f(x)$ must be absolutely integrable in any finite interval $x_1 \leq x \leq x_2$, i.e.,

$$\int_{x_1}^{x_2} |f(x)| \, \mathrm{d}x < \infty.$$

Any function representing a physical quantity satisfies these conditions, but many mathematical functions do not. Several equivalent forms of the Fourier series expansion of a periodic function exist:

$$f(x) = \frac{a_0}{2} + \sum_{n=1}^{\infty} a_n \cos\left(2\pi n \frac{x}{\Lambda} + \alpha_n\right) \tag{9.2a}$$

$$= \frac{a_0}{2} + \sum_{n=1}^{\infty} \left[a_n \cos\left(2\pi n \frac{x}{\Lambda}\right) + b_n \sin\left(2\pi n \frac{x}{\Lambda}\right)\right] \tag{9.2b}$$

$$= \sum_{n=-\infty}^{+\infty} a_n \mathrm{e}^{\mathrm{i}2\pi n \frac{x}{\Lambda}}, \tag{9.2c}$$

where the constant coefficients a_n and b_n are the weighting factors (real or complex) of the terms in the expansion and α_n are the phase constants. The expansions (9.2a) and (9.2b) make use of the sinusoidal and co-sinusoidal functions whereas form (9.2c) uses complex exponentials of the type $\mathrm{e}^{\mathrm{i}2\pi ux}$. The $n = 1$ elementary functions (sinusoidal or exponential) in the expansions have the period of the original function and higher order elementary functions have periods which are integral fractions of this period. The first terms in the expansions (9.2a,b) and $n = 0$ term in Eq. (9.2c) represent the d.c. part of the function. The weighting factors applicable to Eq. (9.2b), obtained from the orthogonality properties of the sinusoidal and co-sinusoidal functions, are given by

$$a_0 = \frac{2}{\Lambda} \int_{-\Lambda/2}^{+\Lambda/2} f(x) \, \mathrm{d}x, \tag{9.3a}$$

$$a_n = \frac{2}{\Lambda} \int_{-\Lambda/2}^{+\Lambda/2} f(x) \cos\left(2\pi n \frac{x}{\Lambda}\right) \mathrm{d}x \tag{9.3b}$$

and

$$b_n = \frac{2}{\Lambda} \int_{-\Lambda/2}^{+\Lambda/2} f(x) \sin\left(2\pi n \frac{x}{\Lambda}\right) \mathrm{d}x. \tag{9.3c}$$

For even $f(x)$,

$$b_n = 0 \quad \text{for all } n > 0$$

and

$$a_n = 0 \quad \text{for all } n > 0$$

when $f(x)$ is odd. The coefficients a_n and b_n are in general non-zero for functions which are neither even nor odd. In analogy with the temporal frequency and its harmonics ($\nu_n = \frac{n}{T}$, n being a positive integer), we define

$$u_n = \frac{n}{\Lambda} \tag{9.4}$$

with dimension of inverse length as the nth spatial frequency. Spatial frequency is the number of times a function varying sinusoidally with a position coordinate repeats itself per unit length. Expressing Eq. (9.2b) in terms of the spatial frequencies,

$$f(x) = \frac{a_0}{2} + \sum_{n=1}^{\infty}\left[a_n \cos(2\pi u_n x) + b_n \sin(2\pi u_n x)\right]. \tag{9.5}$$

The weighting factors a_n and b_n are now associated with the spatial frequency u_n. This series expansion admits only positive spatial frequencies, but Eq. (9.2c) allows negative spatial frequencies $(-\frac{n}{\Lambda})$ as well. Negative frequencies may not always be physically meaningful. For example, for a diffraction grating as we shall see later, the principal maxima on the two sides of the central maximum correspond to positive and negative spatial frequencies. On the other hand, negative frequencies in the time domain may have no physical reality, but must be retained in the mathematical description. In summary, the Fourier series representation of a periodic function, satisfying certain conditions, can be made as close to the original function as desired by adding more and more terms in the expansion, but an exact equivalence between the two is not always guaranteed.

9.2.1 The Rectangle Wave

As an illustration, we develop Fourier series expansion of a periodic function of period Λ, representing an unlimited sequence of one-dimensional rectangle functions (Fig. 9.1). Each rectangle has width $2\Lambda/l$, where l is any real number greater than 2. The amplitude transmission function of a diffraction grating closely resembles this function, except that it involves only a finite number

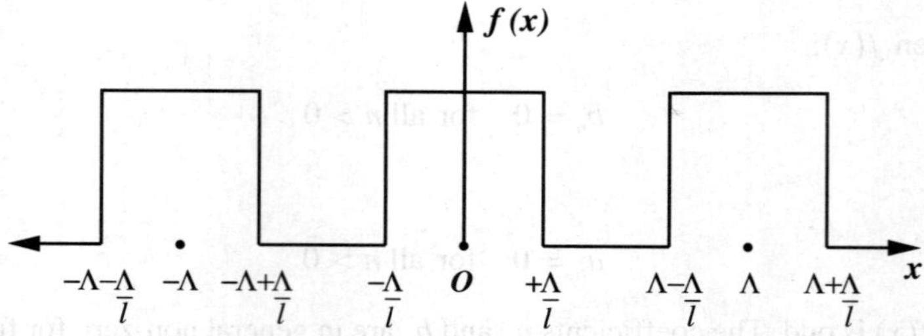

Fig. 9.1: One-dimensional rectangle periodic function.

of repetitions. With O as the origin, the rectangle wave is described by the function

$$f(x) = 1 \quad \text{for} \quad m\Lambda - \frac{\Lambda}{l} \leq x \leq m\Lambda + \frac{\Lambda}{l},$$

$$= 0 \quad \text{for} \quad m\Lambda + \frac{\Lambda}{l} \leq x \leq (m+1)\Lambda - \frac{\Lambda}{l}, \tag{9.6}$$

where $m = 0, \pm 1, \pm 2, \ldots$. The function $f(x)$ being even,

$$b_n = 0 \quad \text{for all } n \tag{9.7a}$$

and

$$a_0 = \frac{4}{l}, \tag{9.7b}$$

$$a_{n\neq 0} = \frac{4}{l}\frac{\sin(2\pi n/l)}{(2\pi n/l)} = \frac{4}{l}\,\text{sinc}\left(\frac{2\pi n}{l}\right). \tag{9.7c}$$

The weighting factors $a_{n\neq 0}$ are zero for integral values of the ratio $\frac{2n}{l}$. For $l = 2$, all $a_{n\neq 0} = 0$ and function $f(x)$ becomes a constant function. For $l = 4$, all $a_{n\neq 0}$ coefficients with even n vanish and for $l = 16$, the coefficients $a_8, a_{16}, \ldots$ are identically zero. For non-integral values of $2n/l$, a_n coefficients are sampled values of the sinc function, where sampling is done at integral values of n. The first few terms in the Fourier decompositions of the periodic rectangle functions for $l = 4$ and 16 are

$$f(x) = \frac{1}{2} + \frac{2}{\pi}\left[\cos(2\pi u_1 x) - \frac{1}{3}\cos(2\pi u_3 x) + \frac{1}{5}\cos(2\pi u_5 x) - \frac{1}{7}\cos(2\pi u_7 x) + \cdots\right] \tag{9.8a}$$

$$= \frac{1}{2} + \frac{1}{\pi}\left[\cos(2\pi u_1 x) + \cos\{2\pi(-u_1)x\} - \frac{1}{3}\cos(2\pi u_3 x)\right.$$
$$\left. - \frac{1}{3}\cos\{2\pi(-u_3)x\} + \cdots\right] \qquad (9.8b)$$
$$= 0.500 + 0.637\cos(2\pi u_1 x) - 0.212\cos(2\pi u_3 x) + 0.127$$
$$\times \cos(2\pi u_5 x) - 0.091\cos(2\pi u_7 x) + 0.071\cos(2\pi u_9 x) + \cdots \qquad (9.8c)$$

and

$$f(x) = 0.125 + 0.244\cos(2\pi u_1 x) + 0.225\cos(2\pi u_2 x)$$
$$+ 0.196\cos(2\pi u_3 x) + 0.159\cos(2\pi u_4 x) + 0.118\cos(2\pi u_5 x)$$
$$+ 0.075\cos(2\pi u_6 x) + 0.035\cos(2\pi u_7 x) - 0.027\cos(2\pi u_9 x)$$
$$+ \cdots, \qquad (9.8d)$$

respectively. A relatively slower decrease in the relative magnitudes of successive weighting factors for the wave with narrower rectangle function should be noted. The ratio a_9/a_0 is 0.108 (11%) for $l = 16$ and 0.071(7%) for $l = 4$.

Figure 9.2a,b shows the repeat periods of the periodic rectangle functions for $l = 4$ and 16, and Fig. 9.2c,d shows the corresponding distributions of the weighting factors (the sampled sinc functions). In these plots, only positive spatial frequencies are shown (Eq. 9.5). However, for this particular example, negative spatial frequencies can be admitted (Eq. 9.8b), allowing a more symmetrical display of the weighting factors (Fig. 9.2e,f).

The weighting factors give the amplitudes and phases (only the signs in the present case) of the spatial frequencies needed to build a periodic function. The negative sign with some of the coefficients in Eqs (9.8) indicates a phase difference of 180° for those spatial frequencies. The distribution of the weighting factors of a function represents its spatial frequency spectrum (Fig. 9.2e,f). The spatial frequencies with zero amplitudes are excluded in the synthesis of a function. For example, for $l = 4$, the spatial frequencies $u = \frac{2}{\Lambda}, \frac{4}{\Lambda}, \frac{6}{\Lambda}, \ldots$ are missing from the spatial frequency spectrum of the rectangle wave. For a fixed period, as the rectangle gets narrower (increasing l), the magnitude of a_0 (representing the d.c. part) decreases and a larger number of higher a_n coefficients begin to have values comparable to that of a_0. Therefore, a narrow function requires a large number of spatial frequencies for its synthesis. Putting it differently, a narrow function possesses a large spatial frequency bandwidth.

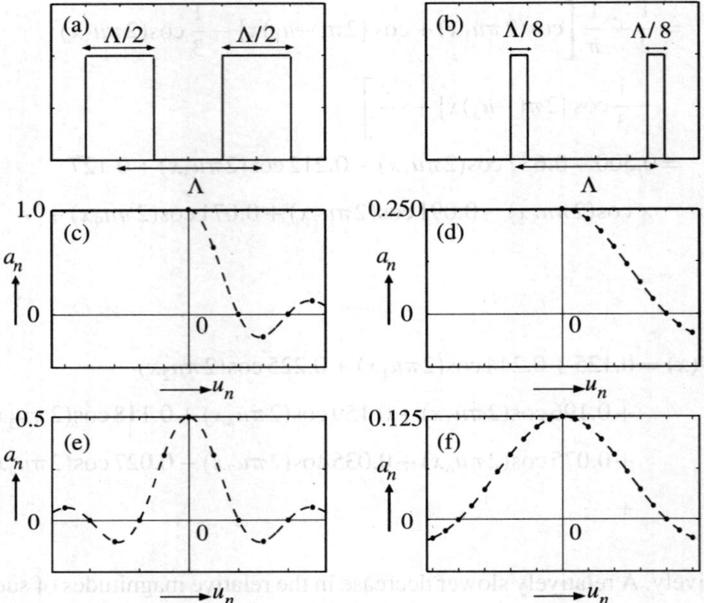

Fig. 9.2: (a, b) Rectangle waves with $l = 4, 16$; distributions of their Fourier coefficients, (c, d) admitting only positive spatial frequencies, (e, f) admitting negative spatial frequencies as well.

The number of terms with non-negligible weighting factors in the Fourier decomposition of a periodic function depends on its detailed structure. Broadly speaking, a smoothly varying function requires a smaller number of terms for its synthesis as compared to a function possessing sharp discontinuities. Figure 9.3 shows an attempt to synthesize a rectangle wave of period 2 and $l = 16$. Retaining terms up to $n = 40$ in the expansion, the synthesized wave (Fig. 9.3a) is a rather poor representation of the rectangle wave. Figure 9.3b, obtained with 10,000 terms in the expansion, seems to reproduce the rectangle wave quite well, except for some discrepancy close to the edges of the rectangle. Figure 9.3c is a zoomed version of Fig. 9.3b showing portions of the synthesized wave very close to a discontinuity. Substantial disagreement (overshooting to the extent of 8.9%) near the edges of the rectangle remains even with 10,000 terms in the expansion. However, the average of the values of the synthesized function just before and just after the discontinuity is in close agreement with the value of the function at the discontinuity.

Note that the Fourier decomposition of a periodic function is not unique. A different choice of the origin in Fig. 9.1 gives another perfectly valid representation

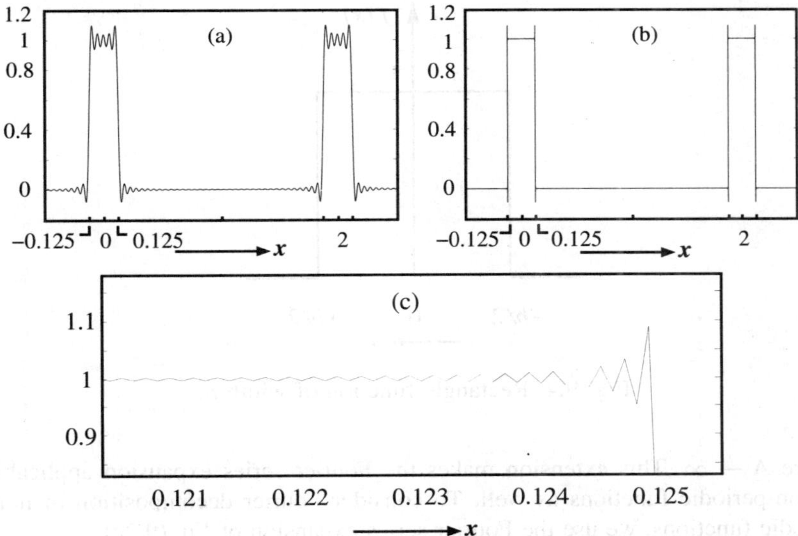

Fig. 9.3: Synthesis of a rectangle wave of period 2 and width 0.250 (a) with 40 terms in the Fourier expansion, (b) with 10,000 terms in the Fourier expansion; (c) zoomed version of (b) showing discrepancy near a discontinuity.

of the rectangle wave. We mention in passing that if the rectangle wave (Eq. 9.6) were to represent the grating transmission, the spatial frequencies u_n and the weighting factors a_n, respectively, give the locations and relative strengths of the principal maxima of the grating diffraction. It may also be noted that making the rectangle function narrower (increasing l in Eq. 9.6) effectively increases the period of the rectangle wave. This has the effect of bringing the spatial frequencies of the rectangle wave closer to each other (compare Fig. 9.2c,d). Extending this argument to the limit, we can say that the spatial frequency spectrum of a wave of period approaching infinity becomes continuous. This brings us to the discussion of the Fourier representation of a non-periodic function.

9.3 FOURIER TRANSFORMS IN ONE DIMENSION

The Fourier series expansion is applicable to periodic functions. A non-periodic function such as the one shown in Fig. 9.4 can be considered to be periodic with infinite period, i.e.,

$$f(x) = f(x + \Lambda),$$

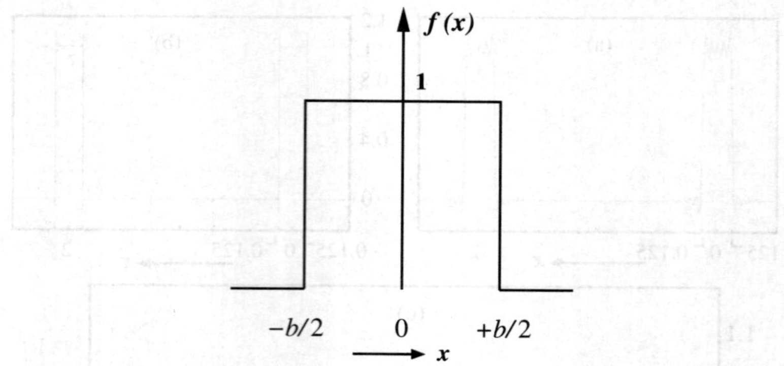

Fig. 9.4: Rectangle function of width b.

where $\Lambda \to \infty$. This extension makes the Fourier series expansion applicable to non-periodic functions as well. To consider Fourier decomposition of non-periodic functions, we use the Fourier series expansion of Eq. (9.2c):

$$f(x) = \sum_{n=-\infty}^{+\infty} a_n \, \mathrm{e}^{\mathrm{i}2\pi u_n x}, \tag{9.2c}$$

where

$$a_n = \frac{1}{\Lambda} \int_{-\Lambda/2}^{+\Lambda/2} f(x) \mathrm{e}^{-\mathrm{i}2\pi u_n x} \, \mathrm{d}x. \tag{9.9}$$

Substituting Eq. (9.9) into Eq. (9.2c), we have

$$f(x) = \sum_{n=-\infty}^{+\infty} \left[\frac{1}{\Lambda} \int_{-\Lambda/2}^{+\Lambda/2} f(x') \mathrm{e}^{-\mathrm{i}2\pi u_n x'} \, \mathrm{d}x' \right] \mathrm{e}^{\mathrm{i}2\pi u_n x}, \tag{9.10}$$

where $u_n = (n/\Lambda)$. As Λ approaches infinity,

$$u_n \to u \quad \Delta u = u_{n+1} - u_n = \frac{1}{\Lambda} \to \mathrm{d}u. \tag{9.11}$$

In this limit, the sum in Eq. (9.10) can be replaced by an integral so that

$$\begin{aligned} f(x) &= \int_{-\infty}^{+\infty} \left[\int_{-\infty}^{+\infty} f(x') \mathrm{e}^{-\mathrm{i}2\pi u x'} \mathrm{d}x' \right] \mathrm{e}^{\mathrm{i}2\pi u x} \, \mathrm{d}u \\ &= \int_{-\infty}^{+\infty} F(u) \mathrm{e}^{\mathrm{i}2\pi u x} \, \mathrm{d}u, \end{aligned} \tag{9.12a}$$

where

$$F(u) = \int_{-\infty}^{+\infty} f(x) e^{-i2\pi ux} \, dx \tag{9.12b}$$

is the Fourier transform of function $f(x)$, written symbolically as

$$F(u) = \mathcal{F}[f(x)]. \tag{9.13a}$$

Equation (9.12a) defines the inverse Fourier transform operation, i.e.,

$$f(x) = \mathcal{F}^{-1}[F(u)] = \int_{-\infty}^{+\infty} F(u) e^{i2\pi ux} \, du. \tag{9.13b}$$

The non-periodic function $f(x)$ has been expressed in terms of the complex exponential functions of continuously distributed spatial frequencies. The product $F(u)du$ represents the weighting factor for the spatial frequencies lying in the interval between u and $u+du$. The function $f(x)$ and its Fourier transform $F(u)$ constitute a Fourier transform pair.

It should be noted that the exponents in Eqs (9.12b) and (9.13b) appear with opposite signs. In literature, considerable variation in notation exists. We have used spatial frequency $u = \frac{1}{\Lambda}$, expressed in cycles/cm (or lines/mm) in the definition of the Fourier transform. Instead, if angular spatial frequency $k = 2\pi u = \frac{2\pi}{\Lambda}$ is used, then

$$F(k) = \int_{-\infty}^{+\infty} f(x) e^{-ikx} \, dx, \tag{9.14a}$$

$$f(x) = \frac{1}{2\pi} \int_{-\infty}^{+\infty} F(k) e^{ikx} \, dk. \tag{9.14b}$$

Yet another notation exists, where

$$F(k) = \frac{1}{\sqrt{2\pi}} \int_{-\infty}^{+\infty} f(x) e^{-ikx} \, dx, \tag{9.15a}$$

$$f(x) = \frac{1}{\sqrt{2\pi}} \int_{-\infty}^{+\infty} F(k) e^{ikx} \, dk. \tag{9.15b}$$

To summarize, the Fourier transform projects the spatial frequency structure of a non-periodic function defined in the spatial coordinate domain. A similar statement can be made for the functions in the time and temporal frequency domains. The Fourier transform is expressed in terms of the complex exponentials with continuously distributed frequencies (positive and negative). This is in contrast to the Fourier series decomposition of a periodic function involving only discrete (harmonic) positive frequencies.

9.3.1 Fourier Transforms of Simple Functions

9.3.1.1 Rectangle Function

The Fourier transform of the rectangle function of unit height (Fig. 9.4) is

$$\begin{aligned} F(u) &= \int_{-\infty}^{+\infty} f(x)\mathrm{e}^{-\mathrm{i}2\pi ux}\,\mathrm{d}x \\ &= \int_{-b/2}^{+b/2} \mathrm{e}^{-\mathrm{i}2\pi ux}\,\mathrm{d}x \\ &= b\,\mathrm{sinc}\,(\pi ub), \end{aligned} \tag{9.16}$$

where b is the width of the rectangle. This transform is real but not always positive. The sinc function (Fig. 9.5) gives the amplitude distribution of the spatial frequencies needed to synthesize the rectangle function. Negative values of the sinc function imply phase reversal for those spatial frequencies. Significant contributions to the Fourier transform of the rectangle function come from the spatial frequencies lying in the interval between $-\frac{n}{b}$ and $+\frac{n}{b}$, where n is a small

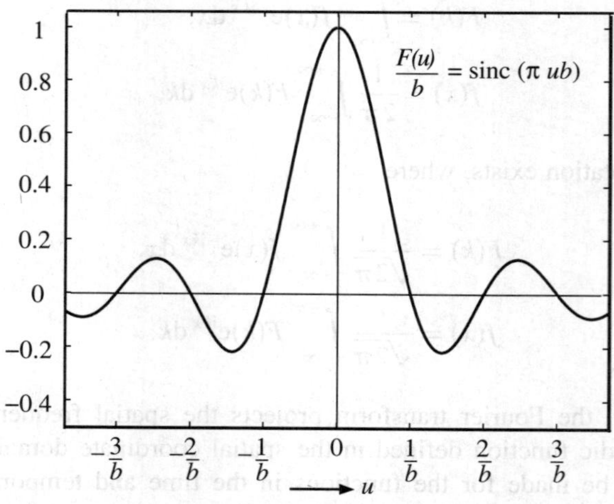

Fig. 9.5: Spatial frequency spectrum of rectangle function of width b.

integer. The sinc function has maximum value of unity for the spatial frequency $u = 0$. The zeroes of the sinc function appear at

$$u = \pm\frac{1}{b}, \pm\frac{2}{b}, \pm\frac{3}{b}, \ldots \tag{9.17}$$

A reciprocal relationship exists between the spatial frequency spread $(2/b)$ of the central lobe of the sinc function and the width of the rectangle function.

A comparison of Eqs (9.7c) and (9.16) suggests an alternate approach to obtain the Fourier transform of a non-repeating function. The spatial frequency spectrum (Fig. 9.2c,d) of the rectangle wave is a sampled version of the continuous spatial frequency spectrum (Fig. 9.5) of the rectangle function. It is therefore possible to generate the Fourier transform of the rectangle function from the knowledge of the spatial frequency spectrum of the corresponding periodic rectangle function. The periodic function can be generated from the non-periodic function by replication, i.e., by treating the non-repeating function as the repeat unit of the periodic function. The question as to what is the minimum sampling needed to get a precise estimate of the Fourier transform of the non-periodic function from the spectrum of the replicated function is answered by Shanon's sampling theorem. This theorem states that if the Fourier transform of a non-periodic function vanishes beyond a certain frequency, then the sampling rate must be at least twice per period of the highest frequency present in the Fourier transform. The frequency which is twice the highest frequency is called the Nyquist frequency. Sampling done at a rate lower than the Nyquist sampling rate can generate spatial frequencies which may not be present in the spatial frequency spectrum of the non-periodic function.

9.3.1.2 The Dirac delta Function

One-dimensional Dirac delta function

$$\delta(x-a) = 0 \quad \text{for } x \neq a \tag{9.18a}$$

has zero value everywhere except at $x = a$. At $x = a$, it approaches infinity in a manner that

$$\int_{-\infty}^{+\infty} \delta(x-a)\,\mathrm{d}x = 1. \tag{9.18b}$$

Its Fourier transform is

$$\begin{aligned} F(u) &= \int_{-\infty}^{+\infty} \delta(x-a)\mathrm{e}^{-\mathrm{i}2\pi ux}\,\mathrm{d}x \\ &= \mathrm{e}^{-\mathrm{i}2\pi ua}. \end{aligned} \tag{9.19}$$

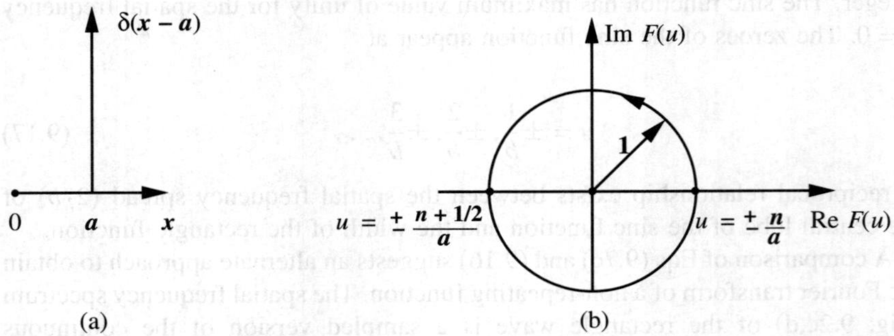

Fig. 9.6: (a) Dirac delta function $\delta(x-a)$, (b) its Fourier transform in the complex plane.

The spatial frequency spectrum of the Dirac delta function located at $x=a$ covers all spatial frequencies from $-\infty$ to $+\infty$ with equal amplitudes and with phases which vary linearly with the spatial frequency. This is shown in the complex plane in Fig. 9.6.

The transform of the delta function located at the origin is, however, real. The transform of two delta functions located at $x=\pm a$ is

$$\begin{aligned} F(u) &= \int_{-\infty}^{+\infty} [\delta(x-a)+\delta(x+a)]\mathrm{e}^{-\mathrm{i}2\pi ux}\,\mathrm{d}x \\ &= 2\cos(2\pi ua). \end{aligned} \tag{9.20}$$

Its inverse also holds, i.e.,

$$\begin{aligned} \mathcal{F}[\cos(2\pi u_0 x)] &= \int_{-\infty}^{+\infty} \cos(2\pi u_0 x)\mathrm{e}^{-\mathrm{i}2\pi ux}\,\mathrm{d}x \\ &= \frac{1}{2}\int_{-\infty}^{+\infty} [\mathrm{e}^{-\mathrm{i}2\pi(u-u_0)x}+\mathrm{e}^{-\mathrm{i}2\pi(u+u_0)x}]\mathrm{d}x \\ &= \frac{1}{2}[\delta(u-u_0)+\delta(u+u_0)]. \end{aligned} \tag{9.21}$$

These features are shown in Fig. 9.7. The transform of the comb function

$$\text{comb}\,(x) = \sum_{n=-N}^{+N} \delta(x-na) \tag{9.22a}$$

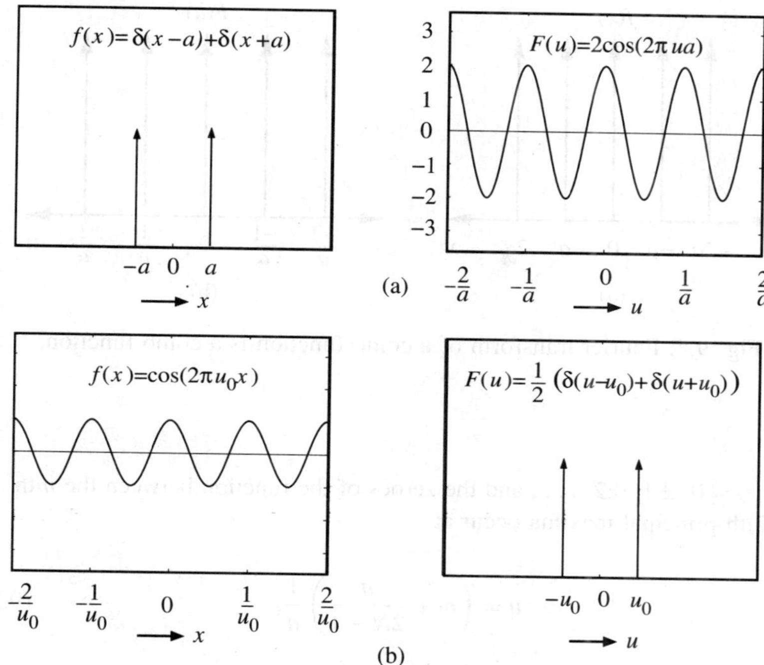

Fig. 9.7: (a) Fourier transform of two delta functions is a cosine function. (b) Fourier transform of a cosine function consists of two delta functions.

consisting of $(2N+1)$ equidistant delta functions is

$$F(u) = \int_{-\infty}^{+\infty} \sum_{n=-N}^{+N} \delta(x-na)\mathrm{e}^{-\mathrm{i}2\pi ux}\,\mathrm{d}x$$

$$= \sum_{n=-N}^{+N} \mathrm{e}^{-\mathrm{i}2\pi una} \tag{9.22b}$$

$$= (2N+1)\frac{\mathrm{sinc}[(2N+1)\pi ua]}{\mathrm{sinc}(\pi ua)}.$$

The principal maxima of this function with peak heights of $(2N+1)$ are located at

$$u = \frac{m}{a}, \tag{9.23}$$

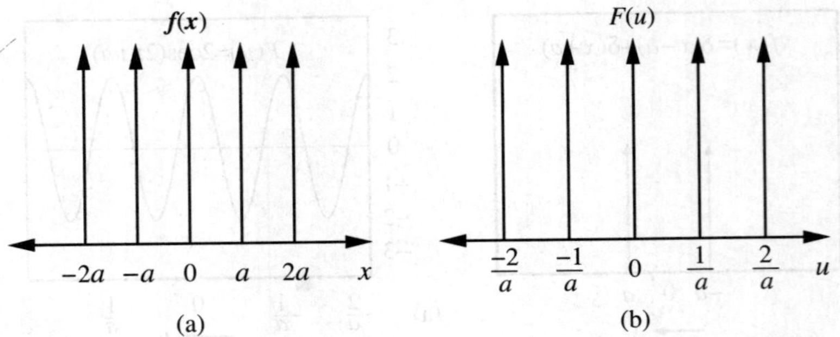

Fig. 9.8: Fourier transform of a comb function is a comb function.

where $m = 0, \pm 1, \pm 2, \ldots$, and the zeroes of the function between the mth and $(m+1)$th principal maxima occur at

$$u = \left(m + \frac{n}{2N+1} \right) \frac{1}{a}, \tag{9.24}$$

where $n = \pm 1, \pm 2, \ldots, \pm 2N$. Weak secondary maxima occur between consecutive zeroes of $F(u)$. For sufficiently large N, the principal maxima become strong and sharp and the secondary maxima become relatively weak. Accordingly, the Fourier transform of a one-dimensional comb function consisting of an infinite array of equally spaced delta functions is a comb function in the spatial frequency domain (Fig. 9.8). Strictly speaking, Fourier transform of a comb function containing a set of infinite delta functions does not exist because the sum in Eq. (9.22a) does not remain finite as $N \to \infty$.

9.3.1.3 Damped Oscillator

We next consider the function

$$\begin{aligned} f(t) &= A_0 \, \mathrm{e}^{-(t/\tau)} \cos(2\pi\nu_0 t) && \text{for } t \geq 0 \\ &= 0 && \text{for } t < 0 \end{aligned} \tag{9.25}$$

in the time domain. This function may represent the electric field radiated by an atom, in which case, τ refers to the life-time of the excited state of the atom.

The transform of this function is

$$\begin{aligned}
F(\nu) &= A_0 \int_0^{+\infty} e^{-(t/\tau)} \cos(2\pi\nu_0 t) e^{-i2\pi\nu t}\, dt \\
&= \frac{A_0}{2} \int_0^{+\infty} e^{-(t/\tau)} \left[e^{i2\pi(\nu_0-\nu)t} + e^{-i2\pi(\nu_0+\nu)t} \right] dt \qquad (9.26)\\
&= \frac{A_0}{2} \left[\frac{1}{\frac{1}{\tau} - i2\pi(\nu_0-\nu)} + \frac{1}{\frac{1}{\tau} + i2\pi(\nu_0+\nu)} \right].
\end{aligned}$$

Second term being small at the optical frequencies can be ignored. Therefore,

$$F(\nu) = \left(\frac{A_0}{2}\right) \frac{1}{\frac{1}{\tau} - i2\pi(\nu_0-\nu)}, \qquad (9.27)$$

$$\begin{aligned}
|F(\nu)|^2 &= \left(\frac{A_0^2}{4}\right) \frac{1}{\frac{1}{\tau^2} + 4\pi^2(\nu_0-\nu)^2} \\
&= \left(\frac{A_0^2\tau^2}{4}\right) \frac{(\delta\nu_0)^2}{(\nu-\nu_0)^2 + (\delta\nu_0)^2},
\end{aligned} \qquad (9.28)$$

where

$$\delta\nu_0 = \frac{1}{2\pi\tau}. \qquad (9.29)$$

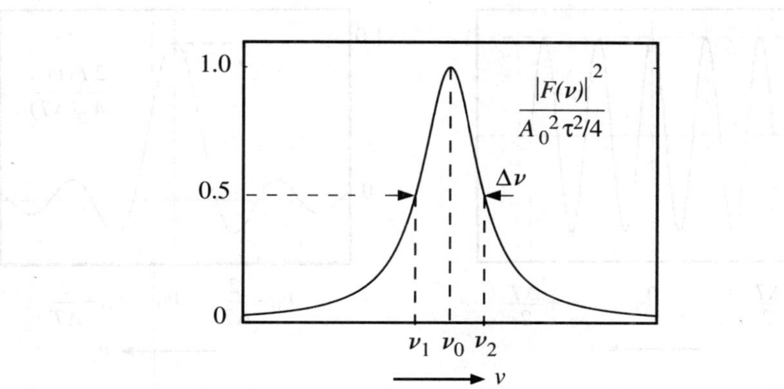

Fig. 9.9: Frequency spectrum of a damped oscillator has Lorentzian profile.

The square modulus of the Fourier transform of the damped oscillator function has Lorentzian profile (Fig. 9.9) with full width at half maximum (FWHM) of

$$\Delta\nu = \nu_2 - \nu_1 = 2\delta\nu_0 = \frac{1}{\pi\tau}. \tag{9.30}$$

9.3.1.4 Truncated Oscillator

The function

$$\begin{aligned} f(t) &= A_0 \cos 2\pi\nu_0 t \quad \text{for } -\frac{\Delta T}{2} \le t \le +\frac{\Delta T}{2}, \\ &= 0 \quad \text{otherwise} \end{aligned} \tag{9.31}$$

describes an oscillator which oscillates without damping for a finite interval of time. Its Fourier transform is

$$\begin{aligned} F(\nu) &= \frac{A_0}{2}\int_{-\Delta T/2}^{+\Delta T/2} (\mathrm{e}^{\mathrm{i}2\pi\nu_0 t} + \mathrm{e}^{-\mathrm{i}2\pi\nu_0 t})\mathrm{e}^{-\mathrm{i}2\pi\nu t}\,\mathrm{d}t \\ &= \frac{A_0}{2}(\Delta T)[\mathrm{sinc}\{\pi(\nu-\nu_0)\Delta T\} + \mathrm{sinc}\{\pi(\nu+\nu_0)\Delta T\}]. \end{aligned} \tag{9.32}$$

The second sinc function may be ignored since its dominant contributions are for negative frequencies. Figure 9.10 shows the truncated oscillator function and its Fourier transform for positive frequencies. The zeroes in the Fourier transform, nearest to the oscillator frequency ν_0, occur at $\nu - \nu_0 = \pm\frac{1}{\Delta T}$.

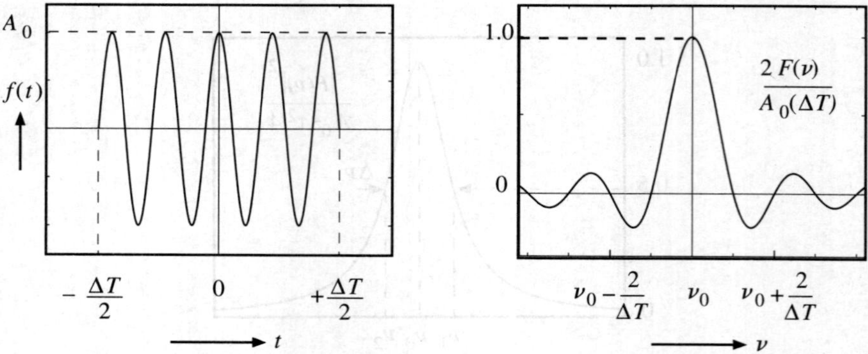

Fig. 9.10: Normalized Fourier transform of the truncated oscillator function is a sinc function.

An oscillator oscillating for a short time emits radiation with a broad frequency spectrum. To emit monochromatic radiation, the oscillator must oscillate for all times. The bandwidth $\Delta\nu$ of a truncated oscillator is defined by the relation

$$\Delta\nu\Delta T = 1. \tag{9.33}$$

9.4 FOURIER TRANSFORMS IN TWO DIMENSIONS

The Fourier transform of a two-dimensional function $f(x, y)$ is

$$F(u, v) = \iint_{-\infty}^{\infty} f(x, y)\mathrm{e}^{-\mathrm{i}2\pi(ux+vy)}\mathrm{d}x\,\mathrm{d}y, \tag{9.34}$$

where u and v defined in the manner of Eq. (9.11) are the spatial frequencies in two dimensions. The transform of a two-dimensional product function

$$f(x, y) = g(x)h(y) \tag{9.35a}$$

is

$$\begin{aligned} F(u, v) &= \int_{-\infty}^{+\infty} g(x)\mathrm{e}^{-\mathrm{i}2\pi ux}\,\mathrm{d}x \int_{-\infty}^{+\infty} h(y)\mathrm{e}^{-\mathrm{i}2\pi vy}\,\mathrm{d}y \\ &= G(u)H(v), \end{aligned} \tag{9.35b}$$

where $G(u)$ and $H(v)$ are the Fourier transforms of the one-dimensional functions $g(x)$ and $h(y)$, respectively. The two-dimensional inverse Fourier transform is likewise defined as

$$\begin{aligned} f(x, y) &= \mathcal{F}^{-1}[F(u, v)] \\ &= \iint_{-\infty}^{\infty} F(u, v)\mathrm{e}^{\mathrm{i}2\pi(ux+vy)}\mathrm{d}u\,\mathrm{d}v. \end{aligned} \tag{9.36}$$

9.4.1 Properties of the Fourier Transforms

The Fourier transform was introduced as an extension of the Fourier series representation of a periodic function in the limit of the period of the function approaching infinity. Therefore, to have a Fourier transform, the function must satisfy all restrictions imposed on a function while defining its Fourier series representation. In particular, for the Fourier transform to exist, the function $f(x, y)$ must be absolutely integrable, i.e.,

$$\iint_{-\infty}^{\infty} |f(x, y)| \mathrm{d}x \, \mathrm{d}y < \infty. \tag{9.37}$$

Some of the important properties of the Fourier transform are given below:

9.4.1.1 Symmetry Properties

For real $f(x, y)$,

$$\begin{aligned} F^*(u, v) &= [\mathcal{F}[f(x, y)]]^* \\ &= \iint_{-\infty}^{\infty} f^*(x, y) \mathrm{e}^{\mathrm{i}2\pi(ux+vy)} \mathrm{d}x \, \mathrm{d}y \\ &= \iint_{-\infty}^{\infty} f(x, y) \mathrm{e}^{-\mathrm{i}2\pi(-ux-vy)} \mathrm{d}x \, \mathrm{d}y \\ &= F(-u, -v). \end{aligned} \tag{9.38}$$

Furthermore,

$$F^*(u, v) = \pm F(u, v) \tag{9.39}$$

if the function is in addition even (+sign) or odd (−sign).

9.4.1.2 Scaling Property

$$\begin{aligned} \mathcal{F}\left[f\left(\frac{x}{a}, \frac{y}{b}\right)\right] &= \iint_{-\infty}^{\infty} f\left(\frac{x}{a}, \frac{y}{b}\right) \mathrm{e}^{-\mathrm{i}2\pi(ux+vy)} \mathrm{d}x \, \mathrm{d}y \\ &= |ab| \iint_{-\infty}^{\infty} f\left(\frac{x}{a}, \frac{y}{b}\right) \mathrm{e}^{-\mathrm{i}2\pi[au(\frac{x}{a})+bv(\frac{y}{b})]} \mathrm{d}\left(\frac{x}{a}\right) \mathrm{d}\left(\frac{y}{b}\right) \\ &= |ab| F(au, bv). \end{aligned} \tag{9.40}$$

A compression in the spatial coordinate domain results in expansion in the spatial frequency domain and vice versa. This feature shows up in the broadening of the Fraunhofer diffraction pattern of an aperture on reducing its size.

9.4.1.3 Shifting Property

$$\begin{aligned}\mathcal{F}[f(x-x_0, y-y_0)] &= \iint_{-\infty}^{\infty} f(x-x_0, y-y_0)\mathrm{e}^{-\mathrm{i}2\pi(ux+vy)}\,\mathrm{d}x\,\mathrm{d}y \\ &= \mathrm{e}^{-\mathrm{i}2\pi(ux_0+vy_0)} \iint_{-\infty}^{\infty} f(x-x_0, y-y_0) \\ &\quad \times \mathrm{e}^{-\mathrm{i}2\pi[u(x-x_0)+v(y-y_0)]}\,\mathrm{d}(x-x_0)\mathrm{d}(y-y_0) \\ &= \mathrm{e}^{-\mathrm{i}2\pi(ux_0+vy_0)}F(u, v).\end{aligned} \tag{9.41}$$

A spatial translation of a function produces a phase shift in its Fourier transform, leaving the square modulus of the Fourier transform unchanged. This is borne out of the fact that a translation of the diffracting aperture in the transverse plane does not modify the intensity distribution in Fraunhofer diffraction. Similarly, it can be shown that a change in the phase of a function shifts the spatial frequency spectrum of its Fourier transform, i.e.,

$$\mathcal{F}[f(x, y)\mathrm{e}^{-\mathrm{i}2\pi(u_0x+v_0y)}] = F(u+u_0, v+v_0). \tag{9.42}$$

9.4.1.4 Linearity Property

$$\mathcal{F}[ag(x, y)+bh(x, y)] = aG(u, v)+bH(u, v), \tag{9.43}$$

where $G(u, v)$ and $H(u, v)$ are the transforms of $g(x, y)$ and $h(x, y)$, respectively, and a, b are arbitrary constants, real or complex. For complementary functions, i.e., for

$$h(x, y) = 1 - g(x, y), \tag{9.44a}$$

the linearity property requires

$$H(u, v) = \delta(u, v) - G(u, v) \tag{9.44b}$$

since

$$\begin{aligned}\mathcal{F}[1] &= \iint_{-\infty}^{\infty} 1\mathrm{e}^{-\mathrm{i}2\pi(ux+vy)}\,\mathrm{d}x\,\mathrm{d}y \\ &= \delta(u, v).\end{aligned} \tag{9.45}$$

Except for the zero spatial frequency, Fourier transforms of complementary functions are identical to within a sign change. Linearity property of the Fourier transform is extensively utilized in Fourier optics.

9.4.1.5 Parseval's Theorem

$$
\begin{aligned}
\iint_{-\infty}^{\infty} |F(u,v)|^2 \mathrm{d}u\,\mathrm{d}v &= \iint_{-\infty}^{\infty} F^*(u,v)F(u,v)\mathrm{d}u\,\mathrm{d}v \\
&= \iint_{-\infty}^{\infty} \left[\iint_{-\infty}^{\infty} f^*(x,y)\mathrm{e}^{\mathrm{i}2\pi(ux+vy)}\mathrm{d}x\,\mathrm{d}y \right] \\
&\quad \times \left[\iint_{-\infty}^{\infty} f(x'y')\mathrm{e}^{-\mathrm{i}2\pi(ux'+vy')}\,\mathrm{d}x'\mathrm{d}y' \right] \mathrm{d}u\,\mathrm{d}v \\
&= \iint_{-\infty}^{\infty}\iint f^*(x,y)f(x',y')\delta(x'-x) \\
&\quad \times \delta(y'-y)\mathrm{d}x\,\mathrm{d}x'\mathrm{d}y\,\mathrm{d}y' \\
&= \iint_{-\infty}^{\infty} f^*(x,y)f(x,y)\mathrm{d}x\,\mathrm{d}y \\
&= \iint_{-\infty}^{\infty} |f(x,y)|^2\mathrm{d}x\,\mathrm{d}y.
\end{aligned}
\tag{9.46}
$$

Parseval's theorem is a statement of energy conservation. As an ilustration, we note that the intensity distribution in Fraunhofer diffraction is proportional to the square modulus of the Fourier transform of the field distribution in the object plane (see Eqs 10.6 and 10.9). Therefore in Fraunhofer diffraction, Parseval's theorem ensures the equality of the energy contents of the field distributions over the object and diffraction planes.

9.5 CONVOLUTION OPERATION

It often happens that a physical quantity actually measured differs non-trivially from what was intended to be measured. This may be due to some inherent but systematic limitation of the instrument used to make the measurement. For example, the finite width of the entrance slit limits the ability of a spectrometer to reproduce the spectral composition of narrow band radiation. The spectral profile recorded by a spectrometer depends on the spectral distribution of the source and also on the spectral response of the spectrometer. In fact, the recorded profile is the convolution of the functions representing the spectral distribution of the source and the spectral response of the instrument. The convolution of functions is an extremely useful concept in optics and elsewhere. We provide here a brief introduction to the convolution operation and its use.

Two functions, continuous or discrete, can be convolved (provided certain conditions are satisfied) to generate a third function which shares the characteristics of the original functions. The convolution of two real and continuous one-dimensional functions $f_1(x)$ and $f_2(x)$ is defined through the integral

$$f(x) = \int_{-\infty}^{+\infty} f_1(x')f_2(x-x')\mathrm{d}x' \tag{9.47a}$$

and is symbolically written as

$$f(x) = f_1(x) * f_2(x). \tag{9.47b}$$

The functions $f_1(x)$ and $f_2(x)$ must be bounded everywhere and be absolutely integrable. The particular form of the argument $(x - x')$ in the second function is often encountered when a shift in the position of the input to a system produces only a shift in the position of the output from the system. Such systems are called shift-invariant systems. Isoplanatism in optics implies shift-invariance of an optical system. The convolution of three one-dimensional functions is defined as

$$\begin{aligned} f(x) &= [f_1(x) * f_2(x)] * f_3(x) \\ &= \left[\int_{-\infty}^{+\infty} f_1(x')f_2(x-x')\mathrm{d}x'\right] * f_3(x) \\ &= \int_{-\infty}^{+\infty}\left[\int_{-\infty}^{+\infty} f_1(x')f_2(x''-x')\mathrm{d}x'\right] f_3(x-x'')\mathrm{d}x''. \end{aligned} \tag{9.48}$$

The convolution operation is commutative:

$$\begin{aligned} f(x) &= f_1(x) * f_2(x) \\ &= \int_{-\infty}^{+\infty} f_1(x')f_2(x-x')\mathrm{d}x' \\ &= \int_{-\infty}^{+\infty} f_2(x'')f_1(x-x'')\mathrm{d}x'' \\ &= f_2(x) * f_1(x). \end{aligned}$$

Similarly, it can be shown that the convolution operation satisfies distributive and associative properties. The convolution operation in two dimensions is defined by the integral

$$f(x, y) = \int\int_{-\infty}^{\infty} f_1(x', y') f_2(x - x', y - y') \mathrm{d}x' \mathrm{d}y' \tag{9.49a}$$

$$= f_1(x, y) * f_2(x, y). \tag{9.49b}$$

To demonstrate the power of the convolution operation, we show how a train of rectangle functions can be generated from the convolution of a rectangle function with a sequence of Dirac delta functions (Fig. 9.11). Let

$$f_1(x) = \delta(x) + \delta(x - a) \tag{9.50}$$

represent two delta functions located at $x = 0$ and $x = a$, and

$$f_2(x) = h(x) \tag{9.51}$$

be a rectangle function of height h and width b. The convolution of $f_1(x)$ and $f_2(x)$ is

$$\int_{-\infty}^{+\infty} f_1(x') f_2(x - x') \mathrm{d}x' = \int_{-\infty}^{+\infty} [\delta(x') + \delta(x' - a)] h(x - x') \mathrm{d}x' \\ = h(x) + h(x - a). \tag{9.52}$$

Thus, the convolution of two delta functions and a rectangle function generates a train of two rectangle functions. Similarly, for sufficiently large N, the

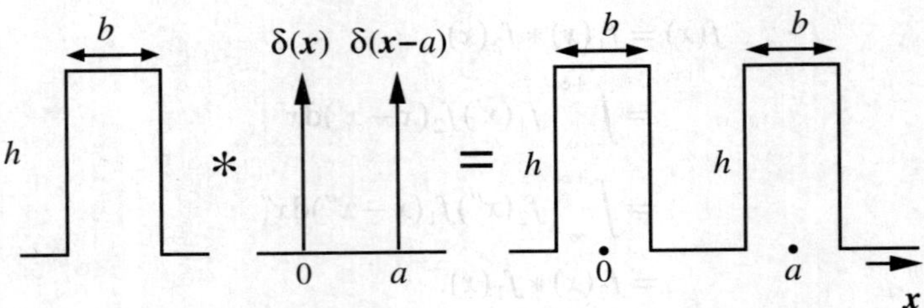

Fig. 9.11: Convolution of a rectangle function with two Dirac delta functions is a train of two rectangle functions.

convolution integral

$$\int_{-\infty}^{+\infty}\left[\sum_{n=-N}^{+N}\delta(x'-na)\right]h(x-x')\mathrm{d}x' \tag{9.53}$$

replicates the rectangle function $h(x)$ into a periodic rectangle function (Fig. 9.1).

9.5.1 Convolution as the Area of Products

The convolution operation is a bit difficult concept to comprehend. To help the reader appreciate what is involved, we digress on the physical interpretation of the convolution operation.

The convolution of functions $f_1(x)$ and $f_2(x)$ can be interpreted in terms of the area of products of the functions $f_1(x')$ and $f_2(x-x')$, where $f_1(x')$ is the function $f_1(x)$ with x replaced by the dummy variable x' (Fig. 9.12a) and function $f_2(x-x')$ is generated by first inverting the function $f_2(x')$ to get $f_2(-x')$ and then translating it by an amount x to the right (Fig. 9.12b). The function $f_2(x-x')$ can also be generated by folding the function $f_2(x')$ about the point $x/2$ (Fig. 9.12c). The functions $f_1(x')$ and $f_2(x-x')$ are then superimposed (Fig. 9.12d). Within the region of overlap of the functions, the product $f_1(x')f_2(x-x')$ is calculated as a function of x'. Figure 9.12e is a plot of this product as a function of x'. The area under this curve is the value of the convolution integral for displacement x of the function $f_2(-x')$. The full range of the convolution function $f(x)$ can be obtained by appropriately displacing the function $f_2(-x')$ to the right and to the left and repeating the above steps. The extent of the overlap between $f_1(x')$ and $f_2(x-x')$ depends on the displacement x and the spreads of the convolving functions. Beyond a certain value of x, the functions may not overlap and the convolution integral vanishes.

To illustrate this procedure, we calculate the convolution of two rectangle functions of unequal heights and widths (Fig. 9.13a). The convolution integral

$$\begin{aligned} f(x) &= f_1(x) * f_2(x) \\ &= \int_{-\infty}^{+\infty} f_1(x')f_2(x-x')\mathrm{d}x' \end{aligned}$$

for any displacement x can be obtained by sliding the inverted function $f_2(-x')$ by an amount x across $f_1(x')$. As long as $f_2(x-x')$ lies fully within $f_1(x')$ as in Fig. 9.13b, the area under the product $f_1(x')f_2(x-x')$ and hence the convolution integral maintains the constant value

$$f(x) = 2bh_1h_2. \tag{9.54a}$$

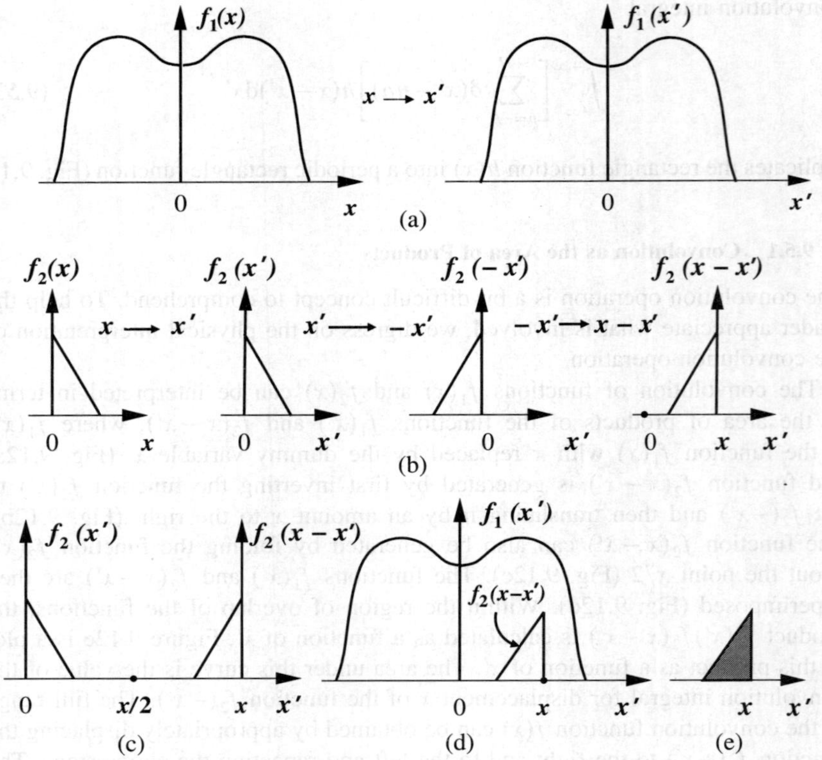

Fig. 9.12: Convolution integral as area of products of $f_1(x')$ and $f_2(x-x')$; area of the shaded figure (e) represents the convolution for a displacement of $f_2(-x')$ by x.

If the function $f_2(x-x')$ is partially outside the function $f_1(x')$ as in Fig. 9.13c, then the convolution integral has the value

$$f(x) = (2b - x'')h_1 h_2, \tag{9.54b}$$

where width x'' of the rectangle $f_2(x-x')$ lies outside $f_1(x')$. Therefore, the convolution of two rectangle functions of unequal widths a and b, obtained by considering all possible displacements of one of the rectangles, is a trapezoid with its base extending from $-(a+b)$ to $+(a+b)$ as shown in Fig. 9.13d. As a rule, the width of the convolved function is the sum of the widths of the convolving functions which are non-zero over finite regions. With few exceptions,

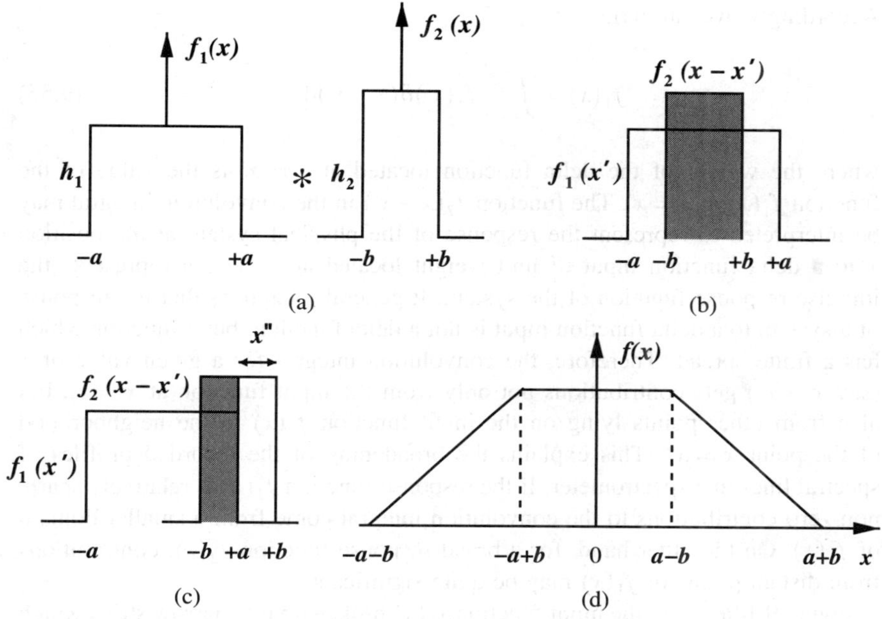

Fig. 9.13: (a) Convolution of two rectangle functions of unequal widths and heights, (b) $f_2(x - x')$ lies wholly within $f_1(x')$, (c) $f_2(x - x')$ lies partially outside $f_1(x')$, (d) convolution of two rectangle functions of unequal widths is a trapezoid.

the convolved function is always broader than either of the convolving functions. As a result, the finite width of the entrance slit in a spectrometer broadens the recorded profiles of the spectral lines. In addition, if neither of the convolving functions is a delta function, the convolution operation smoothens the discontinuities of the convolving functions.

9.5.2 Convolution and Impulse Response

The area of the products of the functions $f_1(x')$ and $f_2(x - x')$ discussed in Section 9.5.1 is not the only interpretation that can be given to the convolution integral. Here is an alternate interpretation which is more in line with our comment in the introduction. The function $f_1(x)$ in the convolution integral may be treated as the input to a physical system. We can imagine $f_1(x)$ to consist of an infinite sequence of continuously distributed weighted delta functions.

Accordingly, we can write

$$f_1(x) = \int_{-\infty}^{+\infty} f_1(x')\delta(x-x')\mathrm{d}x', \tag{9.55}$$

where the weight of the delta function located at $x = x'$ is the value of the function $f_1(x)$ at $x = x'$. The function $f_2(x - x')$ in the convolution integral may be interpreted to represent the response of the physical system at the position x to a delta function input of unit weight located at x', i.e., it represents the impulse response function of the system. It generally happens that the response of a system to a delta function input is not a delta function, but a function which has a finite spread. Therefore, the convolution integral for a given value of x (say $x = x_1$) gets contributions not only from the input function at $x = x_1$, but also from other points lying on the input function $f_1(x)$ in the neighborhood of the point $x = x_1$. This explains the broadening of the recorded profiles of spectral lines in a spectrometer. If the response function $f_2(x)$ is relatively sharp, non-zero contributions to the convolution integral come from a smaller domain of $f_1(x)$. On the other hand, for a broad response function $f_2(x)$, contributions from distant points of $f_1(x)$ may be quite significant.

Figure 9.14a shows the input function $f_1(x)$ broken up into narrow strips which in the limit go over to the appropriately weighted delta functions. Figure 9.14b shows the impulse response function of the system. The contributions to the convolution integral $f(x = x_1)$ from the strips of the input function located at $x = x_3$, x_1, x_2 are shown in Fig. 9.14c. The strips of $f_1(x)$ beyond a certain distance from x_1 do not contribute to the convolution integral $f(x = x_1)$. The contributions from all neighboring strips are added to obtain the value of the convolution integral (Eq. 9.47a) for $x = x_1$. Complete convolution function $f(x)$ can be generated by translating the function $f_2(x)$ across the input function $f_1(x)$.

The convolution of complex functions is defined as

$$f(x) = \int_{-\infty}^{+\infty} h_1(x')\mathrm{e}^{\mathrm{i}\phi_1(x')} h_2(x-x')\mathrm{e}^{\mathrm{i}\phi_2(x-x')}\,\mathrm{d}x', \tag{9.56}$$

where

$$f_1(x) = h_1(x)\mathrm{e}^{\mathrm{i}\phi_1(x)},$$

$$f_2(x) = h_2(x)\mathrm{e}^{\mathrm{i}\phi_2(x)}.$$

The functions $h_1(x)$, $h_2(x)$, $\phi_1(x)$ and $\phi_2(x)$ are real functions.

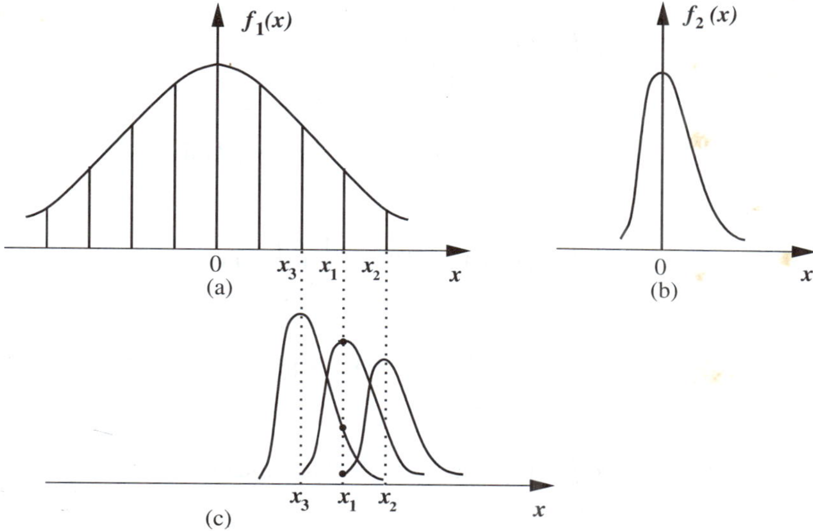

Fig. 9.14: (a) Input function $f_1(x)$ divided into narrow strips, (b) impulse response function $f_2(x)$, (c) contributions to the convolution $f(x = x_1)$ comes from the neighboring strips also.

9.5.3 Convolution Theorems

The Fourier transform of the convolution of two functions is the product of the Fourier transforms of the convolving functions, i.e., if

$$\mathcal{F}[f_1(x, y)] = F_1(u, v),$$
$$\mathcal{F}[f_2(x, y)] = F_2(u, v),$$

then

$$\mathcal{F}[f_1(x, y) * f_2(x, y)] = F_1(u, v)F_2(u, v). \tag{9.57}$$

Proof.

$$\mathcal{F}[f_1(x, y) * f_2(x, y)]$$
$$= \iint_{-\infty}^{\infty} \left[\iint_{-\infty}^{\infty} \mathrm{d}x'\mathrm{d}y' f_1(x', y') f_2(x - x', y - y') \right] \times \mathrm{e}^{-\mathrm{i}2\pi(ux+vy)} \mathrm{d}x\, \mathrm{d}y$$

$$=\int_{-\infty}^{\infty}\!\!\int f_1(x',y')\left[\int_{-\infty}^{\infty}\!\!\int f_2(x-x',y-y')\times e^{-i2\pi(ux+vy)}dx\,dy\right]dx'dy'$$

$$=\int_{-\infty}^{\infty}\!\!\int f_1(x',y')e^{-i2\pi(ux'+vy')}\left[\int_{-\infty}^{\infty}\!\!\int f_2(x-x',y-y')\times e^{-i2\pi\{u(x-x')+v(y-y')\}}d(x-x')d(y-y')\right]dx'dy'$$

$$=\int_{-\infty}^{\infty}\!\!\int f_1(x',y')e^{-i2\pi(ux'+vy')}F_2(u,v)dx'dy'$$

$$=F_1(u,v)F_2(u,v).$$

The converse of the above theorem also holds. The Fourier transform of the product of two functions is the convolution of the Fourier transforms of the functions, i.e.,

$$\mathcal{F}[f_1(x,y)f_2(x,y)]=\int_{-\infty}^{\infty}\!\!\int F_1(u',v')F_2(u-u',v-v')du'dv' = F_1(u,v)*F_2(u,v). \tag{9.58}$$

Proof.

$$\mathcal{F}[f_1(x,y)f_2(x,y)]$$

$$=\int_{-\infty}^{\infty}\!\!\int f_1(x,y)f_2(x,y)e^{-i2\pi(ux+vy)}dx\,dy$$

$$=\int_{-\infty}^{\infty}\!\!\int\left[\int_{-\infty}^{\infty}\!\!\int F_1(u',v')e^{i2\pi(u'x+v'y)}du'dv'\right]\times\left[\int_{-\infty}^{\infty}\!\!\int F_2(u'',v'')e^{i2\pi(u''x+v''y)}du''dv''\right]\times e^{-i2\pi(ux+vy)}\,dx\,dy$$

$$
\begin{aligned}
&= \iint_{-\infty}^{\infty} \iint_{-\infty}^{\infty} \mathrm{d}u'\mathrm{d}v'\mathrm{d}u''\mathrm{d}v'' F_1(u', v')F_2(u'', v'') \\
&\quad \times \iint_{-\infty}^{\infty} \mathrm{e}^{\mathrm{i}2\pi\{(u''+u'-u)x+(v''+v'-v)y\}}\, \mathrm{d}x\, \mathrm{d}y \\
&= \iint_{-\infty}^{\infty} \mathrm{d}u'\mathrm{d}v' F_1(u', v') \iint_{-\infty}^{\infty} F_2(u'', v'') \\
&\quad \times \delta(u''+u'-u)\delta(v''+v'-v)\mathrm{d}u''\mathrm{d}v'' \\
&= \iint_{-\infty}^{\infty} F_1(u', v')F_2(u-u', v-v')\mathrm{d}u'\mathrm{d}v' \\
&= F_1(u, v) * F_2(u, v).
\end{aligned}
$$

We shall have the opportunity to appreciate the power of the convolution theorems in later chapters. Here, we use it to find the Fourier transform of the triangle function. It follows from Fig. 9.13 that the convolution of a rectangle function with its clone is a triangle function. Accordingly, the Fourier transform of the triangle function can be written as

$$
\begin{aligned}
\mathcal{F}[\mathrm{tri}(x)] &= \mathcal{F}[\mathrm{rect}(x) * \mathrm{rect}(x)] \\
&= \mathcal{F}[\mathrm{rect}(x)]\mathcal{F}[\mathrm{rect}(x)] \\
&= \mathrm{sinc}^2(\pi u),
\end{aligned}
\tag{9.59}
$$

where

$$
\begin{aligned}
\mathrm{rect}(x) &= 1 \quad \text{for } |x| \le \frac{1}{2} \\
&= 0 \quad \text{otherwise}
\end{aligned}
$$

and

$$
\begin{aligned}
\mathrm{tri}(x) &= 1 - |x| \quad \text{for } |x| \le 1 \\
&= 0 \qquad\qquad \text{otherwise.}
\end{aligned}
$$

9.6 CONVOLUTION OF DISCRETE FUNCTIONS

Convolution of one-dimensional discrete functions h_k and g_k is the sum

$$f_l = \sum_k h_k g_{l-k}, \tag{9.60}$$

where the discrete function g_k has been first inverted (g_{-k}) about the origin and then translated (g_{l-k}). The sum over k replaces the integration over x' in Eqs (9.47). Convolution of two-dimensional discrete functions is likewise defined as

$$f_{ij} = \sum_{k,l} [h_{kl} g_{i-k,j-l}]. \tag{9.61}$$

Consider two one-dimensional strings, each having identical and equidistant dots along its length. One string lies along the x-axis and the other along the y-axis (Fig. 9.15a). The horizontal string h_k is left undisturbed. The vertical string g_k is first inverted ($k \to -k$) and then displaced. We now look for the overlap between the inverted and displaced string g_{l-k} with the stationary string h_k. The inverted string g_{-k} can be displaced along any direction in the xy plane. Figure 9.15b shows the function h_k, the inverted function g_{-k}, the displaced function g_{l-k}, and the product $h_k g_{l-k}$. Here, the function g_{-k} has been displaced by one unit along the x-axis. For this configuration of strings, the overlap of h_k and g_{l-k} is possible along the x-axis only. The displacements of g_{-k} which

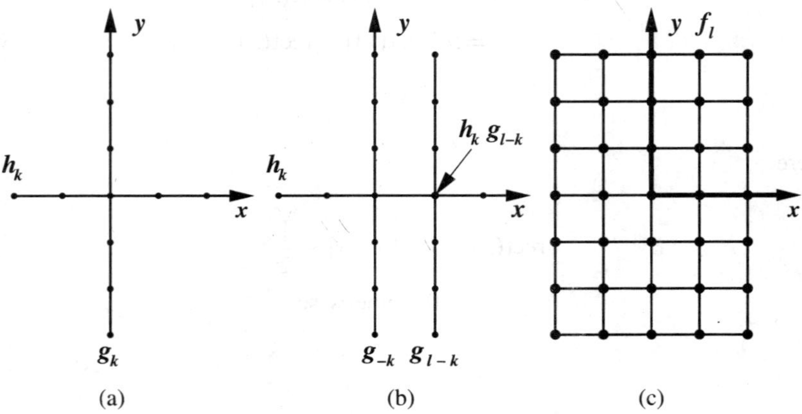

Fig. 9.15: (a) Strings h_k and g_k with equidistant dots, (b) string g_k is first inverted, then displaced by one unit along the x-axis, (c) f_l is the convolution of h_k and g_k.

yield non-zero convolution correspond to $i = 0, \pm 1, \pm 2$, $j = 0, \pm 1, \pm 2, \pm 3$ and any combinations of these displacements, where i and j represent displacements along the x- and y-axes, respectively. The convolution function

$$f_l = \sum_k h_k g_{l-k}$$

in this case is a two-dimensional pattern of dots (Fig. 9.15c). All dots in the pattern have the same size.

The above example clearly demonstrates that the convolution is not the simple product of the convolving functions. Simple product in this case generates only one overlap located at the origin. It is the displacement operation which has generated the pattern of dots. In this example, the role of the folding process is not evident since the convolving functions are even. To see what folding does to the convolution process, let the string g_k have all dots below the origin, so that g_k is no longer symmetric about the origin. Going over the steps as for Fig. 9.15, generates a two-dimensional pattern with all dots located below the x-axis.

9.7 CORRELATION OF FUNCTIONS

The crosscorrelation between two continuous functions $f_1(x)$ and $f_2(x)$ is defined as

$$f(x, y) = \iint_{-\infty}^{\infty} f_1(x', y') f_2^*(x' - x, y' - y) \mathrm{d}x' \mathrm{d}y' \tag{9.62a}$$

$$= \iint_{-\infty}^{\infty} f_1(x'' + x, y'' + y') f_2^*(x'', y'') \mathrm{d}x'' \mathrm{d}y'', \tag{9.62b}$$

where $(x' - x)$ and $(y' - y)$ in Eq. (9.62b) have been replaced by x'' and y'', respectively. The correlation operation involves only the translation and no folding of one of the functions. Attention must be paid to the order in which the two functions appear and to the function which is to be conjugated in the correlation operation. The crosscorrelation between two functions is symbolically denoted as

$$f(x, y) = f_1(x, y) \star f_2(x, y). \tag{9.63}$$

The crosscorrelation operation does not commute:

$$\begin{aligned} f_{12}(x, y) &= \iint_{-\infty}^{\infty} f_1(x''+x, y''+y) f_2^*(x'', y'') \mathrm{d}x'' \mathrm{d}y'' \\ &= \left[\iint_{-\infty}^{\infty} f_2(x'', y'') f_1^*(x''+x, y''+y) \mathrm{d}x'' \mathrm{d}y'' \right]^* \\ &= f_{21}^*(-x, -y). \end{aligned} \tag{9.64}$$

The correlation and convolution operations are related in some manner:

$$\begin{aligned} f_1(x, y) \star f_2(x, y) &= \iint_{-\infty}^{\infty} f_1(x', y') f_2^*(x'-x, y'-y) \mathrm{d}x' \mathrm{d}y' \\ &= \iint_{-\infty}^{\infty} f_1(x', y') f_2^* \left[\frac{(x-x')}{-1}, \frac{(y-y')}{-1} \right] \mathrm{d}x' \mathrm{d}y' \\ &= f_1(x, y) * f_2^*(-x, -y). \end{aligned} \tag{9.65}$$

For real and even $f_2(x, y)$, the convolution and crosscorrelation operations are indistinguishable. Therefore, the earlier example (Section 9.5.1) of the convolution of two rectangle functions may as well be taken as an example of the crosscorrelation between two rectangle functions. The crosscorrelation integral may also be interpreted in terms of the area of the products of the function $f_1(x', y')$ with the shifted function $f_2^*(x'-x, y'-y)$.

As the name suggests, the crosscorrelation function defines quantitatively the correlation or the similarity between two functions. The normalized crosscorrelation between the functions $f_1(x, y)$ and $f_2(x, y)$ is defined as

$$c_{12}(x, y) = \frac{\iint_{-\infty}^{\infty} f_1(x', y') f_2^*(x'-x, y'-y) \mathrm{d}x' \mathrm{d}y'}{\iint_{-\infty}^{\infty} f_1(x', y') f_2^*(x', y') \mathrm{d}x' \mathrm{d}y'}, \tag{9.66}$$

where the integral in the denominator represents the crosscorrelation for zero shift. For $f_2(x, y) = f_1(x, y)$, the crosscorrelation function becomes the autocorrelation function:

$$f(x, y) = \iint_{-\infty}^{\infty} f_1(x', y') f_1^*(x'-x, y'-x) \mathrm{d}x' \mathrm{d}y' \tag{9.67}$$

and the normalized autocorrelation function takes the form

$$c_{11}(x, y) = \frac{\iint_{-\infty}^{\infty} f_1(x', y') f_1^*(x' - x, y' - y) \mathrm{d}x' \mathrm{d}y'}{\iint_{-\infty}^{\infty} |f_1(x', y')|^2 \mathrm{d}x' \mathrm{d}y'}. \tag{9.68}$$

The autocorrelation of a real function is even, irrespective of the function itself being even or not. This is because it does not matter whether a function is shifted to the right or to the left, the overlap of the shifted function with its clone remains the same, i.e.,

$$\begin{aligned} f(-x, -y) &= \iint_{-\infty}^{\infty} f_1(x', y') f_1(x' + x, y' + y) \mathrm{d}x' \mathrm{d}y' \\ &= \iint_{-\infty}^{\infty} f_1(x'' - x, y'' - y) f_1(x'', y'') \mathrm{d}x'' \mathrm{d}y'' \\ &= f(+x, +y). \end{aligned} \tag{9.69}$$

9.7.1 Correlation Theorems

The Fourier transform of the crosscorrelation of two functions is the product of the Fourier transform of the first function with the complex conjugate of the Fourier transform of the second function:

$$\begin{aligned} \mathcal{F}[f_1(x, y) \star f_2(x, y)] &= \iint_{-\infty}^{\infty} \left[\iint_{-\infty}^{\infty} f_1(x + x'', y + y'') \right. \\ &\qquad \left. \times f_2^*(x'', y'') \mathrm{d}x'' \mathrm{d}y'' \right] \mathrm{e}^{-\mathrm{i}2\pi(ux + vy)} \mathrm{d}x \, \mathrm{d}y \\ &= \iint_{-\infty}^{\infty} \left[\iint_{-\infty}^{\infty} f_1(x + x'', y + y'') \mathrm{e}^{-\mathrm{i}2\pi u(x + x'')} \right. \\ &\qquad \left. \times \mathrm{e}^{-\mathrm{i}2\pi v(y + y'')} \mathrm{d}x \, \mathrm{d}y \right] \\ &\qquad \times f_2^*(x'', y'') \mathrm{e}^{\mathrm{i}2\pi(ux'' + vy'')} \mathrm{d}x'' \mathrm{d}y'' \end{aligned} \tag{9.70}$$

$$= F_1(u, v) \int\int_{-\infty}^{\infty} \left[f_2(x'', y'') \mathrm{e}^{-\mathrm{i}2\pi(ux''+vy'')} \mathrm{d}x'' \mathrm{d}y'' \right]^*$$

$$= F_1(u, v) F_2^*(u, v).$$

This is the crosscorrelation theorem. The converse of this theorem also holds, i.e.,

$$\begin{aligned} \mathcal{F}[f_1(x, y) f_2^*(x, y)] &= \int\int_{-\infty}^{\infty} F_1(u', v') F_2^*(u' - u, v' - v) \mathrm{d}u' \mathrm{d}v' \\ &= F_1(u, v) \star F_2^*(u, v). \end{aligned} \tag{9.71}$$

A special case of the crosscorrelation theorem is the autocorrelation theorem. For $f_2(x, y) = f_1(x, y) = f(x, y)$, Eqs (9.70) and (9.71) are reduced to

$$\mathcal{F}[f(x, y) \star f(x, y)] = |F(u, v)|^2 \tag{9.72}$$

and

$$\begin{aligned} \mathcal{F}[|f(x, y)|^2] &= \int\int_{-\infty}^{\infty} F(u', v') F^*(u' - u, v' - v) \mathrm{d}u' \mathrm{d}v' \\ &= F(u, v) \star F^*(u, v). \end{aligned} \tag{9.73}$$

The autocorrelation theorem (Eq. 9.72) states that the Fourier transform of the autocorrelation function is the square modulus of the Fourier transform of the function.

9.7.2 The Wiener–Khinchin Theorem

The counterpart of the square modulus of the Fourier transform ($|F(u, v)|^2$) in the time domain is the spectral density function $|E(\nu)|^2$ (see Eqs 2.23 and 2.28). Equation (9.72) is the statement of the more general theorem called the Wiener–Khinchin theorem. It states that the autocorrelation function and the spectral density function constitute a Fourier transform pair. It is easier to measure and analytically manipulate the autocorrelation function than the spectral density function. The Wiener–Khinchin theorem then allows one to estimate the spectral density function from the Fourier transform of the autocorrelation function. The relevance of the autocorrelation and crosscorrelation functions to coherence properties of quasi-monochromatic light has already been witnessed in Chapter 2. Application of the convolution and correlation techniques to image processing will be taken up in later chapters.

Before concluding, we state that the convolution and correlation integrals defined with integration limits extending from $-\infty$ to $+\infty$ may not be suitable for certain class of functions such as the periodic and the constant functions. In such cases, the following definitions of the convolution and crosscorrelation operations may be useful.

Convolution Operation

$$f_1(x, y) * f_2(x, y) = \lim_{\Lambda\to\infty} \frac{1}{2\Lambda} \int_{-\Lambda}^{\Lambda}\!\!\int f_1(x', y') f_2(x - x', y - y') \mathrm{d}x' \mathrm{d}y'. \quad (9.74)$$

Crosscorrelation Operation

$$f_1(x, y) \star f_2(x, y) = \lim_{\Lambda\to\infty} \frac{1}{2\Lambda} \int_{-\Lambda}^{\Lambda}\!\!\int f_1(x', y') f_2^*(x' - x, y' - y) \mathrm{d}x' \mathrm{d}y'. \quad (9.75)$$

9.8 REFERENCES

9.1 Jack D. Gaskill, Linear Systems, Fourier transforms, and Optics, John Wiley & Sons, New York, 1978.

9.2 R. Bracewell, The Fourier transform and its applications, McGraw-Hill, New York, 1965.

9.3 A. Papoulis, The Fourier Integral and its applications, McGraw-Hill, New York, 1962.

9.9 PROBLEMS

9.1 Find a Fourier series expansion of the triangle wave of Fig. 9.16.

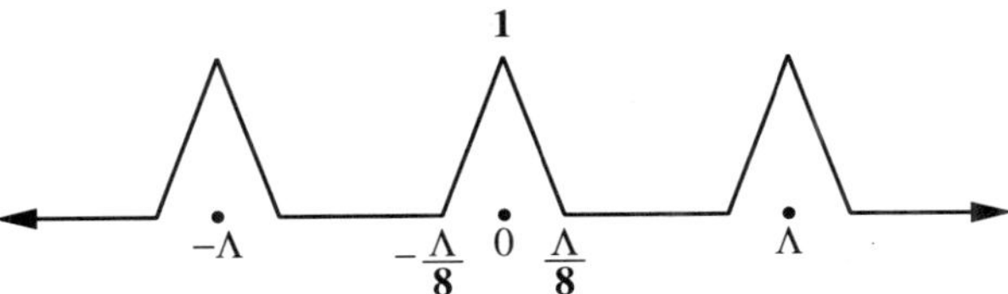

Fig. 9.16.

9.2 Show that the Fourier series expansion of $|\cos 2\pi\nu_0 x|$ is

$$\sum_{-\infty}^{+\infty} \frac{2}{\pi} \frac{(-1)^n}{1-(2n)^2} \mathrm{e}^{\mathrm{i}2\pi n(2\nu_0 x)}.$$

9.3 If you have access to a computer, reproduce Fig. 9.3 (a,b,c) for the rectangle wave.

9.4 Find the Fourier transforms of the following functions.

(a) $f(t) = \mathrm{e}^{-\alpha t}$ for $t \geq 0$, and $= 0$ for $t < 0$.
(b) $f(t) = A_0 \cos^2 2\pi\nu_0 t$ for $-\frac{\Delta T}{2} \leq t \leq +\frac{\Delta T}{2}$, and $= 0$ otherwise
(c) $f(x) = \mathrm{e}^{-\alpha|x|}$
(d) $f(x) = \mathrm{e}^{-\alpha x^2}$
(e) $f(x) = a$ sinc $(\pi a x)$
(f) $f(x, y) = \mathrm{e}^{\mathrm{i}\alpha(x^2+y^2)}$

9.5 Find and sketch the following convolution functions

(a) $f(x) = \text{rect}\,(x-2) * \text{rect}\,(\frac{x+3}{2})$
(b) $f(x) = [\text{rect}\,(x) * \text{rect}\,(x)] * \text{rect}\,(x)$,

where rect $(\frac{x+a}{b})$ represents the rectangle function of unit height and width b, centered at $x = -a$.

9.6 Find sinc $(x) *$ sinc (x).

9.7 Find the self convolution of the function

$$\begin{aligned} f(x, y) &= A \quad \text{for } x^2 + y^2 \leq a^2, \\ &= 0 \quad \text{for } x^2 + y^2 > a^2, \end{aligned}$$

where a and A are positive constants.

9.8 Find and sketch the following crosscorrelations.

(a) $f(x) = \text{rect}\,(x-1) \star \text{rect}\,(x+1)$
(b) $f(x) = [\text{rect}\,(x-1) \star \text{rect}\,(x+1)] \star \text{rect}\,(x-4)$

9.9 Find the convolutions of the following discrete functions

(a) Two one-dimensional strings, each having nine identical and equidistant dots along its length. Both strings are horizontal (Fig. 9.17).

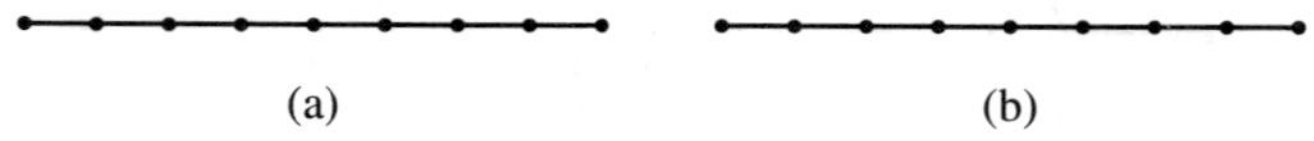

Fig. 9.17.

(b) Two one-dimensional strings, each having seven identical and equidistant dots along its length. One string is horizontal and the other makes an angle of 45° with the horizontal direction (Fig. 9.18).

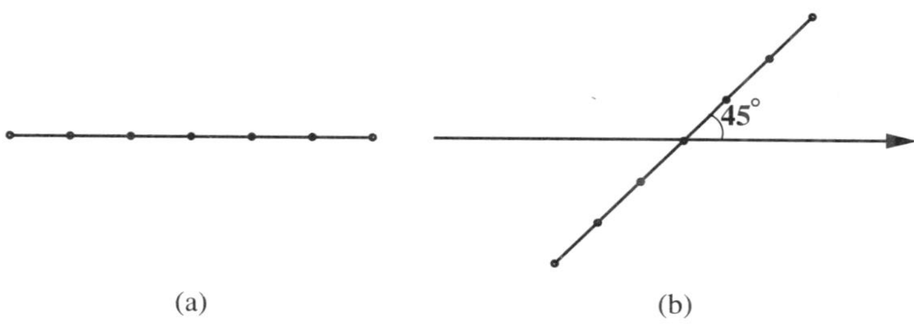

Fig. 9.18.

9.10 Derive Eq. (9.71).

9.11 The truncated oscillator function (Eq. 9.31) can be expressed as the product of a sinusoidal function and a rectangular pulse of width T. Use the convolution theorem to obtain its Fourier transform (Eq. 9.32).

CHAPTER **10**

Fraunhofer Diffraction

10.1 FAR-FIELD DIFFRACTION

When the source and observation points are sufficiently far away from a small diffracting aperture, the phase introduced by the quadratic terms in the diffraction integral (Eq. 7.27) may be a small fraction of 2π radians. This happens, when

$$\frac{p^2}{R_0} \ll \lambda, \tag{10.1}$$

where p determines the extent of the aperture, i.e., the maximum values of the x- and y-coordinates of a point in the aperture and R_0 is the smaller of the R'_0 and R''_0 distances (Fig. 10.1). This is the regime of far-field or Fraunhofer diffraction. Under these conditions, the diffraction integral (Eq. 7.27) reduces to

$$E(P_o) = -\frac{\mathrm{i}a_0}{\lambda} Q \frac{\mathrm{e}^{\mathrm{i}k(R'_0+R''_0)}}{R'_0 R''_0} \iint\limits_{-\infty}^{\infty} t(x, y)\mathrm{e}^{-\mathrm{i}\frac{2\pi}{\lambda}[x(l''-l')+y(m''-m')]}\mathrm{d}x\,\mathrm{d}y \tag{10.2a}$$

$$= -\frac{\mathrm{i}A_0}{\lambda} \iint\limits_{-\infty}^{\infty} t(x, y)\mathrm{e}^{-\mathrm{i}2\pi(ux+vy)}\mathrm{d}x\,\mathrm{d}y, \tag{10.2b}$$

where

$$Q = \frac{1}{2}\left[\cos(\hat{r}'', \hat{n}) - \cos(\hat{r}', \hat{n})\right], \tag{10.3}$$

$$A_0 = a_0 Q \frac{\mathrm{e}^{\mathrm{i}k(R'_0+R''_0)}}{R'_0 R''_0}, \tag{10.4}$$

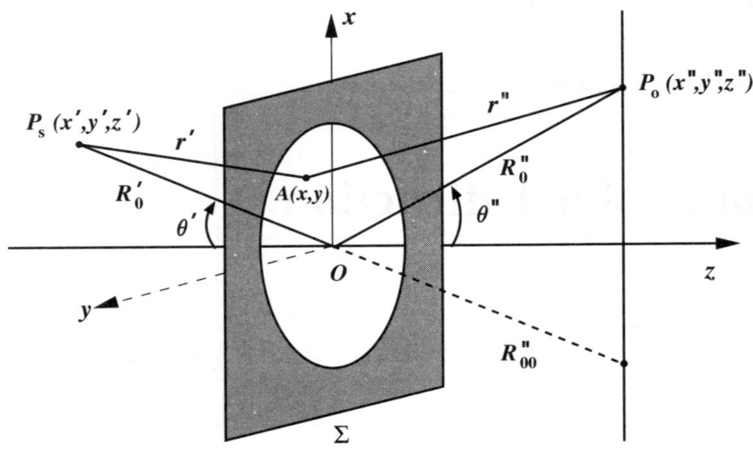

Fig. 10.1: Geometry for Fraunhofer diffraction.

and

$$u = \frac{l'' - l'}{\lambda} = \frac{1}{\lambda}\left(\frac{x'}{R_0'} + \frac{x''}{R_0''}\right), \tag{10.5a}$$

$$v = \frac{m'' - m'}{\lambda} = \frac{1}{\lambda}\left(\frac{y'}{R_0'} + \frac{y''}{R_0''}\right) \tag{10.5b}$$

are the spatial frequencies which determine the positions of the source (x', y') and point of observation (x'', y'') with respect to the aperture. The obliquity factor Q is assumed not to show any significant variation with the position of a point in the aperture. The diffraction integral (Eq. 10.2b) is exactly in the form of the two-dimensional Fourier transform integral (Eq. 9.34). It is therefore possible to express the field and intensity distributions in Fraunhofer diffraction in terms of the Fourier transform of the aperture function:

$$E(u, v) = -\frac{\mathrm{i}A_0}{\lambda}F(u, v), \tag{10.6a}$$

$$I(u, v) = \left(\frac{1}{2}\epsilon_0 c\right)\frac{|A_0|^2}{\lambda^2}|F(u, v)|^2, \tag{10.6b}$$

where

$$F(u, v) = \iint_{-\infty}^{\infty} t(x, y)\mathrm{e}^{-\mathrm{i}2\pi(ux+vy)}\mathrm{d}x\,\mathrm{d}y \tag{10.7}$$

is the Fourier transform of the aperture function. The normalized intensity distribution in Fraunhofer diffraction can be written as

$$\frac{I(u,v)}{I(0,0)} = \left(\frac{R''_{00}}{R''_0}\right)^2 \frac{|F(u,v)|^2}{|F(0,0)|^2}, \tag{10.8}$$

where $I(0,0)$ is the intensity at the center of the diffraction pattern and R''_{00} is the distance of the center of the diffraction pattern from the origin. The diffraction integral in the form

$$E(u,v) = -\frac{\mathrm{i}}{\lambda} Q \frac{\mathrm{e}^{\mathrm{i}kR''_0}}{R''_0} \iint_{-\infty}^{\infty} a_0 \frac{\mathrm{e}^{\mathrm{i}kR'_0}}{R'_0} t(x,y) \mathrm{e}^{-\mathrm{i}2\pi(ux+vy)} \mathrm{d}x\,\mathrm{d}y \tag{10.9}$$

demonstrates the proportionality between the field distribution in Fraunhofer diffraction and the Fourier transform of the field distribution in the aperture plane. The phase factor contained in the proportionality constant is unimportant, unless the diffracted wave is allowed to interfere with some other coherent field as in holography. For a plane wave incident normally ($\theta' = 0$) on the aperture plane,

$$A_0 = \frac{E_0}{2}(\cos\theta'' - 1)\frac{\mathrm{e}^{\mathrm{i}kR''_0}}{R''_0}, \tag{10.10a}$$

$$u = \frac{l''}{\lambda} = \frac{1}{\lambda}\frac{x''}{R''_0}, \tag{10.10b}$$

$$v = \frac{m''}{\lambda} = \frac{1}{\lambda}\frac{y''}{R''_0}. \tag{10.10c}$$

Equation (10.10a) can be obtained by either going back to the Kirchhoff's boundary conditions (Section 7.4.1) and replacing the incident spherical wave by a plane wave, or by taking the limit $R'_0 \to \infty$ and $a_0 \to \infty$ in Eq. (10.4) in a manner that a_0/R'_0 approaches the amplitude E_0 of the plane wave.

10.1.1 Fourier Decomposition of Aperture Function

In the Huygens–Fresnel theory of diffraction, the action of a diffracting aperture may be understood in terms of the modification of the incident wavefront. The modified wavefront propagating in the forward direction carries information

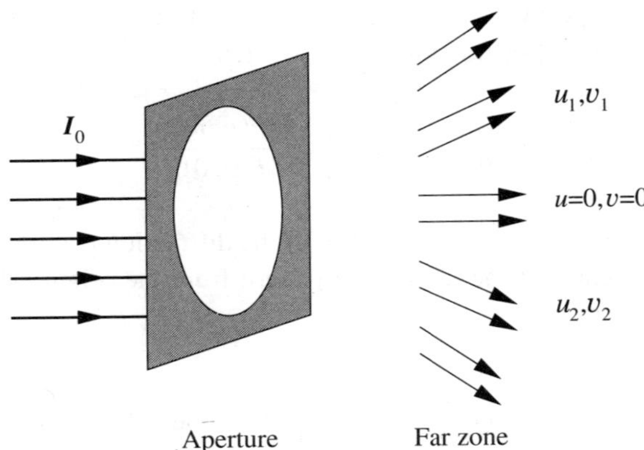

Fig. 10.2: Fourier decomposition of aperture function in terms of plane waves in the far zone.

about the presence of the aperture. A different interpretation to the far-field diffraction is possible in terms of the inverse Fourier transform

$$t(x, y) = \iint_{-\infty}^{\infty} F(u, v) \mathrm{e}^{\mathrm{i}2\pi(ux+vy)} \mathrm{d}u \, \mathrm{d}v. \tag{10.11}$$

With the temporal factor $\mathrm{e}^{-\mathrm{i}2\pi\nu t}$ implied in Eq. (10.11), the aperture transmission function $t(x, y)$ can be thought to represent an infinite set of plane waves describing far-field diffraction (Fig. 10.2). The Fourier transform $F(u, v)$ acts as the amplitude or the weighting factor of a wave in this decomposition. In the absence of the aperture, the incident wave continues unhindered along its original direction of propagation ($u = 0, v = 0$). The presence of the aperture gives rise to additional waves in the far zone along directions specified by the new spatial frequencies $u \neq 0$, $v \neq 0$. These waves collectively describe far-field or Fraunhofer diffraction from the aperture. This interpretation is obviously not available to Fresnel diffraction.

10.1.2 Diffraction with a Lens

Equation (10.1) imposes severe experimental restrictions to observe Fraunhofer diffraction from an aperture. The source and observation points must lie at unmanageably large distances from the diffracting aperture, except when the aperture size is extremely small. A lens kept in the aperture plane can reduce these distances to convenient laboratory distances. A lens possesses remarkable refractive and diffractive properties. It was mentioned in Chapter 4 that a lens converts a paraxial diverging wavefront into a converging image-forming wavefront. However, we did not quite explain there, why a lens does what it actually does. We now describe the action of a lens. To simplify the discussion, the lens is assumed thin and non-absorbing. Figure 10.3 shows an exaggerated view of a section of a thin lens with vertices V_1, V_2 and radii of curvatures r_1 and r_2. We have considered here a biconvex lens but the results can be easily generalized. Consider the ray entering the lens at (x_1, y_1) and leaving at (x_2, y_2). The transverse displacement of a ray in a thin lens is extremely small so that

$$x_1 \approx x_2 = x, \quad y_1 \approx y_2 = y. \tag{10.12}$$

Furthermore, the lens modifies only the phase of the incident wave, leaving its amplitude unchanged. Accordingly, the action of a lens can be described by the equation

$$E_t(x, y) = T(x, y) E_{in}(x, y), \tag{10.13a}$$

where

$$T(x, y) = e^{i\Delta\phi(x,y)}. \tag{10.13b}$$

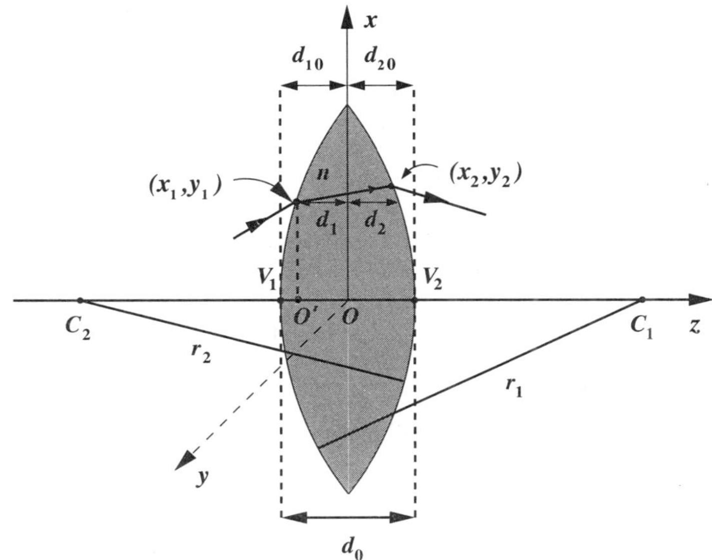

Fig. 10.3: Action of a thin lens.

$E_{\text{in}}(x, y)$ and $E_{\text{t}}(x, y)$ are the incident and transmitted field distributions in the transverse planes passing through the left and right vertices of the lens and $\Delta\phi(x, y)$ is the phase retardation introduced by the lens for a wave entering and exiting it at (x, y). Within the paraxial approximation,

$$\begin{aligned} d_1(x, y) &= O'O = d_{10} - (r_1 - O'C_1) \\ &\approx d_{10} - \frac{x^2 + y^2}{2r_1} \end{aligned} \tag{10.14a}$$

and

$$d_2(x, y) = d_{20} - \frac{x^2 + y^2}{2(-r_2)}. \tag{10.14b}$$

So that

$$\begin{aligned} d(x, y) &= d_1(x, y) + d_2(x, y) \\ &= d_0 - \frac{1}{2}\left(\frac{1}{r_1} - \frac{1}{r_2}\right)(x^2 + y^2), \end{aligned} \tag{10.15}$$

where r_2 is negative in the present case. The phase retardation suffered by a ray between transverse planes passing through the vertices of the lens is

$$\begin{aligned} \Delta\phi(x, y) &= k\,[1\,\{d_0 - d(x, y)\} + nd(x, y)] \\ &= k\,[d_0 + (n - 1)d(x, y)] \\ &= k\left[nd_0 - \frac{x^2 + y^2}{2f}\right], \end{aligned} \tag{10.16}$$

where n is the index of refraction of the material of the lens and f is the focal length of the lens in air, given by

$$\frac{1}{f} = (n - 1)\left(\frac{1}{r_1} - \frac{1}{r_2}\right). \tag{4.26}$$

The lens transformation function then takes the form

$$T(x, y) = \mathrm{e}^{ik\left(nd_0 - \frac{x^2+y^2}{2f}\right)} = \mathrm{e}^{iknd_0}\mathrm{e}^{-ik(x^2+y^2)/2f}. \tag{10.17}$$

The constant phase knd_0, can be ignored. The quadratic phase factor represents the lens transformation.

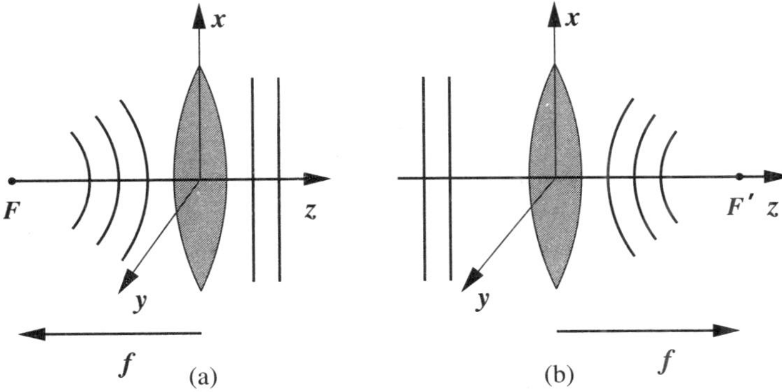

Fig. 10.4: Wavefront modification by a lens; (a) collimating action of a lens, (b) focusing action of a lens.

We first consider a point source at the front focal point of the lens (Fig. 10.4a). The field distributions just in front and just behind the lens are

$$E_{\text{in}}(x, y, 0) = \frac{A}{r}\text{e}^{\text{i}kr} \approx \frac{A}{f}\text{e}^{\text{i}k\left(f+\frac{x^2+y^2}{2f}\right)}, \tag{10.18a}$$

$$E_{\text{t}}(x, y, 0) = T(x, y)E_{\text{in}}(x, y, 0) = \frac{A}{f}\text{e}^{\text{i}kf}, \tag{10.18b}$$

respectively. The field distribution beyond the lens becomes uniform. Therefore, a thin lens converts a spherical wavefront diverging from its front focal point into a plane wavefront. This is the collimating action of a lens. On the other hand, a plane wave incident normally on the lens gives rise to the field distribution

$$E_{\text{t}}(x, y) = E_0\text{e}^{-\text{i}k\frac{x^2+y^2}{2f}} = E_0\text{e}^{\text{i}kf}\text{e}^{-\text{i}k\left(f+\frac{x^2+y^2}{2f}\right)} \tag{10.19}$$

just behind the lens. This field distribution represents, within the paraxial approximation, a spherical wavefront converging to a point a distance f behind the lens. This is the paraxial focusing action of the lens (Fig. 10.4b). The image-forming action of a lens can also be understood in a similar manner. We shall, however, postpone this discussion to Chapter 11.

We now return to the diffraction configuration of Fig. 10.1, but this time with a lens of sufficiently large diameter kept just behind the diffracting aperture. The diffraction takes place at the aperture and the lens subsequently and appropriately retards the phases of the diffracted waves. The amplitude transmission function of the aperture–lens combination is

$$t'(x, y) = \mathrm{e}^{-\mathrm{i}k(x^2+y^2)/2f}\, t(x, y), \tag{10.20}$$

where the first factor on the right-hand side represents the phase retardation due to the lens and $t(x, y)$ is the bare aperture transmission function. Relaxing the Fraunhofer diffraction condition (Eq. 10.1), we return to the Fresnel diffraction integral with the linear phase terms retained, i.e.,

$$E(P_o) = -\frac{\mathrm{i}a_0}{\lambda} Q \frac{\mathrm{e}^{\mathrm{i}k(R_0'+R_0'')}}{R_0' R_0''} \iint_{-\infty}^{\infty} t'(x, y) \times \mathrm{e}^{-\mathrm{i}k\left[x(l''-l')+y(m''-m')-\frac{1}{2}\left(\frac{1}{R_0'}+\frac{1}{R_0''}\right)(x^2+y^2)\right]} \mathrm{d}x\, \mathrm{d}y. \tag{10.21}$$

The remaining quadratic and higher order terms in Eq.(7.28) are assumed small and ignored. Combining Eqs (10.20) and (10.21) gives

$$E(P_o) = -\frac{\mathrm{i}a_0}{\lambda} Q \frac{\mathrm{e}^{\mathrm{i}k(R_0'+R_0'')}}{R_0' R_0''} \iint_{-\infty}^{\infty} t(x, y) \times \mathrm{e}^{-\mathrm{i}k\left[x(l''-l')+y(m''-m')-\frac{1}{2}\left(\frac{1}{R_0'}+\frac{1}{R_0''}-\frac{1}{f}\right)(x^2+y^2)\right]} \mathrm{d}x\, \mathrm{d}y. \tag{10.22}$$

The quadratic exponent vanishes if the source and point of observation lie in conjugate planes of the lens ($\frac{1}{R_0'} + \frac{1}{R_0''} - \frac{1}{f} = 0$),[1] and the diffraction integral reduces to

$$E(P_o) = -\frac{\mathrm{i}a_0}{\lambda} Q \frac{\mathrm{e}^{\mathrm{i}k(R_0'+R_0'')}}{R_0' R_0''} \iint_{-\infty}^{\infty} t(x, y) \mathrm{e}^{-\mathrm{i}2\pi(ux+vy)} \mathrm{d}x\, \mathrm{d}y, \tag{10.23}$$

where the spatial frequencies u and v are as defined in Eqs (10.5) or in Eqs (10.10), depending on the diffraction geometry. This is exactly the integral for the Fraunhofer diffraction (Eq. 10.2), but now the distances R_0' and R_0'' are convenient laboratory distances, not constrained by Eq. (10.1). It must, however, be kept in mind that the conditions of Fraunhofer diffraction are satisfied only in conjugate planes of a lens, and nowhere else. Rephrasing this, it can be said that the Fraunhofer diffraction pattern of the aperture of the lens replaces the point

[1] To be consistent with the sign convention of geometrical optics, R_0' should carry negative sign.

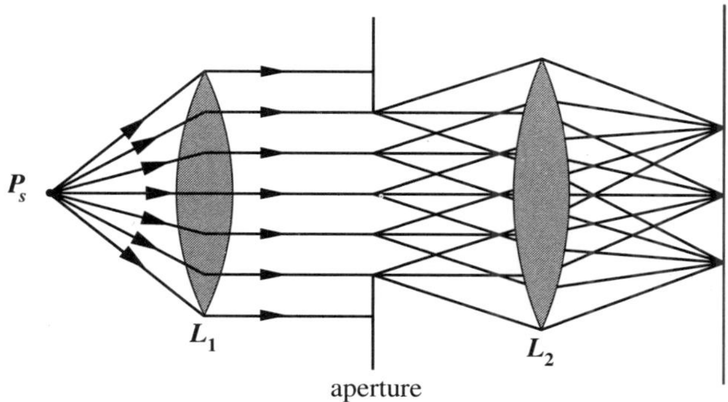

Fig. 10.5: Typical geometry to observe Fraunhofer diffraction.

image (of a point object) of geometrical optics, or alternatively, the Fraunhofer diffraction pattern of the lens aperture represents the diffraction-limited image of a point object. For normal incidence, Fraunhofer diffraction appears in the back focal plane of the lens. For this reason and for the fact that the field distribution in Fraunhofer diffraction is proportional to the Fourier transform of the aperture function, the back focal plane of a lens is called the Fourier transform plane. Figure 10.5 shows a typical configuration to observe Fraunhofer diffraction from an aperture with a lens of sufficiently large diameter.

10.2 DIFFRACTING APERTURES

The Fraunhofer diffraction formalism developed in Section 10.1 will now be applied to some of the commonly encountered diffracting apertures.

10.2.1 Rectangular Aperture

Figure 10.6 shows a rectangular aperture of sides a and b, lying in the plane $z = 0$. The origin O lies at the center of the aperture. The transmission function of the aperture is

$$\begin{aligned} t(x, y) &= 1 \quad \text{for} \quad -\frac{a}{2} \leq x \leq +\frac{a}{2}, \\ & \qquad\qquad -\frac{b}{2} \leq y \leq +\frac{b}{2}, \\ &= 0 \quad \text{elsewhere}. \end{aligned} \tag{10.24}$$

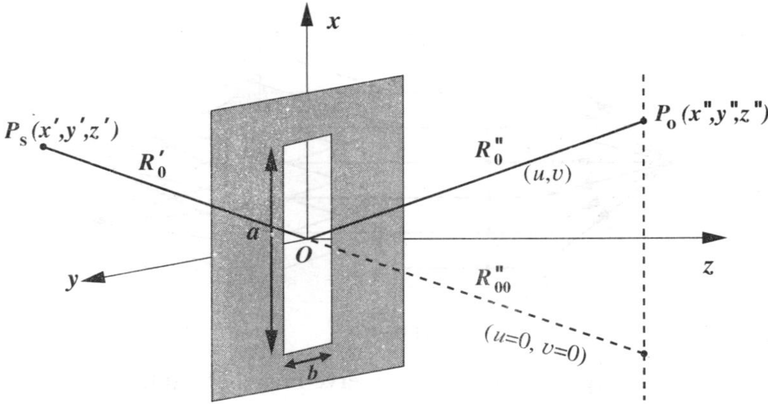

Fig. 10.6: Fraunhofer diffraction from a rectangular aperture.

Its Fourier transform is

$$
\begin{aligned}
F(u, v) &= \iint\limits_{-\infty}^{\infty} t(x, y)\, \mathrm{e}^{-\mathrm{i}2\pi(ux+vy)}\, \mathrm{d}x\, \mathrm{d}y \\
&= \int_{-a/2}^{+a/2} \mathrm{e}^{-\mathrm{i}2\pi ux}\, \mathrm{d}x \int_{-b/2}^{+b/2} \mathrm{e}^{-\mathrm{i}2\pi vy}\, \mathrm{d}y \\
&= ab \operatorname{sinc}(\pi ua) \operatorname{sinc}(\pi vb).
\end{aligned} \tag{10.25}
$$

The field and intensity distributions of Fraunhofer diffraction from a rectangular aperture are

$$
E(u, v) = -\frac{\mathrm{i}A_0}{\lambda} ab \operatorname{sinc}(\pi ua) \operatorname{sinc}(\pi vb), \tag{10.26a}
$$

$$
I(u, v) = I(0, 0) \left(\frac{R_{00}''}{R_0''} \right)^2 \operatorname{sinc}^2(\pi ua) \operatorname{sinc}^2(\pi vb), \tag{10.26b}
$$

respectively, where $I(0, 0)$ is the peak intensity of the central diffraction maximum ($u = 0, v = 0$). The zeroes of the sinc functions, given by the conditions

$$
\pi ua = \pm n\pi, \qquad \pi vb = \pm m\pi, \tag{10.27}
$$

locate the minima of the diffraction pattern at

$$
x'' = \pm n\lambda \frac{R_0''}{a} - \frac{R_0''}{R_0'} x', \qquad y'' = \pm m\lambda \frac{R_0''}{b} - \frac{R_0''}{R_0'} y' \tag{10.28}
$$

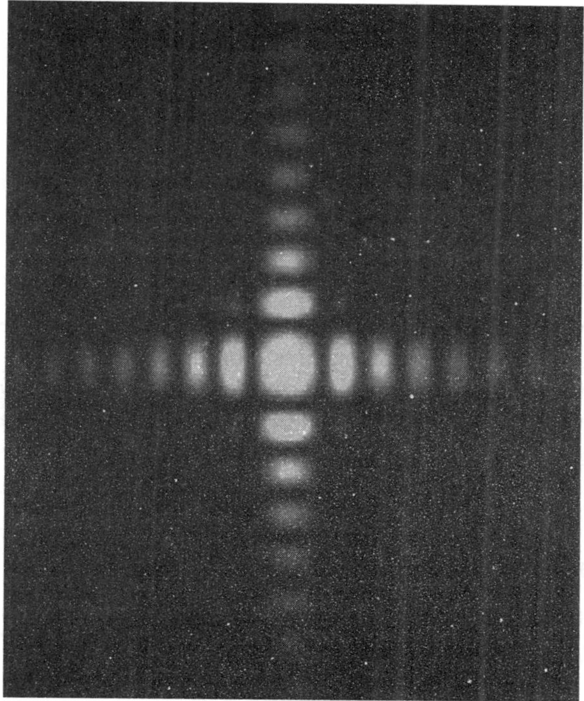

Photo 10.1: Fraunhofer diffraction from a rectangular aperture of sides 0.12 mm × 0.13 mm recorded with 514.5 nm line of an Argon ion laser.

in the plane of observation, where (x', y') are the coordinates of the point source, and n, m take integral values. For a parallel beam incident normally on the aperture, Eq. (10.28) reduces to

$$x'' = \pm n\lambda\frac{R_0''}{a}, \quad y'' = \pm m\lambda\frac{R_0''}{b}.$$

These equations represent dark lines in the plane of observation, parallel to the edges of the rectangular aperture. This is strictly not true since minor variation of R_0'' with the point of observation gives slight curvature to these lines. The central maximum is a rectangular patch of dimensions $2\lambda R_0''/a$ and $2\lambda R_0''/b$ centered on the optical axis. The brightness of this patch is maximum at the center and falls to zero near the edges. The central rectangular patch is surrounded by weak secondary patches. The positions of the peaks of the secondary maxima are obtained from the roots of the transcendental equations:

$$\frac{\mathrm{d}}{\mathrm{d}u}\{\mathrm{sinc}^2(\pi ua)\}=0, \quad \frac{\mathrm{d}}{\mathrm{d}v}\{\mathrm{sinc}^2(\pi vb)\}=0. \tag{10.29}$$

The separations between successive minima of intensity are given by

$$\Delta x''=\lambda\frac{R_0''}{a}, \quad \Delta y''=\lambda\frac{R_0''}{b}. \tag{10.30}$$

We see, once again, an inverse relationship between the aperture dimensions and the spreads of the diffraction maxima. For an aperture, 1 mm on each side, the central diffraction patch is a square of sides 1 mm for $R_0''=100\,\mathrm{cm}$ and $\lambda=500\,\mathrm{nm}$. Photograph 10.1 shows Fraunhofer diffraction pattern of a rectangular aperture of sides $0.12\,\mathrm{mm}\times 0.13\,\mathrm{mm}$ recorded with 514.5 nm line of an Argon ion laser.

10.2.2 Infinitely Long Slit

The Fourier transform of the amplitude transmission function of an infinitely long slit of width b with long edges parallel to the x-axis (Fig. 10.7a) is

$$\begin{aligned} F(u,v) &= \int_{-\infty}^{+\infty} \mathrm{e}^{-\mathrm{i}2\pi ux}\,\mathrm{d}x \int_{-b/2}^{+b/2} \mathrm{e}^{-\mathrm{i}2\pi vy}\,\mathrm{d}y \\ &= b\,\mathrm{sinc}(\pi vb)\delta(u). \end{aligned} \tag{10.31}$$

The field and intensity distributions in the plane of observation are given by

$$E(u,v)=-\mathrm{i}\frac{A_0}{\lambda}F(u,v)=-\mathrm{i}\frac{A_0}{\lambda}b\,\mathrm{sinc}\,(\pi vb), \tag{10.32a}$$

$$\begin{aligned} I(v) &= \left(\frac{1}{2}\epsilon_0 c\right)\frac{|A_0|^2}{\lambda^2}b^2\,\mathrm{sinc}^2(\pi vb) \\ &= I_0\,\mathrm{sinc}^2(\pi vb), \end{aligned} \tag{10.32b}$$

respectively, where the spatial frequency $v=y''/\lambda R_0''$ and I_0 is the peak intensity of the central diffraction maximum $(v=0)$. The remaining intensity maxima are relatively weak (Fig. 10.7b). Their positions can be obtained from $\frac{\mathrm{d}}{\mathrm{d}v}[\,\mathrm{sinc}^2(\pi vb)]=0$. They do not lie exactly halfway between consecutive minima of intensity. Numerical estimates give $I/I_0=0.047$ and 0.017 for the normalized peak intensities of the first two secondary maxima on either side of

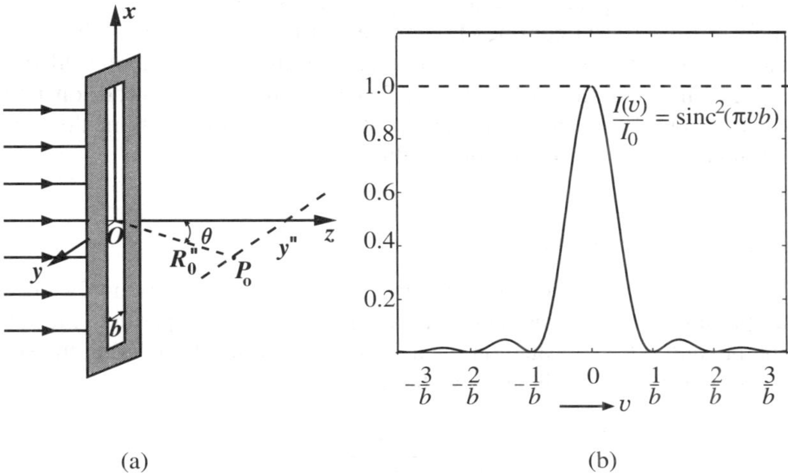

Fig. 10.7: Fraunhofer diffraction from a narrow slit; (a) geometry of diffraction, (b) normalized intensity distribution.

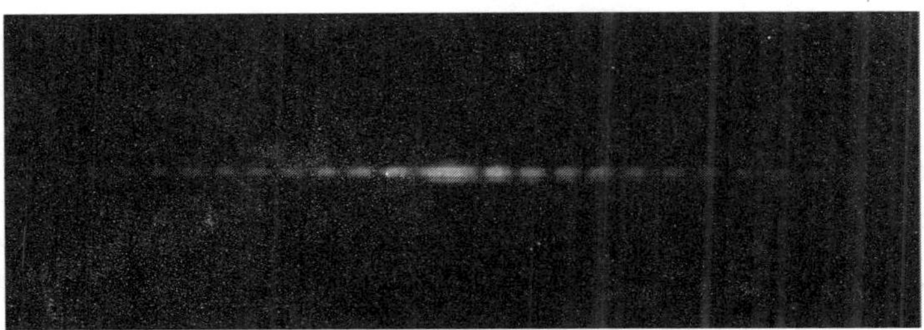

Photo 10.2: Fraunhofer diffraction from a slit of width 0.24 mm recorded with 514.5 nm line of an Argon ion laser.

the central maximum. The positions of the minima of the diffraction pattern can be obtained from the expression

$$\frac{y''}{\lambda R_0''} = \frac{n}{b} \tag{10.33a}$$

which can be put in the more familiar form

$$b \sin\theta = n\lambda, \tag{10.33b}$$

where $\sin\theta = y''/R_0''$ and n takes integral values. The presence of the delta function in Eq. (10.31) confines Fraunhofer diffraction from an infinitely long slit along a line perpendicular to the long edge of the slit. Fraunhofer diffraction from 0.24 mm wide slit recorded with 514.5 nm line of an Argon ion laser is shown in Photo 10.2. The finite spread of the diffraction spots in the vertical direction is due to finite height of the slit.

10.2.3 Circular Aperture

We next consider Fraunhofer diffraction from the most commonly encountered aperture in optical instruments, namely, the circular aperture (Fig. 10.8). The point source P_s is located on the axis of the aperture. Expressing the spatial frequencies in polar coordinates, we have

$$u = \frac{x''}{\lambda R_0''} = \frac{r''\cos\theta''}{\lambda R_0''} = \rho\cos\theta'', \tag{10.34a}$$

$$v = \frac{y''}{\lambda R_0''} = \frac{r''\sin\theta''}{\lambda R_0''} = \rho\sin\theta'', \tag{10.34b}$$

where

$$\rho = \frac{r''}{\lambda R_0''}. \tag{10.35}$$

The amplitude transmission function of the circular aperture is

$$\begin{aligned} t(r,\theta) &= 1 \quad \text{for } r \le a, \\ &= 0 \quad \text{otherwise.} \end{aligned} \tag{10.36}$$

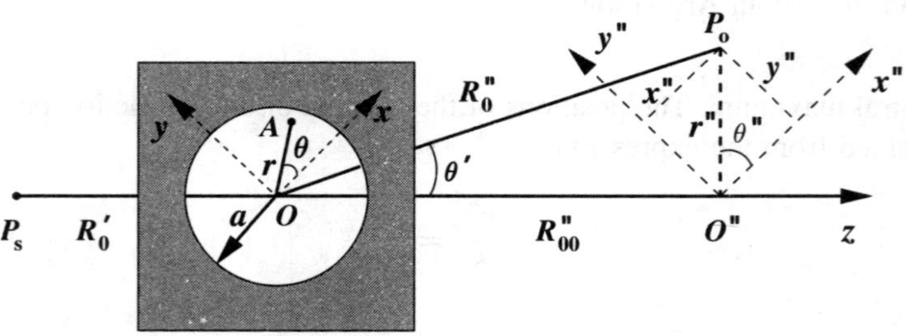

Fig. 10.8: Fraunhofer diffraction from a circular aperture. Source P_s lies on the axis of the aperture.

Its Fourier transform can be expressed as

$$\begin{aligned} F(u, v) = F(\rho, \theta'') &= \int_0^\infty \int_0^{2\pi} t(r, \theta)\, \mathrm{e}^{-\mathrm{i}2\pi(ur\cos\theta + vr\sin\theta)}\, r\,\mathrm{d}r\,\mathrm{d}\theta \\ &= \int_0^a r\left[\int_0^{2\pi} \mathrm{e}^{-\mathrm{i}2\pi\rho r\cos(\theta-\theta'')}\,\mathrm{d}\theta\right]\mathrm{d}r. \end{aligned} \tag{10.37}$$

However, $F(\rho, \theta'')$ cannot depend on angle θ'' because of the rotational symmetry of the configuration. For convenience, we choose $\theta'' = 0$, giving

$$F(\rho) = \int_0^a r\left[\int_0^{2\pi} \mathrm{e}^{-\mathrm{i}2\pi\rho r\cos\theta}\,\mathrm{d}\theta\right]\mathrm{d}r. \tag{10.38}$$

The θ integral falls in the category of Bessel functions. The Bessel function of order n is defined as

$$J_n(x) = \frac{\mathrm{i}^{-n}}{2\pi}\int_0^{2\pi} \mathrm{e}^{\mathrm{i}(n\phi + x\cos\phi)}\,\mathrm{d}\phi. \tag{10.39}$$

It is therefore possible to write

$$\begin{aligned} F(\rho) &= 2\pi\int_0^a rJ_0(2\pi\rho r)\,\mathrm{d}r \\ &= \frac{1}{2\pi\rho^2}\int_0^{2\pi\rho a} (2\pi\rho r)J_0(2\pi\rho r)\,\mathrm{d}(2\pi\rho r). \end{aligned} \tag{10.40}$$

The Bessel functions obey the recursion relation

$$\frac{\mathrm{d}}{\mathrm{d}x}[x^n J_n(x)] = x^n J_{n-1}(x). \tag{10.41}$$

Integrating the recursion relation for $n = 1$, we have

$$x' J_1(x') = \int_0^{x'} xJ_0(x)\,\mathrm{d}x. \tag{10.42}$$

Therefore

$$\begin{aligned} F(\rho) &= \frac{1}{2\pi\rho^2}(2\pi\rho a)J_1(2\pi\rho a) \\ &= 2\pi a^2\frac{J_1(2\pi\rho a)}{2\pi\rho a} \\ &= F(0)\frac{2J_1(2\pi\rho a)}{2\pi\rho a}. \end{aligned} \tag{10.43}$$

In the last step, we have used the property

$$\lim_{2\pi\rho a\to 0}\frac{J_1(2\pi\rho a)}{2\pi\rho a}=1/2. \tag{10.44}$$

The intensity distribution (Eq. 10.8) in the plane of observation takes the form

$$I(\rho)=I(0)\left(\frac{R''_{00}}{R''_0}\right)^2\left|\frac{2J_1(2\pi\rho a)}{2\pi\rho a}\right|^2, \tag{10.45}$$

where $I(0)$ is the intensity at the center of the diffraction pattern ($\rho=0$). Tables of Bessel functions are available. Limited values of $J_1(x)$ are given in Table B1 (Appendix B). The function $\left|\frac{2J_1(2\pi\rho a)}{2\pi\rho a}\right|^2$ is plotted in Fig. 10.9. The Fraunhofer diffraction pattern of a circular aperture is called the Airy pattern after Sir George Briddel Airy, who first obtained Eq. (10.45). The Airy pattern consists of a broad central maximum, called the Airy disk, surrounded by weaker secondary maxima in the form of concentric rings. The minima of the Airy pattern correspond to the roots of $J_1(2\pi\rho a)=0$. The roots of $J_2(2\pi\rho a)=0$ locate the surrounding bright rings. The first three minima of the Airy pattern occur at $2\pi\rho a=1.220\pi$, 2.233π, and 3.238π, respectively. The Airy disk with $r''=0.61\lambda R''_0/a$, where a is the radius of the circular aperture, carries nearly 84% of the incident energy. The first bright ring accounts for an additional 7% of the incident energy. We may rewrite Eq. (10.45) as

$$I(\theta')=I(0)\left(\frac{R''_{00}}{R''_0}\right)^2\left|\frac{2J_1(2\pi\frac{a}{\lambda}\sin\theta')}{2\frac{\pi}{\lambda}a\sin\theta'}\right|^2, \tag{10.46}$$

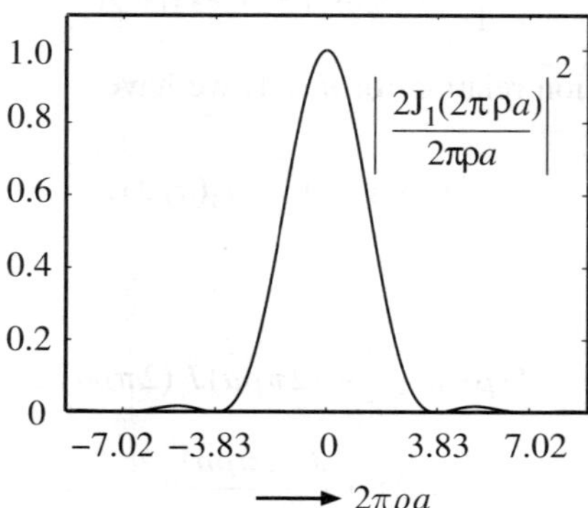

Fig. 10.9: Normalized intensity distribution of Fraunhofer diffraction from a circular aperture.

Photo 10.3: Fraunhofer diffraction from a circular aperture of diameter 0.33 mm recorded with 514.5 nm line of an Argon ion laser.

where θ' is the angle the diffracted ray makes with the z-axis. The first zero of $J_1\left(2\pi\frac{a}{\lambda}\sin\theta'\right)$ determines the size of the Airy disk. Therefore

$$\frac{2\pi}{\lambda}a\sin\theta_0 = 1.22\pi \tag{10.47a}$$

or

$$\sin\theta_0 = 1.22\frac{\lambda}{2a}, \tag{10.47b}$$

where θ_0 is the angular radius of the Airy disk. For small values of λ/a, the half-angular width of the Airy disk is

$$\theta_0 = 1.22\frac{\lambda}{2a} = 0.61\frac{\lambda}{a} \tag{10.48}$$

and the linear diameter of the Airy disk has the value

$$D_{\mathrm{A}} = \left(1.22\frac{\lambda}{a}\right)R_0''. \tag{10.49}$$

When Fraunhofer diffraction is observed in the back focal plane of a lens of focal length f, Eq. (10.49) becomes

$$D_A = \left(1.22\frac{\lambda}{a}\right)f. \tag{10.50}$$

Thus, the image of a point object formed by an aberration-free lens cannot be smaller than the size of the Airy disk with the lens acting as the diffracting aperture as well. Photograph 10.3 shows the Fraunhofer diffraction pattern of 0.33 mm diameter circular aperture recorded with 514.5 nm line of an Argon ion laser.

10.3 APODIZATION

The preceding discussion has shown that the image of a point object is spread out in the form of a diffraction pattern – an Airy pattern for an imaging optic with circular cross-section (Photo 10.3) and a sequence of nearly rectangular patches if the imaging optics has rectangular cross-section (Photo 10.1). As a result, it may be difficult to isolate images of nearby objects. The effect is compounded if one of the objects under observation has much less brightness than its neighbors. This happens, for example, when a telescope is pointed toward a faint star in close proximity of a bright star. For a circular aperture, 16% of the energy resides in the outer rings of the Airy pattern. The presence of the outer rings can impair the resolving capability of the optical system. It is therefore desirable to weaken or eliminate altogether the secondary diffraction maxima to improve system resolution. Apodization ('removal of feet' in Greek) is one of the techniques to weaken the secondary diffraction maxima. One can suppress the secondary diffraction maxima by diluting the edge discontinuity of the diffracting aperture by a suitable modification of the aperture transmission function. We illustrate this procedure with reference to a single slit. Let the slit of width b (Fig. 10.7a) be covered with a filter having the amplitude transmission function

$$\begin{aligned} t(y) &= \cos(\pi y/b) \quad \text{for} -\frac{b}{2} \leq y \leq +\frac{b}{2}, \\ &= 0 \quad \text{elsewhere}. \end{aligned} \tag{10.51}$$

The Fourier transform of the modified aperture function is

$$\begin{aligned} F(v) &= \int_{-b/2}^{+b/2} \cos(\pi y/b) e^{-i2\pi v y} dy \\ &= \left(\frac{2b}{\pi}\right) \frac{\cos(\pi v b)}{1 - 4b^2 v^2}. \end{aligned} \tag{10.52}$$

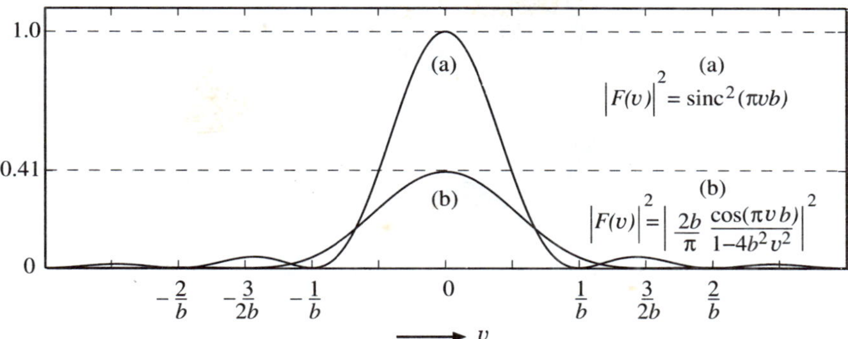

Fig. 10.10: Normalized intensity distribution of Fraunhofer diffraction from (a) unapodized and (b) apodized slits.

This should be compared with the corresponding expression (Eq. 10.31) for the unapodized slit. Figure 10.10 shows this comparison.

The first pair of diffraction minima from the apodized slit occurs at the spatial frequencies $v = \pm 3/2b$ against $v = \pm\frac{1}{b}$ for the unapodized slit. Thus, the central diffraction maximum has broadened on apodization. But the peak irradiance of the first secondary maximum of the apodized slit is only 0.4% of the irradiance of the central peak as compared to an order of magnitude higher value (4.7%) for the unapodized slit. Thus, considerable suppression of the secondary maxima can be achieved by apodization. Note that the Fourier transform of a Gaussian function is a Gaussian function. Therefore, higher diffraction orders are absent if the plane wave in diffraction experiments is replaced by a Gaussian wave, assuming the edges of the aperture do not truncate the transverse profile of the Gaussian wave.

10.4 THE ARRAY THEOREM

We have considered Fraunhofer diffraction from simple and commonly used apertures. Born and Wolf have extended this discussion to elliptical apertures. The apertures of interest in optics and spectroscopy are the multiple apertures. Two-slit or N-slit gratings are some of the examples of multiple apertures. Small particles, like water droplets in the field of a distant light source, act as randomly oriented multiple apertures in space. The description of Fraunhofer diffraction from a single aperture can be extended to multiple apertures with the help of the array theorem. We consider N identical and similarly oriented apertures, distributed randomly or otherwise in the xy plane (Fig. 10.11).

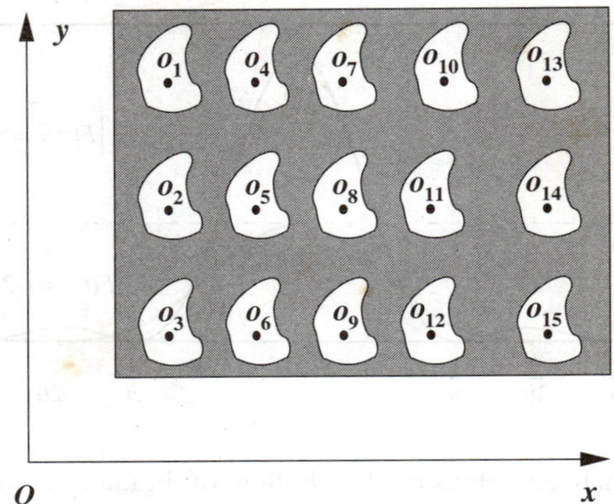

Fig. 10.11: Two-dimensional array of identical apertures.

The actual shape of the apertures is unimportant for the present discussion. Let the similarly located origins (o_1 to o_N) in the apertures have the position coordinates (x_j, y_j) with respect to a fixed coordinate system, where the index j runs from 1 to N. The amplitude transmission function of an array of apertures can be written as

$$\tau(x, y) = \sum_{j=1}^{N} t_j(x - x_j, y - y_j). \tag{10.53}$$

For identical and similarly oriented apertures,

$$\tau(x, y) = t(x - x_1, y - y_1) + t(x - x_2, y - y_2) + \cdots . \tag{10.54}$$

The amplitude transmission function of any one of the apertures with respect to its local coordinates is $t(x', y')$, where $x' = x - x_j$ and $y' = y - y_j$. Equation (10.54) can be expressed as the convolution of the sum of N delta functions with the transmission function of a single aperture (Eq. 9.53), i.e.,

$$\begin{aligned} \tau(x, y) &= \left\{ \sum_{j=1}^{N} \delta(x - x_j, y - y_j) \right\} * t(x, y) \\ &= \int\!\!\int_{-\infty}^{\infty} \sum_{j=1}^{N} \delta(x' - x_j, y' - y_j) t(x - x', y - y') \mathrm{d}x' \mathrm{d}y'. \end{aligned} \tag{10.55}$$

By the convolution theorem (Eq. 9.57), the Fourier transform of this aperture function is

$$F(u, v) = g(u, v)h(u, v),$$

where

$$g(u, v) = \int\int_{-\infty}^{\infty} t(x', y')\mathrm{e}^{-\mathrm{i}2\pi(x'u+y'v)}\mathrm{d}x'\mathrm{d}y' \tag{10.56}$$

is the Fourier transform of the transmission function of any single aperture and

$$h(u, v) = \sum_{j=1}^{N} \mathrm{e}^{-\mathrm{i}2\pi(x_j u+y_j v)} \tag{10.57}$$

is the Fourier transform of N delta functions located at the origins within the apertures. When such an array of apertures is illuminated by monochromatic light, the field distribution of Fraunhofer diffraction (Eq. 10.6a) takes the form

$$E(u, v) = \left\{-\mathrm{i}\frac{A_0}{\lambda} g(u, v)\right\} h(u, v), \tag{10.58}$$

where the factor in the curly brackets gives the field distribution of Fraunhofer diffraction from any one of the apertures in the array. We now state the Array theorem:

The field distribution of Fraunhofer diffraction from an array of similarly oriented, identical apertures is the product of the field distribution of Fraunhofer diffraction from any one of the apertures with the Fourier transform of the set of delta functions distributed in the same manner (random or otherwise) as the apertures in the array.

10.4.1 Two-Slit Aperture

First, we consider an array of two identical infinitely long, parallel slits, each of width b (Fig. 10.12). The coordinates of the centers of the slits are $(0, -a/2)$ and $(0, a/2)$. The Fourier transform of the delta functions, located at the centers of these slits, is

$$h(u, v) = \mathrm{e}^{\mathrm{i}\pi va} + \mathrm{e}^{-\mathrm{i}\pi va} = 2\cos(\pi va) \tag{10.59a}$$

and the Fourier transform of the transmission function of a single slit is

$$g(v) = b \,\mathrm{sinc}\,(\pi vb). \tag{10.59b}$$

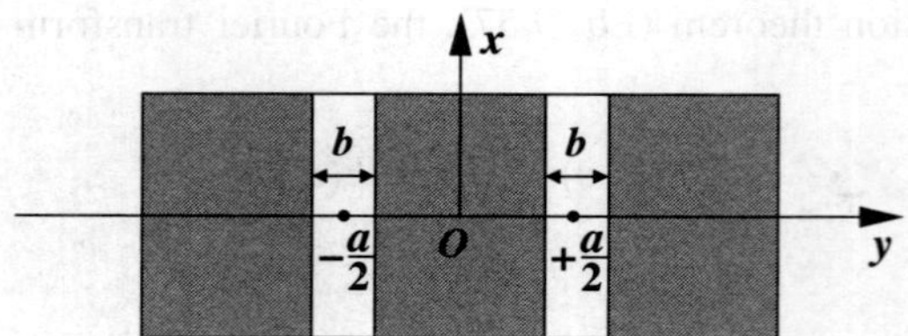

Fig. 10.12: Array of two identical slits.

Substituting Eqs (10.59) into Eq. (10.58) gives the two-slit Fraunhofer diffraction intensity distribution as

$$I(v) = \left(\frac{1}{2}\epsilon_0 c\right) 4b^2 \frac{|A_0|^2}{\lambda^2} \operatorname{sinc}^2(\pi v b) \cos^2(\pi v a) \tag{10.60a}$$

$$= I_0 \operatorname{sinc}^2(\pi v b) \cos^2(\pi v a), \tag{10.60b}$$

where I_0 is the diffracted intensity at the center (P_c) of the diffraction pattern in the plane of observation (Fig. 10.13).

The cosine square factor with

$$v = \frac{1}{\lambda}\left(\frac{y''}{R_0''} + \frac{y'}{R_0'}\right) = \frac{1}{\lambda}(\sin\gamma'' - \sin\gamma') \tag{10.61}$$

is the familiar factor appearing in Young's two-slit intensity distribution (Eq. 6.21) and the $\operatorname{sinc}^2(\pi v b)$ factor describes Fraunhofer diffraction from a single slit (Eq. 10.32b). For infinitesimally narrow slits ($b \to 0$), the sinc function takes nearly unit value everywhere, and Eq. (10.60) reproduces the intensity

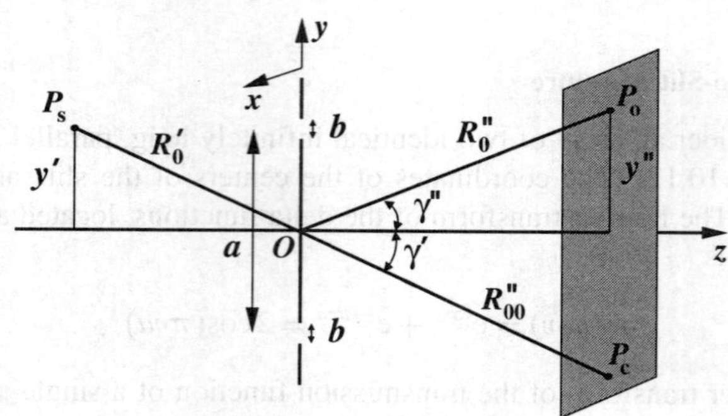

Fig. 10.13: Geometry for two-slit Fraunhofer diffraction.

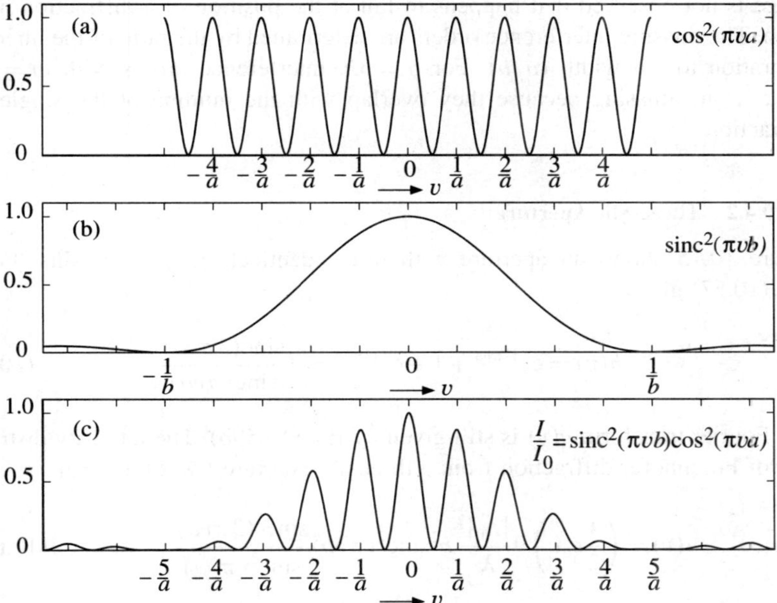

Fig. 10.14: (a) Normalized intensity distribution in two-slit interference with extremely narrow slits. (b) Single slit Fraunhofer intensity distribution for a slit of width b. (c) Normalized two-slit Fraunhofer intensity distribution with inter-slit separation $a = 5b$.

distribution in Young's two-slit interference experiment. Figure 10.14a shows the variation of the interference factor $\cos^2(\pi v a)$ with spatial frequency v. The intensity maxima are located at

$$v = \frac{1}{\lambda}(\sin\gamma''_m - \sin\gamma') = \frac{m}{a}, \quad \text{for } m = 0, \pm 1, \pm 2, \ldots \tag{10.62a}$$

For $b \neq 0$, the single slit diffraction factor $\text{sinc}^2(\pi v b)$ with its zeroes at

$$v = \frac{n}{b}, \quad \text{for } n = \pm 1, \pm 2, \ldots \tag{10.62b}$$

controls the overall intensity distribution in the plane of observation (Fig. 10.14b). Figure 10.14c shows the normalized intensity distribution of two-slit Fraunhofer diffraction (Eq. 10.60). It represents the intensity distribution of Young's interference fringes modulated by the single slit diffraction pattern. An interference fringe is not observed if it happens to fall at the position of a diffraction minimum. The missing interference orders are determined by the ratio of the inter-slit separation to slit width (a/b). For $a = 3b$, interference orders with $m = \pm 3$, $\pm 6, \ldots$ are missing because they overlap with the minima of the single slit diffraction.

10.4.2 Three-Slit Aperture

Figure 10.15 shows an aperture with three identical, equidistant slits. Equation (10.57) gives

$$h(v) = \mathrm{e}^{-\mathrm{i}2\pi va} + 1 + \mathrm{e}^{+\mathrm{i}2\pi va} = 3\frac{\operatorname{sinc}(3\pi va)}{\operatorname{sinc}(\pi va)}. \tag{10.63}$$

The Fourier transform $g(v)$ is still given by Eq. (10.59b). The intensity distribution of Fraunhofer diffraction from a three-slit aperture takes the form

$$I(v) = \left(\frac{1}{2}\epsilon_0 c\right) 9\frac{|A_0|^2}{\lambda^2} b^2 \operatorname{sinc}^2(\pi vb)\frac{\operatorname{sinc}^2(3\pi va)}{\operatorname{sinc}^2(\pi va)} \tag{10.64a}$$

$$= I_0 \operatorname{sinc}^2(\pi vb)\frac{\operatorname{sinc}^2(3\pi va)}{\operatorname{sinc}^2(\pi va)}. \tag{10.64b}$$

Once again, the overall profile of the intensity distribution is governed by the single slit Fraunhofer diffraction factor $\operatorname{sinc}^2(\pi vb)$ and the factor $\operatorname{sinc}^2(3\pi va)/\operatorname{sinc}^2(\pi va)$, depending on the inter-slit separation a, determines

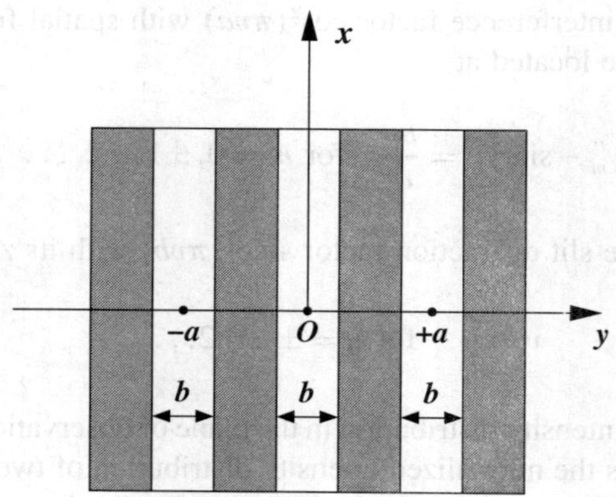

Fig. 10.15: Array of three identical slits.

the extremes in the intensity distribution. The positions of the maxima of the intensity distribution are given by

$$\pi v a = \pm m\pi \tag{10.65}$$

for integral values of m. For reasons which will be apparent shortly, these maxima are called the principal maxima. Note that the condition for the appearance of intensity maxima in three-slit Fraunhofer diffraction is exactly the same as in two-slit Fraunhofer diffraction (Eq. 10.62a). Therefore, the positions of the principal maxima do not change by increasing the number of slits in the aperture as long as the inter-slit separation remains unchanged. This is an important result which has deep significance as we shall see in a moment. The appearance of the factors of 4 and 9 in Eqs (10.60a) and (10.64a) suggests that the intensities of the principal maxima scale as the square of the number of slits in the aperture. We also note that between the mth and $(m+1)$th order principal maxima for the three-slit aperture, the $\mathrm{sinc}^2(3\pi v a)/\mathrm{sinc}^2(\pi v a)$ factor goes through zero twice at $v = \left(m+\frac{1}{3}\right)\frac{1}{a}$ and $v = \left(m+\frac{2}{3}\right)\frac{1}{a}$. There must be an intensity maximum between these two values of the spatial frequency. However, being relatively weak, this maximum is known as the secondary maximum. The secondary maxima do not appear in two-slit diffraction. Figure 10.16 shows the intensity distribution in three-slit Fraunhofer diffraction.

The presence of a secondary maximum between two neighboring principal maxima implies that the three-slit principal maxima are narrower than the two-slit principal maxima for the same inter-slit separation since, as mentioned earlier, the position of the principal maximum of a given order remains unchanged in the two cases. Intuitively, one can anticipate that Fraunhofer diffraction from four slits

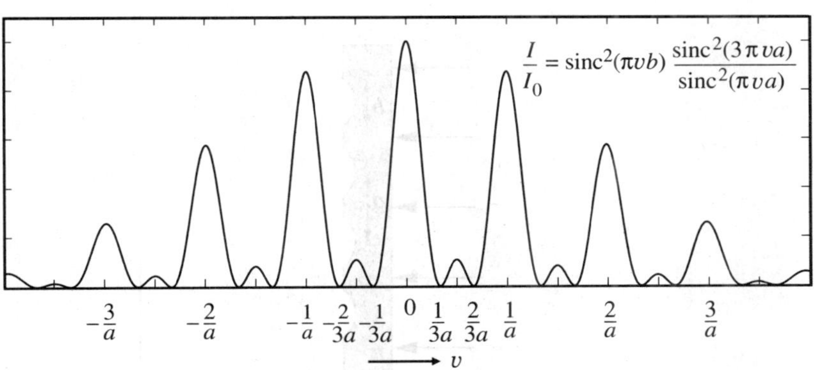

Fig. 10.16: Intensity distribution in three-slit Fraunhofer diffraction $\left(\frac{a}{b}=5\right)$.

will have two secondary maxima between two consecutive principal maxima, with the implication that the principal maxima become sharper and sharper as the number of slits is increased without changing the inter-slit separation. At the same time, the principal maxima grow in intensity because of the N^2 scaling mentioned earlier.

10.5 THE DIFFRACTION GRATING

For the present discussion, a grating may be regarded as an extended array of essentially one-dimensional elements with unchanging inter-element separations. We have now used the term 'elements' and not the slits because practical gratings do not have open apertures. Figure 10.17 shows an exaggerated view of a section of a normally illuminated transmission grating of grating element a. A transmission grating is called an amplitude grating if its aperture function modifies only the amplitude of the light wave passing through it. A phase grating changes only the phase of the light wave. The transmission function of a grating with $N = 2M + 1$ identical and equidistant elements can be written as the convolution of N delta functions with the transmission function of any one of its elements (Eq. 10.55), i.e.,

$$f(y) = \left\{ \sum_{j=-M}^{+M} \delta(y - y_j) \right\} * t(y). \tag{10.66}$$

The Fourier transform of $f(y)$ is

$$F(v) = h(v)g(v), \tag{10.67}$$

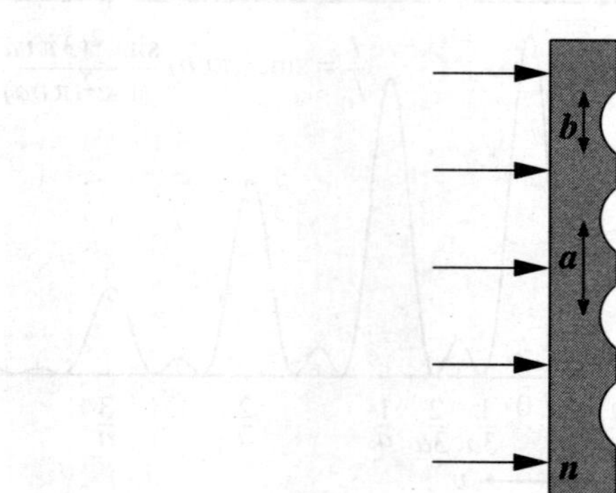

Fig. 10.17: An exaggerated view of a section of a transmission grating.

where

$$h(v) = e^{-i2\pi Mav} + e^{-i2\pi(M-1)av} + \cdots + 1 + \cdots + e^{i2\pi(M-1)av} + e^{i2\pi Mav}$$
$$= N\frac{\text{sinc}\,(N\pi va)}{\text{sinc}\,(\pi va)}, \tag{10.68}$$
$$g(v) = b\,\text{sinc}\,(\pi vb). \tag{10.69}$$

Equation (10.69) may not strictly hold if groove profile of the grating differs substantially from the rectangle function. Neglecting such details, the intensity distribution of Fraunhofer diffraction from a grating can be expressed as

$$I(v) = \left(\frac{1}{2}\epsilon_0 c\right) N^2 \frac{b^2}{\lambda^2}|A_0|^2 \text{sinc}^2(\pi vb)\frac{\text{sinc}^2(N\pi va)}{\text{sinc}^2(\pi va)} \tag{10.70a}$$
$$= I_0\,\text{sinc}^2(\pi vb)\frac{\text{sinc}^2\,(N\pi va)}{\text{sinc}^2\,(\pi va)}. \tag{10.70b}$$

As for the two- and three-slit apertures, the positions of the principal maxima of Fraunhofer diffraction from a grating are also determined by the spatial frequencies

$$v = \frac{m}{a}, \tag{10.71a}$$

where $m = 0, \pm 1, \pm 2, \ldots$. The $(N-1)$ minima between the mth and $(m+1)$th principal maxima correspond to

$$v = \left(m + \frac{n}{N}\right)\frac{1}{a}, \tag{10.71b}$$

with $n = 1, 2, \ldots, (N-1)$, giving $(N-2)$ secondary maxima between two consecutive principal maxima. The exact locations of the secondary maxima may be difficult to obtain, but it may not be too wrong if they are taken to lie halfway between consecutive minima of the intensity distribution, i.e., at

$$v = \left(m + \frac{2n+1}{2N}\right)\frac{1}{a}. \tag{10.71c}$$

The positions of the principal maxima do not change as the number of diffracting elements is increased from 2 to N, but now between two consecutive principal maxima, $(N-1)$ minima and $(N-2)$ secondary maxima of intensity appear. Therefore, for sufficiently large N, the principal maxima of grating diffraction become strong and extremely sharp. A typical grating may have N in excess of 10^5. Therefore, Fraunhofer diffraction from a grating consists of extremely sharp principal maxima of intensity

$$I_P\left(v=\frac{m}{a}\right)=\left(\frac{1}{2}\epsilon_0 c\right)N^2\frac{b^2}{\lambda^2}|A_0|^2\,\text{sinc}^2\left(\pi m\frac{b}{a}\right). \tag{10.72a}$$

Equation (10.71c) yields the peak intensities of the secondary maxima, normalized to the peak intensity of the $m=0$ principal maximum as

$$\frac{I_{\text{sec}}}{I(v=0)}=\left\{\frac{2}{(2n+1)\pi}\right\}^2 \tag{10.72b}$$

The first secondary maximum ($n=1$) carries about 4.5% of the intensity of the $m=0$ principal maximum, irrespective of the number of elements in the grating. However, the secondary maxima near the midway point between the principal maxima with $n\approx N/2$ experience an intensity reduction by a factor of $1/N^2$. It is this aspect of grating diffraction which makes grating instruments indispensable for identifying spectral lines with extremely small wavelength separations. Equation (10.62a), re-written as

$$a(\sin\gamma_m''-\sin\gamma')=m\lambda \tag{10.73a}$$

gives the angular positions of the principal maxima, where the angles γ' and γ'' are as shown in Fig. 10.13. The order of an observable principal maximum cannot exceed $2a/\lambda$. For normal incidence ($\gamma'=0$), Eq. (10.73a) reduces to the more familiar form of the grating equation

$$a\sin\gamma_m''=m\lambda. \tag{10.73b}$$

The spatial frequency width δv_m of the mth order principal maximum can be taken as the difference in the spatial frequencies of the nearest minima on its two sides, i.e.,

$$\delta v_m=\left(m+\frac{1}{N}\right)\frac{1}{a}-\left(m-\frac{1}{N}\right)\frac{1}{a}=\frac{2}{Na}. \tag{10.74a}$$

The corresponding angular width of the principal maximum of mth order, obtained from Eq. (10.61), is

$$\delta\gamma_m''=\frac{\lambda}{\cos\gamma_m''}\delta v_m=\frac{2\lambda}{Na\cos\gamma_m''}. \tag{10.74b}$$

Note that the angular width of the mth order principal maximum varies inversely with the linear width Na of the grating ($\delta\gamma''_m \to 0$ as $Na \to \infty$). It is not dependent on the grating element a as long as the product Na remains constant. For a 10 cm wide grating, used in the visible spectral range, the angular width of a principal maximum can approach 10^{-5} radians. This should be compared with the angular separation

$$\Delta\gamma''_m = \frac{\lambda}{a\cos\gamma''_m} \tag{10.75}$$

between successive principal maxima. This result can be obtained by combining Eq. (10.73a) with the equation

$$a\{\sin(\gamma''_m + \Delta\gamma''_m) - \sin\gamma'\} = (m+1)\lambda. \tag{10.76}$$

The angular separation of successive principal maxima depends on the grating element, and not on the width of the grating. For the 10 cm wide grating mentioned earlier with $N = 10^5$, $\Delta\gamma''_m \approx 1$ radian. The principal maxima of a diffraction grating are therefore quite sharp and far apart. Figure 10.18 shows the calculated intensity distribution of Fraunhofer diffraction from a grating with $N = 20$ and $a/b = 5$.

The $\mathrm{sinc}^2(\pi v b)$ factor appearing in Eqs (10.70) is often called the diffraction factor because it shows up in single slit Fraunhofer diffraction. The $\mathrm{sinc}^2(N\pi v a)/\mathrm{sinc}^2(\pi v a)$ factor is called the interference factor because it takes into account interference among waves diffracted from different slits. This classification should not be taken too seriously because the diffraction factor also

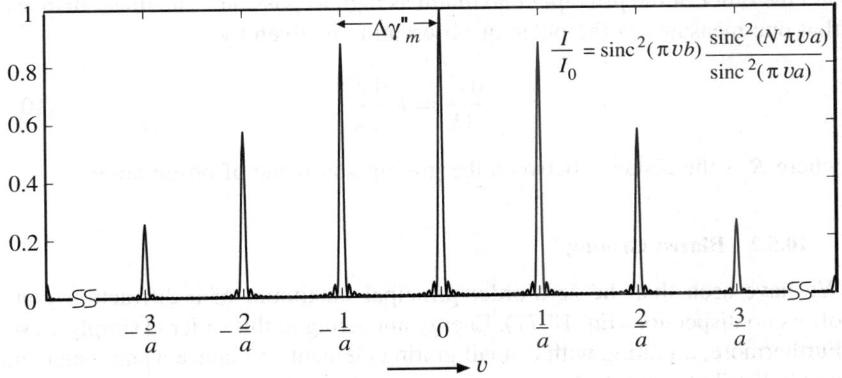

Fig. 10.18: Calculated intensity distribution of Fraunhofer diffraction from a grating with $N = 20$ and $a/b = 5$.

involves interference among waves diffracted from a single slit. The diffraction and interference phenomena may be quite distinct at the fundamental level, but they are hopelessly mixed up in any physical situation. An obstructed wave-front leads to diffraction (bending with respect to the rectilinear propagation) but subsequently, the diffracted waves invariably interfere among themselves.

10.5.1 Grating Dispersion

Diffraction gratings are used to determine the spectral composition of light by recording the variation of the intensity of diffracted light with wavelength. The principal maxima of a given order (except $m = 0$) for different wavelengths appear at different angles (Eqs 10.73). The ability of a grating to separate principal maxima of a given order for two close-lying wavelengths is called dispersion. Larger the separation, higher the dispersion. For $m = 0$, all wavelengths appear at the same angle ($\gamma'' = \gamma'$), and the grating is unable to disperse the spectrum. As such, the $m = 0$ order principal maximum is not of any interest for spectroscopic measurements, where one is primarily interested in dispersing the spectrum. It would be nice if the zero-order diffraction can be eliminated altogether because it carries a substantial fraction of the incident energy without providing any spectral information. An expression for the angular dispersion of a grating can be obtained by differentiating Eq. (10.73), giving

$$\frac{\mathrm{d}\gamma''_m}{\mathrm{d}\lambda} = \frac{m}{a \cos \gamma''_m}. \tag{10.77}$$

For high angular dispersion, i.e., large angular separation of spectral lines with small wavelength difference, the grating element should be as small as possible and the order of the principal maximum as high as possible. The linear dispersion that one measures in the plane of observation is given by

$$\frac{\mathrm{d}y''}{\mathrm{d}\lambda} = R\frac{\mathrm{d}\gamma''_m}{\mathrm{d}\lambda}, \tag{10.78}$$

where R is the distance between the grating and plane of observation.

10.5.2 Blazed Grating

We have seen that the zero-order principal maximum of a diffraction grating offers no dispersion (Eq. 10.77). Energy appearing in this order is simply wasted. Furthermore, a grating with a small grating element and hence a small elemental width distributes incident energy in several principal maxima on both sides of the non-dispersing zeroth order maximum. As a result, the energy available in any one principal maximum is rather small. It is desirable to somehow concentrate most of the diffracted energy in a single principal maximum, preferably of sufficiently high order. This, in fact, can be achieved by suitably modifying the profile of the grating element. The maxima of intensity of two-slit diffraction occur at

$$v = \frac{m}{a}, \quad m = 0, \pm 1, \pm 2, \ldots, \tag{10.62a}$$

and the minima of single slit diffraction are determined by

$$v = \frac{n}{b}, \quad n = \pm 1, \pm 2, \ldots, \tag{10.62b}$$

where a is the separation between the slits and b is the width of each slit. Successive principal maxima of all orders except $m = 0$ will overlap with successive minima of single slit diffraction if slit width b approaches slit separation a. This conclusion holds for the grating as well. But the grating principal maxima are extremely sharp. Accordingly, all principal maxima with the exception of the $m = 0$ principal maximum will vanish if the elemental width is made equal to the grating element. Figure 10.19 shows this behavior.

The above choice, however, does not make a useful device since the $m = 0$ order principal maximum of the grating is non-dispersing. In a blazed grating, the non-vanishing principal maximum is a maximum of order other than zero. Figure 10.20 shows an exaggerated view of the profile of a blazed transmission grating with grooves possessing right prismatic cross-section. The material of the grating, assumed non-absorbing in the spectral range of interest, has index of refraction n. The grating therefore acts as a phase grating. For a sufficiently small angle of the prism (γ_B), called the blaze angle, the grating element a is nearly equal to the elemental width b. The blaze angle is also the angle between the normal to each facet of the grating and the direction of the overall normal to the grating. For simplicity, we have assumed incident light falling normally on the grating. The transmission function of an element of the blazed grating can be written as

$$t(x, y) = e^{i\frac{2\pi}{\lambda}[b \sin \gamma_B + (n-1) y \sin \gamma_B]}, \tag{10.79}$$

where y varies along the inclined surface, as shown in the figure. The first term in the exponent representing a constant phase change may be ignored. The Fourier transform of the transmission function without this factor is

$$\begin{aligned} g(u, v) &= \int_{x=-\infty}^{+\infty} \int_{y=0}^{b} e^{i\frac{2\pi}{\lambda}(n-1) y \sin \gamma_B} e^{-i2\pi(ux+vy)} dx\, dy \\ &= \delta(u) \int_{y=0}^{b} e^{-i2\pi[v - \frac{(n-1)}{\lambda} \sin \gamma_B] y} dy \\ &= b\delta(u) e^{-i\pi(v - v_B) b} \operatorname{sinc}\{\pi(v - v_B) b\}, \end{aligned} \tag{10.80}$$

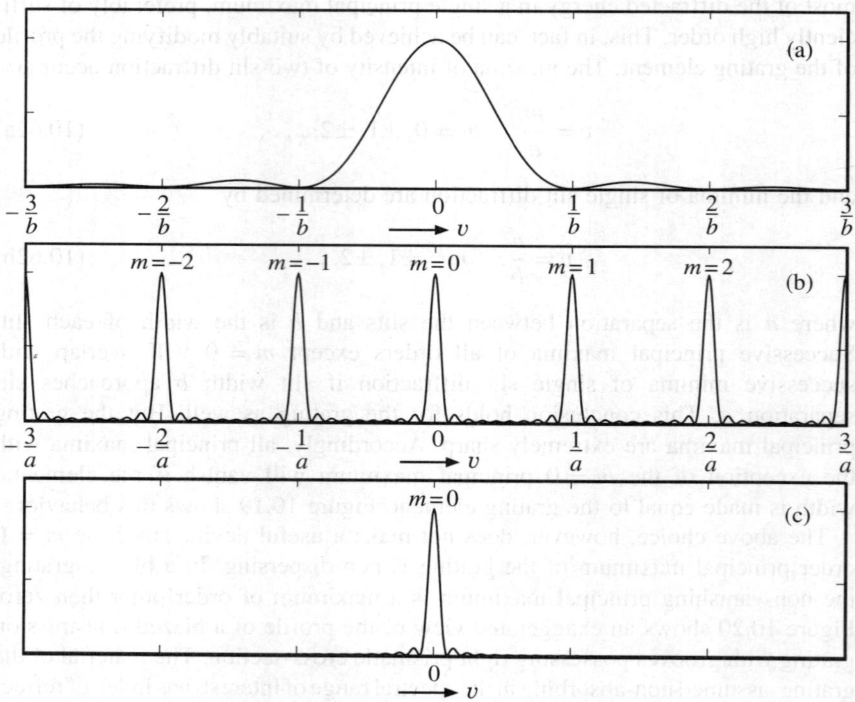

Fig. 10.19: (a) Diffraction factor for a grating with elemental width b. (b) Interference factor for a grating with $N=10$ and $a=b$. (c) Diffraction occurs in $m=0$ order.

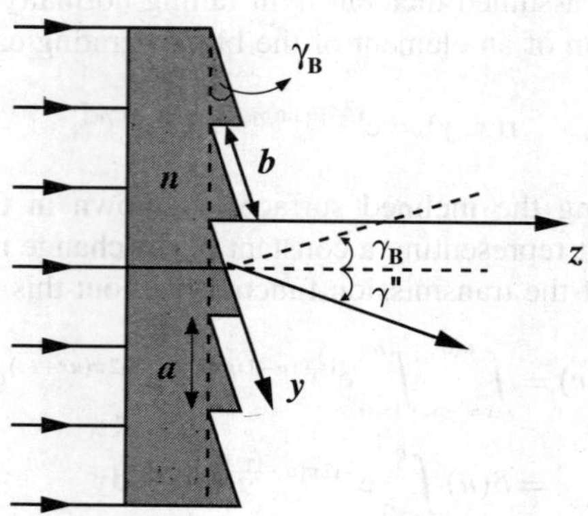

Fig. 10.20: Blazed grating with right prismatic grooves.

where

$$v_{\mathrm{B}} = \frac{n-1}{\lambda} \sin \gamma_{\mathrm{B}}. \tag{10.81}$$

Accordingly, the intensity distribution of Fraunhofer diffraction from a blazed grating takes the form

$$I(v) = \left(\frac{1}{2}\epsilon_0 c\right) \frac{N^2 b^2}{\lambda^2} |A_0|^2 \operatorname{sinc}^2[\pi b(v - v_{\mathrm{B}})] \frac{\operatorname{sinc}^2(N\pi v a)}{\operatorname{sinc}^2(\pi v a)}. \tag{10.82}$$

We see that a blazed grating has exactly the same interference factor as an unblazed grating but the diffraction factor has changed. The single element central diffraction maximum now occurs at the spatial frequency $v = v_{\mathrm{B}}$ and not at $v = 0$. In terms of the angles, the central maximum has shifted from $\gamma'' = 0$ to $\gamma'' = \sin^{-1}[(n-1)\sin \gamma_{\mathrm{B}}]$. The minima of the diffraction factor given by the condition

$$\pi b(v - v_{\mathrm{B}}) = l\pi$$

now occur at

$$v = v_{\mathrm{B}} + \frac{l}{b}, \tag{10.83a}$$

where $l = \pm 1, \pm 2, \ldots$. Since $b \approx a$, the principal maxima for the blazed grating correspond to

$$v = \frac{m}{a} \approx \frac{m}{b}, \tag{10.83b}$$

where $m = 0, \pm 1, \pm 2, \ldots$. Therefore, except for the principal maximum with $v = v_{\mathrm{B}}$, all principal maxima of a blazed grating coincide with the zeroes of the diffraction factor. This is exactly what we set out to achieve.

The wavelength $\lambda (= \lambda_{\mathrm{B}})$ and the blaze angle γ_{B} can be chosen to make the central maximum of the diffraction factor overlap with a certain principal maximum (say m_{B}) of the interference factor, i.e.,

$$v_{\mathrm{B}} = \frac{(n-1)}{\lambda_{\mathrm{B}}} \sin \gamma_{\mathrm{B}} = \frac{m_{\mathrm{B}}}{b}. \tag{10.84}$$

Equation (10.72a) for the peak intensities of the principal maxima now takes the form

$$I\left(v=\frac{m}{b}\right)=\left(\frac{1}{2}\epsilon_0 c\right)\frac{N^2b^2}{\lambda^2}|A_0|^2\operatorname{sinc}^2\{\pi(m-m_{\rm B})\}. \tag{10.85}$$

The principal maximum with $m = m_{\rm B}$ is the only principal maximum which survives in a blazed grating. Figure 10.21 shows the variations of the diffraction factor, the interference factor, and their product for a blazed grating.

A blazed grating possesses much higher diffraction efficiency because it gives the peak intensity of a single element diffraction and the sharpness of a

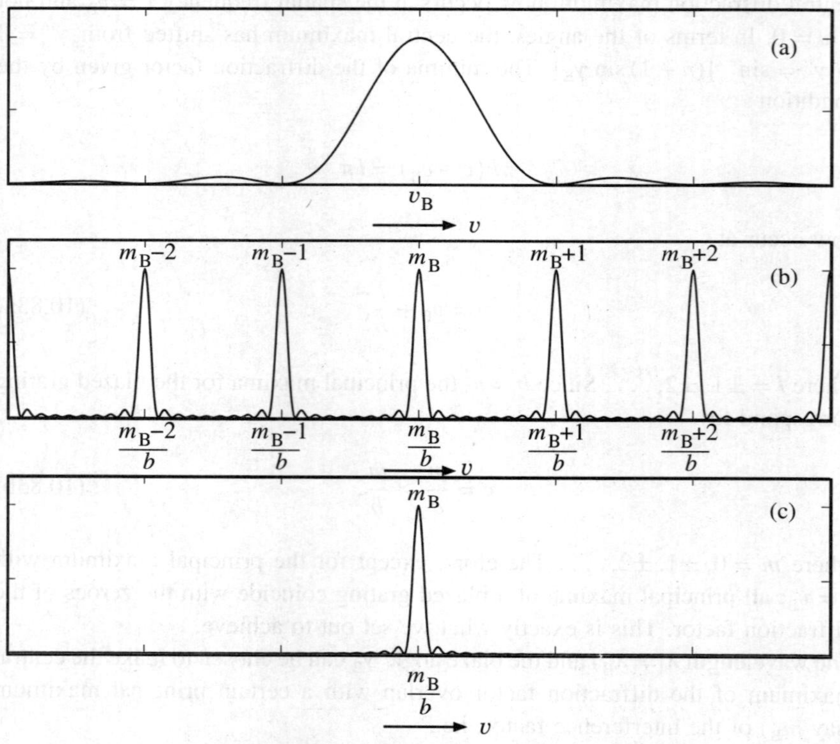

Fig. 10.21: (a) Diffraction factor for a grating with elemental width b. (b) Interference factor for a blazed grating with $N = 10$ and $a = b$. (c) Diffraction occurs in $m = m_{\rm B}$ order of the blazed grating.

multi-element grating. The grating is said to be blazed for wavelength λ_B in order m_B. However, re-writing Eq. (10.84) as

$$m_B\lambda_B = (n-1)b\sin\gamma_B \tag{10.86}$$

reveals that a grating blazed for wavelength λ_B in order m_B is automatically blazed for the wavelengths $\frac{1}{2}\lambda_B, \frac{1}{3}\lambda_B, \ldots$ in $2m_B, 3m_B, \ldots$ orders, respectively. Thus, a single blazed grating can be used in different spectral regions in different orders. Designing a blazed grating with prismatic grooves is not as difficult as it might appear at first sight. The single element central diffraction peak exactly coincides with the direction of the refracted ray.

It must be realized that the width of an element of a blazed grating cannot exactly equal the inter-elemental separation, although the difference between the two can be made small. As a result, the principal maxima in the immediate neighborhood of the principal maximum satisfying Eq. (10.86) carry non-zero irradiance, thereby, reducing the efficiency of a blazed grating. Furthermore, a blazed grating will not be very useful if its use is limited to only the blazing wavelength λ_B. For wavelengths close to λ_B, the m_Bth order principal maximum does not exactly coincide with the peak of the diffraction factor (Fig. 10.21a). Therefore, its irradiance and hence the efficiency of the blazed grating is somewhat reduced. The reduced efficiency for $\lambda \neq \lambda_B$ can be calculated from the modified form of Eq. (10.85):

$$I\left(v=\frac{m}{b}\right) = \left(\frac{1}{2}\epsilon_0 c\right)\frac{N^2b^2}{\lambda^2}|A_0|^2\,\mathrm{sinc}^2\,\{\pi(m-m'_B)\}, \tag{10.87}$$

where Eq. (10.86) allows us to write

$$m'_B = \frac{\lambda_B}{\lambda}m_B.$$

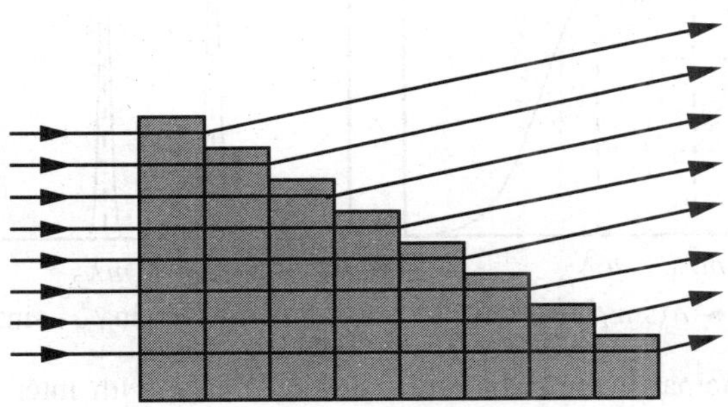

Fig. 10.22: An echelon grating.

The blazed gratings are usually used in low principal orders ($m = 1$–5). However, the echelon gratings, first invented by Michelson, operate in very high orders ($m \sim 1000$) since the path difference between waves diffracted, even at small angles, from successive steps of the echelon is quite large (Fig. 10.22).

10.5.3 Resolving Power of a Grating

Dispersion was defined in terms of the ability of a grating to separate principal maxima of a given order for different wavelengths present in the incident light. Dispersion is an important characteristic of a grating, but it is not a sufficient indicator of the capability or the limitation of the grating or of any optical instrument. The complete profiles, and not just the peaks of the principal maxima, for different wavelengths must be separated. This leads to the concept of the resolving power of a grating as distinct from the dispersion of a grating. If the principal maxima are not sharp, they may remain unresolved even under conditions of high dispersion (Fig. 10.23).

The limit of resolution of a grating is the minimum wavelength separation $\delta\lambda$ between two spectral lines such that their mth order principal maxima are just resolved. There is, however, no unique definition of the term 'just resolved'. The Rayleigh criterion of resolution states that two spectral lines of equal intensity, from an incoherent source, with wavelengths λ and $(\lambda - \delta\lambda)$ are just resolved in the mth order if the peak of the mth order principal maximum for wavelength λ coincides with the minimum nearest to the mth order principal maximum for the wavelength $(\lambda - \delta\lambda)$. The resolving power (RP) of the grating is then

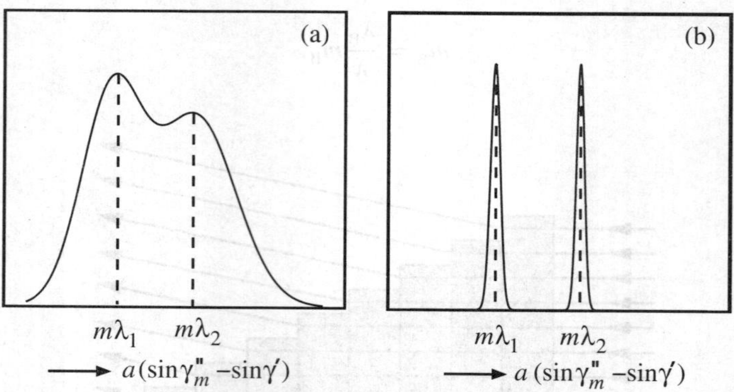

Fig. 10.23: Principal maxima of a diffraction grating with inter-slit separation a; (a) high dispersion, low resolving power, (b) high dispersion, high resolving power.

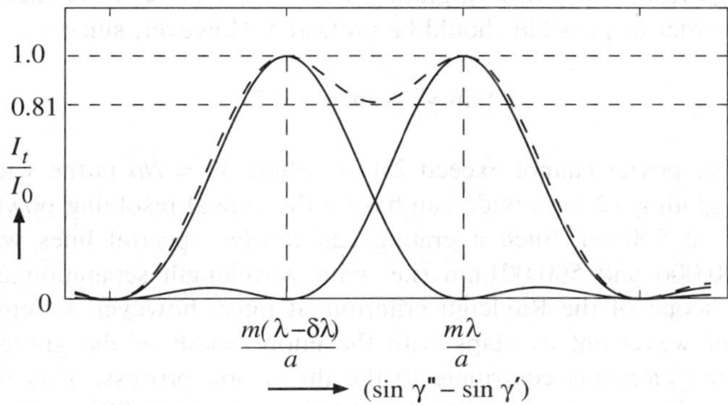

Fig. 10.24: Rayleigh criterion of resolution.

defined by the ratio $\lambda/\delta\lambda$. Figure 10.24 shows the intensity distributions of the principal maxima of order m for the wavelengths λ and $(\lambda - \delta\lambda)$ as a function of $(\sin\gamma'' - \sin\gamma')$.

The angular separation of the peak of the mth order principal maximum from its nearest minimum, obtained from Eq. (10.74b), is

$$\frac{\delta\gamma''_m}{2} = \frac{\lambda}{Na\cos\gamma''_m} \tag{10.88a}$$

and the angular separation between the mth order principal maxima for wavelengths λ and $(\lambda - \delta\lambda)$, calculated from the dispersion relation (Eq. 10.77), is

$$(\delta\gamma''_m)_{\delta\lambda} = \frac{d\gamma''_m}{d\lambda}\delta\lambda = \frac{m}{a\cos\gamma''_m}\delta\lambda. \tag{10.88b}$$

Equating Eqs (10.88a) and (10.88b) to satisfy the Rayleigh criterion of resolution, we obtain

$$\mathrm{RP} = \frac{\lambda}{\delta\lambda} = mN \tag{10.89a}$$

$$= \frac{Na}{\lambda}(\sin\gamma''_m - \sin\gamma'). \tag{10.89b}$$

The right-hand side of Eq. (10.89b) allows one to interpret the resolving power of a grating as the number of wavelengths of light present in the path difference between waves diffracted from the extreme ends of a grating of width Na. To achieve high resolving power, a grating with large number of elements used in as high an order as possible should be preferred. However, since

$$(\sin \gamma''_m - \sin \gamma') \leq 2, \tag{10.90}$$

the resolving power cannot exceed $2W/\lambda$, where $W = Na$ is the width of the grating. A grating 12.5 cm wide can have a theoretical resolving power as high as 500 000 at 500 nm. Such a grating can resolve spectral lines with wavelengths 500.000 and 500.001 nm (i.e. with wavelength separation of 0.01 Å) within the scope of the Rayleigh criterion. It must, however, be ensured that the incident wavefront overlaps with the entire width of the grating so that all N grating elements contribute to the diffraction process. This is possible if light is incident at near-grazing (angle of incidence $\approx 90°$) angle. Alternatively, the light beam can be expanded to cover the entire grating. Figure 10.25 shows Littrow mounting of a blazed reflection grating, commonly used in high-resolution spectrometers. The entrance slit and detector, somewhat displaced from each other, lie in the front focal plane of lens L. The collimated beam falls normally on each facet of the blazed reflection grating G. Diffraction primarily (non-vanishing principal maximum) occurs along the direction of specular reflection. The diffracted light retraces the path of the incident beam (autocollimation). Reflection gratings, being phase gratings, possess higher diffraction efficiencies.

Notwithstanding what has been said above, Eq. (10.89b) shows that a grating having fewer elements with large inter-elemental separations has the same resolving power as a grating with large number of elements and small inter-elemental separations as long as the two have the same overall widths (Na).

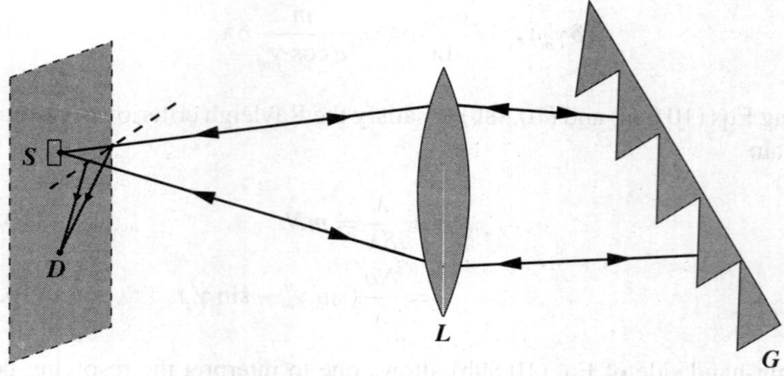

Fig. 10.25: Littrow mounting of a blazed reflection grating; S is entrance slit and D is detector.

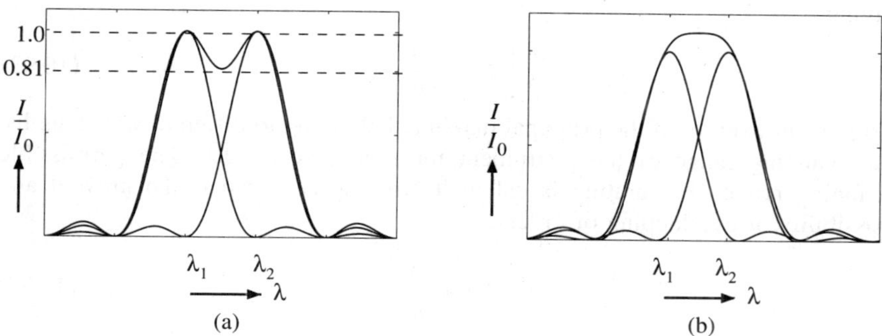

Fig. 10.26: (a) Rayleigh criterion of resolution. (b) Sparrow's criterion of resolution – peaks are allowed to come close to have flat top in the combined profile.

The two gratings will have unequal efficiencies, though. It may be mentioned in passing that Rayleigh criterion is not the only criterion in vogue to specify the limit of resolution of a grating instrument.

Figure 10.26 compares the Rayleigh criterion with another criterion due to C. Sparrow. In the Rayleigh limit of resolution, a dip in the intensity distribution appears between the two peaks (Fig. 10.26a). The dip height is nearly 81% of the height of either of the peaks. In the Sparrow criterion, the two peaks are allowed to come still closer to get a flat top in the intensity distribution (Fig. 10.26b).

10.5.4 Free Spectral Range

A grating instrument like any other wavelength-measuring instrument should be able to unambiguously identify the wavelengths of the spectral lines present in the incident light. In particular, for a diffraction grating, a given principal maximum in the observation plane must correspond to a unique wavelength. This condition can be violated if higher order principal maxima for shorter wavelengths begin to overlap with lower order principal maxima for longer wavelengths (see Eq. 10.86). This puts an upper limit to the useful spectral range of a grating instrument. This limit is reached when the $(m+1)$th order principal maximum for wavelength λ coincides with the mth order principal maximum for wavelength $(\lambda + \Delta\lambda)$, i.e., when

$$(m+1)\lambda = m(\lambda + \Delta\lambda) = a(\sin\gamma''_m - \sin\gamma'), \tag{10.91}$$

giving

$$\Delta\lambda = \frac{\lambda}{m}. \tag{10.92}$$

To prevent overlap of the principal maxima, belonging to different wavelengths, the scanning range of the instrument must not exceed $\Delta\lambda$. The permissible scanning range of a grating is called its free spectral range. To prevent any possibility of overlapping of orders,

$$\Delta\lambda < \frac{\lambda}{m}, \tag{10.93}$$

where λ is the lower wavelength limit of the scan and m is the order of the principal maximum being scanned. Equation (10.92) defines the free spectral range (FSR) of a grating. To keep the free spectral range around a certain wavelength as wide as possible, a low-order principal maximum must be used. This reduces the resolving power of the instrument. Hence, the FSR of a grating can be increased only at the cost of its resolving power and vice versa. A good compromise is to choose large N and a low-order principal maximum for blazing.

10.6 IRREGULARLY POSITIONED APERTURES

We now consider an array of N identical and similarly oriented, but irregularly arranged apertures in two dimensions. The separations among the apertures change randomly (Fig. 10.11). The Fourier transform of the transmission function of such an array of apertures is still given by the product

$$F(u, v) = g(u, v)h(u, v),$$

where

$$g(u, v) = \int\int_{-\infty}^{\infty} t(x, y)\mathrm{e}^{-\mathrm{i}2\pi(ux+vy)}\,\mathrm{d}x\,\mathrm{d}y, \tag{10.94}$$

$$h(u, v) = \sum_{j=1}^{N} \mathrm{e}^{-\mathrm{i}2\pi(x_j u + y_j v)}. \tag{10.95}$$

Since x_j and y_j are now randomly distributed, we have no way of finding this sum. However, the square modulus of $h(u, v)$ is

$$|h(u, v)|^2 = \left(\sum_{j=1}^{N} \mathrm{e}^{-\mathrm{i}2\pi(x_j u + y_j v)}\right)\left(\sum_{k=1}^{N} \mathrm{e}^{\mathrm{i}2\pi(x_k u + y_k v)}\right)$$

$$= \sum_{j=k=1}^{N} e^{-i2\pi[(x_j-x_k)u+(y_j-y_k)v]} + \sum_{j\neq k=1}^{N} e^{-i2\pi[(x_j-x_k)u+(y_j-y_k)v]}$$

$$= N + \sum_{j\neq k=1}^{N} e^{-i2\pi[(x_j-x_k)u+(y_j-y_k)v]}. \tag{10.96}$$

The second term arises due to interference among waves diffracted from different apertures. The signs and magnitudes of the terms in this sum change randomly because of the random distribution of the apertures. For sufficiently large N, positive and negative contributions to the sum may add up to zero. For N not so large, this term is small, but not exactly zero. The intensity distribution of Fraunhofer diffraction from such an array, when illuminated coherently, has the form

$$I(u, v) = \left(\frac{1}{2}\epsilon_0 c\right) \frac{|A_0|^2}{\lambda^2} |g(u, v)|^2 \left[N + \sum_{j\neq k=1}^{N} e^{-i2\pi[(x_j-x_k)u+(y_j-y_k)v]} \right]. \tag{10.97}$$

Ignoring for the moment the interference effects represented by the second term in the square brackets, the diffracted intensity in a given direction from N randomly placed apertures is N times the diffracted intensity due to a single aperture. This should be compared with the N^2 factor for an array of N equally spaced apertures (Eq. 10.70a). Thus, the Fraunhofer diffraction pattern of a finite number of randomly placed apertures has the appearance of the Fraunhofer diffraction pattern of a single aperture, but N times brighter along with some discernible effects due to interference among waves diffracted from different apertures. Commonly observed halos produced by randomly distributed water droplets and aerosol particles, illuminated by a distant light source, are manifestations of this effect. Such halos may be accompanied by speckles, representing interference among waves diffracted from different particles (see Fig. 10.9 in Ref. [10.2]).

10.7 SINUSOIDAL GRATING

Sinusoidal gratings are not relevant for spectroscopic investigations but, as we shall see in a later chapter, they find use in characterizing the performance of lenses and optical systems. A sinusoidal grating has the amplitude transmission function

$$t(x, y) = a + b\cos 2\pi(u_0 x + v_0 y), \tag{10.98}$$

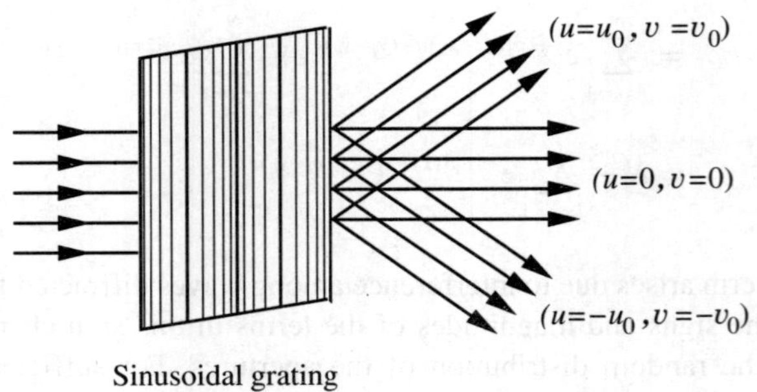

Fig. 10.27: Fraunhofer diffraction from a sinusoidal grating.

where a, b, u_0, v_0 are positive constants. Its Fourier transform is

$$F(u, v) = \int\int_{-\infty}^{\infty} [a + b\cos 2\pi(u_0 x + v_0 y)]\mathrm{e}^{-\mathrm{i}2\pi(ux+vy)}\mathrm{d}x\mathrm{d}y \tag{10.99}$$

$$= a\delta(u, v) + \frac{b}{2}\{\delta(u - u_0, v - v_0) + \delta(u + u_0, v + v_0)\}.$$

The field distribution of Fraunhofer diffraction, obtained by substituting Eq. (10.99) into Eq. (10.6a), is

$$E(u, v) = -\frac{\mathrm{i}A_0}{\lambda}[a\delta(u, v) + \frac{b}{2}\{\delta(u - u_0, v - v_0) + \delta(u + u_0, v + v_0)\}]. \tag{10.100}$$

Thus, Fraunhofer diffraction from a sinusoidal grating appears along only three directions. For illumination with a plane wave, the first term in Eq. (10.100) represents diffraction in the forward direction. This is the zero-order diffraction. The remaining two terms produce diffracted waves along (u_0, v_0) and $(-u_0, -v_0)$ directions (Fig. 10.27).

10.8 TWO PIN-HOLES

As the last example of the array theorem, we consider two identical circular holes illuminated normally by coherent light of wavelength λ (Fig. 10.28).

The intensity distribution of Fraunhofer diffraction for this aperture can be obtained from Eq. (10.58), where $g(u, v)$ is the Fourier transform of the amplitude transmission function of a circular aperture of radius a (Eq. 10.43) and $h(u, v)$ is

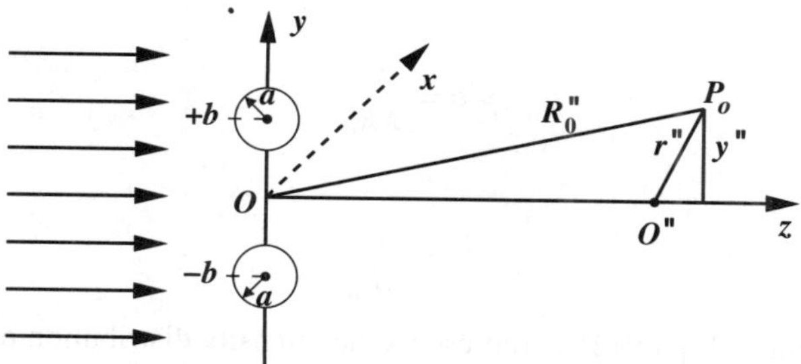

Fig. 10.28: Fraunhofer diffraction from two pin-holes.

the Fourier transform of the Dirac delta functions located at $y = -b$ and $y = +b$ (Eq. 10.59a). Accordingly,

$$I(\rho, v) = I_0 \left| \frac{2J_1(2\pi\rho a)}{2\pi\rho a} \right|^2 \cos^2(2\pi v b), \tag{10.101}$$

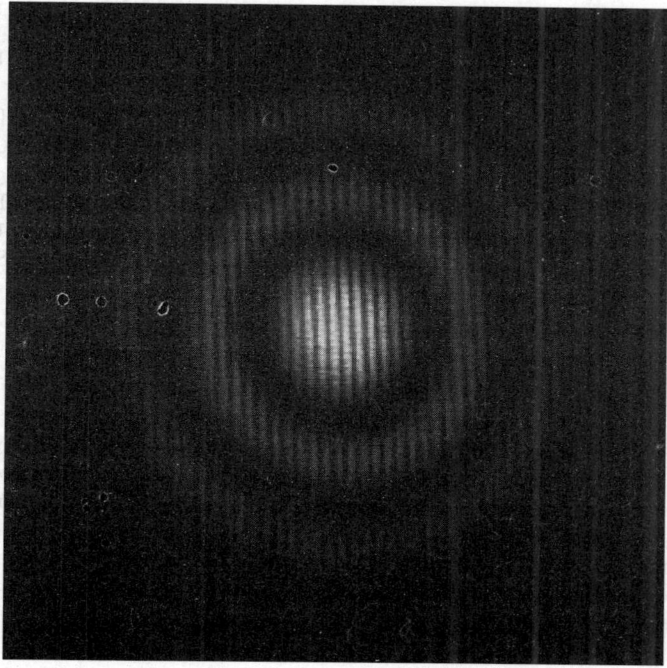

Photo 10.4: Fraunhofer diffraction from two pin holes, each of diameter 0.32 mm, recorded with 514.5 nm line of argon ion laser. The holes were kept 2 mm apart.

where

$$\rho = \frac{r''}{\lambda R_0''} \tag{10.102a}$$

and

$$v = \frac{y''}{\lambda R_0''}. \tag{10.102b}$$

The first factor in Eq. (10.101) represents the intensity distribution of Fraunhofer diffraction from a circular aperture and the second factor, arising due to the presence of two circular holes, is exactly the factor which describes the intensity distribution in Young's interference experiments ($a \to 0$). Fraunhofer diffraction from two pin holes, each of diameter 0.32 mm, recorded with 514.5 nm line of an argon ion laser is shown in Photo 10.4. The holes were kept 2 mm apart. Straight (Young's) interference fringes within the bright portions of the single hole Fraunhofer diffraction pattern can be seen.

10.9 REFERENCES

10.1 Max Born and Emil Wolf, Principles of Optics, 7th ed., Cambridge University Press, Cambridge, 1999.

10.2 Robert D. Guenther, Modern Optics, John Wiley & Sons, New York, 1990.

10.3 S. G Lipson, H. Lipson, and D. S. Tannhauser, Optical physics, 3rd ed., Cambridge University Press, 1995.

10.4 George O. Reynolds, John B. Develis, George B. Parrent, Jr., Brian J. Thompson, The New Physical Optics Notebook, SPIE Optical Engineering Press, 1989.

10.5 Miles V. Klein, Thomas E. Furtak, Optics, 2nd ed., John Wiley & Sons, New York, 1986.

10.6 Eugene Hecht, Optics, 4th ed., Addison-Wesley, Reading, 2001.

10.10 PROBLEMS

10.1 (a) Convince yourself that the transverse displacement of a ray in passing through a thin lens is indeed small. Take $n = 1.5, d_0 = 3$ mm, and angle of incidence of 10°.

(b) Find the range of phase variations introduced by a thin lens of diameter 2 cm and focal length 10 cm. Take $\lambda = 500$ nm.

10.2 Fraunhofer diffraction from a rectangular aperture of sides 0.4 mm × 0.6 mm is investigated with light of wavelength 632.8 nm falling normally on the aperture screen.

(a) Find the least distance of an observation plane from the aperture screen so that the largest quadratic term in the diffraction integral introduces a phase of no more than 5°.

(b) Take the plane of observation 5 m behind the aperture with x'', y'' axes parallel and perpendicular to the long edge of the aperture.

(i) Find the positions and widths of the first secondary maxima on the x'' and y'' axes and determine their peak irradiances as fractions of the peak irradiance of the central diffraction maximum.

(ii) Find the integrated irradiances of the first secondary maxima along the x'' and y'' axes as fractions of the integrated irradiance of the central diffraction maximum.

(iii) Find the ratio of the integrated irradiances of the first and second secondary maxima along the x'' axis.

10.3 Use Eq. (10.23) to obtain the intensity distribution of Fraunhofer diffraction from two long, parallel slits, each of width b and separation parameter d as shown in Fig. 10.29 and verify the result obtained from the Array theorem (Eq. 10.60). Will there be any missing interference fringes if d/b is an integer? Under these conditions, how many fringes appear in the central and first secondary diffraction maxima? Identify the missing orders when the ratio d/b is half integral.

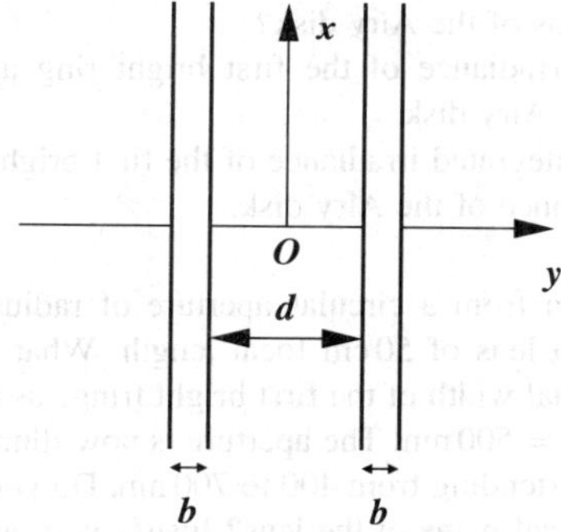

Fig. 10.29.

10.4 Find the intensity distribution of Fraunhofer diffraction from an annular aperture of inner radius a and outer radius $a+b$ illuminated by a monochromatic axial point source. For $a = 0.2$ mm and $b = 0.4$ mm, plot the normalized intensity distribution as a function of the radial distance in the plane of observation located 10 m behind the aperture screen. The point source, emitting 632.8 nm radiation, is 10 m in front of the aperture screen.

10.5 Find the intensity distribution of Fraunhofer diffraction from the crossed aperture, shown in Fig. 10.30, where a and b are small. The slits extend to infinity in all directions.

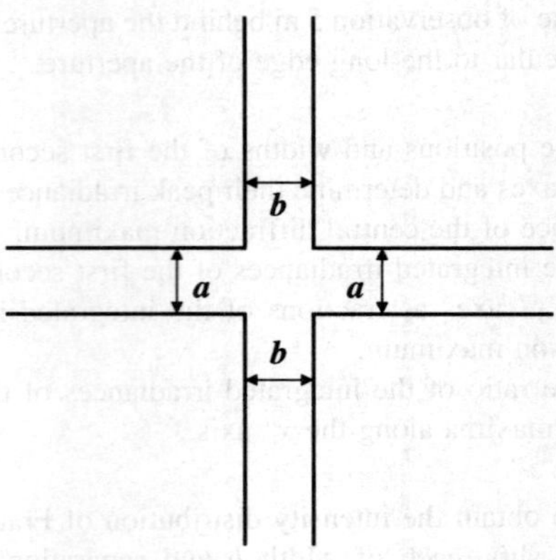

Fig. 10.30.

10.6 Let $a \to 0$ in Problem 10.4 so that the annular aperture goes over to a circular aperture of radius 0.4 mm. The positions of the source and plane of observation remain as in Problem 10.4.

(a) What is the radius of the Airy disk?
(b) Find the peak irradiance of the first bright ring as a fraction of the peak irradiance of the Airy disk.
(c) Determine the integrated irradiance of the first bright ring as a fraction of the integrated irradiance of the Airy disk.

10.7 Fraunhofer diffraction from a circular aperture of radius 1 mm is studied in the back focal plane of a lens of 50 cm focal length. What is the radius of the Airy disk? Express the radial width of the first bright fringe as a fraction of the radius of the Airy disk. Take $\lambda = 500$ nm. The aperture is now illuminated with a collimated beam of white light extending from 400 to 700 nm. Do you expect to see any fringe pattern in the back focal plane of the lens? Justify your answer.

10.8 For the three-slit aperture of Fig. 10.15, plot the intensity distribution of Fraunhofer diffraction in a plane 3 m behind the aperture screen. Take $b = 0.1$ mm and $a = 1$ mm. The aperture is illuminated by a distant axial source emitting light of wavelength 632.8 nm. Find the position of the peak of the secondary maximum between the zeroth and first-order principal maxima. Compare its peak height with that of the zeroth order principal maximum.

10.9 Consider a normally illuminated aperture containing three long slits with widths and separations as shown in Fig. 10.31.

(a) Write the amplitude transmission function of the aperture and obtain the field distribution of Fraunhofer diffraction from it.

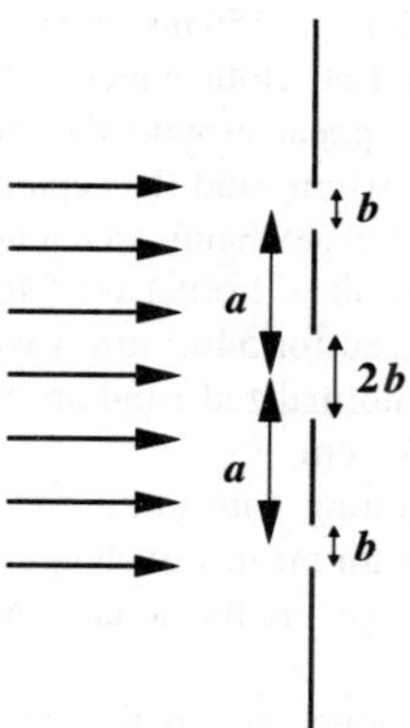

Fig. 10.31.

(b) Sketch the intensity distribution in the plane of observation and locate the three most prominent maxima of intensity.

(c) Show that the field distribution obtained in part (a) goes over to Eq. (10.64) if the middle aperture also had width b.

10.10 Sketch, indicating the salient features, the intensity distributions of Fraunhofer diffraction from the apertures given in Fig. 10.32.

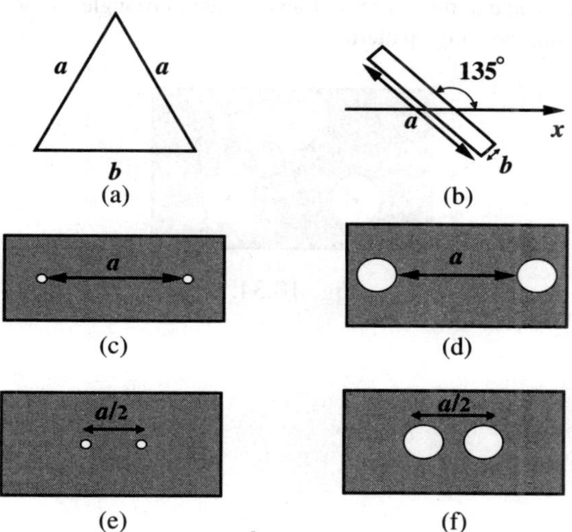

Fig. 10.32.

10.11 A small source emitting light at 550 nm located 50 m away from the observer is seen through a piece of fine cloth which acts as a two-dimensional grating. A number of bright spots appear around the source. If the separation between consecutive bright spots is 10 cm, find the separation of the strands in the cloth.

10.12 A blazed grating is blazed for 589.3 nm wavelength in the second order. Find the normalized irradiance of the $m = 2$ order for 546.1 nm wavelength.

10.13 For a grating ($n = 1.5$) blazed for 546.1 nm wavelength in the second order, find the blazing angle and the normalized irradiance of the $m = 3$ principal order at 589.3 nm. Take $b = 2 \times 10^{-3}$ cm.

10.14 What minimum width a grating with grating element 3×10^{-4} cm must have to resolve two spectral lines with mean wavelength 600 nm, separated by 0.001 nm? What is the free spectral range and the actual wavelength interval(s) in which this grating can be used?

10.15 Sketch the fringe pattern appearing in the intensity distribution of Fraunhofer diffraction produced by two identical holes separated by the diameter of either of the holes (Fig. 10.33).

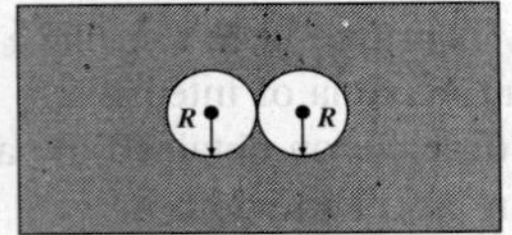

Fig. 10.33.

10.16 Find the intensity distribution of Fraunhofer diffraction from an array of three identical holes located at the vertices of an equilateral triangle as shown in Fig. 10.34. Try sketching the fringe pattern.

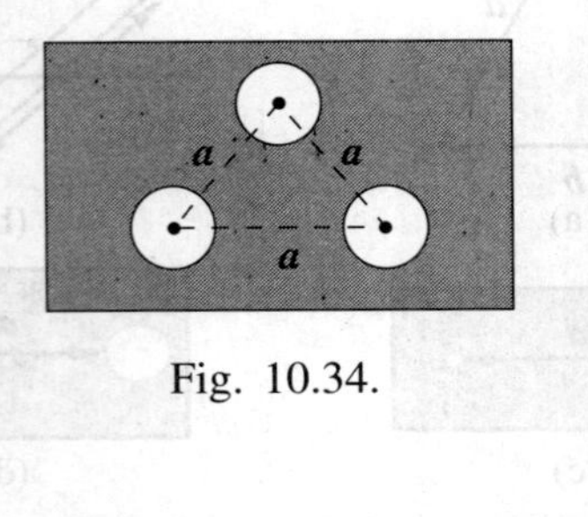

Fig. 10.34.

CHAPTER **11**

Image Formation and Optical Processing

11.1 INTRODUCTION

In the paraxial approximation of geometrical optics, a lens forms a point image of a point object and a line image of a line object (Fig. 11.1). Spherical wavefronts emanating from different points of the object carry with them complete information on the amplitude and phase distributions of the object field. A lens bends and converges these wavefronts to form the image (Fig. 5.1). Optical path lengths of all paths between an object point and its image are exactly equal. Constructive interference among the arriving waves reinforces the field at the image point. The field distribution in the object plane and geometry of the imaging configuration determine the brightness of the image. The location and magnification of the image can be obtained from

$$\frac{1}{v} - \frac{1}{u} = \frac{1}{f} \tag{4.51b}$$

and

$$m = \frac{h'}{h} = \frac{v}{u}, \tag{4.52a}$$

where u and v are the object and image distances from the lens, respectively.

Under ideal conditions, the image field distribution $E(x'', y'')$ of a two-dimensional object (Fig. 11.2) is described, except for the image magnification, by the object field distribution function $E_O(x', y')$, i.e.,

$$E(x'', y'') = \frac{1}{m} E_O\left(x' = \frac{x''}{m}, y' = \frac{y''}{m}\right). \tag{11.1}$$

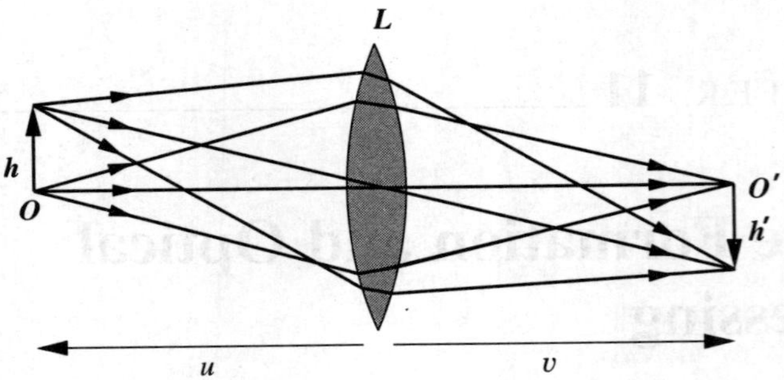

Fig. 11.1: Paraxial image formed by a lens.

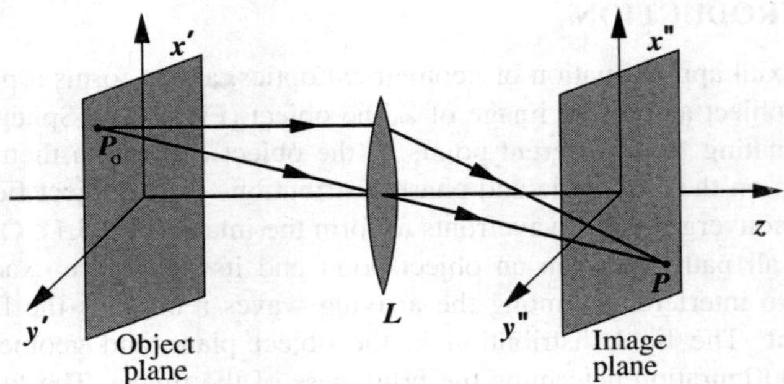

Fig. 11.2: Imaging two-dimensional object by a lens.

This equation relates the field at point (x'', y'') in the image plane to the field at the conjugate point (x', y') in the object plane. Equation (11.1) neglects losses in the process of image formation. A lens with large aperture minimizes the losses and diffraction effects in image formation. But a lens with large aperture causes image degradation as described in Chapter 5. In fact, to reduce image aberrations, aperture stops are often used. Ernst Abbe in the 1870s investigated in depth the effect of the aperture size on the resolution and overall quality of the image formed by a compound microscope. He expected the breakdown of the paraxial approximation with increasing aperture size to adversely affect the quality of the image. He, however, observed larger apertures to generally improve the image resolution. In fact, on reducing the aperture size below a certain limit, he found the image to disappear altogether. His interpretation of these observations laid the foundation of the modern theory of image formation and processing. Diffraction, and not geometrical optics, plays the central role in Abbe's theory of image formation.

11.2 DIFFRACTION THEORY OF IMAGE FORMATION

We have seen in Chapter 10 how the Fourier decomposition

$$t(x, y) = \iint_{-\infty}^{\infty} F(u, v)\mathrm{e}^{\mathrm{i}2\pi(ux+vy)}\mathrm{d}u\,\mathrm{d}v \tag{11.2}$$

of the amplitude transmission function $t(x, y)$ of a coherently illuminated two-dimensional aperture can be interpreted in terms of an infinite set of plane diffracted waves, travelling along directions specified by the spatial frequencies u and v. The product $F(u, v)\mathrm{d}u\,\mathrm{d}v$ is the amplitude or the weighting factor for the waves with spatial frequencies lying in the intervals u, $u+\mathrm{d}u$ and v, $v+\mathrm{d}v$. These waves collectively carry complete object (aperture) information. Image is the result of interference among these waves when brought together. Image plane may be defined as any plane in which the diffracted waves interfere. All diffracted waves must reach the image plane for a faithful reproduction of the object field distribution. Abbe's observations can be understood within the framework of this description of image formation. Low spatial frequencies, carrying information on the gross features (periodicity, overall light distribution, etc.) of the object field distribution and travelling at small angles with the optical axis, are easily collected by the objective of the microscope. On the other hand, higher spatial frequencies carrying fine details (sharpness of edges, etc.) of the object field distribution and travelling at relatively large angles are more likely to be missed by a lens of finite aperture. If an aperture, kept between the object and objective of the microscope, rejects all but the zero-order spatial frequency, only a patch of light, and not the image of the object appears in the image plane. The object phase information remains completely unutilized since the zero spatial frequency wave has no other wave in the image plane to interfere with.

Before forming the image in the image plane, a lens converges these waves in its back focal plane, called the Fourier transform or simply the transform plane (Fig. 11.3).

Each convergence point in this plane is a display of a particular object spatial frequency. The transform plane, as we shall see later, plays an important role in the processing of optical images. Since the object spatial frequencies are separated in this plane, any modification of the image is best carried out in this plane. The diffraction process of image formation described in Fig. 11.3 can be interpreted in terms of two Fourier transform operations in succession. The incident wave is diffracted by the object transparency and the Fourier transform

$$F(u, v) = \iint_{-\infty}^{\infty} E_{\mathrm{O}}(x', y')\mathrm{e}^{-\mathrm{i}2\pi(ux'+vy')}\mathrm{d}x'\mathrm{d}y' \tag{11.3}$$

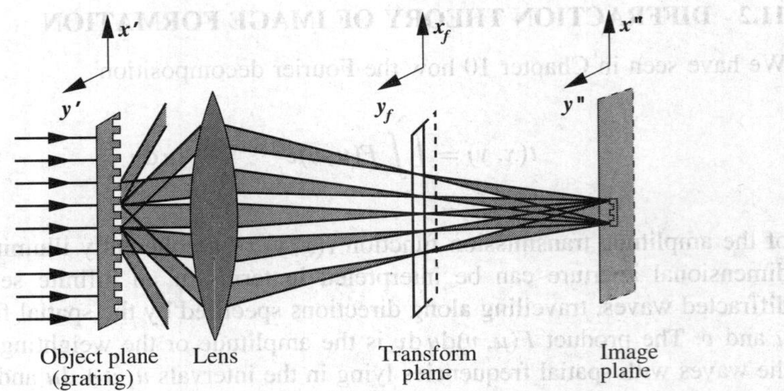

Fig. 11.3: Image formation by a lens as double Fourier transformation.

of the object field distribution $E_{\mathrm{O}}(x', y')$ appears in the back focal plane of the lens. The second stage of image formation begins with the Huygens' wavelets spreading from the back focal plane of the lens and eventually overlapping in the image plane. This process is also a Fourier transform operation provided the image plane is located far away or if a second lens is used to obtain the image (see Fig. 11.5). Therefore, image formation by a lens can be described in terms of the Fourier transform of the Fourier transform of the object field distribution. Accordingly, the image field distribution can be written as

$$\begin{aligned}
E(x'', y'') &= \mathcal{F}[F(u, v)] \\
&= \iint_{-\infty}^{\infty} F(u, v)\mathrm{e}^{-\mathrm{i}2\pi(ux''+vy'')}\mathrm{d}u\,\mathrm{d}v. \\
&= \iint_{-\infty}^{\infty} \mathrm{d}x'\mathrm{d}y'\,E_{\mathrm{O}}(x', y')\left[\iint_{-\infty}^{\infty} \mathrm{e}^{-\mathrm{i}2\pi[u(x'+x'')+v(y'+y'')]}\mathrm{d}u\,\mathrm{d}v\right] \\
&= \iint_{-\infty}^{\infty} E_{\mathrm{O}}(x', y')\delta(x'+x'')\delta(y'+y'')\mathrm{d}x'\mathrm{d}y' \\
&= E_{\mathrm{O}}(x' = -x'', y' = -y''). \qquad (11.4)
\end{aligned}$$

Apart from an overall sign change, this result is in agreement with Eq. (11.1) for $m = -1$. The lens aperture has been tacitly taken to be infinite in the above derivation. In what follows, we systematically develop the diffraction theory of image formation by a lens. The derivation is a bit long, but we want to go through the steps carefully since these results form the basis of many discussions to follow.

11.2.1 Image Formation with one Lens

Figure 11.4 shows an imaging system consisting of just one thin lens. The field distribution immediately behind the object plane ($z=0$) is

$$E_O(x', y', 0) = E_{in} t_O(x', y'), \tag{11.5}$$

where E_{in} is the field incident on the object transparency with amplitude transmission function $t_O(x', y')$. The field distribution just in front of the lens ($z=z_1$), obtained from the generalization of Eq. (7.18c), assuming unit obliquity factor, is

$$E(x, y, z_1) = -\frac{i}{\lambda} \int \int_{\Sigma} E_O(x', y', 0) \frac{e^{ikr'}}{r'} dx'dy', \tag{11.6}$$

where the integration is over the extent of the object transparency $\sum$. Within the Fresnel approximation,

$$r' = z_1 + \frac{1}{2z_1}[(x-x')^2 + (y-y')^2] \tag{11.7}$$

and Eq. (11.6) takes the form

$$E(x, y, z_1) = -\frac{i}{\lambda}\frac{e^{ikz_1}}{z_1} \int \int_{\Sigma} E_O(x', y', 0) e^{\frac{ik}{2z_1}[(x-x')^2+(y-y')^2]} dx'dy' \tag{11.8a}$$

$$= -\frac{i}{\lambda}\frac{e^{ikz_1}}{z_1} \int \int_{\Sigma} E_O(x', y', 0) h_{z_1}(x-x', y-y') dx'dy', \tag{11.8b}$$

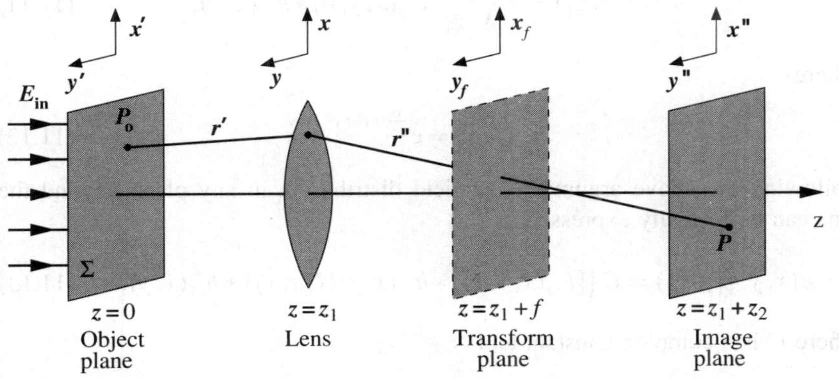

Fig. 11.4: One lens image forming system.

where

$$h_{z_1}(x-x', y-y') = \mathrm{e}^{\frac{ik}{2z_1}[(x-x')^2+(y-y')^2]} \tag{11.9}$$

is the impulse response function of the free space between the object plane and lens. It relates the field at point (x, y), distance z_1 behind the object plane, to the field at the object point (x', y'). Expression (11.8b) may be taken as an input–output relation for a linear optical system. Here, the object field distribution $E_O(x', y', 0)$ is the input to the system and field distribution $E(x, y, z_1)$ is the output from the system. In the present case, the system is the free space between the planes $z = 0$ and $z = z_1$, and its response is characterized by the impulse response function $h_{z_1}(x-x', y-y')$. Later, this concept will be generalized to define the impulse response function of an optical system.

The impulse response function (Eq. 11.9) has been written in a form to emphasize its space invariance. It depends on the differences of the position coordinates $(x-x')$ and $(y-y')$, and not on the position coordinates themselves. The impulse response function of an optical system may, however, be spatially invariant over a limited range of $(x-x')$ and $(y-y')$ values. The integration limits in Eqs (11.8) can be taken from $-\infty$ to $+\infty$, since $E_O(x', y', 0)$ is zero beyond the extent of the object transparency. Accordingly, Eq. (11.8b) can be expressed as the convolution integral

$$E(x, y, z_1) = -\frac{\mathrm{i}}{\lambda}\frac{\mathrm{e}^{ikz_1}}{z_1}\int\!\!\int_{-\infty}^{\infty} E_O(x', y', 0)h_{z_1}(x-x', y-y')\mathrm{d}x'\,\mathrm{d}y', \tag{11.10}$$

written symbolically as

$$E(x, y, z_1) = -\frac{\mathrm{i}}{\lambda}\frac{\mathrm{e}^{ikz_1}}{z_1}E_O(x, y, 0) * h_{z_1}(x, y), \tag{11.11}$$

where

$$h_{z_1}(x, y) = \mathrm{e}^{\frac{ik}{2z_1}(x^2+y^2)}. \tag{11.12}$$

Following the above argument, the field distribution in any plane beyond the lens can be formally expressed as

$$E(x, y, z_1+z_2) = C\left\{[E_O(x, y, z_1) * h_{z_1}(x, y)]T(x, y)\right\} * h_{z_2}(x, y), \tag{11.13}$$

where C is a complex constant and

$$h_{z_2}(x, y) = \mathrm{e}^{\frac{ik}{2z_2}(x^2+y^2)} \tag{11.14}$$

is the impulse response function of the free space between the lens and plane of observation, and

$$T(x, y) = t_L(x, y)e^{-\frac{ik}{2f}(x^2+y^2)} \tag{11.15}$$

is the amplitude transmission function of the lens. For an aberration-free lens, $t_L(x, y) = 1$ within the extent of the lens and zero beyond. However, lens aberrations can modify $t_L(x, y)$ in amplitude as well as in phase. The field distribution in a plane z_2 distance behind the lens, obtained from Eq. (11.13), is

$$\begin{aligned} E(x'', y'', z_1+z_2) &= \left(-\frac{i}{\lambda}\right)^2 \frac{e^{ik(z_1+z_2)}}{z_1 z_2} \iint_{-\infty}^{\infty}\iint_{-\infty}^{\infty} E_O(x', y', 0)e^{\frac{ik}{2z_1}(x-x')^2} \\ &\quad \times e^{\frac{ik}{2z_1}(y-y')^2} t_L(x, y)e^{-\frac{ik}{2f}(x^2+y^2)} e^{\frac{ik}{2z_2}(x''-x)^2} \\ &\quad \times e^{\frac{ik}{2z_2}(y''-y)^2} \, dx' \, dy' \, dx \, dy \qquad (11.16a) \\ &= -\frac{1}{\lambda^2} \frac{e^{ik(z_1+z_2)}}{z_1 z_2} e^{\frac{ik}{2z_2}(x''^2+y''^2)} \iint_{-\infty}^{\infty} dx' \, dy' E_O(x', y', 0) \\ &\quad \times e^{\frac{ik}{2z_1}(x'^2+y'^2)} \iint_{-\infty}^{\infty} t_L(x, y)e^{\frac{ik}{2}\left(\frac{1}{z_1}+\frac{1}{z_2}-\frac{1}{f}\right)(x^2+y^2)} \\ &\quad \times e^{-ik\left[\left(\frac{x'}{z_1}+\frac{x''}{z_2}\right)x+\left(\frac{y'}{z_1}+\frac{y''}{z_2}\right)y\right]} dx \, dy, \qquad (11.16b) \end{aligned}$$

where we have used

$$r'' = z_2 + \frac{1}{2z_2}\left[(x''-x)^2 + (y''-y)^2\right]. \tag{11.17}$$

11.2.1.1 Lens of Large Aperture

It may be useful to first consider an aberration-free lens of infinitely large aperture so that $t_L(x, y) = 1$ for all x, y. The integrals in Eq. (11.16b) can then be evaluated exactly, giving

$$\int_{-\infty}^{+\infty} e^{\frac{-ik}{2}\left(\frac{1}{f}-\frac{1}{z_1}-\frac{1}{z_2}\right)x^2 - ik\left(\frac{x'}{z_1}+\frac{x''}{z_2}\right)x} \, dx = \frac{\sqrt{\pi}}{a} e^{\frac{b^2}{4a^2}}, \tag{11.18a}$$

$$\int_{-\infty}^{+\infty} e^{\frac{-ik}{2}\left(\frac{1}{f}-\frac{1}{z_1}-\frac{1}{z_2}\right)y^2 - ik\left(\frac{y'}{z_1}+\frac{y''}{z_2}\right)y} \, dy = \frac{\sqrt{\pi}}{a} e^{\frac{b'^2}{4a^2}}, \tag{11.18b}$$

where

$$a^2 = \frac{ik}{2}\left(\frac{1}{f} - \frac{1}{z_1} - \frac{1}{z_2}\right), \tag{11.19a}$$

$$b = ik\left(\frac{x'}{z_1} + \frac{x''}{z_2}\right), \tag{11.19b}$$

$$b' = ik\left(\frac{y'}{z_1} + \frac{y''}{z_2}\right). \tag{11.19c}$$

Equation (11.16b) for $a \neq 0$ then takes the form

$$E_\infty(x'', y'', z_1 + z_2) = -\frac{\pi}{\lambda^2 a^2}\frac{e^{ik(z_1+z_2)}}{z_1 z_2} e^{\frac{ik}{2z_2}(x''^2+y''^2)} \iint\limits_{-\infty}^{\infty} E_O(x', y', 0) \times e^{\frac{ik}{2z_1}(x'^2+y'^2)} e^{-\frac{k^2}{4a^2}\left[\left(\frac{x'}{z_1}+\frac{x''}{z_2}\right)^2+\left(\frac{y'}{z_1}+\frac{y''}{z_2}\right)^2\right]} dx'\, dy', \tag{11.20}$$

where $E_\infty(x'', y'', z_1 + z_2)$ is the field distribution in any plane, behind a lens of infinite aperture, satisfying Eq. (11.17). The field distribution in the back focal plane of the lens with $z_2 = f$ and $a^2 = -ik/2z_1$ is

$$E_\infty(x_f, y_f, z_1 + f) = -\frac{i}{\lambda}\frac{e^{ik(z_1+f)}}{f} e^{\frac{ik}{2f}(x_f^2+y_f^2)} \iint\limits_{-\infty}^{\infty} E_O(x', y', 0) \times e^{\frac{ik}{2z_1}(x'^2+y'^2)} e^{-\frac{ikz_1}{2}\left[\left(\frac{x'}{z_1}+\frac{x_f}{f}\right)^2+\left(\frac{y'}{z_1}+\frac{y_f}{f}\right)^2\right]} dx'\, dy' \tag{11.21a}$$

$$= -\frac{i}{\lambda}\frac{e^{ik(z_1+f)}}{f} e^{\frac{ik}{2f}(1-\frac{z_1}{f})(x_f^2+y_f^2)} \iint\limits_{-\infty}^{\infty} E_O(x', y', 0) \times e^{-i2\pi(\frac{x_f}{\lambda f}x'+\frac{y_f}{\lambda f}y')} dx'\, dy' \tag{11.21b}$$

$$= -\frac{i}{\lambda}\frac{e^{ik(z_1+f)}}{f} e^{\frac{ik}{2f}(1-\frac{z_1}{f})(x_f^2+y_f^2)} F\left(\frac{x_f}{\lambda f}, \frac{y_f}{\lambda f}\right), \tag{11.21c}$$

where

$$F\left(\frac{x_f}{\lambda f}, \frac{y_f}{\lambda f}\right) = \iint\limits_{-\infty}^{\infty} E_O(x', y', 0) e^{-i2\pi(\frac{x_f}{\lambda f}x'+\frac{y_f}{\lambda f}y')} dx'\, dy' \tag{11.22}$$

is the Fourier transform of the object field distribution. The quadratic phase factor accompanying the Fourier transform in Eqs (11.21) disappears when the object transparency lies in the front focal plane of the lens. Thus, we have the remarkable result that except for a complex constant, a positive lens of sufficiently large aperture generates in its back focal plane the Fourier transform of the object field distribution in its front focal plane.

We now consider the field distribution in the image plane of geometrical optics satisfying the condition

$$\frac{1}{z_1}+\frac{1}{z_2}=\frac{1}{f}. \tag{11.23}$$

Here, z_1 is measured from the object plane, and not from the lens, hence the sign difference in Eqs (11.23) and (4.51b). With Eq. (11.23), the integrals in Eqs (11.18) reduce to the delta functions, i.e.,

$$\int_{-\infty}^{+\infty} \mathrm{e}^{-\mathrm{i}2\pi\left(\frac{x'}{\lambda z_1}+\frac{x''}{\lambda z_2}\right)x}\,\mathrm{d}x=\delta\left(\frac{x'}{\lambda z_1}+\frac{x''}{\lambda z_2}\right), \tag{11.24a}$$

$$\int_{-\infty}^{+\infty} \mathrm{e}^{-\mathrm{i}2\pi\left(\frac{y'}{\lambda z_1}+\frac{y''}{\lambda z_2}\right)y}\,\mathrm{d}y=\delta\left(\frac{y'}{\lambda z_1}+\frac{y''}{\lambda z_2}\right) \tag{11.24b}$$

and Eq. (11.16b) takes the form

$$\begin{aligned}E_\infty(x'',y'',z_1+z_2) &= -\frac{1}{\lambda^2}\frac{\mathrm{e}^{\mathrm{i}k(z_1+z_2)}}{z_1z_2}\mathrm{e}^{\frac{\mathrm{i}k}{2z_2}(x''^2+y''^2)}\iint_{-\infty}^{\infty} E_\mathrm{O}(x',y',0)\\ &\quad\times \mathrm{e}^{\frac{\mathrm{i}k}{2z_1}(x'^2+y'^2)}\delta\left(\frac{x'}{\lambda z_1}+\frac{x''}{\lambda z_2}\right)\delta\left(\frac{y'}{\lambda z_1}+\frac{y''}{\lambda z_2}\right)\mathrm{d}x'\,\mathrm{d}y'\\ &= \frac{1}{m}\mathrm{e}^{\mathrm{i}k(z_1+z_2)}\mathrm{e}^{\frac{\mathrm{i}k}{2z_2}\left(1-\frac{1}{m}\right)(x''^2+y''^2)}\\ &\quad\times E_\mathrm{O}\left(x'=\frac{x''}{m},y'=\frac{y''}{m},0\right),\end{aligned} \tag{11.25}$$

where

$$m=\frac{v}{u}=-\frac{z_2}{z_1} \tag{11.26}$$

is transverse magnification produced by the lens. Except for quadratic phase modification and magnification factor m, the field at the image point (x'',y'') equals the field at the conjugate point $(x'=x''/m,\ y'=y''/m)$ in the object plane.

11.2.1.2 Lens of Finite Aperture

The aperture function of an aberration-free lens of radius r_0 is

$$t_L(x, y) = 1 \quad \text{for } (x^2 + y^2)^{1/2} \leq r_0, \\ = 0 \quad \text{otherwise.} \tag{11.27}$$

Accordingly, the field distribution in the image plane, obtained from Eqs (11.16b) and (11.23), can be expressed as

$$E(x'', y'', z_1 + z_2) = -\frac{1}{\lambda^2}\frac{e^{ik(z_1+z_2)}}{z_1 z_2} e^{\frac{ik}{2z_2}(x''^2+y''^2)} \times \int\!\!\int_{-\infty}^{\infty}\int\!\!\int_{-\infty}^{\infty} E_O(x', y', 0) e^{\frac{ik}{2z_1}(x'^2+y'^2)} t_L(x, y) \times e^{-i2\pi\left[\left(\frac{x'}{\lambda z_1}+\frac{x''}{\lambda z_2}\right)x+\left(\frac{y'}{\lambda z_1}+\frac{y''}{\lambda z_2}\right)y\right]} \,dx\,dy\,dx'\,dy'. \tag{11.28a}$$

$$= -\frac{1}{\lambda^2}\frac{e^{ik(z_1+z_2)}}{z_1 z_2} e^{\frac{ik}{2z_2}(x''^2+y''^2)} \int\!\!\int_{-\infty}^{\infty} E_O(x', y', 0) \times e^{\frac{ik}{2z_1}(x'^2+y'^2)} \int\!\!\int_{-\infty}^{\infty} t_L(x, y) e^{-i2\pi(x''-mx')\frac{x}{\lambda z_2}} \times e^{-i2\pi(y''-my')\frac{y}{\lambda z_2}} \,dx\,dy\,dx'\,dy' \tag{11.28b}$$

$$= -\frac{1}{\lambda^2}\frac{e^{ik(z_1+z_2)}}{z_1 z_2} e^{\frac{ik}{2z_2}(x''^2+y''^2)} \int\!\!\int_{-\infty}^{\infty} E_O(x', y', 0) \times e^{\frac{ik}{2z_1}(x'^2+y'^2)} F(x'' - mx', y'' - my')\,dx'\,dy', \tag{11.28c}$$

where the Fourier transform

$$F(x'' - mx', y'' - my') = \int\!\!\int_{-\infty}^{\infty} t_L(x, y) e^{-i2\pi(x''-mx')\frac{x}{\lambda z_2}} \times e^{-i2\pi(y''-my')\frac{y}{\lambda z_2}} \,dx\,dy \tag{11.29}$$

at the spatial frequencies $u = (x'' - mx')/\lambda z_2$ and $v = (y'' - my')/\lambda z_2$ describes Fraunhofer diffraction from the lens aperture. This diffraction pattern is centered at the point $x'' = mx'$, $y'' = my'$ in the image plane, where (x', y') is the conjugate point in the object plane and m is the transverse magnification of the image.

11.2.1.3 Coherent Impulse Response Function

The quadratic phase factors $e^{\frac{ik}{2z_1}(x'^2+y'^2)}$ and $e^{\frac{ik}{2z_2}(x''^2+y''^2)}$ in Eqs (11.28) give rise to phase curvatures in the object and image planes, respectively. The latter phase factor is of no significance if intensity distribution in the image plane is all that interests us. However, this factor must be retained if further processing of the image is contemplated. The other phase factor is more troublesome since it appears inside the integral. Invoking the stationarity argument of Section 7.4.2, only a small portion of the object field distribution around the point (x', y') should contribute to the field at the conjugate image point $x'' = mx'$, $y'' = my'$. Accordingly, we may express

$$\begin{aligned} e^{\frac{ik}{2z_1}(x'^2+y'^2)} &\approx e^{\frac{ik}{2z_1}[(\frac{x''}{m})^2+(\frac{y''}{m})^2]} \\ &\approx e^{-\frac{ik}{2mz_2}(x''^2+y''^2)}. \end{aligned} \tag{11.30}$$

Equation (11.28b) then takes the form

$$\begin{aligned} E(x'', y'', z_1+z_2) = {} & m e^{ik(z_1+z_2)} e^{\frac{ik}{2z_2}(1-\frac{1}{m})(x''^2+y''^2)} \\ & \times \iint_{-\infty}^{\infty} E_O(x', y', 0) \iint_{-\infty}^{\infty} t_L(\lambda z_2 \tilde{x}_L, \lambda z_2 \tilde{y}_L) \\ & \times e^{-i2\pi[(x''-mx')\tilde{x}_L+(y''-my')\tilde{y}_L)]} \, d\tilde{x}_L \, d\tilde{y}_L \, dx' \, dy', \end{aligned} \tag{11.31}$$

where

$$\tilde{x}_L = \frac{x}{\lambda z_2}, \quad \tilde{y}_L = \frac{y}{\lambda z_2}. \tag{11.32}$$

For a point source of unit strength in the object plane, Eq. (11.31) describes the impulse response function of an optical system consisting of a single aberration-free lens, i.e.,

$$\begin{aligned} h(x''-mx', y''-my') = {} & m e^{ik(z_1+z_2)} e^{\frac{ik}{2z_2}(1-\frac{1}{m})(x''^2+y''^2)} \\ & \times \iint_{-\infty}^{\infty} t_L(\lambda z_2 \tilde{x}_L, \lambda z_2 \tilde{y}_L) e^{-i2\pi(x''-mx')\tilde{x}_L} \\ & \times e^{-i2\pi(y''-my')\tilde{y}_L} \, d\tilde{x}_L \, d\tilde{y}_L. \end{aligned} \tag{11.33}$$

Apart from some phase modification and a scale factor, the impulse response function of a lens is the field distribution of Fraunhofer diffraction from the aperture of the lens. For a lens of circular aperture, the corresponding intensity distribution consists of bright and dark rings surrounding the Airy disk centered at the image point of geometrical optics. Therefore, the image of a point produced by a lens of finite aperture is the Fraunhofer diffraction pattern of the aperture of the lens, and not a point image of geometrical optics. Diffraction negates one-to-one correspondence between the object and its image. Equation (11.33) describes the coherent impulse response function of a lens since object illumination by monochromatic light has been assumed in the above derivation. The field distribution in the image plane of geometrical optics for an extended two-dimensional object now takes the form

$$E(x'', y'', z_1 + z_2) = \iint_{-\infty}^{\infty} E_{\mathrm{O}}(x', y', 0)h(x'' - mx', y'' - my')\,\mathrm{d}x'\,\mathrm{d}y'. \quad (11.34)$$

With the change of variables

$$\tilde{x} = mx', \quad \tilde{y} = my', \quad (11.35)$$

Eq. (11.31) is transformed to the convolution form:

$$\begin{aligned} E(x'', y'', z_1 + z_2) &= \frac{1}{m} e^{ik(z_1+z_2)} e^{\frac{ik}{2z_2}(1-\frac{1}{m})(x''^2+y''^2)} \\ &\times \iint_{-\infty}^{\infty} E_{\mathrm{O}}\left(\frac{\tilde{x}}{m}, \frac{\tilde{y}}{m}, 0\right) \iint_{-\infty}^{\infty} t_{\mathrm{L}}(\lambda z_2\, \tilde{x}_{\mathrm{L}}, \lambda z_2\, \tilde{y}_{\mathrm{L}}) \quad (11.36a) \\ &\times e^{-i2\pi[(x''-\tilde{x})\tilde{x}_{\mathrm{L}} + (y''-\tilde{y})\tilde{y}_{\mathrm{L}}]}\,\mathrm{d}\tilde{x}_{\mathrm{L}}\,\mathrm{d}\tilde{y}_{\mathrm{L}}\,\mathrm{d}\tilde{x}\,\mathrm{d}\tilde{y} \\ &= \iint_{-\infty}^{\infty} E'_{\mathrm{O}}\left(\frac{\tilde{x}}{m}, \frac{\tilde{y}}{m}, 0\right) h'(x'' - \tilde{x}, y'' - \tilde{y})\,\mathrm{d}\tilde{x}\,\mathrm{d}\tilde{y} \quad (11.36b) \\ &= E'_{\mathrm{O}}(x'', y'') * h'(x'', y''), \quad (11.36c) \end{aligned}$$

where

$$\begin{aligned} h'(x'' - \tilde{x}, y'' - \tilde{y}) &= \iint_{-\infty}^{\infty} t_{\mathrm{L}}(\lambda z_2\, \tilde{x}_{\mathrm{L}}, \lambda z_2\, \tilde{y}_{\mathrm{L}}) \\ &\times e^{-i2\pi[(x''-\tilde{x})\tilde{x}_{\mathrm{L}} + (y''-\tilde{y})\tilde{y}_{\mathrm{L}}]}\,\mathrm{d}\tilde{x}_{\mathrm{L}}\,\mathrm{d}\tilde{y}_{\mathrm{L}} \end{aligned} \quad (11.37)$$

is the redefined impulse response function of the lens, and the modified object field distribution

$$E_O'\left(\frac{\tilde{x}}{m}, \frac{\tilde{y}}{m}, 0\right) = \frac{1}{m} e^{ik(z_1+z_2)} e^{\frac{ik}{2z_2}\left(1-\frac{1}{m}\right)(x''^2+y''^2)} E_O(x', y', 0) \qquad (11.38)$$

differs from the actual object field distribution $E_O(x', y', 0)$ by a phase factor, a magnification factor, and a scale factor. To summarize, the image field distribution has been transformed from a convolution of three functions (Eq. 11.13) to a convolution between two functions. Equation (11.36c) is particularly useful since it is often easier to obtain the image field distribution by taking its Fourier transform and making use of the convolution theorem (see Problems 11.9 to 11.11).

For a lens of infinite aperture, the impulse response function reduces to a delta function and image field distribution of geometrical optics is restored. However, for a lens of finite aperture, the impulse response function is never a sharp point and, as a result, the image field distribution differs from that predicted by geometrical optics. In addition, the convolution operation smoothens the image field distribution, leading to image distortion. The sharp edges of an object may not appear so sharp in its image. The convolution operation also limits the resolution of an optical system. Any image detail, smaller than the width of the impulse response function, will not be resolved. The impulse response function of a square lens of sides a is a sinc function with $2z_2\lambda/a$ as the width of its central lobe. Therefore, an optical system using a square lens of sides a cannot resolve objects with separation less than $2z_2\frac{\lambda}{a}$, where z_2 is the distance of the lens from the image plane. We shall return to these considerations when we discuss the resolution of image-forming systems, later in the chapter.

The image intensity distribution for coherent illumination of the object can be expressed as

$$I(x'', y'', z_1+z_2) = \left(\frac{1}{2}\epsilon_0 c\right) \iint_{-\infty}^{\infty} \iint_{-\infty}^{\infty} E_O'\left(\frac{\tilde{x}_1}{m}, \frac{\tilde{y}_1}{m}\right) h'(x''-\tilde{x}_1, y''-\tilde{y}_1)$$

$$\times E_O'^{*}\left(\frac{\tilde{x}_2}{m}, \frac{\tilde{y}_2}{m}\right) h'^{*}(x''-\tilde{x}_2, y''-\tilde{y}_2) \mathrm{d}\tilde{x}_1 \, \mathrm{d}\tilde{y}_1 \, \mathrm{d}\tilde{x}_2 \, \mathrm{d}\tilde{y}_2 \, . \qquad (11.39)$$

11.2.2 Image Formation with Two Lenses

A two-lens imaging system (Fig. 11.5) is more amenable to image modification and processing as compared to a one-lens system. The lenses in Fig. 11.5 are separated by a distance equal to the sum of their focal lengths. The object transparency is kept in the front focal plane of the first lens and the back focal plane of

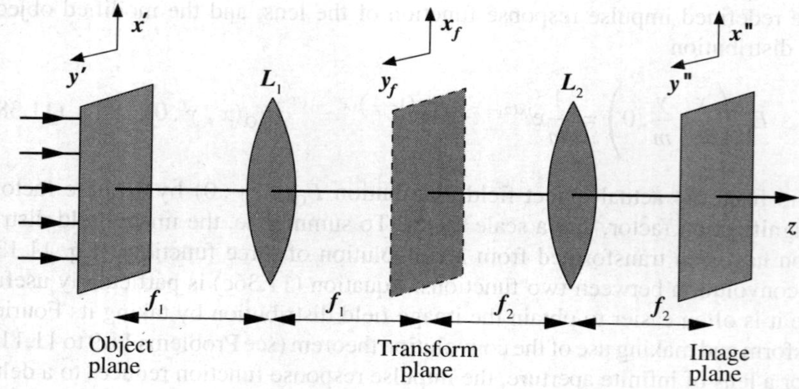

Fig. 11.5: Two-lens image forming system.

the second lens is the image plane. For the present discussion, lens apertures are assumed sufficiently large to intercept most if not all object spatial frequencies. The first lens produces in its back focal plane the Fourier transform of the field distribution in the object plane (Eq. 11.21b), i.e.,

$$E(x_f, y_f, 2f_1) = -\frac{\mathrm{i}}{\lambda}\frac{\mathrm{e}^{\mathrm{i}2kf_1}}{f_1}\int\!\!\int_{-\infty}^{\infty} E_{\mathrm{O}}(x', y')\mathrm{e}^{-\mathrm{i}2\pi(\frac{x_f}{\lambda f_1}x' + \frac{y_f}{\lambda f_1}y')}\mathrm{d}x'\mathrm{d}y', \tag{11.40}$$

where the subscript ∞ in $E_\infty(x_f, y_f)$ has been dropped. The Fourier transform of this distribution appears in the back focal plane of the second lens. Therefore,

$$\begin{aligned}
&E(x'', y'', 2f_1 + 2f_2)\\
&= -\frac{\mathrm{i}}{\lambda}\frac{\mathrm{e}^{\mathrm{i}2kf_2}}{f_2}\int\!\!\int_{-\infty}^{\infty} E(x_f, y_f)\mathrm{e}^{-\mathrm{i}2\pi(\frac{x''}{\lambda f_2}x_f + \frac{y''}{\lambda f_2}y_f)}\mathrm{d}x_f\mathrm{d}y_f\\
&= -\frac{1}{\lambda^2}\frac{\mathrm{e}^{\mathrm{i}2k(f_1+f_2)}}{f_1 f_2}\int\!\!\int_{-\infty}^{\infty} E_{\mathrm{O}}(x', y')\delta\left(\frac{x'}{\lambda f_1} + \frac{x''}{\lambda f_2}\right)\\
&\quad\times\delta\left(\frac{y'}{\lambda f_1} + \frac{y''}{\lambda f_2}\right)\mathrm{d}x'\mathrm{d}y'\\
&= -\frac{f_1}{f_2}\mathrm{e}^{\mathrm{i}2k(f_1+f_2)}E_{\mathrm{O}}\left(x' = -\frac{f_1}{f_2}x'', y' = -\frac{f_1}{f_2}y''\right)\\
&= \frac{\mathrm{e}^{\mathrm{i}2k(f_1+f_2)}}{m}E_{\mathrm{O}}\left(x' = \frac{x''}{m}, y' = \frac{y''}{m}\right),
\end{aligned} \tag{11.41}$$

where $m = -\frac{f_2}{f_1}$. Except for the constant phase factor $e^{2ik(f_1+f_2)}$ and magnification factor m, Eq. (11.41) reproduces the object field distribution. The disturbing quadratic phase factors appearing in one-lens imaging (Eq. 11.28) are absent in the two-lens imaging configuration of Fig. 11.5. Any loss of the object spatial frequencies due to finite apertures of the lenses can be accounted by an effective modification of the spatial frequency spectrum in the Fourier transform plane. This is the subject matter of the next section.

11.3 COHERENT IMAGE PROCESSING

Finite aperture of a lens prevents higher object spatial frequencies from reaching the image plane. In that sense, a lens or any optical system of finite aperture is a low (spatial frequency) pass filter. It rejects higher spatial frequencies, resulting in degradation of the image quality. At the same time, it is possible to design filters which can selectively reject or modify certain object spatial frequencies with desirable effect on the image. Filters also find application in pattern recognition and in making phase objects visible. Image modification can be carried out in the spatial domain by introducing a filter just behind the object transparency to appropriately modify the object field distribution. In spatial frequency filtering, a filter modifies the spatial frequency spectrum of the object in the Fourier transform plane. The two forms of filtering can be shown to be exactly equivalent. Only spatial frequency filtering will be discussed here since in practice it is easier to implement.

11.3.1 Spatial Frequency Filtering

A filter in either domain is a specially prepared transparency to modify the phase and amplitude of the light field passing through it. Figure 11.6 shows an arrangement for coherent image processing in the spatial frequency domain. Lenses L_1 and L_2, each of focal length f, are kept $2f$ distance apart. The coherently illuminated object transparency with amplitude transmission function $f(x', y')$ is kept in the front focal plane of lens L_1 and the spatial frequency filter F is introduced in the transform plane.

Assuming lens L_1 intercepts all object spatial frequencies, the field distribution in the transform plane just behind the spatial frequency filter is

$$E(x_f, y_f) = -\frac{\mathrm{i}}{\lambda}\frac{e^{2ikf}}{f} F\left(\frac{x_f}{\lambda f}, \frac{y_f}{\lambda f}\right) H\left(\frac{x_f}{\lambda f}, \frac{y_f}{\lambda f}\right), \tag{11.42}$$

where

$$H\left(\frac{x_f}{\lambda f}, \frac{y_f}{\lambda f}\right) = \left|H\left(\frac{x_f}{\lambda f}, \frac{y_f}{\lambda f}\right)\right| e^{\mathrm{i}\phi\left(\frac{x_f}{\lambda f}, \frac{y_f}{\lambda f}\right)} \tag{11.43}$$

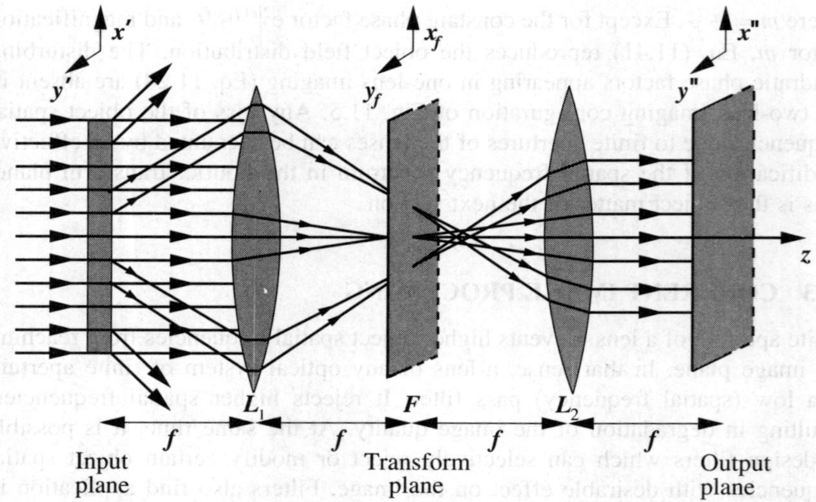

Fig. 11.6: Filtering in the spatial frequency domain; filter F is kept in the transform plane.

is the complex amplitude transmission coefficient of the filter and

$$F\left(\frac{x_f}{\lambda f}, \frac{y_f}{\lambda f}\right) = \mathcal{F}[f(x', y')] \tag{11.44}$$

is the Fourier transform of the object transmission function. The second lens performs the Fourier transform of $E(x_f, y_f)$, yielding the field distribution

$$E(x'', y'') = -\mathrm{e}^{-\mathrm{i}4kf} \int\!\!\int_{-\infty}^{\infty} F\left(\frac{x_f}{\lambda f}, \frac{y_f}{\lambda f}\right) H\left(\frac{x_f}{\lambda f}, \frac{y_f}{\lambda f}\right) \times \mathrm{e}^{-\mathrm{i}2\pi\left(\frac{x_f}{\lambda f}x'' + \frac{y_f}{\lambda f}y''\right)} \mathrm{d}\left(\frac{x_f}{\lambda f}\right) \mathrm{d}\left(\frac{y_f}{\lambda f}\right) \tag{11.45}$$

in the image plane.

As first example of filtering, we consider an infinite one-dimensional square grating (Fig. 11.7a) of grating element a kept in the object plane (plane $x'y'$ in Fig. 11.6). The infinitely sharp diffraction maxima of an infinite grating are located in the transform plane at

$$x_f = \lambda f u = m\lambda f/a, \quad m = 0, \pm 1, \pm 2, \ldots. \tag{11.46}$$

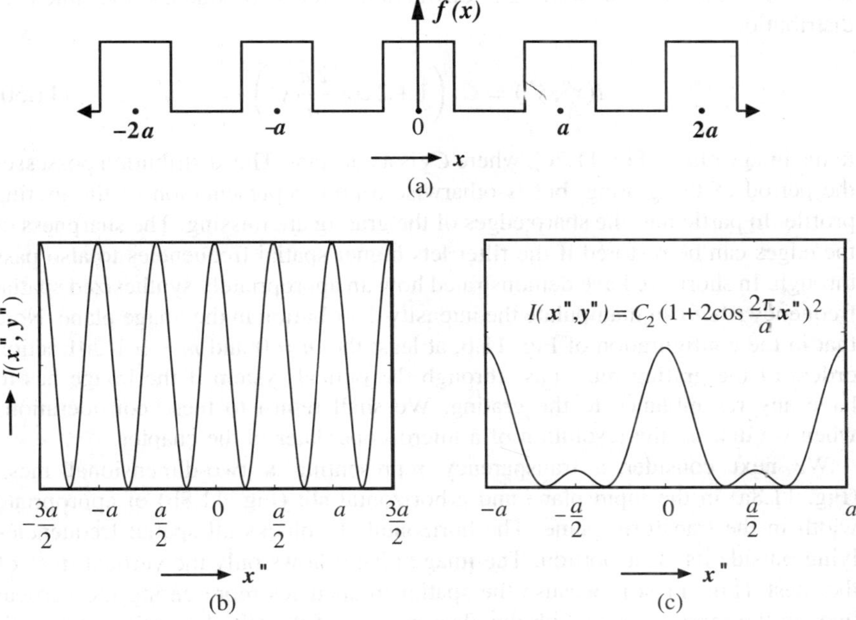

Fig. 11.7: (a) One-dimensional square grating of grating element a kept in object plane. (b) Intensity distribution in image plane when spatial frequency filter transmits only $m = \pm 1$ diffraction orders. (c) Intensity distribution in image plane when filter transmits $m = 0, \pm 1$ diffraction orders.

If the spatial frequency filter blocks all except the zero-order diffraction maximum, i.e., if

$$F\left(\frac{x_f}{\lambda f}, \frac{y_f}{\lambda f}\right) H\left(\frac{x_f}{\lambda f}, \frac{y_f}{\lambda f}\right) = \delta\left(\frac{x_f}{\lambda f}\right), \tag{11.47}$$

then Eq. (11.45) yields uniform illumination in the image plane. If on the other hand, the filter stops all except the $m = \pm 1$ diffraction orders, the intensity distribution

$$I(x'', y'') = C_1 \cos^2\left(\frac{2\pi}{a} x''\right) \tag{11.48}$$

in the image plane displays twice the periodicity of the grating (Fig. 11.7b), where C_1 is a constant. A filter with

$$F\left(\frac{x_f}{\lambda f}, \frac{y_f}{\lambda f}\right) H\left(\frac{x_f}{\lambda f}, \frac{y_f}{\lambda f}\right) = \delta\left(\frac{x_f}{\lambda f}\right) + \delta\left(\frac{x_f}{\lambda f} - \frac{1}{a}\right) + \delta\left(\frac{x_f}{\lambda f} + \frac{1}{a}\right) \tag{11.49}$$

transmits only the $m = 0, \pm 1$ diffraction orders producing the intensity distribution

$$I(x'', y'') = C_2 \left(1 + 2\cos\frac{2\pi}{a}x''\right)^2 \tag{11.50}$$

in the image plane (Fig. 11.7c), where C_2 is a constant. This distribution possesses the period of the grating, but is otherwise a poor representation of the grating profile. In particular, the sharp edges of the grating are missing. The sharpness of the edges can be restored if the filter lets higher spatial frequencies to also pass through. In short, we have demonstrated how an appropriately synthesized spatial frequency filter can manipulate the intensity distribution in the image plane. Note that in the configuration of Fig. 11.6, at least the $m = 0$ and $m = \pm 1$ diffraction orders of the grating must pass through the optical system if the image has to have any resemblance to the grating. We shall return to these considerations when we discuss the resolution of a microscope, later in the chapter.

We next consider a transparency representing a two-dimensional mesh (Fig. 11.8a) in the input plane and a horizontal slit (Fig. 11.8b) of appropriate width in the transform plane. The horizontal slit blocks all spatial frequencies lying outside its clear portion. The image plane shows only the vertical lines of the mesh (Fig. 11.8c), because the spatial frequencies representing the vertical lines in the mesh overlap with the clear portion of the slit. A rotation of the slit by 90° about the optical axis will display only the horizontal lines in the image plane. These are the kind of image-processing experiments, first conducted by AB Porter and Ernst Abbe.

Another interesting application of spatial frequency filtering is the conversion of half-tone images to continuous images. The newspapers carry half-tone pictures. A black and white photograph has different levels of gray – varying from pitch dark (hair) to fair (skin). These levels of gray cannot as such be

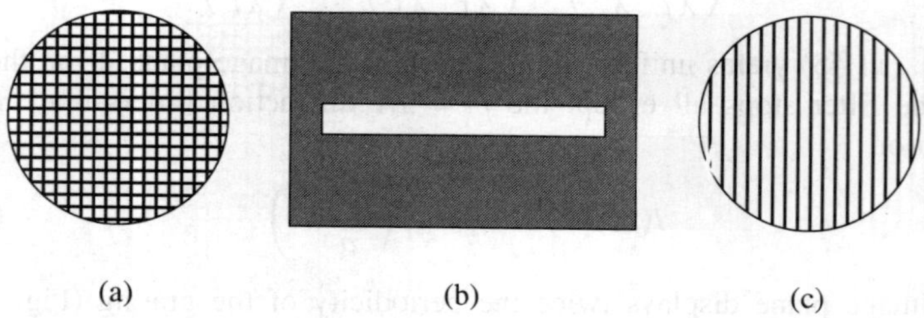

Fig. 11.8: (a) Transparency representing a two-dimensional mesh kept in the object plane. (b) A horizontal slit kept in the transform plane. (c) Only vertical lines of the mesh appear in the image plane.

reproduced on a white paper with black ink. A half-tone picture, prepared from the negative by a special half-tone screen printing process, consists of an array of dots of varying sizes on a white paper. It is the size variation of the dots, and not the dots themselves which carry image information. The dots are larger and more overlapping over the dark portions as compared to the less dark portions of the picture. This effectively creates the illusion of levels of gray. A look at a newspaper picture will reveal the presence of these dots. A filter can be designed to remove the higher spatial frequencies representing diffraction from the network of dots of a half-tone picture, leaving behind low spatial frequencies which display varying opaqueness of the black and white negative.

11.3.1.1 Low Pass Filter to remove Laser Beam Distortion

A laser oscillating in the TEM_{00} mode produces light with a Gaussian beam profile. However, dust particles on the optical elements diffract the laser beam, distorting its profile as it propagates. The distorted beam profile may not be acceptable in certain applications, holography to name one. Diffraction from the dust particles generates high spatial frequencies which travel with relatively large inclinations to the optical axis. Since the transform of a Gaussian function is a Gaussian function, the TEM_{00} mode itself occupies a position around and very close to the optical axis in the transform plane, and the off-axis spatial frequencies representing the beam distortion can be removed by a low pass filter. Figure 11.9 shows schematically the arrangement for cleaning the laser beam. A short focal length (40×) microscope objective (MO) may be employed for this purpose. The spatial frequency filter, essentially an opaque plate with a central hole of suitable size, can be positioned in the transform plane with accurate position translators to allow only the low spatial frequencies to pass through the hole. A second lens (L) collects and collimates the clean laser beam. This

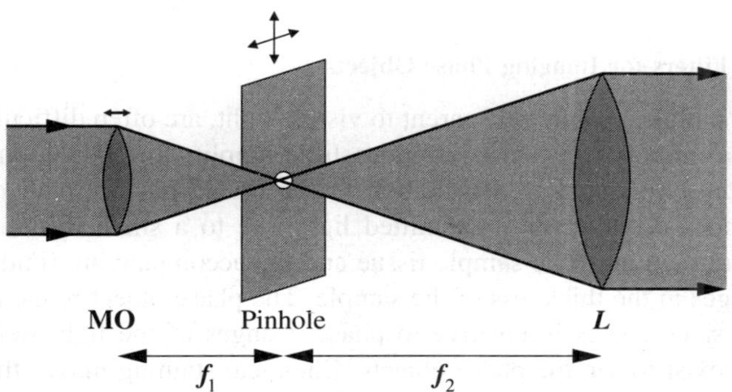

Fig. 11.9: Cleaning laser beam with a pinhole.

arrangement constitutes a beam expander since it gives a clean and expanded laser beam with f_2/f_1 as the beam expansion ratio.

11.3.1.2 High Pass Filter for Dark Ground Imaging

As mentioned earlier, the zero spatial frequency if present alone produces uniform illumination in the image plane. Its removal by a spatial frequency filter provides a dark background in which higher spatial frequencies interfere and produce the image of the object. The dark background techniques are particularly useful for imaging phase objects, as we shall see in the next section. Figure 11.10 shows photographs of a resolution test target before and after filtering the zero spatial frequency. The dark background is clearly visible in Fig. 11.10b.

A dark point or a dark region near the edge of an aperture or an obstacle in an image is dark because all diffracted waves including the zero spatial frequency wave interfere to produce net zero field at that point or in that region. A small object diffracts strongly and a large object diffracts poorly. We may interpret that a dark point in the neighborhood of a small object (a thin line, for example, in Fig. 11.10a) is dark because the zero spatial frequency wave interferes destructively with the resultant of the higher spatial frequencies waves to produce a null field at that point. On removal of the zero spatial frequency, the point is rendered bright. This explains the contrast reversal in Fig. 11.10b for the narrow lines. Diffraction by large objects is confined to regions very close to the edges and hence the contrast reversal is discernible only near the edges of the block and wider lines of the target. The zero spatial frequency can be removed by inserting a transparent plate with an opaque spot of appropriate size at the position of the zero spatial frequency in the transform plane. This is an example of an extreme case of high pass spatial frequency filtering in which all object spatial frequencies, except the lowest one are transmitted by the filter. High pass filters are useful for edge enhancement in images.

11.3.2 Filters for Imaging Phase Objects

Biological samples, being transparent to visible light, are often difficult to examine under a microscope. They introduce little amplitude modulation, resulting in nearly uniform intensity distribution in the image plane. Small differential phase changes occur in the transmitted light due to a small difference in the indices of refraction of the sample tissue and the accompanying fluid, or due to small changes in the thickness of the sample. The phase object remains invisible to the eye since eye is insensitive to phase changes of the light field. Several techniques exist to see the phase objects. Chemical staining makes them differentially absorbing and hence visible but in the process, the active cells of the tissue may get damaged. In the dark background illumination technique discussed

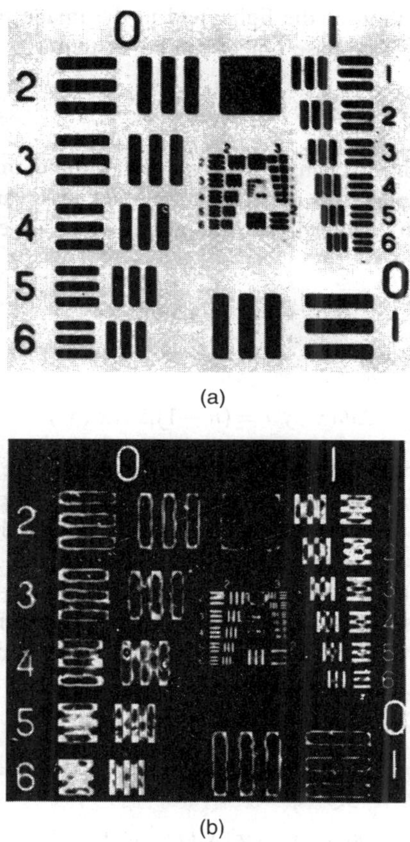

Fig. 11.10: Resolution test target (a) before, (b) after zero spatial frequency filtering – taken from *Optical Transforms*, Ed., H. Lipson, p. 282, Courtesy B. J. Thompson and Academic Press.

in the preceding section, the zero spatial frequency being the strongest wave coming out of the sample is removed. This results in considerably improved image contrast. Similarly, in the Schlieren method, half of the transform plane (excluding the zero spatial frequency) is blocked by a knife edge. This produces intensity variation in the image plane which depends on the rate of change of phase with the thickness of the sample. In phase contrast microscopy, first proposed by Frits Zernike in 1935, the zero spatial frequency is not removed, but its phase is retarded by $\pi/2$ or $3\pi/2$ with respect to the phases of the higher spatial frequencies. As we shall see shortly, it then becomes possible for the zero spatial frequency to interfere with the higher spatial frequencies, giving rise to amplitude variation of the light field in the image plane. The amplitude transmission function of a phase object can be written as

$$f(x', y') = \mathrm{e}^{\mathrm{i}\{\phi_0 - \Delta\phi(x', y')\}}, \tag{11.51}$$

where the average phase change ϕ_0 over the sample may be ignored. The differential phase change $\Delta\phi$ depending on thickness variation of the phase object is usually much smaller than a radian, in which case, Eq. (11.51) can be approximated to

$$f(x', y') = 1 - \mathrm{i}\Delta\phi(x', y'), \tag{11.52}$$

where

$$\Delta\phi(x', y') = (n-1)\Delta d(x', y') \tag{11.53}$$

and $\Delta d(x', y')$ is the point-to-point deviation of sample thickness from the average thickness, and n is the index of refraction of the sample. The unit term in Eq. (11.52) gives rise to the zero spatial frequency and all higher spatial frequencies are generated by the second term. The higher spatial frequencies differ in phase by 90° from the zero spatial frequency. The Fourier transform operation being linear maintains this phase relationship. As a result, no interference takes place between the zero and higher spatial frequencies when brought together in the image plane. The transform of Eq. (11.52) gives

$$\begin{aligned} F(u, v) &= \int_{-\infty}^{\infty}\!\!\int [1 - \mathrm{i}\Delta\phi(x', y')]\mathrm{e}^{-\mathrm{i}2\pi(ux' + vy')}\mathrm{d}x'\,\mathrm{d}y' \\ &= \delta(u, v) - \mathrm{i}\mathcal{F}[\Delta\phi(x', y')], \end{aligned} \tag{11.54}$$

where $\mathcal{F}[\Delta\phi(x', y')]$ is the Fourier transform of $\Delta\phi(x', y')$. The field distribution in the image plane after removing the zero spatial frequency is

$$\begin{aligned} E(x'', y'') &= (-\mathrm{i})\mathcal{F}[\mathcal{F}\{\Delta\phi(x', y')\}] \\ &= C\Delta\phi\left(x'' = \frac{x'}{m}, y'' = \frac{y'}{m}\right), \end{aligned} \tag{11.55}$$

where C is a complex constant. For $m = -1$, the intensity variation

$$I(x'', y'') = I_0[\Delta\phi(x'' = -x', y'' = -y)]^2 \tag{11.56}$$

proportional to the square of the phase change produced by the phase object can be observed in the dark background of the image plane. The image contrast can be improved if the zero spatial frequency is not removed, but its phase and amplitude are suitably modified. A 90° phase retardation of the zero spatial frequency can be introduced by making the spatial frequency filter thicker by $\lambda/4$ at the center. The otherwise transparent filter can also be made somewhat absorbing for the zero spatial frequency. With these modifications, the field distribution in the transform plane can be written as

$$F(u, v)H(u, v) = \mathrm{i}\alpha\delta(u, v) - \mathrm{i}\iint_{-\infty}^{\infty} \Delta\phi(x', y')\mathrm{e}^{-\mathrm{i}2\pi(ux'+vy')}\mathrm{d}x'\mathrm{d}y'. \tag{11.57}$$

The field and intensity distributions in the image plane then become

$$E(x'', y'') = C[\alpha - \Delta\phi(x'' = -x', y'' = -y)] \tag{11.58}$$

and

$$I(x'', y'') = I_0[\alpha - \Delta\phi(x'' = -x', y'' = -y)]^2, \tag{11.59}$$

respectively, where α is the amplitude transmission coefficient of the filter for the zero spatial frequency. By choosing $\alpha \approx \Delta\phi$ in magnitude, the normalized intensity distribution in the image plane can be made to vary from zero to a maximum of $4\alpha^2$, improving image contrast considerably.

11.3.3 Complex Filter

The filter considered in the preceding section to image phase objects by modifying the amplitude and phase of the zero spatial frequency is in fact an example of a complex filter with amplitude transmittance

$$\begin{aligned} H\left(\frac{x_f}{\lambda f}, \frac{y_f}{\lambda f}\right) &= \alpha\,\mathrm{e}^{\mathrm{i}\pi/2} \quad \text{for zero spatial frequency} \\ &= 1 \qquad\quad \text{for higher spatial frequencies.} \end{aligned} \tag{11.60}$$

This filter action was realized by controlling the thickness and absorption coefficient of the filter for the zero spatial frequency. This procedure is obviously too cumbersome if modification of the amplitudes and phases of many or all spatial frequencies is contemplated. We now describe interferometric techniques to synthesize complex filters. Vander Lugt was the first to propose and fabricate such filters. Figure 11.11 shows how Mach-Zehnder and Rayleigh interferometers can be used for this purpose.

In the Mach-Zehnder arrangement (Fig. 11.11a), a collimated beam from the point source S is split by the beam splitter BS1. One beam passes through mask P

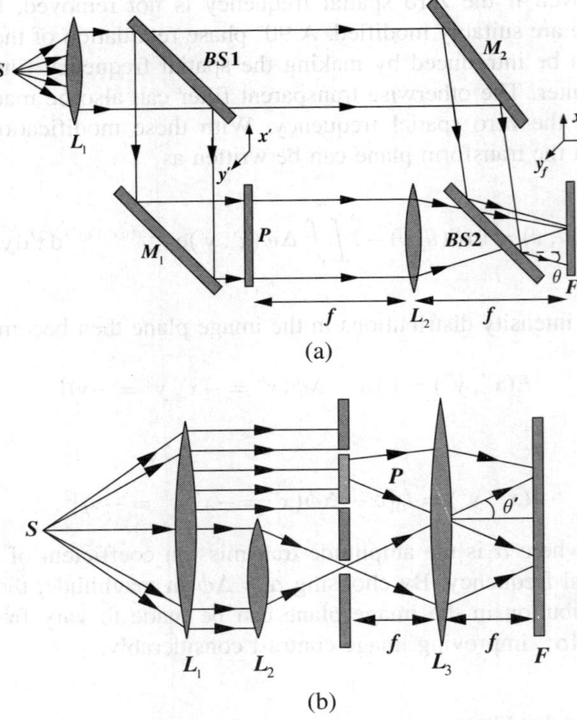

Fig. 11.11: (a) Mach-Zehnder interferometer. (b) Rayleigh interferometer to synthesize complex spatial frequency filters. F is the photographic plate.

which has the desired impulse response for the synthesis of the spatial frequency filter. Lens L_2 generates in its back focal plane the Fourier transform of the field distribution over mask P. Mirror M_2 in the second arm of the interferometer is adjusted so that light from this arm arrives at the back focal plane of L_2 in the form of a plane wave making an angle $(90+\theta)$ with the x_f-axis. This is the reference wave or the carrier wave which interferes with the light arriving from mask P. The photographic plate F kept in the back focal plane of L_2 records this interference pattern.

The field and intensity distributions in the plane of the photographic plate F are

$$E(x_f, y_f) = A_1 \mathrm{e}^{\mathrm{i}\frac{2\pi}{\lambda}(-x_f \sin\theta)} + A_2 S\left(\frac{x_f}{\lambda f}, \frac{y_f}{\lambda f}\right) \tag{11.61}$$

and

$$I(x_f, y_f) = \left(\frac{1}{2}\epsilon_0 c\right)\left[|A_1|^2 + |A_2|^2\left|S\left(\frac{x_f}{\lambda f}, \frac{y_f}{\lambda f}\right)\right|^2 + A_1^* A_2 S\left(\frac{x_f}{\lambda f}, \frac{y_f}{\lambda f}\right) e^{i\frac{2\pi}{\lambda}(x_f \sin\theta)} + A_1 A_2^* S^*\left(\frac{x_f}{\lambda f}, \frac{y_f}{\lambda f}\right) e^{i\frac{2\pi}{\lambda}(-x_f \sin\theta)}\right], \tag{11.62}$$

respectively, where A_1 and A_2 are the complex amplitudes of the light waves in the two arms of the interferometer and

$$S\left(\frac{x_f}{\lambda f}, \frac{y_f}{\lambda f}\right) = \mathcal{F}[s(x', y')] \tag{11.63}$$

is the Fourier transform of the amplitude transmittance of mask P. The photographic plate, after development, when kept in the transform plane of Fig. 11.6 acts as the complex spatial frequency filter with the amplitude transmittance

$$H\left(\frac{x_f}{\lambda f}, \frac{y_f}{\lambda f}\right) = t_0\left(\frac{1}{2}\epsilon_0 c\right)\left[|A_1|^2 + |A_2|^2\left|S\left(\frac{x_f}{\lambda f}, \frac{y_f}{\lambda f}\right)\right|^2 + A_1^* A_2 S\left(\frac{x_f}{\lambda f}, \frac{y_f}{\lambda f}\right) e^{i2\pi\left(\frac{x_f}{\lambda f} f \sin\theta\right)} + A_1 A_2^* S^*\left(\frac{x_f}{\lambda f}, \frac{y_f}{\lambda f}\right) e^{-i2\pi\left(\frac{x_f}{\lambda f} f \sin\theta\right)}\right], \tag{11.64}$$

where t_0 is the constant of proportionality. The exposure of the photographic film has been assumed to lie on the linear portion of the amplitude transmittance versus exposure curve (Fig. 11.12). Equation (11.64) contains one term which is proportional to the Fourier transform of the mask transmittance $s(x', y')$ and another term which is proportional to its complex conjugate. Any desired change in the amplitude and phase of the field distribution behind the filter can be achieved by a judicious choice of the parameters A_1, A_2, and θ. In the above procedure, the complex spatial frequency filter is fabricated by keeping a suitable mask in the spatial domain, and not in the spatial frequency domain.

The field distribution just behind the filter when kept in the transform plane (Fig. 11.6), obtained from Eq. (11.42), is

$$E(x_f, y_f) = CF\left(\frac{x_f}{\lambda f}, \frac{y_f}{\lambda f}\right) H\left(\frac{x_f}{\lambda f}, \frac{y_f}{\lambda f}\right), \tag{11.65}$$

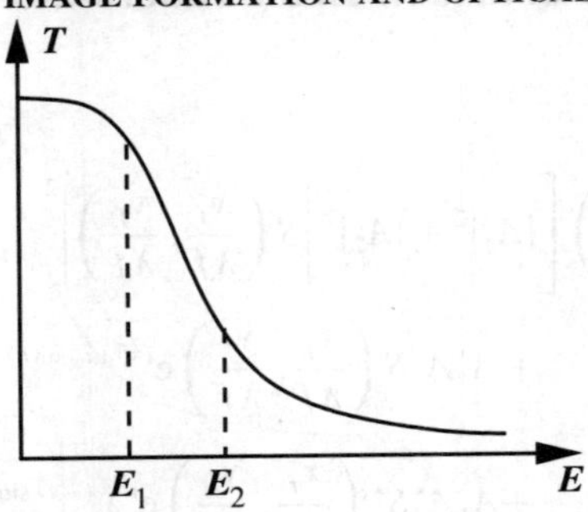

Fig. 11.12: T–E curve of a developed photographic plate; T is its amplitude transmittance and E is product of exposure intensity and exposure time. Between E_1 and E_2, transmittance varies nearly linearly with E.

where $F(\frac{x_f}{\lambda f}, \frac{y_f}{\lambda f})$ is the Fourier transform of the object transparency (Eq. 11.44), C is a complex constant, and $H(\frac{x_f}{\lambda f}, \frac{y_f}{\lambda f})$ is the amplitude transmittance of the spatial frequency filter. The filtered field distribution in the image plane obtained by Fourier transforming Eq. (11.65) is

$$
\begin{aligned}
E(x'', y'') = C_0 \Bigg[& |A_1|^2 \iint_{-\infty}^{\infty} F\left(\frac{x_f}{\lambda f}, \frac{y_f}{\lambda f}\right) e^{-i\frac{2\pi}{\lambda f}(x_f x'' + y_f y'')} dx_f \, dy_f \\
& + |A_2|^2 \iint_{-\infty}^{\infty} F\left(\frac{x_f}{\lambda f}, \frac{y_f}{\lambda f}\right) \left| S\left(\frac{x_f}{\lambda f}, \frac{y_f}{\lambda f}\right)\right|^2 \\
& \times e^{-i\frac{2\pi}{\lambda f}(x_f x'' + y_f y'')} dx_f \, dy_f \qquad (11.66) \\
& + A_1^* A_2 \iint_{-\infty}^{\infty} F\left(\frac{x_f}{\lambda f}, \frac{y_f}{\lambda f}\right) S\left(\frac{x_f}{\lambda f}, \frac{y_f}{\lambda f}\right) \\
& \times e^{-i\frac{2\pi}{\lambda f}\{x_f(x'' - f\sin\theta) + y_f y''\}} dx_f \, dy_f \\
& + A_1 A_2^* \iint_{-\infty}^{\infty} F\left(\frac{x_f}{\lambda f}, \frac{y_f}{\lambda f}\right) S^*\left(\frac{x_f}{\lambda f}, \frac{y_f}{\lambda f}\right) \\
& \times e^{-i\frac{2\pi}{\lambda f}\{x_f(x'' + f\sin\theta) + y_f y''\}} dx_f \, dy_f \Bigg],
\end{aligned}
$$

where C_0 is a suitable complex constant. The first term in Eq. (11.66), being proportional to the Fourier transform of the Fourier transform of the object transmission function, reproduces the object transmission function in the image plane:

$$\mathcal{F}\left[F\left(\frac{x_f}{\lambda f}, \frac{y_f}{\lambda f}\right)\right] = \mathcal{F}\mathcal{F}[f(x', y')] = f(x'' = -x', y'' = -y'). \tag{11.67a}$$

This term will be centered on the optical axis in the image plane if $f(x', y')$ is centered on the optical axis in the object plane. The second term is also centered on the optical axis since $|S(\frac{x_f}{\lambda f}, \frac{y_f}{\lambda f})|^2$ has no phase variation over the transform plane. It can be shown to be proportional to the convolution function

$$\mathcal{F}\left[F\left(\frac{x_f}{\lambda f}, \frac{y_f}{\lambda f}\right)\left|S\left(\frac{x_f}{\lambda f}, \frac{y_f}{\lambda f}\right)\right|^2\right] = \{f(-x, -y) * s(-x, -y)\} * s^*(x, y). \tag{11.67b}$$

These terms are not of much interest for optical processing applications. They represent zero-order diffractions. The third term can be evaluated with the help of the convolution theorem (Eq. 9.57), giving

$$\begin{aligned}
&\mathcal{F}\left[F\left(\frac{x_f}{\lambda f}, \frac{y_f}{\lambda f}\right) S\left(\frac{x_f}{\lambda f}, \frac{y_f}{\lambda f}\right) \mathrm{e}^{\mathrm{i}2\pi\left(\frac{x_f}{\lambda f} f \sin\theta\right)}\right] \\
&= \iint\limits_{-\infty}^{\infty} \iint\limits_{-\infty}^{\infty} \iint\limits_{-\infty}^{\infty} f(x', y') s(x - x', y - y') \\
&\quad \times \mathrm{e}^{-\mathrm{i}2\pi\left(\frac{x_f}{\lambda f} x + \frac{y_f}{\lambda f} y\right)} \mathrm{e}^{-\mathrm{i}2\pi(x'' - f\sin\theta)\frac{x_f}{\lambda f}} \\
&\quad \times \mathrm{e}^{-\mathrm{i}2\pi y'' \frac{y_f}{\lambda f}} \mathrm{d}\left(\frac{x_f}{\lambda f}\right) \mathrm{d}\left(\frac{y_f}{\lambda f}\right) \mathrm{d}x\, \mathrm{d}y\, \mathrm{d}x'\, \mathrm{d}y' \qquad (11.67c) \\
&= \iint\limits_{-\infty}^{\infty} \iint\limits_{-\infty}^{\infty} \delta(x'' - f\sin\theta + x, y'' + y) \\
&\quad \times f(x', y') s(x - x', y - y') \mathrm{d}x\, \mathrm{d}y\, \mathrm{d}x' \mathrm{d}y' \\
&= \iint\limits_{-\infty}^{\infty} f(x', y') s(-x'' + f\sin\theta - x', -y'' - y') \mathrm{d}x' \mathrm{d}y'.
\end{aligned}$$

This term is proportional to the convolution of $f(x, y)$ and $s(x, y)$ and is centered at the off-axis point $(x'' = f\sin\theta,\ y'' = 0)$ in the image plane. Similarly, it can be shown that the fourth term

$$\mathcal{F}\left[F\left(\frac{x_f}{\lambda f}, \frac{y_f}{\lambda f}\right) S^*\left(\frac{x_f}{\lambda f}, \frac{y_f}{\lambda f}\right) \mathrm{e}^{-\mathrm{i}2\pi \frac{x_f}{\lambda f} f \sin\theta}\right]$$

$$= \iint\limits_{-\infty}^{\infty} f(x', y') s^*(x' + x'' + f\sin\theta, y' + y'')\mathrm{d}x'\mathrm{d}y' \qquad (11.67\mathrm{d})$$

is proportional to the crosscorrelation of $f(x, y)$ with $s(x, y)$ and is centered at the off-axis point $(x'' = -f\sin\theta,\ y'' = 0)$ in the image plane. Thus, the field distribution in the image plane is confined to three non-overlapping regions if the carrier spatial frequency $\sin\theta/\lambda$ is sufficiently high. The first two terms (Eqs. 11.67a, b) occupy the central portion of the image plane. The second term is more spread out than the first since it involves the convolution of three functions. The third term representing the convolution function (Eq. 11.67c) lies above the optical axis for the geometry of Fig. 11.11a. The crosscorrelation term (Eq. 11.67d) lies below the optical axis. This is shown in Fig. 11.13. The Rayleigh interferometric scheme (Fig. 11.11b) for the synthesis of a complex spatial frequency filter can be analyzed in a similar manner.

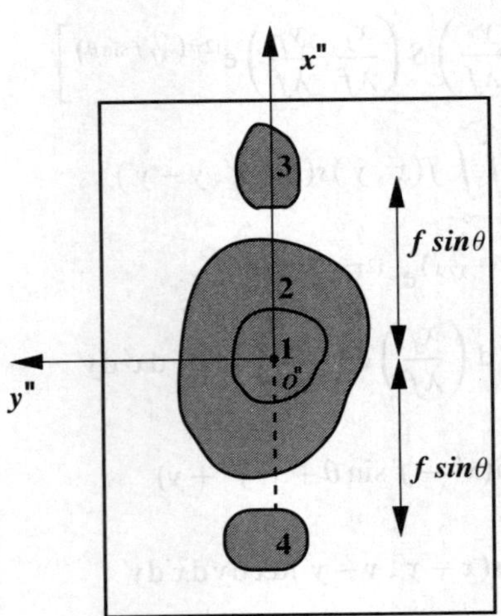

Fig. 11.13: Field distribution in the image plane after filtering by a complex spatial frequency filter.

11.3.4 Matched Filter

A spatial frequency filter is said to be matched to an input signal $s(x, y)$ if its transmittance is proportional to the complex conjugate of the Fourier transform of the signal, i.e., if

$$H\left(\frac{x_f}{\lambda f}, \frac{y_f}{\lambda f}\right) = C' S^*\left(\frac{x_f}{\lambda f}, \frac{y_f}{\lambda f}\right), \tag{11.68}$$

where C' is a constant and $S(\frac{x_f}{\lambda f}, \frac{y_f}{\lambda f})$ is the Fourier transform of $s(x, y)$. A matched filter can help identify a given signal when it appears along with other spatially non-overlapping signals in the input plane. The matched filter is particularly useful to optimize the signal-to-noise ratio when the signal is accompanied with random noise. Let

$$f(x', y') = s(x', y') + n(x', y') \tag{11.69}$$

be the amplitude transmission function of the input transparency in Fig. (11.6), where $s(x', y')$ is the desired signal and $n(x', y')$ is some other signal or simply the noise. On placing a filter matched to the signal $s(x', y')$ in the transform plane, the field generated just behind the filter is

$$\begin{aligned} E(x_f, y_f) &= C'\left[S\left(\frac{x_f}{\lambda f}, \frac{y_f}{\lambda f}\right) + N\left(\frac{x_f}{\lambda f}, \frac{y_f}{\lambda f}\right)\right] S^*\left(\frac{x_f}{\lambda f}, \frac{y_f}{\lambda f}\right) \\ &= C'\left|S\left(\frac{x_f}{\lambda f}, \frac{y_f}{\lambda f}\right)\right|^2 + C' N\left(\frac{x_f}{\lambda f}, \frac{y_f}{\lambda f}\right) S^*\left(\frac{x_f}{\lambda f}, \frac{y_f}{\lambda f}\right). \end{aligned} \tag{11.70}$$

The first term in Eq. (11.70) may show amplitude variation but no phase variation in the Fourier transform plane. It represents a plane wave with weighted amplitude. The second lens (Fig. 11.6) sharply focuses this term as a bright spot in the image plane. Of course, the bright spot is not the image of $s(x', y')$ since the field distribution in the transform plane is no longer described by $S(\frac{x_f}{\lambda f}, \frac{y_f}{\lambda f})$. The phase of $N(\frac{x_f}{\lambda f}, \frac{y_f}{\lambda f})$ in the second term of Eq. (11.70) is not annulled by the filter. As a result, this term appears distributed in the image plane. Thus, a particular signal can be distinguished from other signals by the appearance of a bright spot in the image plane when a filter matched to it is kept in the transform plane.

The field distribution in the image plane, obtained by taking the Fourier transform of Eq. (11.70), is

$$E(x'', y'') = C' \iint_{-\infty}^{\infty} \left[S\left(\frac{x_f}{\lambda f}, \frac{y_f}{\lambda f}\right) S^*\left(\frac{x_f}{\lambda f}, \frac{y_f}{\lambda f}\right) + N\left(\frac{x_f}{\lambda f}, \frac{y_f}{\lambda f}\right) \times S^*\left(\frac{x_f}{\lambda f}, \frac{y_f}{\lambda f}\right) \right] e^{-i\frac{2\pi}{\lambda f}(x_f x'' + y_f y'')} d\left(\frac{x_f}{\lambda f}\right) d\left(\frac{y_f}{\lambda f}\right). \tag{11.71}$$

Using the correlation theorems, this distribution can be expressed as

$$E(x'', y'') = C' \iint_{-\infty}^{\infty} s(x', y') s^*(x' - x'', y' - y'') dx' dy' + C' \iint_{-\infty}^{\infty} n(x', y') s^*(x' - x'', y' - y'') dx' dy'. \tag{11.72}$$

The first term represents the autocorrelation of the signal and second term is the crosscorrelation of the signal with the unwanted signal. The latter term will be particularly small if $n(x', y')$ represents random noise.

11.4 COHERENT OPTICAL PROCESSING

We have seen that a matched filter kept in the transform plane of a coherent image processing setup can pick up a particular signal from other spatially non-overlapping signals. This signal can be in the form of a character, a signature, a photograph, or a pattern in a transparency kept in the input plane. As specific examples, we may want to know how many times a particular alphabet or a particular word appears in a certain composition, or we may be interested in matching a photograph or a signature in a police department or in a bank where a huge database exists. In character recognition, one has to make matched filters for all characters, and in a bank or in a police department for all signatures and photographs which may exist in the database. The identification of the desired signal is accomplished by inserting the signal to be matched in the input plane and the matched filters, sequentially, in the transform plane. For the unmatched filters, crosscorrelation signals are observed in the image plane but for the matched filter, the autocorrelation of the actual signal appears as a bright spot in the image plane. Schwarz' inequality requires the autocorrelation of a function to always exceed its crosscorrelation with a different function. There may be difficulties in matching a filter if the input transparency has different magnification or different orientation with respect to the input for which the matched filter was prepared.

11.5 INCOHERENT IMAGE FORMATION

The discussion so far has been restricted to coherent image formation and processing since a monochromatic plane wave has been used for object illumination. Light sources being partially coherent, monochromatic object illumination must be replaced by quasi-monochromatic illumination (refer to Chapter 2). We now extend this discussion to image formation and processing with spatially incoherent light. We shall not digress on the merits and demerits of the coherent and incoherent imaging schemes, except to mention that an image formed by incoherent light is devoid of any speckle noise, often accompanied in coherent imaging. A linear relationship between the input and output field distributions exists for coherent imaging, but for incoherent imaging, it is the output intensity distribution which is linearly dependent on the input intensity distribution. Completely (spatially) incoherent light fields satisfy the condition

$$\langle E(x_1, y_1, t)E^*(x_2, y_2, t)\rangle = |E(x_1, y_1)|^2\delta(x_2 - x_1, y_2 - y_1), \tag{11.73}$$

where the symbol $\langle\,\rangle$ indicates time averaging. Therefore, for incoherent object illumination, Eq. (11.39) for the time averaged intensity distribution in the image plane gets modified to

$$\begin{aligned} I(x'', y'') &= \left(\frac{1}{2}\epsilon_0 c\right)\iint_{-\infty}^{\infty}\iint_{-\infty}^{\infty}\left\langle E'_{\mathrm{O}}\left(\frac{\tilde{x}_1}{m}, \frac{\tilde{y}_1}{m}\right) E'^{*}_{\mathrm{O}}\left(\frac{\tilde{x}_2}{m}, \frac{\tilde{y}_2}{m}\right)\right\rangle \\ &\quad \times h'(x''-\tilde{x}_1, y''-\tilde{y}_1)h'^*(x''-\tilde{x}_2, y''-\tilde{y}_2)\mathrm{d}\,\tilde{x}_1\,\mathrm{d}\,\tilde{y}_1\,\mathrm{d}\,\tilde{x}_2\,\mathrm{d}\,\tilde{y}_2 \\ &= \left(\frac{1}{2}\epsilon_0 c\right)\iint_{-\infty}^{\infty}\iint_{-\infty}^{\infty}\left|E'_{\mathrm{O}}\left(\frac{\tilde{x}_1}{m}, \frac{\tilde{y}_1}{m}\right)\right|^2 \delta(\tilde{x}_2 - \tilde{x}_1, \tilde{y}_2 - \tilde{y}_1) \\ &\quad \times h'(x''-\tilde{x}_1, y''-\tilde{y}_1)h'^*(x''-\tilde{x}_2, y''-\tilde{y}_2)\mathrm{d}\,\tilde{x}_1\,\mathrm{d}\,\tilde{y}_1\,\mathrm{d}\,\tilde{x}_2\,\mathrm{d}\,\tilde{y}_2 \\ &= \iint_{-\infty}^{\infty} I'_{\mathrm{O}}\left(\frac{\tilde{x}}{m}, \frac{\tilde{y}}{m}\right)|h'(x''-\tilde{x}, y''-\tilde{y})|^2\mathrm{d}\,\tilde{x}\,\mathrm{d}\,\tilde{y} \qquad (11.74\mathrm{a}) \\ &= \frac{I_0}{m^2}\left|f_{\mathrm{O}}\left(\frac{x''}{m}, \frac{y''}{m}\right)\right|^2 * |h'(x'', y'')|^2, \qquad (11.74\mathrm{b}) \end{aligned}$$

where the object transparency is assumed to be normally illuminated with incoherent light of uniform intensity I_0, and $f_{\mathrm{O}}(x, y)$ is the amplitude transmission function of the object transparency. Thus for incoherent object illumination, the intensity distribution in the image plane is the convolution of the intensity distribution in the object plane with the square modulus of the coherent impulse response function of the optical system.

11.6 INCOHERENT OPTICAL PROCESSING

We illustrate incoherent optical processing by evaluating the integral of the product of two functions:

$$I_1 = \int_{-\infty}^{\infty}\int f_1(x, y) f_2(x, y) \mathrm{d}x\,\mathrm{d}y. \tag{11.75}$$

For the procedure to succeed, the functions $f_1(x, y)$ and $f_2(x, y)$ be transferable to object transparencies. Figure 11.14 shows schematically an incoherent optical processing setup, where S is an extended quasi-monochromatic light source. Relevance of the transform plane is lost in incoherent optical processing.

Let the intensity transmittances $T_1(x, y)$ and $T_2(x, y)$ of transparencies T_1 and T_2 represent the functions $f_1(x, y)$ and $f_2(x, y)$, respectively. The transparency

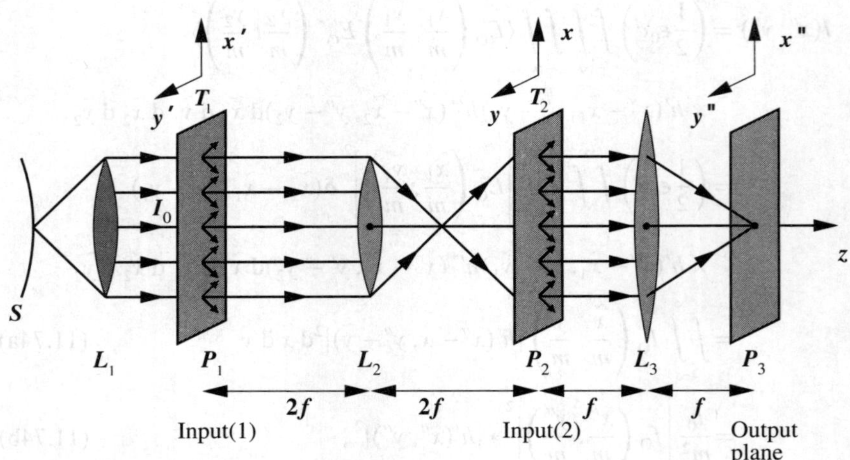

Fig. 11.14: Incoherent optical processing configuration to obtain integral of the product of two functions. S is an extended source.

T_1 is kept in the input plane P_1 with inverted orientation. It is illuminated incoherently but uniformly so that the intensity distribution in plane P_1 is

$$T_1(x', y')I_0 = I_0 f_1(-x', -y'). \tag{11.76}$$

The second transparency with intensity transmittance

$$T_2(x, y) = f_2(x, y) \tag{11.77}$$

is kept in plane P_2. The intensity distribution just behind the second transparency is

$$I(x, y) = I_0[f_1(-x, -y) * |h(x, y)|^2]f_2(x, y), \tag{11.78}$$

where $h(x, y)$ is the coherent impulse response function of the optical system between the planes P_1 and P_2. The impulse response function $h(x, y)$ approaches Dirac's delta function if lens L_2 has sufficiently large aperture to intercept and faithfully transfer all spatial frequencies of the first transparency. For the configuration of Fig. 11.14, an unmagnified and inverted image of transparency T_1 appears in plane P_2. Accordingly, Eq. (11.78) simplifies to

$$I(x, y) = I_0 f_1(x, y) f_2(x, y). \tag{11.79}$$

We now see the reason for keeping transparency T_1 inverted in plane P_1, otherwise the intensity distribution in plane P_2 will be the product $f_1(-x, -y)f_2(x, y)$, and not $f_1(x, y)f_2(x, y)$. The intensity distribution, normalized to the input intensity I_0, measured with a photodiode just behind the second transparency gives the product of the functions $f_1(x, y)$ and $f_2(x, y)$. Finally, lens L_3 produces the Fourier transform

$$I(x'', y'') = C \iint_{-\infty}^{\infty} f_1(x, y) f_2(x, y) \mathrm{e}^{-\mathrm{i}\frac{2\pi}{\lambda f}(xx''+yy'')} \mathrm{d}x\,\mathrm{d}y \tag{11.80}$$

of the product $f_1(x, y)f_2(x, y)$ in plane P_3, where C is a suitable constant. The normalized intensity

$$I_n(x'' = 0, y'' = 0) = \iint_{-\infty}^{\infty} f_1(x, y) f_2(x, y) \mathrm{d}x\,\mathrm{d}y \tag{11.81}$$

at the center of this plane, measured with a photodiode, gives the value of the integral (Eq. 11.75).

A slight modification of this arrangement, appearing in Fig. 11.15, can obtain the convolution and correlation between mathematical functions. In this case, the transparencies T_1 and T_2 representing the functions $f_1(x, y)$ and $f_2(x, y)$, respectively, are juxtaposed in the front focal plane of lens L_2. The intensity distribution just behind the second transparency is

$$I(x', y') = I_0 f_1(x', y') f_2(x', y'). \tag{11.82}$$

One of the transparencies is mounted on an x–y translator so that its position with respect to the other can be shifted. The Fourier transform

$$I(x_f, y_f) = C \int\int_{-\infty}^{\infty} f_1(x', y') f_2(x', y') \mathrm{e}^{-\mathrm{i}2\pi(x'x_f + y'y_f)} \mathrm{d}x'\mathrm{d}y' \tag{11.83}$$

of $I(x', y')$ is produced by lens L_2 in its back focal plane. The intensity at the point $x_f = 0$, $y_f = 0$ in this plane is

$$I(0, 0) = C \int\int_{-\infty}^{\infty} f_1(x', y') f_2(x', y') \mathrm{d}x'\mathrm{d}y'. \tag{11.84}$$

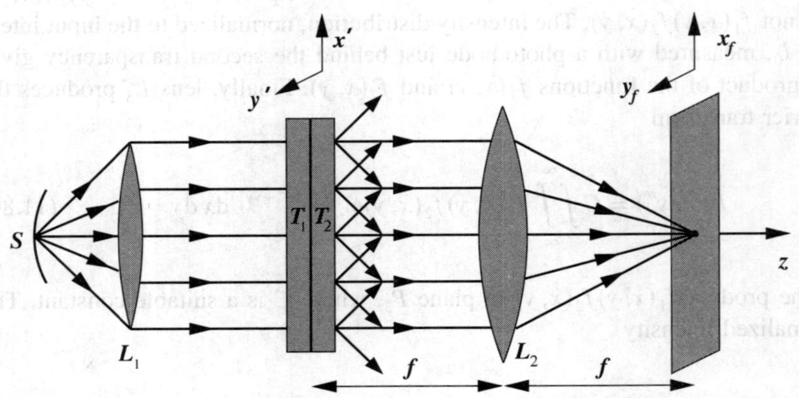

Fig. 11.15: Incoherent optical processing configuration to determine convolution and correlation of two functions. S is an extended source.

As transparency T_1 is displaced with respect to T_2, the changing intensity at the origin of the back focal plane of L_2 generates the crosscorrelation between $f_1(x, y)$ and $f_2(x, y)$:

$$I(0, 0, x, y) = C \int\int_{-\infty}^{\infty} f_1(x' - x, y' - y) f_2(x', y') \mathrm{d}x' \mathrm{d}y'. \tag{11.85}$$

If transparency T_1 is inserted in the inverted orientation and moved across the transparency T_2, the convolution

$$I(0, 0, x, y) = C \int\int_{-\infty}^{\infty} f_1(x - x', y - y') f_2(x', y') \mathrm{d}x' \mathrm{d}y' \tag{11.86}$$

between $f_1(x, y)$ and $f_2(x, y)$ is generated at the origin of the back focal plane of L_2.

11.7 RESOLVING POWER OF IMAGE FORMING SYSTEMS

The resolving power of a spectral instrument is defined in terms of its ability to produce output intensity distribution in which two close-lying spectral lines, present in the spectrum of the source, appear well separated or resolved. It is implied that light fields belonging to different spectral lines are mutually incoherent. Rayleigh criterion was employed to define the resolving power of a grating instrument (Section 10.5.3) and a somewhat different criterion was used in the context of a Fabry–Perot interferometer (Section 6.6.4). The resolving power of an image-forming system is its ability to resolve images of close lying objects. As mentioned earlier, it is the finite spread of the impulse response function of an imaging system which limits its resolution (refer to the discussion following Eq. 11.38).

11.7.1 Incoherent Object Illumination

We first consider the resolving power of an image-forming system such as a telescope or a microscope when the object under examination is either self-luminous or incoherently illuminated. This discussion applies to telescopes in general, but to microscopes only under restricted conditions of object illumination, as for example when an object is observed with a microscope in fluorescent light. Rayleigh criterion can define the resolving power of an image-forming system provided the object illumination is quasi-monochromatic and spatially incoherent. The circular aperture of the exit pupil of an optical system produces, for each point of the object, an Airy pattern in the image plane (Section 11.2). For two point objects to be resolved, their Airy disks must not overlap. From Eq. (10.47b), the angular radius of the Airy disk, for small angles, is

$$\theta_0 \approx \sin\theta_0 = 1.22\frac{\lambda}{d}, \tag{11.87}$$

where d is the diameter of the aperture.

A telescope can resolve two point objects if their angular separation ($\Delta\theta$) is larger than the angular radius of the Airy disk of either of the objects (Fig. 11.16), i.e., if

$$\Delta\theta \geq \theta_0. \tag{11.88}$$

The minimum angular separation (angular limit of resolution) of the objects which can be resolved by a telescope is

$$(\Delta\theta)_{\min} = \theta_0 = 1.22\frac{\lambda}{d}, \tag{11.89}$$

where d may be taken as the diameter of the objective of the telescope.

Equation (11.89) can be combined with Abbe sine condition (Eq. 5.21) to obtain the linear resolution limit of a microscope with incoherent object illumination. Figure 11.17 shows the marginal rays between the object and image planes of lens L, satisfying the sine condition

$$n_0 y_0 \sin\alpha_0 = n y \sin\alpha, \tag{11.90}$$

where y is the image separation of the point objects, a distance y_0 apart in the object plane; n_0 and n are the indices of refraction in the object and image spaces, respectively.

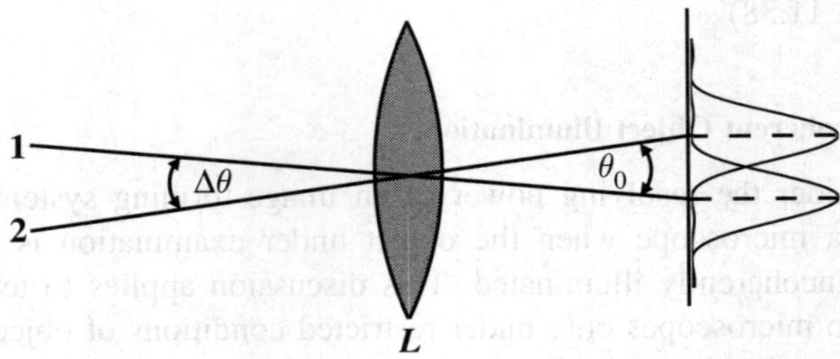

Fig. 11.16: Resolution of a telescope; L is its objective. At the limit of resolution, angular separation between point objects equals angular radius of Airy disk of either of the objects.

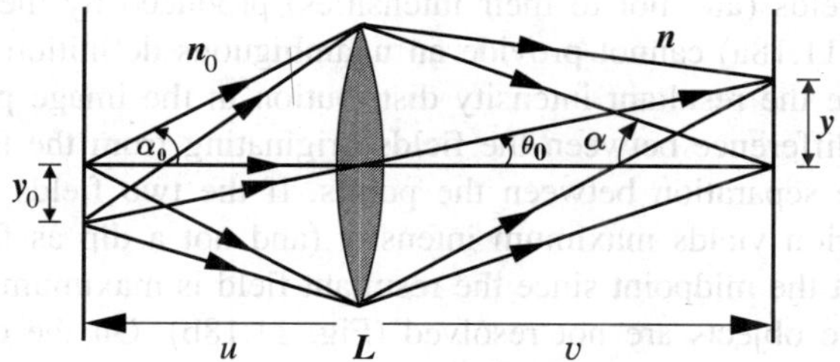

Fig. 11.17: Resolution limit of a microscope under incoherent illumination of the object. L is the objective of the microscope.

Assuming lens L to represent the objective of the microscope, the minimum image separation is given by

$$y_{\min} = v\theta_0 = 1.22\frac{\lambda}{d}v,$$

where d is the diameter of the objective of the microscope and v is the distance of the image plane from the objective of the microscope. With $n = 1$ and $\sin\alpha = d/2v$, the sine condition gives

$$(y_0)_{\min} = \frac{0.61\lambda}{n_0 \sin\alpha_0} = \frac{0.61\lambda}{NA}, \tag{11.91}$$

where $(y_0)_{\min}$ is the minimum separation of the point objects which the microscope can resolve. The numerical aperture (NA) of microscope usually does not exceed 1.6. For incoherent object illumination, this gives the minimum resolvable object separation for a microscope as 190 nm at $\lambda = 500$ nm and 114 nm at $\lambda = 300$ nm.

11.7.2 Coherent Object Illumination

In a microscope, a condenser is often used to illuminate the object. A condenser may be a single lens or a combination of lenses which produces a slightly defocused image of the light source in the object plane of the microscope. Points of the object which lie within the Airy disk, produced by diffraction at the condenser aperture due to a single point of the source, can have a high degree of spatial coherence. The discussion of the previous section, based on incoherent illumination of the object, is therefore inadequate in the context of a microscope. We now consider the resolving power of a microscope under coherent illumination of the object. Rayleigh criterion of resolution applied to the coherent fields (and not to their intensities) produced by the points to be resolved (Fig. 11.18a) cannot provide an unambiguous definition of the image resolution since the resultant intensity distribution in the image plane depends on the phase difference between the fields originating from the two points, in addition to the separation between the points. If the two fields are in phase, Rayleigh criterion yields maximum intensity (and not a dip as for incoherent illumination) at the midpoint since the resultant field is maximum at that point. As a result, the objects are not resolved (Fig. 11.18b). On the other hand, if the fields are 180° out of phase, the resultant field and hence intensity at the midpoint is minimum and the objects should be resolved (Fig. 11.18c). Needless to state that under coherent illumination, Rayleigh criterion may not be the most appropriate criterion for the resolution of a microscope. Sparrow criterion (Fig. 10.26b) may do a little better, but cannot be entirely satisfactory.

Abbe's theory of image formation (Section 11.2) can provide a precise criterion for the resolution of a microscope when object illumination is coherent. We return to our discussion of an infinite square grating of grating element a kept in the input plane of a coherent image processing system (Section 11.3.1 and Fig. 11.7). We recall that in the configuration of Fig. 11.6, the grating is illuminated normally by a plane wave. It was mentioned there that at least the

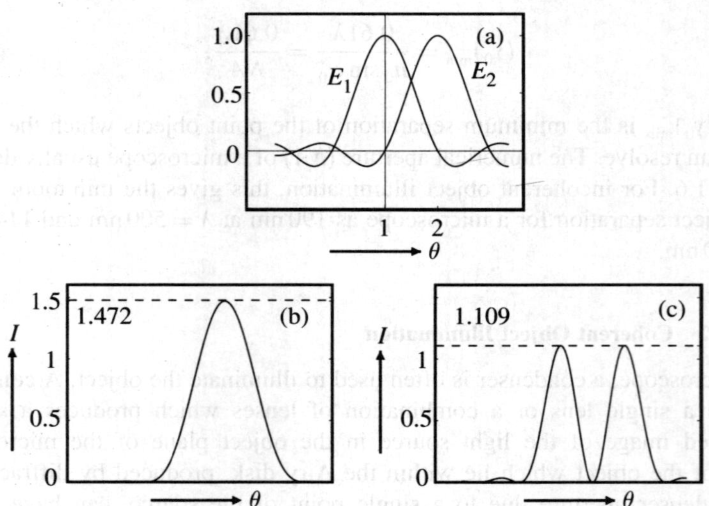

Fig. 11.18: Rayleigh criterion applied to a microscope when object illumination is coherent; field distribution in the image plane (a), intensity distribution in the image plane when point sources are in phase (b) and 180° out of phase (c).

$m = 0$ and $m = \pm 1$ diffraction orders of the grating must reach the image plane for the image to have the periodicity of the grating. Therefore, for a microscope to resolve two neighboring elements of an infinite square grating, the angle (α_0) subtended by each half of the objective of the microscope in Fig. 11.17 must satisfy the condition

$$\sin \alpha_0 \geq \sin \theta_1 = \frac{\lambda}{a}, \tag{11.92}$$

where θ_1 is the angle at which the first diffraction order of the grating appears. Therefore, the least distance between two points that a microscope can resolve (limit of resolution) is

$$(a)_{\min} = \frac{\lambda}{\sin \alpha_0}. \tag{11.93}$$

Equation (11.93) defines the limit of resolution of a microscope when object illumination is coherent. The resolution limit can be extended somewhat by realizing that the image of the grating formed by only $m = 0$ and $m = +1$ (or $m = -1$) orders of diffraction also has the periodicity of the grating. This can be achieved if the grating is illuminated obliquely so that $m = 0$ and $m = -1$ (or $m = +1$) orders are the only diffraction orders of the grating intercepted by the objective of the microscope (Fig. 11.19). Equation (10.73a) gives for the first-order Fraunhofer diffraction,

$$\sin \gamma'' - \sin \gamma' = \frac{\lambda}{a},$$

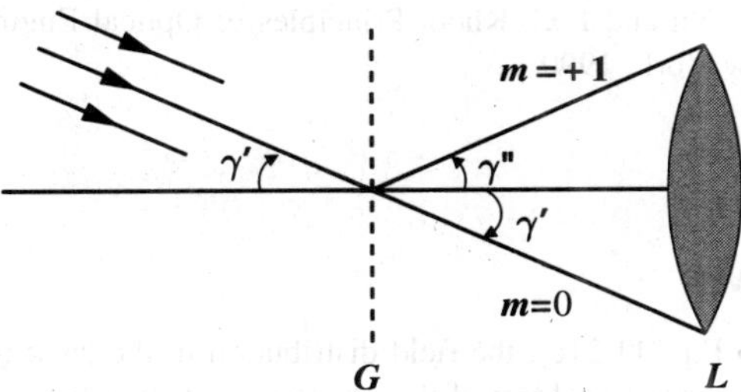

Fig. 11.19: Oblique illumination of the grating G. Only $m = 0$ and $m = +1$ diffraction orders of the grating are intercepted by the objective L of the microscope.

where in the present case, $\gamma'' = -\gamma' = \alpha_0$, and Eq. (11.93) is modified to

$$(a)_{\min} = \frac{\lambda}{2 \sin \alpha_0}.$$

Taking into account the index of refraction of the object space, as for example in the case of an oil-immersion objective (Section 4.3.5), the least distance between the objects that a microscope can resolve under coherent object illumination is

$$(a)_{\min} = \frac{\lambda}{2n_0 \sin \alpha_0} = \frac{\lambda}{2NA}. \tag{11.94}$$

The improved resolution in comparison to Eq. (11.93) is accompanied by a reduction in the contrast since the zero- and first-order diffractions have significantly different amplitudes. In summary, it can be said that the limits of resolution of a microscope under coherent and incoherent illuminations of the object are nearly same.

11.8 REFERENCES

11.1 Joseph W. Goodman, Introduction to Fourier Optics, McGraw-Hill, New York, 1968.

11.2 S. H. Lee (Ed.), Optical Information Processing, Fundamentals, Topics in Applied Physics, Springer-Verlag, Berlin, 1981.

11.3 Francis T. S. Yu, Optical Information Processing, John Wiley & Sons, New York, 1983.

11.4 K. Lizuka, Engineering Optics, Optical Sciences, Springer-Verlag, Berlin, 1985.

11.5 Francis T. S. Yu and I. C. Khoo, Principles of Optical Engineering, John Wiley & Sons, New York, 1990.

11.9 PROBLEMS

11.1 According to Eq. (11.21c), the field distribution in the back focal plane of a lens is the exact Fourier transform of the object field distribution only if the object lies in the front focal plane of the lens. Two arrangements shown in Fig. 11.20 can eliminate the extra phase factor when the object does not lie in the front focal plane of the lens. Find in each case the focal length of the additional lens. The lenses are assumed thin and of sufficiently large apertures.

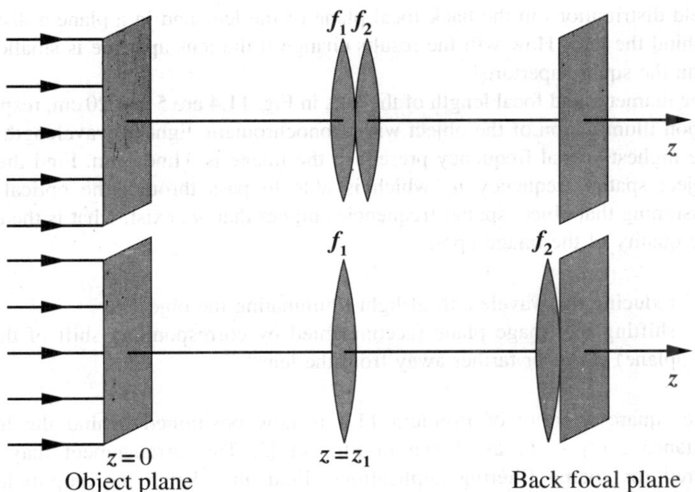

Fig. 11.20.

11.2 Consider Fig. 11.20 without the second lens but the object now lies in the front focal plane of the lens. The intensity distribution in the back focal plane of the lens gives the Fraunhofer diffraction pattern of the aperture. Suppose we measure the intensity distributions in planes somewhat displaced from the back focal plane of the lens. For what maximum range of longitudinal displacements, the intensity distribution is still an accurate measure of the Fraunhofer diffraction pattern of the aperture?

11.3 Find the impulse response function of a diffraction-limited optical system with circular exit pupil of radius a.

11.4 An object in the form of a thin square aperture of sides a is kept just in front of a lens of focal length f (Fig. 11.21). The aperture and lens have a common axis. The diameter of the lens is larger than the sides of the aperture. The aperture is illuminated normally by a plane monochromatic wave of wavelength λ. Find the

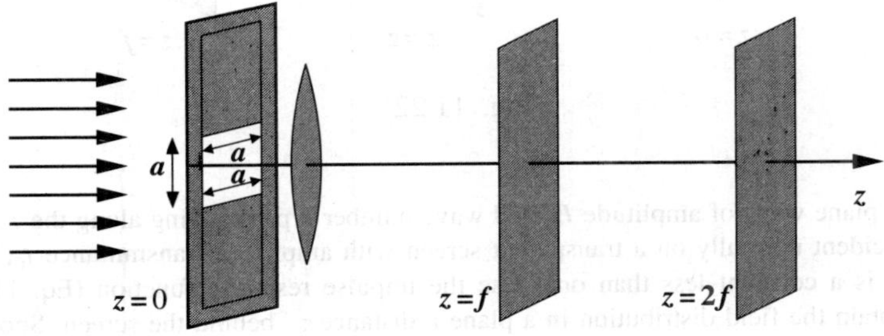

Fig. 11.21.

field distributions in the back focal plane of the lens and in a plane a distance $2f$ behind the lens. How will the results change if the lens aperture is smaller in size than the square aperture?

11.5 The diameter and focal length of the lens in Fig. 11.4 are 5 and 20 cm, respectively. Upon illumination of the object with monochromatic light of wavelength 550 nm, the highest spatial frequency present in the image is 3 lines/mm. Find the highest object spatial frequency u_0 which is able to pass through the optical system. Assuming that object spatial frequencies higher than u_0 exist, what is the effect on the quality of the image upon

(a) reducing the wavelength of light illuminating the object?
(b) shifting the image plane (accompanied by corresponding shift of the object plane) closer or farther away from the lens?

11.6 The square aperture of Problem 11.4 is now positioned behind the lens at a distance $z_1 (z_1 < f)$ as shown in Fig. 11.22. This arrangement may be preferred for spatial filtering applications. Find and sketch the amplitude of the field distribution in the back focal plane of the lens of sufficiently large aperture. Focal length of the lens is 50 cm and $z_1 = 20$ cm. Each side of the square aperture is 1 cm. What is the effect of changing z_1 on the size of the Fourier transform? What value of z_1 gives the largest size of the Fourier transform?

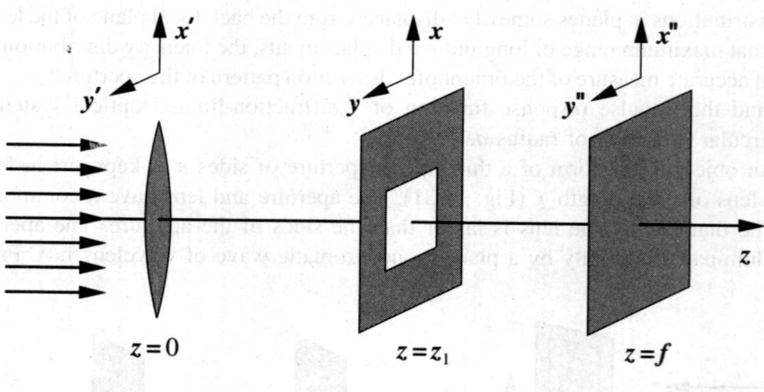

Fig. 11.22.

11.7 A plane wave of amplitude E_0 and wave number k propagating along the z-axis is incident normally on a transparent screen with amplitude transmittance t_0, where t_0 is a constant less than one. Use the impulse response function (Eq. 11.9) to obtain the field distribution in a plane a distance z_1 behind the screen. Show that for a sufficiently large screen, the field distribution in any plane behind the screen, satisfying the Fresnel approximation (Eq. 11.7), approaches a plane wave.

11.8 A transparency with amplitude transmittance

$$t(x, y) = \frac{1}{2}\{1 + \cos 2\pi l(x^2 + y^2)\}$$

kept in the $z = 0$ plane is illuminated normally by a plane wave of amplitude E_0 and wavelength λ, where l is a positive constant of appropriate dimensions. Find the field distribution in a plane a distance $1/2\lambda l$ behind the transparency. Show that such a transparency acts as a transparent plate, a convex lens, and a concave lens simultaneously. Find the focal lengths of the corresponding lenses.

11.9 Consider the diffraction-limited single lens imaging system of Fig. 11.23a. The lens has square cross-section of sides 5 cm and focal length 15 cm. The object is in the form of a square network of fine dots with inter-dot separations of 1 mm along the x' and y' axes (Fig. 11.23b). The object is illuminated normally with a plane wave of wavelength 632.8 nm. Obtain the image field distribution and sketch it as accurately as you can. Be sure to indicate the scales used in the sketches. Will your sketches change qualitatively if the inter-dot separation is reduced to 0.01 mm?

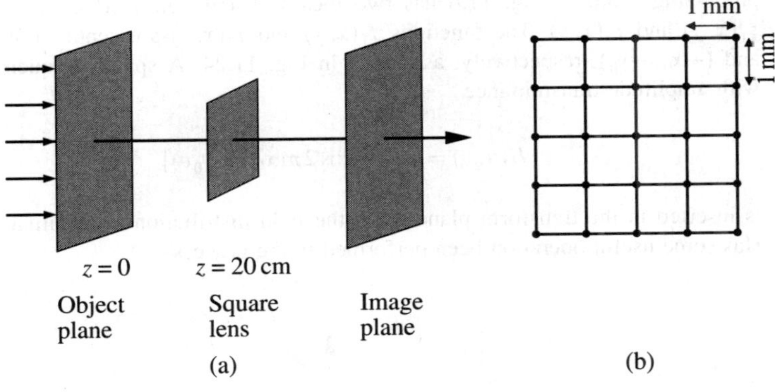

Fig. 11.23.

11.10 Replace the object transparency in Fig. 11.23a by one with the amplitude transmittance

$$t(x, y) = \frac{1}{4}(1 + \sin 2\pi u_0 x),$$

where u_0 is a positive constant. Find and sketch the amplitude of the image field distribution.

11.11 The object transparency in the imaging configuration of Fig. 11.23a is replaced by a square hole of sides 1 cm, symmetrically placed in the object plane. Find analytically or numerically the field distribution in the image plane.

11.12 The field distribution in the object plane is described by the sinc function

$$E(x) = u_0 \operatorname{sinc}(\pi u_0 x).$$

Design a spatial frequency filter of the smallest size which prevents light from reaching the image plane (Fig. 11.6).

11.13 In the spatial frequency filtering setup of Fig. 11.6, $f = 10\,\text{cm}$. A one-dimensional square grating of grating element $a = 5 \times 10^{-4}$ cm kept in the input plane is illuminated by a plane wave of wavelength $\lambda = 500\,\text{nm}$ propagating at 30° to the optical axis. Design a spatial frequency filter which will block all, except the $m = 0$ and $m = -1$ diffraction orders of the grating. Find the intensity distribution in the image plane. What is the period of this distribution? Assume the aperture of the lens to be sufficiently large.

11.14 In the coherent image processing setup of Fig. 11.6, the object is a one-dimensional square grating of grating element a. The zero diffraction order of the grating is blocked in the transform plane. Find and sketch the intensity distribution in the image plane. Assume that if the zero order was not blocked, the grating is exactly reproduced in the image plane.

11.15 The amplitude transmittance of the input transparency in the coherent image-processing setup of Fig. 11.6 has two localized and non-overlapping functions $f_1(x, y)$ and $f_2(x, y)$. The functions $f_1(x, y)$ and $f_2(x, y)$ are centered at (x_0, y_0) and $(-x_0, -y_0)$, respectively, as shown in Fig. 11.24. A spatial frequency filter with amplitude transmittance

$$H(u, v) = \frac{1}{2}[1 + \cos 2\pi(x_0 u + y_0 v)]$$

is inserted in the transform plane. Find the field distribution in the image plane. Has some useful operation been performed in the process?

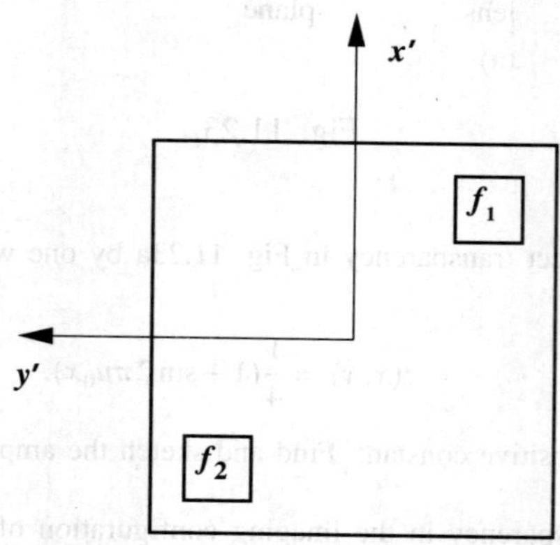

Fig. 11.24.

11.16 The impulse response function of an imaging system has the form

$$h(x, y) = \text{rect}\left[\frac{x+\Delta x}{\Delta x}\right] - \text{rect}\left[\frac{x-\Delta x}{\Delta x}\right].$$

Find image intensity distributions for coherent and incoherent illuminations of an object transparency with the amplitude transmittance

$$t(x, y) = \text{rect}\left[\frac{x+\Delta x}{\Delta x}\right] + \text{rect}\left[\frac{x-\Delta x}{\Delta x}\right].$$

11.17 The Fourier transform of the input function $f(x, y)$ is recorded on a photographic plate (Fig. 11.25). The photographic plate is developed and its positive transparency is inserted in the input plane after removing the original transparency. Assuming the plate has been recorded in the linear portion of the T–E curve of the film (Fig. 11.12), find and interpret the new field distribution in the transform plane.

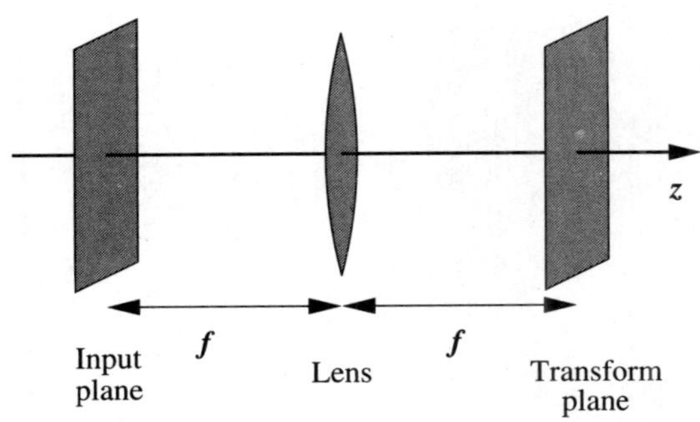

Fig. 11.25.

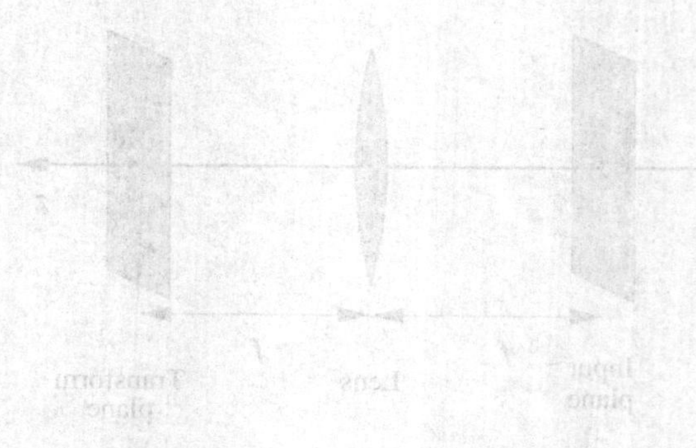

CHAPTER 12

Transfer Functions

12.1 INTRODUCTION

Image formation within the frameworks of geometrical optics and diffraction of light has been described in earlier chapters. We have also considered the resolving capability of an image-forming system, but nothing has been said so far about the quality of the image formed by an optical system. In this chapter, we introduce the transfer functions which characterize the image-forming quality of an optical system. In the paraxial approximation, geometrical optics gives a point image of a point object. Deviations from the paraxial approximation result in degradation of the quality of an image as discussed in Chapter 5. Diffraction theory, on the other hand, generates for a point object, the Fraunhofer diffraction pattern of the aperture of the lens in the image plane of geometrical optics. For an optical system possessing cylindrical symmetry, the image of a point object is the Airy pattern consisting of the bright central disk carrying nearly 84% of image irradiance, surrounded by dark and bright rings. The intensity at the center of the Airy disk is nearly 57 times the maximum intensity in the surrounding rings. For coherent illumination of an extended object, the field distribution in the image plane is the superposition of the field distributions produced by each point of the object. On the other hand, for spatially incoherent object illumination, the intensity distribution in the image plane is the superposition of the intensity distributions produced by each point of the object. The transfer functions should be able to deal with both modes of object illumination. The ability of an optical system to resolve two nearby equally intense but mutually incoherent point objects was described in terms of the Rayleigh criterion of resolution (Section 11.7). For coherent illumination, this criterion lacks definiteness. Even for incoherent illumination, Rayleigh criterion is insufficient to evaluate the image-forming quality of an optical system since it deals with only the radius of the Airy disk and makes no reference to the image contrast. A slightly defocused image can transfer a significant fraction of the energy from the central disk to the surrounding rings accompanied by a substantial change in the image contrast, but little change in the positions of the rings. The introduction of the *Strehl ratio* was the first step in quantifying the image contrast. Strehl ratio is the ratio of the intensity at the center of the Airy disk formed by an optical system to the intensity expected at that point for a diffraction-limited optical system. Strehl ratio of 0.8 and higher is considered satisfactory. Like the Rayleigh criterion, the Strehl ratio is also a one-point indicator of the performance of an optical system. Transfer functions, on the other hand, provide more comprehensive information on the image-forming quality of an optical system in terms of the system's response to the spatial frequency content of the object.

12.2 ISOPLANATISM

For coherent object illumination, the field distribution in the image plane of an aberration-free lens is given by the convolution integral (Eq. 11.36)

$$E_{\mathrm{i}}(x'', y'') = \iint_{-\infty}^{\infty} E'_{\mathrm{o}}\left(\frac{\tilde{x}}{m}, \frac{\tilde{y}}{m}\right) h'(x'' - \tilde{x}, y'' - \tilde{y}) \mathrm{d}\tilde{x}\, \mathrm{d}\tilde{y}, \tag{12.1a}$$

$$= E'_{\mathrm{o}}(x'', y'') * h'(x'', y''), \tag{12.1b}$$

where

$$h'(x'', y'') = \iint_{-\infty}^{\infty} t_{\mathrm{L}}(\lambda z_2 \tilde{x}_{\mathrm{L}}, \lambda z_2 \tilde{y}_{\mathrm{L}}) \times \mathrm{e}^{-\mathrm{i}2\pi(x''\tilde{x}_{\mathrm{L}} + y''\tilde{y}_{\mathrm{L}})} \mathrm{d}\tilde{x}_{\mathrm{L}}\, \mathrm{d}\tilde{y}_{\mathrm{L}} \tag{12.2}$$

is the coherent impulse response function of the lens and

$$E'_{\mathrm{o}}\left(\frac{\tilde{x}}{m}, \frac{\tilde{y}}{m}\right) = \frac{1}{m} \mathrm{e}^{\mathrm{i}k(z_1+z_2)} \mathrm{e}^{\frac{ik}{2z_2}(1-\frac{1}{m})(x''^2+y''^2)} E_{\mathrm{o}}(x', y'), \tag{12.3}$$

where $E_{\mathrm{o}}(x', y')$ is the object field distribution; z_1, z_2 are the object and image distances from the lens, and $m = -z_2/z_1$ is the image magnification. The variables $\tilde{x}_{\mathrm{L}}$, $\tilde{y}_{\mathrm{L}}$, x, and y are as defined in Eqs (11.32) and (11.35) and $t_{\mathrm{L}}(\lambda z_2 \tilde{x}_{\mathrm{L}}, \lambda z_2 \tilde{y}_{\mathrm{L}})$ is the aperture function of the lens or of the exit pupil of the optical system. The intensity distribution in the image plane for coherent illumination of the object is

$$I_{\mathrm{i}}^{\mathrm{coh}}(x'', y'') = \left(\frac{1}{2}\epsilon_0 c\right) \left| \iint_{-\infty}^{\infty} E'_{\mathrm{o}}\left(\frac{\tilde{x}}{m}, \frac{\tilde{y}}{m}\right) h'(x'' - \tilde{x}, y'' - \tilde{y}) \mathrm{d}\tilde{x}\, \mathrm{d}\tilde{y} \right|^2. \tag{12.4}$$

The impulse response function $h'(x''-\tilde{x}, y''-\tilde{y})$ is assumed to be spatially invariant, implying thereby, that the field at an arbitrary point (x'', y'') in the image plane does not depend on its absolute position in this plane, but on its displacement $(x''-mx', y''-my')$ from the paraxial image of the source point (x', y'). Consequently, the field distributions in the image plane produced by two identical point sources in the object plane with position coordinates (x'_1, y'_1) and (x'_2, y'_2) are identical, except for the spatial shift $[\Delta x'' = m(x'_2 - x'_1), \Delta y'' = m(y'_2 - y'_1)]$. This is the condition of *isoplanatism*. In practice, the spatial invariance of the impulse response function $h'(x''-\tilde{x}, y''-\tilde{y})$ of an optical system is satisfied over small regions of the object plane called the *isoplanatism patches*. The aberrations over an isoplanatism patch are stationary with respect to displacements within the patch.

12.3 COHERENT TRANSFER FUNCTION

For coherent object illumination, Eqs (12.1) establish a linear input–output relationship for the optical system. This relationship becomes more transparent when expressed in terms of the spatial frequencies of the input and output field distributions. The spatial frequency spectra of the object and image field distributions are

$$\mathcal{E}_o(u, v) = \iint_{-\infty}^{\infty} E'_o\left(\frac{\tilde{x}}{m}, \frac{\tilde{y}}{m}\right) e^{-i2\pi(u\tilde{x}+v\tilde{y})} d\tilde{x}\, d\tilde{y} \tag{12.5}$$

and

$$\mathcal{E}_i(u, v) = \iint_{-\infty}^{\infty} E_i(x'', y'') e^{-i2\pi(ux''+vy'')} dx''\, dy'', \tag{12.6}$$

respectively, where $u = x/\lambda z_1$, $v = y/\lambda z_1$ for the object field and $u = x/\lambda z_2$, $v = y/\lambda z_2$ for the image field distributions (Fig. 11.4); (x, y) being the coordinate of a point in the plane of the lens aperture. Application of the convolution theorem (Eq. 9.57) to the Fourier transform of Eq. (12.1) yields

$$\mathcal{E}_i(u, v) = g(u, v)\mathcal{E}_o(u, v), \tag{12.7}$$

where

$$g(u, v) = \iint_{-\infty}^{\infty} h'(x'', y'') e^{-i2\pi(ux''+vy'')} dx''\, dy'' \tag{12.8}$$

is the Fourier transform of the space invariant impulse response function of the optical system. The function $g(u, v)$, called the coherent transfer function, relates the complex amplitudes of the spatial frequencies in the object and image field distributions. If $g(u, v) = 1$ for all u and v, the optical system transfers all object spatial frequencies to the image plane with no change in their amplitudes and phases. The spatial frequency spectrum of the image field distribution differs from that of the object field distribution if $g(u, v)$ deviates from unity in magnitude or in phase or in both. Substitution of Eq. (12.2) into Eq. (12.8) gives

$$g(u, v) = \iint_{-\infty}^{\infty} \mathrm{d}\,\tilde{x}_L\, \mathrm{d}\,\tilde{y}_L\, t_L(\lambda z_2\, \tilde{x}_L, \lambda z_2\, \tilde{y}_L)\Big[\iint_{-\infty}^{\infty} \mathrm{e}^{-i2\pi x''(u+\tilde{x}_L)} \times \mathrm{e}^{-i2\pi y''(v+\tilde{y}_L)}\, \mathrm{d}x''\mathrm{d}y''\Big] \tag{12.9a}$$

$$= \iint_{-\infty}^{\infty} \mathrm{d}\,\tilde{x}_L\, \mathrm{d}\,\tilde{y}_L\, t_L(\lambda z_2\, \tilde{x}_L, \lambda z_2\, \tilde{y}_L)\delta(u+\tilde{x}_L)\delta(v+\tilde{y}_L)$$

$$= t_L(-\lambda z_2 u, -\lambda z_2 v). \tag{12.9b}$$

Therefore, the coherent transfer function (CTF) of an optical system is simply its exit pupil function with position variables x, y replaced by $(-\lambda z_2 u)$ and $(-\lambda z_2 v)$, respectively. The negative sign in the argument is not always important since the pupil function usually has a value of 1 or 0.

The pupil functions for circular and rectangular apertures are

$$t_L(x, y) = \mathrm{circ}\left(\frac{\sqrt{x^2+y^2}}{D/2}\right) \tag{12.10a}$$

and

$$t_L(x, y) = \mathrm{rect}\left(\frac{x}{a}\right)\mathrm{rect}\left(\frac{y}{b}\right), \tag{12.10b}$$

respectively, where D is the diameter of the circular aperture and a and b are the sides of the rectangular aperture. The coherent transfer functions of optical systems with circular and rectangular apertures are

$$g(u, v) = \mathrm{circ}\left[\frac{\sqrt{u^2+v^2}}{D/(2\lambda z_2)}\right] = \mathrm{circ}\left[\frac{\sqrt{u^2+v^2}}{u_0}\right] \tag{12.11a}$$

and

$$g(u, v) = \text{rect}\left(\frac{u}{a/(\lambda z_2)}\right) \text{rect}\left(\frac{v}{b/(\lambda z_2)}\right) = \text{rect}\left(\frac{u}{2u_0}\right) \text{rect}\left(\frac{v}{2v_0}\right), \tag{12.11b}$$

respectively, where for the circular aperture, $u_0 = D/2\lambda z_2$ and for the rectangular aperture, $u_0 = a/2\lambda z_2$ and $v_0 = b/2\lambda z_2$. The coherent transfer functions for aberration-free lenses with circular and rectangular apertures are shown in Fig. 12.1. The cutoff spatial frequencies for the circular aperture in any direction in the spatial frequency plane (Fig. 12.1a), expressed in terms of the image and object spatial frequencies, are

$$u_0^{\text{i}} = \frac{D}{2\lambda z_2}, \quad u_0^{\text{o}} = \frac{D}{2\lambda z_1}, \tag{12.12}$$

respectively. The corresponding cutoff spatial frequencies for the rectangular aperture along u and v directions (Fig. 12.1b) are

$$u_0^{\text{i}} = \frac{a}{2\lambda z_2}, \quad v_0^{\text{i}} = \frac{b}{2\lambda z_2} \tag{12.13a}$$

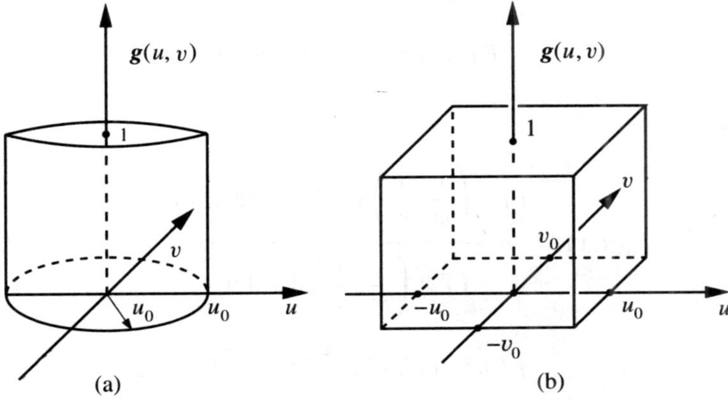

Fig. 12.1: Coherent transfer functions of aberration-free lenses (a) circular cross-section, (b) rectangular cross-section.

and

$$u_0^{\mathrm{o}} = \frac{a}{2\lambda z_1}, \quad v_0^{\mathrm{o}} = \frac{b}{2\lambda z_1}, \tag{12.13b}$$

respectively, where

$$\frac{u_0^{\mathrm{o}}}{u_0^{\mathrm{i}}} = \frac{v_0^{\mathrm{o}}}{v_0^{\mathrm{i}}} = \frac{z_2}{z_1} = -m.$$

12.4 OPTICAL TRANSFER FUNCTION

For incoherent object illumination, the interference terms in Eq. (12.4) vanish, resulting in a linear relationship between the image and object intensity distributions (Eq. 11.74), i.e.,

$$I_{\mathrm{i}}^{\mathrm{incoh}}(x'', y'') = \int_{-\infty}^{\infty}\!\!\int I_{\mathrm{o}}'\left(\frac{\tilde{x}}{m}, \frac{\tilde{y}}{m}\right) |h'(x'' - \tilde{x}, y'' - \tilde{y})|^2 \mathrm{d}\,\tilde{x}\;\mathrm{d}\,\tilde{y} \tag{12.14a}$$

$$= I_{\mathrm{o}}'\left(\frac{x''}{m}, \frac{y''}{m}\right) * |h'(x'', y'')|^2. \tag{12.14b}$$

The square modulus of the impulse response function ($|h'(x'' - \tilde{x}, y'' - \tilde{y})|^2$) is called the point spread function (PSF) of the optical system. Taking the Fourier transform of Eq. (12.14) and making use of the convolution theorem, the analog of Eq. (12.7) for incoherent object illumination is obtained as

$$F_{\mathrm{i}}(u, v) = G(u, v) F_{\mathrm{o}}(u, v), \tag{12.15}$$

where

$$F_{\mathrm{o}}(u, v) = \frac{\int_{-\infty}^{\infty}\!\!\int I_{\mathrm{o}}'\left(\frac{\tilde{x}}{m}, \frac{\tilde{y}}{m}\right) \mathrm{e}^{-\mathrm{i}2\pi(u\tilde{x} + v\tilde{y})} \mathrm{d}\,\tilde{x}\;\mathrm{d}\,\tilde{y}}{\int_{-\infty}^{\infty}\!\!\int I_{\mathrm{o}}'\left(\frac{\tilde{x}}{m}, \frac{\tilde{y}}{m}\right) \mathrm{d}\,\tilde{x}\;\mathrm{d}\,\tilde{y}}, \tag{12.16a}$$

$$F_{\mathrm{i}}(u, v) = \frac{\int_{-\infty}^{\infty}\!\!\int I_{\mathrm{i}}^{\mathrm{incoh}}(x'', y'') \mathrm{e}^{-\mathrm{i}2\pi(ux'' + vy'')} \mathrm{d}x'' \mathrm{d}y''}{\int_{-\infty}^{\infty}\!\!\int I_{\mathrm{i}}^{\mathrm{incoh}}(x'', y'')\, \mathrm{d}x'' \mathrm{d}y''} \tag{12.16b}$$

and

$$G(u, v) = \frac{\iint_{-\infty}^{\infty} |h'(x'', y'')|^2 \, \mathrm{e}^{-\mathrm{i}2\pi(ux''+vy'')} \mathrm{d}x''\mathrm{d}y''}{\iint_{-\infty}^{\infty} |h'(x'', y'')|^2 \, \mathrm{d}x''\mathrm{d}y''} \tag{12.16c}$$

are the normalized Fourier transforms of the object intensity distribution, the image intensity distribution, and the square modulus of the coherent impulse response function of the optical system, respectively. The function $G(u, v)$ is the incoherent transfer function known as the *optical transfer function* (OTF). In general, the OTF is complex, modifying the amplitudes and phases of the object spatial frequencies passing through the optical system. We can express

$$\begin{aligned} G(u, v) &= |G(u, v)| \mathrm{e}^{\mathrm{i}\phi(u,v)} \\ &= M(u, v) \mathrm{e}^{\mathrm{i}\phi(u,v)}, \end{aligned} \tag{12.17}$$

where $M(u, v)$, representing the magnitude of the optical transfer function, is called the *modulation transfer function* (MTF) and the phase factor $\mathrm{e}^{\mathrm{i}\phi(u,v)}$ is called the *phase transfer function* (PTF).

Autocorrelation theorem can be used to relate the coherent and incoherent transfer functions. With Eq. (9.73), the optical transfer function (Eq. 12.16c) can be expressed as

$$G(u, v) = \frac{\iint_{-\infty}^{\infty} g(\xi, \eta) g^*(\xi - u, \eta - v) \, \mathrm{d}\xi \, \mathrm{d}\eta}{\iint_{-\infty}^{\infty} |g(\xi, \eta)|^2 \, \mathrm{d}\xi \, \mathrm{d}\eta}. \tag{12.18}$$

The change of variables

$$\xi \rightarrow \xi + \frac{u}{2}, \qquad \eta \rightarrow \eta + \frac{v}{2}, \tag{12.19}$$

puts the autocorrelation integral in the symmetric form

$$G(u, v) = \frac{\iint_{-\infty}^{\infty} g(\xi + \frac{u}{2}, \eta + \frac{v}{2}) g^*(\xi - \frac{u}{2}, \eta - \frac{v}{2}) \, \mathrm{d}\xi \, \mathrm{d}\eta}{\iint_{-\infty}^{\infty} |g(\xi, \eta)|^2 \, \mathrm{d}\xi \, \mathrm{d}\eta}. \tag{12.20}$$

This is the desired result connecting the coherent and incoherent transfer functions. Identifying the coherent transfer function with the lens aperture function (Eq. 12.9), Eq. (12.20) takes the form

$$G(u, v) = \frac{\iint\limits_{-\infty}^{\infty} t_{\mathrm{L}}(\xi - \frac{\lambda}{2}z_2 u, \eta - \frac{\lambda}{2}z_2 v) t_{\mathrm{L}}^*(\xi + \frac{\lambda}{2}z_2 u, \eta + \frac{\lambda}{2}z_2 v)\, \mathrm{d}\xi\, \mathrm{d}\eta}{\iint\limits_{-\infty}^{\infty} |t_L(\xi, \eta)|^2 \,\mathrm{d}\xi\, \mathrm{d}\eta}. \qquad (12.21)$$

The autocorrelation integral in the numerator represents the area of overlap of two identical but displaced apertures with centers at $(-\frac{1}{2}\lambda z_2 u, -\frac{1}{2}\lambda z_2 v)$ and $(\frac{1}{2}\lambda z_2 u, \frac{1}{2}\lambda z_2 v)$. The denominator of Eq. (12.21) gives the overlap area when the centers of the apertures coincide. The optical transfer function $G(u, v)$ possesses the following properties:

$$G(0, 0) = 1, \qquad (12.22a)$$

$$G(-u, -v) = G^*(u, v), \qquad (12.22b)$$

$$|G(u, v)| \leq |G(0, 0)|. \qquad (12.22c)$$

The last property follows from the Schwarz' inequality (page 99).

12.5 OTF OF A DIFFRACTION-LIMITED OPTICAL SYSTEM

Consider an aberration-free, centered optical system with exit pupil of unit radius and aperture function

$$\begin{aligned} t_{\mathrm{L}}(\xi, \eta) &= 1 \quad \text{for } \sqrt{\xi^2 + \eta^2} \leq 1 \\ &= 0 \quad \text{otherwise.} \end{aligned} \qquad (12.23)$$

Direct evaluation of the correlation integral in Eq. (12.21) for this aperture function is not difficult, but here we find its value from the area of overlap of the displaced apertures. From Fig. 12.2a, this displacement is

$$\begin{aligned} OO' &= [(OP)^2 + (PO')^2]^{1/2} \\ &= \lambda z_2 (u^2 + v^2)^{1/2}. \end{aligned} \qquad (12.24)$$

The displacement OO' can be in any direction in the plane of the aperture. However, without loss of generality, we take the centers of the apertures to be

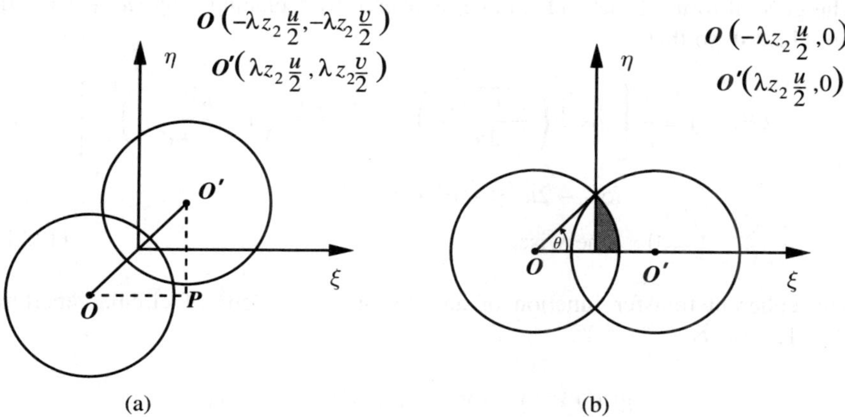

Fig. 12.2: Autocorrelation of a circular aperture. (a) Displacement in arbitrary direction. (b) Displacement along one of the axes.

displaced along the ξ-axis. The area of overlap of the displaced apertures is four times the shaded area in Fig. (12.2b), giving

$$\iint_{-\infty}^{\infty} t_{\mathrm{L}}\left(\xi - \frac{\lambda}{2}z_2 u,\, \eta - \frac{\lambda}{2}z_2 v\right) t_{\mathrm{L}}^{*}\left(\xi + \frac{\lambda}{2}z_2 u,\, \eta + \frac{\lambda}{2}z_2 v\right) \mathrm{d}\xi\, \mathrm{d}\eta$$

$$= 4\left[\frac{\theta}{2} - \frac{\lambda}{4}z_2 u\left(1 - \frac{\lambda^2}{4}z_2^2 u^2\right)^{1/2}\right]. \tag{12.25}$$

The normalization integral in the denominator of Eq. (12.21) equals π. Therefore,

$$G(u,0) = \frac{2}{\pi}\left[\cos^{-1}\left(\frac{u}{2u_0}\right) - \frac{u}{2u_0}\sqrt{1 - \left(\frac{u}{2u_0}\right)^2}\,\right] \quad \text{for } -2u_0 \le u \le 2u_0$$
$$= 0 \quad \text{otherwise}, \tag{12.26}$$

where, as defined earlier,

$$u_0 = \frac{1}{\lambda z_2} \quad \text{for } \frac{D}{2} = 1$$
$$= \frac{D/2}{\lambda z_2} \quad \text{for } \frac{D}{2} \neq 1. \tag{12.27}$$

The general form of the OTF can be recovered by replacing u by $(u^2+v^2)^{1/2}$ in Eq. (12.26), so that

$$G(u,v)=\frac{2}{\pi}\left[\cos^{-1}\left(\frac{\sqrt{u^2+v^2}}{2u_0}\right)-\frac{\sqrt{u^2+v^2}}{2u_0}\left(1-\frac{u^2+v^2}{4u_0^2}\right)^{1/2}\right]$$

$$\text{for } -2u_0\le\sqrt{u^2+v^2}\le 2u_0$$

$$=0 \quad \text{otherwise.} \tag{12.28}$$

The coherent transfer function of an aberration-free lens of circular aperture (Eq. 12.11a) is

$$g(u,v)=1 \quad \text{for } -u_0\le\sqrt{u^2+v^2}\le u_0$$

$$=0 \quad \text{otherwise.} \tag{12.29}$$

Variations of the transfer functions with spatial frequency are shown in Fig. 12.3 for an aberration-free lens of circular cross-section. The coherent transfer function maintains unit value and then abruptly falls to zero at the cutoff spatial frequencies ($\pm u_0$). The OTF, on the other hand, falls gradually from unit value at zero spatial frequency to zero at the cutoff spatial frequencies ($\pm 2u_0$). Object spatial frequencies beyond the cutoff frequencies are not transmitted by the lens. Thus, the coherent and incoherent transfer functions not only characterize an optical system in terms of its cutoff spatial frequencies, but they also quantify the performance of the optical system at any given spatial frequency.

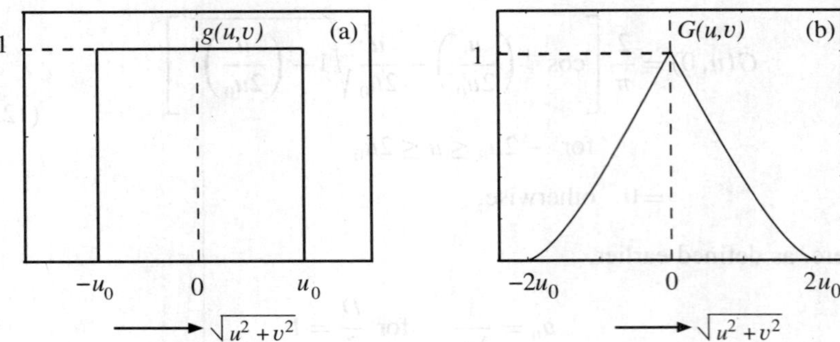

Fig. 12.3: Spatial frequency dependence of (a) coherent and (b) incoherent transfer functions for an aberration-free lens of circular cross-section.

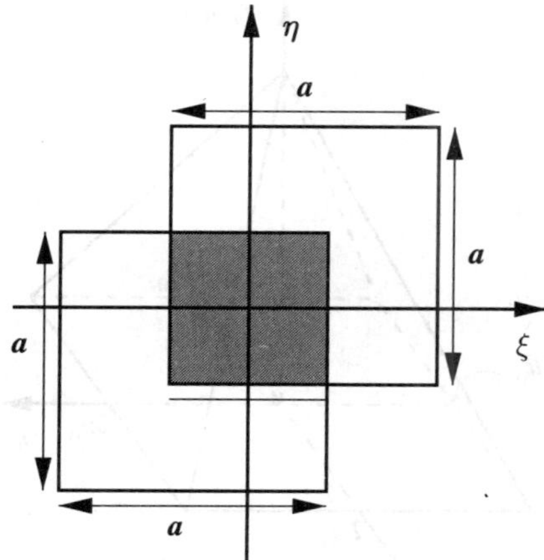

Fig. 12.4: Autocorrelation of a square aperture of sides a.

The OTF of a square aperture of sides a, obtained with reference to Fig. 12.4, is

$$\begin{aligned} G(u, v) &= \frac{(a - \lambda z_2 u)(a - \lambda z_2 v)}{a^2} \\ &= \left(1 - \frac{\lambda}{a} z_2 u\right)\left(1 - \frac{\lambda}{a} z_2 v\right) \\ &= \Lambda\left(\frac{u}{2u_0}\right)\Lambda\left(\frac{v}{2u_0}\right) \quad \text{for } |u| \leq 2u_0, |v| \leq 2u_0 \\ &= 0 \quad \text{otherwise,} \end{aligned} \tag{12.30}$$

where u_0 is the cutoff frequency for the coherent transfer function (Eq. 12.13a) and the triangle function $\Lambda(x)$ is defined as

$$\begin{aligned} \Lambda(x) &= 1 - |x| \quad \text{for } |x| \leq 1 \\ &= 0 \quad \text{otherwise.} \end{aligned} \tag{12.31}$$

The variation of the OTF of a rectangular lens is shown in Fig. 12.5. Note that in the above examples, the cutoff spatial frequencies of the incoherent transfer functions are twice as large as the corresponding cutoff frequencies of the coherent transfer functions. This should not be construed to imply that a diffraction-limited optical system always performs better under incoherent object illumination. This need not be the case. In fact, juxtapositioning the plots in Fig. (12.3a,b) for coherent and incoherent transfer functions can mislead the reader. It should be kept in mind that

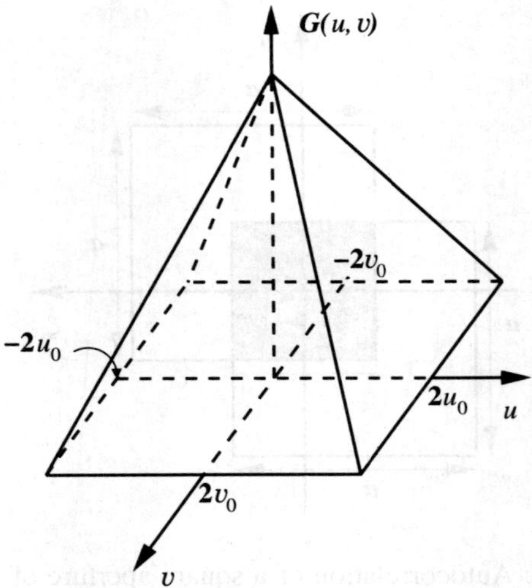

Fig. 12.5: Incoherent transfer function of a lens of rectangular cross-section.

the coherent transfer function $g(u, v)$ represents the transfer characteristics of the amplitude distribution, whereas the incoherent transfer function $G(u, v)$ refers to the transfer characteristics of the intensity distribution, and hence a direct comparison between the two transfer functions makes no sense at all. Instead, we should compare the frequency spectra of the image intensity distributions in the two cases.

The frequency spectrum of the intensity distribution in the image plane under incoherent object illumination can be obtained by taking the Fourier transform of Eq. (12.14), giving

$$\begin{aligned}\mathcal{F}[I_\mathrm{i}^\mathrm{incoh}(x'', y'')] &= \mathcal{F}[I'_\mathrm{o} * |h'|^2] \\ &= \mathcal{F}[I'_\mathrm{o}]\mathcal{F}[|h'|^2] \\ &= \left(\frac{1}{2}\epsilon_0 c\right) \mathcal{F}[E'_\mathrm{o}E'^*_\mathrm{o}]\mathcal{F}[h'h'^*],\end{aligned} \tag{12.32}$$

where $\mathcal{F}$ symbolizes the Fourier transform operation. With the autocorrelation theorem (Eq. 9.73), this result can be expressed as

$$\begin{aligned}\mathcal{F}[I_\mathrm{i}^\mathrm{incoh}(x'', y'')] &= \left(\frac{1}{2}\epsilon_0 c\right) \{\mathcal{F}[E'_\mathrm{o}] \star \mathcal{F}^*[E'_\mathrm{o}]\} \{\mathcal{F}[h'] \star \mathcal{F}^*[h']\} \\ &= \left(\frac{1}{2}\epsilon_0 c\right) \{\mathcal{E}_\mathrm{o}(u, v) \star \mathcal{E}^*_\mathrm{o}(u, v)\} \{g(u, v) \star g^*(u, v)\}\},\end{aligned} \tag{12.33}$$

where $\mathcal{E}_o(u, v)$ and $g(u, v)$ are the Fourier transforms of the object field distribution $E'_o(\tilde{x}, \tilde{y})$ and the impulse response function $h'(x'', y'')$, respectively. The spatial frequency spectrum of the image intensity distribution for coherent object illumination can be obtained by re-writing Eq. (12.1b) as

$$\begin{aligned} E^{\text{coh}}(x'', y'') &= E'_o(x'', y'') * h'(x'', y'') \\ &= E'_o * h'. \end{aligned} \tag{12.34}$$

Therefore,

$$\begin{aligned} \mathcal{F}[I^{\text{coh}}(x'', y'')] &= \left(\frac{1}{2}\epsilon_0 c\right) \mathcal{F}\left[(E'_o * h')(E'_o * h')^*\right] \\ &= \left(\frac{1}{2}\epsilon_0 c\right) \mathcal{F}[E'_o * h'] \star \mathcal{F}^*[E'_o * h'] \\ &= \left(\frac{1}{2}\epsilon_0 c\right) \{\mathcal{F}[E'_o]\mathcal{F}[h']\} \star \{\mathcal{F}[E'_o]\mathcal{F}[h']\}^* \\ &= \left(\frac{1}{2}\epsilon_0 c\right) [\mathcal{E}_o(u, v) g(u, v)] \star [\mathcal{E}_o(u, v) g(u, v)]^* . \end{aligned} \tag{12.35}$$

The spatial frequency spectra of the image intensity distributions under incoherent and coherent object illuminations are indeed quite different. One needs to take specific examples to appreciate this difference. This task is left to problems (Problem 12.3). We merely state here that the quality of optical imaging under coherent and incoherent object illuminations depends critically on how the intensity and phase change over the object. Depending upon the system constraints, one of the imaging schemes may be preferred over the other.

12.6 TRANSFER FUNCTIONS OF ABERRATED OPTICAL SYSTEMS

We have so far considered transfer functions of aberration-free optical systems. The aberrations may produce additional changes in the amplitudes and phases of the spatial frequencies passing through the optical system. However, if the aberrations are not too severe, the changes in the amplitude may be of lesser concern. We consider here aberrations which primarily introduce phase modifications. The effect of the aberrations can be incorporated through the modified exit pupil function:

$$P(x_s, y_t) = t_P(x_s, y_t) e^{i \frac{2\pi}{\lambda} W(x_s, y_t)}, \tag{12.36}$$

where $t_{\rm P}(x_{\rm s}, y_{\rm t})$ is the pupil function in the absence of aberrations and $W(x_{\rm s}, y_{\rm t})$ is the aberration function (Eq. 5.3), expressed in the sagittal ($x_{\rm s}$) and tangential ($y_{\rm t}$) coordinates (Fig. 5.7). We have replaced the (ξ, η) coordinates by $(x_{\rm s}, y_{\rm t})$ coordinates since the geometrical aberrations are best described in these variables. We may continue to assume

$$\begin{aligned} t_{\rm P}(x_{\rm s}, y_{\rm t}) &= 1 \quad \text{within the extent of the exit pupil} \\ &= 0 \quad \text{otherwise.} \end{aligned} \tag{12.37}$$

The coherent transfer function of an aberrated optical system is obtained by substituting Eq. (12.36) into Eq. (12.9b), giving

$$g(u, v) = t_{\rm P}(-\lambda z_2 u, -\lambda z_2 v) e^{i\frac{2\pi}{\lambda}W(-\lambda z_2 u, -\lambda z_2 v)} \tag{12.38a}$$

$$= t_{\rm P}\left(-\frac{u}{u_0}, -\frac{v}{v_0}\right) e^{i\frac{2\pi}{\lambda}W(-\frac{u}{u_0}, -\frac{v}{v_0})}, \tag{12.38b}$$

where the cutoff spatial frequencies u_0, v_0 are defined in the manner of Eq. (12.27). The corresponding incoherent transfer function can be obtained by combining Eqs (12.20) and (12.38). For real aberration function $W(x_{\rm s}, y_{\rm t})$, the incoherent transfer function for an aberrated optical system takes the form

$$G_{ab}(u, v) = \frac{1}{t_0}\Bigg[\iint_{-\infty}^{\infty} t_{\rm P}\left(x_{\rm s} + \frac{u}{2u_0}, y_{\rm t} + \frac{v}{2v_0}\right) t_{\rm P}\left(x_{\rm s} - \frac{u}{2u_0}, y_{\rm t} - \frac{v}{2v_0}\right) \times e^{i\frac{2\pi}{\lambda}\left\{W\left(x_{\rm s}+\frac{u}{2u_0}, y_{\rm t}+\frac{v}{2v_0}\right) - W\left(x_{\rm s}-\frac{u}{2u_0}, y_{\rm t}-\frac{v}{2v_0}\right)\right\}} \mathrm{d}x_{\rm s}\, \mathrm{d}y_{\rm t}\Bigg], \tag{12.39}$$

where

$$t_0 = \iint_{-\infty}^{\infty} |t_{\rm P}(x_{\rm s}, y_{\rm t})|^2 \,\mathrm{d}x_{\rm s}\,\mathrm{d}y_{\rm t}. \tag{12.40}$$

Schwarz' inequality requires the MTF (magnitude of $G_{ab}(u, v)$) of an aberrated optical system to be always less than the MTF of a diffraction-limited optical system, i.e.,

$$|G_{ab}(u, v)| < |G(u, v)|_{\text{diff.limited}}, \tag{12.41}$$

except at the zero spatial frequency where MTF has unit value by definition and at the cutoff spatial frequency where MTF has zero value in both cases. It may also happen that the MTF of an aberrated optical system goes through zero value more than once before vanishing completely at and beyond the cutoff spatial frequency.

12.6.1 OTF of a Defocused Optical System

Defocusing is really not an aberration (see Section 5.4.2), but for the present demonstration we treat it so. As this example will show, finding the OTF in the presence of aberrations is not an easy task. Let the image plane of a centered, aberration-free optical system be somewhat defocused. Assuming

$$t_P(x_s, y_t) = 1$$

for the exit pupil of unit radius, Eq. (12.39) reduces to

$$G(u, v) = \frac{\iint_{OR} e^{\frac{i2\pi}{\lambda}[W(x_s+\frac{u}{2u_0}, y_t+\frac{v}{2v_0})-W(x_s-\frac{u}{2u_0}, y_t-\frac{v}{2v_0})]}\mathrm{d}x_s\,\mathrm{d}y_t}{\iint_{OR} 1\mathrm{d}x_s\,\mathrm{d}y_t}, \tag{12.42}$$

where OR in the limits stands for the overlap region. The defocusing aberration function, obtained from Eqs (5.3) and (11.16b), is

$$\begin{aligned} W(x_s, y_t) &= {}_0C_{20}(x_s^2 + y_t^2) \\ &= \frac{1}{2}\left(\frac{1}{z_1} + \frac{1}{z_2} - \frac{1}{f}\right)(x_s^2 + y_t^2). \end{aligned} \tag{12.43}$$

To simplify calculation, let the aperture be displaced along the x_s-direction (Fig. 12.2b). Accordingly,

$$\begin{aligned} G(u,0) &= \frac{1}{\pi}\iint_{OR} e^{i\frac{4\pi}{\lambda}{}_0C_{20}\frac{u}{u_0}x_s}\,\mathrm{d}x_s\,\mathrm{d}y_t \\ &= \frac{1}{\pi}\left[\iint_{OR} \cos(bx_s)\mathrm{d}x_s\,\mathrm{d}y_t + i\iint_{OR} \sin(bx_s)\mathrm{d}x_s\,\mathrm{d}y_t\right], \end{aligned} \tag{12.44}$$

where $b = \frac{4\pi}{\lambda}{}_0C_{20}\frac{u}{u_0}$. By symmetry, the second integral vanishes and

$$G(u,0) = \frac{4}{\pi}\iint_{\Delta} \cos(bx_s)\mathrm{d}x_s\,\mathrm{d}y_t, \tag{12.45}$$

where Δ represents the area of the shaded region in Fig. 12.2b. On the curved boundary of the shaded region (Fig. 12.2b), the condition

$$\left(x_s + \frac{u}{2u_0}\right)^2 + y_t^2 = 1 \qquad (12.46)$$

holds. Integrating Eq. (12.45) over x_s from $x_s = 0$ to $x_s = \sqrt{1 - y_t^2} - \frac{u}{2u_0}$, we obtain

$$G(u, 0) = \frac{4}{\pi b} \int_0^{\sqrt{1-(\frac{u}{2u_0})^2}} \sin\left[b\left(\sqrt{1 - y_t^2} - \frac{u}{2u_0}\right)\right] \mathrm{d}y_t. \qquad (12.47)$$

The optical transfer function $G(u, 0)$ is real, but not necessarily positive. Analytical evaluation of integral (12.47) in terms of the Bessel functions can be tried, but such integrals are best handled numerically. Figure 12.6 shows the results of numerical integration of Eq. (12.47). In this figure, the OTF is

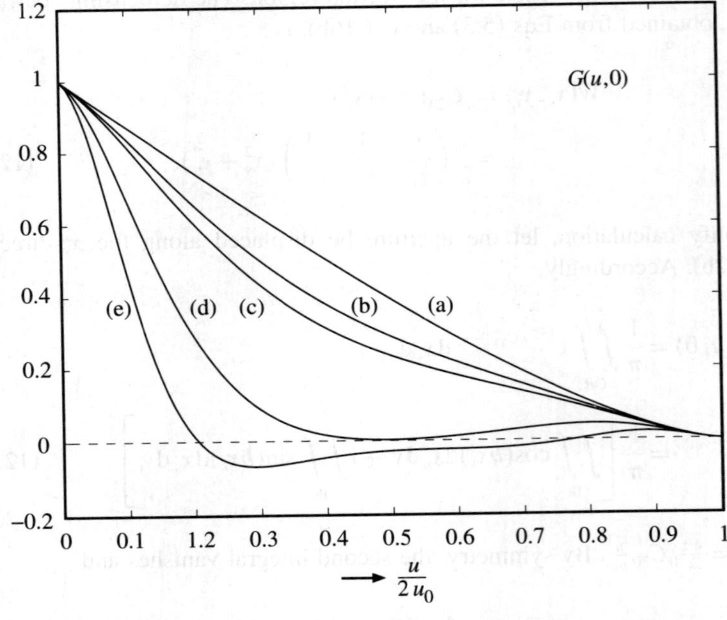

Fig. 12.6: OTF of a defocused diffraction-limited optical system for ${}_0C_{20} = 0$ (a), $\frac{\lambda}{4}$(b), $\frac{\lambda}{\pi}$(c), $\frac{2\lambda}{\pi}$(d), $\frac{3\lambda}{\pi}$(e).

plotted as a function of the normalized spatial frequency $(u/2u_0)$ for various values of the defocusing parameter ${}_0C_{20}$, expressed as multiples of λ/π. We have specifically included a plot for ${}_0C_{20} = \lambda/4$, which corresponds to the Rayleigh criterion for satisfactory performance of an optical imaging system. As the figure shows, the OTF of a defocused optical system indeed falls below the OTF of a focused optical system $({}_0C_{20} = 0)$ without any change in the maximum spatial frequency transmitted by the system. For defocusing aberration with ${}_0C_{20} = \frac{2\lambda}{\pi}$, the OTF falls to zero at nearly half the cutoff spatial frequency. For higher values of the defocusing parameter, the OTF changes sign for certain ranges of spatial frequencies. The negative OTF corresponds to a phase modification of exactly π radians, leading to reversal of the image contrast. Under these conditions, the bright portions of the object appear dark and vice versa. This is an example of spurious resolution.

In conclusion, the determination of the OTF begins with the knowledge of the exit pupil function of the optical system. Equation (12.36) gives the exit pupil function of an optical system when aberrations introduce only phase modifications. The exact exit pupil function may be obtained by interferometric techniques or by ray tracing. Once the exit pupil function is known, the OTF is obtained as the autocorrelation of the exit pupil function (Eq. 12.21) or as the Fourier transform of the square modulus of the impulse response function (Eq. 12.16c).

12.7 IMAGING SINUSOIDAL OBJECT MODULATION

We now show that the intensity distribution in the image plane of an optical system is sinusoidal for a sinusoidal intensity distribution in the object plane, albeit with modified amplitude and shifted phase. Let the intensity distribution of an incoherently illuminated object be described by a single spatial frequency along some general direction in the object plane (Fig. 12.7). This distribution can be equivalently described by the spatial frequencies u_0 and v_0 along the x' and y' axes, respectively, i.e.,

$$I_{\mathrm{o}}(x', y') = I_0[1 + a\cos 2\pi(u_0x' + v_0y')], \tag{12.48}$$

where I_0 and a are real constants. It is assumed that the spatial frequencies u_0 and v_0 do not exceed the corresponding cutoff spatial frequencies of the optical system. With $|a| < 1$, $I_{\mathrm{o}}(x', y')$ takes only non-negative values. For unit magnification, the intensity distribution in the image plane, given by Eq. (12.14a), is

$$I_{\mathrm{i}}(x'', y'') = \iint\limits_{-\infty}^{\infty} I_0[1 + a\cos 2\pi(u_0x' + v_0y')]|h'(x'' - x', y'' - y')|^2 \mathrm{d}x'\,\mathrm{d}y'. \tag{12.49}$$

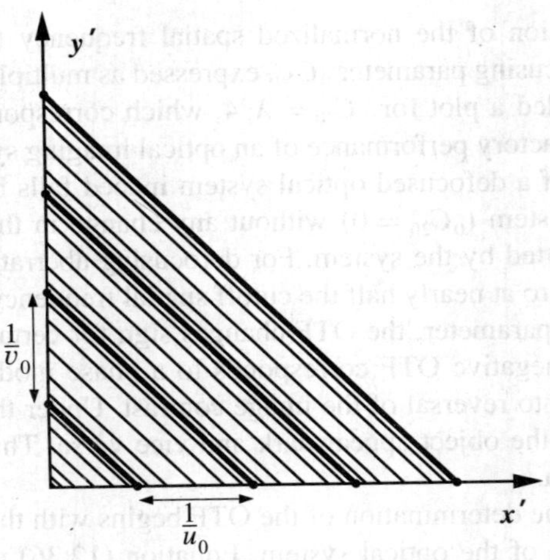

Fig. 12.7: Two-dimensional sinusoidal intensity distribution.

For the paraxial image with unit magnification, $x' = x''_0$, $y' = y''_0$. We can therefore replace the object intensity distribution in Eq. (12.49) by the paraxial image intensity distribution

$$I_{\mathrm{p}}(x''_0, y''_0) = I_0[1 + a\cos 2\pi(u_0 x''_0 + v_0 y''_0)]. \tag{12.50}$$

This equation does not describe the intensity distribution in the image plane (it will do so only in the limit of geometrical optics). Here, it is no more than a convenient representation for the object intensity distribution. With this conceptual manipulation, the integration over the object plane in Eq. (12.49) can be replaced by integration over the image plane, so that

$$I_{\mathrm{i}}(x'', y'') = \int\limits_{-\infty}^{\infty}\!\!\int I_0[1 + a\cos 2\pi(u_0 x''_0 + v_0 y''_0)] \times |h'(x'' - x''_0, y'' - y''_0)|^2 \mathrm{d}x''_0\, \mathrm{d}y''_0. \tag{12.51}$$

Application of the convolution theorem to Eq. (12.51) gives

$$F^0_{\mathrm{i}}(u, v) = I_0 \mathcal{F}[1 + a\cos 2\pi(u_0 x''_0 + v_0 y''_0)]G^0(u, v) \tag{12.52a}$$

$$= I_0\left[\delta(u)\delta(v) + \frac{a}{2}\{\delta(u - u_0)\delta(v - v_0) + \delta(u + u_0)\delta(v + v_0)\}\right] G^0(u, v). \tag{12.52b}$$

Standard results of the Fourier transform theory have been used to go from Eq. (12.52a) to (12.52b). $F_i^0(u, v)$ is the Fourier transform of the image intensity distribution (Eq. 12.16b without the denominator) and $G^0(u, v)$ is the Fourier transform of the square modulus of the impulse response function (Eq. 12.16c without the denominator). The intensity distribution in the image plane is the inverse Fourier transform of Eq. (12.52b). Therefore,

$$
\begin{aligned}
I_i(x'', y'') &= I_0 \iint_{-\infty}^{\infty} [\delta(u)\delta(v) + \frac{a}{2}\{\delta(u-u_0)\delta(v-v_0) \\
&\quad + \delta(u+u_0)\delta(v+v_0)\}] G^0(u, v) e^{i2\pi(ux''+vy'')}\, du\, dv \\
&= I_0[G^0(0,0) + \frac{a}{2}\{G^0(u_0, v_0) e^{i2\pi(u_0x''+v_0y'')} \\
&\quad + G^0(-u_0, -v_0) e^{-i2\pi(u_0x''+v_0y'')}\}] \\
&= I_0[G^0(0,0) + a|G^0(u_0, v_0)| \cos 2\pi\{u_0x'' + v_0y'' \\
&\quad + \phi(u_0, v_0)\}] \\
&= I_0[1 + a|G(u_0, v_0)| \cos 2\pi\{u_0x'' + v_0y'' + \phi(u_0, v_0)\}], \qquad (12.53)
\end{aligned}
$$

where we have used

$$G^0(-u_0, -v_0) = [G^0(u_0, v_0)]^* \qquad (12.54a)$$

and

$$G^0(u_0, v_0) = |G^0(u_0, v_0)| e^{i2\pi\phi(u_0, v_0)}. \qquad (12.54b)$$

The constant factor $G^0(0, 0)$ has been absorbed in I_0 in Eq. (12.53). We note that the image intensity distribution is indeed described by the spatial frequencies of the object intensity distribution, but with modified amplitude and phase. For unit magnification, as in the present example, there is one-to-one correspondence between the object and image spatial frequencies. We also note that defining the contrast of an intensity distribution as

$$m = \frac{I_{max} - I_{min}}{I_{max} + I_{min}},$$

the ratio of the contrasts of the image and object intensity distributions is the magnitude of the optical transfer function; hence the name modulation transfer function given to $|G(u, v)|$.

12.8 MEASUREMENT OF OTF

The measurement of the OTF of an optical system is a tedious task, beset with several practical problems: precise centering of the optical elements is one, the necessity of employing a large number of sinusoidal gratings to cover a reasonable span of spatial frequencies is another, and so on. Here, we give only the rudiments of the experimental techniques used to determine the OTF of optical systems. Figure 12.8 shows the basic setup, consisting of a sinusoidal grating (SG) illuminated uniformly but incoherently, the optical system to be tested, a long and narrow slit (S) oriented parallel to the grating edge and placed in the image plane, and a photodiode (PD) kept just behind the slit.

The image intensity distribution can be recorded by uniformly translating the slit, along with the photo-diode, parallel to itself. For improved resolution, the slit should be narrow. To reduce the problem to one dimension, the long edges of the grating and slit are assumed sufficiently long. The intensity distribution (Eq. 12.49) in the image plane is then given by

$$I(x'') = I_0 \int_{-\infty}^{+\infty} (1 + a\cos 2\pi u_0 x')|h'(x'' - x')|^2 \,\mathrm{d}x', \tag{12.55}$$

where a and u_0 are, respectively, the amplitude and spatial frequency of the sinusoidal grating and $|h'(x'' - x')|^2$ is the line spread, and not the point spread function of the optical system. As shown in Section 12.7, the image intensity distribution (Eq. 12.53) can be written as

$$I(x'') = I_0[1 + |G(u_0)|a\cos 2\pi\{u_0 x'' + \phi(u_0)\}], \tag{12.56}$$

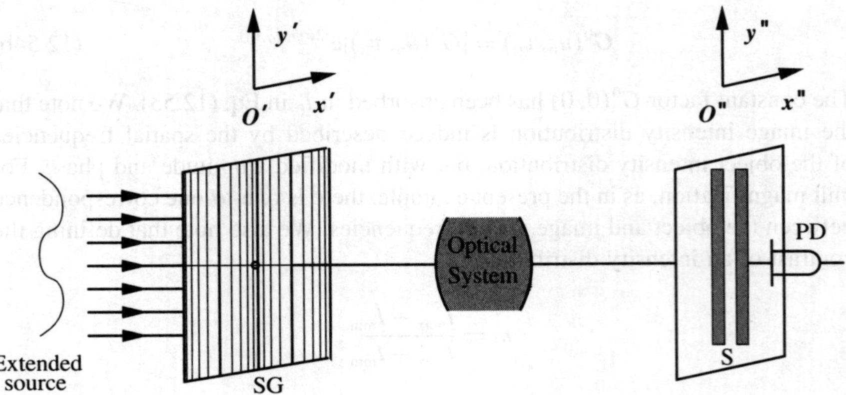

Fig. 12.8: Experimental setup to obtain OTF of an optical system; SG is a sinusoidal grating, S is narrow slit, PD is photodetector.

where $|G(u_0)|$ is the MTF of the optical system and $2\pi\phi(u_0)$ is the phase change at the spatial frequency u_0. The intensity distribution recorded by the photodiode is the convolution of the image intensity distribution (Eq. 12.56) with the line spread function $S(x''_D - x'')$ of the slit, i.e.,

$$I(x''_D) = I_0 \int_{-\infty}^{+\infty} [1 + |G(u_0)| a \cos 2\pi\{u_0 x'' + \phi(u_0)\}] S(x''_D - x'')\, dx'', \quad (12.57)$$

where x''_D is the displacement of the slit from the origin of the coordinate system in the image plane. Following the treatment of Section 12.7, the intensity distribution recorded by the photodiode can be shown to have the form

$$I(x'') = I_0[1 + |G_s(u_0)||G(u_0)| a \cos 2\pi\{u_0 x'' + \phi(u_0) + \phi'(u_0)\}], \quad (12.58)$$

where $|G_s(u_0)|$ is the MTF of the slit and $2\pi\phi'(u_0)$ is the phase change, if any, introduced by the slit alone at the spatial frequency u_0. The product of the MTF of the optical system and that of the slit can be obtained by dividing the amplitude of the recorded intensity distribution in the image plane by the amplitude of the intensity distribution in the object plane. The slit MTF can be obtained in a separate measurement without the optical system in position. The same measurement yields $\phi'(u_0)$ also. It will be necessary to use sinusoidal gratings with varying spatial frequencies to fully characterize the image-forming quality of an optical system.

12.9 REFERENCES

12.1 Joseph W. Goodman, Introduction to Fourier Optics, McGraw-Hill, New York, 1968.

12.2 S. H. Lee in Optical Information Processing–Fundamentals, Ed. S. H. Lee, Topics in Applied Physics, **48**, Springer-Verlag, Berlin, 1981.

12.3 K. Lizuka, Engineering Optics, Optical Sciences, Springer-Verlag, Berlin, 1985.

12.4 Charles S. Williams and Orville A. Becklund, Introduction to the Optical Transfer Function, John Wiley & Sons, New York, 1989.

12.10 PROBLEMS

12.1 Consider a diffraction-limited image-forming setup consisting of a lens of aperture diameter 5 cm and focal length 10 cm. The object placed 15 cm in front of the lens is illuminated by 632.8 nm light from a He–Ne laser. Find the highest resolvable spatial frequencies in the object and image field distributions.

12.2 Find the optical transfer function $G(u, 0)$ of a diffraction-limited optical system with exit pupil in the form of a square of sides a with its central portion blocked by a symmetrically placed opaque square screen of sides $\frac{a}{4}$ (Fig. 12.9). Sketch $G(u, 0)$ as a function of u.

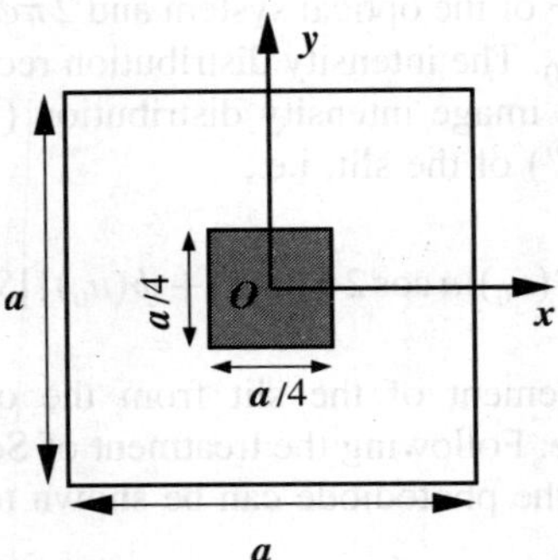

Fig. 12.9.

12.3 Using Eqs (12.33) and (12.35), obtain the spatial frequency spectra of the image intensity distributions under coherent and incoherent illuminations of the following object field distributions. The optical system is diffraction-limited with coherent cutoff spatial frequency of 1500 cycles/cm.

(a) $E_o(x', y') = \cos 2\pi v_0 x'$; $v_0 = 1000$ cycles/cm,
(b) $E_o(x', y') = |\cos 2\pi v_0 x'|$; $v_0 = 1000$ cycles/cm,
(c) $E_o(x', y') = \frac{1}{2}(1 + \cos 2\pi v_0 x')$; $v_0 = 1000$ cycles/cm.

Show that the coherent illumination performs better in case (a) and poorer in case (b). Comment on the quality of the images produced by the coherent and incoherent illuminations in case (c).

12.4 In Problem 12.3 (a,b,c), what maximum values of the coherent cutoff spatial frequencies will lead to uniform illumination in the image plane. Your answer must cover coherent and incoherent object illuminations.

12.5 An optical system produces the intensity distribution

$$I(x'', y'') = I_0\left(1 + 0.4\cos 2\pi\left(v_0 x'' + \frac{1}{6}\right)\right)$$

in the image plane when the object intensity distribution is

$$I(x', y') = I_0\left(1 + 0.7\cos 2\pi\left(v_0 x' - \frac{1}{6}\right)\right).$$

Find the modulation transfer function (MTF), the phase transfer function (PTF), and the optical transfer function (OTF) at the spatial frequency v_0.

12.6 Obtain and sketch numerical solutions of Eq. (12.47) when the defocusing parameter has values: ${}_0C_{20} = \frac{\lambda}{4}, \frac{2}{\pi}\lambda$.

12.7 Find the OTF of a defocused optical system with exit pupil of square cross-section.

12.8 Find the optical transfer functions $G(u, 0)$ and $G(0, v)$ of a diffraction-limited optical system with exit pupil having two clear square apertures as shown in Fig. 12.10. Each square is of sides a and the distance between the centers of the squares is $3a$. Sketch $G(u, 0)$ and $G(0, v)$.

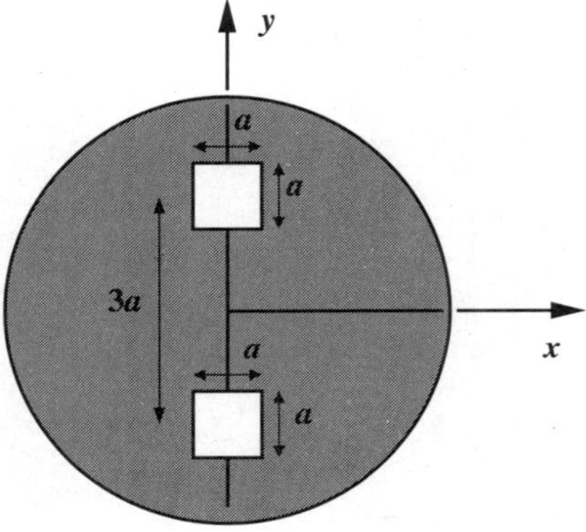

Fig. 12.10.

12.9 Do Problem 12.8 if each of the squares is replaced by a circle of diameter a. The distance between the centers of the circles remains $3a$.

12.10 Let the object transparency of Problem 12.3a be coherently illuminated by a plane wave of wavelength 500 nm propagating in the $x'z$ plane at an angle θ to the z-axis as shown in Fig. 12.11. Find the maximum value angle θ can have and still intensity variations can be observed in the image plane.

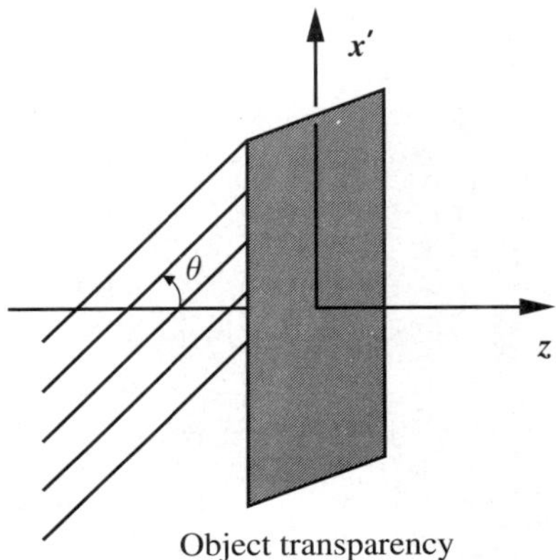

Fig. 12.11.

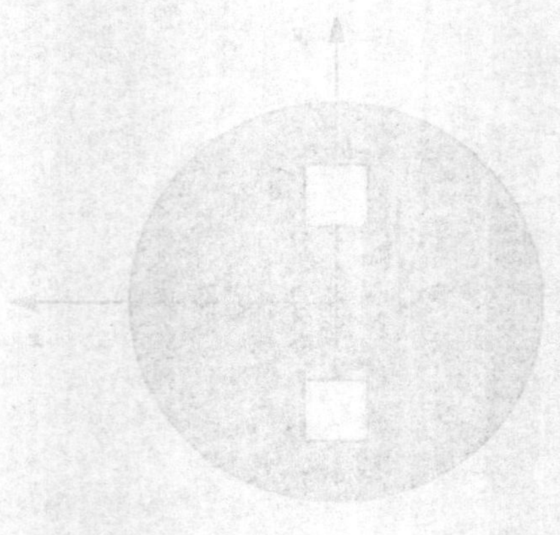

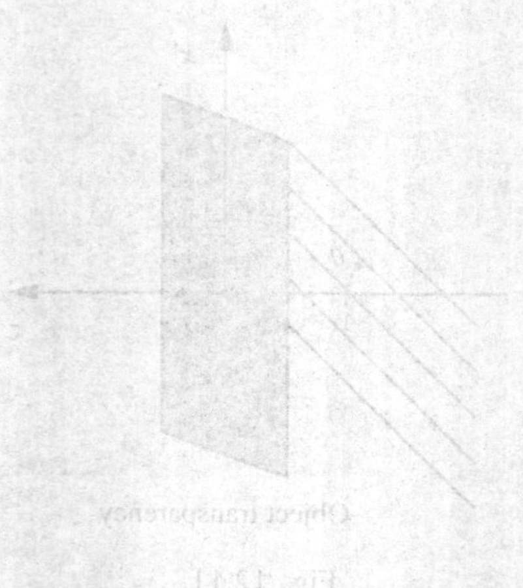

CHAPTER 13

Holography

13.1 INTRODUCTION

Image formation of two-dimensional (2D) objects was discussed in Chapter 11. A sharp and bright image of a 2D object can be recorded on a photographic film kept in the conjugate plane of an aberration-free lens. Imaging 3D objects poses problems. Ideally, the plane of the film can be conjugate to only one transverse plane of a 3D object. Rays from a given point on this plane reach the conjugate point in the plane of the film in phase (recall Fermat's principle). This holds for all points on this object plane, irrespective of the object illumination being coherent or incoherent. The image of this plane is therefore sharp and bright. Rays emanating from a point lying on any plane other than object plane form a defocused image of that point in the plane of the film. The optical path lengths of these rays are unequal. The phase information of a 3D object contained in the optical path lengths of the rays arriving from different planes of the object is therefore lost, and only the intensity distribution of the 3D object gets recorded in the film. This results in the loss of the depth perception in an ordinary photograph of a 3D object. Unlike the film, the eyes see a 3D object as a 3D object through parallax.

Nevertheless, it is possible to record the phase and amplitude distributions of a coherently illuminated 3D object in a single plane if light diffracted by the 3D object is made to interfere with a coherent reference wave in that plane. This is exactly what is done in the lens-less imaging process called holography, invented by Gabor in 1948. Holography, meaning 'whole writing' in Greek, reproduces the amplitude and phase distributions of a coherently illuminated 3D object in its image. In the absence of a lens, there is no unique pair of conjugate planes in this imaging scheme. The depth perception is therefore not lost in holographic imaging. Holography is a two-step process. In the first step, called hologram recording, the amplitude and phase distributions of the object field are recorded on a high-contrast photographic film in the form of a stable interference pattern produced by the object wave and a coherent reference wave. The object wave is the light diffracted by the object when illuminated coherently and the

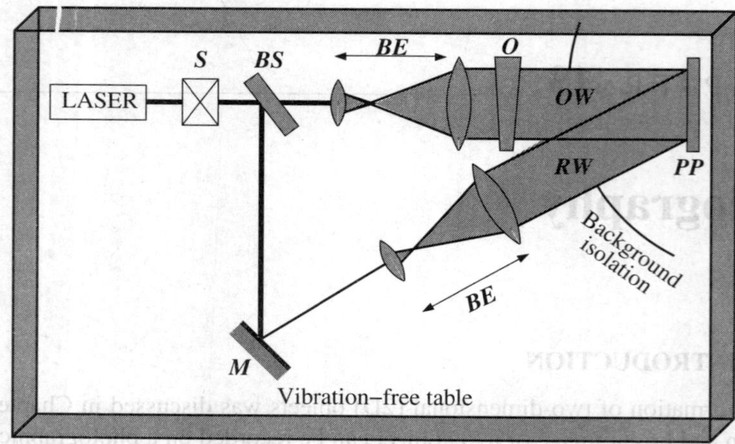

Fig. 13.1: Typical setup for recording an off-axis hologram; *S* shutter, *BS* beam splitter, *BE* beam expander, *O* object, *OW* object wave, *M* mirror, *RW* reference wave, *PP* photographic plate.

reference wave is usually a quasi-monochromatic plane or spherical wave. The entire holographic apparatus is mounted on a vibration-free table to secure a stable interference pattern (Fig. 13.1).

No optical component in a holographic setup should move with respect to any other component by more than a fraction of the wavelength of light. The developed film (negative or positive) is called the hologoram. It does not carry the image of the object, but carries a permanent signature of the object in the form of an intricate interference pattern. A hologram can be envisioned as a diffraction grating with a highly complex transmission profile. In the second step of holographic imaging, called wavefront reconstruction, the hologram when illuminated with the reconstruction wave, preferably the same as the reference wave (or its spatial phase conjugate wave) used in the first step, reconstructs the original wavefront diffracted by the object during the recording of the hologram. Actually, the hologram generates not only the original diverging object wavefront, but also its spatial complex conjugate. From the term original, it is implied that this reconstructed wavefront resembles in all respects the diverging wavefront originating from the object during the recording of the hologram. This wavefront therefore gives rise to a virtual image at the original position of the object if the geometries of the recording and reconstruction processes are identical, except that the object is absent during the reconstruction. The reconstructed conjugate wavefront is converging and forms a real image of the object.

A theoretical framework which can describe hologram recording and wavefront reconstruction has already been introduced in the context of complex filters in Section 11.3.3. But even at the risk of some repetition, we take the traditional route to develop the subject matter ab initio, primarily to expose the reader to the problems and solutions of practical holography. Our treatment of holography will closely follow Yu's presentation [13.1]. Actually, Gabor was not initially interested in 3D imaging, but once he succeeded in recording a hologram, he realized the significance of his invention. His original aim, at the time of undertaking this investigation, to improve the electron microscope images through wavefront reconstruction, however, remained unrealized. Gabor was handicapped due to the non-availability of good coherent light sources at that time. He faced difficulty in isolating the real and virtual reconstructed images. Development of coherent light sources in the form of lasers and their introduction to holography by Leith and Upatnicks has made holography relevant today in diverse fields of human activity.

13.2 ON-AXIS HOLOGRAPHY

To understand the simultaneous appearance of real and virtual images in holography, we take an approach which is closer to our usual notion of image formation with lenses.

13.2.1 Hologram Recording

For simplicity, we first consider the recording of a hologram of a point object. An extended object can be regarded as a collection of point objects. Let the point object O be situated on the axis of the photographic plate at a distance z_1 from it (Fig. 13.2a). The reference wave is a monochromatic plane wave $R(A_2, k_1)$, incident normally on the photographic plate.

The spherical wave emitted by the point object interferes with the reference wave everywhere, in particular, in the plane of the photographic plate. It is obvious but may still be pointed out that unlike in the image plane of a lens, light from the point object (and also from an extended object) in holography reaches every point of the photographic plate. Consequently, every portion of the hologram acquires complete information on the amplitude and phase distributions of the object field in the form of an interference pattern. This seems to introduce a great deal of redundancy in holographic imaging, but the images reconstructed from a hologram of large size are brighter and possess higher resolution. The arrangement of Fig. 13.2a is somewhat similar to the one originally employed by Gabor to record a hologram (Fig. 13.2b). He used an optical filter and a pin-hole to improve coherence of his light source. Gabor used a small semi-transparent

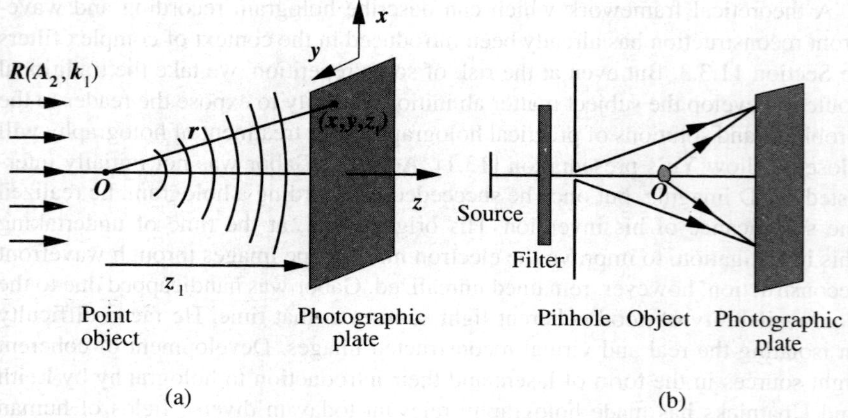

Fig. 13.2: (a) On-axis hologram recording of a point object with a plane reference wave. (b) Gabor's arrangement, O is a semi-transparent object.

object. Light transmitted by the object acts as the reference wave and light diffracted by the object constitutes the object wave.

Suppressing the time dependence, the complex scalar field distribution in the plane of the photographic plate in Fig. 13.2a is

$$E(x, y, z_1) = \frac{A_1}{r} e^{ik_1 r} + A_2 e^{ik_1 z_1}, \tag{13.1}$$

where A_1 is the amplitude of the object wave at unit distance from the point object and A_2 is the amplitude of the reference wave. For a stable interference pattern, no temporal changes in any of the variables in Eq. (13.1) can be permitted during the recording of the hologram, and hence the use of vibration-free tables in holography. Random changes, of the order of the wavelength of light, in the path lengths of the interfering waves may destroy the interference pattern altogether. Within the quadratic approximation

$$r = z_1 + \frac{x^2 + y^2}{2z_1}, \tag{13.2}$$

the field and intensity distributions over the photographic plate can be expressed as

$$E(x, y, z_1) = \frac{A_1}{z_1} e^{ik_1\left(z_1 + \frac{x^2+y^2}{2z_1}\right)} + A_2 e^{ik_1 z_1} \tag{13.3}$$

and

$$I(x, y, z_1) = \left(\frac{1}{2}\epsilon_0 c\right)\left[\frac{|A_1|^2}{z_1^2} + |A_2|^2 + \frac{A_1 A_2^*}{z_1} e^{\frac{ik_1}{2z_1}(x^2+y^2)} + \frac{A_1^* A_2}{z_1} e^{\frac{-ik_1}{2z_1}(x^2+y^2)}\right] \tag{13.4a}$$

$$= \left(\frac{1}{2}\epsilon_0 c\right)\left[\frac{|A_1|^2}{z_1^2} + |A_2|^2 + 2\frac{|A_1||A_2|}{z_1} \times \cos\left\{\frac{k_1}{2z_1}(x^2+y^2) + \phi_0\right\}\right], \tag{13.4b}$$

respectively, where ϕ_0 is the constant phase difference between the two waves. Without introducing any significant discrepancy, the amplitude factor $\frac{1}{r}$ of the spherical wave has been replaced by $\frac{1}{z_1}$. This intensity distribution is, indeed, dependent on the phases with which the light waves from the object arrive at different points of the photographic plate. The interference pattern created in the plane of the photographic plate consists of circular fringes which are not equally spaced. The fringes tend to crowd together as one moves away from the center of the photographic plate.

The film exposure is given by the product $(I\Delta t)$, where Δt is the time for which the film is exposed and I is the intensity distribution over the film during recording. The holographic film must have high resolving capability to record rapid (spatial) intensity variations of the interference pattern, especially towards the edges of the hologram. The grain size of these films is small, requiring relatively long exposure times, unless the source is a powerful one, as for example a pulsed laser. The film exposure can be optimized to obtain the amplitude transmittance of the hologram varying linearly with the intensity during exposure. The bias irradiance level (see Fig. 11.12) is provided by the relatively stronger reference wave in comparison to the object wave. After development, the photographic plate becomes the hologram with amplitude transmittance

$$T(x, y, z_1) = T_0 - \alpha I \Delta t$$

$$= A_0 + B_0\, e^{\frac{ik_1}{2z_1}(x^2+y^2)} + B_0^*\, e^{-\frac{ik_1}{2z_1}(x^2+y^2)} \tag{13.5a}$$

$$= A_0 + 2|B_0| \cos\left\{\frac{k_1}{2z_1}(x^2+y^2) + \phi_0\right\}, \tag{13.5b}$$

where

$$A_0 = A + B\left(\frac{|A_1|^2}{z_1^2} + |A_2|^2\right), \tag{13.6a}$$

$$B_0 = B\frac{A_1 A_2^*}{z_1}. \tag{13.6b}$$

The constants A and B are dependent on the actual conditions of hologram recording and characteristics of the photographic film; B is positive if positive transparency is used as the hologram. The first term of Eq. (13.5a) suggests the hologram acting as a semi-transparent plate, attenuating the wave passing through it. The remaining two terms make the hologram mimic the actions of concave and convex lenses (Eq. 10.17), each of focal length z_1. No wonder, the hologram generates simultaneously the real and virtual images of the point object. Note that for another point object, a distance z_2 in front of the photographic plate during recording, the same hologram will also act as concave and convex lenses, each of focal length z_2. Thus a hologram can be envisioned as a collection of many lenses, built into one with as many focal lengths, capable of producing sharp and bright images of 3D objects. Within this interpretation, a hologram can be regarded as a Fresnel zone plate (Section 8.4) with positive and negative lensing actions and also acting as an attenuator. Equation (13.5b), on the other hand, allows the hologram to be interpreted as a sinusoidal grating, which upon coherent illumination generates two diffraction orders in addition to the zero order (see Section 10.7).

A hologram acts as a 2D hologram when the thickness of the emulsion layer in the photographic plate is smaller than the separation between consecutive fringes of the interference pattern established in the photographic plate. For the present, this condition is assumed to hold.

13.2.2 Wavefront Reconstruction

To reconstruct the object wavefront, the hologram recorded in Fig. 13.2a is trans-illuminated with a plane coherent wave of amplitude E_0 and wave number $\left(k_2 = \frac{2\pi}{\lambda_2}\right)$ which may be different from the wave number of the wave used in making the hologram (Fig. 13.3). The location of the point object during the recording of the hologram is also shown (point O in the plane $z = 0$) for reference.

From Eq. (11.11), the field distribution in a plane, a distance z_2 behind the hologram, can be expressed as the convolution of the field distribution just

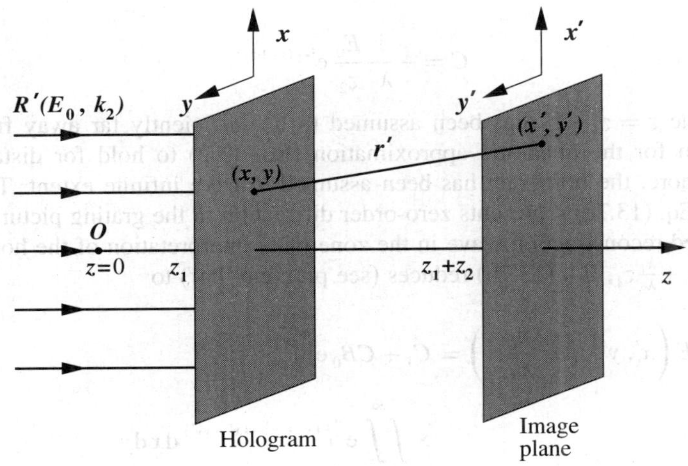

Fig. 13.3: Wavefront reconstruction with a plane reference wave. The object O at $z = 0$ is shown only for reference.

behind the hologram with the impulse response function of the space between the planes $z = z_1$ and $z = z_1 + z_2$, i.e.,

$$E(x', y', z_1 + z_2) = -\frac{\mathrm{i}}{\lambda_2} E_0 \frac{\mathrm{e}^{\mathrm{i}k_2(z_1+z_2)}}{z_2} T(x', y', z_1) * h_{z_2}(x', y') \tag{13.7a}$$

$$\begin{aligned} &= C \iint_{-\infty}^{\infty} T(x, y, z_1)\, \mathrm{e}^{\frac{\mathrm{i}k_2}{2z_2}[(x'-x)^2+(y'-y)^2]}\, \mathrm{d}x\, \mathrm{d}y \\ &= CA_0 \iint_{-\infty}^{\infty} \mathrm{e}^{\frac{\mathrm{i}k_2}{2z_2}[(x'-x)^2+(y'-y)^2]}\, \mathrm{d}x\, \mathrm{d}y \\ &\quad + CB_0\, \mathrm{e}^{\frac{\mathrm{i}k_2}{2z_2}(x'^2+y'^2)} \iint_{-\infty}^{\infty} \mathrm{e}^{\frac{\mathrm{i}}{2}\left(\frac{k_1}{z_1}+\frac{k_2}{z_2}\right)(x^2+y^2)} \\ &\quad \times \mathrm{e}^{-\mathrm{i}\frac{k_2}{z_2}(xx'+yy')}\, \mathrm{d}x\, \mathrm{d}y \\ &\quad + CB_0^*\, \mathrm{e}^{\frac{\mathrm{i}k_2}{2z_2}(x'^2+y'^2)} \iint_{-\infty}^{\infty} \mathrm{e}^{\frac{\mathrm{i}}{2}\left(-\frac{k_1}{z_1}+\frac{k_2}{z_2}\right)(x^2+y^2)} \\ &\quad \times \mathrm{e}^{-\mathrm{i}\frac{k_2}{z_2}(xx'+yy')}\, \mathrm{d}x\, \mathrm{d}y, \end{aligned} \tag{13.7b}$$

where

$$C = -\frac{\mathrm{i}}{\lambda_2}\frac{E_0}{z_2}\,\mathrm{e}^{\mathrm{i}k_2(z_1+z_2)}. \tag{13.8}$$

The plane $z = z_1 + z_2$ has been assumed to be sufficiently far away from the hologram for the quadratic approximation (Eq. 13.2) to hold for distance r'. Furthermore, the hologram has been assumed to have infinite extent. The first term in Eq. (13.7b) represents zero-order diffraction in the grating picture or the attenuated reconstruction wave in the zone plate interpretation of the hologram. For $z_2 = +\frac{\lambda_1}{\lambda_2}z_1$, Eq. (13.7b) reduces (see problem 9.4f) to

$$\begin{aligned} E\left(x', y', z_1 + \frac{\lambda_1}{\lambda_2}z_1\right) &= C_1 + CB_0\,\mathrm{e}^{\frac{ik_1}{2z_1}(x'^2+y'^2)} \\ &\quad\times \iint\limits_{-\infty}^{\infty} \mathrm{e}^{\frac{ik_1}{z_1}(x^2+y^2-xx'-yy')}\,\mathrm{d}x\,\mathrm{d}y \\ &\quad + CB_0^*\,\mathrm{e}^{\frac{ik_1}{2z_1}(x'^2+y'^2)} \iint\limits_{-\infty}^{\infty} \mathrm{e}^{-\frac{ik_1}{z_1}(xx'+yy')}\,\mathrm{d}x\,\mathrm{d}y \\ &= C_1 + C_2\,\mathrm{e}^{\frac{ik_1}{4z_1}(x'^2+y'^2)} + C_3\delta(x', y'), \end{aligned} \tag{13.9}$$

where C_1, C_2, and C_3 are complex constants. The delta function (third term) in Eq. (13.9) gives rise to a real on-axis image of an on-axis point object, a distance $\frac{\lambda_1}{\lambda_2}z_1$ behind the hologram, where z_1 is the distance of the object from the photographic plate during recording. The real image will be exactly a distance z_1 behind the hologram if the recording and reconstruction wavelengths are same. The second term in Eq. (13.9) represents, within the paraxial approximation, a diverging spherical wave originating from the on-axis virtual image lying in front of the hologram. This is borne out by the fact that the middle term of Eq. (13.7b) reduces to a constant times the delta function $\delta(x', y')$ for $z_2 = -\frac{\lambda_1}{\lambda_2}z_1$. Figure 13.4 shows the real image, the virtual image, and the transmitted reconstruction wave generated by an on-axis recorded hologram.

Since the line joining the real and virtual images is collinear with the axis of the hologram, seeing either image without the background of the other image and that of the transmitted reconstruction wave is not possible. In the grating interpretation, the three diffraction orders overlap in on-axis holography. On-axis holographic imaging is therefore not very useful. Nevertheless, it finds application in viewing point scatterers such as the aerosol particles (see Problem 13.1). The reconstructed images can be separated from each other and from the coherent background of the reconstruction wave if the hologram is recorded with an off-axis reference wave. But, before we discuss the off-axis holography, we

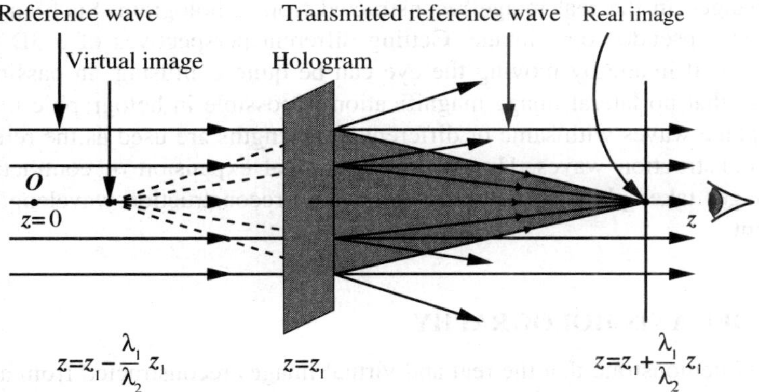

Fig. 13.4: Reconstructed virtual and real images from an on-axis recorded hologram.

comment on the nature of the holographic images. Figure 13.5 shows four points A, B, C, D, lying on an extended object. The reconstructed virtual images of these points are coincident with their respective object points if same reference wave is used in hologram recording and wavefront reconstruction. The virtual image is therefore normal or orthoscopic. The relative positions of different parts of an orthoscopic image are similar to those found in the actual 3D object. The reconstructed real images A', B', C', D' lie behind the hologram. Viewed from behind the real image, object point A is behind and object point C is in front of the object points B and D. The virtual image obviously maintains these relative orientations. On the other hand, in the real image, point A' is seen in front and point C' is seen behind the points B' and D'. Therefore, the back of a 3D object seen in the real holographic image appears in front and vice versa, i.e., the object appears inside out. Similarly, the right–left directions of the object are also

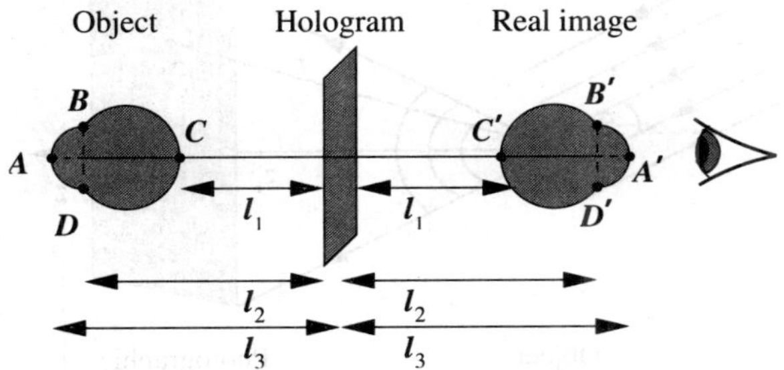

Fig. 13.5: Holographic real image of an extended object is pseudoscopic.

interchanged in the real image reconstructed from a hologram. Such an image is called a pseudoscopic image. Getting different perspectives of a 3D object from its real image by moving the eye can be quite confusing. In passing, we mention that no lateral image magnification is possible in holographic imaging when plane waves with same or different wavelengths are used as the reference and reconstruction waves. However, longitudinal expansion or contraction of the images takes place when the reference and reconstruction wavelengths are different.

13.3 OFF-AXIS HOLOGRAPHY

We now demonstrate that the real and virtual images reconstructed from a hologram recorded with an oblique reference wave can be separated. For the present discussion, same reference wave is employed for hologram recording and wavefront reconstruction. In Fig. 13.6, the reference wave makes an angle $(-\theta)$ with the axis of the photographic plate.

The field and intensity distributions in the plane of the photographic plate are

$$E(x, y, z_1) = \frac{A_1}{z_1} e^{ik\left(z_1 + \frac{x^2+y^2}{2z_1}\right)} + A_2 e^{ik(z_1 \cos\theta - x \sin\theta)}, \tag{13.10}$$

$$I(x, y, z_1) = \left(\frac{1}{2}\epsilon_0 c\right)\left[\frac{|A_1|^2}{z_1} + |A_2|^2 + \frac{A_1 A_2^*}{z_1} e^{ikz_1(1-\cos\theta)} e^{ik\left(\frac{x^2+y^2}{2z_1} + x\sin\theta\right)} + \frac{A_1^* A_2}{z_1} e^{-ikz_1(1-\cos\theta)} e^{-ik\left(\frac{x^2+y^2}{2z_1} + x\sin\theta\right)}\right], \tag{13.11}$$

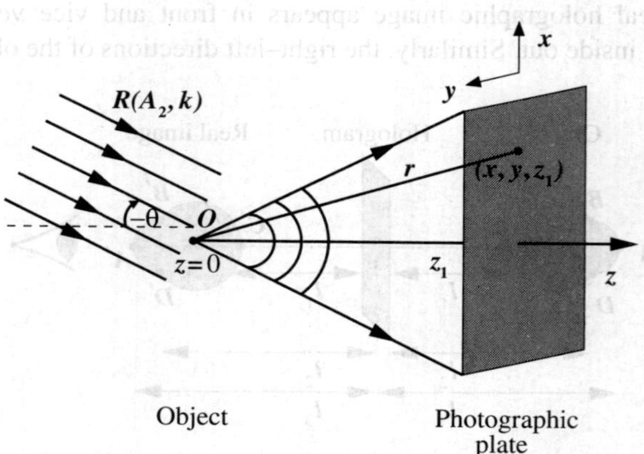

Fig. 13.6: Hologram recording with an off-axis reference wave.

respectively, where A_1 is the amplitude at unit distance of the spherical wave originating from the point object O and A_2 is the amplitude of the plane reference wave. Equation (13.5a) for the amplitude transmittance of the hologram now takes the form

$$T(x, y, z_1) = A_0 + B_1 \mathrm{e}^{\mathrm{i}k\left(\frac{x^2+y^2}{2z_1}+x\sin\theta\right)} + B_1^* \mathrm{e}^{-\mathrm{i}k\left(\frac{x^2+y^2}{2z_1}+x\sin\theta\right)}, \qquad (13.12)$$

where

$$B_1 = \frac{A_1 A_2^*}{z_1} B \mathrm{e}^{\mathrm{i}kz_1(1-\cos\theta)}. \qquad (13.13)$$

On reconstructing the wavefront with the same reference wave (Fig. 13.7), the field distributions in the plane of the hologram and in a plane a distance z_2 behind the hologram are

$$E(x, y, z_1) = E_0 \mathrm{e}^{\mathrm{i}k(z_1\cos\theta - x\sin\theta)} T(x, y) \qquad (13.14)$$

and

$$\begin{aligned} E(x', y', z_1+z_2) &= -\frac{\mathrm{i}}{\lambda}\frac{\mathrm{e}^{\mathrm{i}kz_2}}{z_2} E(x', y', z_1) * h_{z_2}(x', y') \\ &= -\frac{\mathrm{i}}{\lambda}\frac{\mathrm{e}^{\mathrm{i}kz_2}}{z_2} \int\!\!\int_{-\infty}^{\infty} E(x, y, z_1) \mathrm{e}^{\frac{\mathrm{i}k}{2z_2}\left[(x'-x)^2+(y'-y)^2\right]} \mathrm{d}x\,\mathrm{d}y, \end{aligned} \qquad (13.15)$$

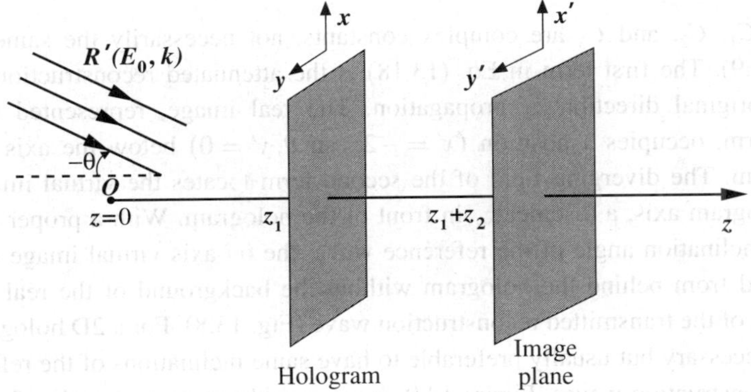

Fig. 13.7: Wavefront reconstruction with an oblique reconstruction wave.

respectively. Substituting Eqs (13.12) and (13.14) into Eq. (13.15), we obtain

$$\begin{aligned} E(x', y', z_1+z_2) &= CA_0 \iint_{-\infty}^{\infty} e^{\frac{ik}{2z_2}\left[(x'-x)^2-2z_2 x\sin\theta+(y'-y)^2\right]}\mathrm{d}x\,\mathrm{d}y \\ &+ CB_1 \iint_{-\infty}^{\infty} e^{\frac{ik}{2z_1}\left[x^2+y^2+\frac{z_1}{z_2}\{(x'-x)^2+(y'-y)^2\}\right]}\mathrm{d}x\,\mathrm{d}y \\ &+ CB_1^* \int_{-\infty}^{+\infty} e^{-\frac{ik}{2z_1}\left[x^2+4z_1 x\sin\theta-\frac{z_1}{z_2}(x'-x)^2\right]}\mathrm{d}x \\ &\times \int_{-\infty}^{+\infty} e^{-\frac{ik}{2z_1}\left[y^2-\frac{z_1}{z_2}(y'-y)^2\right]}\mathrm{d}y, \end{aligned} \tag{13.16}$$

where

$$C = -\frac{\mathrm{i}}{\lambda}E_0\frac{e^{ik(z_1\cos\theta+z_2)}}{z_2}. \tag{13.17}$$

After a few algebraic manipulations, the integrals in Eq. (13.16) can be solved, giving the field distribution in the plane a distance z_1 behind the hologram as

$$E(x', y', 2z_1) = C_1 e^{-ikx'\sin\theta} + C_2 e^{\frac{ik}{4z_1}(x'^2+y'^2)} + C_3\delta(x'+2z_1\sin\theta, y'), \tag{13.18}$$

where C_1, C_2, and C_3 are complex constants, not necessarily the same as in Eq. (13.9). The first term in Eq. (13.18) is the attenuated reconstruction wave in its original direction of propagation. The real image, represented by the third term, occupies a position ($x' = -2z_1\sin\theta$, $y' = 0$) below the axis of the hologram. The diverging field of the second term locates the virtual image on the hologram axis, a distance z_1 in front of the hologram. With a proper choice of the inclination angle of the reference wave, the on-axis virtual image can be observed from behind the hologram without the background of the real image and that of the transmitted reconstruction wave (Fig. 13.8). For a 2D hologram, it is not necessary but usually preferable to have same inclinations of the reference and reconstruction waves. Figure 13.9 shows wavefront reconstruction from the same hologram with a reconstruction wave making an angle $(+\theta)$ with the axis

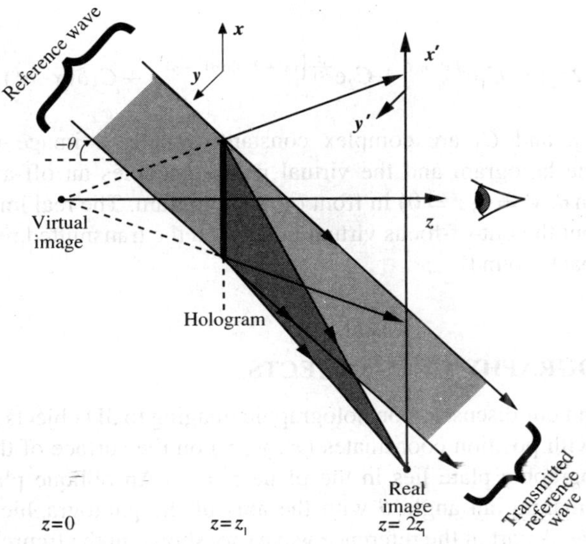

Fig. 13.8: Reconstructed images from an off-axis recorded hologram. Inclinations of the reference and reconstruction waves are same.

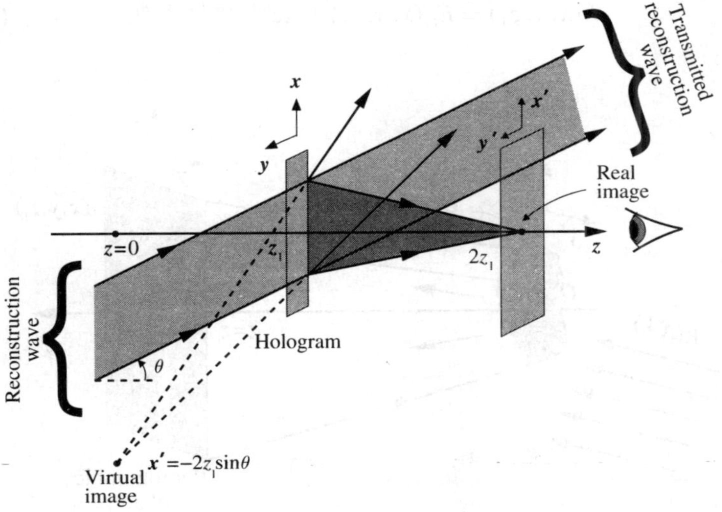

Fig. 13.9: Reconstructed images with a reconstruction wave at $(+\theta)$ from a hologram recorded with a reference wave at $(-\theta)$.

of the hologram. In this case, the field distribution in the plane $z = 2z_1$ has the form

$$E(x', y', 2z_1) = C_1 e^{ikx' \sin\theta} + C_2 e^{\frac{ik}{4z_1}\left[(x'+2z\sin\theta)^2 + y'^2\right]} + C_3 \delta(x', y'), \qquad (13.19)$$

where C_1, C_2, and C_3 are complex constants. The real image now lies on the axis of the hologram and the virtual image occupies an off-axial position ($x' = -2z_1 \sin\theta$, $y' = 0$, $z = 0$) in front of the hologram. The real image can now be seen without the out-of-focus virtual image and the transmitted reconstruction wave in the background.

13.4 HOLOGRAPHY OF 3D OBJECTS

We now extend our discussion on holographic imaging to 3D objects (Fig. 13.10). Q is a point with position coordinates (x', y', z') on the surface of the 3D object O. The photographic plate lies in the plane $z = z_1$. An oblique plane wave of amplitude A making an angle θ with the axis of the photographic plate is the reference wave. A part of the reference wave (not shown in the figure) illuminates the object O.

The field distribution in the plane of the photographic plate is

$$E(x, y, z_1) = E_O(x, y, z_1) + Ae^{ik(z_1 \cos\theta + x \sin\theta)}, \qquad (13.20)$$

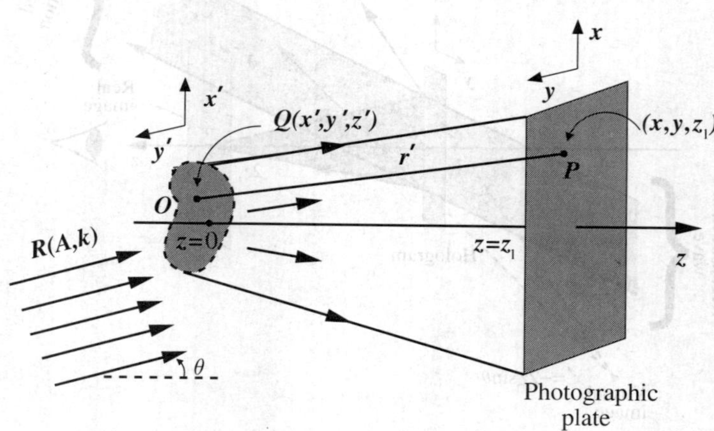

Fig. 13.10: Hologram recording of a 3D object with a plane reference wave $R(A, k)$.

where the object wave $E_O(x, y, z_1)$ arriving at the photographic plate can be expressed as the convolution of the field distribution $E_O(x', y', z')$ on the surface of the object with the impulse response function of the space between the object and the photographic plate (Eq. 11.11), i.e.,

$$E_O(x, y, z_1) = -\frac{\mathrm{i}}{\lambda}\frac{\mathrm{e}^{ikz_1}}{z_1}\iint_{S_O} E_O(x', y', z')\mathrm{e}^{\frac{ik}{2(z_1-z')}\left[(x-x')^2+(y-y')^2\right]}\mathrm{d}S'. \quad (13.21)$$

The integration is over the surface of the object as seen from the photographic plate. Ignoring the factor $(\frac{1}{2}\epsilon_0 c)$, the intensity distribution in the plane of the photographic plate is

$$\begin{aligned} I(x, y, z_1) = {} & |A|^2 + |E_O(x, y, z_1)|^2 + A^*\mathrm{e}^{-ik(z_1\cos\theta + x\sin\theta)} \\ & \times E_O(x, y, z_1) + A\mathrm{e}^{ik(z_1\cos\theta + x\sin\theta)}E_O^*(x, y, z_1). \end{aligned} \quad (13.22)$$

After developing the photographic film, the amplitude transmittance of the hologram, assuming linearity of the T–E plot, is

$$\begin{aligned} T(x, y, z_1) = {} & A_0 + B_0|E_O(x, y, z_1)|^2 + B_1\mathrm{e}^{-ikx\sin\theta} \\ & \times E_O(x, y, z_1) + B_1^*\mathrm{e}^{ikx\sin\theta}E_O^*(x, y, z_1), \end{aligned} \quad (13.23)$$

where A_0, B_0, and B_1 are suitable constants. Upon illumination of the hologram with the same reference wave as used in the recording (Fig. 13.11), the field distributions appearing in planes just behind and a distance z_2 behind the hologram are

$$E(x, y, z_1) = A\mathrm{e}^{ik(z_1\cos\theta + x\sin\theta)}T(x, y, z_1) \quad (13.24)$$

and

$$\begin{aligned} E(x'', y'', z_1 + z_2) = {} & -\frac{\mathrm{i}}{\lambda}\frac{\mathrm{e}^{ikz_2}}{z_2}A\,\mathrm{e}^{ik(z_1\cos\theta + x\sin\theta)} \\ & \times T(x'', y'', z_1) * h_{z_2}(x'', y'') \end{aligned} \quad (13.25a)$$

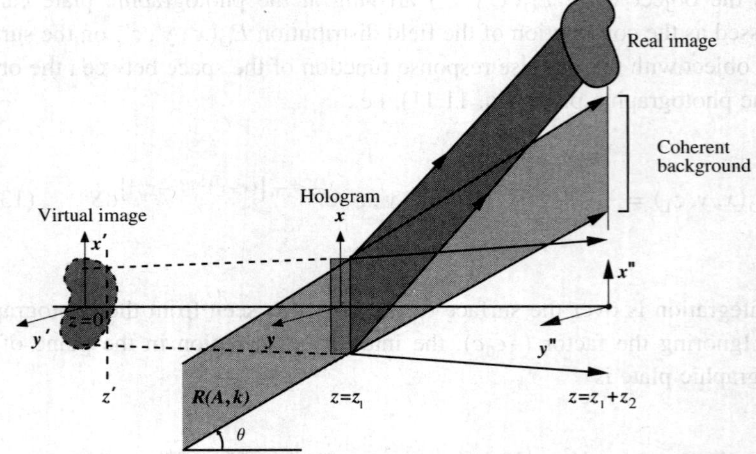

Fig. 13.11: Image reconstruction of a 3D object. Reference and reconstruction waves are identical.

$$
\begin{aligned}
&= A_0' \int\!\!\int_{-\infty}^{\infty} \mathrm{e}^{\frac{ik}{2z_2}[(x''-x)^2+(y''-y)^2+2z_2 x \sin\theta]} \mathrm{d}x\,\mathrm{d}y \\
&\quad + B_0' \int\!\!\int_{-\infty}^{\infty} |E_{\mathrm{O}}(x,y,z_1)|^2 \\
&\qquad \times \mathrm{e}^{\frac{ik}{2z_2}[(x''-x)^2+(y''-y)^2+2z_2 x \sin\theta]} \mathrm{d}x\,\mathrm{d}y \\
&\quad + B_1' \int\!\!\int_{-\infty}^{\infty} E_{\mathrm{O}}(x,y,z_1) \mathrm{e}^{\frac{ik}{2z_2}[(x''-x)^2+(y''-y)^2]} \mathrm{d}x\,\mathrm{d}y \\
&\quad + B_1'^{*} \int\!\!\int_{-\infty}^{\infty} E_{\mathrm{O}}^{*}(x,y,z_1) \\
&\qquad \times \mathrm{e}^{\frac{ik}{2z_2}[(x''-x)^2+(y''-y)^2+4z_2 x \sin\theta]} \mathrm{d}x\,\mathrm{d}y,
\end{aligned}
\tag{13.25b}
$$

respectively, where A_0', B_0', and B_1' are suitably chosen complex constants. The first term in Eq. (13.25b) is the transmitted reconstruction wave in its original direction of propagation. The second term also represents zero-order diffraction since $|E_{\mathrm{O}}(x, y, z_1)|^2$ is real, though somewhat spread out. We now show that the third term generates the virtual image. Substitution of Eq. (13.21) into the third term of Eq. (13.25b) gives

$$E_v(x'', y'', z_1 + z_2) = -\frac{\mathrm{i}}{\lambda}\frac{\mathrm{e}^{ikz_1}}{z_1} B_1' \mathrm{e}^{\frac{ik}{2z_2}(x''^2 + y''^2)} \int\int_{-\infty}^{\infty} E_O(x', y', z')$$
$$\times \mathrm{e}^{\frac{ik}{2(z_1 - z')}(x'^2 + y'^2)} \left[\int\int_{-\infty}^{\infty} \mathrm{e}^{\frac{ik}{2}\left(\frac{1}{z_1 - z'} + \frac{1}{z_2}\right)(x^2 + y^2)} \right. \tag{13.26}$$
$$\left. \times \mathrm{e}^{-ik\left[x\left(\frac{x'}{z_1 - z'} + \frac{x''}{z_2}\right) + y\left(\frac{y'}{z_1 - z'} + \frac{y''}{z_2}\right)\right]} \mathrm{d}x\, \mathrm{d}y \right] \mathrm{d}x'\, \mathrm{d}y'.$$

We have replaced integration over the surface of the object by integration over the transverse planes of the object in succession. We have also let the limits of integration in the object plane to extend from $-\infty$ to $+\infty$. For $z_2 = -(z_1 - z')$, i.e., in the plane $z = z'$, Eq. (13.26) reduces to

$$E_v(x'', y'', z') = C_2 E_O(x'' = x', y'' = y', z = z'), \tag{13.27}$$

where C_2 is a complex constant. Thus, apart from a complex constant multiplier, the virtual image reproduces the field distribution of each plane of the object. Similarly, the fourth term in Eq. (13.25b) can be shown to generate the real image of the object plane $z = z'$ at a distance $z_1 - z'$ behind the hologram with the field distribution

$$E_r(x'', y'', 2z_1 - z') = C_3 E_O^*(x'' = x' + 2(z_1 - z')\sin\theta, y'' = y', z = 2z_1 - z') \tag{13.28}$$

where C_3 is a complex constant. The real image of the object is centered about the off-axial point $(x'' = 2(z_1 - z')\sin\theta, y'' = 0, z = 2z_1)$. Thus, looking from behind the hologram, a virtual 3D image of the object can be seen in the exact location of the original object without any background. Had we used a different wavelength for reconstruction, the virtual image would be somewhat shifted from the position of the object. For the reconstruction wave making an angle $(-\theta)$ with the axis of the hologram (as in Fig. 13.8), the real image with field distribution

$$E_r(x'', y'', 2z_1 - z') = C_3' E_O^*(x'' = x', y'' = y', z = 2z_1 - z') \tag{13.29}$$

occupies an axial position behind the hologram and the virtual image moves to an off-axial position. The real image appears at the original position of the object if the reconstruction wave is the phase conjugate of the reference wave used in the recording of the hologram (Fig. 13.12). The phase conjugate of a plane

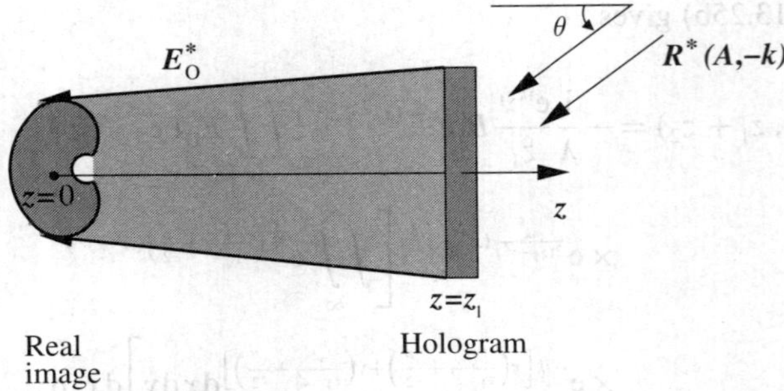

Fig. 13.12: Reconstruction of the real image with the conjugate of the reference wave used in recording.

reference wave is identical to the reference wave, except that its direction of propagation is reversed ($\vec{k} \to -\vec{k}$). We note that the reconstructed real images (Eqs 13.28 and 13.29) do not exactly reproduce the object field distribution, but a distribution which is the complex conjugate of the spatial part of the object field distribution. For this reason, the reconstructed real image is also called the conjugate image. We mention in passing that in the reconstruction process, a hologram can produce the wave $E^*(x, y, z)$ which is the phase conjugate of the original wave $E(x, y, z)$. The phase conjugate waves have some interesting properties (see Section 14.6).

13.5 MAGNIFICATION IN HOLOGRAPHIC IMAGING

Holographic images generated with plane reference and reconstruction waves have unit lateral magnifications (see Eqs 13.27 and 13.29). Spherical reference and reconstruction waves, on the other hand, can produce image magnifications in holography. This may be of interest in the microscopy of small biological samples. A magnified 3D image of a microorganism can be frozen for later examination. We now consider hologram recording and reconstruction with spherical waves. Let the reference point $P_R(x_2, y_2, z_2)$ in Fig. 13.13 act as the source of the spherical reference wave for recording the hologram of the point object $P_O(x_1, y_1, z_1)$. Points P_O and P_R are coherently illuminated with a wave of wave number $k_1 = \frac{2\pi}{\lambda}$. The field distribution in the plane of the photographic plate, within the quadratic approximation, is given by

$$E(x, y, z_0) = \frac{A_1}{l_1} e^{ik_1\left[l_1 + \frac{(x-x_1)^2+(y-y_1)^2}{2l_1}\right]} + \frac{A_2}{l_2} e^{ik_1\left[l_2 + \frac{(x-x_2)^2+(y-y_2)^2}{2l_2}\right]} \tag{13.30}$$

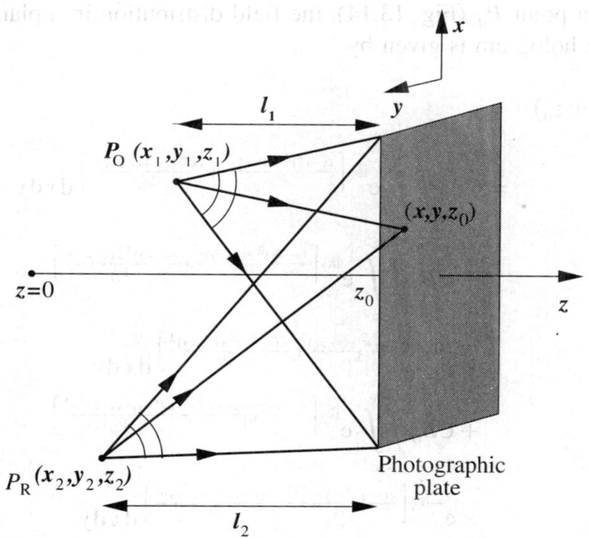

Fig. 13.13: Recording hologram of a point object with spherical reference wave.

and the corresponding intensity distribution in units of $\left(\frac{1}{2}\epsilon_0 c\right)$ is

$$\begin{aligned}I(x, y, z_0) &= \frac{|A_1|^2}{l_1^2} + \frac{|A_2|^2}{l_2^2} + \frac{A_1 A_2^*}{l_1 l_2}\, e^{ik_1(l_1 - l_2)} \\ &\quad \times e^{ik_1\left[\frac{(x-x_1)^2+(y-y_1)^2}{2l_1} - \frac{(x-x_2)^2+(y-y_2)^2}{2l_2}\right]} \\ &\quad + \frac{A_1^* A_2}{l_1 l_2}\, e^{-ik_1\left[(l_1-l_2)+\frac{(x-x_1)^2+(y-y_1)^2}{2l_1} - \frac{(x-x_2)^2+(y-y_2)^2}{2l_2}\right]},\end{aligned} \tag{13.31}$$

where $l_1 = z_0 - z_1$, $l_2 = z_0 - z_2$, and A_1 and A_2 are the complex amplitudes of the object and reference waves at unit distances from P_O and P_R, respectively. After development of the photographic plate, the linear amplitude transmittance of the hologram can be expressed as

$$\begin{aligned}T(x, y, z_0) &= A_0 + B_0\, e^{ik_1\left[\frac{(x-x_1)^2+(y-y_1)^2}{2l_1} - \frac{(x-x_2)^2+(y-y_2)^2}{2l_2}\right]} \\ &\quad + B_0^*\, e^{-ik_1\left[\frac{(x-x_1)^2+(y-y_1)^2}{2l_1} - \frac{(x-x_2)^2+(y-y_2)^2}{2l_2}\right]},\end{aligned} \tag{13.32}$$

where A_0 and B_0 are suitable constants. On illuminating the hologram with the spherical wave of wave number k_2 and amplitude A_3 at unit distance from the reconstruction point P'_R (Fig. 13.14), the field distribution in a plane a distance z'_0 behind the hologram is given by

$$
\begin{aligned}
&E(x'', y'', z_0+z'_0)\\
&\quad = CA_0 \iint_{-\infty}^{\infty} e^{ik_2\left[\frac{(x-x_3)^2+(y-y_3)^2}{2l_3}+\frac{(x''-x)^2+(y''-y)^2}{2z'_0}\right]} \mathrm{d}x\,\mathrm{d}y\\
&\quad + CB_0 \iint_{-\infty}^{\infty} e^{ik_2\left[\frac{(x-x_3)^2+(y-y_3)^2}{2l_3}+\frac{(x''-x)^2+(y''-y)^2}{2z'_0}\right]}\\
&\quad \times e^{ik_1\left[\frac{(x-x_1)^2+(y-y_1)^2}{2l_1}-\frac{(x-x_2)^2+(y-y_2)^2}{2l_2}\right]} \mathrm{d}x\,\mathrm{d}y\\
&\quad + CB_0^* \iint_{-\infty}^{\infty} e^{ik_2\left[\frac{(x-x_3)^2+(y-y_3)^2}{2l_3}+\frac{(x''-x)^2+(y''-y)^2}{2z'_0}\right]}\\
&\quad \times e^{-ik_1\left[\frac{(x-x_1)^2+(y-y_1)^2}{2l_1}-\frac{(x-x_2)^2+(y-y_2)^2}{2l_2}\right]} \mathrm{d}x\,\mathrm{d}y
\end{aligned}
\tag{13.33a}
$$

$$
\begin{aligned}
&= CA_0\, e^{ik_2\left[\frac{x_3^2+y_3^2}{2l_3}+\frac{x''^2+y''^2}{2z'_0}\right]}\\
&\times \iint_{-\infty}^{\infty} e^{\frac{ik_2}{2}\left(\frac{1}{l_3}+\frac{1}{z'_0}\right)(x^2+y^2)}\, e^{-ik_2\left[x\left(\frac{x_3}{l_3}+\frac{x''}{z'_0}\right)+y\left(\frac{y_3}{l_3}+\frac{y''}{z'_0}\right)\right]} \mathrm{d}x\,\mathrm{d}y\\
&+ CB_0\, e^{ik_1\left[\frac{x_1^2+y_1^2}{2l_1}-\frac{x_2^2+y_2^2}{2l_2}\right]} e^{ik_2\left[\frac{x_3^2+y_3^2}{2l_3}+\frac{x''^2+y''^2}{2z'_0}\right]}\\
&\times \iint_{-\infty}^{\infty} e^{\frac{i}{2}\left[\frac{k_1}{l_1}-\frac{k_1}{l_2}+\frac{k_2}{l_3}+\frac{k_2}{z'_0}\right](x^2+y^2)}\\
&\times e^{-ix\left(k_1\frac{x_1}{l_1}-k_1\frac{x_2}{l_2}+k_2\frac{x_3}{l_3}+k_2\frac{x''}{z'_0}\right)}\\
&\times e^{-iy\left(k_1\frac{y_1}{l_1}-k_1\frac{y_2}{l_2}+k_2\frac{y_3}{l_3}+k_2\frac{y''}{z'_0}\right)} \mathrm{d}x\,\mathrm{d}y\\
&+ CB_0^*\, e^{-ik_1\left[\frac{x_1^2+y_1^2}{2l_1}-\frac{x_2^2+y_2^2}{2l_2}\right]} e^{ik_2\left[\frac{x_3^2+y_3^2}{2l_3}+\frac{x''^2+y''^2}{2z'_0}\right]}\\
&\times \iint_{-\infty}^{\infty} e^{-\frac{i}{2}\left[\frac{k_1}{l_1}-\frac{k_1}{l_2}-\frac{k_2}{l_3}-\frac{k_2}{z'_0}\right](x^2+y^2)}\\
&\times e^{-ix\left(-k_1\frac{x_1}{l_1}+k_1\frac{x_2}{l_2}+k_2\frac{x_3}{l_3}+k_2\frac{x''}{z'_0}\right)}\\
&\times e^{-iy\left(-k_1\frac{y_1}{l_1}+k_1\frac{y_2}{l_2}+k_2\frac{y_3}{l_3}+k_2\frac{y''}{z'_0}\right)} \mathrm{d}x\,\mathrm{d}y,
\end{aligned}
\tag{13.33b}
$$

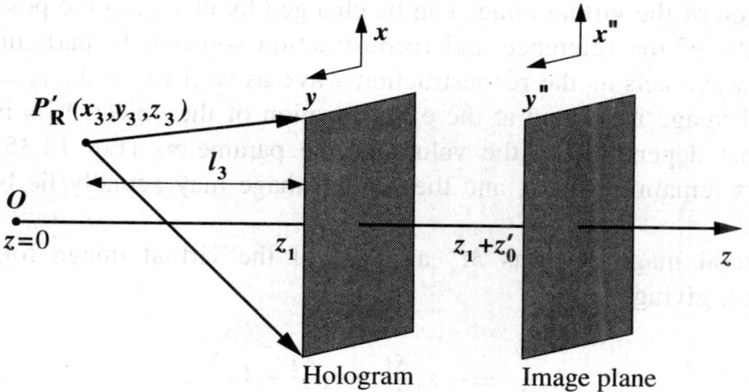

Fig. 13.14: Wavefront reconstruction with a spherical wave.

where

$$C = -\frac{\mathrm{i}}{\lambda_2}\frac{A_3}{l_3}\frac{\mathrm{e}^{\mathrm{i}k_2(l_3+z_0')}}{z_0'}. \tag{13.34}$$

The first term in Eq. (13.33b) represents zero-order diffraction and will not be discussed any further. The second term can lead to the virtual image if the coefficient of (x^2+y^2) becomes zero, i.e., if

$$\frac{k_2}{l_v} = \frac{k_1}{l_2} - \frac{k_1}{l_1} - \frac{k_2}{l_3}, \tag{13.35}$$

where $z_0' = l_v$ is expected to be negative for the virtual image. Under these conditions, the second term in Eq. (13.33b) reduces to

$$E_v(x'', y'', z_0 + l_v) = C_2\delta\left(k_1\frac{x_1}{l_1} - k_1\frac{x_2}{l_2} + k_2\frac{x_3}{l_3} + k_2\frac{x''}{l_v},\right.$$
$$\left. k_1\frac{y_1}{l_1} - k_1\frac{y_2}{l_2} + k_2\frac{y_3}{l_3} + k_2\frac{y''}{l_v}\right), \tag{13.36}$$

where C_2 is a suitable complex constant. The distance of the virtual image from the hologram, obtained from Eq. (13.35), can be expressed as

$$\frac{1}{l_v} = \frac{\lambda_2}{\lambda_1}\left(\frac{1}{l_2} - \frac{1}{l_1}\right) - \frac{1}{l_3} \tag{13.37a}$$

or as

$$l_v = \frac{\lambda_1 l_1 l_2 l_3}{\lambda_2 l_1 l_3 - \lambda_2 l_2 l_3 - \lambda_1 l_1 l_2}. \tag{13.37b}$$

The position of the virtual image can be changed by changing the positions and wavelengths of the reference and reconstruction sources. In particular, if the reference wave acts as the reconstruction wave as well ($\lambda_1 = \lambda_2, l_2 = l_3$), then the virtual image is formed at the exact location of the object. It is interesting to note that depending on the values of the parameters (Eq. 13.35), l_v may not always remain negative, and the virtual image may actually lie behind the hologram.

The lateral magnifications M_x^v and M_y^v of the virtual image follow from Eq. (13.36), giving

$$k_2\frac{x''}{l_v} = -k_1\frac{x_1}{l_1} + k_1\frac{x_2}{l_2} - k_2\frac{x_3}{l_3}, \tag{13.38a}$$

$$k_2\frac{y''}{l_v} = -k_1\frac{y_1}{l_1} + k_1\frac{y_2}{l_2} - k_2\frac{y_3}{l_3}. \tag{13.38b}$$

Let the lateral displacements of the virtual image for small lateral displacements Δx_1 and Δy_1 of the point object be $\Delta x''$ and $\Delta y''$, respectively, then

$$M_x^v\left(=\frac{\Delta x''}{\Delta x_1}\right) = M_y^v\left(=\frac{\Delta y''}{\Delta y_1}\right) = \frac{\lambda_2}{\lambda_1}\frac{l_v}{l_1} = \frac{1}{1-\frac{l_1}{l_2}+\frac{\lambda_1}{\lambda_2}\frac{l_1}{l_3}}. \tag{13.39}$$

For

$$\frac{k_2}{z_0'} = \frac{k_2}{l_r} = \frac{k_1}{l_1} - \frac{k_1}{l_2} - \frac{k_2}{l_3}, \tag{13.40}$$

the third term in Eq. (13.33b) generates the real image with the field distribution

$$\begin{aligned} E_r(x'', y'', z_0 + l_r) = C_3\delta\bigg(&-k_1\frac{x_1}{l_1} + k_1\frac{x_2}{l_2} + k_2\frac{x_3}{l_3} + k_2\frac{x''}{l_r}, \\ &-k_1\frac{y_1}{l_1} + k_1\frac{y_2}{l_2} + k_2\frac{y_3}{l_3} + k_2\frac{y''}{l_r}\bigg), \end{aligned} \tag{13.41}$$

where C_3 is a suitable complex constant. Eq. (13.40), re-written as

$$\frac{1}{l_r} = \frac{\lambda_2}{\lambda_1}\left(\frac{1}{l_1} - \frac{1}{l_2}\right) - \frac{1}{l_3} \tag{13.42a}$$

locates the real image at

$$l_r = \frac{\lambda_1 l_1 l_2 l_3}{\lambda_2 l_2 l_3 - \lambda_2 l_1 l_3 - \lambda_1 l_1 l_2} \tag{13.42b}$$

with lateral magnifications

$$M_x^{\mathrm{r}} = M_y^{\mathrm{r}} = \frac{1}{1 - \frac{l_1}{l_2} - \frac{\lambda_1}{\lambda_2}\frac{l_1}{l_3}}. \tag{13.43}$$

Note that the lateral magnifications for the real and virtual images are different. The longitudinal magnifications of the virtual and real images, obtained from Eqs (13.37b) and (13.42b), are

$$M_z^v = -\frac{\partial l_v}{\partial l_1} = \frac{\lambda_1 \lambda_2 l_2^2 l_3^2}{(\lambda_2 l_1 l_3 - \lambda_2 l_2 l_3 - \lambda_1 l_1 l_2)^2}, \tag{13.44}$$

$$M_z^{\mathrm{r}} = \frac{\partial l_{\mathrm{r}}}{\partial l_1} = \frac{\lambda_1 \lambda_2 l_2^2 l_3^2}{(\lambda_2 l_2 l_3 - \lambda_2 l_1 l_3 - \lambda_1 l_1 l_2)^2}, \tag{13.45}$$

respectively. Combining Eqs (13.39) and (13.44) and Eqs (13.43) and (13.45), we obtain relationships between the corresponding longitudinal and lateral magnifications:

$$M_z^v = \frac{\lambda_1}{\lambda_2}(M_x^v)^2 = \frac{\lambda_1}{\lambda_2}(M_y^v)^2, \tag{13.46a}$$

$$M_z^{\mathrm{r}} = \frac{\lambda_1}{\lambda_2}(M_x^{\mathrm{r}})^2 = \frac{\lambda_1}{\lambda_2}(M_y^{\mathrm{r}})^2. \tag{13.46b}$$

In conclusion, we note that the lateral and longitudinal magnifications depend on the object distance (l_1). This leads to distortion in the reconstructed images of a 3D object. Furthermore, the longitudinal and lateral magnifications are in general different, causing additional image distortions. These distortions can be minimized by a proper choice of the positions of the reference and reconstruction sources. The image magnifications can also be changed by using different wavelengths during recording and reconstruction. In the limit of the plane reference and reconstruction waves ($l_2 \to \infty$, $l_3 \to \infty$) and $\lambda_1 = \lambda_2$, $M_x = M_y = M_z = 1$.

13.5.1 Lensless Fourier Transform Hologram

A hologram obtained when the photographic plate records Fresnel diffraction from the object is called a Fresnel hologram. Thus far, we have considered only Fresnel holograms. A Fraunhofer hologram is obtained when the photographic plate is sufficiently far away from the object to record the far-field or Fraunhofer diffraction from the object. A Fourier transform hologram, on the other hand, records the Fourier transform of the object field distribution. Recording and reconstruction from a Fourier transform hologram are shown in Fig. 13.15,

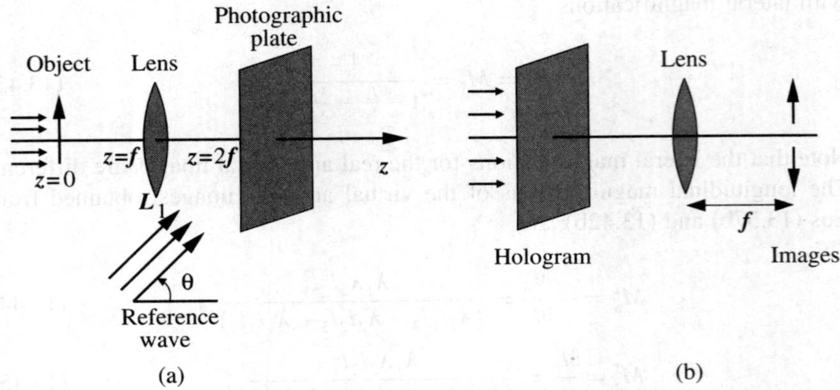

Fig. 13.15: (a) Recording, and (b) reconstruction from a Fourier transform hologram.

where lens L_1 generates the Fourier transform of the object field distribution in the plane of the photographic plate. The image reconstruction from a Fourier transform hologram also requires a lens. The reconstructed images are real and lie in the back focal plane of the lens, symmetrically placed about the axis of the Fourier transform hologram.

It is possible to record a Fourier transform hologram of an object without the use of a lens. For the configuration of hologram recording (Fig. 13.13), where the object and reference points lie in the same transverse plane ($l_1 = l_2 = l$), Eq. (13.32) for the amplitude transmittance of the hologram gives

$$T(x, y, l) = A_0 + B_0\,\mathrm{e}^{\frac{i\pi}{\lambda l}\{x_1^2+y_1^2-x_2^2-y_2^2+2(x_2-x_1)x+2(y_2-y_1)y\}} + B_0^*\,\mathrm{e}^{-\frac{i\pi}{\lambda l}\{x_1^2+y_1^2-x_2^2-y_2^2+2(x_2-x_1)x+2(y_2-y_1)y\}} \quad (13.47a)$$

$$= A_0 + 2|B_0|\cos\left[2\pi\left\{\left(\frac{x_2-x_1}{\lambda l}\right)x + \left(\frac{y_2-y_1}{\lambda l}\right)y\right\} + \phi(x_1, x_2, y_1, y_2) + \phi_0\right]. \quad (13.47b)$$

The characteristic quadratic phase variation of Fresnel holograms (Eqs 13.5 and 13.32) is absent in Eqs (13.47). Instead, in the plane of the hologram, the phase varies linearly with the position coordinates. On reconstruction, Fig. 13.14 and Eqs (13.37a) and (13.42a) for the present configuration ($l_1 = l_2 = l$) give $l_v = l_r = -l_3$, i.e., the real and virtual reconstructed images lie in the plane of the reconstruction source. If the reconstruction is done with a plane wave ($l_3 = \infty$) and a lens is kept behind the hologram, the reconstructed images will lie in the

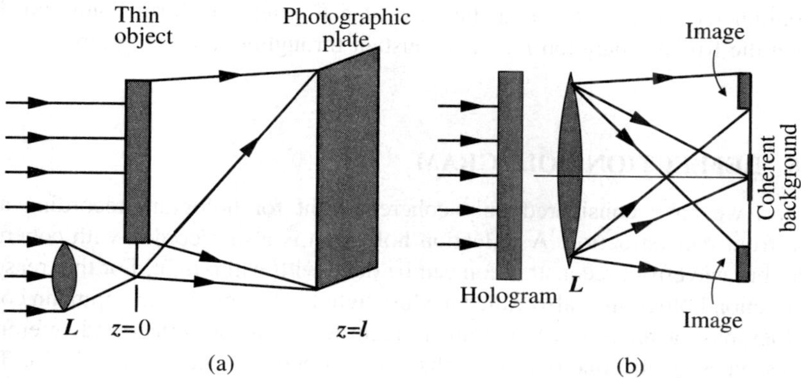

Fig. 13.16: (a) Recording, and (b) reconstruction from a lensless Fourier transform hologram.

back focal plane of the reconstruction lens. Furthermore, under these conditions, Eqs (13.36) and (13.41) predict the reconstructed images to be symmetrically located about the axis of the hologram. This is exactly what happens for a Fourier transform hologram (Fig. 13.15b). But, here, the hologram is recorded without a lens, and hence the name lensless Fourier transform hologram. The standard configurations for recording and reconstruction from a lensless Fourier transform hologram of a thin extended object are shown in Fig. 13.16.

For the Fourier transform hologram (Eq. 13.47), the fringe separation in any direction remains same throughout the hologram and the photographic film is not required to resolve more fringes per unit distance in the outer regions of the hologram as it happens for a Fresnel hologram. This results in increased resolution of images, reconstructed from Fourier transform holograms.

13.5.2 Resolution of a Hologram

In the previous section, a reference was made to hologram resolution. This needs to be elaborated. The resolution of a hologram, as of any optical system, depends on its aperture size. For a circular hologram of diameter d, the angular resolution limit (Eqs 11.89 and 11.93) is of the order of λ/d. Larger the diameter of the hologram, smaller the details that the hologram can resolve. However, it does not always help to increase the size of a hologram. It was mentioned in Section 13.2 that the separations of the interference fringes in the plane of the hologram decrease as one moves away from the center of the hologram. Reduced fringe separations imply higher spatial frequencies. The photographic film may have poor response at these high spatial frequencies, making the outer regions of the hologram redundant, except in the case of a Fourier transform hologram, for which the fringe separation remains constant throughout the hologram.

13.6 REFLECTION HOLOGRAM

So far, we have considered only coherent light for hologram recording and wavefront reconstruction. A reflection hologram is also recorded with coherent light, but wavefront reconstruction can be done with white light. For that reason, a reflection hologram is also called a white light hologram. As in Lippmann color photography, a reflection hologram is recorded with the object and reference waves entering the photographic plate from opposite sides (Fig. 13.17). The photographic plate used for recording a reflection hologram contains a relatively thick emulsion layer supported on a glass substrate. For the present discussion, only a point object is considered but the analysis can be extended to a 3D object. With origin O located at the position of the point object, the front and back surfaces of the photographic film lie at $z = z_1$ and $z = z_1 + \Delta z$, where Δz is the thickness of the emulsion layer. The field distribution in the plane $z = z_1 + z'$ of the photographic plate can be expressed as

$$E(x, y, z_1 + z') = A_1 e^{ik_1[-(z_1+z')\cos\theta + x\sin\theta]} + \frac{A_2}{z_1} e^{ik_1\left[z_1+z'+\frac{x^2+y^2}{2(z_1+z')}\right]}, \qquad (13.48)$$

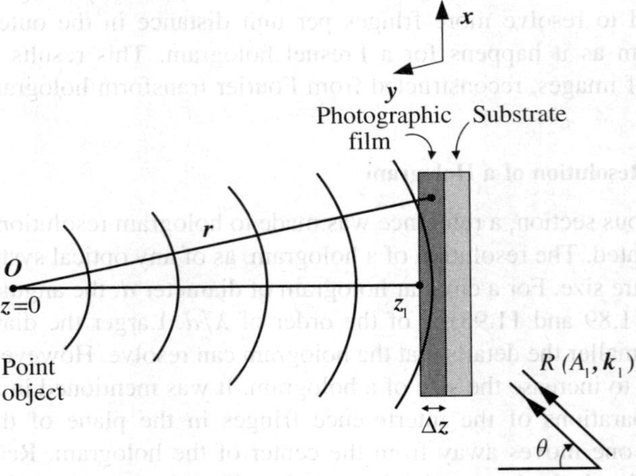

Fig. 13.17: Recording reflection hologram of a point object.

where $0 \le z' \le \Delta z$, A_1 is the amplitude of the reference wave, A_2 is the amplitude of the spherical wave at unit distance from the point object, and the distance r in Fig. 13.17 has been approximated to

$$r = z_1 + z' + \frac{x^2 + y^2}{2(z_1 + z')}. \tag{13.49}$$

The corresponding intensity distribution in this plane of the photographic plate, ignoring the factor $\frac{1}{2}\epsilon_0 c$, is

$$\begin{aligned} I(x, y, z_1 + z') &= |A_1|^2 + \frac{|A_2|^2}{z_1^2} + \frac{A_1^* A_2}{z_1} e^{ik_1\left[(z_1+z')(1+\cos\theta) - x\sin\theta + \frac{x^2+y^2}{2(z_1+z')}\right]} \\ &\quad + \frac{A_1 A_2^*}{z_1} e^{-ik_1\left[(z_1+z')(1+\cos\theta) - x\sin\theta + \frac{x^2+y^2}{2(z_1+z')}\right]} \\ &= |A_1|^2 + \frac{|A_2|^2}{z_1^2} + \frac{2}{z_1}|A_1||A_2|\cos k_1[(z_1 + z') \\ &\quad \times (1 + \cos\theta) - x\sin\theta + \frac{x^2 + y^2}{2(z_1 + z')} + \phi_0], \end{aligned} \tag{13.50}$$

where ϕ_0 is the constant phase difference between the two waves. For $z = z_1 + z'$, where $0 \le z' \le \Delta z$, Eq. (13.50) generates intensity distributions in different planes of the emulsion. Because of the standing wave character of the interference pattern, the intensity and hence the emulsion exposure shows periodic variation with z'. The planes in the photographic plate with similar exposure conditions lie approximately $\lambda/2$ distance apart for small angle of inclination of the reference wave. Therefore, the planes of maximum concentration of Ag atoms in the hologram, corresponding to the planes of maximum exposure in the photographic plate, are nearly perpendicular to the hologram axis and $\lambda/2$ distance apart for small θ. The reflection hologram acts as a volume hologram to the reconstructing reference wave, much like a crystal appears to the incoming X-rays. The waves scattered from different crystallographic planes interfere destructively, unless the X-rays are incident at Bragg angle (Fig. 13.18), satisfying the condition

$$2d\sin\alpha = n\lambda, \tag{13.51}$$

where d is the separation between the crystallographic planes, α the Bragg angle, λ the wavelength of X-rays, and n is an integer. Assuming linearity in the T–E

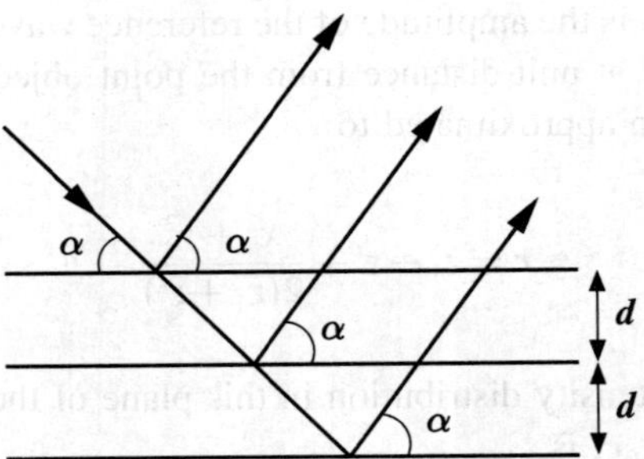

Fig. 13.18: Bragg scattering of X-rays from crystallographic planes.

plot of the photographic emulsion (see Fig. 11.12), the amplitude reflectance of the layer within the hologram at $z = z_1 + z'$ can be expressed as

$$
\begin{aligned}
R(x, y, z_1 + z') = A_0 + B_0 \mathrm{e}^{\mathrm{i}k_1\left[(z_1+z')(1+\cos\theta) - x\sin\theta + \frac{x^2+y^2}{2(z_1+z')}\right]} \\
+ B_0^* \mathrm{e}^{-\mathrm{i}k_1\left[(z_1+z')(1+\cos\theta) - x\sin\theta + \frac{x^2+y^2}{2(z_1+z')}\right]},
\end{aligned}
\tag{13.52}
$$

where A_0 and B_0 are suitable constants. Figure 13.19 shows wavefront reconstruction from a reflection hologram with a collimated beam of white light of amplitude A incident in the direction of the reference wave during recording.

From the spectrum of white light, only the wavelength at which the hologram was recorded satisfies the Bragg condition. The field distribution of reflected light in the layer at $z = z_1 + z'$ of the hologram can be expressed as

$$
E(x, y, z_1 + z') = A\,\mathrm{e}^{\mathrm{i}k_1[-(z_1+z')\cos\theta + x\sin\theta]} R(x, y, z_1 + z'),
\tag{13.53}
$$

giving the field distribution of reflected light in the plane $z = z_1 + z' + z_2$ as

$$
\begin{aligned}
E(x'', y'', z_1 + z' + z_2) = -\frac{\mathrm{i}}{\lambda_1}\frac{\mathrm{e}^{\mathrm{i}k_1 z_2}}{z_2} A \int\!\!\int_{-\infty}^{\infty} \mathrm{e}^{\mathrm{i}k_1[-(z_1+z')\cos\theta + x\sin\theta]} \\
\times \Bigg[A_0 + B_0 \mathrm{e}^{\mathrm{i}k_1\left[(z_1+z')(1+\cos\theta) - x\sin\theta + \frac{x^2+y^2}{2(z_1+z')}\right]} \\
+ B_0^* \mathrm{e}^{-\mathrm{i}k_1\left[(z_1+z')(1+\cos\theta) - x\sin\theta + \frac{x^2+y^2}{2(z_1+z')}\right]} \Bigg] \\
\times \mathrm{e}^{\frac{\mathrm{i}k_1}{2z_2}\left[(x''-x)^2 + (y''-y)^2\right]}\,\mathrm{d}x\,\mathrm{d}y.
\end{aligned}
\tag{13.54}
$$

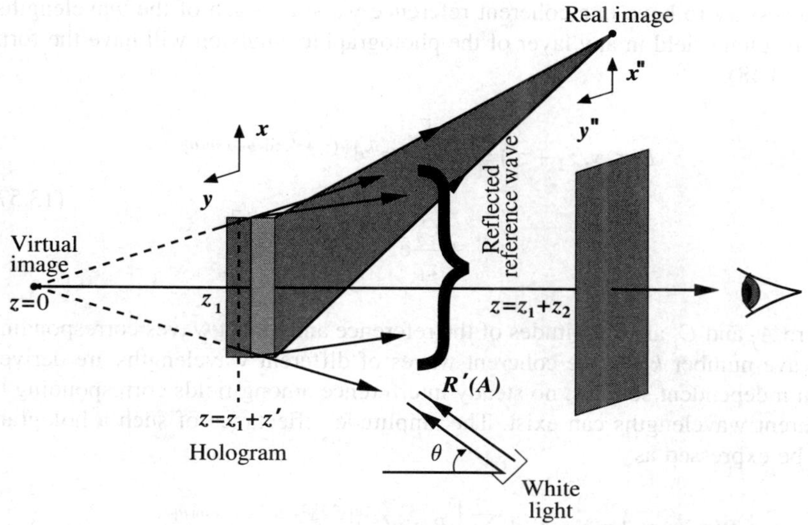

Fig. 13.19: Wavefront reconstruction from a reflection hologram with white light.

For $z_2 = z_1 + z'$, the above distribution reduces to

$$E(x'', y'', 2(z_1 + z')) = C_1(z')\mathrm{e}^{\mathrm{i}k_1 x'' \sin\theta} + C_2(z')\mathrm{e}^{\frac{\mathrm{i}k_1}{4(z_1+z')}(x''^2 + y''^2)} + C_3(z')\delta(x'' - 2(z_1 + z')\sin\theta, y''), \tag{13.55}$$

where $C_1(z')$, $C_2(z')$, and $C_3(z')$ are suitable complex constants. The first term in Eq. (13.55) is the component of white light reflected by the hologram layer at $z = z_1 + z'$ with $k = k_1$. The second term originates from the virtual image located on the axis of the hologram at the exact location of the original point object. All layers within the hologram produce virtual images exactly at the position of the original object. The third term generates the real image at the off-axial position $x'' = 2(z_1 + z')\sin\theta, y'' = 0$. The reflected field distributions are shown in Fig. 13.19. The net field of the virtual image is the superposition of fields produced by different layers of the hologram, i.e.,

$$E_v(z = 0) = \int_0^{\Delta z} C_2(z')\,\mathrm{d}z'. \tag{13.56}$$

A reflection hologram can also be recorded by illuminating the object with two or more coherent waves of different wavelengths, simultaneously. It will also be necessary to have one coherent reference wave for each of the wavelengths. The resultant field in any layer of the photographic emulsion will have the form (Eq. 13.48),

$$E(x, y, z_1 + z') = \sum_j \left[A_j e^{ik_j[-(z_1+z')\cos\theta + x\sin\theta]} + \frac{C_j}{z_1} e^{ik_j\left[z_1+z'+\frac{x^2+y^2}{2(z_1+z')}\right]} \right], \tag{13.57}$$

where A_j and C_j are amplitudes of the reference and object waves corresponding to wave number k_j. Since coherent waves of different wavelengths are derived from independent sources, no steady interference among fields corresponding to different wavelengths can exist. The amplitude reflectance of such a hologram can be expressed as

$$R(x, y, z_1 + z') = A_0 + \sum_j \left[B_j e^{\frac{ik_j}{2(z_1+z')}[x^2+y^2-2(z_1+z')x\sin\theta]} + B_j^* e^{-\frac{ik_j}{2(z_1+z')}[x^2+y^2-2(z_1+z')x\sin\theta]} \right], \tag{13.58}$$

where A_0 and B_j are complex constants. Upon illumination with white light, such a hologram generates multi-color images in reflected light – one for each wavelength used in the recording of the hologram.

Since a reflection hologram is a volume hologram, the direction of the reconstruction wave must exactly coincide with the direction of the reference wave during hologram recording, otherwise the Bragg condition remains unsatisfied. Several scenes can be stored in the same hologram by changing the direction of the reference wave for different scenes. All these scenes can be retrieved from the hologram by reconstructing with white light of changing direction. A reflection hologram can therefore be used as a holographic memory.

13.7 RAINBOW HOLOGRAPHY

A transmission hologram recorded at one wavelength can be viewed at another wavelength. However, the position of a reconstructed image, usually quite far from the hologram, varies with the wavelength of the reconstruction wave (see Sections 13.2.2 and 13.5). White light cannot be used for image reconstruction from a normal transmission hologram because the wavelength-dependent shifts of the image completely obscure the image details. A rainbow hologram is a

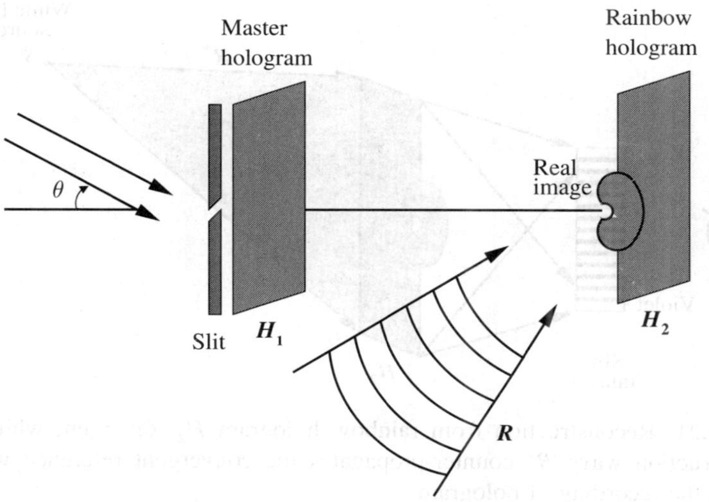

Fig. 13.20: Recording of a rainbow hologram. Master hologram H_1 is illuminated through a narrow horizontal slit. The real image shown in the figure is the object image formed by H_1. The reference wave R is convergent coherent light.

specially prepared transmission hologram recorded with monochromatic light which can be viewed with white light. In rainbow holography, first a transmission hologram of the object, called the master hologram (or the primary hologram), is recorded in the usual manner. The hologram H_1 in Fig. 13.20 is the master hologram. A second hologram H_2, called the rainbow hologram, is recorded in the following manner. The master hologram is illuminated, just as in the normal reconstruction process, by the conjugate of the reference wave used in its recording, except that the reconstruction wave is restricted by an opaque screen with a narrow horizontal slit kept in front of the master hologram, as shown in the figure. Thus, only a part of the master hologram gets illuminated, reducing the image resolution and brightness to some extent. The master hologram produces the real image of the object as shown in the figure. The photographic plate H_2 is kept very close, but just behind this image. The hologram of this real image is now recorded on the photographic plate H_2 with a convergent reference wave R derived from the same coherent wave which illuminates the primary hologram H_1. The photographic plate H_2 after development is the rainbow hologram.

For reconstruction, the rainbow hologram is illuminated by divergent white light counter-propagating to the convergent coherent wave R used during the recording of the hologram. This is shown in Fig. 13.21. The rainbow hologram

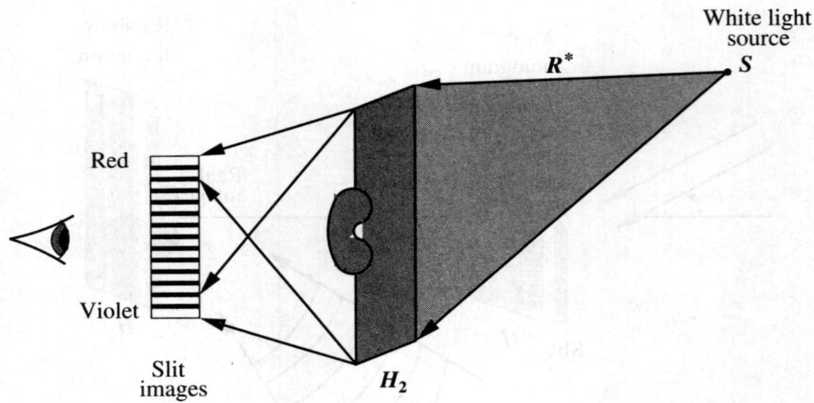

Fig. 13.21: Reconstruction from rainbow hologram H_2; divergent white light reconstruction wave R^* counter-propagates the convergent reference wave R used in the recording of hologram.

generates multiple real images of the object, one for each wavelength of white light. These images lie very close to the rainbow hologram since the object for the rainbow hologram, i.e., the image formed by the master hologram was very close to hologram H_2 during recording. The wavelength-dependent shifts of these images for different wavelengths of white light are minimized since these images lie very close to the rainbow hologram. Furthermore, these images are real orthoscopic images of the original object because these are real images of the pseudoscopic image formed by the master hologram. At the same time, the rainbow hologram generates the same number of real images of the slit somewhat away from it. The slit images for different wavelengths are transversely shifted from each others (see Eq. 13.43). Figure 13.21 shows a spread of the slit images for different colors. Through the image of the slit, formed by a particular color of white light, an orthoscopic real image of the object in only that color will be visible. By moving the eye up and down to see through different slit images, real orthoscopic images of the object in different colors can be seen. This is the rainbow effect. In rainbow holography, the vertical parallax is lost, but the horizontal parallax is still available.

13.8 HOLOGRAPHIC INTERFEROMETRY

Among the myriad applications (some realized, others waiting to be exploited) of holography, holographic interferometry is perhaps the most significant. Classical interferometry is confined to optically flat and specularly reflecting surfaces.

Holographic interferometry, on the other hand, can be applied to diffusely reflecting rough surfaces. Another advantage of holographic interferometry lies in the fact that not all interfering wavefronts need be real time wavefronts. Holographic interferometry deals with some or all holographically generated interfering light fields.

13.8.1 Double Exposure Holographic Interferometry

A hologram of an unstrained object is first recorded. The object is then subjected to some form of stress and a second hologram is recorded on the same photographic plate, ensuring in the process that the object and photographic plate remain in their original positions. The intensity distributions in the plane of the photographic plate during the two exposures are

$$\begin{aligned} I_1(x,y,z) &= \left(\frac{1}{2}\epsilon_0 c\right)[|E_{01}(x,y,z)+E_{\mathrm{r}}(x,y,z)|^2] \\ &= \left(\frac{1}{2}\epsilon_0 c\right)[|E_{01}(x,y,z)|^2+|E_{\mathrm{r}}(x,y,z)|^2 \\ &\quad +E_{01}(x,y,z)E_{\mathrm{r}}^*(x,y,z)+E_{01}^*(x,y,z)E_{\mathrm{r}}(x,y,z)] \end{aligned} \tag{13.59}$$

and

$$\begin{aligned} I_2(x,y,z) = \left(\frac{1}{2}\epsilon_0 c\right)[|E_{02}(x,y,z)|^2+|E_{\mathrm{r}}(x,y,z)|^2+E_{02}(x,y,z) \\ \times E_{\mathrm{r}}^*(x,y,z)+E_{02}^*(x,y,z)E_{\mathrm{r}}(x,y,z)], \end{aligned} \tag{13.60}$$

respectively, where $E_{01}(x, y, z)$ and $E_{02}(x, y, z)$ are the object fields incident on the photographic plate during the two exposures, and $E_{\mathrm{r}}(x, y, z)$ is the field of the reference wave. The linear amplitude transmittance of the photographic plate after development is

$$\begin{aligned} T(x,y,z) = A_0 + B_0[\{E_{01}(x,y,z)+E_{02}(x,y,z)\}E_{\mathrm{r}}^*(x,y,z) \\ +\{E_{01}^*(x,y,z)+E_{02}^*(x,y,z)\}E_{\mathrm{r}}(x,y,z)], \end{aligned} \tag{13.61}$$

where A_0 and B_0 are real constants. The doubly exposed hologram is illuminated with the reference (or its spatial conjugate) wave used in recording the hologram. These two reconstruction waves produce least aberrations in the reconstructed images. With the reference wave also used as the reconstruction wave, the field distribution just behind the hologram is given by

$$\begin{aligned} E(x,y,z) = {} & A_0 E_r(x,y,z) + B_0\{E_{01}(x,y,z) + E_{02}(x,y,z)\} \\ & \times |E_r(x,y,z)|^2 + B_0\{E_{01}^*(x,y,z) + E_{02}^*(x,y,z)\} \\ & \times E_r^2(x,y,z). \end{aligned} \tag{13.62}$$

The field distribution in any plane behind the hologram can be obtained as described in Section 13.4. The second term in Eq. (13.62) gives rise to the virtual image in the original position of the object if the reconstruction is done in the recording geometry. From Eq. (13.27), the field distribution of the virtual image can be written as

$$E_v(x',y',z') = C\{E_{01}(x',y',z') + E_{02}(x',y',z')\}, \tag{13.63}$$

where C is a complex constant. Since the object movement during the stress is quite small, the two object field distributions differ in phase, and not in amplitude. Accordingly, we can write

$$E_{01}(x',y',z') = |E_O(x',y',z')|\,\mathrm{e}^{-\mathrm{i}\phi_1(x',y')}, \tag{13.64a}$$

$$E_{02}(x',y',z') = |E_O(x',y',z')|\,\mathrm{e}^{-\mathrm{i}\phi_2(x',y')}. \tag{13.64b}$$

The intensity distribution of the virtual image then takes the form

$$I_v(x',y',z') = 2|C|^2 I_O(x',y',z')[1 + \cos\{\phi_2(x',y') - \phi_1(x',y')\}], \tag{13.65}$$

where $I_O(x',y',z')$ is the intensity distribution of the unstrained object. If the object remains unstrained during the second exposure also ($\phi_2(x',y') = \phi_1(x',y')$), then the virtual image possesses the intensity distribution of the original object.

The strain ($\phi_2(x',y') \neq \phi_1(x',y')$) during the second exposure gives rise to interference fringes superimposed on the virtual image. The contours of the fringes reflect the nature of the strain produced in the object. In particular, the portions of the object which remain undisplaced during the strain show bright fringes. A similar fringe pattern, superimposed on the real image, can also be seen if the reconstruction is done with the conjugate of the reference wave used in the recording. Double exposure holographic interferometry finds use in non-destructive testing of materials.

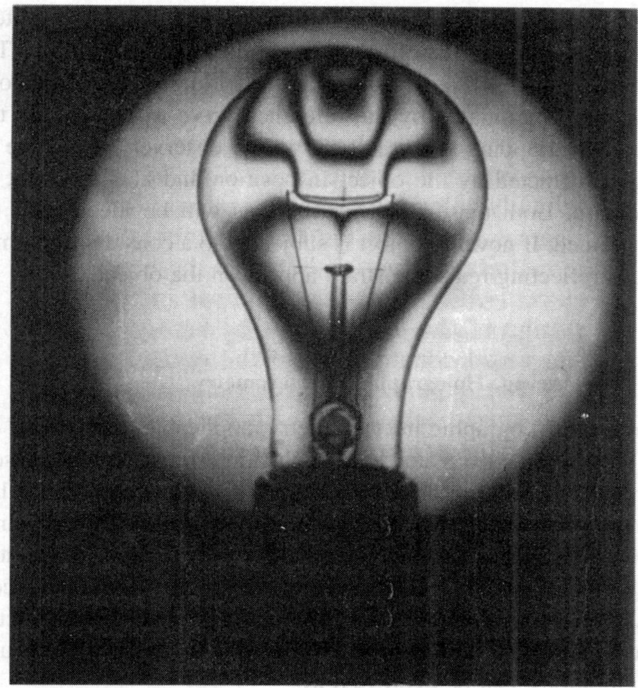

Fig. 13.22: Double exposure holographic interferogram of incandescent lamp before and after switching it on – taken from *Handbook of Optical Holography*, Ed., H. J. Caulfield, p. 472, Courtesy Gerald Brandt and Academic Press.

Another interesting example of double exposure holographic interferometry is shown in Fig. 13.22 (Courtesy, Gerald Brandt and Academic Press). Here the object is the incandescent lamp and the exposures are taken before and after switching it on. The heat produced by the filament changes the index of refraction of the ambient gas, creating additional phase changes for the second exposure. The interference between the reconstructed wavefronts shows the contours of refractive index (and hence thermal) changes around the filament.

13.8.2 Real-Time Holographic Interferometry

In real-time holographic interferometry, a hologram of the unstrained object is first recorded. This hologram must be placed in the exact position of the photographic plate during the recording of the hologram which is quite difficult. The photographic plate is therefore usually processed in position. The object must also remain in its fixed position and be illuminated continuously. The hologram is then illuminated by the reference wave to reconstruct the virtual image exactly overlapping with the object. The observer behind the hologram receives light diffracted by the object in position and also the light diffracted by the hologram. Both these field distributions will be identical if the object remains unstrained. If now the object is subjected to a constant or a time-varying stress, fringes reflecting real-time strain appear on the object.

13.8.3 Time-Average Holographic Interferometry

The time-average holographic interferometry, applicable to vibrating objects, is similar to the multiple-exposure holographic interferometry discussed earlier. The hologram of a vibrating object is recorded for a time ΔT, much larger than the period of vibration of the object. This is equivalent to recording a large number of sub-holograms of the object, one for each state of its vibration. Since all these sub-holograms are recorded under coherent conditions, the reconstructed wavefronts interfere producing fringes superimposed on the reconstructed images of the object. The distribution of the field over a planar object, undergoing sinusoidal vibrations, can be expressed as

$$E_{\rm O}(x, y, t) = |E_{\rm O}(x, y)|\,{\rm e}^{-{\rm i}\{\phi(x,y)+kd(x,y)\cos\omega t\}}, \tag{13.66}$$

where $\phi(x, y)$ describes the phase distribution of the scattered field for the stationary object and $d(x, y)$ gives the amplitude distribution of sinusoidal vibration of angular frequency ω. For sufficiently large ΔT as compared to the period of vibration (T) of the object, the intensity distribution in the plane of the hologram is essentially determined by the intensity averaged over one period of vibration, i.e.,

$$\begin{aligned} I(x, y) &= \langle I(x, y, t)\rangle_T \\ &= |E_{\rm O}(x, y)|^2 + |E_{\rm r}(x, y)|^2 + |E_{\rm O}(x, y)|\,{\rm e}^{-{\rm i}\phi(x,y)} E_{\rm r}^*(x, y) \\ &\quad \times \frac{1}{T}\int_0^T {\rm e}^{-{\rm i}kd(x,y)\cos\omega t}\,{\rm d}t + |E_{\rm O}(x, y)|{\rm e}^{{\rm i}\phi(x,y)} E_{\rm r}(x, y) \\ &\quad \times \frac{1}{T}\int_0^T {\rm e}^{{\rm i}kd(x,y)\cos\omega t}\,{\rm d}t. \end{aligned} \tag{13.67}$$

The integral

$$\mathcal{J}_0 = \frac{1}{T}\int_0^T e^{ikd(x,y)\cos\omega t}\,dt$$
$$= \frac{1}{2\pi}\int_0^{2\pi} e^{ikd(x,y)\cos\omega t}\,d(\omega t)$$

can be replaced by the Bessel function (Eq. 10.39)

$$J_0(x) = \frac{1}{2\pi}\int_0^{2\pi} e^{ix\cos\phi}\,d\phi$$

of zero order.

On illuminating the hologram with the reference wave or its phase conjugate, the intensity distribution of a reconstructed image will have the form

$$I(x', y') = I_O(x', y')J_0^2\{kd(x', y')\}, \tag{13.68}$$

where $I_O(x', y')$ is the image intensity distribution of the object in equilibrium. The fringes superimposed on the image will have the characteristic variation of $J_0^2(kd(x', y'))$, shown in Fig. 13.23. The zeroes and maxima of J_0 determine the contours of the dark and bright fringes, respectively. The central bright fringe corresponds to the zero of the argument of J_0, i.e., to the nodes of the vibrating object. Successive bright fringes are considerably weaker.

Figure 13.24 (Courtesy – J Shamir and Academic Press) shows the vibrational modes of a guitar observed by time-averaged holographic interferometry.

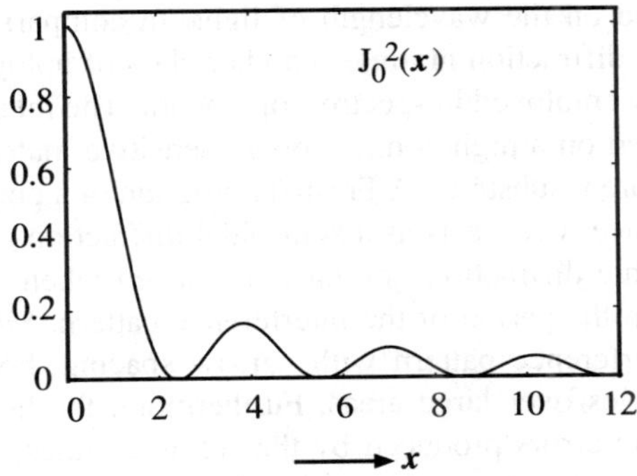

Fig. 13.23: Variation of square of Bessel function of zero order.

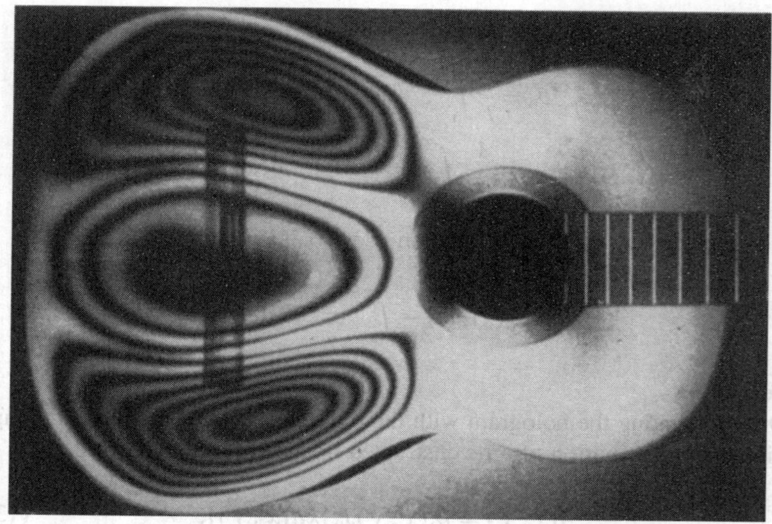

Fig. 13.24: Vibrational modes of a guitar by time-averaged holographic interferometry – taken from *Optical Transforms*, Ed., H. Lipson, p. 333, Courtesy J. Shamir and Academic Press.

13.9 HOLOGRAPHIC OPTICAL ELEMENTS

It has already been stated that a Fresnel hologram of a point object acts as a lens (Section 13.2.1). One needs to record the holographic interference pattern on a suitable and stable recording material such as hardened dichromated gelatin on a transparent substrate. Holographic lenses are used for only special applications such as the over-head display devices. The imaging characteristics of a holographic lens depend on the wavelength of light. In comparison to holographic lenses, holographic diffraction gratings, another class of holographic optical elements, are routinely employed in spectroscopic work. The interference pattern, in this case, is recorded on a high-contrast photo-sensitive material such as a photoresist on a transparent substrate. A Fresnel hologram of a point object, recorded with a plane reference wave, acts as a sinusoidal diffraction grating (Eq. 13.5b). A square holographic diffraction grating is produced when the photo-sensitive layer is thinner than the period of the interference pattern. Since it is quite easy to generate an interference pattern with narrow spacing, holographic gratings can have fine grooves over large areas. Furthermore, the holographic gratings avoid the systematic errors produced by the ruling engines, which give rise to ghost lines in the spectrum recorded with ruled gratings. However, the groove profile is more difficult to control in holographic gratings.

13.10 REFERENCES

13.1 Francis T. S. Yu, Optical Information Processing, John Wiley & Sons, New York, 1983.

13.2 P. Hariharan, Optical holography, Cambridge University Press, Cambridge, 1984.

13.3 Robert J. Collier, Christoph B. Burckhardt, Lawrence H. Lin, Optical Holography, Academic Press Inc., New York, 1971.

13.4 H. J. Caulfield (Ed.), Handbook of Optical Holography, Academic Press, New York, 1979.

13.5 Yu I. Ostrovsky, M. M. Butusore, G. V. Ostrovskaya, Interferometry by Holography, Springer-Verlag, Heidelberg, 1980.

13.6 Robert Jones and Catherine Wykes, Holographic and Speckle Interferometry, Cambridge University Press, Cambridge, 1983.

13.7 J. Shamir, Optical Transforms (Ed. H. Lipson), Academic Press London, 1972.

13.11 PROBLEMS

13.1 Find the amplitude transmittance of an on-axis hologram of a point object when the distance between the object and photographic plate is large enough for the Fraunhofer approximation to hold. Show that for a Fraunhofer hologram, the background of the reconstructed real image is not much of a hindrance to view the point scatterers such as the aerosol particles in the virtual image.

13.2 Show that in a hologram with amplitude transmittance described by Eq. (13.5b), the fringe separation for large distances from the center of the hologram varies approximately inversely with the distance from the center of the hologram.

13.3 The off-axis hologram of a point object recorded in Fig. 13.6 is illuminated as in Fig. 13.7, except that the reconstruction wave has wavelength different from the wavelength of the reference wave used in the recording of the hologram. The direction of propagation of the reconstruction wave is the same as in Fig. 13.7. Obtain the field distributions behind the hologram and locate the positions of the reconstructed images. Take the recording wavelength as 550 nm. Find the longitudinal and transverse spreads of the image positions if the reconstruction wave has wavelength spread from 400 to 750 nm. Take $z_1 = 30$ cm and $\theta = 30°$.

13.4 An off-axis hologram of a point object is recorded as in Fig. 13.6 with a monochromatic plane reference wave of wavelength 488.0 nm making an angle of 30° with the axis of the photographic plate. The hologram is illuminated by a point monochromatic source of wavelength 632.8 nm kept 50 cm in front of the hologram and 5 cm above the axis of the hologram. Obtain the field distributions behind the hologram. Find the positions and magnifications (lateral and longitudinal) of the reconstructed images.

13.5 Consider the hologram recording and reconstruction configurations of Figs 13.10 and 13.12, respectively. Show that the real image reconstructed by the spatial conjugate of the reference wave is formed in the original position of the object. Is this image pseudoscopic or orthoscopic?

13.6 Consider the hologram recording configuration of Fig. 13.25. The small object O lies 30 cm in front of the photographic plate and 5 cm above the axis of the photographic plate. The reference wave of 457.9 nm diverging from the reference point P_R illuminates the object as well.

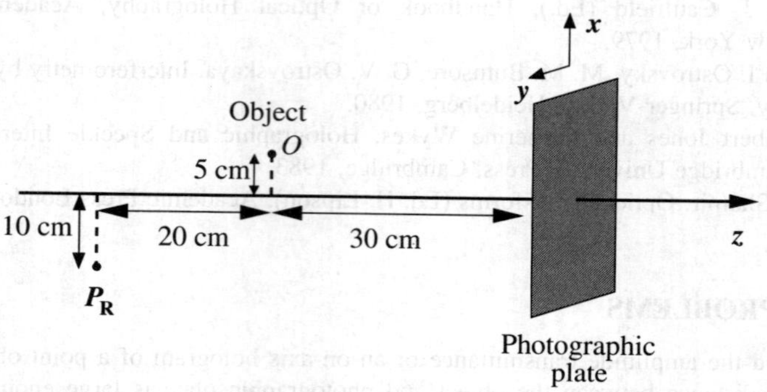

Fig. 13.25.

(a) Choose a suitable origin of coordinates and find the linear amplitude transmittance of the hologram. You may assume the object and reference point to lie in the xz plane.

(b) The hologram is illuminated with 632.8 nm line of a He–Ne laser diverging from the reconstruction point also lying in the xz plane, 75 cm in front of the hologram and 10 cm above its axis. Compute the positions and magnifications (lateral and longitudinal) of the reconstructed images.

(c) Compute the new positions and magnifications of the reconstructed images if the following changes are made.

   (i) The reference and reconstruction points are moved back by 1 m each from their respective positions without changing their distances from the axis of the hologram.

   (ii) Only the object is moved back by 20 cm without changing its distance from the axis of the photographic plate.

(d) Find the positions and magnifications in all the above cases if the reference and reconstruction wavelengths are made same.

13.7 The reflection hologram of Fig. 13.17 is illuminated with the reconstruction wave which is the phase conjugate of the reference wave used in its recording (i.e. with propagation vector $-\vec{k}$). Find the field distributions behind the hologram and determine the positions of the reconstructed images.

13.8 Find the amplitude transmittance of the hologram recorded in the configuration of Fig. 13.16a. Comment if this hologram records the Fourier transform of the object field distribution.

CHAPTER **14**

Nonlinear Optics

14.1 INTRODUCTION

Our description of optics (read linear optics) thus far has been constrained by Eq. (1.9a)

$$\vec{P}(\vec{r}, t) = \epsilon_0 \chi^{(1)} \vec{E}(\vec{r}, t), \tag{1.9a}$$

which restricts the polarization $\vec{P}(\vec{r}, t)$ to have linear dependence on the electric field $\vec{E}(\vec{r}, t)$. This holds for weak light fields, but for light fields not so weak yet sufficiently weak, the more general Eq. (1.8)

$$\begin{aligned} P_i &= \left[\epsilon_0 \chi_{ij}^{(1)} E_j\right] + \epsilon_0 \left[\chi_{ijk}^{(2)} E_j E_k + \chi_{ijkl}^{(3)} E_j E_k E_l + \cdots\right] \\ &= \left[\left(\vec{P}_{\mathrm{L}}\right)_i\right] + \left[\left(\vec{P}_{\mathrm{NL}}\right)_i\right] \end{aligned} \tag{1.8}$$

with implied summation over repeated indices prevails, where $\vec{P}_{\mathrm{L}}$ and $\vec{P}_{\mathrm{NL}}$ are the linear and nonlinear polarizations, respectively. This is the regime of nonlinear optics [14.1–6]. Each component of the nonlinear polarization $\vec{P}_{\mathrm{NL}}$ may depend on quadratic and higher order products of the components of the amplitude of the electric field, making nonlinear optics, except perhaps for the vacuum, a universal phenomenon. Of course, some media may show discernible nonlinear effects at relatively low optical field strengths while others may need intense light fields produced by pulsed lasers to exhibit the nonlinear behavior. Quantum mechanics must be used for a proper description of nonlinear optics but that is beyond the scope of this book. Here, we shall describe nonlinear optics through Maxwell's equations (Eqs 1.10). In linear optics the index of refraction and the absorption coefficient of a medium are constant at a given temperature and frequency, but in nonlinear optics the index of refraction and to some extent the absorption coefficient of a medium begin to depend on the strength of the light field. For media with absorption frequencies much above the light frequencies, light fields comparable in strength to the atomic fields ($E_{\text{at}} \sim e/4\pi\epsilon_0 a_0^2$, where $a_0 = \hbar^2/me^2$ is the Bohr radius of the hydrogen atom) are needed to generate the lowest order nonlinear polarization equal in strength to the linear polarization. Whereas $E_{\text{at}} \sim 10^7$ V/cm, the electric field strength of a laser beam of intensity $2.5\,\text{W/cm}^2$ is only about 1 V/cm. Thus even with laser sources, nonlinear optical effects may remain small perturbations over linear optical effects. Under resonant excitation, optical nonlinearity of a medium is associated with the ability of the light field to transfer a significant fraction of the atomic population from the ground to the excited states. This may be accomplished with relatively weaker light fields [14.7]. We shall extend the wave equation (Eq. 1.11a)

$$\nabla^2 \vec{E} - \mu\epsilon \frac{\partial^2 \vec{E}}{\partial t^2} = 0 \tag{1.11a}$$

of linear optics to incorporate the nonlinear polarization $\vec{P}_{\text{NL}}$ as a source term to describe some of the commonly observed nonlinear optical phenomena, such as second-harmonic generation, sum- and difference-frequency generations, parametric amplification, optical phase conjugation, etc. In these processes, the role of the medium is important but only passive. It simply facilitates interaction among the coherent waves to generate new coherent waves without influencing the frequencies of the new waves. The classical explanation for the generation of the new waves stipulates acceleration of the atomic electrons not only at the frequencies of the input fields but also at their sum and difference frequencies. However, the quantum mechanical explanation is much neater. Two or more light photons coalesce, conserving energy to generate a photon of the sum frequency. In the difference-frequency generation, a high-energy photon is destroyed (absorbed) and simultaneously two low-energy photons are created (emitted). The presence of the photons in the medium at one of the low frequencies stimulates the difference-frequency generation, although their presence is not absolutely essential. Needless to state that the superposition principle is invalidated in nonlinear optics.

There are other nonlinear optical processes such as the stimulated Raman and Brillouin scattering processes in which the medium plays a more active role in determining the actual frequencies of the new waves. In these processes, the medium also participates in the conservation of the overall energy. These processes are best understood in the quantum mechanical description of nonlinear optics, hence their exclusion from our consideration. The observation of second-harmonic light at 347.1 nm by Franken et al. [14.8] when light from a ruby laser at 694.2 nm was passed through a quartz crystal is taken to herald the emergence of the field of nonlinear optics, although optical pumping of atoms by resonant light, a nonlinear optical process indeed, was achieved before the lasers came into existence [14.9].

14.2 NONLINEAR POLARIZATION

In Section 1.9, our treatment of dispersion based on the Lorentz model of an atom yielded polarization which varies linearly with the electric field (Eq. 1.105). The harmonic restoring force ($-m\omega_0^2\vec{r}$) used in that derivation (Eq. 1.103) restricts the strength of the light field to low values, otherwise the restoring force may not remain harmonic. The scalar form of Eq. (1.103), modified to the lowest order of anharmonicity, is

$$\frac{\mathrm{d}^2x}{\mathrm{d}t^2}+\gamma\frac{\mathrm{d}x}{\mathrm{d}t}+\omega_0^2x+ax^2=\frac{q}{m}E'(t), \tag{14.1}$$

where $E'(t)$ is the local field (Eq. 1.104) experienced by the oscillating electron of charge q, mass m, and a is a constant which goes to zero in the harmonic limit. This equation is applicable to noncentrosymmetric media only because it uses a restoring force ($-m\omega_0^2x-max^2$) which lacks the inversion symmetry.[1] In particular, this equation cannot be applied to isotropic and cubic media. For centrosymmetric media, the corresponding restoring force ($-m\omega_0^2x-mbx^3$) involves a cubic term in place of the square term. We should note that Eq. (14.1) is nonlinear and the strength of the nonlinearity is determined by the anharmonicity constant a. The nonlinear term enables the light fields present in the medium to interact with each other and generate in the process fields which may not be present in the incident light. In linear optics, waves can interfere but cannot produce new waves. Let the input field consist of two monochromatic plane waves, so that

$$E'(t)=\frac{1}{2}\left[E'(\omega_1)\,\mathrm{e}^{-\mathrm{i}\omega_1 t}+E'(\omega_2)\,\mathrm{e}^{-\mathrm{i}\omega_2 t}+\mathrm{cc}\right], \tag{14.2}$$

where $E'(\omega_1)$ and $E'(\omega_2)$ are amplitudes of the local fields of frequencies ω_1 and ω_2, respectively. $E'^*(\omega_1)=E'(-\omega_1), E'^*(\omega_2)=E'(-\omega_2)$, and cc stands for complex conjugate. The spatial dependence of the fields has been suppressed.

[1] A force possessing inversion symmetry changes sign but not the magnitude when position vector $\vec{r}$ changes to $(-\vec{r})$.

For off-resonance excitation ($\omega_1, \omega_2 \ll \omega_0$) of the medium, the nonlinear term is generally small ($ax^2 \ll \omega_0^2 x$) and it is possible to express the solution of Eq. (14.1) in the form

$$x(t) = x^{(1)}(t) + x^{(2)}(t) + x^{(3)}(t) + \cdots, \tag{14.3}$$

where the dominant term $x^{(1)}(t)$ is the solution of Eq. (14.1) with $a = 0$. The remaining terms written in decreasing order of magnitude are expected to be much smaller. Substituting

$$x = x^{(1)}(t) = \frac{1}{2}\left[x^{(1)}(\omega_1)\,\mathrm{e}^{-\mathrm{i}\omega_1 t} + x^{(1)}(\omega_2)\,\mathrm{e}^{-\mathrm{i}\omega_2 t} + \mathrm{cc}\right]$$

into Eq. (14.1) with $a = 0$ gives

$$\begin{aligned}(-\omega_1^2 - \mathrm{i}\gamma\omega_1 + \omega_0^2)x^{(1)}(\omega_1)\mathrm{e}^{-\mathrm{i}\omega_1 t} + (-\omega_2^2 - \mathrm{i}\gamma\omega_2 + \omega_0^2)x^{(1)}(\omega_2)\mathrm{e}^{-\mathrm{i}\omega_2 t} + \mathrm{cc} \\ = \frac{q}{m}\left[E'(\omega_1)\mathrm{e}^{-\mathrm{i}\omega_1 t} + E'(\omega_2)\mathrm{e}^{-\mathrm{i}\omega_2 t} + \mathrm{cc}\right].\end{aligned} \tag{14.4}$$

Equating coefficients of $\mathrm{e}^{-\mathrm{i}\omega_1 t}$ and $\mathrm{e}^{-\mathrm{i}\omega_2 t}$ on both sides, we obtain

$$x^{(1)}(\omega_1) = \frac{qE'(\omega_1)/m}{\omega_0^2 - \omega_1^2 - \mathrm{i}\gamma\omega_1}, \quad x^{(1)}(\omega_2) = \frac{qE'(\omega_2)/m}{\omega_0^2 - \omega_2^2 - \mathrm{i}\gamma\omega_2}. \tag{14.5}$$

Therefore

$$x^{(1)}(t) = \frac{1}{2}\left[\frac{qE'(\omega_1)/m}{\omega_0^2 - \omega_1^2 - \mathrm{i}\gamma\omega_1}\mathrm{e}^{-\mathrm{i}\omega_1 t} + \frac{qE'(\omega_2)/m}{\omega_0^2 - \omega_2^2 - \mathrm{i}\gamma\omega_2}\mathrm{e}^{-\mathrm{i}\omega_2 t} + \mathrm{cc}\right]. \tag{14.6}$$

Suppressing the spatial dependence, the linear polarization generated in the medium can be expressed as

$$P_{\mathrm{L}}(t) = \frac{1}{2}\left[P_{\mathrm{L}}(\omega_1)\mathrm{e}^{-\mathrm{i}\omega_1 t} + P_{\mathrm{L}}(\omega_2)\mathrm{e}^{-\mathrm{i}\omega_2 t} + \mathrm{cc}\right], \tag{14.7}$$

where $P_{\mathrm{L}}^*(\omega_1) = P_{\mathrm{L}}(-\omega_1)$, $P_{\mathrm{L}}^*(\omega_2) = P_{\mathrm{L}}(-\omega_2)$. The amplitudes of the linear polarizations generated at the frequencies ω_1 and ω_2 are

$$\begin{aligned}P_{\mathrm{L}}(\omega_1) &= Nqx^{(1)}(\omega_1) = \frac{(Nq^2/m)\,E'(\omega_1)}{\omega_0^2 - \omega_1^2 - \mathrm{i}\gamma\omega_1} = N\alpha^{(1)}(\omega_1)\,E'(\omega_1), \\ P_{\mathrm{L}}(\omega_2) &= Nqx^{(1)}(\omega_2) = \frac{(Nq^2/m)\,E'(\omega_2)}{\omega_0^2 - \omega_2^2 - \mathrm{i}\gamma\omega_2} = N\alpha^{(1)}(\omega_2)\,E'(\omega_2),\end{aligned} \tag{14.8}$$

where N is the number of electrons per unit volume of the medium and the linear or the first-order molecular polarizabilities at the frequencies ω_1 and ω_2 are given by

$$\alpha^{(1)}(\omega_1) = \frac{(q^2/m)}{\omega_0^2 - \omega_1^2 - i\gamma\omega_1}, \quad \alpha^{(1)}(\omega_2) = \frac{(q^2/m)}{\omega_0^2 - \omega_2^2 - i\gamma\omega_2}. \tag{14.9}$$

14.2.1 Second-Order Nonlinear Polarization

We express the nonlinear interaction term ax^2 as

$$ax^2 = a\left[x^{(1)} + x^{(2)} + x^{(3)} + \cdots\right]^2 = a(x^{(1)})^2 + 2ax^{(1)}x^{(2)} + \cdots. \tag{14.10}$$

Equation (14.6) gives

$$\begin{aligned}(x^{(1)})^2 =& \frac{1}{4}\left[a_1 e^{-i\omega_1 t} + a_1^* e^{i\omega_1 t} + a_2 e^{-i\omega_2 t} + a_2^* e^{i\omega_2 t}\right]^2 = \frac{1}{2}(a_1 a_1^* + a_2 a_2^*)\\ &+ \frac{1}{4}\left[a_1^2 e^{-i2\omega_1 t} + a_2^2 e^{-i2\omega_2 t} + 2a_1 a_2 e^{-i(\omega_1+\omega_2)t} + 2a_1 a_2^* e^{-i(\omega_1-\omega_2)t} + \text{cc}\right],\end{aligned} \tag{14.11}$$

where

$$a_1 = \frac{qE'(\omega_1)/m}{\omega_0^2 - \omega_1^2 - i\gamma\omega_1}, \quad a_2 = \frac{qE'(\omega_2)/m}{\omega_0^2 - \omega_2^2 - i\gamma\omega_2}. \tag{14.12}$$

The second- and higher order terms in Eq. (14.10) are considerably smaller than the first term. The second-order term $x^{(2)}(t)$ is obtained by solving the equation

$$\frac{d^2x^{(2)}}{dt^2} + \gamma\frac{dx^{(2)}}{dt} + \omega_0^2 x^{(2)} = -a(x^{(1)})^2. \tag{14.13}$$

It follows from Eqs (14.11) and (14.13) that $x^{(2)}(t)$ must have terms which oscillate at the frequencies $2\omega_1$, $2\omega_2$, $(\omega_1+\omega_2)$, $(\omega_1-\omega_2)$ and 0. Accordingly, we can write

$$\begin{aligned}x^{(2)}(t) =& x^{(2)}(0) + \frac{1}{2}\left[x^{(2)}(2\omega_1)e^{-i2\omega_1 t} + x^{(2)}(2\omega_2)e^{-i2\omega_2 t}\right.\\ &\left.+ x^{(2)}(\omega_1+\omega_2)e^{-i(\omega_1+\omega_2)t} + x^{(2)}(\omega_1-\omega_2)e^{-i(\omega_1-\omega_2)t} + \text{cc}\right],\end{aligned} \tag{14.14}$$

where $x^{(2)}(0)$ is the nonoscillating part of $x^{(2)}(t)$, $x^{(2)}(2\omega_1)$ is the amplitude of the term which oscillates at frequency $2\omega_1$, and so on. Substituting Eq. (14.14) into Eq. (14.13) and equating coefficients of the various exponential terms on both sides, we get

$$x^{(2)}(0)=\frac{1}{2}\frac{(-a)(q/m\omega_0)^2 E'(\omega_1)E'^*(\omega_1)}{(\omega_0^2-\omega_1^2-\mathrm{i}\gamma\omega_1)(\omega_0^2-\omega_1^2+\mathrm{i}\gamma\omega_1)}$$

$$+\frac{1}{2}\frac{(-a)(q/m\omega_0)^2 E'(\omega_2)E'^*(\omega_2)}{(\omega_0^2-\omega_2^2-\mathrm{i}\gamma\omega_2)(\omega_0^2-\omega_2^2+\mathrm{i}\gamma\omega_2)}, \tag{14.15a}$$

$$x^{(2)}(2\omega_{\mathrm{i}})=\frac{1}{2}\frac{(-a)(q/m)^2 E'(\omega_i)E'(\omega_i)}{(\omega_0^2-4\omega_i^2-\mathrm{i}2\gamma\omega_i)(\omega_0^2-\omega_i^2-\mathrm{i}\gamma\omega_i)^2}, \tag{14.15b}$$

$$x^{(2)}(\omega_1+\omega_2)=\frac{(-a)(q/m)^2 E'(\omega_1)E'(\omega_2)}{[\omega_0^2-(\omega_1+\omega_2)^2-\mathrm{i}\gamma(\omega_1+\omega_2)]}$$

$$\times\frac{1}{(\omega_0^2-\omega_1^2-\mathrm{i}\gamma\omega_1)(\omega_0^2-\omega_2^2-\mathrm{i}\gamma\omega_2)}, \tag{14.15c}$$

$$x^{(2)}(\omega_1-\omega_2)=\frac{(-a)(q/m)^2 E'(\omega_1)E'^*(\omega_2)}{\left[\omega_0^2-(\omega_1-\omega_2)^2-\mathrm{i}\gamma(\omega_1-\omega_2)\right]}$$

$$\times\frac{1}{(\omega_0^2-\omega_1^2-\mathrm{i}\gamma\omega_1)(\omega_0^2-\omega_2^2+\mathrm{i}\gamma\omega_2)} \tag{14.15d}$$

The second-order nonlinear polarization can be expressed as

$$P_{\mathrm{NL}}^{(2)}(t)=P_{\mathrm{NL}}^{(2)}(0)+\frac{1}{2}\Big[P_{\mathrm{NL}}^{(2)}(2\omega_1)\mathrm{e}^{-\mathrm{i}2\omega_1 t}+P_{\mathrm{NL}}^{(2)}(2\omega_2)\mathrm{e}^{-\mathrm{i}2\omega_2 t}$$
$$+P_{\mathrm{NL}}^{(2)}(\omega_1+\omega_2)\mathrm{e}^{-\mathrm{i}(\omega_1+\omega_2)t}+P_{\mathrm{NL}}^{(2)}(\omega_1-\omega_2)\mathrm{e}^{-\mathrm{i}(\omega_1-\omega_2)t}+\mathrm{cc}\Big].$$

The amplitudes of the various polarizations are as given below:

$$P_{\mathrm{NL}}^{(2)}(0)=Nqx^{(2)}(0)=N\left[\alpha^{(2)}(0,\omega_1,-\omega_1)E'(\omega_1)E'^*(\omega_1)\right.$$
$$\left.+\alpha^{(2)}(0,\omega_2,-\omega_2)E'(\omega_2)E'^*(\omega_2)\right], \tag{14.16a}$$

$$P_{\mathrm{NL}}^{(2)}(2\omega_i)=Nqx^{(2)}(2\omega_i)=N\alpha^{(2)}(2\omega_i,\omega_i,\omega_i)E'(\omega_i)E'(\omega_i),$$

$$P_{\mathrm{NL}}^{(2)}(\omega_1+\omega_2)=Nqx^{(2)}(\omega_1+\omega_2) \tag{14.16b}$$

$$=N\alpha^{(2)}(\omega_1+\omega_2,\omega_1,\omega_2)E'(\omega_1)E'(\omega_2),$$

$$P_{\mathrm{NL}}^{(2)}(\omega_1-\omega_2)=Nqx^{(2)}(\omega_1-\omega_2) \tag{14.16c}$$

$$=N\alpha^{(2)}(\omega_1-\omega_2,\omega_1,\omega_2)E'(\omega_1)E'^*(\omega_2), \tag{14.16d}$$

where the second-order molecular polarizabilities are given below:

$$\alpha^{(2)}(0,\omega_1,-\omega_1)=\frac{(-a)\left(q^3/2m^2\omega_0^2\right)}{\left(\omega_0^2-\omega_1^2-\mathrm{i}\gamma\omega_1\right)\left(\omega_0^2-\omega_1^2+\mathrm{i}\gamma\omega_1\right)},\tag{14.17a}$$

$$\alpha^{(2)}(0,\omega_2,-\omega_2)=\frac{(-a)\left(q^3/2m^2\omega_0^2\right)}{\left(\omega_0^2-\omega_2^2-\mathrm{i}\gamma\omega_2\right)\left(\omega_0^2-\omega_2^2+\mathrm{i}\gamma\omega_2\right)},\tag{14.17b}$$

$$\alpha^{(2)}(2\omega_i,\omega_i,\omega_i)=\frac{(-a)\,q^3/2m^2}{\left(\omega_0^2-4\omega_i^2-\mathrm{i}2\gamma\omega_i\right)\left(\omega_0^2-\omega_i^2-\mathrm{i}\gamma\omega_i\right)^2},\tag{14.17c}$$

$$\alpha^{(2)}(\omega_1\mp\omega_2,\omega_1,\omega_2)=\left[\frac{(-a)q^3/m^2}{(\omega_0^2-(\omega_1\mp\omega_2)^2-\mathrm{i}\gamma(\omega_1\mp\omega_2))}\times\frac{1}{(\omega_0^2-\omega_1^2-\mathrm{i}\gamma\omega_1)(\omega_0^2-\omega_2^2\pm\mathrm{i}\gamma\omega_2)}\right]\tag{14.17d}$$

Thus as a result of the nonlinear interaction, applied fields at the frequencies ω_1 and ω_2 generate polarizations in the medium at the frequencies $2\omega_1$, $2\omega_2$, $(\omega_1\mp\omega_2)$, and 0. These polarizations (oscillating dipoles) in turn radiate new fields at the second harmonics, and sum and difference frequencies. It is interesting to note that the oscillating fields generate dc fields via the nonlinear interaction. The creation of zero-frequency polarization is called optical rectification.

At this point we make an observation, the relevance of which will become apparent as we proceed. We note that in Eqs (14.16) for the nonlinear polarizations, positive signs with the frequencies in the arguments of $\alpha^{(2)}$ are accompanied with the product of the amplitudes of the electric fields at those frequencies, but the complex conjugate of the electric field amplitude appears whenever a frequency in the argument of $\alpha^{(2)}$ carries negative sign. For example in the difference-frequency generation term (Eq. 14.16d), the product of the field amplitudes contains $E'^*(\omega_2)$ as ω_2 in the argument of $\alpha^{(2)}(\omega_1-\omega_2)$ has negative sign. This feature is shared by the higher order polarizations as well.

Equations (14.8) and (14.16) express the polarizations generated in a medium in terms of the microscopic polarizabilities and the local electric fields. Equation (1.8), on the other hand, links polarization to the macroscopic susceptibilities of the medium and the applied electric fields. The local and applied electric fields differ in dense media (Eq. 1.104). We now reconcile the two definitions of polarization. The results of Eqs (14.8) and (14.16) can be generalized in the form

$$\begin{aligned}P(\omega)=N\big[&\alpha^{(1)}(\omega)E'(\omega)+\alpha^{(2)}(\omega,\omega_1,\omega_2)E'(\omega_1)E'(\omega_2)\\&+\alpha^{(3)}(\omega,\omega_1,\omega_2,\omega_3)E'(\omega_1)E'(\omega_2)E'(\omega_3)+\cdots\big],\end{aligned}\tag{14.18a}$$

where the first term on the right-hand side gives the linear polarization at frequency ω generated by a local field of amplitude $E'(\omega)$ oscillating at the same frequency. The strength of the linear polarization is determined by the linear polarizability $\alpha^{(1)}(\omega)$. The second term gives the second-order nonlinear polarization generated in the medium at frequency ω in the presence of local electric fields of frequencies ω_1 and ω_2; $\alpha^{(2)}(\omega, \omega_1, \omega_2)$ is the corresponding second-order polarizability. Similar explanations can be offered for the higher order terms as well. It should be understood that once an optical field at frequency ω has been generated through any of the nonlinear processes, linear polarization at frequency ω (the first term in Eq. 14.18a) is generated in the medium even though there is no input field at this frequency. By substituting in the first term on the right-hand side of Eq. (14.18a) the expression (Eq. 1.104) for the local field in terms of the applied field, we obtain

$$P(\omega) = N\alpha^{(1)}(\omega)\left[E(\omega) + \frac{P(\omega)}{3\epsilon_0}\right] + N\alpha^{(2)}(\omega, \omega_1, \omega_2)\, E'(\omega_1)\, E'(\omega_2) + N\alpha^{(3)}(\omega, \omega_1, \omega_2, \omega_3)\, E'(\omega_1)\, E'(\omega_2)\, E'(\omega_2) + \cdots \tag{14.18b}$$

Collecting the polarization terms on the left-hand side gives

$$P(\omega) = N\alpha^{(1)}(\omega)\frac{E(\omega)}{1 - \frac{N\alpha^{(1)}(\omega)}{3\epsilon_0}} + \frac{1}{1 - \frac{N\alpha^{(1)}(\omega)}{3\epsilon_0}}\left[N\alpha^{(2)}(\omega, \omega_1, \omega_2) \times E'(\omega_1)E'(\omega_2) + N\alpha^{(3)}(\omega, \omega_1, \omega_2, \omega_3)E'(\omega_1)E'(\omega_2)E'(\omega_3)) + \cdots\right]. \tag{14.18c}$$

In going from Eq. (14.18b) to Eq. (14.18c), we seem to have replaced the local field $E'(\omega)$ in the first term by $(E(\omega)/(1 - \frac{N\alpha^{(1)}(\omega)}{3\epsilon_0}))$. The local fields appearing in all terms and not just in the first term of Eq. (14.18a) should have been expressed in terms of the applied fields, but doing so would enormously increase the computational difficulties. Therefore, we ignore contributions to the local fields from the higher order terms, in which case, we can make the replacement

$$E'(\omega_i) = \frac{E(\omega_i)}{1 - \frac{N\alpha^{(1)}(\omega_i)}{3\epsilon_0}} \tag{14.19}$$

in all terms of Eq. (14.18c), giving

$$P(\omega) = \left[1 - \frac{N\alpha^{(1)}(\omega)}{3\epsilon_0}\right]^{-1} \left[N\alpha^{(1)}(\omega) E(\omega) + \frac{N\alpha^{(2)}(\omega, \omega_1, \omega_2) E(\omega_1) E(\omega_2)}{\left[1 - \frac{N\alpha^{(1)}(\omega_1)}{3\epsilon_0}\right]\left[1 - \frac{N\alpha^{(1)}(\omega_2)}{3\epsilon_0}\right]} + \cdots \right]. \tag{14.20}$$

Now since the applied fields and not the local fields appear in Eq. (14.20), we can compare it with Eq. (1.8), reproduced here as

$$P(\omega) = \epsilon_0 \left[\chi^{(1)}(\omega) E(\omega) + \chi^{(2)}(\omega, \omega_1, \omega_2) E(\omega_1) E(\omega_2) + \cdots\right], \tag{14.21}$$

giving the desired relationships among the macroscopic susceptibilities and the microscopic polarizabilities:

$$\chi^{(1)}(\omega) = \frac{N\alpha^{(1)}(\omega)/\epsilon_0}{1 - \frac{N\alpha^{(1)}(\omega)}{3\epsilon_0}}, \tag{14.22a}$$

$$\chi^{(2)}(\omega, \omega_1, \omega_2) = \frac{N\alpha^{(2)}(\omega, \omega_1, \omega_2)/\epsilon_0}{\left(1 - \frac{N\alpha^{(1)}(\omega)}{3\epsilon_0}\right)\left(1 - \frac{N\alpha^{(1)}(\omega_1)}{3\epsilon_0}\right)\left(1 - \frac{N\alpha^{(1)}(\omega_2)}{3\epsilon_0}\right)}, \tag{14.22b}$$

$$\chi^{(n)}(\omega, \omega_1, \omega_2, \ldots, \omega_n) = \frac{N\alpha^{(n)}(\omega, \omega_1, \omega_2, \ldots, \omega_n)/\epsilon_0}{\left(1 - \frac{N\alpha^{(1)}(\omega)}{3\epsilon_0}\right)\left(1 - \frac{N\alpha^{(1)}(\omega_1)}{3\epsilon_0}\right)\left(1 - \frac{N\alpha^{(1)}(\omega_2)}{3\epsilon_0}\right)\cdots\left(1 - \frac{N\alpha^{(1)}(\omega_n)}{3\epsilon_0}\right)}, \tag{14.22n}$$

where the polarizabilites $\alpha^{(2)}$ for the second-order nonlinear processes are given in Eqs (14.17). The higher order polarizabilities $\alpha^{(n)}$ can be defined in a similar manner. The first frequency in the arguments of $\alpha^{(n)}$ and $\chi^{(n)}$ for $n > 1$ is the frequency at which the nonlinear polarization is created in the medium and the remaining frequencies in the arguments are the frequencies of the fields which generate this polarization. We shall further sharpen this notation as we proceed.

To get a feel for the strengths of the nonlinear polarizations produced in an optically transparent medium, we consider the nonlinear polarization at twice the frequency of the applied field. From Eqs (14.8) and (14.16), we find

$$\begin{aligned}\frac{P^{(2)}}{P^{(1)}} &= \frac{P(2\omega)}{P(\omega)} = \frac{Nqx^{(2)}(2\omega)}{Nqx^{(1)}(\omega)} \\ &= \frac{(-a)(q/2m)E'(\omega)}{\left(\omega_0^2-4\omega^2-\mathrm{i}2\gamma\omega\right)\left(\omega_0^2-\omega^2-\mathrm{i}\gamma\omega\right)}.\end{aligned} \tag{14.23}$$

For the optically transparent media the absorption frequencies lie in the ultra-violet, so that $\omega_0 \gg 2\omega$, in which case the denominator in Eq. (14.23) can be replaced by ω_0^4, and Eq. (14.23) reduces to

$$\frac{P(2\omega)}{P(\omega)} = \left|\frac{aq}{2m\omega_0^4}\right| E'(\omega), \tag{14.24}$$

where ω_0 is the lowest frequency of absorption of the medium. Based on our comment in the introduction, an estimate of the anharmonicity constant a can be made by equating the first-and second-order polarizations produced in a medium when the applied fields approach the atomic fields. Under these conditions, Eq. (14.24) gives

$$\left|\frac{aq}{2m\omega_0^4}\right| E_{\text{at}} \approx 1, \tag{14.25}$$

so that

$$\frac{P(2\omega)}{P(\omega)} \sim \frac{E'(\omega)}{E_{\text{at}}},$$

where E_{at} may be taken as the electric field experienced by the electron in the hydrogen atom and $E'(\omega)$ is the local electric field in the medium in the presence of the light beam. Infact, it can be shown that

$$\frac{P^{(n+1)}}{P^{(n)}} \sim \frac{E'(\omega)}{E_{\text{at}}}, \tag{14.26}$$

where $P^{(n)}$ is the nth-order polarization. For typical light fields, $\frac{E'(\omega)}{E_{\text{at}}} \sim 10^{-7}$. Thus, the nonlinear polarizations are indeed very small and hence the relevance of powerful laser sources for nonlinear optical studies. However, for resonant and nearly resonant light fields, the denominator in Eq. (14.23) can become quite small, making it possible to observe nonlinear effects with modest light fields.

We conclude this discussion by demonstrating that the susceptibility of a second-order nonlinear process can be expressed in terms of the first-order susceptibilities and in the process obtain their orders-of-magnitude values. For second-harmonic generation, Eqs (14.22) give

$$\begin{aligned}\chi^{(2)}(2\omega,\omega,\omega) &= \frac{N\alpha^{(2)}(2\omega,\omega,\omega)/\epsilon_0}{\left(1-\frac{N\alpha^{(1)}(2\omega)}{3\epsilon_0}\right)\left(1-\frac{N\alpha^{(1)}(\omega)}{3\epsilon_0}\right)^2} \\ &= \frac{N\alpha^{(2)}(2\omega,\omega,\omega)/\epsilon_0}{\left[N\alpha^{(1)}(2\omega)/\epsilon_0\chi^{(1)}(2\omega)\right]\left[N\alpha^{(1)}(\omega)/\epsilon_0\chi^{(1)}(\omega)\right]^2} \\ &= \left(\frac{\epsilon_0}{N}\right)^2 \frac{\alpha^{(2)}(2\omega,\omega,\omega)}{\left(\alpha^{(1)}(2\omega)\right)\left(\alpha^{(1)}(\omega)\right)^2}\chi^{(1)}(2\omega)\left(\chi^{(1)}(\omega)\right)^2. \end{aligned} \tag{14.27}$$

Substituting values of $\alpha^{(1)}(\omega), \alpha^{(1)}(2\omega), \alpha^{(2)}(2\omega,\omega,\omega)$ from Eqs (14.9) and (14.17) into Eq. (14.27) yields

$$\frac{\alpha^{(2)}(2\omega,\omega,\omega)}{\alpha^{(1)}(2\omega)\left(\alpha^{(1)}(\omega)\right)^2} = (-a)\frac{m}{2q^3}, \tag{14.28}$$

giving

$$\chi^{(2)}(2\omega,\omega,\omega) = \left|\frac{am\epsilon_0^2}{2N^2q^3}\right|\chi^{(1)}(2\omega)\left(\chi^{(1)}(\omega)\right)^2, \tag{14.29}$$

where $\chi^{(1)}(2\omega)$ is the linear susceptibility at twice the frequency of the input field. Similar expressions can be obtained for the sum- and difference-frequency generations. Equation (14.25) gives an approximate value of the anharmonicity constant as

$$a \sim \frac{m\omega_0^4}{qE_{\text{at}}}. \tag{14.30}$$

For off-resonance excitation of the medium and neglecting the difference between the local and applied fields, Eqs (14.9) and (14.22a) give

$$\chi^{(1)}(\omega) \sim \chi^{(1)}(2\omega) \approx \frac{Nq^2}{\epsilon_0 m\omega_0^2}. \tag{14.31}$$

Substituting Eqs (14.30) and (14.31) into Eq. (14.29) gives

$$\chi^{(2)}(2\omega, \omega, \omega) = \frac{q}{m\omega_0^2 d}, \tag{14.32}$$

where we have replaced E_{at} by $q/4\pi\epsilon_0 d^2$ and N by $1/d^3$, d may be taken as the inter-atomic distance in the medium. Using $m = 9.1 \times 10^{-31}$ kg, $\omega_0 = 10^{16}$ rad/s, $d = 2 \times 10^{-10}$ m, $\epsilon_0 = 8.85 \times 10^{-12}\,\mathrm{C^2\,N^{-1}\,m^{-2}}$, $q = 1.6 \times 10^{-19}$ C gives

$$\chi^{(1)}(\omega) \sim 1, \tag{14.33}$$

$$\chi^{(2)}(2\omega, \omega, \omega) \sim 10^{-12}\ \mathrm{m/V}. \tag{14.34}$$

Equation (14.29) shows that the ratio $\frac{\chi^{(2)}(2\omega,\omega,\omega)}{\chi^{(1)}(2\omega)\left(\chi^{(1)}(\omega)\right)^2}$ is nearly constant for most media. This result is known as Miller's rule.

14.2.2 Third-Order Nonlinear Polarization

Calculation of the third-order nonlinear polarization is too lengthy to be attempted here, but it is quite easy to get a feel for what to expect from the next higher order solution of Eq. (14.1). The next term $(x^{(3)}(t))$ in Eq. (14.3) is obtained by solving the homogeneous part of Eq. (14.1) with ax^2 term replaced by $2a(x^{(1)}(t))(x^{(2)}(t))$ (see Eq. 14.10). We shall not perform this calculation, but it immediately follows from Eqs (14.6) and (14.14) that the product $(x^{(1)}(t))(x^{(2)}(t))$ has terms which oscillate at the frequencies $\omega_1, \omega_2, 3\omega_1, 3\omega_2, (\omega_1 + 2\omega_2), (2\omega_1 + \omega_2), (2\omega_1 - \omega_2)$, and $(2\omega_2 - \omega_1)$. Accordingly, nonlinear polarizations at all of these frequencies are generated in the medium through the third-order nonlinear interaction between the applied optical fields of frequencies ω_1 and ω_2. These polarizations radiate new fields at all of these frequencies; in particular, third harmonics are generated at the frequencies $3\omega_1$ and $3\omega_2$. We mention in passing that although the third-order nonlinear polarization is generated when the medium is excited with intense fields at one or two frequencies, the most general case of third-order nonlinear polarization arises when three or more optical fields at different frequencies are applied. For details, the interested reader may consult *Nonlinear Optics* by Robert W. Boyd [14.1].

14.2.3 Higher Order Nonlinear Polarizations

Our treatment of nonlinear optics thus far concerns only the hypothetical scalar fields. We must now consider nonlinear optical interactions among vector electric fields. Fortunately, the results of the previous sections though obtained for scalar fields hold for vector fields as well, but we need to put them in the proper perspective. Furthermore, we must take note of the crystalline environment of the atoms since nonlinear optical interactions are more often investigated in crystalline solids. Anisotropy of the solid media has already been discussed in Chapter 1 (Section 1.10). First expression of Eq. (1.106) and Eq. (1.119) suggest that the first-order susceptibility $\chi^{(1)}$ is a tensor of the second rank with nine elements. The second-order susceptibility $\chi^{(2)}$ is a tensor of the third rank with 27 elements and the third-order susceptibility $\chi^{(3)}$ has 81 elements. It is quite obvious that our notation while dealing with vector fields is going to get very elaborate and complicated. That is precisely the reason why we started with the scalar fields. Extending Eq. (14.7) to higher order polarizations

$$\vec{P}(t) = \vec{P}^{(1)}(t) + \vec{P}^{(2)}(t) + \vec{P}^{(3)}(t) + \cdots + \vec{P}^{(n)}(t), \tag{14.35}$$

we may write

$$\vec{P}^{(1)}(t) = \frac{1}{2}\left[\vec{P}^{(1)}(\omega)\,\mathrm{e}^{-\mathrm{i}\omega t} + \vec{P}^{(1)}(-\omega)\,\mathrm{e}^{\mathrm{i}\omega t}\right], \tag{14.36a}$$

$$\vec{P}^{(2)}(t) = \frac{1}{2}\left[\vec{P}^{(2)}(\omega)\,\mathrm{e}^{-\mathrm{i}\omega t} + \vec{P}^{(2)}(-\omega)\,\mathrm{e}^{\mathrm{i}\omega t}\right], \tag{14.36b}$$

$$\vec{P}^{(n)}(t) = \frac{1}{2}\left[\vec{P}^{(n)}(\omega)\,\mathrm{e}^{-\mathrm{i}\omega t} + \vec{P}^{(n)}(-\omega)\,\mathrm{e}^{\mathrm{i}\omega t}\right], \tag{14.36n}$$

where $\vec{P}^{(1)}(t)$ is the linear polarization and the remaining Eqs (14.36b–n) represent nonlinear polarizations. In writing the above equations, the amplitudes of the oscillating polarizations are assumed to satisfy the condition $\vec{P}^{(n)*}(\omega) = \vec{P}^{(n)}(-\omega)$, making the polarizations $\vec{P}^{(n)}(t)$ as real quantities. A formal representation of the nth-order nonlinear polarization at frequency ω may take the form

$$\vec{P}^{(n)}(\omega, t) = \epsilon_0 \chi^{(n)}(\omega, \omega_1, \omega_2, \ldots, \omega_n) : \vec{E}(\omega_1, t)\,\vec{E}(\omega_2, t) \cdots \vec{E}(\omega_n, t), \tag{14.37}$$

where $\omega = \omega_1 + \omega_2 + \cdots + \omega_n$, and $\vec{E}(\omega_i, t)$ for $i = 1, 2, \ldots, n$ are the electric fields present in the medium at the frequencies $\omega_1, \omega_2, \ldots, \omega_n$; $\chi^{(n)}$ is the electric susceptibility tensor of the $(n+1)$th rank. However, more relevant quantities in the present context are the components of the amplitudes of the polarizations which can be expressed as

$$P_i^{(1)}(\omega) = \epsilon_0 \sum_j \chi_{ij}^{(1)}(\omega) E_j(\omega), \tag{14.38a}$$

$$P_i^{(2)}(\omega) = \frac{\epsilon_0}{2} \sum_{jk} \chi_{ijk}^{(2)}(\omega, \omega_1, \omega_2) E_j(\omega_1) E_k(\omega_2), \tag{14.38b}$$

$$P_i^{(n)}(\omega) = \frac{\epsilon_0}{2^{n-1}} \sum_{jk\cdots p} \chi_{ijk\cdots p}^{(n)}(\omega, \omega_1, \omega_2, \ldots, \omega_n) E_j(\omega_1) E_k(\omega_2) \cdots E_p(\omega_n), \tag{14.38n}$$

where $i = x, y, z$ and $E_j(\omega_1), E_k(\omega_2), \ldots, E_p(\omega_n)$ can be any of the Cartesian components E_x, E_y, E_z of the applied electric fields at different frequencies. The frequencies $\omega_1, \omega_2, \ldots, \omega_n$ can be rearranged but ω must equal the sum of $\omega_1, \omega_2, \ldots, \omega_n$. As a matter of notation, the order of the frequencies $\omega_1, \omega_2, \ldots, \omega_n$ associated with the electric field components $E_j(\omega_1), E_k(\omega_2), \ldots, E_p(\omega_n)$ is kept the same as the order of the frequencies in the argument of $\chi_{ijk\cdots p}^{(n)}(\omega_1, \omega_2, \ldots, \omega_n)$. The summation over $j, k, \ldots, p$ ensures that contributions to the ith component of the nth-order polarization at frequency ω from all Cartesian components of the electric fields belonging to all different frequencies have been systematically included. The electric field components appearing in Eq. (14.38n) can be arranged in any order provided the order of their subindices $(j, k, \ldots, p)$ follows the order of the subindices of $\chi_{ijk\cdots p}^{(n)}(\omega_1, \omega_2, \ldots, \omega_n)$. A term like $\chi_{ijk}^{(2)}(\omega, \omega_1, \omega_2) E_k(\omega_1) E_j(\omega_2)$ cannot appear in Eq. (14.38b) for $n = 2$ because the orders of j, k indices in $\chi_{ijk}^{(2)}(\omega, \omega_1, \omega_2)$ and in the product $E_k(\omega_1)\, E_j(\omega_2)$ of the field components are different.

Any permutation of the field components in Eqs (14.38) within the above constraint does not constitute an additional contribution to $P_i^{(n)}(\omega)$ and hence must be excluded from the sum. For example, if the term $\chi_{ijk}^{(2)}(\omega, \omega_1, \omega_2) E_j(\omega_1) E_k(\omega_2)$ has been included in the ith component of the second-order polarization, then the term $\chi_{ikj}^{(2)}(\omega, \omega_2, \omega_1) E_k(\omega_2) E_j(\omega_1)$, being only a rearrangement of the above term, cannot appear in the sum. More specifically for the sum-frequency generation,

$$P_i^{(2)}(\omega = \omega_1 + \omega_2) = \frac{\epsilon_0}{2} \sum_{jk} \Big[\chi_{ijk}^{(2)}(\omega, \omega_1, \omega_2) E_j(\omega_1) E_k(\omega_2) + \chi_{ijk}^{(2)}(\omega, \omega_2, \omega_1) E_j(\omega_2) E_k(\omega_1) \Big], \tag{14.39a}$$

but for the second-harmonic generation,

$$P_i^{(2)}(2\omega) = \frac{\epsilon_0}{2}\sum_{jk} \chi_{ijk}^{(2)}(2\omega, \omega, \omega)\, E_j(\omega)\, E_k(\omega). \tag{14.39b}$$

Each term in Eqs (14.38) can be calculated in exactly the same manner as the scalar terms derived in the previous sections, though the number of terms for the higher order polarizations can indeed be very large as the following examples demonstrate. For the first-order polarization,

$$\begin{aligned} P_i^{(1)}(\omega) &= \epsilon_0 \sum_j \chi_{ij}^{(1)}(\omega)\, E_j(\omega) \\ &= \epsilon_0 \left[\chi_{ix}^{(1)}(\omega)\, E_x(\omega) + \chi_{iy}^{(1)}(\omega)\, E_y(\omega) + \chi_{iz}^{(1)}(\omega)\, E_z(\omega)\right]. \end{aligned} \tag{14.40}$$

Because of the anisotropy of the crystalline environment, all nine elements $\chi_{ix}^{(1)}, \chi_{iy}^{(1)}, \chi_{iz}^{(1)}$ for $i = x, y, z$ may be different and nonzero. In the second-order polarization

$$P_i^{(2)}(\omega) = \frac{\epsilon_0}{2}\sum_{jk} \chi_{ijk}^{(2)}(\omega, \omega_1, \omega_2)\, E_j(\omega_1)\, E_k(\omega_2), \tag{14.41}$$

we shall have to deal with 27 elements of $\chi^{(2)}(\omega, \omega_1, \omega_2)$ if the order of the frequencies in its argument is not changed. Allowing that change increases the number of elements to 162, since ω, ω_1, ω_2 can be arranged in six different ways. But while rearranging the frequencies, we must make sure that the first frequency in the argument of $\chi_{ijk\cdots p}^{(n)}(\omega, \omega_1, \omega_2, \ldots, \omega_n)$ must equal the sum of the remaining frequencies. This may necessitate some changes in the signs of the frequencies as we shall see later. There are some symmetry considerations which reduce the number of independent elements of the susceptibility tensors. We make a brief mention of these symmetries.

14.3 SYMMETRY PROPERTIES OF THE SUSCEPTIBILITY TENSORS

14.3.1 Susceptibility Tensors for Negative Frequencies

The complex conjugate of Eq. (14.38n) gives

$$P_i^{(n)*}(\omega) = \frac{\epsilon_0}{2^{n-1}} \sum_{jk\cdots p} \chi_{ijk\cdots p}^{(n)*}(\omega, \omega_1, \omega_2, \ldots, \omega_n)\, E_j^*(\omega_1)\, E_k^*(\omega_2) \cdots E_p^*(\omega_n). \tag{14.42}$$

Since $P^{(n)}(t)$ and $E(t)$ are real, $P^{(n)*}(\omega) = P^{(n)}(-\omega)$, $E^*(\omega_i) = E(-\omega_i)$ and Eq. (14.42) becomes

$$P_i^{(n)}(-\omega) = \frac{\epsilon_0}{2^{n-1}} \sum_{jk\cdots p} \chi_{ijk\cdots p}^{(n)*}(\omega, \omega_1, \omega_2, \ldots, \omega_n) \times E_j(-\omega_1)E_k(-\omega_2)\cdots E_p(-\omega_n). \tag{14.43}$$

On replacing ω by $(-\omega)$ and ω_i by $(-\omega_i)$ in Eq. (14.38n), we obtain

$$P_i^{(n)}(-\omega) = \frac{\epsilon_0}{2^{n-1}} \sum_{jk\cdots p} \chi_{ijk\cdots p}^{(n)}(-\omega, -\omega_1, -\omega_2, \ldots, -\omega_n) \times E_j(-\omega_1)E_k(-\omega_2)\cdots E_p(-\omega_n). \tag{14.44}$$

A comparison of Eqs (14.43) and (14.44) yields

$$\chi_{ijk\cdots p}^{(n)}(-\omega, -\omega_1, -\omega_2, \ldots, -\omega_n) = \chi_{ijk\cdots p}^{(n)*}(\omega, \omega_1, \omega_2, \ldots, \omega_n). \tag{14.45a}$$

Therefore, susceptibilities for the negative frequencies can be expressed in terms of the susceptibilities for the positive frequencies. Furthermore, extrapolation of Eqs (14.9) and (14.22) suggests that as long as the excitation frequencies are sufficiently small in comparison to the lowest absorption frequency of the medium, that is for nearly nonabsorbing media, susceptibility of any order becomes real, in which case, Eq. (14.45a) reduces to

$$\chi_{ijk\cdots p}^{(n)}(-\omega, -\omega_1, -\omega_2, \cdots, -\omega_n) = \chi_{ijk\cdots p}^{(n)}(\omega, \omega_1, \omega_2, \ldots, \omega_n). \tag{14.45b}$$

14.3.2 Full Permutation Symmetry

The full permutation symmetry allows all frequencies in the argument of the susceptibility tensor $\chi_{ijk\cdots p}^{(n)}(\omega, \omega_1, \omega_2, \ldots, \omega_n)$ including the one at which the polarization is generated to be rearranged as long as the Cartesian subindices $(i, j, k, \ldots, p)$ are also rearranged in the same order. In a rearrangement in which the first frequency is exchanged with some other frequency, the signs of both these frequencies in the new arrangement must be reversed to ensure that the first frequency in the new arrangement is equal to the sum of the remaining frequencies. For example if the first frequency ω is exchanged with ω_2, then according to the full permutation symmetry,

$$\chi_{ijkl\cdots p}^{(n)}(\omega, \omega_1, \omega_2, \omega_3, \ldots, \omega_n) = \chi_{kjil\cdots p}^{(n)}(-\omega_2, \omega_1, -\omega, \omega_3, \ldots, \omega_n). \tag{14.46a}$$

With the reality condition (Eq. 14.45b), the above equality changes to

$$\chi^{(n)}_{ijkl\cdots p}(\omega, \omega_1, \omega_2, \omega_3, \ldots, \omega_n) = \chi^{(n)}_{kjil\cdots p}(\omega_2, -\omega_1, \omega, -\omega_3, \ldots, -\omega_n). \tag{14.46b}$$

In particular for second-order susceptibility tensor, we can write

$$\chi^{(2)}_{ijk}(\omega, \omega_1, \omega_2) = \chi^{(2)}_{jki}(\omega_1, -\omega_2, \omega) = \chi^{(2)}_{kji}(\omega_2, -\omega_1, \omega) \tag{14.46c}$$

for the sum-frequency generation with $\omega = \omega_1 + \omega_2$, but for the second-harmonic generation,

$$\chi^{(2)}_{ijj}(2\omega, \omega, \omega) = \frac{1}{2}\chi^{(2)}_{jji}(\omega, -\omega, 2\omega). \tag{14.46d}$$

Let us see what kinds of nonlinear interactions the two susceptibilities appearing in Eq. (14.46b) represent. Following our observation in the new paragraph starting after Eqs (14.17), these susceptibilities will give rise to the following polarizations:

$$P_i(\omega) = \frac{\epsilon_0}{2^{n-1}}\chi^{(n)}_{ijkl\cdots p}(\omega, \omega_1, \omega_2, \omega_3, \ldots, \omega_n) E_j(\omega_1) E_k(\omega_2) \times E_l(\omega_3) \cdots E_p(\omega_n), \tag{14.47}$$

$$P_k(\omega_2) = \frac{\epsilon_0}{2^{n-1}}\chi^{(n)}_{kjil\cdots p}(\omega_2, -\omega_1, \omega, -\omega_3, \ldots, -\omega_n) E^*_j(\omega_1) E_i(\omega) \times E^*_l(-\omega_3) \cdots E^*_p(-\omega_n). \tag{14.48}$$

Equation (14.47) represents a nonlinear process in which one photon at each of $\omega_1, \omega_2, \omega_3, \ldots, \omega_n$ frequencies is destroyed and simultaneously a photon of frequency ω is created (Fig. 14.1a). Equation (14.48), on the other hand, represents a nonlinear process in which one photon of frequency ω is destroyed and simultaneously one photon at each of $\omega_1, \omega_2, \omega_3, \ldots, \omega_n$ frequencies is created (Fig. 14.1b). The first frequency in the argument of $\chi^{(n)}$ for $n > 1$ is always the frequency at which the nonlinear polarization is generated and hence is the frequency of a created photon. Among the remaining frequencies in the argument, those carrying positive signs belong to the photons which are destroyed and those carrying negative signs belong to the photons which are created in the nonlinear process. Equivalently, the complex conjugated field components in the product accompanying $\chi^{(n)}$ represent photons which are created and the field components which are not conjugated represent photons which are destroyed in a nonlinear process.

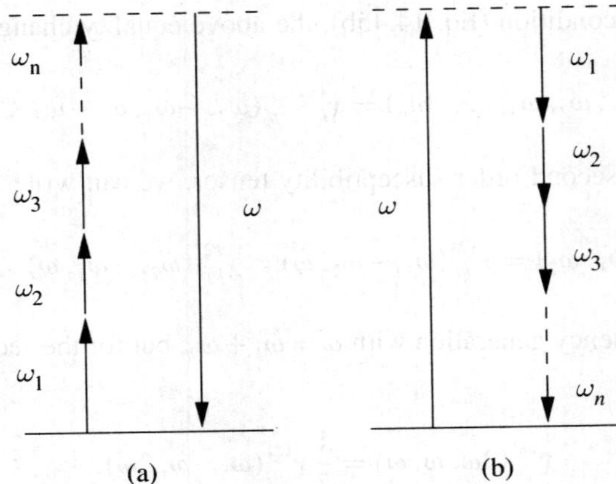

Fig. 14.1: Quantum mechanical description of a nonlinear process (a) in which one photon at each of $\omega_1, \omega_2, \omega_3, \ldots, \omega_n$ frequencies is destroyed and one photon of frequency ω is created, (b) in which one photon of frequency ω is destroyed and one photon at each of $\omega_1, \omega_2, \omega_3, \ldots, \omega_n$ frequencies is created. The up- (down-) directed arrows represent destroyed (created) photons.

14.3.3 Kleinman's Symmetry

As long as the excitation frequencies remain much below the lowest absorption frequency of the medium, the susceptibility tensors exhibit only weak dependence on the frequencies appearing in their arguments. In Kleinman's symmetry, this dependence is neglected altogether. As a result, in the context of the third-rank susceptibility tensor, the full permutation symmetry in the presence of Kleinman's symmetry yields

$$\begin{aligned}\chi^{(2)}_{ijk}(\omega, \omega_1, \omega_2) &= \chi^{(2)}_{ikj}(\omega, \omega_1, \omega_2) = \chi^{(2)}_{jki}(\omega, \omega_1, \omega_2) \\ &= \chi^{(2)}_{jik}(\omega, \omega_1, \omega_2) = \chi^{(2)}_{kij}(\omega, \omega_1, \omega_2) = \chi^{(2)}_{kji}(\omega, \omega_1, \omega_2).\end{aligned} \tag{14.49}$$

We have not rearranged the frequencies in the arguments of $\chi^{(2)}$ in Eq. (14.49) as required by the full permutation symmetry because Kleinman's symmetry makes $\chi^{(2)}$ independent of the frequencies. It should be understood that the Kleinman's symmetry is an approximation but whenever it holds, the number of independent elements of the susceptibility tensors are considerably reduced. For example, as we shall see, it reduces the number of independent elements of $\chi^{(2)}$ from 27 to 10.

The crystal symmetry further reduces the number of independent elements of the susceptibility tensors. We shall, however, not go into these details, but just show that the susceptibility tensors $\chi^{(n)}$ for even n vanish for the centrosymmetric crystals. These crystals possess centers of inversion, i.e., it is possible to choose an origin such that any site within the unit cell with position vector $\vec{r}$ is exactly equivalent to the site with position vector $(-\vec{r})$. It follows that in such crystals, the generated polarization simply reverses its direction on reversing the directions of all applied electric fields. Rewriting Eq. (14.38n) before and after reversing the directions of the applied electric fields, we obtain

$$P_i^{(n)}(\omega) = \frac{\epsilon_0}{2^{n-1}} \sum_{jk\cdots p} \chi_{ijk\cdots p}^{(n)}(\omega, \omega_1, \omega_2, \ldots, \omega_n) E_j(\omega_1) E_k(\omega_2) \cdots E_p(\omega_n), \tag{14.50a}$$

$$-P_i^{(n)}(\omega) = \frac{\epsilon_0}{2^{n-1}} \sum_{jk\cdots p} \chi_{ijk\cdots p}^{(n)}(\omega, \omega_1, \omega_2, \ldots, \omega_n)(-E_j(\omega_1))$$

$$\times (-E_k(\omega_2)) \cdots (-E_p(\omega_n)),$$

$$= \frac{\epsilon_0}{2^{n-1}} \sum_{jk\cdots p} \chi_{ijk\cdots p}^{(n)}(\omega, \omega_1, \omega_2, \ldots, \omega_n) E_j(\omega_1) E_k(\omega_2) \cdots E_p(\omega_n), \tag{14.50b}$$

when n is even. Therefore for even n, Eqs (14.50a) and (14.50b) can be reconciled only if

$$\chi^{(n)}(\omega, \omega_1, \omega_2, \ldots, \omega_n) = 0. \tag{14.51}$$

In particular, $\chi^{(2)}(\omega, \omega_1, \omega_2) = 0$ for the centrosymmetric crystals, disallowing second-harmonic generation in such crystals.

Before concluding this section we introduce the contracted notation of expressing the elements of a susceptibility tensor. We define[2]

$$d_{ijk}^{(2)} = \frac{1}{2}\chi_{ijk}^{(2)}, \tag{14.52}$$

where Kleinman's symmetry has been used to suppress the argument of $\chi^{(2)}$. In addition, since the last two subindices of $\chi_{ijk}^{(2)}$ and hence of $d_{ijk}^{(2)}$ can be freely exchanged, they can be replaced by a single subindex. Therefore, we can write

$$d_{ijk}^{(2)} = d_{il}, \tag{14.53}$$

where the index l is defined in the following manner:

$$\begin{array}{llllll} (jk): & 11 & 22 & 33 & (23),(32) & (13),(31) & (12),(21) \\ (l): & 1 & 2 & 3 & 4 & 5 & 6 \end{array}$$

[2] For the general case, the d-tensor is defined as $d^{(n)} = (2)^{-n+1+s}\chi^{(n)}$, where s is the number of dc fields present in the input.

Table 14.1. d_{il} (in 10^{-12} m/V) values of some nonlinear crystals.

$LiNbO_3$	$d_{22} = 2.6 \pm 1$	$d_{31} = -5.4 \pm 0.5$	$d_{33} = -49 \pm 9$
$BaTiO_3$	$d_{15} = 17.7 \pm 1.5$	$d_{31} = -18.8 \pm 1.5$	$d_{33} = -7.1 \pm 0.5$
KH_2PO_4 (KDP)		$d_{36} = 0.51 \pm 0.02$	

It is then possible to replace the $d_{ijk}^{(2)}$ tensor by the d_{il} matrix having many common elements as the following example shows. Since all the subindices of $d_{ijk}^{(2)}$ can be freely exchanged (see Eq. 14.49), we must have

$$d_{13} = d_{133} = d_{313} = d_{35}.$$

The complete d_{il} matrix having only 10 independent elements can be shown to have the form

$$d_{il} = \begin{bmatrix} d_{11} & d_{12} & d_{13} & d_{14} & d_{15} & d_{16} \\ d_{16} & d_{22} & d_{23} & d_{24} & d_{14} & d_{12} \\ d_{15} & d_{24} & d_{33} & d_{23} & d_{13} & d_{14} \end{bmatrix}. \tag{14.54}$$

The matrix notation of nonlinear polarization for second-harmonic generation is

$$\begin{pmatrix} P_x^{(2)}(2\omega) \\ P_y^{(2)}(2\omega) \\ P_z^{(2)}(2\omega) \end{pmatrix} = \epsilon_0 \begin{pmatrix} d_{11} & d_{12} & d_{13} & d_{14} & d_{15} & d_{16} \\ d_{21} & d_{22} & d_{23} & d_{24} & d_{25} & d_{26} \\ d_{31} & d_{32} & d_{33} & d_{34} & d_{35} & d_{36} \end{pmatrix} \begin{pmatrix} E_x^2(\omega) \\ E_y^2(\omega) \\ E_z^2(\omega) \\ 2E_y(\omega)E_z(\omega) \\ 2E_z(\omega)E_x(\omega) \\ 2E_x(\omega)E_y(\omega) \end{pmatrix}. \tag{14.55}$$

Table 14.1 gives d_{il} elements for some commonly used nonlinear crystals (taken from [14.6]).

14.4 WAVE EQUATION FOR NONLINEAR MEDIA

To describe propagation of light waves in a nonlinear medium, we express the displacement field (Eq. 1.6a) as

$$\begin{aligned} \vec{D} &= \epsilon_0 \vec{E} + \vec{P} \\ &= \epsilon_0 \vec{E} + \vec{P}_{\mathrm{L}} + \vec{P}_{\mathrm{NL}} \\ &= \epsilon_0 (1 + \chi^{(1)}) \vec{E} + \vec{P}_{\mathrm{NL}} \end{aligned}$$

$$= \epsilon \vec{E} + \vec{P}_{\mathrm{NL}}, \tag{14.56}$$

where

$$\epsilon = \epsilon_0 (1 + \chi^{(1)}) \tag{1.9c}$$

is the linear permittivity of the medium and $\vec{P}_{\mathrm{NL}}$ is the nonlinear polarization generated in the medium in the presence of the electric field $\vec{E}$. Following steps which led to Eq. (1.11a), Maxwell's equations

$$\nabla \times \vec{E} = -\frac{\partial \vec{B}}{\partial t}, \quad \nabla \times \vec{B} = \mu \frac{\partial \vec{D}}{\partial t}, \tag{1.10c,d}$$

and Eq. (14.56) yield the inhomogeneous wave equation

$$\nabla^2 \vec{E}(\vec{r}, t) - \mu \epsilon \frac{\partial^2 \vec{E}(\vec{r}, t)}{\partial t^2} = \mu \frac{\partial^2 \vec{P}_{\mathrm{NL}}(\vec{r}, t)}{\partial t^2}, \tag{14.57}$$

which describes wave propagation in a source-free, nonlinear medium of linear permittivity ϵ and permeability μ. For optically transparent media, $\mu \sim \mu_0$, where μ_0 is permeability of the vacuum. The nonlinear polarization term on the right-hand side of Eq. (14.57) can be treated as a source term with sources distributed throughout the nonlinear medium. These sources radiate new waves which reach a given point in the medium with different phases. Because of this phase variation, the interference among the waves can lead to energy flowing back and forth among the nonlinearly generated and applied optical fields. For n optical fields of frequencies $\omega_1, \omega_2, \ldots, \omega_n$ entering the nonlinear medium and generating nonlinear polarization at frequency ω_{n+1}, we must solve $(n+1)$ wave equations of the type

$$\nabla^2 \vec{E}(\vec{r}, t, \omega_i) - \mu \epsilon(\omega_i) \frac{\partial^2 \vec{E}(\vec{r}, t, \omega_i)}{\partial t^2} = \mu \frac{\partial^2 \vec{P}_{\mathrm{NL}}(\vec{r}, t, \omega_i)}{\partial t^2} \tag{14.58}$$

for $i = 1, 2, \ldots, (n+1)$, where $\epsilon(\omega_i)$ is the linear permittivity of the medium at frequency ω_i.

14.5 SECOND-ORDER NONLINEAR PROCESSES

Consider two monochromatic plane waves

$$E_i(z, t, \omega_1) = \frac{1}{2}\left[E_i(\omega_1) \mathrm{e}^{\mathrm{i}(k_1 z - \omega_1 t)} + \mathrm{cc}\right],$$

$$E_j(z,t,\omega_2)=\frac{1}{2}\left[E_j(\omega_2)\,\mathrm{e}^{\mathrm{i}(k_2z-\omega_2t)}+\mathrm{cc}\right], \tag{14.59}$$

incident normally on a nonlinear, nonabsorbing medium confined between the planes $z=0$ and $z=L$. For definiteness, one of the incident waves is polarized along the x direction and the other along the y direction. For the second-order nonlinearly generated polarization at frequency ω, the three waves propagating in the z direction inside the nonlinear medium can be described by the fields

$$\begin{aligned}
E_i(z,t,\omega_1)&=\frac{1}{2}\left[E_i(z,\omega_1)\,\mathrm{e}^{\mathrm{i}(k_1z-\omega_1t)}+\mathrm{cc}\right],\\
E_j(z,t,\omega_2)&=\frac{1}{2}\left[E_j(z,\omega_2)\,\mathrm{e}^{\mathrm{i}(k_2z-\omega_2t)}+\mathrm{cc}\right],\\
E_k(z,t,\omega)&=\frac{1}{2}\left[E_k(z,\omega)\,\mathrm{e}^{\mathrm{i}(kz-\omega t)}+\mathrm{cc}\right],
\end{aligned} \tag{14.60}$$

where $E_i(z,\omega_1)$ and $E_j(z,\omega_2)$ are the amplitudes of the waves of frequencies ω_1 and ω_2, respectively, and $E_k(z,\omega)$ is the amplitude of the nonlineariy generated wave which, for sufficiently large L, also propagates in the z direction. The polarization of the nonlinearly generated wave can be along x or y directions. Because of the nonlinear interaction, the amplitudes of the three waves vary spatially as they propagate in the nonlinear medium but the sum of the intensities of the three waves should remain constant for the nonabsorbing medium under consideration. The frequencies ω_1, ω_2, ω have been included in the arguments of the field amplitudes merely to specify the frequencies of the respective waves. They are not to be taken as the variables. Since no x and y dependences of the amplitudes are being considered, we need to solve the following three wave equations:

$$\begin{aligned}
\frac{\partial^2 E_i(z,t,\omega_1)}{\partial z^2}-\mu\epsilon_1\frac{\partial^2 E_i(z,t,\omega_1)}{\partial t^2}&=\mu\frac{\partial^2 P_i^{(2)}(z,t,\omega_1)}{\partial t^2},\\
\frac{\partial^2 E_j(z,t,\omega_2)}{\partial z^2}-\mu\epsilon_2\frac{\partial^2 E_j(z,t,\omega_2)}{\partial t^2}&=\mu\frac{\partial^2 P_j^{(2)}(z,t,\omega_2)}{\partial t^2},\\
\frac{\partial^2 E_k(z,t,\omega)}{\partial z^2}-\mu\epsilon\frac{\partial^2 E_k(z,t,\omega)}{\partial t^2}&=\mu\frac{\partial^2 P_k^{(2)}(z,t,\omega)}{\partial t^2},
\end{aligned} \tag{14.61}$$

where $\epsilon_1, \epsilon_2, \epsilon$ are the linear permittivities of the medium at the frequencies $\omega_1, \omega_2, \omega$, respectively. The second-order nonlinear polarizations $P_i^{(2)}(z, t, \omega_1)$, $P_j^{(2)}(z, t, \omega_2)$, $P_k^{(2)}(z, t, \omega)$ can be expressed as

$$\begin{aligned} P_i^{(2)}(z, t, \omega_1) &= \frac{1}{2}\left[P_i^{(2)}(z, \omega_1)\,\mathrm{e}^{-\mathrm{i}\omega_1 t} + \mathrm{cc}\right], \\ P_j^{(2)}(z, t, \omega_2) &= \frac{1}{2}\left[P_j^{(2)}(z, \omega_2)\,\mathrm{e}^{-\mathrm{i}\omega_2 t} + \mathrm{cc}\right], \\ P_k^{(2)}(z, t, \omega) &= \frac{1}{2}\left[P_k^{(2)}(z, \omega)\,\mathrm{e}^{-\mathrm{i}\omega t} + \mathrm{cc}\right]. \end{aligned} \tag{14.62}$$

Substituting Eqs (14.60) and (14.62) into Eqs (14.61) gives

$$\begin{aligned} \frac{\mathrm{d}^2\left[E_i(z, \omega_1)\,\mathrm{e}^{\mathrm{i}k_1 z}\right]}{\mathrm{d}z^2} + \mu\epsilon_1\omega_1^2 E_i(z, \omega_1)\,\mathrm{e}^{\mathrm{i}k_1 z} &= -\mu\,\omega_1^2 P_i^{(2)}(z, \omega_1), \\ \frac{\mathrm{d}^2\left[E_j(z, \omega_2)\,\mathrm{e}^{\mathrm{i}k_2 z}\right]}{\mathrm{d}z^2} + \mu\epsilon_2\omega_2^2 E_j(z, \omega_2)\,\mathrm{e}^{\mathrm{i}k_2 z} &= -\mu\,\omega_2^2 P_j^{(2)}(z, \omega_2), \\ \frac{\mathrm{d}^2\left[E_k(z, \omega)\,\mathrm{e}^{\mathrm{i}kz}\right]}{\mathrm{d}z^2} + \mu\epsilon\omega^2 E_k(z, \omega)\,\mathrm{e}^{\mathrm{i}kz} &= -\mu\,\omega^2 P_k^{(2)}(z, \omega). \end{aligned} \tag{14.63}$$

14.5.1 Sum-Frequency Generation

The nonlinear polarizations appearing on the right-hand sides of Eqs (14.63) can be obtained from Eq. (14.38b) in conjunction with our comment in the discussion following Eq. (14.48) or by a comparison with Eqs (14.16). For sum-frequency generation, we obtain

$$\begin{aligned} P_i^{(2)}(z, \omega_1) &= \frac{\epsilon_0}{2}\sum_{jk}\chi_{ijk}^{(2)}(\omega_1, -\omega_2, \omega)E_j^*(z, \omega_2)\,E_k(z, \omega)\,\mathrm{e}^{\mathrm{i}(k-k_2)z}, \\ P_j^{(2)}(z, \omega_2) &= \frac{\epsilon_0}{2}\sum_{ki}\chi_{jki}^{(2)}(\omega_2, \omega, -\omega_1)E_k(z, \omega)\,E_i^*(z, \omega_1)\,\mathrm{e}^{\mathrm{i}(k-k_1)z}, \\ P_k^{(2)}(z, \omega) &= \frac{\epsilon_0}{2}\sum_{ij}\chi_{kij}^{(2)}(\omega, \omega_1, \omega_2)E_i(z, \omega_1)\,E_j(z, \omega_2)\,\mathrm{e}^{\mathrm{i}(k_1+k_2)z}, \end{aligned} \tag{14.64}$$

where $\omega = \omega_1 + \omega_2$. A few comments on these equations may be in order. The equation for the nonlinear polarization $P_k^{(2)}(z, \omega)$ at the sum frequency $\omega = \omega_1 + \omega_2$ is essentially the Eq. (14.38b) except for some rearrangement of the i, j, k indices. The tensor $\chi_{kij}^{(2)}(\omega, \omega_1, \omega_2)$ implies sum-frequency generation since $\omega = \omega_1 + \omega_2$. The polarizations $P_i^{(2)}(z, \omega_1)$ and $P_j^{(2)}(z, \omega_2)$ at the frequencies ω_1 and ω_2, respectively, are however created by difference-frequency generation since $\omega_1 = \omega - \omega_2$ and $\omega_2 = \omega - \omega_1$, and hence the appearance of tensors $\chi_{ijk}^{(2)}(\omega_1, -\omega_2, \omega)$ and $\chi_{jki}^{(2)}(\omega_2, \omega, -\omega_1)$ in the first two of Eqs (14.64). A comparison with Eq. (14.16d) shows why the field amplitudes $E_j(z, \omega_2)$ and $E_i(z, \omega_1)$ are complex conjugated in these equations. We note that

$$\begin{aligned}&\frac{\mathrm{d}^2}{\mathrm{d}z^2}\left[E_i(z, \omega_1)\mathrm{e}^{\mathrm{i}k_1 z}\right] + \mu\epsilon_1\omega_1^2 E_i(z, \omega_1)\mathrm{e}^{\mathrm{i}k_1 z}\\ &= \left[\frac{\mathrm{d}^2 E_i(z, \omega_1)}{\mathrm{d}z^2} + 2\mathrm{i}k_1\frac{\mathrm{d}E_i(z, \omega_1)}{\mathrm{d}z} + \left(\mu\epsilon_1\omega_1^2 - k_1^2\right)E_i(z, \omega_1)\right]\mathrm{e}^{\mathrm{i}k_1 z}\\ &\approx 2\mathrm{i}k_1\mathrm{e}^{\mathrm{i}k_1 z}\frac{\mathrm{d}E_i(z, \omega_1)}{\mathrm{d}z}.\end{aligned}$$

Similarly

$$\begin{aligned}\frac{\mathrm{d}^2}{\mathrm{d}z^2}\left[E_j(z, \omega_2)\mathrm{e}^{\mathrm{i}k_2 z}\right] + \mu\epsilon_2\omega_2^2 E_j(z, \omega_2)\mathrm{e}^{\mathrm{i}k_2 z} &= 2\mathrm{i}k_2\mathrm{e}^{\mathrm{i}k_2 z}\frac{\mathrm{d}E_j(z, \omega_2)}{\mathrm{d}z},\\ \frac{\mathrm{d}^2}{\mathrm{d}z^2}\left[E_k(z, \omega)\mathrm{e}^{\mathrm{i}kz}\right] + \mu\epsilon\omega^2 E_k(z, \omega)\mathrm{e}^{\mathrm{i}kz} &= 2\mathrm{i}k\mathrm{e}^{\mathrm{i}kz}\frac{\mathrm{d}E_k(z, \omega)}{\mathrm{d}z}.\end{aligned} \tag{14.65}$$

In obtaining Eqs (14.65), we have used the slowly varying amplitude approximation

$$\frac{\mathrm{d}^2 E(z, \omega)}{\mathrm{d}z^2} \ll k\frac{\mathrm{d}E(z, \omega)}{\mathrm{d}z} \tag{14.66}$$

and the results (see Eq. 1.18a)

$$k_1^2 = \mu\epsilon_1\omega_1^2, \quad k_2^2 = \mu\epsilon_2\omega_2^2, \quad k^2 = \mu\epsilon\omega^2. \tag{14.67}$$

According to the slowly varying amplitude approximation, the variation of the amplitude of a wave over a distance of the order of the wavelength of light in the direction of propagation is small. However, significant changes in the amplitude can take place over macroscopic distances. Substituting Eqs (14.64) into Eqs (14.63) and making use of Eqs (14.65), we obtain the equations which describe the variations of the amplitudes of the three waves in the nonlinear medium as

$$\begin{aligned}\frac{\mathrm{d}E_i(z, \omega_1)}{\mathrm{d}z} &= \frac{\mathrm{i}\omega_1}{4cn_1}\sum_{jk}\chi_{ijk}^{(2)}(\omega_1, -\omega_2, \omega)E_j^*(z, \omega_2)E_k(z, \omega)\mathrm{e}^{\mathrm{i}\Delta kz},\\ \frac{\mathrm{d}E_j(z, \omega_2)}{\mathrm{d}z} &= \frac{\mathrm{i}\omega_2}{4cn_2}\sum_{ki}\chi_{jki}^{(2)}(\omega_2, \omega, -\omega_1)E_k(z, \omega)E_i^*(z, \omega_1)\mathrm{e}^{\mathrm{i}\Delta kz},\\ \frac{\mathrm{d}E_k(z, \omega)}{\mathrm{d}z} &= \frac{\mathrm{i}\omega}{4cn}\sum_{ij}\chi_{kij}^{(2)}(\omega, \omega_1, \omega_2)E_i(z, \omega_1)E_j(z, \omega_2)\mathrm{e}^{-\mathrm{i}\Delta kz},\end{aligned} \tag{14.68}$$

where n_1, n_2, and n are the linear indices of refraction of the medium at the frequencies ω_1, ω_2, and ω, respectively (see Eq. 1.18b), and

$$\Delta k = k - k_1 - k_2 \tag{14.69}$$

is the wave vector mismatch and (Δkz) is the phase mismatch between the nonlinearly generated wave $E_k(z, \omega)$ and the nonlinear polarization $P_k^{(2)}(z, \omega)$ which sustains it. We note that the sum-frequency wave $E_k(z, t, \omega)$ is generated even in the absence of perfect phase matching $(\Delta k = 0)$, albeit with reduced efficiency. Klienman's symmetry makes the $\chi^{(2)}$ tensors appearing in Eqs (14.68) real and independent of the frequencies in their arguments. In addition, an effective $\chi^{(2)}$ can take care of the summations over the field components, so that Eqs (14.68) become

$$\frac{\mathrm{d}E_i(\omega_1)}{\mathrm{d}z} = \mathrm{i}\alpha\frac{\omega_1}{n_1}E_j^*(\omega_2)E_k(\omega)\mathrm{e}^{\mathrm{i}\Delta kz}, \tag{14.70a}$$

$$\frac{\mathrm{d}E_j(\omega_2)}{\mathrm{d}z} = \mathrm{i}\alpha\frac{\omega_2}{n_2}E_k(\omega)E_i^*(\omega_1)\mathrm{e}^{\mathrm{i}\Delta kz}, \tag{14.70b}$$

$$\frac{\mathrm{d}E_k(\omega)}{\mathrm{d}z} = \mathrm{i}\alpha\frac{\omega}{n}E_i(\omega_1)E_j(\omega_2)\mathrm{e}^{-\mathrm{i}\Delta kz}, \tag{14.70c}$$

where

$$\alpha = \frac{1}{4c}\chi_{\text{eff}}^{(2)} = \frac{1}{2c}d_{\text{eff}}^{(2)}, \tag{14.71}$$

and c is the speed of light in the vacuum. To simplify the notation, we have dropped z from the arguments of the field amplitudes. Exact solutions of Eqs (14.70) are difficult to obtain because of the coupling among the amplitudes of the three waves. Before considering special solutions of Eqs (14.70), we derive some general results concerning second-order nonlinear processes in a nonabsorbing, nonlinear medium. The intensity of the wave of frequency ω_1 is (see Eq. 1.46)

$$I(\omega_1) = \frac{1}{2}\epsilon_0 n_1 c E_i(\omega_1)E_i^*(\omega_1).$$

Therefore

$$\frac{\mathrm{d}I(\omega_1)}{\mathrm{d}z} = \frac{1}{2}\epsilon_0 n_1 c\left[E_i(\omega_1)\frac{\mathrm{d}E_i^*(\omega_1)}{\mathrm{d}z} + E_i^*(\omega_1)\frac{\mathrm{d}E_i(\omega_1)}{\mathrm{d}z}\right]. \tag{14.72}$$

Substituting Eq. (14.70a) into Eq. (14.72) gives

$$\begin{aligned}\frac{dI(\omega_1)}{dz} &= \frac{1}{2}\epsilon_0 c\alpha\omega_1 \left[-iE_i(\omega_1)E_j(\omega_2)E_k^*(\omega)\,e^{-i\Delta kz}\right.\\ &\qquad \left.+iE_i^*(\omega_1)E_j^*(\omega_2)E_k(\omega)\,e^{i\Delta kz}\right]\\ &= \epsilon_0 c\alpha\omega_1 I_{im}\left[iE_i^*(\omega_1)E_j^*(\omega_2)E_k(\omega)\,e^{i\Delta kz}\right]. \end{aligned} \tag{14.73a}$$

Similarly,

$$\frac{dI(\omega_2)}{dz} = \epsilon_0 c\alpha\omega_2 I_{im}\left[iE_i^*(\omega_1)E_j^*(\omega_2)E_k(\omega)\,e^{i\Delta kz}\right], \tag{14.73b}$$

$$\frac{dI(\omega=\omega_1+\omega_2)}{dz} = -\,\epsilon_0 c\alpha\omega I_{im}\left[iE_i^*(\omega_1)E_j^*(\omega_2)E_k(\omega)\,e^{i\Delta kz}\right], \tag{14.73c}$$

where I_{im} refers to the imaginary part of the quantity within the brackets. Adding Eqs (14.73a,b,c) gives

$$\frac{d}{dz}\left[I(\omega_1)+I(\omega_2)+I(\omega=\omega_1+\omega_2)\right]=0. \tag{14.74}$$

Therefore in sum-frequency generation, the three waves merely exchange energy as they propagate in the nonabsorbing, nonlinear medium without any loss in the overall intensity of the waves. This is the statement of energy conservation. Furthermore, we can recast Eqs (14.73) in the form

$$\frac{1}{\omega}\frac{dI(\omega)}{dz} = -\frac{1}{\omega_1}\frac{dI(\omega_1)}{dz} = -\frac{1}{\omega_2}\frac{dI(\omega_2)}{dz}. \tag{14.75}$$

Since $I(\omega)=n\hbar\omega$, where n is the number of photons of frequency ω and energy $\hbar\omega$ crossing unit area in unit time, Eq. (14.75) has the obvious interpretation that the rate of creation of the photons of the sum frequency $\omega=\omega_1+\omega_2$ equals the rates of destructions of the photons of frequencies ω_1 and ω_2. This is the statement of Manley–Rowe relations. We now solve Eqs (14.70) first when both incident waves are strong and then when one incident wave is strong and the other is weak. The latter case corresponds to the nonlinear process known as upconversion.

When the incident waves are strong and efficiency of sum-frequency generation sufficiently low, the incident waves propagate in the nonlinear medium without significant depletion in the their intensities. Therefore with $E_i(\omega_1)$ and $E_j(\omega_2)$ treated as constants, Eq. (14.70c) can be integrated to give the amplitude of the sum-frequency wave upon emergence from the nonlinear medium as

$$E_k(\omega_1+\omega_2, z=L) = \mathrm{i}(\omega_1+\omega_2)\frac{\alpha}{n}E_i(\omega_1)E_j(\omega_2)\int_0^L \mathrm{e}^{-\mathrm{i}\Delta k z}\,\mathrm{d}z$$

$$= \mathrm{i}(\omega_1+\omega_2)\frac{\alpha}{n}L\,\mathrm{e}^{-\mathrm{i}\frac{\Delta k}{2}L}E_i(\omega_1)E_j(\omega_2)\mathrm{sinc}\left(\frac{\Delta kL}{2}\right), \tag{14.76}$$

giving the intensity of the emerging sum-frequency wave as

$$I(\omega_1+\omega_2, z=L) = I_0\,\mathrm{sinc}^2\left(\frac{\Delta kL}{2}\right), \tag{14.77}$$

where

$$I_0 = \frac{(\omega_1+\omega_2)^2L^2I(\omega_1)I(\omega_2)}{2n_1n_2n\epsilon_0c^3}(d_{\mathrm{eff}}^{(2)})^2,$$

$$\mathrm{sinc}\left(\frac{\Delta kL}{2}\right) = \frac{\sin(\Delta kL/2)}{\Delta kL/2},$$

and

$$I(\omega_1) = \frac{1}{2}\epsilon_0n_1c\,|E_i(\omega_1)|^2, \quad I(\omega_2) = \frac{1}{2}\epsilon_0n_2c\,|E_j(\omega_2)|^2$$

are the intensities of the incident waves. Normalized intensity (I/I_0) variation of the sum-frequency wave is plotted in Fig. 14.2. We note that the efficiency

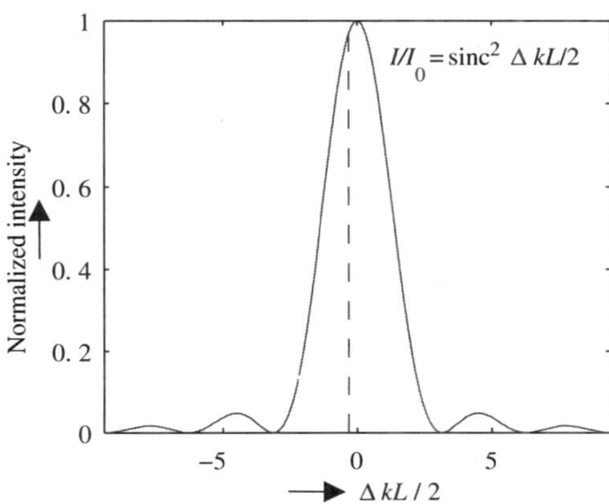

Fig. 14.2: Normalized intensity variation of the sum-frequency signal.

of sum-frequency generation decreases with increasing $(\Delta k L)$ due to increased phase mismatch between the sum-frequency wave and the driving nonlinear polarization, resulting in the flow of energy from the sum-frequency wave back to the incident waves.

14.5.1.1 Phase Matching

Maximum efficiency of sum-frequency generation occurs when $\Delta k = k - k_1 - k_2 = 0$. This is the condition for perfect phase matching. When this condition is achieved, sum-frequency generation for collinear incident waves is confined to the forward direction only (Fig. 14.3a). For $\Delta k \neq 0$, sum-frequency generation is spread over an angle

$$\theta \approx \frac{\Delta k}{k} = \frac{2\pi/L}{2\pi/\lambda} = \frac{\lambda}{L}, \tag{14.78}$$

where L is the thickness of the nonlinear medium (Fig. 14.3b). The fact that the sum-frequency wave is generated even when $\Delta k \neq 0$ implies that although energy conservation holds, momentum conservation is not strictly obeyed in nonlinear optical processes. This is so because in quantum mechanics, the momentum of a photon with propagation vector $\vec{k}$ is $\hbar\vec{k}$, where $\hbar = h/2\pi$, h is Planck's constant. For momentum conservation in sum-frequency generation, $\hbar\Delta k = \hbar(\vec{k} - \vec{k}_1 - \vec{k}_2)$ must be zero. The seemingly small angular spread (λ/L) for a macroscopic thickness of the nonlinear medium can considerably reduce the efficiency of sum-frequency generation. Perfect phase matching requires a nonlinear medium of infinite extent. It is therefore necessary to achieve phase matching by other means. For collinear incident waves, perfect phase matching for sum-frequency generation occurs when $k = k_1 + k_2$ or when

$$(\omega_1 + \omega_2)n(\omega_1 + \omega_2) = \omega_1 n(\omega_1) + \omega_2 n(\omega_2), \tag{14.79}$$

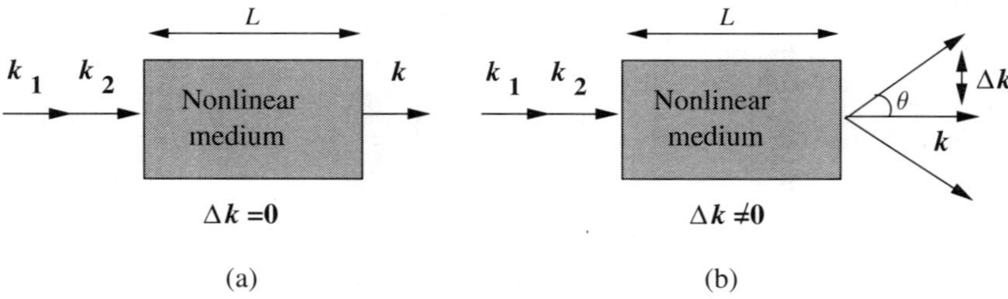

Fig. 14.3: Sum-frequency generation for collinear waves (a) in the forward direction only under perfect phase-matching condition, (b) has finite angular spread in the absence of phase matching.

where $n(\omega_1)$, $n(\omega_2)$, and $n(\omega_1+\omega_2)$ are the linear indices of refraction of the medium at the frequencies ω_1, ω_2, and $\omega_1+\omega_2$, respectively. It is impossible to satisfy the above condition in singly refracting media (see Problem 14.3) because of the monotonic increase in the index of refraction with frequency due to normal dispersion (see Fig. 1.21). However, index matching may be possible in birefringent media (see Sections 1.10.3 and 1.10.4). In uniaxial crystals, the index of refraction experienced by the extraordinary wave polarized in the plane containing its direction of propagation and the optic axis of the crystal varies from the ordinary index n_o to the extraordinary index n_e as the direction of propagation changes from along to perpendicular to the optic axis. On the other hand, the ordinary wave polarized perpendicular to the plane of the optic axis and the direction of propagation experiences no refractive index variation. Therefore, a proper choice of the polarization directions of the incident and sum-frequency waves in a birefringent medium may achieve index matching. In positive uniaxial crystals with $n_e > n_o$, perfect phase matching for collinear waves may be achieved in the following two ways.

Type I Phase Matching
Both incident waves are extraordinary waves and the sum-frequency wave is an ordinary wave satisfying the condition

$$n_o(\omega_1+\omega_2) = \frac{\omega_1}{\omega_1+\omega_2} n_e(\omega_1) + \frac{\omega_2}{\omega_1+\omega_2} n_e(\omega_2), \tag{14.80}$$

where n_o and n_e refer to the ordinary and extraordinary indices of refraction of the birefringent medium, respectively.

Type II Phase Matching
In this scheme, one of the incident waves is an extraordinary wave and the other is an ordinary wave and the sum-frequency wave is also an ordinary wave satisfying the condition

$$n_o(\omega_1+\omega_2) = \frac{\omega_1}{\omega_1+\omega_2} n_o(\omega_1) + \frac{\omega_2}{\omega_1+\omega_2} n_e(\omega_2). \tag{14.81}$$

Type I and II phase matching can also be achieved in negative uniaxial crystals with $n_e < n_o$.

14.5.2 Upconversion

We now consider sum-frequency generation when one of the incident waves is strong and the other is weak. This may correspond to a situation in which a weak infrared signal and strong visible laser light interact in a nonlinear medium to generate visible light at the sum frequency. This process is called upconversion because one might think that the nonlinear interaction has effectively shifted the infrared radiation to visible light, where it can be detected with higher sensitivity of the visible detectors. We assume that phase matching has somehow been achieved. For low efficiency upconversion, the laser light of frequency ω_1 and amplitude $E_i(\omega_1)$ emerges from the nonlinear medium with essentially undiminished amplitude. We need to solve the remaining two equations (Eqs 14.70 with $\Delta k = 0$) for the infrared wave of frequency ω_2 and amplitude $E_j(\omega_2)$ and the upconverted wave of frequency ω and amplitude $E_k(\omega)$:

$$\frac{dE_j(\omega_2)}{dz} = i\frac{\omega_2}{n_2}\alpha E_i^*(\omega_1)E_k(\omega), \tag{14.82a}$$

$$\frac{dE_k(\omega)}{dz} = i\frac{\omega}{n}\alpha E_i(\omega_1)E_j(\omega_2). \tag{14.82b}$$

By differentiating Eq. (14.82a) and substituting into Eq. (14.82b) and vice versa, we obtain

$$\frac{d^2E_j(\omega_2)}{dz^2} = -\frac{\omega\omega_2}{nn_2}\alpha^2 |E_i(\omega_1)|^2 E_j(\omega_2), \tag{14.83a}$$

$$\frac{d^2E_k(\omega)}{dz^2} = -\frac{\omega\omega_2}{nn_2}\alpha^2 |E_i(\omega_1)|^2 E_k(\omega). \tag{14.83b}$$

For the upconverted wave with $E_k(\omega) = 0$ at $z = 0$, the solutions of these equations are

$$E_j(\omega_2) = E_0 \cos(\beta z), \tag{14.84a}$$

$$E_k(\omega) = E_0' \sin(\beta z), \tag{14.84b}$$

where

$$\beta = \sqrt{\frac{\omega\omega_2}{nn_2}}\alpha |E_i(\omega_1)| = \frac{1}{2c}\sqrt{\frac{\omega\omega_2}{nn_2}} |E_i(\omega_1)| d_{\text{eff}}^{(2)},$$

$$E_0' = i\sqrt{\frac{n_2\omega}{n\omega_2}}\frac{E_i(\omega_1)}{|E_i(\omega_1)|}E_0,$$

so that the ratio of the amplitudes of the upconverted and infrared signal waves is

$$\frac{E_0'}{E_0} = i\sqrt{\frac{n_2\omega}{n\omega_2}}\frac{E_i(\omega_1)}{|E_i(\omega_1)|}. \tag{14.85}$$

Since the frequency ω of the upconverted signal is in the visible and ω_2 is in the infrared, the upconverted wave under phase-matched conditions has larger

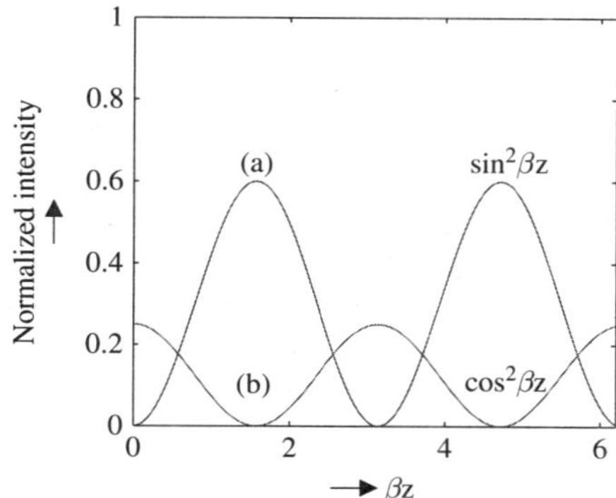

Fig. 14.4: Normalized intensity variation of the (a) upconverted wave, (b) infrared signal under phase-matched conditions (vertical scale arbitrary).

amplitude as compared to the amplitude of the infrared signal. Normalized intensity variations of the two waves in a nonlinear medium when phase matching has been achieved are shown in Fig. 14.4. The infrared and upconverted waves continuously exchange energy as they advance in the nonlinear medium. In the absence of phase matching, the intensity variations are qualitatively similar to those shown in Fig. 14.4, but with considerably reduced efficiency of upconversion.

14.5.3 Second-Harmonic Generation

Second-harmonic generation is a nonlinear process of great practical importance. It is routinely employed to obtain visible and ultraviolet radiations from infrared and visible light emitting lasers. For example, the fundamental wavelength ($1.06\,\mu$m, where $1\,\mu\text{m} = 10^{-6}\,$m) of emission of the Nd:YAG laser lies in the infrared spectral region. Visible light at $0.53\,\mu$m from this laser is obtained by second-harmonic generation. We continue to assume that the absorption frequencies of the nonlinear medium are far above the frequencies of the incident (usually called the pump wave or simply the pump) and nonlinearly generated second-harmonic waves, so that the susceptibility tensor $\chi^{(2)}$ is real and obeys full permutation symmetry. Assuming perfect phase matching and ignoring for the moment the polarization states of the waves, Eqs (14.70) in the present context ($\omega_1 = \omega_2 = \omega$, $\omega_1 + \omega_2 = 2\omega$) reduce to

$$\frac{\mathrm{d}E(\omega)}{\mathrm{d}z} = \mathrm{i}\frac{\omega}{4n(\omega)c}\chi_{\text{eff}}^{(2)}(\omega, -\omega, 2\omega)E^*(\omega)E(2\omega), \tag{14.86a}$$

$$\frac{\mathrm{d}E(2\omega)}{\mathrm{d}z} = \mathrm{i}\frac{2\omega}{4n(2\omega)c}\chi^{(2)}_{\mathrm{eff}}(2\omega, \omega, \omega)E^2(\omega), \tag{14.86b}$$

where $n(\omega)$ and $n(2\omega)$ are the linear indices of refraction of the medium at the frequencies ω and 2ω, respectively. We have used the tensor $\chi^{(2)}(\omega, -\omega, 2\omega)$ in Eq. (14.86a) because this equation applies to the nonlinearly generated field $E(\omega)$ from the field $E(2\omega)$ by a process in which a photon of the nonlinearly generated second-harmonic wave of frequency 2ω is destroyed and two photons of frequency ω are created, whereas in Eq. (14.86b), two photons of frequency ω are destroyed and one photon at the second-harmonic frequency 2ω is generated and hence the use of $\chi^{(2)}(2\omega, \omega, \omega)$ tensor in this equation. With

$$\chi^{(2)}(2\omega, \omega, \omega) = \frac{1}{2}\chi^{(2)}(\omega, -\omega, 2\omega), \tag{14.46d}$$

Eqs (14.86) can be rewritten as

$$\begin{aligned}\frac{\mathrm{d}E(\omega)}{\mathrm{d}z} &= \frac{\mathrm{i}\beta}{n(\omega)}E^*(\omega)E(2\omega),\\ \frac{\mathrm{d}E(2\omega)}{\mathrm{d}z} &= \frac{\mathrm{i}\beta}{n(2\omega)}E^2(\omega),\end{aligned} \tag{14.87}$$

where

$$\beta = \frac{\omega}{4c}\chi^{(2)}(\omega, -\omega, 2\omega). \tag{14.88}$$

From energy conservation,

$$\frac{1}{2}I(\omega) + \frac{1}{2}I(\omega) + I(2\omega) = I_0, \tag{14.89}$$

where the pump wave of intensity $I(\omega)$ is treated as two waves, each of intensity $\frac{1}{2}I(\omega)$ and I_0 is a constant. Following Boyd [14.1], we rewrite Eq. (14.89) as

$$I(\omega) + I(2\omega) = I_0\left(\varepsilon^2(\omega) + \varepsilon^2(2\omega)\right), \tag{14.90}$$

or equivalently as

$$\frac{1}{2}n(\omega)c\epsilon_0\,|E(\omega)|^2 + \frac{1}{2}n(2\omega)c\epsilon_0\,|E(2\omega)|^2 = I_0\left(\varepsilon^2(\omega) + \varepsilon^2(2\omega)\right), \tag{14.91}$$

where $\varepsilon(\omega)$ and $\varepsilon(2\omega)$ are real and satisfy the condition

$$\varepsilon^2(\omega) + \varepsilon^2(2\omega) = 1. \tag{14.92}$$

We now define the complex field amplitudes $E(\omega)$ and $E(2\omega)$ as

$$\begin{aligned} E(\omega) &= \sqrt{\frac{2I_0}{n(\omega)c\epsilon_0}}\,\varepsilon(\omega)\,e^{i\phi_\omega}, \\ E(2\omega) &= \sqrt{\frac{2I_0}{n(2\omega)c\epsilon_0}}\,\varepsilon(2\omega)\,e^{i\phi_{2\omega}}. \end{aligned} \tag{14.93}$$

Substituting Eqs (14.93) into Eqs (14.87) gives

$$\begin{aligned} \frac{d\varepsilon(\omega)}{dz} &= i\beta\sqrt{\frac{2I_0}{n^2(\omega)n(2\omega)c\epsilon_0}}\, e^{i(\phi_{2\omega}-2\phi_\omega)}\varepsilon(\omega)\varepsilon(2\omega), \\ \frac{d\varepsilon(2\omega)}{dz} &= i\beta\sqrt{\frac{2I_0}{n^2(\omega)n(2\omega)c\epsilon_0}}\, e^{-i(\phi_{2\omega}-2\phi_\omega)}\varepsilon^2(\omega). \end{aligned} \tag{14.94}$$

Since $\varepsilon(\omega)$ and $\varepsilon(2\omega)$ are real and $\varepsilon(2\omega)$ is likely to grow during propagation in the nonlinear medium, we choose $\phi_{2\omega} - 2\phi_\omega = \pi/2$, so that

$$\begin{aligned} \frac{d\varepsilon(\omega)}{dz} &= -\beta\sqrt{\frac{2I_0}{n^2(\omega)n(2\omega)c\epsilon_0}}\,\varepsilon(\omega)\varepsilon(2\omega), \\ \frac{d\varepsilon(2\omega)}{dz} &= \beta\sqrt{\frac{2I_0}{n^2(\omega)n(2\omega)c\epsilon_0}}\,\varepsilon^2(\omega). \end{aligned} \tag{14.95}$$

Substituting Eq. (14.92) into second of Eqs (14.95) yields

$$\frac{d\varepsilon(2\omega)}{dz} = \beta\sqrt{\frac{2I_0}{n^2(\omega)n(2\omega)c\epsilon_0}}\,(1 - \varepsilon^2(2\omega)). \tag{14.96}$$

Integrating Eq. (14.96) over the thickness of the nonlinear medium (from $z = 0$ to $z = L$), we obtain

$$\int_0^{\varepsilon(2\omega)} \frac{d\varepsilon(2\omega)}{1 - \varepsilon^2(2\omega)} = \gamma \int_0^L dz,$$

giving

$$\varepsilon(2\omega, z = L) = \tanh(\gamma L), \tag{14.97}$$

where we have assumed zero amplitude of the second-harmonic wave in the plane $z = 0$, and

$$\gamma = \beta\sqrt{\frac{2I_0}{n^2(\omega)n(2\omega)c\epsilon_0}}$$
$$= \frac{\omega}{4n(\omega)c}\sqrt{\frac{2I_0}{n(2\omega)c\epsilon_0}}\chi^{(2)}(\omega, -\omega, 2\omega). \tag{14.98}$$

The intensity of the second-harmonic wave as it emerges from the nonlinear medium, obtained from Eqs (14.93) and (14.97), is

$$I(2\omega, z = L) = I_0 \tanh^2(\gamma L), \tag{14.99a}$$

and intensity of the pump wave as it emerges from the nonlinear medium is

$$I(\omega, z = L) = I_0 - I(2\omega, z = L) = I_0 \operatorname{sech}^2(\gamma L), \tag{14.99b}$$

where I_0 is the intensity with which the pump wave enters the nonlinear medium. Figure 14.5 shows the normalized intensity variations of the pump and second-harmonic waves with the thickness of the nonlinear medium. The figure shows the entire energy of the pump wave eventually appearing in the second-harmonic

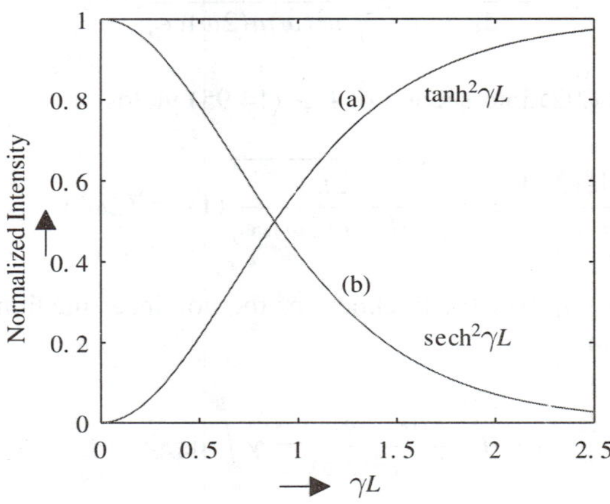

Fig. 14.5: Normalized intensity variations of the (a) second-harmonic wave, (b) pump wave under phase-matched conditions.

wave, but in practice the efficiency of second-harmonic generation is much lower. Lack of perfect phase matching further lowers the conversion efficiency.

The phase-matching condition (Eq. 14.79) when applied to second-harmonic generation requires

$$n(2\omega) = n(\omega), \tag{14.100}$$

a condition impossible to satisfy in singly refracting media since the index of refraction increases monotonically with frequency due to normal dispersion. However, in a uniaxial crystal, as mentioned earlier, the index of refraction for the extraordinary wave depends on the angle that its direction of propagation makes with the optic axis of the crystal (Fig. 14.6). This dependence can be obtained from Eq. (1.135b)

$$v_p'' = v_o^2 \cos^2\theta + v_e^2 \sin^2\theta, \tag{1.135b}$$

after expressing the phase velocities in terms of the indices of refraction, i.e., after making the changes

$$v_p'' = \frac{c}{n_e(\theta)}, \qquad v_o = \frac{c}{n_o}, \qquad v_e = \frac{c}{n_e},$$

giving

$$\frac{1}{n_e^2(\theta)} = \frac{\cos^2\theta}{n_o^2} + \frac{\sin^2\theta}{n_e^2}, \tag{14.101}$$

where $n_e(\theta = 0°) = n_o$ and $n_e(\theta = 90°) = n_e$. To achieve the type I phase-matching condition (Eq. 14.100) in positive uniaxial crystals ($n_e > n_o$), the pump wave is taken as an extraordinary wave polarized in the plane of its direction of

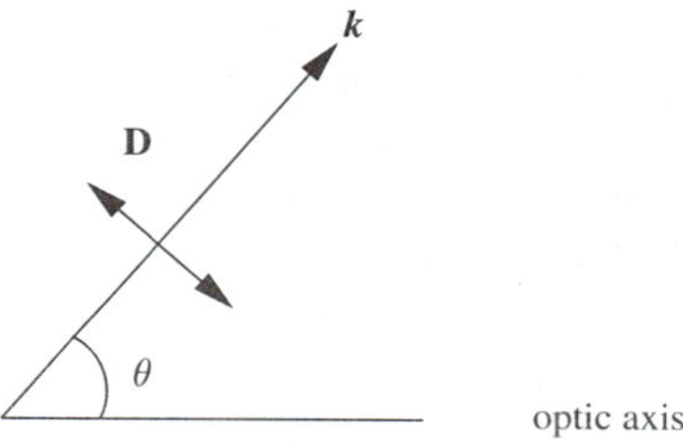

Fig. 14.6: Extraordinary wave propagating at an angle θ to the optic axis.

propagation and the optic axis of the crystal. The second-harmonic wave is the ordinary wave polarized perpendicular to the plane containing the optic axis and the common direction of propagation of the pump and second-harmonic waves. For the phase-matching ($n_o(2\omega) = n_e(\omega)$) angle θ_{ph}, Eq. (14.101) becomes

$$\frac{1}{n_o^2(2\omega)} = \frac{\cos^2\theta_{ph}}{n_o^2(\omega)} + \frac{\sin^2\theta_{ph}}{n_e^2(\omega)}, \tag{14.102}$$

giving

$$\sin^2\theta_{ph} = \frac{(n_o(\omega))^{-2} - (n_o(2\omega))^{-2}}{(n_o(\omega))^{-2} - (n_e(\omega))^{-2}}. \tag{14.103}$$

Usually the phase angle θ_{ph} is neither zero nor 90°. Therefore the obliquely incident pump wave, being an extraordinary wave, walks away from the second-harmonic wave (ordinary wave) despite the two waves having collinear propagation vectors. This happens because the direction of the Poynting vector of the pump wave inside the nonlinear medium deviates from the direction of the Poynting vector of the second-harmonic wave. The latter coincides with their common direction of propagation, but the former does not since the pump wave inside the nonlinear medium is an extraordinary wave (see Section 1.10.5 on double refraction). The path taken by a wave coincides with its Poynting vector, hence the 'walk-off effect'. It may be possible to choose a nonlinear medium with phase-matching angle close to 90°. The remaining change in the index of refraction to achieve phase matching at 90° may be obtained by controlling the temperature of the nonlinear medium since the index of refraction varies with temperature.

14.5.4 Parametric Amplification

Parametric amplification is a second-order nonlinear process in which a weak signal (signal wave) propagating in a nonlinear medium is amplified in the presence of a strong signal (pump wave) of higher frequency and generating in the process the difference-frequency wave, often called the idler wave. This nonlinear process is particularly useful to generate coherent waves in the far-infrared spectral region, where coherent radiation is otherwise difficult to generate. The nonlinear process involved in parametric amplification is actually the difference-frequency generation. Notwithstanding that, the growth of the pump wave in parametric amplification must involve sum-frequency generation since the pump wave has the highest frequency among the three waves. The signal and idler waves, however, grow through difference-frequency generation. Therefore equations describing parametric amplification, obtained from Eqs (14.68), are

$$\begin{aligned}\frac{dE_P(z,\omega_1)}{dz} &= \frac{i\omega_1}{4cn_1}\chi^{(2)}_{eff}(\omega_1,\omega_2,\omega)E_S(z,\omega_2)E_I(z,\omega)e^{-i\Delta kz},\\ \frac{dE_S(z,\omega_2)}{dz} &= \frac{i\omega_2}{4cn_2}\chi^{(2)}_{eff}(\omega_2,\omega_1,-\omega)E_P(z,\omega_1)E_I^*(z,\omega)e^{i\Delta kz},\\ \frac{dE_I(z,\omega)}{dz} &= \frac{i\omega}{4cn}\chi^{(2)}_{eff}(\omega,\omega_1,-\omega_2)E_P(z,\omega_1)E_S^*(z,\omega_2)e^{i\Delta kz},\end{aligned} \tag{14.104}$$

where $E_P(z,\omega_1)$, $E_S(z,\omega_2)$, $E_I(z,\omega)$ are the amplitudes of the pump wave of frequency ω_1, the signal wave of frequency ω_2, the idler wave of the difference frequency $\omega=\omega_1-\omega_2$, respectively, and

$$\Delta k = k_P - k_S - k_I. \tag{14.105}$$

Effective tensors have replaced summations in Eqs (14.68). Full permutation symmetry allows us to write

$$\chi^{(2)}_{eff}(\omega_1,\omega_2,\omega) = \chi^{(2)}_{eff}(\omega_2,\omega_1,-\omega) = \chi^{(2)}_{eff}(\omega,\omega_1,-\omega_2) = \chi^{(2)}_{eff}. \tag{14.106}$$

Further, we may assume low efficiency of parametric amplification so that the pump wave is not depleted during propagation in the nonlinear medium. For perfect phase matching, Eqs (14.104) are reduced to

$$\frac{dE_S(z,\omega_2)}{dz} = \frac{i\omega_2}{4cn_2}\chi^{(2)}_{eff}E_P(\omega_1)E_I^*(z,\omega), \tag{14.107a}$$

$$\frac{dE_I(z,\omega)}{dz} = \frac{i\omega}{4cn}\chi^{(2)}_{eff}E_P(\omega_1)E_S^*(z,\omega_2), \tag{14.107b}$$

where $E_P(\omega_1)$ is the undepleted amplitude of the pump wave. Differentiating Eq. (14.107a) and substituting into Eq. (14.107b) and vice versa yields

$$\begin{aligned}\frac{d^2E_S(z,\omega_2)}{dz^2} &= \beta^2 E_S(z,\omega_2),\\ \frac{d^2E_I(z,\omega)}{dz^2} &= \beta^2 E_I(z,\omega),\end{aligned} \tag{14.108}$$

where

$$\beta = \frac{1}{4c}\sqrt{\frac{\omega\omega_2}{nn_2}}\chi^{(2)}_{eff}\left|E_P(\omega_1)\right|. \tag{14.109}$$

Since the idler wave is not present among the incident waves, it must have the form

$$E_I(z, \omega) = E_I(\omega)\sinh(\beta z). \tag{14.110a}$$

Differentiating Eq. (14.110a) and substituting into Eq. (14.107b) gives

$$E_S(z, \omega_2) = E_S(\omega_2)\cosh(\beta z), \tag{14.110b}$$

and

$$E_I(\omega) = i\sqrt{\frac{n_2\omega}{n\omega_2}}\frac{E_P(\omega_1)}{|E_P(\omega_1)|}E_S(\omega_2), \tag{14.111}$$

where $E_S(\omega_2)$ is the amplitude with which the signal wave enters the nonlinear medium and n is the linear index of refraction of the medium at the difference frequency $\omega = \omega_1 - \omega_2$. The growths of the signal and idler waves during propagation in the nonlinear medium are shown in Fig. 14.7. If the parametric amplification is carried out with the nonlinear medium kept within a resonator (see Fig. 4.29) possessing highly reflecting mirrors at the signal wave frequency or at the idler wave frequency or at both, then the device becomes a parametric oscillator.

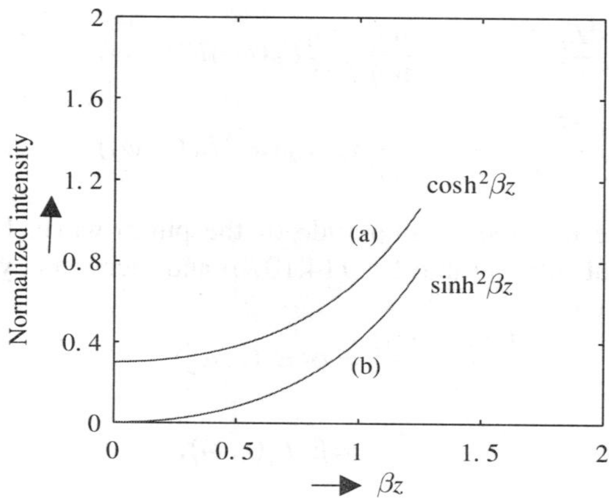

Fig. 14.7: Growth of the (a) signal wave, (b) idler wave in phase-matched parametric amplification with undepleted pump wave(vertical scale arbitrary).

14.6 OPTICAL PHASE CONJUGATION

Optical phase conjugation is a nonlinear process in which the medium generates a wave whose spatial phase is the complex conjugate of the spatial phase of one of the incident waves. The phase-conjugate wave of special interest is the one which in addition counter-propagates the incident wave, i.e., if the incident wave is

$$\vec{E}_{\text{in}}(\vec{r},t) = \vec{E}_0(\vec{r})\,e^{i(\vec{k}\cdot\vec{r}-\omega t)}, \tag{14.112}$$

then its phase-conjugate wave is

$$\vec{E}_{\text{pc}}(\vec{r},t) = a\vec{E}_0^{*}(\vec{r})e^{i(-\vec{k}\cdot\vec{r}-\omega t)}, \tag{14.113}$$

where a is a constant which may exceed one. In a way, the nonlinear medium in optical phase conjugation acts as a mirror because a mirror can also reverse the direction of propagation of the incident wave, but there is a subtle difference between the counter-propagating wavefronts produced by an ordinary mirror and by what may be called a phase-conjugate mirror. Figure 14.8a,b shows diverging wavefronts incident on the ordinary (M) and phase-conjugate (PCM) mirrors. Upon reflection from the ordinary mirror, the wavefront continues to diverge but with a reversed curvature (see dotted curves in Fig. 14.8a). The wavefront reflected by the phase-conjugate mirror is reversed with respect to the wavefront reflected by the ordinary mirror (compare dotted curves in Fig. 14.8a,b). For that reason, optical phase conjugation is also called wavefront reversal. But the phase-conjugate wavefront, though travelling backward, actually replicates the incident wavefront, converging precisely at the source point O (Fig. 14.8b). Therefore, optical phase conjugation can be used to precisely locate an object in space, provided scattered light from the object reaches a phase-conjugate mirror. Optical phase conjugation also has the capability to remove any phase distortion that the medium, such as a turbulent atmosphere, might have inflicted on the wavefront during propagation. Figure 14.8c shows that the portions of the wavefront which are advanced during passage through a distorting medium are equally retarded (and vice versa) on reflection from the phase-conjugate mirror (compare the solid and dotted curves in front of the phase-conjugate mirror in Fig. 14.8c). Consequently, the wavefront becomes distortion free as it emerges from the phase distorter on the return trip (the dotted lines in front of the phase distorter in Fig. 14.8c).

We now briefly outline the theory of optical phase conjugation. Our intention here is to demonstrate the generation of the phase-conjugate wave in a nonlinear process, avoiding mathematical complications to the extent possible. Optical phase conjugation is a special case of degenerate four-wave mixing (Fig. 14.9).

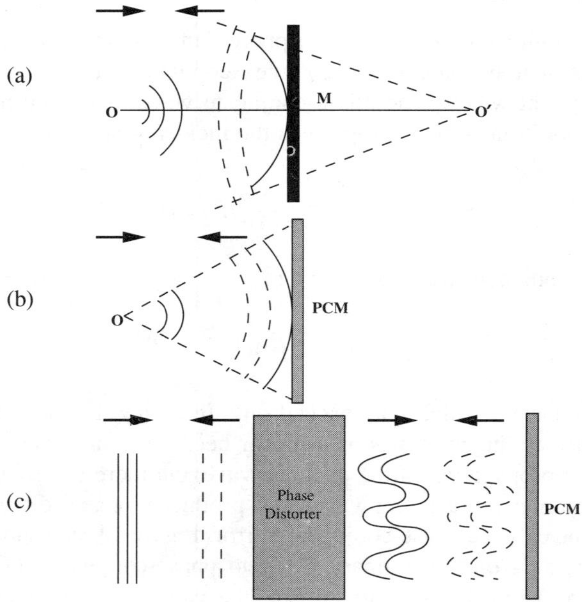

Fig. 14.8: Reflection from (a) an ordinary mirror (M), (b) a phase conjugate mirror (PCM), (c) distortion removal in optical phase conjugation. Solid (dotted) lines and curves are sections of incident (reflected) wavefronts.

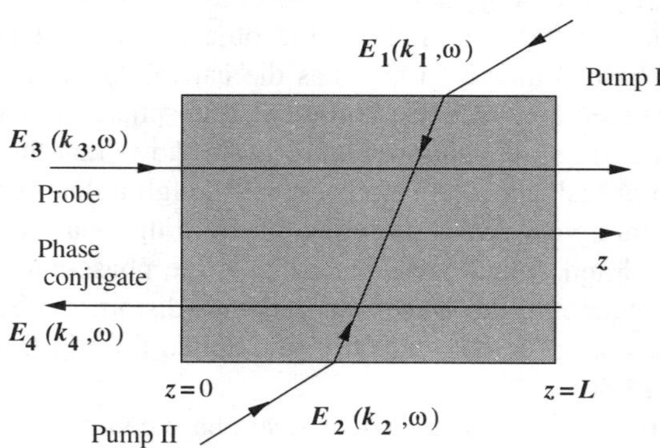

Fig. 14.9: Degenerate four-wave mixing configuration for optical phase conjugation.

Three waves of the same frequency are incident on the medium confined between the planes $z = 0$ and $z = L$, and the medium generates the fourth wave at the frequency of the incident waves. The term degenerate here refers to the fact that all four waves have the same frequency. The counter-propagating waves $\vec{E}_1(\vec{k}_1, \omega)$ and $\vec{E}_2(\vec{k}_2, \omega)$ are called the pump waves. Usually only one pump wave is incident, the other pump wave is obtained by retro-reflection of this wave. The third incident wave $\vec{E}_3(\vec{k}_3, \omega)$, called the probe wave, is weaker than the pump waves. The phase-conjugate wave $\vec{E}_4(\vec{k}_4, \omega)$ generated by the medium counter-propagates the probe wave $\vec{E}_3(\vec{k}_3, \omega)$. The equations describing the propagation of these waves in the nonlinear medium are very similar to those apearing in sum-frequency generation or in parametric amplification (Sections 14.5.1 and 14.5.4), except that the nonlinear process involved in optical phase conjugation is of third order due to the presence of four waves in the medium. For low-efficiency optical phase conjugation, the pump waves may be assumed to remain undepleted. The phase-matched equation for the growth of the probe wave, obtained by an extension of Eqs (14.104), is

$$\frac{dE_3(\omega)}{dz} = \frac{i\omega}{4cn}\chi^{(3)}[E_1(\omega)E_2(\omega)E_4^*(\omega)\,e^{i(\vec{k}_1+\vec{k}_2-\vec{k}_4-\vec{k}_3).\vec{r}} + \{E_1(\omega)E_1^*(\omega)+E_2(\omega)E_2^*(\omega)+E_3(\omega)E_3^*(\omega)+E_4(\omega)E_4^*(\omega)\}\,E_3(\omega)] \tag{14.114a}$$

$$= \frac{i\omega}{4cn}\chi^{(3)}\left[E_1(\omega)E_2(\omega)E_4^*(\omega) + \left\{|E_1(\omega)|^2+|E_2(\omega)|^2\right\}E_3(\omega)\right] \tag{14.114b}$$

$$= i\alpha E_4^*(\omega) + i\beta E_3(\omega), \tag{14.114c}$$

where

$$\alpha = \frac{\omega}{4cn}\chi^{(3)}E_1(\omega)E_2(\omega), \tag{14.115}$$

$$\beta = \frac{\omega}{4cn}\chi^{(3)}\left(|E_1(\omega)|^2+|E_2(\omega)|^2\right), \tag{14.116}$$

and $\chi^{(3)} = \chi^{(3)}(\omega, \omega, \omega, -\omega)$ is the third-order susceptibility (real for a nonabsorbing medium) and

$$\Delta\vec{k} = \vec{k}_1 + \vec{k}_2 - \vec{k}_4 - \vec{k}_3 = 0 \tag{14.117}$$

since $\vec{k}_1 + \vec{k}_2 = 0$ for the counter-propagating pump waves and $\vec{k}_3 + \vec{k}_4 = 0$ for the counter-propagating probe and phase-conjugate waves. In writing Eq. (14.114b), we have ignored contributions from the relatively weak probe and phase-conjugate waves. The first term in Eq. (14.114a) can be interpreted to describe the nonlinear process in which one photon from each of the pump waves is destroyed and simultaneously one photon each is added to the probe and phase-conjugate waves. The remaining terms in this equation involve nonlinear processes in which one photon is created and one destroyed from each of the four waves along with simultaneous creation and destruction of one photon each from the probe wave. There are no other terms which are frequency and phase matched with the probe wave. Substituting

$$E_3(\omega) = E_3'(\omega)\mathrm{e}^{\mathrm{i}\beta z}, \quad E_4(\omega) = E_4'(\omega)\mathrm{e}^{-\mathrm{i}\beta z}, \tag{14.118}$$

into Eq. (14.114c) yields

$$\frac{\mathrm{d}E_3'(\omega)}{\mathrm{d}z} = \mathrm{i}\alpha E'^{*}_4(\omega). \tag{14.119a}$$

In a similar manner, we obtain

$$\frac{\mathrm{d}E_4'(\omega)}{\mathrm{d}z} = -\mathrm{i}\alpha E'^{*}_3(\omega). \tag{14.119b}$$

The phase-conjugate wave propagates in the negative z direction, hence the minus sign in Eq. (14.119b). Differentiating Eqs (14.119) gives

$$\frac{\mathrm{d}^2E_3'(\omega)}{\mathrm{d}z^2} = -|\alpha|^2 E_3'(\omega), \quad \frac{\mathrm{d}^2E_4'(\omega)}{\mathrm{d}z^2} = -|\alpha|^2 E_4'(\omega). \tag{14.120}$$

The solutions of these equations are

$$E_3'(\omega) = E_3(0)\cos(|\alpha|z) + B\sin(|\alpha|z), \quad E_4'(\omega) = C\cos(|\alpha|z) + D\sin(|\alpha|z), \tag{14.121}$$

where the probe wave enters the nonlinear medium with amplitude $E_3(0)$. The phase-conjugate wave has zero amplitude in the plane $z = L$. Therefore,

$$C = -D\tan(|\alpha|L).$$

For Eqs (14.121) to be consistent with Eq. (14.119b), we must have

$$D = -\mathrm{i}E_3^*(0), \quad B = E_3(0)\tan(|\alpha|L),$$

giving

$$\begin{aligned} E_3'(\omega) &= E_3(0)\left[\cos(|\alpha|z) + (\tan(|\alpha|L))\sin(|\alpha|z)\right], \\ E_4'(\omega) &= -\,\mathrm{i}E_3^*(0)\left[\sin(|\alpha|z) - (\tan(|\alpha|L))\cos(|\alpha|z)\right]. \end{aligned} \tag{14.122}$$

The amplitude of the phase-conjugate wave, apart from a phase factor, on emerging from the plane $z = 0$ is

$$E_4(\omega, z = 0) = \mathrm{i}E_3^*(0)\tan(|\alpha|L), \tag{14.123}$$

and the amplitude of the probe wave, apart from a phase factor, on leaving the nonlinear medium at $z = L$ is

$$E_3(\omega) = \frac{E_3(0)}{\cos(|\alpha|L)}. \tag{14.124}$$

The amplitude of the emerging phase-conjugate wave can exceed the amplitude of the incident probe wave because the phase-conjugate wave draws energy from the pump waves.

14.7 OPTICAL KERR EFFECT AND SELF-FOCUSING

The index of refraction of a material is modified in the presence of a strong beam of light. Distortion of the electronic charge distribution, creation of density changes in the manner of electrostriction observed with dc fields, orientation of the polar molecules of the medium are some of the mechanisms responsible for the light-induced refractive index changes. Most of these mechanisms can be described in terms of the third-order nonlinear polarization induced by the light field. The third-order nonlinear polarization produced by a linearly polarized light wave of frequency ω propagating in a nonabsorbing, isotropic medium is given by

$$P^{(3)}(\omega) = \epsilon_0 \chi^{(3)}(\omega, \omega, \omega, -\omega)E(\omega)E(\omega)E^*(\omega). \tag{14.125}$$

The nonlinear process involved in this refractive index modification is quite similar to the degenerate four-wave mixing described in Section 14.6, except that here we are dealing with a single wave propagating in the nonlinear medium.

The process involves destruction of two photons and simultaneous creation of two photons, all of the same frequency ω. The net polarization produced in the medium at frequency ω is

$$P(\omega) = P^{(1)}(\omega) + P^{(3)}(\omega) = \epsilon_0 \left[\chi^{(1)} + \chi^{(3)} |E(\omega)|^2\right] E(\omega), \qquad (14.126)$$

where $P^{(1)}(\omega)$ is the linear polarization at frequency ω. The frequency dependence of the $\chi^{(3)}$ has been suppressed. The effective refractive index of the medium can be expressed as (see Eq. 1.9c)

$$\begin{aligned} n &= \left[1 + \chi^{(1)} + \chi^{(3)} |E(\omega)|^2\right]^{\frac{1}{2}} \\ &= \left[n_0^2 + \chi^{(3)} |E(\omega)|^2\right]^{\frac{1}{2}} \qquad (14.127) \\ &= n_0 + \frac{\chi^{(3)}}{2n_0} |E(\omega)|^2 = n_0 + n_2 I(\omega), \end{aligned}$$

where

$$n_2 = \frac{\chi^{(3)} |E(\omega)|^2}{n_0^2 c \epsilon_0}, \qquad (14.128)$$

and n_0 is the linear index of refraction of the medium at frequency ω. In view of the smallness of $\chi^{(3)}$, binomial expansion in which only the first term is retained has been used in the above derivation. Since the light-induced refractive index change is quadratic in the electric field, this effect is called the optical Kerr effect in analogy with the Kerr electrooptic effect associated with the dc fields. This nonlinearly generated change in the refractive index does not cause any change in the polarization state of a linearly or circularly polarized light wave propagating in an isotropic medium, but the state of polarization of elliptically polarized light is modified during propagation in an isotropic medium.

A light beam with a Gaussian profile (see Fig. 1.2), such as the one coming from a laser operating in the TEM_{00} mode, has maximum intensity along its axis. Therefore for positive n_2, such a light beam experiences a decreasing index of refraction of the medium for points away from the axis of the light beam. This behavior is somewhat similar to what a light beam experiences while traversing a positive lens. The optical path length through a positive lens is maximum at the center and least near the periphery. Thus for a light beam with transversally decreasing intensity profile, the medium acts like a positive lens and the beam gets focused during propagation. This is known as self-focusing (Fig. 14.10a). However, due to its finite cross-section, the light beam also has the tendency to

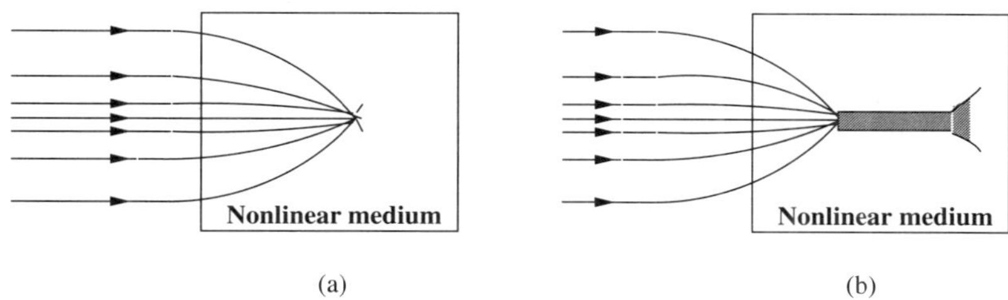

Fig. 14.10: (a) Self-focusing, (b) beam-trapping of a light beam with a Gaussian profile in a nonlinear medium.

spread because of diffraction which increases as the beam gets narrower due to self-focusing. It is in fact possible that the two competing processes may balance each other, resulting in the beam maintaining its reduced cross-section over a finite thickness of the medium. This is called beam-trapping (Fig. 14.10b). Self-focusing can lead to optical breakdown of the medium due to high intensities created around the focal point.

14.8 THE ELECTROOPTIC EFFECT

Refractive index change produced by an optical field was discussed in Section 14.7. Low-frequency and dc electric fields can also modify the refractive index of a material by displacing the ions from their equilibrium positions. The refractive index change produced by dc and low-frequency electric fields is called the electrooptic effect. The linear electrooptic effect, also called the Pockel effect, is described in terms of the second-order nonlinear polarization

$$P_i^{(2)}(\omega) = \epsilon_0 \sum_{jk} \chi_{ijk}^{(2)}(\omega, \omega, 0) E_j(\omega) E_k(0), \tag{14.129}$$

where $E_k(0)$ may represent the dc or the low-frequency electric field and $E_j(\omega)$ is the optical field at which the change in the index of refraction of the material is being investigated. The linear electrooptic effect is absent in isotropic and centrosymmetric media since $\chi^{(2)} = 0$ in these media (see Eq. 14.51). However, the quadratic electrooptic or the Kerr effect can be observed in all media. The third-order nonlinear polarization which describes this effect is given by

$$P_i^{(3)}(\omega) = \epsilon_0 \sum_{jkl} \chi_{ijkl}^{(3)}(\omega, \omega, 0, 0) E_j(\omega) E_k(0) E_l(0). \tag{14.130}$$

The electrooptic effect is infact a nonlinear optical phenomenon and the refractive index change can be expressed in terms of the nonlinear susceptibilities as was done in Section 14.7, but this is usually not done. Instead, the electrooptic effect is described in terms of the electric field-induced changes in the index ellipsoid (see Section 1.10.2)

$$\frac{D_x^2}{u\epsilon_x} + \frac{D_y^2}{u\epsilon_y} + \frac{D_z^2}{u\epsilon_z} = 1, \tag{14.131}$$

where D_x, D_y, D_z are the components of the displacement field along the principal axes of the real and symmetric permittivity (dielectric) tensor ϵ_{ij}, u is the energy density and $\epsilon_x = \epsilon_{xx}$, $\epsilon_y = \epsilon_{yy}$, $\epsilon_z = \epsilon_{zz}$ are the principal dielectric constants. The index ellipsoid when expressed in terms of the principal refractive indices takes the form

$$\frac{x^2}{n_{xx}^2} + \frac{y^2}{n_{yy}^2} + \frac{z^2}{n_{zz}^2} = 1, \tag{14.132}$$

where $x = D_x/\sqrt{\mu\epsilon_0}$, $y = D_y/\sqrt{\mu\epsilon_0}$, $z = D_z/\sqrt{\mu\epsilon_0}$ and $n_{xx}^2 = \epsilon_x/\epsilon_0$, $n_{yy}^2 = \epsilon_y/\epsilon_0$, $n_{zz}^2 = \epsilon_z/\epsilon_0$. The index ellipsoid referred to axes other than the principal axes has the general form

$$\frac{x^2}{n_{xx}^2} + \frac{y^2}{n_{yy}^2} + \frac{z^2}{n_{zz}^2} + \frac{2yz}{n_{yz}^2} + \frac{2zx}{n_{zx}^2} + \frac{2xy}{n_{xy}^2} = 1, \tag{14.133}$$

where for a nonabsorbing medium, $n_{xx}, n_{yy}, n_{zz}, n_{yz}, n_{zx}, n_{xy}$ are the six real and independent elements of the refractive index tensor. Application of the electric field modifies the refractive index tensor and hence the shape and orientation of the index ellipsoid. The electric field-induced change in the refractive index is given by the tensor equation

$$\left(\frac{1}{n_{ij}^2}\right)_{E_0} = \left(\frac{1}{n_{ij}^2}\right)_0 + \sum_k r_{ijk} E_k(0) + \sum_{kl} p_{ijkl} E_k(0) E_l(0), \tag{14.134}$$

where $\left(\frac{1}{n_{ij}^2}\right)_0$ is the inverse of the square of the refractive index tensor element n_{ij} in the absence of the electric field and $\left(\frac{1}{n_{ij}^2}\right)_{E_0}$ is the corresponding quantity in the presence of the electric field. The r_{ijk} and p_{ijkl} tensors describe the linear and quadratic electrooptic effects, respectively. The contracted notation of indices (Eq. 14.53) can be used here as well since the refractive index tensor n_{ij} is symmetric. The linear electrooptic effect in the contracted notation is described by the matrix equation

$$\Delta\left(\frac{1}{n^2}\right)_i = \left(\frac{1}{n_{ij}^2}\right)_{E_0} - \left(\frac{1}{n_{ij}^2}\right)_0 = \sum_k r_{ik} E_k(0), \tag{14.135}$$

where $i = 1, 2, \ldots, 6$. Accordingly the equations of the index ellipsoids, not restricted to the principal-axis systems, before and after the application of the electric field take the forms

$$\begin{aligned}&\left(\frac{1}{n^2}\right)_1 x^2 + \left(\frac{1}{n^2}\right)_2 y^2 + \left(\frac{1}{n^2}\right)_3 z^2 + 2\left(\frac{1}{n^2}\right)_4 yz \\ &\quad + 2\left(\frac{1}{n^2}\right)_5 zx + 2\left(\frac{1}{n^2}\right)_6 xy = 1,\end{aligned} \tag{14.136a}$$

and

$$\begin{aligned}&\left[\left(\frac{1}{n^2}\right)_1 + \Delta\left(\frac{1}{n^2}\right)_1\right] x^2 + \left[\left(\frac{1}{n^2}\right)_2 + \Delta\left(\frac{1}{n^2}\right)_2\right] y^2 \\ &\quad + \left[\left(\frac{1}{n^2}\right)_3 + \Delta\left(\frac{1}{n^2}\right)_3\right] z^2 + 2\left[\left(\frac{1}{n^2}\right)_4 + \Delta\left(\frac{1}{n^2}\right)_4\right] yz \\ &\quad + 2\left[\left(\frac{1}{n^2}\right)_5 + \Delta\left(\frac{1}{n^2}\right)_5\right] zx + 2\left[\left(\frac{1}{n^2}\right)_6 + \Delta\left(\frac{1}{n^2}\right)_6\right] xy = 1,\end{aligned} \tag{14.136b}$$

respectively, where the $\Delta\left(\frac{1}{n^2}\right)_i$ corrections due to the presence of the electric field are given by the matrix equation

$$\begin{pmatrix} \Delta\left(\frac{1}{n^2}\right)_1 \\ \Delta\left(\frac{1}{n^2}\right)_2 \\ \Delta\left(\frac{1}{n^2}\right)_3 \\ \Delta\left(\frac{1}{n^2}\right)_4 \\ \Delta\left(\frac{1}{n^2}\right)_5 \\ \Delta\left(\frac{1}{n^2}\right)_6 \end{pmatrix} = \begin{pmatrix} r_{11} & r_{12} & r_{13} \\ r_{21} & r_{22} & r_{23} \\ r_{31} & r_{32} & r_{33} \\ r_{41} & r_{42} & r_{43} \\ r_{51} & r_{52} & r_{53} \\ r_{61} & r_{62} & r_{63} \end{pmatrix} \begin{pmatrix} E_x \\ E_y \\ E_z \end{pmatrix} \tag{14.137}$$

The r_{ij} coefficients are called the linear electrooptic coefficients. For crystals with the point group symmetry $\bar{4}\,2m$ [14.10], such as the KDP crystal, the r_{ij} matrix

$$r_{ij} = \begin{pmatrix} 0 & 0 & 0 \\ 0 & 0 & 0 \\ 0 & 0 & 0 \\ r_{41} & 0 & 0 \\ 0 & r_{41} & 0 \\ 0 & 0 & r_{63} \end{pmatrix} \tag{14.138}$$

has only three nonzero electrooptic coefficients. Therefore for such crystals

$$\begin{aligned} &\Delta\left(\frac{1}{n^2}\right)_1 = 0, \quad \Delta\left(\frac{1}{n^2}\right)_2 = 0, \quad \Delta\left(\frac{1}{n^2}\right)_3 = 0, \\ &\Delta\left(\frac{1}{n^2}\right)_4 = r_{41}E_x, \quad \Delta\left(\frac{1}{n^2}\right)_5 = r_{41}E_y, \quad \Delta\left(\frac{1}{n^2}\right)_6 = r_{63}E_z. \end{aligned} \tag{14.139}$$

Furthermore for the uniaxial crystals,

$$\left(\frac{1}{n^2}\right)_1 = \left(\frac{1}{n^2}\right)_2 = \frac{1}{n_o^2}, \quad \left(\frac{1}{n^2}\right)_3 = \frac{1}{n_e^2}, \tag{14.140}$$

where n_o and n_e are the ordinary and extraordinary indices of refraction of the medium (see Section 1.10.3). Therefore, the index ellipsoid

$$\frac{x^2}{n_o^2} + \frac{y^2}{n_o^2} + \frac{z^2}{n_e^2} = 1 \tag{14.141a}$$

for a uniaxial crystal in its principal-axis system with z axis coinciding with the optic axis of the crystal (see Section 1.10.3) is transformed to

$$\frac{x^2}{n_o^2} + \frac{y^2}{n_o^2} + \frac{z^2}{n_e^2} + 2r_{41}E_x yz + 2r_{41}E_y zx + 2r_{63}E_z xy = 1, \tag{14.141b}$$

by the application of the electric field.

14.9 ELECTROOPTIC MODULATORS

Electrooptic modulators can be designed to modulate the amplitude and phase of a light wave. Figure 14.11 shows a typical configuration of an electrooptic intensity modulator using the uniaxial crystal KDP, cut perpendicular to its optic axis (see Section 1.10.3). For longitudinal electrooptic modulation, a potential

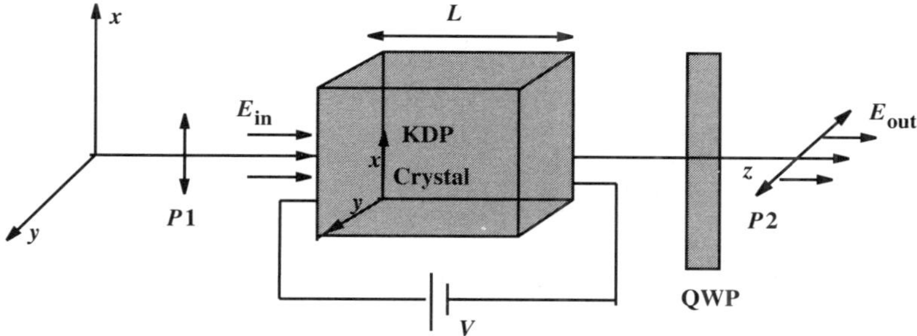

Fig. 14.11: A typical configuration for longitudinal electrooptic modulation; $P1$ and $P2$ are crossed polarizers, QWP is a quarter-wave plate.

difference of V volts is applied across the end faces of the crystal by making them conducting with thin layers of conducting coatings. The KDP crystal is preceded by the polarizer $P1$ with its transmission direction coinciding with the x principal axis (in the absence of electric field) of the KDP crystal. Light transmitted by the KDP crystal passes through a quarter-wave plate (see Section 3.3.2 after Eq. 3.29b), followed by the polarizer $P2$ with transmission direction crossed with that of the polarizer $P1$. For the following discussion, we ignore the presence of the polarizers and the quarter-wave plate in Fig. 14.11.

With the electric field applied along the optic axis (also the z axis), Eq. (14.141b) of the index ellipsoid reduces to

$$\frac{x^2}{n_o^2}+\frac{y^2}{n_o^2}+\frac{z^2}{n_e^2}+2r_{63}E_z xy=1. \tag{14.142}$$

Obviously, the principal axes x, y, z of the index ellipsoid in the absence of the electric field (Eq. 14.141a) are no longer the principal axes of the index ellipsoid in the presence of the longitudinal electric field (Eq. 14.142). However, the substitution

$$x=\frac{y'+x'}{\sqrt{2}}, \quad y=\frac{y'-x'}{\sqrt{2}}, \quad z=z' \tag{14.143}$$

transforms the index ellipsoid (Eq. 14.142) to its principal-axis form

$$\frac{x'^2}{n_{x'}^2}+\frac{y'^2}{n_{y'}^2}+\frac{z'^2}{n_e^2}=1, \tag{14.144}$$

where

$$\frac{1}{n_{x'}^2} = \frac{1}{n_o^2} - r_{63}E_z, \tag{14.145a}$$

$$\frac{1}{n_{y'}^2} = \frac{1}{n_o^2} + r_{63}E_z. \tag{14.145b}$$

For $r_{63}E_z \ll 1$, Eqs (14.145) reduce to

$$n_{x'} = n_o + \frac{1}{2}n_o^3 r_{63}E_z, \quad n_{y'} = n_o - \frac{1}{2}n_o^3 r_{63}E_z. \tag{14.146}$$

The uniaxial crystal has become slightly biaxial since $n_{x'} \neq n_{y'}$(see Section 1.10.4). Sections of the normal surfaces (see Section 1.10.2 and Figs 1.27 and 1.28) in a plane perpendicular to the optic axis of the crystal with and without the electric field are shown in Fig. 14.12. In the absence of the electric field, the section is a circle so that the index of refraction for any direction of polarization of a wave propagating along the optic axis is the ordinary refractive index n_o, but in the presence of the electric field, the section is an ellipse with semi-major and minor axes proportional to the indices of refraction $n_{x'}$ and $n_{y'}$ (for $n_{x'} > n_{y'}$), respectively. However, in the presence of a longitudinal electric field in KDP ($r_{63} = -10.5 \times 10^{-12}$ m/V) or any other uniaxial crystal with negative r_{63}, a wave polarized along x' principal axis of the index ellipsoid travels faster than a wave

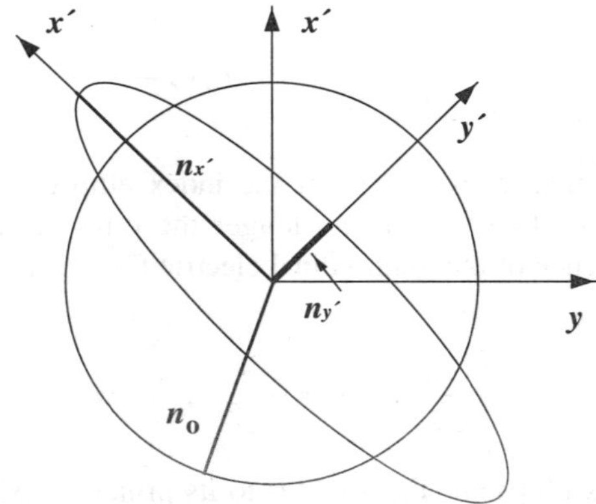

Fig. 14.12: Sections of the normal surfaces of a uniaxial crystal with (ellipse) and without (circle) the longitudinal electric field.

polarized along the y' principal axis of the ellipsoid. Such a crystal behaves like a phase retarder or a phase plate, introducing a phase retardation (see Eq. 3.28)

$$\Delta\psi = \frac{2\pi}{\lambda_v}\left(n_{x'} - n_{y'}\right) L = \frac{2\pi}{\lambda_v} n_o^3 r_{63} V = \pi \frac{V}{V\pi} \tag{14.147}$$

after the wave has traveled a distance L in the crystal, where $V = E_z L$ is the applied potential difference between the end faces of the crystal, λ_v is the wavelength of light in vacuum and the half-wave voltage

$$V_\pi = \frac{\lambda_v}{2n_o^3 r_{63}} \tag{14.148}$$

is the voltage required to produce a phase retardation of π radians. With the applied voltage equal to V_π volts, the KDP crystal rotates the plane of polarization of the linearly polarized wave by 90°. However, the linear state of polarization of the incident wave can be converted into any state of polarization by appropriately adjusting the voltage across the crystal.

14.9.1 Electrooptic Intensity Modulator

We now return to Fig. 14.11 with the polarizers and the quarter-wave plate in their respective positions. The quarter-wave plate, with its slow axis along y' axis (see Eq. 14.143), introduces an additional phase retardation (called the bias phase retardation) of $\pi/2$ radians. Therefore the net phase retardation of the wave in passing through the KDP crystal and the quarter-wave plate is

$$\Delta\phi = \frac{\pi}{2} + \pi \frac{V}{V_\pi}. \tag{14.149}$$

The wave transmitted by the polarizer $P1$ may have the form

$$\vec{E}_{\text{in}} = \frac{\vec{E}_0}{\sqrt{2}} e^{i(kz-\omega t)} + \text{cc}, \tag{14.150}$$

where cc stands for complex conjugate. With the transmission direction of polarizer $P1$ along the x principal axis of the crystal, the amplitude of the wave entering the KDP crystal is $\frac{E_0}{\sqrt{2}}\left(\frac{\hat{x}'+\hat{y}'}{\sqrt{2}}\right)$ since $\hat{x} = \frac{\hat{x}'+\hat{y}'}{\sqrt{2}}$. Let the phase retardations suffered by the components of the wave polarized along the x' and y' axes in traversing the KDP crystal and the quarter wave plate be $\phi_{x'}$ and $\phi_{y'}$, respectively, then the amplitude of the wave reaching the polarizer $P2$ is

$$\begin{aligned}\vec{E} &= \frac{E_0}{2}\left[e^{i\phi_{x'}}\hat{x}' + e^{i\phi_{y'}}\hat{y}'\right] = \frac{E_0}{2}e^{i\phi_{x'}}\left[\hat{x}' + e^{i(\phi_{y'}-\phi_{x'})}\hat{y}'\right] \\ &= \frac{E_0}{2}e^{i\phi_{x'}}\left[\hat{x}' + e^{i\Delta\phi}\hat{y}'\right],\end{aligned} \tag{14.151}$$

where

$$\phi_{y'} - \phi_{x'} = \Delta\phi = \frac{\pi}{2} + \pi\frac{V}{V_\pi}. \tag{14.152}$$

Neglecting the unimportant (in the present context) overall phase factor $e^{i\phi_{x'}}$, the amplitude of the wave leaving the polarizer $P2$, having its transmission direction along $\hat{y}(=\frac{\hat{y}'-\hat{x}'}{\sqrt{2}})$, is

$$\vec{E}_{\text{out}} = \frac{E_0}{2}\left(\hat{x}' + e^{i\Delta\phi}\hat{y}'\right)\left(\frac{\hat{y}'-\hat{x}'}{\sqrt{2}}\right) = \frac{E_0}{2\sqrt{2}}\left(-1 + e^{i\Delta\phi}\right),$$

giving

$$|E_{\text{out}}|^2 = \frac{|E_0|^2}{2}\sin^2\frac{\Delta\phi}{2}. \tag{14.153}$$

Therefore the intensity transmittance T of the modulator is

$$T = \frac{|E_{\text{out}}|^2}{|E_{\text{in}}|^2} = \sin^2\frac{\Delta\phi}{2} = \sin^2\left(\frac{\pi}{4} + \pi\frac{V}{2V_\pi}\right). \tag{14.154}$$

The variation of the transmittance of the modulator with the applied voltage is plotted in Fig. 14.13. With zero voltage across the modulator, half the intensity of the incident wave is blocked by the modulator. Figure 14.13 shows that the introduction of the quarter-wave plate generates nearly linear dependence of the transmittance over a certain range of the applied voltages. If the low-frequency ac voltage

$$V(t) = V_0 \sin\omega_0 t \tag{14.155}$$

instead of the dc voltage is applied across the KDP crystal, then the intensity transmittance of the modulator for $\frac{\pi V_0}{V_\pi} \ll 1$ takes the form

$$\begin{aligned}T &= \sin^2\left(\frac{\pi}{4} + \frac{\pi V_0}{2V_\pi}\sin\omega_0 t\right) \\ &\approx \frac{1}{2}\left(1 + \frac{\pi V_0}{V_\pi}\sin\omega_0 t\right).\end{aligned} \tag{14.156}$$

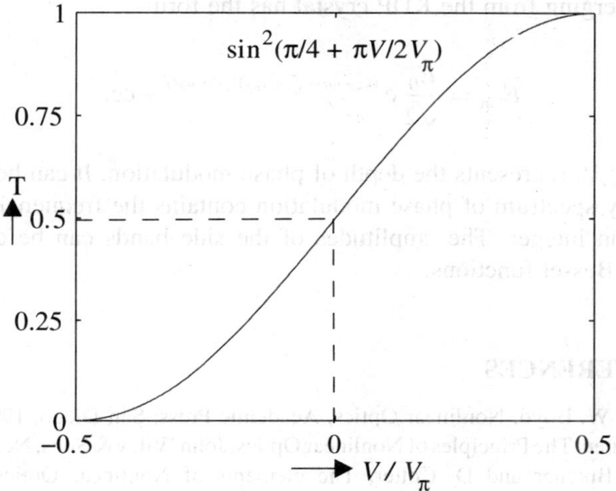

Fig. 14.13: Variation of the transmittance of an electrooptic intensity modulator with voltage.

14.9.2 Electrooptic Phase Modulator

Consider the configuration of Fig. 14.11 without the quarter-wave plate and the polarizer $P2$. The polarizer $P1$ is rotated until its transmission direction coincides with one of the principal axes (x' or y') of the KDP crystal in the presence of the longitudinal electric field. Since the wave entering the KDP crystal is polarized along one of its principal axes, the wave emerges from the KDP crystal in its initial state of polarization. However, the refractive index experienced by the wave changes from the ordinary index n_o to an index of refraction $n_{x'}$ (if the transmission direction of the polarizer P1 is along x'axis) on applying the potential difference across the KDP crystal. Therefore the phase shift produced by the applied voltage is

$$\Delta\phi = \frac{2\pi}{\lambda_0}(n_{x'} - n_o)\,L = \frac{\pi}{\lambda_0} n_o^3 r_{63} V. \tag{14.157}$$

Thus, the combination of the polarizer $P1$ and the KDP crystal in the presence of a longitudinal electric field acts as an electrooptic phase modulator, producing a voltage-dependent shift in the phase of a light wave passing through it. For the applied voltage

$$V(t) = V_0 \sin\omega_0 t, \tag{14.158}$$

the wave emerging from the KDP crystal has the form

$$\vec{E}_{\text{out}} = \frac{\vec{E}_0}{\sqrt{2}} \mathrm{e}^{\mathrm{i}(kz-\omega t+\frac{\pi}{\lambda_0}n_o^3 r_{63} V_0 \sin \omega_0 t)} + \text{cc}, \tag{14.159}$$

where $\frac{\pi}{\lambda_0} n_o^3 r_{63} V_0$ represents the depth of phase modulation. It can be shown that the frequency spectrum of phase modulation contains the frequencies $\omega \pm n\omega_0$, where n is an integer. The amplitudes of the side bands can be expressed in terms of the Bessel functions.

14.10 REFERENCES

14.1 Robert W. Boyd, Nonlinear Optics, Academic Press, San Diego, 1992.

14.2 Y. R. Shen, The Principles of Nonlinear Optics, John Wiley & Sons, New York, 1984.

14.3 B. N. Butcher and D. Cotter, The elements of Nonlinear Optics, Cambridge University Press, 1990.

14.4 G. C. Baldwin, An Introduction to Nonlinear Optics, Plenum Press, New York, 1969.

14.5 N. Bloembergen, Nonlinear Optics, Benjamin, New York, 1964.

14.6 Christopher C. Davis, Lasers and Electro-optics, University Press, Cambridge, 1996.

14.7 Sharma K. K., Divakar Rao, and Ravindra Kumar G., Nonlinear optical interactions in dye doped solids, Opt. Quant. Electron, **26**, (1994) 1–23.

14.8 P. A. Franken, A. E. Hill, C. W. Peters, and G. Weinreich, Phys. Rev. Lett. **7**, (1961) 118.

14.9 Brossel J., Kastler A., and Winter J., On ground state of the Na optical creation of an inequality of population between Zeeman sublevels of the ground state of atoms, J. Phys. Radium **13**, (1952) 668.

14.10 George F. Koster, John O. Dimmock, Robert G. Wheeler, Hermam Statz, Properties of the Thirty-two point Groups, M.I.T. Press, 1963.

14.11 PROBLEMS

14.1 Determine the ratio $\frac{\chi^{(2)}(\omega_1+\omega_2,\omega_1,\omega_2)}{\chi^{(1)}(\omega_1+\omega_2)\chi^{(1)}(\omega_1)\chi^{(1)}(\omega_2)}$ for sum-frequency generation.

14.2 Using the data from Table 14.1, make an order of magnitude estimate of the nonlinear polarization for second-harmonic generation when 1 W of 488.0 nm line of an Argon ion laser is incident on a KDP crystal. Compare it with the linear polarization produced by the laser beam. The radius of the laser beam may be taken as 1 mm.

14.3 Prove that the phase-matching condition for sum-frequency generation (Eq. 14.79) cannot be satisfied in singly refracting media.

14.4 Make an order of magnitude estimate of the anharmonicity constant a.

APPENDIX-A

Table A.1. Partial list of Fresnel integrals.

w	$C(w)$	$S(w)$	w	$C(w)$	$S(w)$	w	$C(w)$	$S(w)$
0	0	0	2.6	0.3889	0.55	5.2	0.4389	0.4969
0.1	0.1	0.0005	2.7	0.3925	0.4529	5.3	0.5078	0.4405
0.2	0.1999	0.0042	2.8	0.4675	0.3915	5.4	0.5572	0.514
0.3	0.2994	0.0141	2.9	0.5624	0.4101	5.5	0.4784	0.5537
0.4	0.3975	0.0334	3.0	0.6057	0.4963	5.6	0.4517	0.47
0.5	0.4923	0.0647	3.1	0.5616	0.5818	5.7	0.5385	0.4595
0.6	0.5811	0.1105	3.2	0.4663	0.5933	5.8	0.5298	0.546
0.7	0.6597	0.1721	3.3	0.4057	0.5193	5.9	0.4486	0.5163
0.8	0.7228	0.2493	3.4	0.4385	0.4296	6.0	0.4995	0.447
0.9	0.7648	0.3398	3.5	0.5326	0.4152	6.1	0.5495	0.5165
1.0	0.7799	0.4383	3.6	0.588	0.4923	6.2	0.4676	0.5398
1.1	0.7638	0.5365	3.7	0.5419	0.575	6.3	0.476	0.4555
1.2	0.7154	0.6234	3.8	0.4481	0.5656	6.4	0.5496	0.4965
1.3	0.6386	0.6863	3.9	0.4223	0.4752	6.5	0.4816	0.5454
1.4	0.5431	0.7135	4.0	0.4984	0.4205	6.6	0.469	0.4631
1.5	0.4453	0.6975	4.1	0.5737	0.4758	6.7	0.5467	0.4915
1.6	0.3655	0.6389	4.2	0.5417	0.5632	6.8	0.4831	0.5436
1.7	0.3238	0.5492	4.3	0.4494	0.554	6.9	0.4732	0.4624
1.8	0.3336	0.4509	4.4	0.4383	0.4623	7.0	0.5455	0.4997
1.9	0.3945	0.3733	4.5	0.526	0.4343	7.1	0.4733	0.536
2.0	0.4883	0.3434	4.6	0.5672	0.5162	7.2	0.4887	0.4573
2.1	0.5816	0.3743	4.7	0.4914	0.5671	7.3	0.5393	0.5189
2.2	0.6363	0.4557	4.8	0.4338	0.4968	7.4	0.4601	0.5161
2.3	0.6266	0.5532	4.9	0.5002	0.4351	7.5	0.516	0.4607
2.4	0.555	0.6197	5.0	0.5636	0.4992	7.6	0.5156	0.5389
2.5	0.4574	0.6192	5.1	0.4998	0.5624	7.7	0.4628	0.482

APPENDIX-B

Table B.1. Partial list of Bessel Function $J_1(x)$.

x	$J_1(x)$	x	$J_1(x)$	x	$J_1(x)$
0	0	2.6	0.4708	5.2	−0.3432
0.1	0.0499	2.7	0.4146	5.3	−0.3460
0.2	0.0995	2.8	0.4097	5.4	−0.3453
0.3	0.1483	2.9	0.3754	5.5	−0.3414
0.4	0.196	3.0	0.3391	5.6	−0.3343
0.5	0.2423	3.1	0.3009	5.7	−0.3241
0.6	0.2867	3.2	0.2613	5.8	−0.3110
0.7	0.329	3.3	0.2207	5.9	−0.2951
0.8	0.3688	3.4	0.1792	6.0	−0.2767
0.9	0.4059	3.5	0.1374	6.1	−0.2559
1.0	0.4401	3.6	0.0955	6.2	−0.2329
1.1	0.4709	3.7	0.0538	6.3	−0.2081
1.2	0.4983	3.8	0.0128	6.4	−0.1816
1.3	0.522	3.9	−0.0272	6.5	−0.1538
1.4	0.5419	4.0	−0.066	6.6	−0.1250
1.5	0.5579	4.1	−0.1033	6.7	−0.0953
1.6	0.5699	4.2	−0.1386	6.8	−0.0652
1.7	0.5778	4.3	−0.1719	6.9	−0.0349
1.8	0.5815	4.4	−0.2028	7.0	−0.0047
1.9	0.5812	4.5	−0.2311	7.1	0.0252
2.0	0.5767	4.6	−0.2566	7.2	0.0543
2.1	0.5683	4.7	−0.2791	7.3	0.0826
2.2	0.556	4.8	−0.2985	7.4	0.1096
2.3	0.5399	4.9	−0.3147	7.5	0.1352
2.4	0.5202	5.0	−0.3276	7.6	0.1592
2.5	0.4971	5.1	−0.3371	7.7	0.1813

APPENDIX-B

Table B.1. Partial list of Bessel Function $J_1(x)$

x	$J_1(x)$	x	$J_1(x)$	x	$J_1(x)$
0	0	2.6	0.4708	5.2	−0.3432
0.1	0.0499	2.7	0.4146	5.3	−0.3460
0.2	0.0995	2.8	0.4097	5.4	−0.3453
0.3	0.1483	2.9	0.3754	5.5	−0.3414
0.4	0.196	3.0	0.3391	5.6	−0.3343
0.5	0.2423	3.1	0.3009	5.7	−0.3241
0.6	0.2867	3.2	0.2613	5.8	−0.3110
0.7	0.329	3.3	0.2207	5.9	−0.2951
0.8	0.3688	3.4	0.1792	6.0	−0.2767
0.9	0.4059	3.5	0.1374	6.1	−0.2559
1.0	0.4401	3.6	0.0955	6.2	−0.2329
1.1	0.4709	3.7	0.0538	6.3	−0.2081
1.2	0.4983	3.8	0.0128	6.4	−0.1816
1.3	0.522	3.9	−0.0272	6.5	−0.1538
1.4	0.5419	4.0	−0.066	6.6	−0.1250
1.5	0.5579	4.1	−0.1033	6.7	−0.0953
1.6	0.5699	4.2	−0.1386	6.8	−0.0652
1.7	0.5778	4.3	−0.1719	6.9	−0.0349
1.8	0.5815	4.4	−0.2028	7.0	−0.0047
1.9	0.5812	4.5	−0.2311	7.1	0.0252
2.0	0.5767	4.6	−0.2566	7.2	0.0543
2.1	0.5683	4.7	−0.2791	7.3	0.0826
2.2	0.556	4.8	−0.2985	7.4	0.1096
2.3	0.5399	4.9	−0.3147	7.5	0.1352
2.4	0.5202	5.0	−0.3276	7.6	0.1592
2.5	0.4971	5.1	−0.3371	7.7	0.1813

INDEX